THE

OLD AND NEW

MONONGAHELA.

—— BY ——

JOHN S. VAN VOORHIS, A. M., M. D.

BELLEVERNON, PA.

JANAWAY PUBLISHING
Santa Maria, California

Notice

In many older books, foxing (or discoloration) occurs and, in some instances, print lightens with wear and age. Reprinted books, such as this, often duplicate these flaws, notwithstanding efforts to reduce or eliminate them. The pages of this reprint have been digitally enhanced and, where possible, the flaws eliminated in order to provide clarity of content and a pleasant reading experience.

The Old and New Monongahela

Copyright © 1893 John S. Van Voorhis

Originally published
Pittsburgh, Pennsylvania
1893

Reprinted with new index by:

Janaway Publishing, Inc.
732 Kelsey Ct.
Santa Maria, California 93454
(805) 925-1038
www.janawaygenealogy.com
2017

ISBN: 978-1-59641-375-7

Made in the United States of America

CONTENTS.

Monongahela Valley	5
Early White Settlers	6
Early Navigation	8
Monongahela Navigation Company	8
Steamboat Packets	9
Transportation by Wagons	11
Early Farming	11
Whiskey and Stillhouses	14
Historical Address by J. S. Van Voorhis, M. D.	15
Letter from George P. Fulton	29
The Dedication of Public School House, Monongahela City	33
The New School House Destroyed by Fire	34
Address of Prof. George P. Fulton at the Re-dedication of the Public School House in Monongahela City	35
Re-dedication of the School House in Monongahela City	40
Old Time School Houses	40
Life of William Colhoun	42
Old Time Schools	51
Schools in Later Days	57
Horse Shoe Church, Williamsport, Monongahela City	60
Rev. John Kerr	66
The Church on the Hill	69
Rev. A. H. Kerr	74
Reminiscences of 1840	75
Mrs. Jane Fulton Power	77
Dr. George E. Lytle	78
Mrs. Margaret Lowry Everhart	79
Mrs. Sarah F. Stevenson	80
William J. Markell	81
Historical Address of J. S. Van Voorhis, M. D., November 15th, 1892, on the One Hundredth Anniversary of Monongahela City, Pa.	83
West Monongahela	116
Monongahela only	117
Monongahela City Methodist Episcopal Church	118
Cyrus Underwood	135
Ira R. Butler	137
Elias Watkins	144
Richard Stockdale	146
Mark Borland	147
Hon. Alexander Hervey Houston	149
Aunt Margaret Philips	150

Contents.

The Black—Bentley—King Families	151
William Jones Family	156
The Alexander Family	160
Mrs. Rose Ann Davidson	160
Joseph Alexander	164
Death of William Wickerham in 1879	165
Death of John King in 1881	168
Death of Dr. Wm. H. King	170
John E. Shaffer, M. D.	171
The Walker Family	176
Samuel Frew	180
Death of Mrs. Sarah Wilson	180
Scott Family	182
Moses Scott	185
Hon. James Scott	186
Van Voorhis Family	186
Hon. Daniel Van Voorhis	191
Isaac Van Voorhis	199
Death of Mrs. James H. Van Voorhis	212
Mrs. Lizzie Van Voorhis Cunningham	213
The Smith Family—Dr. Bela Smith	216
George P. Fulton	226
Prof. George P. Fulton's Mother	228
Death of Mrs. Mary Finley	231
The Hair Family—James Hair	233
Death of Uriah Hair	238
The Late Rev. G. M. Hair	238
The Sample Family	240
Alexander Wilson	241
The Gordon Family	245
Jesse Martin	250
The McFarland Family	252
The McGrew Family	254
The Beazell Family—B. F. Beazell	255
James K. Marshall	260
The Teeple Family	261
Gen. John M. Davis	265
The Frye Family	268
Dr. Mathew Porter Morrison	274
The Death of Joseph S. Morrison, Esq.	275
A Tender Memory	277
Death of Maj. A. P. Morrison	278
Mrs. Eliza Morrison Alexander	280
The Morrison Family	280
Hon. T. R. Hazzard	281
Dr. Wilson dead	285
Dr. R. F. Biddle	286

Contents.   V.

Mrs. M. J. Biddle.	289
Samuel Pollock dead	290
J. Sutton Wall	290
One Hundred Years	293
Bellevernon	299
The Presbyterian Church of Bellevernon	321
The Cunningham Family	326
Bellevernon Sabbath School	329
Methodist Episcopal Church of Bellevernon	332
Stewards in Bellevernon M. E. Church	343
Free Will Baptist Church	347
Disciple Church of Bellevernon	351
The First School in Bellevernon	352
The New Brick School House in Bellevernon	359
Bellevernon Academy	361
Post Office and Telegraph	363
Newspapers	365
Glass Works and Business Men in Bellevernon	366
The Grand Army Post	368
I. O. O. F.	373
Other Lodges	375
Natural Gas History (1887)	376
Bellevernon Electric Heat and Light Company	377
Bellevernon Water Company	377
Bellevernon Bridge Company	377
First National Bank of Bellevernon	377
Cleveland Coal Company	378
Romana Land Company	379
Washington and Westmoreland Ferry Company	379
The Militia, Fourth of July, Temperance, Centennial and Railroads	379
North Bellevernon	383
Gibsonton	388
Gibsonton in 1890	392
Natural Gas	397
Glass—Works of R. C. Schmertz & Co.	403
Extracts from Bellevernon *Enterprise*—S. F. Jones, Robert J. Linton, Thomas L. Daly and J. S. Van Voorhis	406
Bellevernon—"All things come to him who waits"	410
Address of Welcome delivered by Dr. J. S. Van Voorhis, October 15, 1889, at the Opening of the McKeesport & Bellevernon Railroad to Bellevernon	418
An Opening Opened and Big Day of Celebration	426
Nathaniel Everson and Miscellaneous Matters	430
Speers	435
Louis M. Speer	437
Death of Col. William F. Speer	442
David Furnier	443

Corwin 449
J. Westley Corwin... 451
Death of Mrs. Sarah A. Springer... 452
J. B. Gould... 453
William Eberheart... 456
Dr. David Porter.. 459
Captain Woolsey.. 460
Springer Family... 460
Andrew Dunlevy.. 464
Hazelbaker... 465
Thomas Ward and Frederick Cooper... 467
Captain Joseph Shepler.. 468
Crossed Over the River—Mrs. Robert J. Linton....................... 471
Rehoboth.. 473
Death of Mrs. Anna M. Baker... 474
Hon. George Plumer.. 475
Gibsonton Cemetery.. 479
Long Branch.. 479
Speers.. 479
Stockdale.. 479
Glassport.. 480
Col. Sam. B. Bentley... 480
Mrs. Jane Van Voorhis... 482
Building and Loan Associations in Bellevernon......................... 483
Charleroi.. 485
Robert McKean.. 485

ERRATA.

Page 148, fifth line from bottom, read 1883 not 1833.

Page 220, twelfth line from bottom, read Harriet, daughter of Dr. Smith, married John Fuller, late of Connellsville, Pa., instead of daughter of Dr. Smith Fuller.

Wherever the name Beezel occurs, it should read Beazell.

On page 144, Elias Watkins instead of Watson.

Page 186, sixth line from bottom, read Castellum, not Casteltum.

In eighteenth line from bottom read Ibela instead of Kela.

Wherever Daily read Daly.

MONONGAHELA VALLEY.

From different sources amid the mountains of West Virginia the Monongahela River arises, and running in a northerly direction at Pittsburgh, in Pennsylvania, it joins the Allegheny to form the Ohio. It is situated principally between 41° and 42° north latitude and in the 89° degree of longitude west of Greenwich. Its water flows gently from pure mountain springs and in its course to the mouth fails to gather the malarial poison. The valley for the most part is bordered with moderately high mountains and hills which abound in every variety of minerals, timber, and especially in bituminous coal, petroleum and natural gas. The coal formation susceptible of being mined is estimated at 400 square miles. Petroleum and natural gas are of recent discovery and their development into practical use of very modern date and limited extent. The soil of the valley is rich in fertility and capable of producing grain and vegetation of almost every variety. The forests originally abounded in chestnut, pine, cedar, oaks, maple, ash, walnut, hickory, poplar, beech, but of late years timber has been literally wasted to make lumber and obtain space for the productions in agriculture.

The principal towns of the valley in Pennsylvania are New Geneva, Brownsville, Fayette City and Bellevernon in Fayette County; Greensboro, in Greene County; Millsboro, Fredericktown, West Brownsville, California, Coal Centre, Allenport, West Bellevernon, Charleroi, Lock No. 4, Columbia and Coal Bluff, in Washington County, besides Monongahela, recently formed into a city. In Westmoreland County are situated Gibsonton Mills, North Bellevernon and Webster. Within the limits of Allegheny County, outside of the City of Pittsburgh, are located Carrollton, Elizabeth and West Elizabeth,

Coal Valley, Dravosburg, McKeesport, Duquesne, Port Perry, Braddock and Homestead. The Monongahela River is made up, besides the large branches in West Virginia, from the Cheat River, Dunkard Creek, Ten Mile, Dunlap's Creek, Big Redstone, Pike Run, Little Redstone, Maple Creek, Pigeon Creek, Mingo Creek, Peters Creek and Youghiogheny River.

At what period the first white people came into the valley is not definitely known, but it is a well established fact that the whites as now considered were not the primitive settlers; of the aborigines, we have no history other than relics which abound, and traditional stories handed down from generation to generation. Mounds, graveyards and battlefields containing skeletons, war implements and other peculiar relics are found to abound in the valley. They to a good degree differ from those generally conceded to belong to the Indian tribes. The forts as they are called in modern day, were intelligently located for effective service for both offensive and defensive warfare. These forts were for the most part fixed at points not easily accessible by an enemy, whilst the battlefields and burial places were chosen plateau grounds which the defensive had prepared in advance of the approach of the attacking party. Those killed on the field were buried in a mound, many of which still remain. The forts were erected in an elliptical form and the dead killed inside were buried in a circle on the inner edge of the fortifications. They were laid in a trench on the left hip in a semi-sitting posture with the face looking to the east. An earthen pipe and bowl were interred with the body, but rarely is found any war instrument, for the reason it is supposed, that such would be useful in battle again, and mainly because the passage to the land of the great spirit was only to be accomplished by peace measures.

EARLY WHITE SETTLERS.

Prior to the expedition of General Braddock the valley was very sparsely settled, but the unfortunate career of this General seemed to have given a new impetus to this part of Western

Pennsylvania, or Virginia, as it was originally called. The road over which this unfortunate man traveled in marching to his fatal battlefield on the Monongahela is still marked and well known in history. The early immigrants were generally from the eastern states, although many came direct from foreign countries. The Scotch-Irish were among the most prominent settlers, and did much by their manners and strict habits to give caste to the different settlements. The early settlers encountered many and very hazardous dangers and difficulties which in modern times cannot be fully estimated. Block houses for refuge and defense were established in every community into which in times of threatened danger families resorted. These houses were different from Indian forts. They were built of round logs, compact and capable of resisting the arrow of the enemy. Guns, generally held by the whites, were used in defense and proved superior to the war implements of the attacking party.

On landing in their new home the first duty was to erect a cabin for shelter, and then to select a suitable spot to cultivate for use when the stores carried with them were exhausted. The cabin was built of round logs, the interstices were chunked and daubed with common clay, or catan clay, which was a mixture of clay and grass, or straw. The chimney was on the outside and made of split logs at the bottom or fireplace, so called, and the top was of smaller split sticks, the whole being well daubed with clay mortar. The fireplace was lined with stone and mortar so as as to prevent it catching fire. The floor, where there was any, was made of split logs hewn in shape to closely fit together. One window furnished the light, and one door hung on wooden hinges, with a latch and string, the mode of entrance. The latter drawn in was the lock to prevent entrance. The latchstring hanging out was always a token of welcome to the cabin. The furniture was for the most part rude and made impromptu; the chairs and tables were homemade. The grand old chest, brought from the east, was ample for clothing. The cupboard ware was pewter, and the bed and bedding were brought with them. There was no bedstead save that made by the few tools on hand from split timber. Immigration generally took place in the spring of the year, so that the first crop to be raised was corn and flax, the former to provide food for man and beast and the latter for clothing. The cabin was always located near a spring from which could be obtained water for the household and stock. The early settlers differed very much in the choice of location, some preferring the high and others the low lands. Along the creeks sites for sawmills were the choice of those who had a genius for water machinery, although the original mills were the wind mill and the tramp mill.

EARLY NAVIGATION.

The primitive mode of navigation on the Monongahela consisted in the simple Indian canoe, propelled by an oar or oars according to the taste of the owner. The canoe was beautifully constructed by the unskilled hand and his bark, thus built was the pride of the untutored heart. Generally they were made from a solid section of a tree hewn into shape by the rude tomahawk. Sometimes the material was of bark and nicely ornamented. The successor to the canoe was the skiff, as it is now called. The original freight crafts were constructed in the form of rafts of logs, but on the coming into date of the saw mills, the flatboat or broad horn took their place. The flatboats served a good purpose for many years and were superseded in the early part of the present century by the keelboat. Keelboats gave place in due time to steamboats. The first steamboat was built in the valley at West Brownsville but by whom and when is not fully settled. The Enterprise, it is generally believed, was the first constructed in the valley.

MONONGAHELA NAVIGATION COMPANY.

After several attempts to have the general government permanently improve the navigation of the Monongahela, without any practical success the "Monongahela Navigation Company" was authorized by an Act of Assembly of the State of Pennsylvania, March 31, 1836. The only improved condition of navigation heretofore had been the construction of chutes and wing-walls at the different shoal points. The improvement by this company proposed was a series of locks and dams. No. 1 and 2 were put in use in October 1841. Nos. 3 and 4 were completed for use to Brownsville, November 13, 1844. Other locks and dams have been completed at different times until, with the aid of the government improvement, below Morgantown W. Va., navigation is easy and complete to that point. The slackwater is now in perfect working order, (1893) so that the steamboat company run its boats from Pittsburg to Morgantown at all seasons of the year.

This 8th day of November 1889, the locks and dams are complete to Morgantown, W. Va., the steamboat James G. Blaine passed up from Pittsburgh to that place being the first to make the trip.

Steamboat Packets.

Prior to the completion of the slackwater to Brownsville there were no regular packets on the river. The Liberty, Exchange, Oella, Massachusetts, Export and that class of boats did duty as carriers of freight and passengers whenever the depth of water would allow. The Pittsburgh and Brownsville Packet Company was organized in 1844 by Adam Jacobs, G. W. Cass, J. K. Moorhead, J. L. Dawson, I. C. Woodward and others.

The Consul was the first boat built for the company; she was commanded by Captain Samuel Clark. Shortly afterward the Louis McLane was put on the line, under the command of Captain Adam Jacobs. These boats in 1850 were superseded by the Baltic, Captain Jacobs, and the Atlantic, Captain James Parkinson. In the year 1851 the Redstone was placed on the line, with I. C. Woodward as captain. After a short term of service she was sold and a few months afterwards she exploded her boilers near Cincinnati, killing the engineer and several others.

In 1852 the Jefferson and Luzerne were put in the trade to take the place of the Baltic and Atlantic. Captain Morgan Mason was put in command of the Jefferson and Elisha Bennet the Luzerne. In 1856 the Telegraph, Captain I. C. Woodward, was built. The slackwater now being finished above Brownsville, the Jefferson, Captain G. W. Clark, was put above to connect with the Telegraph and Luzerne.

In 1859 the Gallatin, Captain Clark, and Dunbar, Captain Bennett, were built. The Dunbar was in service only a very short time when she was sold to parties in the lower Ohio. The Franklin, with Bennett as captain came out in 1860. In 1864 the Fayette was placed on the line, Captain S. C. Speers on the roof. In 1866 the E. Bennett was put on the line, with Captain M. A. Cox in command. At that time the company were running four boats. In 1868 the Peoples' Line, which had been operating for a few months with their boats Elector and Chieftain, was consolidated with the old line, after which the style and corporate title of the company was the Pittsburgh, Brownsville and Geneva Packet Company, and by this arrangement the Elector and Chieftain were added to the line. The Geneva was built in 1871 and was in the trade 14 years.

The stern-wheel boat John Snowden came into service in 1876, Captain Peter Donaldson in charge. In a short time she was sold to Captain L. N. Clark, of Pittsburgh, who turned her into an excursion boat. The Bennett and Chieftain were lost in the disastrous ice breakup in 1877. In 1878 the Germania came out, in charge of Captain R. R. Abrams. The James G. Blaine was built in 1882, M. A. Cox master, and has been in continual service ever since. The Adam Jacobs made her maiden trip September 15, 1885, Captain M. A. Cox in command. This boat was the first to carry the electric light, and now, 1893, with the Blaine and Germania, constitutes the fleet in the line. Before the completion of the Pennsylvania railroad to Pittsburgh the Monongahela was on the great route between the west and the east. The packet company was a very important link in the route, and the number of through passengers carried by its boats prior to 1852 would astonish the modern enthusiast.

TRANSPORTATION BY WAGONS.

Before the time of railroads between the east and west of the Allegheny mountains, the freight business to the Monongahela was carried on by means of the Conestoga road wagons drawn by six horses. By this way the freight to Pittsburgh was carried exclusively, but after the completion of the Pennsylvania canal, transportation was divided between the canalboat and the wagon. As early as 1817 12,000 wagons, in twelve months, passed over the Allegheny mountains from Philadelphia and Baltimore, each with from four to six horses, carrying from thirtyfive to forty hundred weight. The cost was about $7 per 100 weight, in some cases $10. To transport one ton of freight between Philadelphia and Pittsburgh, therefore, would cost about $140, and in so doing two weeks, at least, of time would be consumed. Now, by the Pennsylvania railroad, a ton between these same cities will only cost $2.87. In 1817 it cost $14 to carry a barrel of flour from Pittsburgh to Philadelphia, and now the charge is only twenty-eight cents. At that time the merchant paid $7 per 100 for his dry goods hauled from Philadelphia to Pittsburgh, the same weight now carried for fourteen cents.

The early immigrants carried much of their household goods on horseback, and for years after their arrival at their new home they were compelled to make frequent pilgrimages to the east in order to obtain salt, iron, and such like for their use. Families combined and sent one or more to procure these things for all. The roads over which traveling was accomplished were Indian trails, and in many places these were very hard to find.

EARLY FARMING.

The primitive farming was done either with oxen or horses, as it suited the taste and ability of the owner. The ground after being cleared was soft and easily turned up by the home-made plow, consisting of a straight beam and handles, with a wooden mould-board, the share and coulter alone being iron. The harrow was triangular in shape, as often we see in modern days, but the teeth were of wood and the frame of hewn timber. The gears were principally at first such as were brought with the settler from the east, but the new ones, and repairing was made from ropes, home-made out of tow, which was the second quality of flax.

Sowing of grain was done broadcast, in which the modern invention of drilling is not generally admitted to be an improvement. Small grain was gathered with the sickle. After the country was somewhat opened up a system of reaping was adopted. The fields were run out at the time of sowing in what was called lands eight feet wide. Two full hand reapers were expected to cut this width and keep up with the gang or else be docked in their pay. The best reaper was selected as the leader and the rest had to follow not far behind until the end of the *through*. It was a beautiful sight to look upon a gang of twenty or more reapers. Not unfrequently even the leader would retire to the shade, having "given out" as it was called, but in modern parlance such a condition is considered a *sunstroke*. At the end of the *through*, which extended across the field, one-half of the reapers took up all the sickles and carried them back half way to the starting point, where, on the arrival of the other half the sickles were taken up, thus the grain cut was bound into sheaves by the time the gang reached the beginning. The two on each land always put their grain in one grip so as to facilitate the binding.

Generally before another round was made, cool water from an adjacent spring and whiskey from the green glass bottle were handed around and each partook freely to brace up the physical nature, yet a drunken man in the harvest field was a rare occurence and looked upon as very disgraceful conduct. Women on many farms were as expert reapers as men. The scarcity of men laborers called the women into service in order to save the grain. A days work in the harvest field was from daylight to dark.

The barn was generally erected of round logs in double form. The barn roof was made with clap-boards at first, then of straw and finally of shingles. The clap-boards were rived or split by a tool called a frow, from the best of oak timber. These boards were kept in place by what was called knees and weight poles. The straw-roof was made of rye straw bound in small bundles by a bark withe and these tied neatly to the wood-work of the roof. The straw-roof well put on was more lasting than any other roof and to this day, we occasionally meet with one over half century old.

In addition to the barn, there was erected on some farms what was known as the barracks, this was about 20 feet square with an open floor on which to rest the grain and at each corner an upright post at least twenty feet high, on these corners a movable roof was placed. By a lever and pins this roof could be raised at will, so that as the grain was built up inside, it would be moved so as to allow more or less room.

All these improvements were done pretty much by the household itself and the voluntary assistance of the neighbors. The tools consisted principally of an axe, hand axe, hand and cross-cut saw, draw knife, a frow, a few augers and a gimlet, and perhaps a hammer. Nails were not used in the beginning, but wooden pins. Some of the more wealthy settlers brought with them a few shoemaker's tools so that their own mending could be done.

Threshing was done with the flail during the winter.

The original settlers in western Pennsylvania based their titles to farms on the tomahawk right. Having selected a desirable spot they encircled it with a line marked by blazing trees with an axe. There was no attention to angles, degrees and chains, the sole object being to designate the boundaries of the tract without reference to the number of acres. Lines thus indicated were held sacred by all parties and to this day are legal. These irregular lines have given rise to ill shaped farms, and even now small tracts are found not included, and hence we have vacant land subject to entry by anyone who will take legal means to obtain a title from the State. In those days, sections, half sections and quarter sections were unknown and even county and township lines were run according to circumstances.

WHISKY AND STILLHOUSES:

The sale of grain of all kinds was very limited, and unless made into whisky there was little demand for it. This was a staple production. A stillhouse for its manufacture was erected on nearly every farm. The primitive stillhouse was always located below some never-failing spring, from which cold water could be taken by dugout troughs. Cold water, then as now, was essential to the distillery process. The house was built of round logs, with clapboard roof. Two copper stills fixed in a stone furnace constituted the capacity of the house on which was based the license to distill, but sometimes there were more than two, as could be seen from the licenses. In 1791 there were 272 stills in Washington county. The whisky insurrection in 1794 arose from the imposition of an excessive tax upon distilled liquors, which affected Washington county especially. Resistance for a time to the law gave rise to a great deal of trouble, the U. S. army having to be called into active duty before the insurgents submitted. The whole thing was finally settled by way of a compromise. The use of spirits as a beverage in olden time was a prevailing custom. Late as sixty years ago it was considered a breach of etiquette not to set out the bottle when friends and even ministers called on a visit. The green-glass, long-necked quart bottle was kind of a household god. It was present on nearly every occasion. At weddings, corn-huskings, wood-choppings, log-rollings, flax-pullings, manure frolics, sheep-washing, fish-gigging, house and barn raisings, it was an essential element.

HISTORICAL ADDRESS.

[Historical address delivered by J. S. Van Voorhis, M. D. at the dedication of the new school house in Monongahela City, Pa., July 1, 1881, together with a letter from Prof. Geo. P. Fulton.]

The history of Education in this vicinity, in common with other matters of local interest, is shrouded in uncertainty, only a few vague and general items being preserved. Looking upon our ancestors from a present standpoint, they appear to have lived merely for their day only, caring little for the wants and desires of the future. They were content when satisfied that they and their offspring had whereof to eat, drink and wherewithal to be clothed. In fact, their immediate necessities were so urgent as to call for the greater part of their time in efforts secure for them what was termed in those days "a living." Faith in the precepts of the Bible in its truest *version* was innate to the first settlers of our valley; the strongest Puritanical ideas being the literature upon which they founded their hopes of the future, never doubting that time and labor would in the end verify the prophetic saying, "The wilderness and the solitary place shall be glad for them, and the desert shall rejoice and blossom as the rose." Until about the close of the last century individual culture consisted chiefly in learning to farm in the most primitive manner, which included a very limited knowledge of the art of raising grain and the manufacture of home-made clothing. The favored few, who were privileged to literary attainment, were in full proportion at reaching the point of reading, writing and ciphering to the Single Rule of Three. Houses erected especially for school purposes were unknown. If, perchance, some itinerant individual, representing himself to be a schoolmaster, should happen along, an impromptu school house was obtained in the shape of some log cabin vacated by the tenant as unfit to occupy. The predecessor of the Parkisons, whose name we have mislaid, on his arrival found the site on which this rapidly growing city is located to be a dense forest of sugar and walnut trees, untouched by the hand of art or science. Cotemporary with this settlement, was the region around the old Horse Shoe Bottom meeting-house filled with immigrants. Here the older Powers, Moodys, Colvins, McComas, Witherows, Rices, Fryes, &c., founded their homes. This church, erected at the close of the revolution, was the first in this region, and its organization gave at once new life and vigor to the settlers, and its force of character culminated in awaking a desire for more than a homespun education. The influence of that congregation rapidly grew into such magnitude as to make it a centre of a higher state of civilization. Its power attracted the immigrant on his way thitherward in his search for a new home, which was found by many in the circle of country of which the church was the centre. So rapidly was this region taken up by new-comers that it for a time overshadowed the river settlements. From all information we can gather, it is evident that the first school at which settlers of this city attended, was located in an old log house that stood near where John Witherow's blacksmith shop now stands, and is supposed to have been the original residence of the older McComas. To add more to this influence, on the 19th day of October, 1796, Mr. Samuel Ralston, a licentiate from the Presbytery of New Castle, was called to preach to this congregation. He was a foreigner by birth and education. He was a man not only filled with the Holy Ghost, but he was adorned with the highest literary attainments found in the old world. In his every day life he exemplified the value of education, and impressed the minds of his people that it followed hand in hand with religion. The good of his teachings soon cropped out in the establishment of other schools. During the winter seasons another school was opened in the vicinity of the residence of the late Dutton Shannon, another at Parkison's Ferry, in an old log house of primitive style—by this we mean of unhewn logs. It was a dwelling once, used as such, situate in a grove of sugar trees on the lot on which stands the residence of Michael Yohe, near the old Presbyterian Church, not far from the lot on which this beautiful house has been erected. Shades of the departed !

thy spirits may yet linger around this sacred spot whilst we dedicate another temple to the god of science.

Up to this time, and many years afterwards, there was no organized effort to establish a uniform system of schools, the first attempt in that direction being the assessment and collection of a poor tax on the richer to pay the schooling of the poorer class of citizens. This new notion had many disadvantages and not any virtues. It fixed at once a discrimination in personal character which was then and is now distasteful to the full-blooded American.

Schools were taught in several of the old-time houses beside the famous old log house already named. A Mrs. McKeever, an elderly lady, in 1819 had a school in an old house where the depot now stands. Among her scholars were Joseph Warne, well known in this vicinity. Edward Tower, father of G. H. and Theo. Tower, of Elizabeth, taught a school not long afterwards in the old red house that stood on the lot on which the People's Bank now stands.

A Mr. Victor also taught in the same house. He also had Mr. Joseph Warne for a scholar. This teacher boarded with Mr. James Warne, who built and lived in the house so long occupied by the late Joseph Wilson on Main street. Orlando H. Gold taught about the year 1830 in the old red house on the river bank, long known as the house in which the late Samuel Black kept his first store. The building has long since disappeared. Among his scholars were W. J. Alexander, the worthy President of your Board of Directors, Charles Bebee, Samuel C. King, Wash. Spence, Samuel Guthrie, Wm. Devore, Robert McGrew, Franklin Manown and many other formerly well-known boys.

Mr. Joseph Grieves, a man of delicate constitution—who lived near the toll-gate up the pike—also taught in the old red house on the river bank, the above-mentioned boys constituting many of his scholars. For some reason, during the progress of his school he packed up his paraphernalia, consisting of rod, ferule and dinner basket, and moved his quarters to the red house, where the People's Bank now stands, he, in common with his patrons, having a peculiar taste for a red house. In after years no doubt many of them were gratified to see brick substituted, whether on account of the red color or not, we can only have our opinion. In a recent interview with Moses Arthurs, now a resident of this city and perhaps with us to-night, he informed us that he taught a school in 1831 in an old house which stood on the river bank on the upper corner of the lot on which the old Huston mansion then stood—above the old wharf. Mr. B. F. Bentley was one of his scholars, if we are not mistaken.

In the year 1834 Mr. E. A. Talbot opened a school in the old Methodist Church, a part of which can still be seen near the new wharf, and Miss Clarke, an aunt of S. C. and W. H. Wilson, taught a school during the same year in the old house formerly known as the Dorcas Cooper house, opposite the present residence of Richard Stockdale, on Main street. To this school of Miss Clarke Mr. Underwood first sent his children after his arrival in the place. Under her teaching my old friend and schoolmate "Uncle Abe," learned his first lesson of wisdom, and perhaps to the early impressions of her rulings may be attributed the fact that to this day he has eschewed matrimony. Mr. Watson, well known among the boys as *Blue Beard*, also kept school in this house. It seemed in those days that no kind of a building except an old house could be used for a school house. The idea of erecting a school house was not even among the possibilities. Such, in a general way, was the condition of school matters in this vicinity prior to the adoption of the common school system of 1834, and let it ever be to its credit that the township embracing Williamsport was among the first to accept the provisions of the law. By the Act of Assembly dated March 28, 1781, the county of Washington was divided into thirteen townships, one of which number was called Fallowfield, and included within its territory the district now known as Monongahela City. All schools to which we have alluded were within its limits until the formation of

Carroll, September 30, 1834. It will be noticed that Miss Clarke and Mr. Watson were the last to teach in the town whilst it was connected with old Fallowfield. Before the school system was organized, Carroll Township was formed and Williamsport was within its limits and under its jurisdiction for all purposes.

The first election in the new township was held at the house of Joseph Hamilton, who kept the hotel now known as the Miller House, on Main street. At this election a Board of School Directors was elected for the first time. On this Board devolved the duty of organizing the Township for school purposes. This was no easy task. We can recall but the names of David Williams, uncle of your honorable Secretary, Isaac Van Voorhis, my venerated father, and Geo. Morrison, now residing in Uniontown, as members of that Board. The Board, for the time being, divided the Township into convenient sub-districts, as required by law, using for school-houses whatever old buildings could be obtained. An old house on the hillside, to the left of the road leading from Yerty's Run to Galbreath's, furnished one in which a one-armed man was teacher. He being barred out at one time at the approach of the holidays, forced an entrance through the clapboard roof and soon settled the boys with a severe *drubbing*, as it was called. He was a strict but succesful teacher introducing many new and practical ideas not dreamed of in old time philosophy. This school was finally merged into the one in the stone house at the forks of the run, Col. A. T. Gregg, now in this audience, aided in building, and in which house he taught the first school, thus carrying into practice the homeopathic dogma, "*Similia similibus curantur.*" On the hill, above the present residence of Wm. Blythe, may yet be seen traces of a log cabin, which, condemned by common consent as unfit for any other use, was selected as a suitable school house. It was a retired spot, not even a road, much less a house, within sight; no wonder the proprietor was constantly complaining of the depredations of such boys as McCarty Williams, Robert Phillips, James Stockdale, Robert Van Voorhis, &c., who, not alive to his finer feelings, displayed a good deal of faith in old time NIHILISM, having no disposition to ignore the doctrine well cherished everywhere, that the "boy had no pent-up UTICA to contract his power" to roam undisturbed, not being met in those days at every crossing by the huge sign of danger as now, bearing the inscription, TRESPASSERS, BEWARE, or if, by chance some such bug-bear passed before them, it was quickly demolished by the finger-stone—the boys' native arm of defence. The only thing that forced the old-time boy to a hasty retreat was the bumble-bee and yellow-jacket. In this school, as already intimated, our friend Robt. Phillips was a scholar, and methinks I can see him yet, as he sat cross-legged on a split log bench, with slate and pencil, intent on working out a sum in pounds, shillings and pence, or proving to those around him, in his peculiar style, how he had solved the question, "that if two and two make four, four and four would make eight." In this waste cabin an irishman named Lewis first taught; he was succeeded by Sampson and Paull. Lewis was Irsh indeed, and his pupils were very much inclined to imitate his *twang*, calling have *have*, sounding the A long instead of A short. The town was divided into two sub-districts, one being a double district. The upper end, including Catsburg, attended school in a frame house which stood on the island near where the foundry now stands, being owned at that time by the heirs of the late Elias Watkins. For one term at least this school was taught by the late Thos. Collins, Esq. The lower end of town occupied the old Methodist Church for a time as a school house. E. A. Talbot seems to have been the first teacher in this house under the new system. He was succeeded in 1835 by a Mr. Prescott. He was a relative of the celebrated historian, and and was a man of more than ordinary literary attainments.

After grave consideration the Board of Directors determined to erect in each district a brick or stone house. The houses built in town under this resoultion was the three-roomed house of which the late Alex. Scott was contractor, still standing on the old Presbyterian Church lot, and the one on the island long since passed into the river. In the latter house we think Thos. Collins was the first teacher. These houses were occupied for the first time in the winter of 1836, having been built during the preceding summer. We feel almost certain that Nimrod Gregg, brother of Col. A. T. Gregg, taught one of the schools in the double house during this winter, and that a Mr. Dunn taught the other one. Mr. Dunn was a Yankee schoolmaster. He was fresh from Yankee land, and full of new ideas in the school business. He was soon impressed with the fact that he was in a strange land and surrounded by habits and customs requiring no little moral courage to break into, and as much physical nerve to introduce a new departure. He took in the situation readily. He came among them as *Mr.* not *Master* Dunn, and as such he would have them recognize him. He intended to teach, not keep school; that he only had one rule, and that was obedience to *his* will. His rule was founded, no doubt, on the moral lesson taught in the words of the poet:

> "I am monarch of all I survey;
> My right there is none to dispute,
> I make the little ones to obey,
>   And manage the big ones to boot."

Which being translated, means that he would use the rod to the smaller and his boot to the larger scholars.

Mr. Dunn's career as a teacher was a success. His Scholastic attainment and gentlemanly deportment, together with natural kindness, won for him the esteem of all with whom he came in contact. He was the first to introduce prizes as rewards of merit, and the first school prizes ever given were taken by three sisters of your worthy President.

By the Act of April, 1837, the town of Williamsport was incorporated into a borough under the name and style of Monongahela city, and thereafter the schools were placed under the control of a Board of Directors elected exclusively by the voters in the new borough. The late T. R. Hazzard succeeded Dunn as teacher, and carried out more fully new improvements in the art of teaching. He was a fine scholar, a kind friend and a generous benefactor. To him, more than any one individual, is this community indebted for its well known educational spirit. He taught the first classical academy in the town. Among his pupils were many who are now holding or have held important positions in church and State. Under his teachings a new spirit on the subject of education seemed to take hold of the people, giving rise to a desire for an advance in the cause, with the selection of teachers of a higher order of literary worth. Shortly after his retirement from teaching in the old house, the question of examining teachers as to their qualifications was raised, and to render the matter practical, the late Dr. R. F. Biddle and A. W. Davidson, editor of the Carroll *Gazette*, were appointed a Board of Examiners.

Among the many other teachers in the old double house were Joseph S. Morrison, now a distinguished member of the Pittsburgh bar, and R. F. Cooper. Cooper had been among Hazzard's earliest pupils, at the age of sixteen having read at a public exhibition his masterly literary production entitled, "Mutability of all things." To him and his teachings your speaker owes his earliest thirst for literature. As a teacher, penman, writer, printer, editor and soldier, he had few equals. His criticism at the early part of the late war on the tactics of the United States army, as printed in the Philadelphia *North American*, elicited commendation from the highest military authorities of the nation. On the graves of Hazzard and Cooper let us not forget to strew flowers and shed tears of regret over their early demise. Friends, teachers, though dead, thy virtues live.

The rapid growth of the borough soon necessitated the erection of a new school building. In the year 1852 the Board of Directors, consisting of our venerable friend, Cyrus Underwood, as President, and the late Alexander Wilson as Secretary, with Joseph Alexander, H. H. Finley, Wilson

Thompson and Alex. Scott as members, resolved to build a new school house, which gave the town the brick house across the street from this house. The lot was purchased from Henry Fulton. The house cost $7,000. Johnson Baird and Wm. Wilson did the stone and brick work, whilst the veteran contractor, Wm. Coulter—with us to-night—did the carpenter work. It was opened for school in the fall of 1853. Andrew Brown, now of the "Forks" and T. R. Hazzard, just returned from West Newton, were the first teachers, the former having been the last to teach in the old building. Too much credit cannot be given President Underwood for his untiring industry and foresight in moulding public opinion and carrying the enterprise to a successful issue. He was born in Baltimore, Md., August 28, 1807. He first settled in this place in 1834, where he has resided ever since, excepting three years he served as recorder of the county. He and H. H. Finley are the only surviving members of that Board of Directors. We are glad to see them both here to-night. Kind friends, faithful Christians, human benefactors, we bid you God speed.

The Union school was organized in the fall of 1854, with James H. Moore as Principal, and Miss Webster, Miss Bebee and Miss Hodgson as assistants. Mr. Moore is deceased. His wife, formerly Miss Webster, is now Principal of one of the public schools of Indianapolis. This Union school, under the supervision of a principal, was a new thing among the people, and for a time the plan had many prejudices to overcome, but ere the close of the first term it was pronounced a success by the bitterest enemy. Owing to many diversified circumstances the principal and teachers were very often changed, a policy of questionable propriety. Recently, however, the reverse obtains. We cannot recall the names of all who have in this building taught school. We record here that Prof. Jennings was the last principal in that building, and that his reputation is such as insure us in openly declaring that his career has been successful, and that the very walls of the old building join in echoing his praise.

By the provisions of the act incorporating the borough into a city, its boundaries were considerably enlarged, adding thereby much to the population, and increasing the number of scholars in the public schools. This fact had much to do in originating the necessity of this grand edifice, now under the process of dedication. This building needs no eulogy from me; it speaks for itself in tones that will reverberate through generations yet unborn. When this valley, with its hundred villages, smoking with the fires of industry, shall quake with the thunderings of the iron horse as it drives with lightning speed its human freight from ocean to ocean, this house will be pointed to as the proudest monument to science between the rising and setting sun. Long after the drapery of the grave shall have enshrouded them, the names of Williams, Beaver, King, Hammond, Shepler, Linn, Blythe, Teeters, Alexander, Coulter, Hartrick and others connected therewith, will have an abiding place in the future. The contractors, too, Neil Blythe & Co., will not be forgotten, when future generations shall make up their jewels of rejoicing. We cannot refrain from turning aside for a moment and pointing you to some interesting features in the life of our old friend and schoolmate, Wm. Coulter. More than half a century ago we together attended the old Colhoon school, near the late residence of Abe Hull. He has been so long identified with this community in all its interests, and especially in that of its public schools, that his nature has had much to do in moulding the disposition and tastes of the people. He was born November 11, 1817, in Catsburg, in the old house still standing on the corner of the street leading to the cemetery. He came on the stage of life, it will thus be seen, about the time in the history of that village when "Biddie Caldwell" held queenly sway. He first attended school in an old house long since passed into the river, near the residence of the late Judge Hill. His next school was that of Miss Burke, who kept in an old house on the Bollman lot, near the residence of the late Noble Woodward. Among the scholars were his brother Ralph and Joseph Woodward. He also attended John Dunning's school, kept in the red house already named, where the Peoples Bank stands. In 1827 he attended school in the old house in the rear of the grocery of D. H. Williams, where Gabriel Silverthorn lived long ago. Early in 1828 he attended the old Colhoon school. In 1830 he went to school to a man named Hepburn, who, with his two daughters, taught a semi-graded school in the old Dorcas Cooper house. Mrs. Margaret Sloan was one of the scholars, and has very vivid recollections of the teachers. After the adoption of the common school system he was a scholar at the Irish Lewis school on Marshall's hill. The last school he ever attended was taught by Moses Arthurs, on the Yough river, near Robbin's mill. At the close of this school he considered himself a graduate in the "Single Rule of Three," and congratulated himself, no doubt, that after years of hard study in many schools of learning, he had at length acquired sufficient proficiency in that Rule as to qualify him for the carpenter trade. He began to learn his trade with a Mr. Kelly, but made poor progress, owing to the fact that Kelly did not have anything to do. This did not suit the young apprentice as well as it would boys now-a-days, so he left Kelly and engaged with Amos Robbins to learn the millwright trade. It soon, however, struck William that curves, wheels and spindles would not lead rapidly to wealth, so he suddenly, with rule and square, set out for himself on his first track, and how well he has pursued it ever since, let the result of skill all over this neighborhood bear the testimony. He is with us to-night, and although his first love of a schoolhouse has been superceded, he delights to dwell on the beauties of this grand palace. He has been a school director in his native town back to the time to which memory runneth not to the contrary. He has seen the old building across the way come and answer its day. Although in appearance he looks hale and robust, a twinkle of the eye readily detects the fact that the weight of years is upon him. God bless you Wm. Coulter.

Independent of the common school system, the influence of

the select and academical schools acted no little part in creating that educational spirit which has given your city so widespread reputation for its literary taste. Over half a century ago, Dr. Ralston, at his residence near Ginger Hill, heard the late Samuel Hare, Aaron Williams and Samuel Williams recite their first lessons in Greek and Latin. Then followed the academies of Hazzard and E. S. Blake in the old church on the river bank; of J. D. Mason, in the old church on the hill, and of J. P. Thompson, in the old carriage factory where your humble servant learned to decline "Stella," and conjugate the Greek verb TUPTO, TUPSO, TETUPHA, ETUPON. Then followed the schools of McFarland and the Morrison brothers and the select school of Mary J. Cooper, now Mrs. Biddle, whose presence greets us to-night. There, too, was Miss Celia Gillet, daughter of the late Rev. N. H. Gillet, of Rehoboth. She, with her father and mother, have passed to the better land, whilst Miss Lizzie Lockhart is here to-night. Miss Haines, a lady from Canonsburg, taught a select school for a time in the old church on the river bank; so, also, did Rev. Samuel Hudson, now a distinguished minister in the Cumberland Church. Miss Haines had among her scholars Miss Eliza J. Warne, now the wife of John Watkins, of Missouri; Miss Hindman and Miss Campbell, of Finleyville, Miss Rebecca Van Voorhis, now of Spearville, Kansas, and many others whose names we cannot recall.

From these schools in this vicinity were sent forth many who have taken an important part in the drama of life. J. W. F. White, once a pupil, is now a judge in Pittsburgh, A. H. Kerr is an able minister in St. Peters, Minnesota; John McFarland was a pioneer minister in Missouri, and died a few years ago near Greenfield, Dade county; J. C. Cooper is a prominent physician of Philadelphia; W. F. Hamilton is one of the most talented ministers in the Synod of Wheeling; John H. Storer and James H. Manown have long been prominent physicians of West Virginia; A. J. Davis is a physician in the East End, Pittsburgh; Joseph S. and A. P. Morrison are lawyers of high standing in Pittsburgh; James Fleming is a successful physician in Franklin, Ohio; George T. Miller is a wealthy coal dealer in this valley, near Lock No. 2; he is the father of Rev. Miller, of the Presbytery of Blairsville; Dr. W. H. King was one of the most distinguished surgeons and physicians in Western Pennsylvania; he died a few years since in the prime of manhood; his remains are sleeping calmly in the beautiful cemetery overlooking his native town; Francis Gardner remains in *statu quo* on the farm in the bend of the river below Elkhorn; James Scott, one of Hazzard's early pupils, studied medicine with Dr. Biddle in the little old office that stood where Hoffman's store now is. He first practiced his profession in Greenfield, Pa. moved to Ohio, where as physician and politician, he has always occupied a high position. For many years he was a leading member of the Ohio Legislature; was consul at Honolulu for a term, and is now again a member of the legislature, where, as Nestor of that body, he is recognized as the leading spirit. He is a brother of the late Alex. Scott, of this city. Thomas Hodgson, grandson of the good old J. R. Shugart, is a talented and successful minister in the M. E. Church. Cyrus B. King is a physician in Allegheny, and at this time one of the visiting surgeons of the West Penn Hospital. Geo. P. Fulton, at the age of seventeen, devoted himself to teaching, and has pursued it ever since, except whilst in the army during the war. He has just been elected for the eleventh time Principal of the Hiland public schools, East End, in city of Pittsburgh. Thomas P. Gordon, son of the late Judge Gordon, was the first college graduate in the town, having graduated at Jefferson College in 1833. He was a minister, and died at his post of duty in Terre Haute, Indiana. He was the only native of this city who ever received the honorary degree of D. D. He was a brother of Mrs. Sloan, who is a resident of this city. Want of physical vigor alone prevents her presence to-night. May her last be the crowning years, and may the happy thought of a well-spent life be her consolation. Thomas T. Williams, was a school boy at Blake & Hazzard's; is now a successful medical practitioner at White College, Greene county, Pa., where for twenty-three years he has physicked Democrats and Republicans to their stomach's content. Dr. J. M. H Gordon has long been a physician in Fayette county. Alonzo Linn, brother of Dr. Linn, a worthy member of your Board, was one of Hazzard's scholars; he graduated at Jefferson College; studied divinity; was licensed to preach by the Presbytery of Redstone; is now Vice-President and Professor of Greek in Washington and Jefferson College, and is looked upon as one of the most learned Greek scholars in the nation. M. P. Morrison is your oldest resident physician, and if my eyesight does not deceive me, the frosty tinge noticeable on his head should remind him that it is not good for man to be alone. The mild and genial James P. Fulton is preaching to the pioneer sinners of Harper, Kansas, after having served his Master in that capacity for over a quarter century in the old Keystone State. Robert Officer is a successful business man in Baltimore, Md., and Uncle Abe Underwood is still a resident of your city, and looks but little older than he did when a student in the old carriage factory, forty-one years ago. There, too, is my old friend, Frank Manown; he has seen the old log school house, the old red house, the old brick house, the new brick house over the street, and the present palace. He claims to be one of the oldest resident scholars. His early education consisted in plying the oar at the old ferry. In his early days he was much engaged in mercantile and other pursuits, but for a long season his occupation has been that of a farmer and attending to the wants of those around him—kind and generous to a fault. He and C. C. Johnson, of Pittsburgh, are the only survivors of those who occupied what was known as the bachelor's pew in the old Presbyterian Church at the foot of the hill. At the close of his day's labor, he still can be seen in his regular walk over the bridge to spend a few hours with his friends in the city.

A peculiar fondness for education has ever characterized the citizens of this city, and thus their early literary spirit gave hem an advance hold on the dominant idea of the present day. Let us not, then, mourn over the departure of ancient manners and customs supplanted by the American idea. This is the motive power of the present day. By it we have assumed a proud position as a nation among the constellation of States; by it we have utilized the electric spark to annihilate time and space; by it the late Col. Scott pushed the iron horse freighted with human thought from the rising of the sun to the going down thereof in eighty hours; by it the western wilds and sandy deserts have been converted into fields of ever-blooming flowers; by it we can signal the coming storm, and tell what a day may bring forth; by it we have solved the problem of self-government, which defied the genius of sixty centuries; by it we are reminded that he only "shall receive the blessing from the Lord and righteousness from the GOD of his SALVATION who hath clean hands and a pure heart; who hath not lifted up his soul unto vanity nor sworn deceitfully."

LETTER FROM GEORGE P. FULTON.

HILAND PUBLIC SCHOOL,
Pittsburgh, Pa., July 1st, 1881.

Directors of Monongahela City Public Schools:

GENTLEMEN,—I have the honor to acknowledge the receipt of your invitation "to be present at and aid in the dedication of the public school building" in your city this evening.

The many duties attending the closing of the term in our own schools will prevent me from gratifying a long-cherished hope of meeting again my old friends, and participating in the reunion the occasion will afford to the "boys" and "girls" who answered the school-bells of more than a quarter of a century ago.

In contemplating your joyous meeting, my heart truly yearns for a glimpse of the old footprints of youth and home that were once mine, around and within the precincts of my native town. The fathers that in my youthful days were the guardians of your municipality have all passed away from earth and its conflicts, and have now no part in all the "pomp that decks the summer hills, save that their graves are green."

The generation next succeeding these are now the old men who go about your town with frosty brows, garrulous of the "good times" when the raftman's horn awoke the echoes of the hills and the wild duck and the yellow perch held their favorite haunts by the "Island" and its winding creek hard by.

The boys of that day, who then pressed up Beebe's alley and around past the Presbyterian Church into Captain Cooper's school, with the golden dust of the yellow fennel on our bare feet, or afterwards attended Mr. Joseph S. Morrison's academy on the river bank, held over the room where dwelt Mrs. Noble and her dog, are no longer the *lads* who threw "fireballs" through the streets every time that the Hon. George V Lawrence was elected, or built bon-fires on the grave-yard hill when we would hear men talking of good news from the armies of Scott and Taylor in the war with Mexico. We were *full* of that war, for Sparks Cooper—the brave *old* Sparks—was he not in it, and had we not seen on a Fourth of July, Captain Washington's artillery from Carlisle Barracks go through our place on its journey to that distant field of strife?

Not to make mention of the school girls of that day would be to withhold the utterance of our happiest and purest recollections. They "piped unto us when we danced" to our flagellations, and even shared our quarrels. Did they not, with their own white hands, weave the wreaths of pine and myrtle with which we decked our church for the yearly exhibition, and "read their essays" and adorned our ranks with their youthful beauty. Many of them will, doubtless, be with you this evening as the honored mothers of a duteous train of younglings to be reared under the fostering influences of the new school, while of others we must reflect in sadness, that—

> "The mossy marbles rest
> On the lips that we have press'd
> In their bloom,
> And the names we loved to hear,
> Have been carved for many a year
> On the tomb."

I have to regret that I am not fully informed as to the names of all who comprise your present School Board. I can see in fancy the honored President, in inextinguishable youth, gracing the night's array, the friend of the boys of '81 as he was the mentor and model of spotless manhood to the boys of 1842.

Of my former *schoolmates* on your Board, Secretary Williams is scanning the spacious building that his energy and tireless spirit aided so much to project and build, atoning in part for unpunished acts of demolition, chronicled against him in the school-house by the river, where he strung bells and rung them during the meditations of our study hours, put the then "smallest boy," Chill now Major, Hazzard, out of the house, through the window, and terrified his mates from their beds at night by alarms of ghosts and spirits evolved from his rollicking brain.

There, too, is Captain Wilson (Clark), who once on a time could boast of swimming, with three other Leanders, from Baird's to Eccles' wharf, without a rest, and who was with me "up the creek" when Michael Dooley was drowned, and Doctor George Lynn, the faithful student, who came from over the bridge, with Will. Pierce, John Wilson, Curry and William Ketcham. How I recall him invoking on "speech days," "Glenara," from the "Highland Glen," or imploring "Pizarro" for a hearing ear.

Last but not least in my affections, I can see my old friend and army comrade, Doctor William King, towering manly and strong as when in youth he trod the hills of the "Jersey settlement," or in later years followed the flag of his country in our strife for the Union, and won rank and honor in the 155th Regiment Pennsylvania Volunteers.

I trust that the new edifice may be dedicated to the fostering of a sturdy brood of townsmen, who will be equally well taught in the uses of the body, the mind and the heart; that it may be consecrated as the people's school, the poor man's college, the rich man's safeguard and the great hope of all classes of society.

From its rooms may there ever go forth legions of stalwarts who will be strong enough to earn their bread, wise enough to know their duty, and brave enough to *do* it.

May the generation to be trained in the new house be better taught than the ancients of the town, as they will have better opportunities, and be equal to them in honesty, purity, social and public virtue, and are the elements of exalted character.

I close with a sentiment uttered by the late Col. Sam. Black in an address once delivered in your own county: "Let us all, with one accord, say, 'God bless the common school system. For it is to the wintry condition of the world what the sunshine of spring, the rain of heaven and the distilled dews of the night are to the earth in her struggles to bring forth through ribs of frost the bud, the leaf and the flower.'"

I remain, very respectfully,

Your obedient servant,

GEO. P. FULTON.

THE DEDICATION.

The school building was dedicated July 1st, 1881, by Rev. Dr. Higbee, State Superintendent.

REPORT OF BUILDING COMMITTEE.

WHAT IT COST.

Captain T. H. Williams, Chairman of the Building Committee, made the following report :

Paid John Kennedy for 100 feet square of ground	$ 3,213 67
Damage to tenants on same	250 00
Wallace estate for one lot	65 97
	$3,529 64
Contract with Neel, Blythe & Co , of our city, for the entire completion of the building	17,750 00
Contract with Kelly & Jones, of Pittsburgh, for steam heating apparatus	2,536 27
Contract with Keystone School-Church Furniture Co., for the entire seating of building	2,700 00
Contract with Mitchell, Vance & Co., New York, for chandeliers	220 00
Contract with Solomon Meredith for one 75-barrel cistern to supply water for boilers	75 00
Wm. Nelson & Sons, stone buttresses for front steps	125 00
Drum & Steen, architects	230 00
	$27,165 91

We issued on June 30, 1880, $17,300 bonds at 16 years, bearing 6 per cent. interest, which we sold at a premium of 3 per cent. We issued on April 1, 1881, $6,000 6 per cent. bonds, running 20 years, which we sold at a premium of 7 per cent., making a total bonded indebtedness of $23,000—bonds purchased by our own citizens.

T. H. WILLIAMS,   WM. J. ALEXANDER,
  Secretary.   *President.*

Quite a large number of prominent educators were in attendance during the dedication, among whom were Rev. Dr. Higbee, State Superintendent, Prof. George J. Lucky, City Superintendent of Pittsburgh, Rev. George P. Beard, President of the State Normal School at California, Prof. J. H. Darling, Superintendent of Allegheny Schools, Prof. G. E. Hemphill, Superintendent of Allegheny ward schools, Prof. Teal, County Superintendent of Greene County, Prof. E. W. Mouck, Superintendent of Washington County.

THE NEW SCHOOL HOUSE DESTROYED BY FIRE.

This beautiful school building was of short life. On Friday morning, March 2, 1883, the whole building was destroyed by fire. We extract from the *Daily Republican* the particulars of the fire. The *Republican* of the 3d says:

"We have to record the most disastrous fire that ever occurred in this city About 4 o'clock Mr. Simmons in company with some fellow miners going to work discovered the block, corner Main and Fourth streets, on fire. It seemed to them to be just under or just back of the stairway leading to the *Record* printing office and R. F. Cooper's photograph rooms. The building in which the fire originated was built last spring, and was a wooden tinder box, made of pine lumber and filled with paint ; a mere shell, which was soon in so hot a blaze that it was impossible to pass up Main street between it and the Central Block. The flames soon spread to the wagon shops adjacent, and that too blazed like a straw pile. It was soon evident that unless something was speedily done the new school house must fall a prey to the flames. A feeble effort was made to tear the shops down, but the utter lack of appliances and the fast encroaching heat soon rendered all attempt in this direction *futile*. Then the cry went up 'The school house is afire,' and soon the tongue of flame licking the cornice and eating its way into the roof sent a shudder through the thousands of on-lookers, and for a while paralyzed all efforts. Could it be possible ? Must that splendid building, the pride of our hearts, the magnificent School Building, pronounced by the State Superintendent 'the finest in the state,' must it be given a prey to the relentless flames? Alas, it is too true."

ADDRESS.

[Address delivered at the Re-dedication of the Public School House, Monongahela City, Pa., September 27, 1883, by Prof. George P. Fulton, of the Hiland Public School, Pittsburgh, Pa. :]

To ask me to speak here to-night is like calling upon a man to respond to a toast at the marriage feast of his step-mother. The bride is young and fair, as all brides are. His father's face beams on the throng of smiling guests. The table is spread and the light is gleaming on china and glassware and silver. The limpid golden notes of the marriage bell ringing over all. But can the son of the woman who is dead, of the wife whose place is being taken by the stranger, speak in accord with all this? Will there not more likely rise up in his memory the scenes of that other day, the outgoing of that other wife—his mother? This bride is fair, but his mother's face was more rarely pale that day.

Many of these same guests were there. Their jests were neither so light nor so loud, but the clasp of their hands was closer and the bells rang then. Can he speak to the toast of this new bride when his heart is full of the other? Do not ask him. He sees the dark pall loom across the lights of revelry and through all the merry jest and compliment of the banquet rings a sound as of the far-off tolling of a bell. His face is set toward the feast but his heart turns backward to the funeral. So mine to-night. I turn my face to this fine, large building, with its wide halls and spacious rooms and artistic furnishings. This commodious structure which your intelligence and thrift have builded, and your affection and forethought are dedicating to your children, but my eyes are full of another picture. I have in my mind two other school houses—nay, three—for some of the boys are doubtless here. The grey-bearded boys of Carroll, who recall the old brick school house that stood between Baird's and Beckett's, that we attended under the tutilage of Mrs. Moses Arthurs, in the days when your honored citizen, T. H. Baird, Esq., was the jolly skipper of the steamer "Harlem," and the Hon. Geo. W. Lawrence was first taking his seat in the legislative halls of Pennsylvania. Not so spacious nor so handsome in your eyes as this one—the old double house where Captain R. F. Cooper led our bare feet over the thorny paths of primary learning, and the academy by the river where the gentle Morrison and Storer ruled up stairs and Mrs. Noble's dog "held savage sway below." "We may build more splendid habitations but we cannot buy with gold the old associations."

Build your new school house of the brightest bricks, lay the walls true and set angles square, adorn them with mullion and pilaster and buttress, but they will lack the lettering of the dear old names which made the walls of the double house and the academy read like a muster roll.

Call the rolls of the old schools over and hear how the scattered responses come from every quarter of the globe. That faithful historian, my beloved friend and brother, Dr. Van Voorhis, who loves to garner precious memories and indite on perpetual tablets the recollections of his native valley, gave in the exercises of your dedication two years ago a roll of the school boys, a few of whose names at least some of the "oldsters" here to-night will be glad to hear repeated.

"J. W. F. White," call that one softly, or peradventure a tipstave will take you into custody for contempt of court. White has gone from the wooden bench the Doctor mentions to the bench of the Common Pleas Court of Allegheny County. It is Judge White now.

"James Scott." Hear it echo out in Ohio. They hear of nothing but the Scott law there. "Jim Scott was one of the oldsters," as Frank, and Pat, and Orr, and John, and Mose, and Joe, were of the youngsters of your speaker's day. He had his training under the vigilant eyes and the kind and generous ministrations of the lamented Hazzard. He studied medicine and moved to Ohio, where no outsider can succeed, except a few from Washington county with the pith and fibre of these hills in their physique. He was elected to the legislature, represented his country at Honolulu for a term, came back, was again elected to the legislature, and is now famous as the author of the new law to tax the liquor traffic in that State. Coming from so healthy a community as this, it is wonderful how the boys who have gone out from these schools have ran to physic.

"A. J. Davis," of old Carroll stock, is a practicing physician in the community in which I teach.

"J. C. Cooper." He has for years been toning up the vital organs and regulating the digestion of a large circle of clients in Philadelphia.

"M. P. Morrison." The children of his schoolmates have been making wry faces at his rhubarb and jalap here in Monongahela for thirty years.

"W. H. King," there is no answer from his lips. He sleeps in the cemetery, but his name is famous among the foremost surgeons of Western Pennsylvania.

"Jas. M. H. Gordon," a physician and a soldier, has of late gone down to rest, and the glistening night dew now weeps o'er his churchyard pillow. Of our personal friends and playmates of a later generation, there is Cyrus King winning a name and competency in Allegheny City. George Linn, prosperous and domiciled under the very shadow of the hills over which we together loved to roam, and Thomas T. Williams, doctoring Democrats at White Cottage in the County of Greene. But I will not weary you by going over all the names that come thronging to my tongue. It would be but to tell you where your fathers and your uncles are. The boys of the past are the men of the present. They have rolled down their pantaloons and wear shoes now all the year round. We cannot claim them as boys now, but they have given us no reason to blush for them as men. They have done honor to their honest breeding; some in the physician's office, some in the counting room, some in the courts and many in the pulpit, for the schools of Monongahela city have given to the ministry some of the grandest, the noblest men that ever went out under the white banner of the son of God.

But there are those of my school fellows here to-night who have not preached, nor stirred the mystic potion in the Æsculapian chaldron and who may have plead in youth at other "Bars" than those of justice, who have yet acted well their part in this town of yours, to whom I give my warmest salutation. I may not name them, but you will recognize them as your foremost citizens, sitting at your Council Boards, and directors of your schools. They have given their best energies to the enhancement of the wealth and resources of their native town, have reared churches in amends for youthful irreverency and built school houses in expiation of their designs on those they may once have wished to burn. Very many of the old boys of the advanced class are gone : violets blossom now above the graves of the old masters. The old directors are dust. Pardon me if I have dwelt at wearisome length on these men of earlier days. It seemed to me that they should have a share in the words spoken here to-night.

> "Not to the living only be it said,
> But to the other living called the dead,
> Whose dear paternal images appear
> Not wrapped in gloom, but robed in sunshine here;
> Whose simple lives, complete and without flaw
> Were part and parcel of great nature's law.
> Who said not to their Lord, as if afraid,
> ' Here is thy talent in a napkin laid,'
> But labored in their sphere as men who live
> On the delight that work alone can give.
> Peace be to them ; eternal peace and rest,
> And the fulfillment of the great behest :
> ' Ye have been faithful over a few things,
> Over ten citiies shall ye reign as kings.'"

It was their lot to strike the axe into the edge of the wilderness, to pass along the way of life when ignorance sat at every gate, a blind and helpless Bartimeus. What in their light to see was given to their hands to do, they did it well. You who have clearer light to your eyes and more adequate machinery to your hands are expected to do better. They had the clay and the log, you have the brick and the plank. You have the wisdom that they taught you.

If I may be pardoned the personal comparison, they had the foot-prints of Chill Hazzard's bare-feet upon the school room floor, and the marks of the chewed paper wads upon the ceiling, you have his head joined to your councils, and the more powerful paper weapon which he wields now to aid you. Do not make the mistake of supposing that there is less necessity for work. Machinery will not run itself. Maps and globes of themselves will not teach anybody anything even in this fine school house. Do not go home after this dedication and sit down content that you have contributed so much money. You can stint and economise and lower the tax a little. A dollar paid out to support a public school is a dollar put at interest for the benefit of your children, and you owe it to them. You have brought them into this struggling, fighting world and they have a right to demand that you furnish them weapons forthwith. The old flint lock will not do. They were good enough in our father's day, but we require something better and our children will need the best. The old Concord coaches offered wonders in the way of speed to our ancestors, but we travel by steam now, and those who come after us are getting ready to do everything by electricity. Steam is too slow for them and they look to you to furnish the machinery.

You have done well to build this beautiful school house. You have done bravely, in view of your misfortune, in your last costly structure. But do not go home and canonize yourselves. You have done no more than your duty to your children, as your parents did by you. The future will belong, as every age has, to the educated men. By what you have done here as fathers and what will be done within these walls hereafter, you simply file your children's claim for a share in it. As citizens you pay your debt to the government which protects you by doing the best and most that within you lies to guarantee to your country an intelligent and patriotic citizenship in the future. The school house is the cornerstone of liberty and its bells chime the forward march of civilization and improvement. You have laid the one deep in the abiding rock and swung the other high to the winds of heaven. You have a right to be pleased with yourselves and with your work, and there is not one among this company who has more reason to be proud and gratified than I who owe so much to the early advantages which the liberality of your fathers gave me.

RE-DEDICATION OF THE SCHOOL HOUSE IN MONONGAHELA CITY.

The *Daily Republican* of September 28, 1883, gives an elaborate account of the dedication of this school house, re-built on the same site and embracing much of the brickwork of the one burned March 2, 1883. State Superintendent Higbee, J. D. Moffat, President of Washington and Jefferson College, Professor Lucky, Professor Douthett and Dr. J. S Van Voorhis, delivered very interesting addresses, in addition to Professor Fulton, inserted in full above. W. J. Alexander, President of the Board of Directors, before closing the exercises, remarked "that it was half-past ten o'clock and plenty of good dishes on the table not served. So in dire need he was compelled to close, having omitted several names from the programme, fortunatety, however, of gentlemen whose local residence will enable us to hear them again.

OLD TIME SCHOOL HOUSES.

On the old road in Fallowfield Township, Washington county, Pa., leading from Hair's old mill to the Pittsburgh and Brownsville State road, near where Dickey's school house lately stood, near the farm line of the late Moses Colvin may yet be seen a few relics of what was, over sixty years ago, an old dilapidated house, converted into a primitive school house It was erected of round oak logs, one story high ; about 18 by

20 feet in size, roofed with clap-boards held in place by what were called "weight poles" extending a little beyond the length of the roof ; these poles were kept at proper spaces apart by what were called "knees ;" these were pieces of timber either round or split, about 3 feet in length. The clap-boards were about 6 feet long and 6 inches wide, split like unshaven shingles of now-a-days, but of uniform thickness and width. The ceiling was laid loose with inch boards and the floor in the same manner. The space between the logs was filled with "puncheons" and the open space filled with clay mortar. The huge fire place was made of split logs, interlaid with flat stones laid at an angle of 45 degrees, and daubed with a mortar called "catan" clay. The chimney was "topped" out with split sticks plastered with the same kind of mortar. If the chimney smoked it was attributed to the wind "beating down." The door was hung on wooden hinges and made throughout without nails. The wooden latch with its flaxen string were the fastenings of every day use. But, to make secure, was accomplished by the wooden bolt which could only be displaced by a practised manipulation of the wire key made at the nearest blacksmith shop. The windows were on the sides, midway between the ceiling and the floor. They were made by taking out on each side a log for about two-thirds the length, and to keep out the cold and admit light, in the absence of glass, greased paper was used instead of panes of glass. The paper being more frequently used on account of its cheapness. Along these windows, fastened to the log wall, were the boards on which the advanced scholars did their writing. The benches used for seats for the scholars were made of split logs with the split side up—and no backs to lean against. The fire was a wood fire—no coal being yet used. Such is a meagre description of an old time school house, where, in old Fallowfield township, the older Moodys, Witherows, Colvins, Hairs, Van Voorhis', McComas', Powers, Evans and others were accustomed to congregate to be taught their first lessons of wisdom.

The younger generation of these fathers also "went to school" here, and among the least was the writer, who "went" his first day to school in this house, when Miss Crawford was "mistress" of the school. The lady teacher was then called mistress, not *schoolmarm*. In due course of time, this old-time school house had to be abandoned, and the friends of education in that vicinity, in order to have the school in a more central location, erected a house similar to the former on a three-cornered piece of ground donated for the purpose by the late Daniel Van Voorhis, near the residence of Van Shannon, near a double sugar tree, just before turning down the run, opposite the entrance into Shannon's barnyard. At that time this sugar tree was quite small, and it acted in a clear day as kind of timepiece, for when the shadow of the school house reached this tree it was time to "let out." The first teacher in this house was Thomas Heslep, of the well known family in "Horse Shoe." Here in this time-honored house William Colhoun taught for many years the youngsters of the older families. He was a good master, severe in his discipline but successful in *beating* what he did know into the minds of others. He was a great tobacco chewer and always had the floor near his seat well besmeared with the juice of the weed.

Life of William Colhoun.

William Colhoun was born in Donegal, Ireland, four miles from Letter-Keeney, June 10, 1796. He was a son of Andrew Colhoun, who was born, lived and died in the same house in which William was born. No one of the family except William ever came to this country. He emigrated to America in 1818. Sailed from Londonderry in May 7 of that year for Quebec, and was six weeks making the voyage. His destination was Chambersburg, Pennsylvania, where he had two uncles. They had built and were operating a paper mill in connection with a large store, in which he expected to obtain employment as a clerk. There being no large vessels to sail for Philadelphia for two or three weeks, his company, consisting of three persons, concluded to take a schooner.

The officers agreed to lash their baggage fast on deck and cover it with canvas. For a time all seemed well, but the little vessel was overtaken by storm and capsized off the coast of Nantucket, where it lay for twenty-six hours, the captain and sailors sticking to the rigging on the outside and within was the little company of passengers, among whom was an old sailor, who having found a hatchet, took in the situation, sailor-like, and in a short time had a plank cut from the bottom of the vessel, and from the opening thus made he ordered the company to pass to the outside, after which he had the hole stopped with bedding. He then cut off the mast and the vessel righted itself. Everything on deck was washed overboard and lost, together with its sails and mast. The vessel with its officers and little company of passengers floated at the will of the waves until the next day, when they were taken up and landed at Amboy, New Jersey. William Colhoun lost all he had except what he had on his person and a few guineas in his pocket. He had with him in his baggage $2,400 worth of linen. It was the custom for emigrants on leaving Ireland to invest their surplus money in fine linen and by coming through Canada they avoided the high duty to a good extent that would have been imposed on them in sailing directly to the United States. He made his way at once to his uncles, where he expected to find employment, but found most of the customers of the store were Dutch and required the service of a clerk to suit that vernacular.

Disappointed, but not discouraged, the young Irishman made rapid pace to his cousin William, in Clarksville, Greene county, in whose store he remained two years. At the expiration of this time, Samuel Clark, proprietor of the town, and his brother, Robert Clark, of Brownsville, sent him to New Orleans with a flat boat loaded with flour and whiskey. The late Captain Samuel Clark, son of the above Robert Clark, was one of the crew attached to the flat boat. They left Millsborough in February, 1821, and returned in due time, coming up on the first steamboat that ever run on the lower Mississippi; that being her second trip up. The boat could not get further than Louisville, at which point they embarked on a small boat for Cincinnati. Here they found the river too low for any boat, and they were compelled to buy horses on which they made the rest of the journey by way of Zanesville, where Colhoun had a cousin in the person of the wife of the Rev. Culbertson, a Presbyterian minister, with whom they tarried a day. On his return he obtained employment in the then small town of Washington as a clerk in the store of the late Alexander Reed, father of C. M. Reed, esq., who kept store on the same corner which his son now occupies. Colhoun now had his residence for the first time in Washington county. He was married in 1823 to Ruth Clark, daughter of John and Hannah Clark, who lived midway between Millsborough and Clarksville. She was born in the same township February 28, 1795. After close confinement in Reed's store for two years, William's health began to fail. Not being able to work at manual labor, the physicians advised him to teach a country school where he would be compelled to walk daily not less than five miles. As near as we can find out it was about this time he got married, and moved to a house on the farm of Mr. Harmon, near David Kerr's, on Pigeon creek, in which neighborhood he taught his first school. He in succession lived and taught school at Benjamin Parkinson's, near Dunningsville, at William Jones's, near Ginger Hill, and whilst living here he taught at the Dutch meeting house school house. From the farm of William Jones he moved to John McKelvey's, on Mingo, near John Witherow's, a brother of the late Samuel Witherow, who was the father of John Witherow, of the old blacksmith stand near Curtin school house. In the Spring of 1829 he moved to the old house that stood where the present residence of Robert Coulter now stands, then owned by the late Daniel Van Voorhis, and so long occupied by his son Abraham, now of Illinois. It was during this summer that he taught his first school in the famous old log school house near the present residence of Van Shannon, on Taylor's Run. This house was the first building erected especially for school purposes in all that neighborhood, and perhaps in all the old township of Fallowfield. The school houses generally in Western Pennsylvania at that time were "waste houses," unfit for any other purpose. This log house, was the successor of the old house that stood on the old road leading to Hair's mill, in which Thomas Heslep, of Horse Shoe, and a Miss Crawford taught. This first log school house was built by general consent, and subscription paid by labor in building it.

While teaching his first term in this house he boarded in the family of the late Daniel Van Voorhis; was one of the guests at the wedding of Newton Van Voorhis and Nancy Cooper, which took place May 28th, 1829. About this time Bowman Shepler was a terror in the neighborhood, in the way of mischief and tricks, especially on wedding occasions. He was invited to this wedding ostensibly as a relative, but really for the purpose of appeasing his mischief working propensities. Bowman was not slow to take in the situation, and the result was the taking off the cartwheels and concealing them, with the crowbar, which were not found until the mowing of the meadow in hay harvest. Colhoun's health began to decline while teaching in the old log house. The physicians advised him to seek some outdoor employment in the summer. Uncle Danny Van Voorhis, true to his inborn philanthrophy, came to his rescue, and offered him ground to farm. But he was no farmer. Uncle Danny says, "I will let you have horses to work with and you can get persons who owe you for schooling to plough for you until you learn how yourself."

The advice and aid were accepted and for years thereafter he did some farming in the summer and taught six months in the winter. His teaching was very well received, and especially in the old log house. His integrity and perfect honesty won for him the esteem of all with whom he came in contact. His deportment and influence as a teacher wielded no little power in moulding an educational spirit which in after years aided so much in the adoption of the public school system.

During his first teaching in the old log house, among the subscribers to the school none are now living.

Moses Colvin lived in the old house that stood near the late residence of his grandson, Jay Colvin. Stephen Colvin resided in the old stone house near Hair's old mill, owned by his son, Lewis Colvin, at his death. Alexander McAllister, father of William McAllister, lived on the farm now owned by Enoch Colvin. Simon Wilson resided in the old house which has given way to the beautiful mansion of John Wilson near the Horse-shoe Church. Philomen Boyle, the older, lived and died in the house recently occupied by his son Felix. Henry Spharr made his home on the farm now owned by our genial friend David L. Fournier. Robert Moody was a scholar—his father lived in the old house that stood near where Newton Van Voorhis now resides. Samuel Withrow carried on the blacksmithing at the stand where his son John now pursues the same business. Leech Loyd, Charles Behanna, and Edward Sprouls, the shoemaker, lived successively in the old log house that stood near the present residence of Van. Shannon, recently owned by Abe. Hull. Alex. Frazier, now deceased, of Rostravor township, Westmoreland county, had a blacksmith shop near Shannon's site, whilst Behanna lived in the old house. David Behanna, now of Catsburg, and Nelson Evans had the only fist fight that ever occurred in this school. It happened in some way during a game of town ball. During one winter Isaiah, son of Elwood Sprouls, had his leg broken whilst riding down the hill in a big sled. He was nicknamed Zedick, and was, and is no doubt to-day, if living, a queer fellow.

Zedick in some kind of a scuffle having bitten severely one of the scholars on the arm, concluded that it would be the better part of valor to escape the coming wrath of the master by absenting himself. For days he concealed himself in the old cabin just above the school house, neither going home nor to school. The boys at noon would start him up from his lair, and then chase him fox-like to the woods. He finally flanked his pursuers by returning and submitting to a severe whipping as a penalty for the wrong committed.

James Dickey sent his daughter Elizabeth to the Colhoun school, both in the old log and the Dickey house. His wife was a daughter of the late Daniel McComas, whose father, William McComas, came to this country from Maryland at a very early day. Dickey's wife had a brother who moved to Ohio many years ago. His wife is still living near Rex Mills, Muskingum county, Ohio, and though nearly one hundred years old, she has very distinct recollection of spinning flax in the family of Captain Daniel Van Voorhis ; of being present at the wedding of the older Colvins and Fryes, and more recently at the marriage of Newton Van Voorhis.

Among the patrons of the Colhoun school was Daniel Evans, the wagon maker, who lived on the old road that once led from Van Shannon's to John Wilson's. He was poor, but his son Dan and daughter Sarah were the most apt scholars in the school. The Crossans were scholars ; they lived in the old house that stood on the run not far below John Wilson.

Philip Crabb sent his sons Philip and Henry. Philip died many years ago. Henry married a Miss Mitchell and lives at Lock No. 4, surrounded by all the comforts of life, bearing the name of being one of the most skillful steamboat engineers on the western rivers. Abram Frye, better known as West's Abe Frye, was among the most liberal supporters. He lived, owned and kept tavern at the house now occupied by the heirs of the late Washington Cooper. His wife was Elizabeth, daughter of Samuel West, who lived near where Wm. Beazel now resides. They had nine children ; the three oldest were scholars, viz : Samuel, Orilla, and Mary Anna. Samuel married Nancy, daughter of the late Apollos Speers ; their daughter, Mary E., is the wife of Wm. H. Jackman, of Wayne Co., Ohio. Orilla married J. Brinton Nixon ; moved to Mount Union, Ohio, where she died in 1875, and he died in 1877. Mary Ann married Thos. Neblack in 1842. He died many years ago and his wife January 16, 1883. W. H. H. Degarmo seemed to be the orphan scholar and butt of the school. His marriage was a good one. His eldest son is a prominent minister in the Presbyterian church; the old gentleman is still living, and has been for many years a resident of the vicinity of Rex Mills, in Muskingum county, Ohio. William Colhoun having resided in the Horse Shoe neighborhood for over five years, most of which time he taught in the famous old log house, concluded to change his residence to the old house so long occupied by Isaac Frye before he emigrated to the west. This house stood near the present residence of Mrs. Tuman, in Fallowfield township. Whilst living here he taught in an old log house just below his residence, thus foregoing for one time his habit of walking a distance to school. This improvised school house was said to have been the primitive residence of the older Abraham Frye, who came to that vicinity in 1771 or thereabouts. Among his scholars here were such well known persons as Elder Samuel Frye, John Frye, Solomon Frye, the poet, Lucy Scott, now the wife of John Spahr, and after whom was named the beautiful village of Lucyville, on the Monongahela. The Cooper boys were also scholars, whose father, Valentine Cooper, resided on the farm where the late Thomas Redd lived, at the mouth of Maple Creek. Here Rezin Frye, now of Bellewood, received many a lesson that added much to his success in life. The next year William Colhoun moved to the Ringland farm, near Jonestown. Whilst living here he taught most of the time during the winter in an old log house that stood on the farm of the late Simeon Jackman, in Allen township. This house was of more modern style, being built of hewed logs. It was the same house in which Robert Gaily, the blacksmith, subsequently lived. It was situated very near the present residence of Addison Cummings. Robert Gaily married Rachel Spahr, sister of John Spahr. Having carried on the blacksmithing for some time at this stand, he concluded to move to Pittsburgh, where he met with more than ordinary success in his business. He subsequently moved to Clarion county, where in the oil business he accumulated a fortune. A few months ago he returned to the vicinity of his early life and is now in West Bellevernon.

Colhoun's next move was to the Peter Sheplar farm, on Maple creek, now owned by heirs of Esq. Swabe. The common school system was now in full operation, brick and stone houses taking the place of old waste houses for school purposes. The famous old house on the run had to give way to the Dickey house, on the Brownsville road. Colhoun taught more or less during three years in this house. He moved next in order to the farm of Jerome Grable, on Pigeon creek; taught two terms in the Greer McIlvain district; two terms in the Benjamin Dickey school house, near Ginger Hill, and the balance of the time, whilst living here, he taught at the Dickey house near Colvin's, referred to above, which was the outgrowth of the school he taught in the old log house, and around which cluster so many reminiscenses of the past. In 1844 he determined to leave the vicinity of his first love and those with whom he had so long associated as patrons and scholars. In the Spring of this year he moved to the Cook farm, near the old Brown Ferry, in Rostraver township, Westmoreland county. It is said that former tenants had so run down this farm that nothing but briars and other rubbish would grow on the soil. The people pitied Colhoun and said, "Why he will never pay his rent." Not long after his coming into their midst, some of the neighbors noticed day after day, the old gentleman and his boys tinkering, as they called it, for days in a field that former tenants had considered not worth ploughing. One day, a certain one now living, concluded to go over and see what all that kind of work meant. On coming to the field an unusual sight met his eyes. Briars, thorns, stumps, fence corners were torn in tatters and ready to be burned—the oldest boy was ploughing a furrow about six inches wide and ten inches deep, turning up a rich soil that had not been dreamed of in the philosophy of the former tenants. The neighborhood was astonished in the Fall at the wonderful crop; after that year he was regarded not only as the best school master, but that he could teach any man how to farm. Whilst living on this farm he taught more or less in the new school house over the Monongahela river, very near the old house in which he had taught when living in the house on Jackson Frye's farm. He walked, as usual, and crossed the river in his own skiff, which he kept locked not far above the present Rostraver coal works. He was quite a gunner, and very generally carried his fowling piece as he walked to school. One morning, as he drew near the river, he espied a flock of ducks. He fired into them, and was no little astonished to find that he had killed 10 at one shot. Henceforth he was reckoned a crack sportsman, as well as teacher and farmer.

Having by farming and teaching realized some means; his family also arriving at mature age, Colhoun became somewhat restless and determined to seek a new home in what was called at that time the West. In the Fall of 1849, he sought out and purchased from John Bigham 120 acres of land in Adams township, Geurnsey county, Ohio, to which he moved his family in the Spring of 1850. On this farm he lived until he died June 24, 1871. He died of cancer in the face. He never taught school in Ohio.

In early life he was rather erect in his stature, measuring in height perhaps five feet ten inches. He alway wore a swallow-tail coat, blue in color, and trimmed with brass buttons. His hair was dark and bushy, with toilet not always up to fashion. He was strikingly temperate as to ardent spirits, but an inveterate tobacco chewer. He had by constant habit worn out the Irish brogue, and pronounced the English emphatically correct. He was a fine penman, speller, and in arithmetic had no superior in his day. He was always a Democrat; never held any office; he refused all offices "both small or great;" he claimed that the general result of office was to give trouble and make enemies. His wife died April 30, 1881, on the old homestead in Adams township, Geurnsey county, Ohio, of old age.

They had eight children, viz: John, Maria, Jane, Rebecca, Ruth, Andrew, William and Elizabeth. Andrew married Jane Carr, of Ostrander, Delaware county, Ohio. He died February 1, 1865, in the same county, leaving two children. John married Tillie L. Monroe, and have no children. Jane married John Hutchinson and have had six children, of whom Ann died in 1879. Elizabeth married Geo. C. Duff; have no children. William married Jane Bean, of Ostrander, and have five children. In the spring of 1860 father Colhoun had purchased 227 acres of land near the village of Ostrander, in Sciota township, Delaware county, to which William and Andrew moved in 1860, and on which William and his unmarried sisters, Maria, Rebecca and Ruth, now live.

OLD TIME SCHOOLS.

Personally we were well acquainted with Colhoun, having been one of his scholars for several years. He taught in the school house above described for many terms, which extended from three to nine months. The terms were from one dollar and a half to two dollars for three months. The teacher boarding generally around among the patrons. For those who were unable to pay provision was made in the way of a poor fund assessed by law on the rich class. Taking up school at the appointed time was announced by calling out on the part of the teacher, "Books," in a loud tone, which was responded to promptly, and a tardiness to be in place was severely punished.

The books used in those days were the United States Spelling Book, the English Reader, the Introduction and Western Calculator. The scholars were well drilled in spelling, and the result was seen in the good spellers, that would cast into the shade the "new fangled" notions of teaching orthography now-a-days. The goose quill furnished the material from which the master made the pens for the scholars. The ink was home made from maple bark, sumac, white oak, &c., and occasionally appeared an ink made from what was called "ink powder," but it was regarded as an outside "material," not to be trusted, as it would *fade*. The home-made ink was supposed to be unfading, and it really seems so, as the writer has in his possession manuscripts thus written over one hundred years old and not any signs of fade. The paper used in olden times was unruled. It was ruled by a home-made ruler, so called, and a pencil manufactured impromptu from a bar of lead. Cyphering on the slate was done with a pencil obtained from the nearest soapstone. The rocks from which this material was taken was named the *slates*. The soapstone was chiseled into pencils with the famous "Barlow knife," or the "Elevy" knife, with a red bone handle, containing two blades. The latter was the rich man's son's knife. The copy was set by the master, whose competency was measured much according to his proficiency in making good pens and setting copies. The house was heated by a huge wood fire within the fireplace, the back wall and jams of which were well lined with stone and mortar so as to be secure from fire. This fireplace was about seven feet wide, so that quite large sticks of wood could be used as fuel.

Notwithstanding the open condition of the house, this fireplace afforded all the heat required to make the scholars comfortable. The female scholars were dressed in woolen frocks, long sleeved and close necked, with home-made stockings and upper leather shoes, whilst the boys were clothed in home-spun cloth and the comfortable flannel warmus, corresponding to the blouse of the present day. There was no recess in Colhoun's school but the usual hour at noon for amusements, which consisted in town's ball, corner ball, paddle ball and three-cornered cat. Black man's base, "pussy wants a corner" and such like were indulged in by both boys and girls. The playground, called the "camp," was the grove of sugar trees across the run from the school house, where can be seen stumps that mark the old bases of ball playing long ago. At the door, inside, was a paddle hung on a tow string, on the one side was pasted the word "in" and on the other the word "out," when, by permission, a scholar retired during school hours, the paddle was turned so as to show "out," and when the scholar returned, it was so changed as to show "in." The school was governed altogether by the physical force of the ferule and rod. Kind words were few and terror and fear reigned within every scholar, both great and small. It was within the code of honor that the teacher should, during Christmas and New Years' holidays, be "barred out," and allowed to regain his place in the school house on agreeing to treat to apples and gingerbread. The treat generally was only apples and they were distributed by throwing them helter-skelter over the floor. And such gingerbread, when it was given, the like of which can no more be produced, since old Grand-Daddy Rose and Mother Huttenour have gone. Master Colhoon one morning, just before Christmas, arrived at the door and found the latch-string pulled in and silence reigning within. He at once took in the situation; he was barred out. After rubbing his hands a moment, he at once resolved on *barring* the scholars in. Going to a near wood pile, he carried from thence huge logs, placed them against the door on the outside, which soon created no little commotion within, and in a short time the door was flung open —the scholars dispersed. The latch-string was again hung out and "Books" called, to which all responded, and thus ended the last barring out of Master Colhoon in the old school house.

The patrons of Colhoon's school were scattered over quite a large district, embracing many of the older families. Among these was Daniel Evans, the wagon and wheelbarrow maker; he lived on the old road leading from the late residence of Abe Hull to the old Horse Shoe Meeting House—a road long since abandoned. His sons Nelson, Daniel, Oliver and Simon, with the daughter, Sarah, were scholars. Nelson is still living as far as we know; the others left this country some fifty years ago. Daniel was very expert in figures, and was regarded by the school as well as by the neighborhood as a young man of extra talent, but as far as we can learn his after life did not crop out as was anticipated. Robert Moody, son of Samuel Moody, was a scholar. His father lived in the old house where now stands the residence of the late Newton Van Voorhis. Robert's father was a member of the old Horse Shoe Meeting House congregation, his name appearing on the subscription paper for the support of Dr. Ralston early as November 28, 1805.

Samuel Witherow was the blacksmith for more than half a century in that neighborhood, and was a son of William Witherow, of still earlier days. Samuel sent to this school his sons Noah, Alexander, John and Samuel Finley, besides two or three daughters. Alexander and Noah died many years ago. Finley, as he was called at school, is a shoemaker, residing on the Brownsville road near the paternal blacksmith-shop. John, after going through a long batchelorhood, married, and remains to-day a fixture at the old shop where successfully he still carries on the business after the manner of his father. This blacksmith shop has a widespread reputation, being one of the oldest in the neighborhood. It was a shop when iron and salt was transported from east of the mountains on horseback. Whenever iron and salt became scarce families associated in sending in turn a train of horses equipped with packsaddles, and thus the supply was kept up. With these exceptions all other things were raised or made at home. The use of iron was pretty much limited to horse shoeing and the making of what few nails the richer people might really need. Cast iron was used in the form of kettles required so much in the making of maple sugar—the only sugar then known to the inhabitants.

One of the Witherow girls married John Boyd and died years ago in Carroll township. Of the others we have no information. Philip Crabb sent his sons Henry and Philip. He lived in the old house above the residence of the late Esq. Swabb. The old gentleman was among the primitive market men to Williamsport. He did not often fail to go with his marketing on Saturday. He always wore a round-crowned, white wool hat, and carried his marketing in a round-bottom basket, on a horse which traveled in a half-trot pace. He owned for a long time the farm on which the late Isaac Teeple died—in Carroll township. Crabb died many years ago on the homestead in Fallowfield, leaving a widow who married Peter W. Shepler. His son Philip died not long after Colhoon quit teaching in that neighborhood. Henry became a steamboat engineer and has followed his trade on the Monongahela most of his life. He has earned the reputation of not only being an honest and upright man, but of being one of the most trustworthy engineers on the Monongahela or Ohio rivers. He married a Miss Mitchell and now resides at his own home, near Lock No. 4, in comfort and in the enjoyment of the good will of all those around him. His head is fast showing the effects of time and the exposure incident to his steamboat life.

Abraham Frye, generally known as "West's Abe. Frye," was another patron. He lived on the farm now owned by the heirs of Washington Cooper. He for many years kept a tavern which was known as the Fallowfield house, where the elections were held from time immemorial to us later day people. The private muster, too, was held here on the first Monday of May in each year. He had several sons and daughters who were scholars of the old school. Samuel, Abraham, Florilla and one other daughter, whose name the writer cannot recall. Florilla married J. Benton Nixon, and lived in Mount Union, Ohio, but whether living now we cannot say. Abe. Frye, the father, having moved to a house above Speers' ferry, his son Samuel courted and married Nancy Speers, daughter of the late Apollas Speers, granddaughter of Rev. Henry Speers and great-granddaughter of the older Henry Speers, who died near the present site of Bellevernon in 1773. Shortly after the marriage of Samuel the whole family removed to Sandusky, Ohio. The family seemed to have gone from memory in this country until a few years ago William Jackman returned to his father's homestead in Allen township, bringing with him his wife in the person of Mary daughter of Samuel Frye.

As Daniel Evans was the pride of the school, so was Harrison DeGarmo, its butt. Not as smart, perhaps, as some other scholars, he was the target for the rude in manner. He was picked at, teased and plagued without stint. He was always getting into trouble, was constantly under the eye of the teacher and often, no doubt, punished without deserving, yet the scholars were his friends. He carried his dinner in a reticule which was ample cause for trouble. This article of use conformed to the modern satchel. He was an orphan boy raised by one Jimmy Thompson, who lived in the house still standing below the residence of David L. Furnier. Harrison's after life cropped out far better than many who at school caused his young soul so much vexation. He married a lady named Dunlevy in the "Forks of Yough," passed through the late war as a soldier with honor and now lives with his son, H. C. DeGarmo, near Freeland, Muskingum county, Ohio. His wife died in 1887, and one of his sons was killed on the B. & O. Railroad not long after his mother's death. Salathiel, the oldest son, is a Presbyterian minister located somewhere in the West. He is poor but in respectable circumstances and awaiting patiently the gratitude of the government which, in due time, will grant him a justly merited annuity for his patriotic services.

The Crossan family lived in the old cabin which stood near the entrance to the residence of Wash. Shannon on Taylor's run, below the brick house of John Wilson. Robert and Thomas were scholars. The only peculiarity of the family consisted in having a drunkard's reputation and the story was common in school that the Crossans were raised on "mush and whisky."

The playground of this school was on the land of Moses Colvin, who sent his son Vincent and Jonathan Grant of his household to this school. Stephen Colvin lived in the stone house near Hare's old mill. His sons, Abraham and Stephen, with Sarah, Mary and Betsy, were among the scholars of Colhoon. David L. Furnier and sister Susan of the household of Henry Spharr were in this school. Henry Spharr lived on the farm on which David L. Furnier recently died. Furnier's wife was Betsy Colvin. John and Isabel Wilson were children of Simon Wilson who resided a long lifetime on the farm on which John lived and died, situated near the old Horseshoe meeting house. James and Elizabeth Dicky belonged to the school. Their father, James Dicky, resided most of his life on what was known in early days as the McComas farm near Witherow's shop. Edward Sprouls for a while lived in the old house where now stands the residence of one of the sons of the late Dutton Shannon. He was a shoemaker by trade and did the cobbling for most of his neighbors. His sons and daughters were scholars in the school. He finally settled near Bentleysville, where he died many years ago. Some of his family still are in the vicinity of that town. The Hairs, Van Voorhis and a host of others were patrons and scholars at this school, some of whom we will trace in a future part of this work. William Colhoon's successor in this school was a gentleman from the east, kind of semi-blooded Yankee named Joseph Styles, *Mister* not Master Styles. He wore a tall, white fur hat, a white starched dickey with high collar, kept in place about his neck with a stock made of satin and bristles buckled at the nape of the neck, a fine blue broad-cloth dress coat with brass buttons, and boots of calf-skin, made to shine with lampblack and white of an egg. In all that region he was the first to introduce the study of grammar and geography. His scholars in these branches were Daniel and Sarah Evans.

Schools in Later Days.

In the winter of 1834 the Legislature passed the act establishing our present system of public schools. Previous to that time the territory now embracing Monongahela City and Carroll township was included in Fallowfield, one of the original townships into which Washington county was divided at its formation, March 28, 1781. Carroll was formed September 30, 1834, from parts of Fallowfield and Nottingham townships; was originally called Knox, but the Court, Judge Thomas H. Baird, presiding, for some reason changed it to Carroll. This township embraced Williamsport, now Monongahela City, within its limits, as a school district. It remained thus a part of the township until the name of Williamsport was changed to that of Monongahela City, April 1, 1837.

Prior to the formation of Carroll the citizens of Williamsport, and the territory taken from Fallowfield, voted at the tavern of Abraham Frye, on the Brownsville road, beyond the Witherow blacksmith shop; but in the act creating Carroll, the elections were ordered to be held at the hotel then owned and kept by the late Joseph Hamilton, grandfather of the present editor of the *Republican*. At the first township election a board of school directors was elected, on whom devolved the altogether new duty of starting this system of schools, based on an equitable assessment of tax, out of which the cost of the schools were to be paid. We can only recall the names of David Williams and Isaac Van Voorhis as original members of that board. The directors for the time being divided the new township into convenient districts, as required by the law, using whatever buildings could be obtained for schoolhouses. An old log house which stood in a field to the left of the road leading from Taylor's run to Wm. Galbraith's, furnished one, where a one-armed man was teacher for the first term; being barred out, as was the custom, he forced an entrance through the clapboard roof and settled the boys with a severe "overgoing." It was a rule that if a master once gained admission he could not again be barred out during the term.

This master was a severe but successful teacher, introducing some new practical ideas that were not dreamed of in old time philosophy. On the hill, above the late Wm. Blythe's residence, may yet be seen traces of an old log cabin, which being condemned by common consent as unfit for any other use, was secured for a school house. It was then owned by James K. Marshall. It was a retired spot, not even a road, much less a house within sight; no wonder the proprietor was constantly complaining of the depredations of the boys. In this waste cabin an Irishman named Lewis and another man of the name of Sampson were teachers for a time. Lewis was Irish indeed, and his scholars were prone to follow his *twang* and call have have, sounding the *a* long instead *a* short. His great failing, however, was his inclination to drink too much strong drink. Sam son was a strong, sober man overrunning with conceit, wherewithal not a bad teacher. Among the scholars at this school were James Marshall, now dead, long a resident of Beaver county in after years; his brother, John, now living in the same vicinity where he was born; Capt. Robert Philips, a well known steamboat man and long a citizen of Monongahela city; McCarty and Thomas Williams, W. J. Markell, the Stockdale boys and girls, the families of Abram and Isaac Van Voorhis. The town of Williamsport was divided into two districts. The upper end attended school in a frame house still standing near where Keller's foundry stood in after years. For one term at least Thos. Collins, Esq., was the teacher. The scholars from the lower end of the town attended school in the old Methodist Church near the present wharf; the building since converted into a dwelling and finally demolished. At that time only a few persons were on what has always been known as the Island, besides those connected with the glass works on the point, traces of which still remain.

The brick row now owned by Wm. Coulter was not yet built. The old frame building opposite this row was the brewery of Samuel Devore. The old frame house near the school house referred to was the residence of the widow of the late Elias Watkins, who was a brother of the first wife of Abraham Van Voorhis. The old frame house, burned years ago, above the brick, known in early days as the Swartz house, was the residence of Asher Van Kirk, who carried on the chairmaking business. The old tavern house near the mouth of the creek was among the first buildings on the island after its sale to James Manown. By this sale the ferry went into the hands of James Manown and was no longer the Parkison Ferry. After grave consideration the Carroll board of directors determined to erect in each sub-district a stone or brick school house. The Harlem house on the Judge Baird farm, the Columbia, the Horse Shoe, on the road from the Baptist church to Columbia, the stone house at the forks of the road above Markell's distillery, one near Ginger Hill, one on the farm of Samuel Keenan, one on the farm of Isaac Van Voorhis, the double house adjoining the old Presbyterian church in Williamsport and the one on the island, long since passed into the river, were the houses erected under the resolution. The one in Catzburg was afterwards determined upon, as the population increased. It may be that a house was built near the Dutch meeting house under the first resolution. The stone school house, now converted into a two-storied dwelling, was built by Elgy Van Voorhis, now an extensive farmer and cattle dealer in Greene county. The plastering was done by Col. A. T. Gregg, who taught the first school in the house. The one on the farm of Van Voorhis was built by the late David Phillips, brother of Capt. Robert Phillips; the price was $200.00. Cheapness was the great desideratum in building, and the history of these houses attested the impolicy of such an idea. These houses as to comfort were in advance of their predecessors, having board seats and glass in the windows, with shutters, also a chimney for a stove, an innovation on the time-honored fireplace. The people as well as directors began to select teachers in some measure on account of their qualifications, although no formal examination was required. The next series of school houses in this township was frame, excepting the stone one on the Brownsville road near the residence of the late Francis Nelson.

HORSE SHOE BOTTOM CHURCH, WILLIAMSPORT (MONONGAHELA CITY.)

From the Centennial sermon preached by the Rev. W. O. Campbell, July 2, 1876, we make the following extracts as published in the *Valley Record* of July 15, 1876:

We are informed that one of the peculiarities of Presbyterianism in Western Pennsylvania, about the time when this government was inaugurated, was its rural character. The people were an agricultural people. They cleared out the wilderness, they tilled the soil, they pursued the same avocation here that they had followed at home. The first Presbyterian churches were not established in the nucleus of the towns and cities, but in the country places. The Horseshoe Bottom Church, of which this is regarded as the true linial descendant, was built in 1785, three and a half miles from this place, on the ridge road leading to Brownsville, on a farm owned by Simon Wilson. It was a log church and additions were made to it until it had sixteen corners; part of its foundation is still visible. When that church was built "there was not a church or chapel, preacher or priest of any kind in the City of Pittsburgh," although the city had been partially laid out since 1765. The Church of Horseshoe Bottom preceded the First Church of Pittsburgh by one year. But the country churches of Montour's Raccoon, Cross Creek Buffalo, Chartiers and Pigeon Creek were then large and flourishing. The ministers residing in the country occasionally supplied the viliages and hamlets with preaching. The only Presbytery in this part of the county was the Presbytery of Redstone. There was no village from Pittsburgh to Brownsville, and none from Pittsburgh to Wheeling, except a small hamlet at Beaver. The first record history gives us of this church is found in the minutes of the meeting of the Presbytery of Redstone, held at Pigeon Creek in 1786, one year after the Horseshoe Bottom Church was built, and is as follows: "The Presbytery conceive that the supplication of Mingo Creek, Horseshoe Bottom and Pike Run congregations for a man to preside in drawing up a call for Mr. H. Morrison, Jr., cannot be granted for the reason that they are entire strangers to Mr. Morrison, and know not whether ever he was regularly licensed to preach the gospel, nor has he shown his credentials to any member of the Presbytery." In 1789 the first General Assembly held its meeting, composed of twenty-three ministers and elders, and had for its moderator, Dr. John Witherspoon. Again, October 16th, 1792, this church, in conjunction with Mingo Creek, presented a call to the Rev. William Swan, which was declined. Another call was made out for Rev. Mr. Mercer in 1793, which appears to have been as unsuccessful as the others. In that year the Presbytery of Ohio was formed out of portion of the Presbytery of Redstone, and this church was transferred to it. While it was without a pastor it was supplied occasionally by members of the Presbytery. The Rev. Samuel Ralston, D. D., received a call from this and the Mingo Creek congregation in November, 1796, which he accepted. In 1807 the organization was transferred to Williamsport, as this place was then called. About this time Mr. James Hair was chosen the first elder of the church. Dr. Ralston preached his first sermon in a small school house which stood in the rear of the church building that was occupied before we came to this one. He preached two years in that house in the winter season; in summer he preached in a tent in what was known as Bentley's sugar grove. In 1815 it was resolved to build a small brick church 31x35 feet, on the hill just above the church building lately occupied. In 1816, April 20th, the services of Dr. Ralston were secured for one-third of his time. In August, 1816, the first communion was held in the new church, the pastor being assisted by Rev. Matthew Brown, D. D., and the elder by Mr. Benjamin Williams, of Mingo; forty-five members sat down at the table of the Lord. In the same month Messrs. James McGrew, Jesse Martin and Robert McFarland were elected and ordained elders. James McGrew died in 1855, September 26th, aged 80, having served thirty-nine years. Jesse Martin died May 27th, 1848, having served thirty-two years. Robert McFarland died in 1835, having served nineteen years. James Hair died in 1826, having served about twenty years. The first Sabbath-school held in this town was organized by Jesse Martin and James Gordan, who reported July 25th, 1823, about 100 scholars. In 1834 Dr. Ralston resigned his charge here and gave all his time to Mingo. He preached here and at Horseshoe thirty-eight years. At a meeting of the Presbytery of Ohio, at Mingo Church, April 20th, 1837, the name of this church was changed to that of the First Presbyterian Church of Monongahela City.

Dr. Ralston died Sept. 25th, 1851, being 94 years old, a

man of logical mind and good classical and scholarly attainments, of great faith and power. This church owes much gratitude, praise and love to the memory of this good man, and to the memory of those good elders who have long since gone to their reward for the labors and sacrifices in its behalf. Dr. Ralston was succeeded by Rev. Mr. Moore, a stated supply, who labored here about six months. On July 30th, 1835, at a congregational meeting, of which Aaron Kerr was chairman and Joseph Wilson secretary, it was unanimously resolved that a new church building should be erected, and a committee composed of James Gordan, Esq., James Manown, Esq., and Jesse Martin was appointed to procure a lot for the purpose. The committee appointed to take subscriptions for the new church was composed of Samuel Hill, Esq., Isaac Van Voorhis, James Mercer, Dr. Biddle and Jesse Applegate. The building committee was James Gordan, Esq., James McGrew, Esq., and Samuel Hill, Esq. Mr. Hill becoming the contractor for the building was, at his own request, removed and James Manown, Esq., substituted in his place. The cost of the building was $2.100. The dedication sermon was preached by Rev. Dr. Elliott, of the Western Theological Seminary. Rev. Geo. D. Porter began preaching to the congregation two-thirds of his time Oct. 15th, 1835. Feb. 12th, 1836, Mr. Aaron Kerr was installed, and Messrs. Isaac VanVoorhis and James Gordan were ordained and installed elders. Mr. Kerr afterwards removed to Cross Creek, and died June 1st, 1866, being 86 years old. Mr. Van Voorhis died June 4th, 1875, in the 82nd year of his age, known to us as a good man full of faith and the Holy Ghost. Mr. Porter ceased preaching here in February, 1838. The Rev. Mr. Chambers succeeded him as stated supply, remaining about six months. Oct. 28th, 1839, Rev. Jno. Kerr was invited to take the pastoral charge of the congregation two-thirds of his time. He was ordained and installed April 22nd, 1840, and remained until April, 1862, a period of 22 years. During this time the church grew from a membership of 90 to 205, the years of greatest increase being in 1842 thirty-six members, in 1848 forty, in 1857 twenty-seven. In 1843 Mr. Henry Fulton was elected and installed elder. He afterwards removed to Washington, and died April 13th, 1869, aged 85 years. June 29th, 1857, the following persons were installed elders: Messrs. Jos. Kiddoo, John Power and James Dickey. Mr. James Curry was ordained elder at the same time. Mr. Dickey died Sept. 9th, 1864, and Mr. Kiddoo Aug. 11th, 1870. April 7th, 1862, a call was made out for the services of Rev. S. G. Dunlap. He was installed Dec. 6th, 1862, and remained pastor until Sept. 29th, 1866, about four years. Under his ministrations fifty-five were added on examination in 1863 and twenty-eight in 1864. Mr. Dunlap died in 1871 at Orrville, Ohio. Dec. 6th, 1862, Mr. E. W. Tower was installed, and Messrs. John Wright, Francis I. Gardner and David Moore were ordained elders of the church. Mr. Tower was drowned in the Monongahela River Feb. 19th, 1869, and Mr. Moore died May 11th, 1867. Dec. 30th, 1866, the congregation voted a call to Rev. J. S. Stuchell, who was installed May 10th, 1867, and continued pastor until April 1st, 1870, a period of three years. Mr. Stuchell died Oct. 1875. Oct. 26th, 1867, Messrs. Wm. C. Shaw, D. D. Yohe and Samuel Hindman were ordained elders. Mr. Yohe died Aug. 7th, 1868. Oct. 1st, 1871, a call was made out for the present pastor. He began his labors as pastor elect Oct. 16th, was installed Nov. 6th, 1871. At a congregational meeting held January 20th, 1868, it was resolved to build a new house of worship, and committees were appointed to procure a site and solicit subscriptions. The building committee were Messrs. Aaron Brawdy, H. H. Finley, T. R. Hazzard, Esq., John Patterson, James Stockdale, Wm. J. Alexander, Jas. H. VanVoorhis and Francis I. Gardner. The present house of worship was built at a total cost of about $32,000.00. The lecture room was dedicated by divine service March 17th, 1872, the first sermon being in the text John 2, 19. The house was brought to its present state of completion the next year, and dedicated June 8th, 1873, the pastor

The Old and New Monongahela. 65

preaching the sermon from Is. 56, 7, and Mark 11, 17. He was assisted in the service by the other pastors of the town, also by his predecessor, Rev. J. S. Stuchell, who preached in the evening. Messrs. Jas. Van Voorhis and John Patterson were elected and ordained, and Mr. Hindman was installed elder January 21st, 1872. During the present pastorate the new church building has been built and dedicated to God, 50 members have been received on profession of faith and 83 on certificate, making a total of 133, an average of 22 each year; a Ladies' Foreign Missionary Society has been organized and maintained with a good degree of success; the contributions to the Boards of the church have been increasing, the greatest amount ever given by this church being that given last year, $755. The years which came nearest to that were 1853–'54 and '55. The contribution of 1853 was $680, that of '54 $535, that of '55 $736. The growth of the church in spirituality, in the knowledge of the truth, and in grace, in harmony and peace, in stability and strength, has, I think, been manifest; the attendance upon the Sabbath day is increased in numbers and regularity. While the prayer meeting is not at all what it should be, we have both reason to regret the poor progress we have made and we have reason to rejoice at the good progress made. We may bless God and go forward. When we think of the condition of the church as it was six years ago, its divisions, its despondency, its depression, the poverty of its sanctuary, and look upon this church and congregation, its unity, its united strength, its increased powers of endurance, the every way improved aspect of its life, its increased interest in and attention to the word, its beautiful house of worship, why we can scarcely recognize our old selves. Yet our progress is not such as we should have made, and our ongoings are not so great as our short comings. But notwithstanding we have great reason for gratitude to God, and for encouragement for the future.

In two days more forty millions of people will rejoice over the one hundredth anniversary of this Nation's birth. Before another Sabbath the Nation will have entered on the second century of its career. The State and Church, entirely separate in their organization, happily they are not separate in their sympathy, they are not here as elsewhere antagonistic. Sundered in organization each has to acknowledge that it has received many blessings from the other. Happy the church which is so entirely left to the enjoyment of its liberties and the free exercise of its consecrated powers; happy the state that has received so many benign influences from the religion of the church; happy the people that are so untrammeled as we in the enjoyment of our liberties and the exercise of all lawful powers! We will search the pages of history in vain to find a Nation that has entered upon its second century with so fair a prospect, with so rich an inheritance. When we remember our forefathers who wrought so wisely, who fought so manfully, devout be our gratitude to God who inspired them with wisdom and courage. Let us be consecrated anew to the cause of that religion which gave us, and which alone can perpetuate so great liberties.

NOTE.—Alexander Wilson was installed an elder in 1840. He came from the First Church of Minersville, Allegheny county, over which Rev. S. M. Sparks presided. He was for many years the Superintendent of the Sabbath School and was mainly instrumental in building it up.

Rev. W. F. Hamilton, nephew of Samuel Ralston, D. D , and now Professor in Washington and Jefferson College, was here as a supply during Rev. John Kerr's absence in the south, about the year 1851.

Rev. James P. Fulton, son of elder Henry Fulton, was also in charge of the church as supply in 1850.

Rev. W. O. Campbell, who was installed pastor of this church November 16, 1871, resigned his pastorate, and, on the 2d day of February, 1886, Rev. Jas. M. Maxwell was called, and on June 6, 1886, was duly installed.

REV. JOHN KERR.

[Written for the REPUBLICAN by request.]

Although not unexpected, our citizens were startled at the announcement on Monday of the death on Sabbath morning,

March 20, 1892, of Rev. John Kerr, which occurred at his home in Parnassus, Westmoreland county, Pa. He was the oldest minister, as to ordination, in the Allegheny Presbytery.

Rev. John Kerr was the son of James Kerr, who came from Northampton county to Washington county in 1800. He was married to Hannah Mason in 1803. The deceased was their fifth child, and was born in Florence, Washington county, Pa., December 25, 1813. He commenced his classical studies in the fall of 1828, in the private school of Thomas Levingston, near Florence, Pa. He was a student in the Cross Creek Academy for three sessions; he entered Washington College in the autumn of 1830, in the Freshman Class; graduated in 1834, and immediately entered the Western Theological Seminary. During the next winter he took charge of the New London Academy in Chester county, Pa. Mr. Kerr also assisted during the winter of 1837–8 in the Florence Academy. In October, 1838, he was licensed to preach by the Presbytery of Washington at its meeting in Cross Creek. During the winter after he was licensed he supplied various vacant churches, especially the Mill Creek Church, where he was urged to accept a call which he declined, preferring to take charge of the Kittanning Academy, preaching in the meantime at Manor, Crooked Creek and Apollo. Calls was presented at the fall meeting of Presbytery from that field and Monongahela City. The latter call he accepted, and was ordained and installed pastor of this church by the Presbytery of Ohio, April 22, 1840. He labored in the Monongahela City church for twenty-two years, declining in the meantime a call from the Fourth Church of Pittsburgh. He declined especially on account of the strong and united remonstrance against his removal to any other field of labor. In 1862 he resigned his pastorate. During his labors in this church the membership increased from 90 to 205.

His next field was as stated supply, and pastor-elect for three years, of the church of Raccoon. He declined this call in order to engage in city mission work under the care of the Pittsburgh Presbytery, in which he continued until

December 14, 1869. January 17, 1872, he was installed pastor of the Valley Church, Allegheny, from which charge he was released in July, 1874, and removed to his late residence.

In later years he supplied different churches up the Allegheny, and by his personal efforts several new church buildings were erected, the last one being at Natrona, where, said he, "I expect to finish my mission and ministerial work on earth." He was married in April, 1840, to Miss Anne B. Campbell, daughter of the Rev. Allen D. Campbell. The deceased was the father of six children: B. B. Kerr, Allen C. Kerr and J. M. Kerr, all in business in Pittsburgh. Thomas Kerr is an attorney in New York; John Kerr is a minister in Joliet, Ill.; his daughter Ella married Rev. J. E. Wright, of Germantown, Pa., and his daughter Euphemia is deceased. She was the wife of Dr. C. B. King, a native of this city.

We can hardly realize that the friend and preacher of our youth has passed away—he whom everybody loved. During his pastorate in this city, he was held in high esteem by old and young. He was not only valued as a minister but equally so as a citizen and Christian gentleman. His heart and feelings were warm, and his disposition so mild and pliable that none feared to approach him. Settling in this city amidst the exciting times of 1840, he never failed to do well his work as a minister of the gospel, so as to hold together in unity his co-workers and church membership. He had around him as advisers such men as elders Gordon, McGrew, Martin, Van Voorhis, Fulton, Wilson, Kiddoo and Power. They, too, have all passed away excepting Power, and are to-day enjoying together the glories of the immortal state. He not only identified himself with the interests of the church, but incorporated himself and his interests into everything that tended to advance the good of his adopted city and neighborhood. The twelve members of his graduating class are deceased, we think, excepting Rev. Hamilton, the Indian missionary. Among the class was such names as Prof. Murry, Dr. W. L. Lafferty, E. S. Graham and Robert Woods.

The wife of the deceased survives him. The remains were interred in the Allegheny cemetery. Blessed be the memory of such a man. For much of this sketch we are indebted to the College Annual and to a personal interview with the deceased not many years ago. V.

THE CHURCH ON THE HILL.

At 11 o'clock A. M., Sabbath day, over sixty years ago, let us enter the old brick Presbyterian Church on the hill, standing in about the centre of the graveyard lot, and take in the surroundings. The edifice was nearly square ; the carpenter work was done by Benjamin Ferguson, and the interior was finished with pine, unpainted; the inside was divided by aisles, one running up and down the river from door to door and one leading from the door, fronting the river, back to the pulpit; on the right and left in going in from the inner door the seats were at right angles until reaching the main aisle running from the doors, where the seats were at angles to this aisle. The pews, as they are now called, had doors on the end next the aisle; the owner of, at least one, kept his pew locked, and on one occasion, having forgotten his key, had, to his own discomfiture, jump into his seat. The pulpit was high toward the ceiling, and a stairway on each side leading to the interior, where a smoothly planed pine boat-seat furnished accommodations to the preacher or preachers ; cushioned chairs and sofas were unknown quantities. The acoustic facilities of an audience room were then believed to be in the height of the pulpit or platform, having no ideas of the angles of incidence and reflection. In front of the pulpit was located the *clark's* desk. Benjamin Furguson was "clark" for a long time. At the proper time he would rise up, place his elbow on the front of the desk, holding in his hand Watt's hymn-book, line out the hymn and start the singing in which all joined in spirit if not with understanding, believing singing to be an essential part of worship. Mr. Ferguson removed west before the old church disappeared, leaving behind a name cherished by all who knew him.

In a seat on the right and in front of the pulpit was Aaron Kerr and his family. The old gentleman, leaning on his ivory-headed cane, occupied the outer end of the pew, so as to give his stiff limb more comfort by extending it into the aisle. His family consisted of his wife and several sons and daughters. He was for years a member of the legislature from Washington county. During his legislative career he acquired something of a reputation in a little speech in which he declared boldly that "a man should not be disfranchised because he had a black streak down his back." This expression at that time was condemned, but its outcropping has been the adoption of universal suffrage, without respect to race or color. He was a member of the Constitutional Convention of 1838, and was highly esteemed. He was installed as an elder in this church February 12, 1836, when James Gordon and Isaac Van Voorhis were ordained and installed.

Many years ago he removed to Cross Creek, where he died June 1, 1866. His oldest daughter, Susan, was first married to a Dr. Todd, of West Newton, Penn'a., and her last husband was Jesse Applegate, of Allegheny county. She died in Claysville, Pa., February 23, 1884. His daughter Phœbe married James G. Hair, who died at Claysville, Pa., August 10, 1885. She still lives. Amanda married a Rev. Reed, who died many years ago, leaving a daughter Lizzie, who married John McCullough, who was a son of Hon. James McCullough, of Canonsburg, Pa. Amanda was married to a Mr. Hanna as her second husband. They are both dead.

Aaron H. Kerr, son of A. Kerr, studied Latin and Greek with Prof. J. D. Mason in this old church, and subsequently with Prof. J. P. Thompson, in the old carriage factory, in an upstairs room. Among the students in this academy were Rev. John McFarland, who died years ago in Greenfield, Dade county, Mo.; Abram Underwood, lately deceased; Dr. A. J. Davis, of East End, Pittsburgh; Francis Gardner, of Forward township, Allegheny county; Dr. J. H. Storer, of Treadelphia, West Va.; Dr. J. H. Manown, of Kingwood, West Va.; Dr.

J. S. Van Voorhis, of Bellevernon, Fayette county; J. S. Morrison, now deceased, a distinguished member of the Pittsburgh bar; Dr. James C. Fleming, of Franklin, Ohio; Robert Officer, of Baltimore, and S. B. Bently, of Monongahela City. A. H. Kerr graduated in old Jefferson College, in the class of 1843, and also was a graduate of the Western Theological Seminary, died February 27, 1890, in Minnesota. He was a distinguished educator, and minister of St. Peter's, Minnesota. Hampton was another son of Aaron Kerr. He was long a successful merchant of Cross Creek, Washington county, and died a few years since in that place. Joseph was another son of Aaron Kerr. He died April 11, 1891, at Chicago, Illinois.

Isaac Van Voorhis and John Hair, with their families, occupied the back seat to the left of the pulpit. Of these we will have more to say in another part of this work. Just in front of their seat the venerable form of Grand-daddy McCain, with his family, could be seen. The family have all passed to the better land. Margaret married James Hull, who lived for many years in the old log house which stood near the present dwelling of Wm. Booth, on Taylor's Run, in Carroll. For a few years prior to his death, which took place in 1848, he lived on the farm recently owned by his son Abram in Fallowfield, now in possession of one of the Shannon boys. Hugh McCain was a blacksmith, had his shop, in 1834, on Second street, above the People's bank; but, in after years, had it in Catzburg, where he died many years since. Henry McCain was a stiller by trade, and as such worked many winter seasons for the late Isaac Van Voorhis in the old log still-house that stood on the present farm of John Van Voorhis, in Carroll.

The later history of the old Horseshoe Bottom Congregation and the early history of the Williamsport Meeting House congregation, were so intimately interwoven that their interests were for a time identical. This was especially true in a financial way. William Irwin, of Parkison's Ferry, took an important part, with Michael Power and Samuel Moody, in managing the money matters. Among the archives of that old church is the following subscription paper. Some of the names are written in the subscriber's own writing and others not:

November the 28, 1805.

James Prine	$2 50
Robert Williams	2 50
Daniel Vorehas	3 00
Henry Blythe	1 50
Moses Carr	2 00
William Witherow	2 00
William Fenton	2 17
Jacob Crabs	2 00

Subscribed December 19, 806.

James Hair	$3 00
William Prian	1 00
John Foraker	1 00

Then is added below a subscription in pounds, shillings and pence:

Henry Shepler	17s.	6d.
James McKnight	7s.	6d.
Hannah Power	18s.	9d.
John Power	18s.	9d.
Jen McCutcheon	7s.	6d.

On the back of this paper is written, in Dr. Ralston's own writing, the following: "April 5th, 1806. Received from Samuel Moody seven pound, one shilling and ten pence one half penny in stipends for the year 1805." Elder James Hair had, during the summer of 1806, removed from Berkeley county, Va., and among his first duties was to subscribe to the support of the gospel and deposit the certificate of himself and wife from the church of Middletown, under the signature of Father Joseph Glass, pastor. From this period to 1811, we have no record of either the spiritual or financial condition of the congregation, only that in some way, or by some means, the place of preaching was changed to Parkison's Ferry.

In the old Horse Shoe Church there was no pew rent, but the subscriptions were called stipends and pronounced "*stee-pins*." Seats were free to all, but each family was naturally inclined to occupy the same seat, and hence gradually was originated the idea of families each renting by the year a seat called "pews" first in the old church on the hill, where the pew-rent system was adopted. As Esq. Hair was one of the giants in the Williamsport congregation, so Michael Power was the *giant* in the old Horse Shoe Church, where, during his life, he delighted to worship. He lived on the high hill above the residence of one of the Shannons, on a part of the farm now owned by the heirs of Moses Colvin, deceased. His barn standing on the highest part of the hill, shortly before his death, was burned with all its contents. On hearing of the fire, Dr. Ralston remarked to a friend that "the individual who fired that sainted man's barn would die on the gallows." Subsequent events in the eyes of the neighborhood verified the prediction. His remains, together with a countless host of other earlier settlers, lie in the graveyard adjoining the old church. Wm. Irwin, although living in Parkison's Ferry, took an active part in the old Horse Shoe congregation, and was permitted to see the church on the hill grow in number and spiritual strength, and for years in it he occupied a pew. He built and resided for some years in the brick house now occupied as a boarding house by Mrs. Kerr on Main street in Monongahela City. This house was built on Lot No. 1 in the original plan of the town, and it was the first brick house in the town. In what year it was built we cannot say, but we think in 1802. William Witherow was a cooper by trade and followed his occupation in a shop not far from the present residence of his grandson, John Witherow, in Fallowfield. Whiskey barrels, churns, buckets, tubs, wash tubs and *phlakestands* for still-houses were the kind of vessels generally made. Flour and apple barrels were in little demand.

We have as early as September 17, 1814, a record that shows he was a cooper, in our possession, being an old account book. He was the father of Samuel, David, Benjamin and James. Samuel was the father of John Witherow, the well-known blacksmith on the Brownsville road. He was a blacksmith, as well as his son John. who still holds the old shop and is one of the substantial fixtures in Fallowfield.

Henry Shepler was another old Horseshoe subscriber. He lived and died on the farm now owned by Wm. Rogers on Maple creek. His wife was the daughter of the older Samuel Frye. Shepler, with his brother-in-law. Samuel Frye, owned the old mill on Maple creek, where now stands the mill of Henry Cooper. Shepler had two sons. Bowman, celebrated for his love of mischief, moved west long ago, where he died. Peter lived on the farm now owned by the heirs of Wm. Swab, on Maple creek. He removed west about 1860, and has been dead many years.

Rev. Aaron Harvey Kerr

Died at Rochester, Minnesota, February 27th, 1890. He was born in Washington county, Pa., January 1st, 1819. His father was the late Aaron Kerr, Esq., who for so many years represented Washington county in the Legislature, and who for years kept store and lived in the brick house on Main street in Monongahela City, now owned by Mrs. Stuart, nearly opposite the Episcopal church. The deceased was familiarly known as Harvey. He was a brother of Rev. Joseph Kerr, of Fairfield, Iowa, of Hampton Kerr, of Cross Creek, Washington county, Pa. He was also a brother of Mrs. Susan Applegate, Mrs. Phœbe Hair and Mrs. Amanda Hanna, all well known in this community.

Harvey was a student of the academy taught by Rev. J. D. Mason, in the old church on the hill, and of the academy of J. P. Thomson, in the old carriage factory. He graduated from Jefferson College in the Class of 1843, studied theology in the Western Theological Seminary, was licensed by the Presbytery of Ohio, April, 1846, He preached as a pioneer in many of the early churches of the west, and was for a time connected with the educational interests of St. Peter's, Minnesota. He was married October 13, 1847, to Elizabeth, daughter of the late Hon. Walter Craig, of Cross Creek, Washington county, Pa. The writer of this article was a schoolmate at the Old Factory school, and knew him well. In youth he was a man of fine physical appearance, tall, erect. and full of vigorous nerve, fond of a joke, but always carried his religion with him. He was one of the good of his day, and his many friends of fifty years ago, will learn of his death with regret. He was not only a soldier of the late war,, but a soldier nearly all his life in the army of the Lord. Blessed be his memory.

[From the DAILY REPUBLICAN, July 3, 1888.]

REMINISCENCES OF 1840.

Last Sunday's *Leader* is quite off on its guess work history of the Harrisons, as it relates to Western Pennsylvania, in the campaign of 1840. It speaks of Andrew Jackson Ogle as "Spooney Ogle," who earned a national reputation by exposing the extravagance of the White House in Van Buren's day. It was Charles Ogle, an uncle of Jack Ogle. In 1840 Jack Ogle was not a full grown man. He made his first speech from the balcony of the Monongahela House, in Pittsburgh, in 1844, in favor of Henry Clay. He was elected to Congress from the Somerset, Fayette and Greene district in 1848, defeating John L. Dawson. In 1850 he in turn was defeated by Dawson. He was appointed by Fillmore Charge de Affairs to Denmark, but died before he arrived in that country. Charles Ogle served in the 25th and 26th Congress. His celebrated spoon speech gave him a high rank in the campaign. The *Leader* names as speakers in that campaign, among others, S. T. Hurd, editor of the Washington *Reporter*, J. W. F. White, J. M. Kirkpatrick. In 1840 Hurd was not a resident of Washington, and never was editor of the *Reporter*. John Bausman was its editor at that time, and with it printed the "Rolling Ball," as a campaign paper. John M. Kirkpatrick did not graduate at Jefferson College until 1846. J. W. F. White was a student in Allegheny College in that campaign and Rippey, D. N. White and Collier were not active politicians in that day. Rippey was too young and of the age of the other two I cannot say. Andrew Stewart was then in the prime of his life. The more prominent whig speakers of the 1840 campaign in this county were the Hon. T. M. T. McKennan, Hon. Joseph Lawrence, William McDaniel, and the local lights in this vicinity were Dr. R. F. Biddle, Wm. Mills and R. F. Cooper, Esq., at that time acting editor of the Carroll *Gazette*, which had deserted its neutral ground and came out boldly for Tippecanoe and Tyler too. In Allegheny county Hons. Walter Forward, A. W. Loomis, W. W. Irwin, F. C. Flannigan, W. B. McClure and Cornelius Daragh were very active in the cause. In Westmoreland, Edgar Cowan, then a resident of West Newton, was the rising speaker in the Whig cause. He made his first speech in the streets of West Newton from a canoe, on a wagon. That speech gave him the start as a stump-speaker. The campaign was opened in Monongahela City by the great mass-meeting at 'Squire Wall's in Elizabeth township, near Wm. Penn school house. The procession left Hamilton's hotel, preceded by eight men carrying a bark canoe made by the Indians, and the property of Jack McFarland, who had long been a trader among the Indian tribes, in what was then called the far west. It was very light for its size, and about thirty feet long, and of a tan color, neatly made. Dr. Biddle carried a miniature log cabin and some one, whose name we cannot recall, carried on a pole a live coon. The meeting was immense and the pies and cakes were without measure. Cider for the multitude was furnished free by old Abe Applegate. The speakers were F. C. Flannigan and W. W. Irwin—well known as "Pony" Irwin—a member of Congress and Minister to Denmark. A full description of this meeting was written by R. F. Cooper of the Carroll *Gazette* with special references to the "old dame with her brood" on Main street, who were so conspicuous in their criticism of the procession as it passed up the street. The Washington *Examiner*, edited by Grayson and Kaine, also had a Loco Foco view of the whole affair. It was after this great meeting that T. R. Hazzard became a "Straightout" from the Loco Foco Democratic party and remained in opposition to that party to the day of his death.

The great debate of the local campaign was held in the old church on the hill. The participants were Dr. John Wishart and Wm. Montgomery, Democrats, against Edgar Cowan and Joseph Lawrence, Whigs. There was a daylight and night session of the debate. The discussion was a very able one, but it was conceded that the Whigs had the better of the fight. The writer has a few manuscript copies of some of the more popular songs of that campaign.

Mrs. Jane Fulton Power.

Died at her late residence in Monongahela City, Pa., March 23, 1891.

She was born in West Newton, Pa., November 15, 1814. She was the daughter of the late Henry Fulton, who was a ruling elder for many years in the Presbyterian church of this city. She united with the Presbyterian church of Sewickley at the age of thirteen years, under the ministrations of Rev. A. O. Patterson. She was married to John Power, September 13, 1836, by the Rev. Wm. Annan. Her husband survives in his 80th year. The family of Henry Fulton has been signally and peculiarly connected with the Presbyterian church. His oldest son, Abram, was an elder, and his daughter Jane, the deceased, married an elder, and his granddaughter, Rebecca—daughter of Abram—married Rev. Alonzo Linn, L. L. D., Professor in Washington and Jefferson College. Another granddaughter is the wife of Rev. J. H. Sherrard, of Ohio, whose daughter Jennie is the wife of Rev. Ewing, a foreign missionary. Henry Fulton's daughter Rebecca was the wife of Wm. J. Power who for many years was a ruling elder in the Pigeon Creek congregation, where at this date two of his sons are serving that church in the same office.

Henry Fulton's son, James P., is a Presbyterian minister in Kansas, Harper county, and his grandson, Wm. S., son of James P., is the pastor of one of the churches in Lexington, Ky. Rev. Robert H. Fulton, D. D., the youngest son of Henry Fulton, is pastor of Northminster church, Philadelphia.

Henry Fulton had three daughters married to ministers. Sarah, now deceased, was the wife of Rev. J. H. Stevenson, D. D., of Mount Carmel, Illinois, Nancy married Rev. R. T. Price, of Scio, Ohio, and Almira is the wife of Rev. E. P. Lewis, of St. Paul, Minnesota. Margaret is the wife of James Means, for many years a ruling elder in Lebanon Church, Allegheny county, and his son, Henry F., is a minister lately in charge of the churches of Fairfield and Union, in the Presbytery of Blairsville. Henry Fulton's son, George P., deceased, was one of the most successful educators in Western Pennsylvania.

Mrs. Power, wherever she abode in life, was looked upon as one of God's own children. Her faith never wavered. It was an anchor to her soul, sure and steadfast.

Dr. George E. Lytle.

This estimable young man and physician died at Gallatin, Tenn., March 6, 1891, at the home of his sister, Mrs. Frank Pierce. He was 35 years of age, the son of Perry A. Lytle, Esq., of Forward township. He was educated at Washington and Jefferson College, read medicine with Dr. Linn, graduated from Jefferson Medical College, of Philadelphia, in 1876, and afterwards took a special course on the eye. He opened an office here in 1876, and has since been in the active practice of his profession, until failing health obliged him to seek relief in a milder southern climate. Some months ago he went to North Carolina, but still failing, he went thence to Tennessee and, sending for his mother, died at his sister's home, with his friends about his bedside.

George Elmer Lytle was the son of Perry A. Lytle, Esq., of Forward township, born August 26, 1856, read medicine with Dr. George A. Linn, of this city, received his diploma as Doctor of Medicine from Jefferson Medical College of Philadelphia, began practice when 20 years of age, and returned to Philadelphia a few years later to take a special course on the eye. He was a successful practitioner from the very beginning, was popular in social circles, he had the confidence of his clientele, and in his specialty of the Eye had already won an enviable reputation.

Doctor Lytle was a member of the Presbyterian Church, he was a Mason and a Knight Templar. He held membership in Henry M. Phillips' Blue lodge, in Monongahela chapter of Holy Royal Arch Masons, and in Pittsburgh Commandery No. 1. He was a member of the Order of Forresters; was in the Junior Order of American Mechanics, and was honored by being Chief Marshal of the fine parade of 1889. He was a member of the Order of Solon, and of Guild No. 1 of Royal Americans. The Doctor was very fond of the military. He entered service as hospital stewart of the Tenth Regiment National Guards in 1876, and had risen to the rank of Major and Surgeon of the Tenth, which commission he held at his death. The regiment had no more popular officer.

Doctor Lytle was intelligent and bright, sympathetic, companionable and honorable. He had a fund of humor that was irresistable, and his wit sparkled under the pleasant society of a circle of friends where he was always welcome. He will be missed from our city where he was much esteemed, and from many homes where he was the accepted family physician.

Mrs. Margaret Lowrey Everhart

Died in her home on State street, in the City of Chicago, Ill., on Tuesday, April 28th, 1891.

She was a daughter of Mr. James and Mary Plumer Smith, who removed from Pittsburgh to Blairsville in the spring of 1827.

He had met with heavy losses in his business and in trading in the Sciota country of Ohio, which finally overwhelmed him, and soon after, August, 1829, he died in Blairsville, and his family returned to Robbstown, Westmoreland county, near which the father of Mrs. Smith, the Hon. George Plumer, resided.

Amongst the kindly tributes of friendly condolence at the funeral services of Mrs. Everhart, was one of rarely beautiful flowers from Mr. George M. Lyon and his sister, now resident in Chicago. Their grandfather and grandmother, Mr. and Mrs. George Mulhollan and the Hon. John Cunningham were the ever kind and sympathizing friends of Mr. and Mrs. Smith in their day of trouble in Blairsville, the remembrance of which has always been gratefully cherished by the writer.   G. P. S.

Mrs. Sarah F. Stevenson,

Wife of Rev. Jos. H. Stevenson, D. D., died Tuesday, May 26th, 1891, at her late residence in Mount Carmel, Wabash county, Illinois.

She was born in West Newton, Westmoreland county, Pa. She was a daughter of Henry Fulton, a well known elder in the Presbyterian Church in Western Pennsylvania. Her mother was Elizabeth Plumer, daughter of Hon. George Plumer, who represented Westmoreland county in Congress for several terms. He was one of the substantial elements in the early settlement of Western Pennsylvania. His integrity as a citizen and his great moral worth as a representative are still cherished by the descendants of his constituents.

The deceased graduated from the Washington Female Seminary in the Class of 1857, from which institution two of her daughters have since graduated. She united in early life with the Presbyterian Church of Monongahela City, Pa., during the ministrations of Rev. John Kerr. We cannot portray her Christian character in a truer light than by inserting here a few extracts from Rev. Dr. Spilman's remarks at the funeral of the deceased:

"Mrs. Stevenson inherited from her parents a deep, strong, religious nature, which developed by the converting grace of God experienced in childhood, and carefully trained and instructed in a Christian home of a positive type. Her strong, logical mind grasped the doctrines of the Presbyterian Church with more than ordinary clearness and intelligence. She was a Christian by the grace of God and a Presbyterian from intelligent conviction and loving choice. Her religious life was rather quiet than demonstrative. Its current ran deep, and strong, and constant. Her spirit was reverent. To her the spiritual side of life was very real; the love of God was real; salvation was real; Christian obligation was real. She loved the Bible. To her it was the word of God; it was the daily food of her soul. She loved the house of God with its worship and holy fellowship, and never failed to attend its services when her strength permitted. The interests of Christ's kingdom lay constantly on her heart. The cause of missions deeply interested her, hence she could not rest without a missionary society in the church. Salvation meant so much to her, and her sympathy with Christ and for the perishing world was so deep and tender, that she felt a Christian woman must pray and labor and give constantly for the cause of missions. The deceased was a model minister's wife, deeply concerned in all that pertained to the welfare of her husband's charge. The spiritual life of the church, and especially the care of the sick and the poor, received her tenderest thoughts. The friends who weep in this presence to-day and strew her casket with flowers, whose fragrance is fitly emblematical of the perfume of her beautiful and useful life, will add your testimony to the truth of what I say. But I have occasion to know that Mrs. Stevenson is held in like loving, grateful remembrance by other congregations who have felt the benediction of her Christian life. They in bereavement mingle their tribute of tears and flowers with yours to-day.

J. S. V.

[From the DAILY REPUBLICAN.]

WILLIAM J. MARKELL

Died at his late residence in Monongahela City, Saturday December 3, 1892. He was born in 1824, in Greensboro, Greene county, Pa., second son of William and Eliza Markell. The family came to Monongahela City in 1830. In 1842 William went into the general merchandise store as clerk, then kept by his brother, John S. Markell. He remained in that capacity until 1847.

In that year he went into the glass business for one year and then went on the Muskingum river as clerk on a steamer, but he soon afterwards accepted the captaincy of an Ohio river packet, and boated in that capacity for ten years, closing as part owner and captain of the Hartford and Endeavor respectively. Mr. Markell went west in 1858, and was as far out as Pike's Peak, and in other parts of the then new silver country.

Mr. Markell was postmaster of this place from 1857 to 1860, and was succeeded by R. M. Clark at the election of Mr. Lincoln. After his return from the west he engaged in the tobacco business, then he was clerk at Mr. Kern's store, in the People's Bank building, and in 1875 in partnership with Elijah Harrison he purchased the distillery at Mingo, which they operated in partnership for several years, when Markell bought the Josiah Taylor distillery and brewery, which he operated alone for several years.

Another of our older citizens sleeps with the dead. A man whose sixty-two years' residence in our city had made him one of the best known among the business men of the town. As postmaster under President Buchanan, his official life was characterized by probity and courtesy. Socially Mr. William J. Markell was full of humor, he always saw the pleasanter side, and the quiet chuckle of his fun pointed many a joke. He was a member of the Protestant Episcopal church, of the Masonic lodge, and was by political faith a Democrat of the Jacksonian kind.

He had been over the sea twice, and seemed to enjoy telling of his observations in Europe, as well as of the halcyon days of his steamboat life, and the experience of his trip to Pike's Peak in the early sixties.

He was married twice, first in 1852 to Margaret Dougherty, by whom he had four sons, William, Edward, Charles and Lewis, all of this city. After his wife's death he again married, in 1880, to Mary Kern, by whom he has two children, Eliza and Norman Keys Markell.

In his later life Mr. Markell had suffered from the prostration of a paralysis. His family has been tender and kind, his wife a loving minister at his bedside in all the hours of his illness and suffering.

HISTORICAL ADDRESS

Delivered by J. S. VAN VOORHIS, M. D., November 15, 1892, on the One Hundredth Anniversary of Monongahela City, Pa.

Abraham Decker originally laid claim to the land on which the upper part of Monongahela City is located. The title was based on a Virginia entry and confirmed by patent No. 3783, bearing the date of August 26th, 1769. Having passed the researches and dispute between the states of Virginia and Pennsylvania, the Board of Property finally declared the title to be valid.

In the year 1770 the Parkisons arrived from the east in search of a home in the wilds of the Monongahela Valley and selected the Decker plateau as a most desirable site, and in course of time secured the title to Joseph, as above stated. Of the Parkisons, there were five brothers, viz: Joseph, Thomas, James, Benjamin and William. It is in Joseph we have the most interest. Our information is that Joseph Parkison married Miss Margaret Weaver, a regular descendent in the Pennsylvania Dutch line. They had as children, James, David, William and Mary.

The Deckers had reared their primitive cabin a short distance above the spring on what is now the Van Voorhis homestead, on Pigeon Creek, and consequently Joseph Parkison on his arrival was compelled either to dwell in a tent or enjoy the hospitality of the Deckers. The Devore Ferry, authorized in 1775, was in operation on the arrival of Parkison. It was known as Devore's Ferry until 1782, when the landing of

Devore on the north side, and that of Parkison on the south, near the mouth of Pigeon Creek, was established by law as Parkison's Ferry. Prior to this date Devore seems to have had kind of a private ferry, worked to suit his own will. Devore had at an early date a store near his landing, which was a branch of the great store of David Furnier, located just below Bellevernon of the present day.

It was about this time in the history of the settlement that the pioneers realized the necessity of a postoffice. Brownsville, Bassett Town (now Washington), and Pittsburgh, were the nearest postoffices. The office was granted and named Parkison's Ferry. It is very probable that the keen eye of Joseph Parkison saw in the Ferry money at no distant day. A public road had, in 1781, been laid out from the town now called Washington to the mouth of what is now First street, though in the town originally known as Ford street, named so on account of that point of the river being, in low water, forded by the traveler. The established ferry and the newly laid out road soon attracted the attention of the public and resulted in giving the point an importance which in a very short time induced Joseph Parkison to erect on the new road his inn, which the older citizens will recollect stood back from what is now Main street, but fronting the public road, which run diagonally from the mouth of Ford street across the bottom land and up the hill westward.

It was located on the second lot up from Stewart's alley. The old part of the building was log, but the new addition, with its well remembered porch extending to Main street, was frame. The log part of this house was, beyond all question, the first erected on the site of the town, but not the first on the Decker tract, as we have already stated. The original settlers generally in the valley selected their new homes out from the river. The value of the river was overlooked in the terror of Indian depredations, which were more frequent on the river, where their wigwams were located. Joseph Parkison, with no fear of the Indian, entered into the business to succeed.

The increased trade and travel on this route, to and from the east, of which Joseph Parkison was more cognizant than any other person, owing to his position as inn keeper, was the potent incentive to his laying out of the new town of Williamsport, named as such in honor of his son William. After having the ground surveyed and a plot thereof made, he offered the lots at public sale, as will be seen by an advertisement in an October, 1792, issue of the Pittsburgh *Gazette*, from which we extract the following :

"The subscriber has laid out a part of his farm on the Monongahela river, in the county of Washington, at the mouth of Pigeon creek, opposite Devore's Ferry, into lots for a town, the sale of which will begin on the premises on the 15th day of November next."

WASHINGTON Co., Oct. 20, 1792.

JOSEPH PARKISON.

The sale was not very successful, owing not so much to it being a new enterprise as to the fact that difficulties still existed, growing out of the issuing of Pennsylvania patents and Virginia certificates. In 1796 however, the Board of Property decided that Joseph Parkison was the legal owner of the tract of land on which the town was laid. In pursuance of such decision, the patent issued August 26th, 1769, to Abraham Decker, was given May 11th, 1796, to Joseph Parkison. Encouraged by this decision and confident of success, Parkison determined once more to offer for sale additional lots in the town. The notice of this sale for August 26, 1796, was published in the *Telegraphe*, a newspaper printed in Washington, Pa., by Messrs. Wm. Hunter & Co. The notice was in the form of a proclamation and on account of its interesting and novel features, we will read it entire :

"WHEREAS, the subscriber has layed out lotts for a town on his plantation, near the mouth of Pigeon creek, on the 26th of August, Instant, notice is hereby given to all those who incline to become purchaser or purchasers of said lott or lotts of this special condition, that every of said purchaser or purchasers of said lott or lotts are to be prevented from erecting or causing to be erected, any craft, boat or canoe for the conveying of passengers across the Monongahela river, but the same is hereby reserved to the subscriber or his heirs or assigns, so far as the claim of the subscriber extends. The hiest bidder for each lott or lotts to be the buyer. Any person or persons purchasing any lott or lotts are to pay one third of the purchase money by the third day of September next, one third part by the 26th of November next, and the remaining third part to be paid on or before the 26th of February next, when the purchaser will receive a sufficient title for each lott or lotts, subject to the payment of one dollar per annum on each lott, to be payable the 1st of October each year, first year due October, 1797.

Any person or persons inclining to have their deed or deeds before the above described time, may, on payment of the purchase money, immediately receive them. Notes and security will be required for the first payment, and failure of making the second payment, the first will be forfeited to the proprietor, and on failure of the third payment, the first and second to be forfeited and the lotts to revert to the owner. Each lott is 60 feet in front and 200 feet deep. The streets 60 feet wide, and the alleys extending from the river to the hill, 15 feet wide, the cross alleys, from 15 to 25 feet wide, according to the situation of the ground.

August 26th, 1796.   JOSEPH PARKISON."

In the general plan of the town, a lot of ground was reserved in the centre for a market house and also a lot for a school house and meeting house. By way of publicity to the sale of lots, Esquire DePew certified that the town was laid out and lots sold and some built upon, as witnessed his hand and seal January 11th, 1797. At this sale of August 26th, 1796, twenty-four lots were sold at prices ranging from $22 to $239, the total being $1,385. On the laying out of the town, the old road was superceded by Main street, or Market street as it was originally named. Traces of the old road as it passed up the hill can still be seen. The earliest road viewers did not realize that it was just as near to go around a hill as to run over the summit, hence all the ancient road paths crossed the top of the hill rather than go around it.

The original plot of the town extended from Ford, now First street, to almost Race, now Third street. The original Parkison & Froman line cut one lot above Race at the river and two lots at the upper end on the hill. The tract of land adjoining the new town at Race, now Third street, was patented to Paul Froman and sold by him to Adam Wickerman March 13th, 1792. On this same tract, or part thereof, Adam Wickerman laid out Georgetown in 1807. The Georgetown plot was made a part of Williamsport by the act of Adam Wickerman in the following paper :

"I, Adam Wickerman, do certify that this plot is made agreeable to my direction and that I do acknowledge it as a part of Williamsport, formerly cawled Georgetown, as witness my hand seal this 23d day of February, 1816."

The towns had been in separate plots under different names for nearly ten years, and we can readily imagine the rivalry and conflicting interests that would spring up between the two villages. Prior to this date the lot holders had insisted on and finally required of Wickerman that he should record it as Williamsport. This paper was signed by such lot holders as John Cooper, Patrick Burke, John R. Shugart, Joseph Butler, W. P. Biles, John Shouse, Michael Miller, Peter Shouse, James Manown, Joseph Hamilton, Thomas Gordon and others of no less influence. East Williamsport was laid out in 1811, by James Mitchell, an early river trader and active progressive business man, and was well known as Esquire Mitchell. The addition has always been more generally known as Catsburg, named in honor of Kitty Caldwell and her kittens, whose history can be related in full by Ex-Mayor R. C. King. That part of the town known as the Island, though owned by Parkison, was not included within the original town plot. The Island made by Pigeon creek on two sides and the Monongahela river on the other, did not foreshadow flattering prospects for an extension of the town, yet in time, and for a time, it has been a busy hive of industry.

Parkison owned the Island without improving very much until January 5th, 1829, at which time it was sold to James Manown by Sheriff Henderson. By this sale the right of the Washington county side of the ferry passed to the same purchaser. The ravine which reached the river at the mouth of Ford, now First street, has almost disappeared. Either by inheritance or otherwise, the Allegheny side of the ferry passed into the Manown family. The Manowns operated the ferry until 1838, when the building of the bridge rendered it useless. On many of the lots in the Georgetown addition ground rent was fixed, but in the original Parkison plot only a small portion of the lots was finally subject to such an incumbrance.

In the original design of the town a public square was reserved for a market house, and Parkison intended also a lot for a meeting house and a school house. How far his ideas were executed we shall know by the sequel. The square was reserved at the crossing of Market, changed to Main street and Washington, now Second street; besides the street crossings, a certain number of feet at each corner was included within the square. The buildings of Joseph Brown, of the Nucleus Hall Association, of R. C. King and the People's Bank now occupy ground intended to be included within the public square.

The primitive Market House stood in part on this square on Main, just below Second street. Our notes do not show at what time or by what means or by whom it was built. We do know that it was there in 1834, and it is very likely that it was erected soon after the incorporation of the town of Williamsport into a borough by the act of April 8th, 1833. In course of time this building was removed to Second street above Main. The building was erected on brick pillars, and in not many years after its removal the boys had so far destroyed the columns as necessitated its taking away. The building and object were both failures. The beef shops and wagons have long since taken the place of Market Houses.

The reserve for a meeting house never cropped out, only in consideration of a certain sum of money Joseph Parkison and Adam Wickerman, in July, 1814, did convey to certain trustees for building a meeting house, the tract of land known in part as lot No. 72, on which was afterward erected a brick church building by contributions from all denominations, and on which was located the primitive graveyard, in which were buried a large number of the older citizens of the town and surrounding country, and in which, we regret to say, are the remains of many of the older fathers neglected because unremembered. The lot for a school house was forgotten and the scholars of the impromptu schools had to find shelter for training in whatever shanty could be found unfitted for any other purpose.

By an act of Assembly approved by Gov. Wolfe, April 3d, 1833, Williamsport was incorporated into a borough. The act appointed the third Friday in May for the first election, and thereafter the third Friday of March each year, at the tavern of Joseph Caldwell. The elections ordered by the act of incorporation related merely to Borough officers, not changing the township officers, as the new borough remained in Fallowfield and Nottingham until September 30th, 1834, and in Carroll until 1842. By whom the first election was held we can not ascertain, neither do we know who were chosen officers, only as we gather from the proceedings relating to the death of Joseph Parkison. On the death of Joseph Parkison, the Monongahela *Patriot* of April 29th, 1834, published in Williamsport, states:

"DIED—In this borough on Monday night, April 28th, 1834, at the advanced age of 94 years, Mr. Joseph Parkison. Mr. P. was well known to many as the original proprietor of this place, from whom it received the name of Parkison's Ferry. Although his death was long looked for, it has cast a gloom over our citizens. The following testimony of respect from our town authorities, to the memory of the deceased, was handed in a few moments before our paper went to press.

TRIBUTE OF RESPECT.

WHEREAS, we have learned with deep regret of the death of our aged and esteemed fellow citizen, Joseph Parkison, the original proprietor of this town, Therefore

Resolved, That as testimony of respect to the memory of the deceased, we will attend his funeral this afternoon at 4 o'clock, and that it be recommended to the citizens generally to attend on said occasion.

By order of the council of the borough of Williamsport.

AARON KERR, President.
JOHN BAUSMAN, Secretary.''

The philology of the name would indicate that Joseph Parkison was of English descent, but of his early history we have very little information. He was born in 1740, seven years before General Washington visited Western Pennsylvania, and fifteen years before Braddock's defeat on the Monongahela river. He immigrated to this region in the 30th year of his age. He settled here at a time when the spirit of the Revolution was quietly pervading the American heart. He laid out his new town in perfect faith of the greatness and perpetuity of the new nation born at the close of the war of Independence. He died after seeing his town arise from a wilderness to take a proud position among the flourishing villages in Western Pennsylvania.

In early life Parkison was a tall, bony, muscular man, dressed rather fashionable in the costume of his day, with knee buckles and shoe buckles, such as these. In his older days he wore side whiskers, and the well known que of the times. Some of the older citizens can recall him changed to an old, bent in form man, sitting on the porch, trembling with nearly a century of years and waiting the summons to pass through the gate to the beyond. Instead of neglect marking his grave, the citizens should long since have erected over it a monument in commemoration of his deeds of daring in establishing the town in a wilderness, now a garden of ever blooming flowers.

In 1833 the name of the postoffice was changed to Williamsport, and April 1st, 1837, it took the present name of Monongahela City—it ought to have been Parkison City. We have failed to obtain from the department the name of the first postmaster at Parkison's Ferry, but it is conceded that as Joseph Parkison was instrumental in obtaining the office, he must have been appointed postmaster, and, in addition, from the fact that he had a store in connection with his inn. On the arrival of the late Ira Butler and his father's family, in 1805, Adam Hailman was postmaster, and in 1813 he was still in the office. Hailman died February 24th, 1813. He was succeeded by Mr. White, father of J. W. F. White, now a distinguished judge in Allegheny county. He was succeeded by Geo. Wythe, for many years a business man in the town.

We cannot recall all the successors to Wythe, but we are all familiar with the names of Jesse Martin, W. S. Mellinger, J. W. Smith, W. J. Markell, R. M. Clark, Chill Hazzard, Jas. H. Moore, W. C. Robinson and W. W. Bentley. Postage on letters in the early days of the town was rated according to the distance, three cents, six and one-quarter, twelve and one-half, eighteen and three-quarters and twenty-five cents for a single sheet, no matter how large. The custom was not to prepay the postage, and it was considered a breach of etiquette to prepay. The mail in Parkison, Hailman and White's time was carried on horseback by post-boys, as they were called. The old fashioned saddle bags contained the mail.

Although the town had been incorporated for nine years, yet it never had severed its connection with Carroll township as a general voting district. Before the formation of Carroll township, September 30th, 1834, a part of the citizens of the town of Williamsport voted with Fallowfield, at the tavern house of Abram Frye, on the farm now owned by heirs of Washington Cooper, on the Pittsburgh and Brownsville State road, and the remaining citizens voted with Nottingham township. From

September, 1834, to May 26th, 1842, the voting place of Carroll and the borough was at the tavern of Joseph Hamilton, known as the City Hotel, and stood where now is T. S. McCurdy's hardware store. After the separation the voting place of the town remained at the same place, but the citizens of Carroll voted for a time in a little brick office of Thomas Collins, Esq., near the corner of Main and Cemetery streets, in Catsburg.

In after years the poling place was removed to the Rose-Thompson house, up the turnpike, a short distance outside the borough. In the borough, in the course of time, the place of holding elections was moved to the Teeters hotel, corner Second and Railroad streets. The ground on which the hotel stood is now owned by the railroad company. On the incorporation of the borough into a city, by Act of Assembly of March 24th, 1873, three wards were formed, each of which constituted a voting district. At the first city election John Holland was choosen mayor, and Hon. S. H. Huston is mayor at the present time.

The city embraces a large extent of territory in comparison with the original design of Parkison. The early business of the town was transacted on a trading scale, generally only a very small amount of cash being current. The exports and imports were transported by means of the pack horse. About the time the town received its new impetus, after the second sale of lots, the river became utilized as a means of transportation by crude crafts, called flatboats or broadhorns, now known as coalboats. William Parkison was, no doubt, the first to build such boats at his yard in the "gut," as it was called, at the mouth of Ford street. These crafts, loaded with whiskey, flour, etc., were floated to the lower markets.

The flat, for local use, succeeded such crafts. Their destiny was Pittsburgh and up river trading points. They were returned by being pushed with the old time pike pole. The keelboat succeeded the flat and was used until displaced by the steamboat. The keelboats always landed at the mouth of Pigeon creek, which was not only a convenient landing, but a safe harbor. Steamboats never made this point a landing place. They first landed at the Chess wharf, at the mouth of Ferry, now Fourth street. The Limetown packet, Ploughman, commanded by Captain Joe Chester, was the first to make regular landings at this wharf. Then followed the Export, of which I. C. Woodward was Captain; here, also, the Dr. Pollock boat, the Moxahala, and others made landings, until the completion of the Slackwater.

In 1845 the Consul and Louis McLane entered the regular packet line, and had their landing at the Chess wharf, until the town council had it removed to the mouth of Washington, now Second street. Another avenue of trade was opened up by the Washington and Williamsport turnpike. The company was chartered by Act of March 18th, 1816. It is still called a turnpike in name. It was constructed under very great financial difficulties, and was only completed by the State coming to its aid with a liberal subscription to the stock. For many years this turnpike was on the great route from east to the west. The older citizens will call to mind the thousands of foreign imigrants who, in the old Conestoga road wagon, wended their way west, where their descendents now make up the empire of states between the Ohio and Mississippi rivers.

This westward move of imigration was at its height between 1830 to 1840. At this period, for the most part, Conrad Crickbaum and Frank Manown were running the Ferry at the mouth of Pigeon creek. Crickbaum did the work and Frank took care of the cash, and it would be wonderful if in that period Frank had not become an adept in the Dutch vernacular. On the turnpike was established a line of coaches, called stages, each of which could carry nine passengers and the mail.

These stages were very substantially and nicely finished. They were drawn by four horses, managed by a driver on a seat constructed on the upper and front part. We can only call to mind two of the prominent drivers, Bob Backhouse, and Samuel Burgess. The stage office and horses were kept at the tavern of Joseph Hamilton, long known as the City Hotel. The first survey through the town for a railroad was by B. H. Latrobe, in 1835. The line was run along Coal street and across Pigeon creek, in the rear of the Applegate property, in Catsburg.

Opposition in the Legislature, and the cry that the passage through Washington county of a railroad would ruin Pittsburgh and make the grass to grow over the National pike, prevented the company from getting the right of way. After several unsuccessful efforts, the railroad company finally constructed its road around Washington county, leaving Pittsburgh to seek other channels of transit to the east, and thus the town of Williamsport, through the whims of a few would be philanthropists, was deprived of railroad facilities for thirty-eight years.

In 1850, May 15th, the Hempfield railroad company was incorporated with the view of constructing a railroad from Greensburg to Wheeling. It was to cross the river just below Third street. After a large sum of money had been expended the work was abandoned. In 1873 the Pittsburgh, Virginia & Charleston railroad was opened to this city. The late Dr. W. L. S. Wilson was appointed agent and sold the first ticket to Maj. A. P. Foster, now of Florida. Dr. Wilson held the position until his death, September 6th, 1886. He was a genial officer, a good citizen and amiable gentleman. His early death was not only a loss to the railroad company, but to the town in which he had so long resided.

The completion of the McKeesport & Belle Vernon railroad in October, 1889, on the east shore of the Monongahela river, added another avenue to the growing trade of this city, whose 100th anniversary we celebrate to-day. January 4th and 5th, 1832, petitions were presented by Messrs. Waugh and Patterson, of Washington county, and Gebhart of Somerset, in the Legislature, in favor of incorporating a company to build a bridge across the Monongahela at Williamsport. The act proposed an appropriation in its aid, which gave rise to a very active opposition in both houses, but through the efforts of the members from Somerset, Washington, Westmoreland and

Allegheny counties, it was passed, carrying with it an appropriation of $15,000, which was approved by Gov. Wolfe, March 16th, 1832.

This bridge was built of pine frame on stone piers. It stood on the site of the present bridge. The old bridge was burned in 1883 or '84, and the present iron one erected in 1887. In 1800 Joseph Parkison was the inn keeper, and in connection therewith he had a trading mercantile store, in which certain goods were kept to be sold for cash or produce, such as grain whiskey, furs in the shape of skins. Iron and salt transported from east of the mountains on pack horses were very common commodities.

A tavern, store and blacksmith shop in old times constituted a town. Tradition credits Parkison with being, in his early day, a shrewd, successful Indian trader. At the close of the last century (1794) Samuel Black appeared in the town as a merchant and down river trader. He built the house long known as the red house, on the river bank just below First street. The very site of the building has long since been washed away by the ravages of the river. He was very successful in business, and at his death in 1846, was considered one of the most wealthy men in the county. He was a man of large stature and always wore a que.

Daniel DePue was the Esquire of his day. He lived in the old log house on the point at the mouth of Pigeon creek. His peculiar signature is attached to many of the older deeds. His first commission was dated March 12th, 1792.

William Irwin was also a merchant, had his store in a log room on the corner of First street. He, in 1802, built the old part of the house now occupied by Mrs. Kerr, and it was the first brick house in the town. He died in 1822, and was buried in the old graveyard on the hill, where his remains and those of his wife are to this day. His son John married Margaret Guthrie, niece of the late Joseph Wilson, of whom others will speak. At the beginning of this century James Warne and William Parkison were associated as merchants.

In 1805 James Warne married Mary, daughter of Joseph Parkison and sister to his business partner. Not long after his marriage Warne built the house on Main street, above Stewart's alley, so many years the residence of Joseph Wilson. In this house all of Warne's children were born, excepting one. James Warne, in 1820, purchased from James Parkison the farm above Catsburg, on which he resided until his death in 1855. His son, Joseph P., now owns it.

William Parkison, son of Joseph Parkison, and business partner of James Warne, owned, in early days, the farm long known as the Black homestead, on the pike, in what is now called Bellevidere. He built the old mansion still standing on the turnpike. In front of this mansion on the meadow land, William had a race course in circular form, through the woodland. This race ground gave rise to the name of Race, now Third street, in the town of Williamsport, laid out by his father.

In October, 1805, Benjamin Butler, with his family, arrived in the town on his way west, but he having died the first night after his arrival, the family abandoned the idea of going any further, and settled here. The arrival of the family and the death of the father created no little stir. Other particulars will no doubt be related by the committee on genealogy. Business and the social status of the town received a new impulse through the Butler family.

Adam Wickerman, proprietor of Georgetown, was an active business man in early days. He was the father of William Wickerman, Mrs. Mary Chess and Mrs. John Bausman, who is still alive and resides in Washington, Pa.

George Trout built, prior to 1805, and kept the tavern on Main street, afterwards so long carried on by Joseph Caldwell.

Nathan Chalfant was a boatbuilder.

A. B. Chess was farmer and trader; he built the old frame tavern on the river bank above Ferry street, known as Chess' tavern.

But time will fail us to tell, in detail, of Dr. Rose, Acneas

Graham, Frederick Layman, Thomas Officer, Drs. King, Pollack and Brooks, Esq. Mitchell, James Gordon, Wm. Hunter, John Eckles, J. and R. McGrew, John Watkins, Washington Palmer, who built the City Hotel, W. P. Biles, John Shouse, Peter Shouse, Robert Beebee, Joseph Hamilton, Jesse Martin, Benjamin Furguson and many others more or less prominent. We will refer only to a few.

Joseph McClure was the first cabinet maker in the town. He made the coffin in which was buried the older Benjamin Butler. His shop stood just below the old City Hotel, in which Joseph Hamilton so long had his shop, and in which the late Jefferson M'Lain passed most of his mechanical life, and in which were made the larger part of the coffins interred in the old graveyard.

Thomas Wells was the first saddle and harness maker.

Charles Bollman located in the town about 1810. He had a store in the first place in a log building near the bank of the river, a short distance below Ford street. Two houses were between this store room and the red house already mentioned. In one of these houses Dick Manks, the Parkison ferryman, lived, and the other was occupied in later years by Wm. Waddell, the wheelbarrow maker. Dick Manks is universally conceded to have been the first colored man settled in the town, even antedating Charlie the beer man, and Elijah and Thomas Bowman. Bollman in after years erected a brick house on Main, two doors above Second street. On the corner next to the alley, he had a store room, to which he removed his store. About 1830 his dwelling and store room and goods were burned, this being the first fire in the town. The house and store room were rebuilt, but the marks of the fire can yet be seen on the front brick work.

Joel Butler built the brick house now owned and occupied by Mrs. A. J. Stewart. James P. Stewart owned it, we think, from the days of Butler. In this house Aaron Kerr lived and had a store for many years.

Joseph Wilson, successor to H. Wilson & Son, had a store

for nearly half a century on Main street, just below the Parkison tavern.

The good old Jesse Martin had the postoffice and a shoe shop for many years on the corner of Main and Second streets, where now stands the Odd Fellows building. He also kept the office on the Dick King corner, where Sutman's shoe shop now is. He lived for many years in the brick house just below, which has been displaced by the new house built by his grandson, the late James C. Scott, in which is now the clothing store of W. C. Rolinson.

The old glass works on coal street, below Washington, now Second street, were erected by Warne, Parkison & Co., in 1816. The company consisted of James Warne, William Parkison, Joel and Benjamin Butler. For convenience in their business, the company issued a currency in the shape of bank notes, known better as shinplasters, redeemable in goods or current bank notes at their store. These notes were of the denomination of $6\tfrac{1}{4}$, or fips; $12\tfrac{1}{2}$, or levys; 25 and 50 cents. This effort to make glass was a failure. The works were sold by the sheriff to Samuel Black, and J. and R. McGrew, which after being repaired, were leased to Wm. Ihmsen.

Sometime prior to 1834, Wm. Ihmsen erected what was called the new factory, on the Island. He operated both of these factories until the day of his death. He was considered the most extensive and successful glass man of his day. In 1834, in the old factory, were blowers as follows: John Shouse, John Caldwell, John Tevis, Wash. Spence, Chas. Rose, Nat. McCalla and H. D. Cooper. John S. Markell was apprenticed to Nat. McCalla. Rollers were then made 24 by 30 inches and now 87 by 52 inches.

In later years Samuel Black erected a glass works at Dry Run. It never was much of a success. The glass factory at the lower end of the town, now in operation under O'Leary, is the last effort to make glass in this city. Wm. Ihmsen, Henry Ihmsen, John S. Markill, A. L. Williams, Smith and Herron were the more prominent glass manufacturers in former days.

The old hotel now owned by Gregg Brothers was kept by Caleb Harvey, A. L. Williams, Stephen Earnest 1840 to '45 and Jacob Weltner. We have not any knowledge who originally carried on the Chess tavern other than at one time, George Rose, the older, had it rented; then it was converted into a cabinet shop, where Abe Elliot and John Brownlee did work for Cyrus Huston. It was in this room where Huston and lawyer T. J. Fox Alden had their headquarters during the long litigation with A. B. Chess, in determining the title to the farm on which the lower part of this city is now built, and which had been willed to Mrs. Chess by her father, Adam Wickerman.

George Rose also kept a tavern and cake and beer stand in the old frame house which stood on what is now Brown's corner, Main and Second streets.

The tavern already mentioned, built by George Trout on Main street, short distance below the Episcopal church, had in its day several landlords, such as George Trout, Joseph Caldwell, A. T. Gregg and John Chessrown. The old City Hotel, which has already been mentioned, was built by Washington Palmer, in 1811, just before he went into the army with Captain James Warne's company. Joseph Hamilton, Henry Wilson, Caleb Harvey and W. H. Miller were landlords in this tavern.

Abram Teeters had a tavern for many years at the corner of Second and Railroad streets. After his death it was kept by his son, Dan Teeters. The house was used for a depot after the building of the railroad, and on the completion of the present depot, the old tavern house was torn away.

The brick house, corner Main and Fourth streets, was erected by James Mercer prior to 1834. He used the corner for a store room, in which he kept the first exclusive shoe store in town. He was drowned at the wharf, mouth of Fourth street, by his horse plunging into the river. After his death the house was used as a tavern by Mrs. Backhouse, Shively Hazelbaker, Abram Fulton, Jas. P. Shepler, T. B. Wilgus and the present landlord, and perhaps others whose names we cannot recall.

John Lamb, in early days, carried on a tan yard over the creek where David Woodward, whose wife was a Butler, lived to the day of his death, he having married his wife previous to emigrating from the east with the Butler family. I think his son Noble lived in this house most, if not all of his life. David's son, Joseph, still lives, and has for many years resided in Catsburg, he to-day is one of the substantial mechanics of the town, a living link between the past and present Butler family.

John Cooper removed from West Newton, in old time called Robbstown, to this place in 1810, and purchased from Adam Wickerman the lots now occupied by the residence of the late James P. Shepler, and the old school house, on which he erected a tannery. His wife's maiden name was Miss Sparks. They were married March 2nd, 1809. John Cooper died March 1st, 1820, leaving a widow and sons Richard Sparks, Hezekiah D., John S. and Robert F., and one daughter, Mary Jane, who married the late Dr. R. F. Biddle, and is the only surviving child of John Cooper.

Mrs. Cooper married John Shouse March 28th, 1828. He died at the Valley Inn, on the pike, now called Baidland Post Office, August 13th, 1834, leaving one son, W. H. Shouse, now of Cincinnati, Ohio, and one daughter, Fannie C., wife of Rev. J. P. Fulton, of Harper, Kansas.

The sons of John Cooper inherited much of the military spirit of their grandfather, Richard Sparks, who had been a soldier in the Indian and Revolutionary Wars, and was at the close of the Revolution a Colonel in the United States army. He died in the south whilst on duty.

Richard S., son of John Cooper, served as a soldier in the Mexican War, and was for years Captain of the old Jackson Guards, of which the late Washington Eckles was fifer and Noble Woodward drummer. He died November 13th, 1857. Hezekiah received his title from being captain in a militia company which did corn stalk service at the stone tavern stand of Alexander Campbell, on the pike above the toll gate, and at Ginger Hill.

R. F. Cooper was not only a man of learning, but one of the most accomplished military men of the state. He died in the United States service in 1864.

James Gordon, for years in connection with a store had a tan yard on Main Street, above Bollman's alley. He built the brick house, corner of Main and Bollman's alley, in which he lived for many years. The same yard in after years was operated by John J. Linn, Henry Fulton and Richard Stockdale. Matthew Fleming, in the forties, had a small tannery on the river bank just below the present knitting factory. He abandoned the tan yard to accept the position of toll keeper of the bridge.

Æneus Graham was an early resident of the town. He was a tailor by trade, a wise and good man. He had his tailor shop first in the old building two doors above the Cocain Hotel on Second street, and afterward for a time on the corner where now stands the Odd Fellows' building. He removed to the brick building, corner of Third and Main streets, now owned by Mrs. Phillips. He erected this house and lived in it to the day of his death. His wife was a daughter of Daniel DePue and mother of S. B. Bentley's first wife.

Frederick Layman, the tailor, emigrated from Germany and came direct to Williamsport in 1807, where he resided all of his long life. He lived at first in the old house that stood where now is located the brick house occupied by Mrs. H. D. Cooper in the latter part of her life. It is situated on Main street, three doors above the Peoples Bank. Some time prior to 1834, Frederick Layman built the brick house on the north east corner of Main street and Church alley, in which he died, we think, in 1846. This building is now owned by John S. Markell.

The first suit of clothes Layman made in this country was for Major James Warne, and also the last suit he made was for him. He finished the suit in the evening and was dead before morning. He was the father of Wm. Layman, who died not many years ago in the Third ward of this city. William was the father of Wilson and Fred Layman, formerly citizens of this place. Frederick Layman also owned at his death a tract of land on Pigeon creek, adjoining Stockton.

Wm. P. Biles was an early settler in the town and was the first citizen who pretended to practice law in the place. He was also a singing master. He lived for years in the old house which stood on Main Street, a little west of Mark Borland's residence. Biles, though not educated in the classics, yet was a man of genius and made himself heard when conducting suits before the old time Esquires. It is said he had two prices for conducting a law suit, two dollars and a half if the client found the witnesses, and five if he found them. In all he was a peculiar character.

J. R. Shugart and Henry Rabe were old time saddlers, but for the last half a century R. M. Clark has been the fixed saddle and harness maker.

Before and sometime after 1834, Samuel Devore had a brewery on Main street, the remains of which can yet be seen opposite the brick row in the "gut," as it used to be called.

Billy Savage was the old time stone cutter. He lived on the Island and made most of the old time stone tombstones, many of which lay scattered in the old graveyard.

James McCalla was a gunsmith. He built and lived in the house for many years occupied by the late Rev. John Kerr, corner Fifth and Main streets, also by Hon. G. V Lawrence. It is now owned by Wm. Devore.

J. & R. McGrew were the hatters for nearly a half a century. They carried on the business at the corner where the Odd Fellows building now stands. The firm was dissolved by the death of Robert, the junior partner, somewhere in the latter thirties, Their wool hats were famous for wear, much to the discomfort of the boys who clamored for a new hat every winter, which could not be afforded. To satisfy their desires the old hat was ironed over by J. & R. McGrew, which for a time gave it a very fine glossy appearance. The old wool hat had one great advantage in the fact that the boys could not tear it with their teeth, and their only hope was in punching it in holes. That ended its use, except as a muzzle to the horse in corn plowing time.

In later years Alex. Wilson was a very active man. He settled in this city about 1845, where he gradually extended his business until he became the largest dealer in the county in wool, grain and produce generally. His store was in the old building where now is located Landefeld's new store rooms. He removed in 1857 to Heyworth, Illinois, where he died June 14th, 1862. His remains lay aside of those of his wife, in the Monongahela cemetery, where a beautiful monument perpetuates their memory.

The first drug store in the town was kept by Dr. George Morgan, in the brick house opposite M'Gregor's block, on Main street, in which James Dickey, the cabinet maker, in later years, resided.

Mrs. Jane Biddle, Mrs. John Philips, Mrs. Ellen Bowman, Mrs. Nancy Smith, Wm. Coulter, Joseph P. Warne, S. B. Bently and Joseph Woodward are the oldest residents of this city.

Asher Vankirk was the chair maker of olden time. His shop was located on the Island on the lot on which is the residence of Mrs. Walter Applegate. The building was destroyed by fire many years ago. After the retirement of Vankirk from the business, the shop was carried on by Wm. McMahon until his removal to the State of Indiana, where he died.

In olden time when our grandmothers had a grate to set, or a chimney to top out, or a bake oven to build, they always sent for "Pap,, George Mumbower.

The town has always been famous for its many skilled carpenters. The Butler Brothers, John Eckles, John Watkins, Joseph Hamilton, Benjamin Ferguson, Enoch Pierce, John Watson and others whose names we can not recall, were among the skilled mechanics of early day. In these latter days their number is legion. The Coulters, the Blythe boys, the Yoho brothers, Joseph Woodward, Jefferson M'Lain and the

Stockdale brothers have taken high rank as contractors and skilled workmen.

Thomas Collins was a potter by trade, and with James Collins carried on the pottery business in a building that stood on Cemetery street, in Catsburg. Thomas Collins was born in Uniontown, Pa., December 10th, 1803. He learned his trade in Greensboro, Pa. In what year he came to Monongahela City we are not informed. He taught the first public school in this place, which was in the winter of 1834-35, and in an old house on the Island still standing. Among his scholars were John Anawalt and Frank Manown. He was superintendent of the first Methodist Sunday School organized in the town. He was elected justice of the peace in 1839, being one of the first under the Constitution of 1838. He was elected and served five terms. He died at his residence on Waverly hill, this city, December 24th, 1873. He was buried at Ginger hill. At the time of his death he was a member of the Lutheran church.

Among the first efforts at manufacturing in old times was the carding machine and fulling mill. Benjamin Parkison, grandfather of A. R. Parkison, had such a mill run by the tramp wheel at the mouth of Mingo. Prior to this mill, carding wool was done by the settlers with a hand card. Common material for wearing apparel was made by hand, in the shape of woolsey-linsey, a composite of wool and flax. At Dry Run, in 1834-37, Matthew Murdy & Co. had a carding machine. Samuel Devore, in 1837, had a small carding machine in the rear of the old Parkison lot.

About the year 1834, C. W. & Wm. Bryant erected what has long been called the old carriage factory on Main street. On its completion in 1834, the firm removed their iron store from the shop one door west of the City Hotel, in which Jacob Cort immediately commenced to manufacture copper and tinware.

The Bryants were the first in the town to make plows and wagons on an extensive scale, and to keep a general assortment of Iron, especially Juniata iron.

In 1834 Mrs. S. Guthrie carried on the millinery and mantua making next door to Joseph Wilson's store on Main street. Miss A. Flemming had a similar shop on Ferry street next door to James Mercer's store. Mrs. James Officer also carried on the same business on Third street below the railroad, and continued long after the former had quit the business. The cards of Mrs. Guthrie and Miss Flemming both appear in the Monongahela *Patriot*, April 29th, 1834.

Robert Walker, in the latter forties, had a woolen factory on or near the site of Blythe & Co.'s planing mill on Fifth street near the river. It was burned in June, 1853.

William Johnson, at an early date. erected the first saw mill in the town. It stood below the site of the same planing mill.

There was another saw mill as late as 1837 above the same planing mill, owned and operated for a time by William Mills. It was the first to saw lumber by steam for the boat yard of Robert Beebe. Timber for building boats had been before this time sawed by hand with the whip saw.

As William Mills had erected a saw mill for the boat yard, so William Ihmsen, Vankirk and McAllister built one at the mouth of Pigeon creek, in Catsburg, to furnish boards for glass boxes for his two factories. This mill, after the death of Ihmsen, passed to other owners and operators. Just before the late war Mr. Cunningham built a few steamboat hulls at this mill. Mr. James Smith, we believe, was the last owner before it was dismantled.

David Bolton manufactured augers over a half a century ago in the old house that was located at the upper end of the street leading from the creek bridge in Catsburg. He moved to the vicinity of Ginger Hill, where he died. He was a brother-in-law of the late Judge Hill.

The beginning of the Monongahela Manufacturing Company, now located in the Third ward, was started by James W. Downer, in 1872. The business was carried on by Downer, Samuel Hindman and Col. David Lackey, until 1877, at which time Downer and Lackey retired and Major W. H. Morrison was taken into the firm and the business was carried on by Hindman and Morrison until 1881, when R. B. Abrams was added to the firm, which was changed to Morrison, Abrams & Co. In 1883 the company was merged into the Monongahela Manufacturing Company, which still exists. The whole plant was burned June, 1890. The present extensive brick plant was erected immediately after the fire, excepting the carpenter and blacksmith shops, which were erected in 1892.

The telegraph was established originally to this city by way of West Newton, in 1864. O. C. House sent the first message over the line to Pittsburgh, by way of West Newton. At Pittsburgh connection was made with the U. S. Telegraph Company. The message cost 55 cents for ten words. The Monongahela Valley Company was organized in 1864, by J. L. Shaw, and under his management as President the line was extended all along the valley. This, with the West Newton line, was merged into the Pacific and Atlantic, which, in 1877, was sold to the Western Union Company.

The first telegraph operator at this city was McNulty, from 1864 to '66; then North, 1866-'67; then Scott, 1867-'68; Adams, 1869; J. A. Wilson, 1869 to January, 1876; A. Park Wilson, 1876 till his death in October, 1881; W. H. Lewis, 1881 to 1887. In October, 1872, the office was moved from Wilson's drug store, on Main street, below Second, to the railroad station. In this drug store the office was first opened. Since the death of Dr. Wilson, George Oehle has been agent and operator, with others under him. Others will give in detail:—

The Valley Saw and Planing Mill of Blythe & Co., established in 1850 by Wm. and Joseph Brown; the extensive mills of Yohe Brothers; the paper mill established by Samuel D. Culbertson in 1850; the City Flouring Mill, erected in 1845, by Henry Shearer and John Shepler; The Monongahela City Steam Granite and Marble Works, established by R. M. Gee in 1852; the steam docks, put in operation by Joseph Tuman, Shadrick Heyser, George Grove and Cyrus Lynn; Graham's

Foundry, established in 1879 by E. V. Graham, the present proprietor; the gas company; natural gas company; telephone; water works and sewerage system; electric light; the public schools; churches and academies.

Philip Catlin was the first barber in the city, as far as we can ascertain. In 1834 he had his shop in the barroom of Joseph Caldwell's tavern. Among his old successors were Wm. Ralph, now a minister, Daniel Baizor and B. W. Adams. Then followed Catlin and Strange. At the dissolution of this firm, Alfred Catlin took a shop of his own. Alfred was a son of Vachel Catlin, of West Newton, and brother of Captain, Wm. Catlin, of this city. About 1871 Captain Wm. Catlin and W. H. Jones formed a partnership, which was dissolved in 1873, each one opening a shop. In 1874 Stephen B. Batch opened his present shop on Second street.

About 1870 Baizor took into partnership Joseph A. Jones. This firm was dissolved by the death of Baizor, which occurred July 30th, 1881. Joseph R. Brooks then formed a firm with Joseph A. Jones, under the name of Jones & Brooks. In January, 1891, Brooks retired from the firm, and Joseph A. Jones and W. H. Jones entered into a partnership under the name of Jones & Jones, who opened up one of the finest shops in the valley, at No. 257 West Main street. Joseph A. Jones died December 9th, 1891. The barbers of to-day in the city are S. B. Batch, James R. Brooks, Captain Wm. Catlin and W. H. Jones. Lizzie, wife of Philip Catlin, is still living and resides in East End, Pittsburgh.

My friend, Samuel Fox, of Fallowfield, has kindly furnished me with an original copy of the articles of association of a bank, entitled "The Monongahela and Williamsport Manufacturing Company," to be established in 1816, as shown by the date of the articles. Books of subscription to the stock were to be opened November 21st, 1816, in Williamsport, at the house of Joseph Parkison; in Elizabethtown, at the house of John Walker; also at Ginger hill, Thomas Carson's Columbia, Robbstown and Garret Walls' The only signature to this copy of the articles is that of John Grable, grandfather, we presume, of John M. Grable, of this city.

The proposed capital was $100,000. In order to facilitate the organization, a president and twelve directors were self-constituted to serve until the regular election, May, 1817. These officers were president, James Mitchell; directors, Major James Warne, John Cooper, James McGrew, William Parkison, W. P. Biles, James P. Stuart, Joel Butler, Garret Wall, Robert McFarland, William Findlay, Aaron Applegate, and Major John Grable. What was the final outcome of this attempt to form a bank we are not able to gather, but tradition makes it a failure.

In after years, in the early forties perhaps, Major A. L. Williams, at the old Manown tavern, issued a currency in the form of shin plasters, as they were called, redeemable at his bar and at the store of Charles Bollman. This undoubtedly was the first and only bank of issue in the town, and it was of short life.

The banking house of Alexander & Co. was the first real bank in the city. It was established in 1850, when the mercantile firm consisted of Joseph and son, W. J. Alexander, under the title of J. Alexander & Son, which had existed since 1843. The firm in 1850 was reorganized with the same partners, under the name of Alexander & Co., which still exists, although the names of James S. Alexander and Joseph A. Herron have been added and Joseph Alexander died June 20th, 1871.

The banking business was opened in the rear end of the store room which stood on the site of the present McGregor block. The building in which the bank is now located, corner of Main and Third streets, was erected in 1870. The bank is one of the most solid in the state, and its members, by their gentlemanly manners, sterling and long tried integrity, have won the confidence of the business men in every part of the nation.

The Peoples Bank was established in 1870, with a paid up

capital of $100,000. The late A. C. Sampson was its first president. Hon. J. B. Finley is the present president. This too is a substantial, prosperous institution. Its president is one of the most enterprising men of the city, and his life seems to be devoted to the advancement of its welfare. The new bridge, the telephone, the electric light, water works, the gas works and street improvements, all bear the impress of his progressive spirit.

The Pittsburgh *Gazette* was the first newspaper printed in Western Pennsylvania, and in 1786 was delivered to subscribers along the Monongahela river by one John Blair, who advertised in the *Gazette* August 30th, 1786, that he would pass up and down said river, from Pittsburgh to Casting's (Castener's) Ferry, with a boat every week, all subscribers along the river and neighborhood could have their papers brought to them every week at a reasonable rate. It was in this paper Parkison advertised his first sale of lots.

The first paper printed in this town was the *Williamsport Chronicle*. A copy dated January 23d, 1813, is still in possession of Mrs. Rebecca V. Stewart, of Speareville, Kansas. In it we find the following marriage notice :

"Married.—On Thursday evening, January 20th, by Rev. Ralston, Joseph Hamilton, of Ginger Hill, and Miss Peggy Ferguson."

These were the parents of Rev. W. F. Hamilton, D. D., and grandparents of Editor Col. Chill Hazzard, of the *Monongahela Republican*. It also records the marriage of Joseph Caldwell and Catherine Swartz, by Rev. Mercer. It makes reference to David Hickman as a jolly old fellow who lived an easy life, and, amongst other things, pulled teeth for a living, using rude pinchers, made by Benjamen Langhead, who, as the paper says, kept a Smith shop on Market street, next door to James Freeman's shoe shop, where Dr. Roberts formerly lived. David Hickman was no doubt the first resident dentist in the town.

The *Village Informant* was published first in 1818, by Joseph Clingan. We have part of a copy of this paper as printed in 1819, but by some means it has been so mutilated as to be of little service. It contained the obituary notice of grandfather Daniel Van Voorhis.

The next paper in the town was the *Pennsylvanian*, published by John Bausman, at the northwest corner of Main street, if any one can tell where that is. We present to you a copy, Vol. 2, No. 71, dated November 21st, 1829, It contains the marrriage notice of Wm. Blythe to Miss Mary Marshall, Thursday, November 19th, 1818. It contains among other advertisements, that of James Mills, who wants his customers to pay so that he could go forward with Elias Watkins in building a steam mill for the interest of the community at large. The mill was finished and after many years was sold to a man named Coulson, in whose time it was burned. The mill was situated on the river bank, opposite mouth of First street. The dwelling still stands.

The *Pennsylvanian* seems to have merged into the *Williamsport Patriot*, the first number of which was issued on the 11th day of November, 1833. Its editor was also John Bausman. On the 15th day of April, 1834, Bausman sold the *Patriot* to Samuel G. Bailey and John W. Hammond, who changed its name to the *Monongahela Patriot*, a copy of which, No. 49, dated April 29th, 1834, I herewith exhibit. This paper was sold to A. W. Davidson, who changed its name to the *Carroll Gazette*, a shor ttime before, or after the Ritner-Wolfe campaign for Governor.

We recall very well the fact that it printed week after week the constitution of 1838, and why it was so often in the paper was the wonder of my boyhood. Mr. Davidson's health gave way about 1840, and the late R. F. Cooper became acting editor, as well as school teacher during the winter in the brick school house near the toll gate on the pike. Many an article he wrote for that paper in the school house whilst the scholars enjoyed their dinner time. The *Gazette* ceased in 1840.

The *Neutral Ground*, by John McNeal, was first issued in 1841, and was of short life.

Rev. W. H. H. Barnes, in 1844, started kind of a temperance paper, which was a failure in every particular.

The *Monongahela Republican* has outlived every other attempt to publish a paper in the town. Since its first issue by Solomon Alter, Esq., July 7th, 1848, it has been the persistent advocate of improvement in the valley, and especially in this city. It has passed through shade and sunshine until to-day it takes rank among the most prominent newspapers in Western Pennsylvania. It has been owned and edited by the Hazzards since 1855. Col. Chill Hazzard is its present editor and proprietor.

The *Valley Record*, first published by Wm. M. Boggs, March 4th, 1876, had for years been a spirited and well gotten up paper. After several changes, it has finally been merged into the *Monongahela Democrat* published and edited by the Monongahela Democrat Publishing Company. The first number, dated October 3rd, 1892, is full of spirit and bright hopes of the future. Judging from the character and ability of the managers, we predict for it a prosperous career.

This city can boast that many of her citizens from time to time have held important positions of trust in the great arena of life. Aaron Kerr was elected to the Legislature in 1824-25-26-27-28 and in 1840, and was also a member of the constitutional convention of 1838.

Geo. V. Lawrence has been an active politician since 1842. He was elected to the Legislature in 1843-46-58-59. In 1848 he was elected to the State Senate over his opponent, the late William Montgomery. He was re-elected to the Senate in 1860, of which body he was Speaker in 1863. He was again elected to the Senate in 1874-76-78. In 1864-66-82 he was elected a member of Congress. In 1872 he was elected a delegate at large to the Constitutional convention. He has just been elected once more to the Legislature. Thus for fifty years he has been identified with national and state politics, and it is a happy thought that his course in public life has always been devoted to progress and the right.

In 1843 the self-educated O. B. M'Fadden, a resident of the town, was elected with G. V Lawrence to the Legislature. The question of a new county was the means which elected these two gentlemen in the same vicinity and of opposite politics. Mr. McFadden was a man of rare natural talent, and with an unbounded energy he was enabled to succeed in almost every step in life. Deserting his tannery in Beallsville, he studied law and was admitted to the Washington bar the same year in which he was elected to the Legislature. In 1845 he was elected prothonotary as successor to E. L. Blaine, father of the distinguished James G. Blaine. At the expiration of his term he emigrated to Washington Territory, where, under a democratic administration, he was appointed a judge of the United States Court, from which position he retired to become a delegate to Congress. He died in that far-off country many years ago. His wife was a daughter of the old tavern keeper, Joseph Caldwell.

John Storer represented Washington county in the Legislature in 1842. He was the father of Dr. John H. Storer, Mrs. Dr. J. H. Connolly, and Mrs. Sarah, wife of C. C. Johnson, a former active business man of the town. Johnson was born in New York state. He brought to the town the first one-horse buggy, as the Butlers did the first two-horse carriage.

Jesse Martin, the old postmaster, was elected to the Legislature in 1841.

Jacob Cort was elected a representative in 1847-48. He for years carried on the tin and copper business one door west of the City Hotel and in the old frame house that stood on what is now called Brown's corner. He moved west, where he died many years ago.

J. S. VanVoorhis, your humble historian, represented Washington county in 1857.

J. B. Finley was a member of the house in 1887-89-91.

T. R. Hazzard was also a member of the late constitutional convention. He was a native of New York, immigrated to this city about the year 1838, where he resided nearly all the remainder of his life. He was perhaps the most successful academic teacher in the valley. He established the first academy in this city, and from it and other similar institutions with which he was connected, went forth to fight the battles of life, many who have attained high positions in literary and professional life. Of such we may mention Chief Justice M'Elvain, of Ohio, Dr. James H. Manown, of Kingwood, W. Va., Major R. C. Walker, of Montana, Dr. J. C. Cooper, of Philadelphia, Rev. William F. Hamilton, D. D., Hon. D. L. Letherman, of Washington county, Dr. J. H. Storer, of West Virginia, Dr. Robert Niccolls, of California, J. S., M. P. and A. P. Morrison, of this city, Dr. O. J. Porter, of Westmoreland county, W. G. Johnson, Esq., of Pittsburgh, Dr. James Flemming, of Ohio, A. H. Kerr, of Minnesota, William Fuller, the millionaire cattle dealer, of Philadelphia, and others of no less note.

Hazzard in his day did more for the cause of scientific and classical education than any other man in the valley. It was the work of his life. As an editor, under trying circumstances, he succeeded in building up the Monongahela *Republican* to be a first-class newspaper, which has for nearly a half century been a household god in the families of the valley. He died in 1877. He was admitted to the Washington county bar in 1840.

James Gordon became a resident in 1810. He served as Justice of the peace for thirty-five years. He was in 1845 appointed an associate Judge by Governor Shunk. He was elected a member of the Electoral college in 1828, and as such voted for General Jackson. In 1813 he was a county commissioner and in 1857 was a member of the Board of Revenue commissioners.

Samuel Hill was also an associate Judge.

Thomas H. Baird and Ianthus Bentley were elected and served with honor as District attorneys of Washington county. Bentley moved to Colorado, where he died a few years ago.

Sheshbazzar Bentley, Jr., father of Ianthus, was elected commissioner and sheriff of Washington county.

Cyrus Underwood and Alvin King were elected Recorder, and R. F. Cooper Clerk of Courts.

Hon. James Scott was another Monongahela boy of distinction. Although never a resident, yet was for years a fixture in this city. He was born in Mingo, April 15th, 1815. He received his literary education in the common schools and in the Rev. Marshall's Academy and in Washington College. He studied medicine with Dr. R. F. Biddle, in the old office which stood on corner of Main street and Church alley, where now George A. Hoffman has his hardware store. He graduated at the Cincinnati Medical College. In 1841 he practiced a short time in Greenfield, now Coal Centre, Washington county, Pa. He subsequently removed to Lebanon, Ohio, where he resided the remainder of his days. In course of time he abandoned the medical profession and adopted that of law. He became prominent in politics and served in the Legislature of Ohio for near twenty years. During Grant's administration he was appointed Secretary of the Territory of Washington, and on the death of the incumbent was confirmed as Governor. He was also U. S. Consul to the Sandwich Islands. His rare talent carried with it an ambition that knew nothing but to succeed. He died December 16th, 1888, at his home in Lebanon, Ohio.

Among the medical men in the nation is Dr. W. A. Hammond, once a boy in this city. He was born at Annapolis, Md., August 28th, 1828, and at the age of four years immigrated to this city with his father, Dr. J. W. Hammond. He, with James S. Alexander and others, played many a game of "Knucks" in the old market house. He was Surgeon general at the beginning of the late rebellion and is now on the retired list. He is still hale and hearty.

In ministers of the gospel, this city has sent forth such men as Samuel Hair, Thomas P. Gordon, G. M. Hair, Joseph Kerr, A. H. Kerr, John Goucher, W. F. Hamilton, Thomas Hodgeson, James P. Fulton, Robert H. Fulton, John McFarland, O. M. Todd.

Joseph P. Warne, William Coulter, S. B. Bentley and Mrs. Jane Biddle have always had a continuous residence within the limits of this city, and are perhaps more conversant with its early history than any other persons.

Coulter was born in the old house on the corner of Main and Second streets, Catsburg, in 1817. We have traced his career on another occasion.

S. B. Bentley was born in 1826, in the house known in later days as the old M. E. Church, on the bank of the river. S. B. Bentley has all his life been identified with the interests of his native Monongahela City. His recollections of the past are very vivid; he can recall readily the names and doings of all the active business men of his day. He has been from his youth a member of the Methodist E. Church, and to his persistent and prayerful efforts is indebted much of the standing of that useful and influential branch of the church in this city.

Prior to 1840 we had no certain means to ascertain certainly the population of this city. From that date we count on its separate population, although the increase must be attributed, to a certain degree, to the extension of its boundaries.

The population was in 1832.................. 600
" " 1840 752
1850.................. 977
1860.................. 999
1870.................. 1,078
1880.................. 2,904
1890.................. 4,065

We are indebted to the *Monongahela Democrat*, in its first issue, for the following summary of the present business status of the city:

It has 2 railroads—the Pennsylvania and Lake Erie systems, 10 churches, elegant school buildings, 16 schools—9 months in the year and 1,000 scholars, 1 roller flour mill, 3 livery stables, 2 hotels, 2 sale stables, 2 machine shops, 2 founderies, 1 paper mill, 2 planing mills, 3 lumber yards, 2 docks, 1 river toll bridge, 1 fire engine, 1 hose company, 1 hook and ladder company, 1 city hall, 1 city jail, 3 insurance agencies, 2 banks 1 local building and loan association, 4 national building and loan associations, 2 coal works in city limits and dozens near by, 2 brick works, 1 water works, 1 electric light plant, natural gas, artificial gas, city sewerage and paved streets (vitrified brick) in course of construction, 1 window glass factory, 1 electric experiment station, 1 haulage engine factory, 1 carborundum works, 1 manilla paper factory, pick handle factory, 1 lampwick factory, 1 miner's lamp factory, 1 pitcar factory, 1 real estate office, 1 opera house, 3 newspapers, 2 dailies, 2 weeklies, 1 monthly, 3 photograph galleries. It has 5 lawyers, 9 physicians, 4 dentists, 3 journalists, 4 notaries public 9 bankers, 3 insurance agents, 8 ministers."

Such the past and such the present of your prosperous and rapidly growing city. What the future shall be depends upon your continued energy, determination and public spirit, and that of the generations to come. The forefathers in looking into the future failed to anticipate such results in 100 years as confront the present inhabitants of this city.

It takes no flight of fancy or prophetic genius to foreshadow its outcome in another 100 years. You have the elements to make it a metropolitan city, and it requires no stretched imagination to assert that within that period 50,000 people will be imbraced within its limits, doing honor to the memory of the man who dared in the wilderness to lay the foundation of such a city—and that man's name was PARKISON.

WEST MONONGAHELA.

This town is situated immediately below and adjoining Monongahela City. It was located and laid out into lots, suitable avenues and streets by H. Higenbotham in 1893. It is on the south side of the Monongahela river and has a long river front of deep water. It is on the Pittsburgh, Virginia & Charleston railroad, with a good prospect of being on a branch of the Baltimore & Ohio railroad. A company is already organized to construct an electric road passing through the town, and the facilities of natural gas, electric light and water works are within reach at any time.

The town is situated on a beautiful plateau, capable of easy drainage and free from all marsh. For manufacturing purposes there are no better sites in the valley. Already the Thomas Wightman Glass Co. has located its extensive works in the town and are rapidly completing a plant which will employ 300 hands. Other capitalists are about erecting plants of various kinds. The proprietor has a coal frontage of 15,000 acres, an amount sufficient to furnish fuel for ages to come.

Mr. H. Higenbotham is a man of indomitable energy and business force, having started in the battle of life on his own resources at the age of eleven years. He was born in Masontown, Fayette county, Pa. He is the son of Theodore Higenbotham, who was the son of Samuel Higenbotham, an early settler in that country. Mr. H. Higenbotham has an abiding faith in the future greatness of the Monongahela valley. His new enterprise is already a success and foreshadows a near future when this town will be dotted over with manufactories of every variety, adding untold wealth to the capitalist and constant employment to skill and labor.

Monongahela Only.

In postoffice circles there will be no Monongahela City after April 1st, 1893, but thereafter when writing to Col. Hazzard's town the place should be designated as plain Monongahela. The following from the *Monongahela Republican* explains itself:

POSTOFFICE DEPARTMENT,
WASHINGTON, D. C., Feb. 13th, 1893.

You are respectfully informed that an order has been made changing the name of Monongahela City to Monongahela, to take effect April 1st, 1893.

E. E. RATHBORNE,
Fourth Assistant P. M. General.

THE MONONGAHELA CITY METHODIST EPISCOPAL CHURCH.

The early history of this church is not very satisfactory, owing to the absence of records. In 1812 two local preachers, brothers, named Riggs, organized a class at the house of Samuel Baxter, who then lived on the farm lately owned by Ira Butler, Esq., but now by Hiram Rabe, in Horseshoe, as a certain part of Carroll township is called. The class was composed of the two Riggs, Samuel Baxter and wife, and some of their children, and John R. Shugart and wife. A short time prior to the organization of this class another was formed at Father Preston's, and the two in due time became appointments under the title of the Beallsville circuit. It was in 1813, however, that the first class was formed in the town, the records of which are lost.

Among the members of this class were John R. Shugart and wife, who left the other class for convenience sake. Mrs. Shugart was a daughter of Samuel Baxter, above named. She died, as well as her husband, many years ago, and are yet remembered as pillars in the church. Mr. Shugart for long years carried on the saddle and harness business on the corner of Main and Third streets, now occupied by the large brick building belonging to J. B. Boyer heirs. He was a good workman, a good citizen and a good christian. Polly Baxter, a sister of Mrs. Shugart, was another member of this town class. Mrs. Vandever, at whose house the class held its first meeting, with her two daughters, belonged to the same class. Mrs. Vandever lived in a house owned by William Wickerham, corner of Race, now Third street, and Cherry alley. One of her daughters married Peter Shouse, the well-known boat builder of early days; his wife went with him to the Presbyterian church. The other daughter married Robert Bebee, also a boat builder. Mrs. Elizabeth McNary was also a member of this class. She was a sister of the late William P. Biles, who in his later days was kind of a lawyer. He lived in an old house on Main street, near the present residence of Dr. C. B.

Wood. A short time after the class was formed Æneas Graham and wife joined it. She was the daughter of Daniel DePue, Esq., who was commissioned Justice of the Peace March 12, 1793, by Governor Thomas Mifflin. His peculiar signature is attached to many of the old acknowledgments of deeds. In a short time after the class had got under fair headway Robert Bebee joined it.

This class really was the successor of the Riggs' class, and both were properly merged into one. The class was led by the preacher who held his first services in the house of Mrs. Vandever, where the class held its meetings. The leading of the class by the preacher was soon abandoned, and Æneas Graham was elected leader and to have the spiritual care of the little flock, from which nucleus has grown the present large and influential congregation.

If the spirits of the saved are permitted to hover around the living, then is his spirit near that church where the outcroppings of his early training are visibly seen in the multitude who have come into the fold of Christ through the means of this church.

The rapid increase of the class under the leadership of Mr. Graham soon required larger accommodations. Robert Bebee gave it a room in his dwelling, then on the bank of the river, afterward owned by Jonathan Pierce, known as the Wilson row, in honor of Alexander Wilson, who formerly was a prominent merchant in town, living in the house on Main street now occupied as storerooms and owned by Mark Borland and Landefeld. This room was also the place of preaching. It was, however, soon too small, and the class and preaching was removed to the old log school house where the Presbyterians also had their preaching, on which afterwards a public school house of three rooms was erected, the school house still remaining and used as a dwelling house. The old log school house becoming unfit to occupy, the roof leaking and windows broken, the place of preaching was removed to an old house once used as a barracks for troops on Main street, on a lot now owned by Daniel Swickard. Besides this place, the class and preaching were very often held in private houses in the neighborhood. William Jones, of whom we have written in another place, was a member of this class. The next place of preaching was in the brick church on the hill, which was built on a general subscription, the Presbyterians having an exclusive right to occupy it every third Sabbath, the balance of the time it could be used by any evangelical denomination.

The Methodist E. Church rapidly increased its membership by conversions and otherwise, especially by members moving into town from other places, among whom were Rev. John White, father of Judge J. W. F. White, of Pittsburgh, and Wm. Ihmsen, with Andrew, James and Wm. Mills. In 1827 the congregation purchased the house which, in a remodeled style, for many years stood just below the Second street wharf, on the bank of the river, but now torn down. The house originally had a brick first story. This was taken down and a gallery and wings were added to the old building. Soon after taking possession of this church, the Sabbath school was first organized, the late Thomas Collins being chosen superintendent. The matter of having a church of their own seemed to infuse new life into the congregation, so that in the year 1833 it had grown into such a position that they asked the conference to send them a station preacher, which was responded to by sending them Rev. Charles Cooke. At the second Quarterly Conference, held in December, 1833, it was resolved to make an effort to build a new church, and a committee was appointed, which afterwards constituted a Board of Trustees, to see what could be done in the way of raising money and selling the old church. This committee consisted of Joseph Alexander, Wm. Ihmsen and Wm. Mills. The next Quarterly Conference met March 18, 1834, and was composed of Charles Elliot, Presiding Elder; Rev. Charles Cooke, preacher in charge; Dr. David Johnson, local preacher; Wm. Mills and David Sherbondy, Stewards; Ira R. Butler, Cyrus Black, Wm. Ihmsen, Joseph Warne, Æneas Graham, Asher Vankirk and

John Hull, leaders. At this meeting the trustees, the number of which had been increased by the addition of Wm. Ihmsen, John R. Shugart and A. L. Williams, reported that they had raised by subscription eleven hundred dollars; that Wm. Ihmsen had donated a lot on the corner of Race, now Third street, and Spring alley, 50 by 80 feet, and that they had sold the old church for 125,000 brick, to be delivered at four dollars per thousand. The report was received and the Trustees were ordered to contract for the building of a brick house 44 by 62 feet with a gallery. They contracted with Samuel Devore to build it so far as to enclose in and lay the floors for $1,600. We are not informed who laid the brick, but Charles Reding did the carpenter work. The job was a good one, and at the day of its removal there was not a crack in it. During its existence a storm blew in the western gable end, but that was not the fault of the work. Whilst fixing in place the upper joists the late Andrew Clark was injured by falling through two tier of joist to the ground. His injuries were so severe as to ever afterwards prevent him from walking. He lived on the pike above Ginger Hill, was Postmaster for a while and Justice of Peace for many years, and was always considered a man of sterling integrity. The building committee of this church have all passed away. Wm. Ihmsen, so long identified with the business of the town, died long ago, leaving Joseph Wilson one of his executors. Wm. Mills married Lucinda Speer, of Bellevernon, Pa. He carried on the mercantile business for some years in the firm of Mills & Storer, in the old storeroom above the present residence of Dr. George A. Linn, on Main street, and in other places in town, either alone or in company. He was quite a politician, taking an active part in the campaign of 1840; was a candidate for the Legislature, but suffered defeat. He moved to Washington where he was a member of the firm of Mills & Baily; was also in business alone on the corner of Main and Wheeling streets; studied law and was admitted to the Washington bar in August, 1855; moved shortly after this date to Davenport, Iowa, where he remained until his death.

Among the active leaders who took part in the building of this church none were more interested than Æneas Graham. He died May 7, 1848, and his remains were interred in the old graveyard. He was one of the good of earth. He was long one of the pillows in the church, and was looked upon by saint and sinner as a model Christian gentleman. Small in stature, neat in attire, erect in his gate, pleasant in manner, intelligent in mind, kind in his domestic circle and honest in his dealings among men. He was a tailor by trade. He built the brick house now owned by Mrs. Phillips, corner of Main and Third streets, and in it for many years carried on the merchant tailoring business. His daughter Sarah was the first wife of S. B. Bentley, who survives her. Another daughter married the late Joel Ferree; both are dead. Ashur Vankirk was another leader of that day. His wife was a daughter of James Manown. He carried on the chairmaking business at that time on the "Island," as it was called. He died in McKeesport not many years since.

In order to complete the history of the Methodist E. Church we take the liberty of inserting, entire, the proceeding had on the Semi-Centennial celebration, as published in the *Monongahela Republican*, September 24, 25, 1883.

MAKING HISTORY.

That was a happy inspiration of Father Underwood, that this being the 50th year of the establishment of this church as a station it were well to celebrate the event. Pastor Nesbitt arranged a program, and yesterday both morning and evening services were devoted to historical papers and memorial addresses. A neatly printed programme was served bearing some of the *old* hymns, which during the services the choir sang to old-time melodies. The first paper was read by Mrs. Vandella Fell Wickerham upon

PLACES OF WORSHIP.

The beginning of Methodism at Parkisons Ferry, afterwards Williamsport, now Monongahela City, were humble but full of promise. For thirteen years after its origin it had no place of worship it could call its own, but tabernacled in private dwellings or in rented buildings. It is interesting to note the places where its meetings were held.

1st. In 1813 Mrs. Vandever, living on the corner of Race street and Cherry alley, opened her house for class meetings and preaching.

2d. After about three years the meetings were transferred to an upper room in the home of Robert Bebee on the river bank. They continued there until they out-grew the capacity of the room.

3d. Then a log house on Main street that had been used as a barracks for troops was rented and used as a house of worship.

4th. From this the society transferred its meetings to the old "log school house" that long stood on spring alley.

5th. The fifth place used for holding its meetings was the old union church on the hill. An incident that occurred there aroused in the members an ambition to have a house of their own.

6th. As the result, in 1826, a private dwelling standing on the bank of the river, was purchased, remodeled and fitted up as a place of worship. This was occupied for nine years, and then the growth of the society required a more commodious building.

7th. In 1834 a new church was commenced on the corner of Race and Chess streets, on a lot donated to the society by Wm. Ihmsen. That building was completed in the spring of 1835, and dedicated in May of that year by the pastor, Rev. Charles Cooke. For thirty-two years worship was conducted there.

8th. The present building is the third house of worship owned by the society, and the eighth place where it has held regular meetings. The initial steps towards securing this site and putting up this building were taken in 1864, when Rev. Ezra Hingely was pastor. The building committee appointed by the Quarterly conference was composed of O. C. House, R. M. Clark, Daniel Pierce, Alexander Scott, E. L. King, R. Stockdale, Joseph Alexander, James Williams, John Blythe, Cyrus Underwood, Robert Coulter, Joel T. Ferree, Isaac Jones, Col. Joseph Taylor, C. R. Stuckslager and S. P. Keller. The present site was purchased from Messrs. John and Henry Shæfer. In 1867 the lecture room was finished, opened, dedicated and used, and in 1878 the main audience room. Rev. Dr. W. A. Davidson officiated in the dedication of the lecture room and the pastor and Rev. A. B. Leonard in that of the main audience room. The building and lot cost about $45,000. It is now about seventy years since Methodism was planted in this place, and this fine building is a monument both of its spirit and its activity.

Mr. Cyrus Underwood then spoke of the fragmentery character of the records; the almost successful efforts now to put tradition on record, connected by the best data obtainable; of such character were the chapters in Dr. Creigh's history, in Boyd Cunningham's later history and in Doctor Van Voorhis' historical sketches, published in the *Republican*. He said: I came first here from Brownsville, in December, 1831, and in 1834 moved here permanently, during Rev. Cooke's pastorate; was a class leader from 1834 to 1854. He referred to a disputed point on the membership of the first class, but thought the matter tolerably certain now. When Brant built his grist mill to meet the growing wants of the town he employed two brothers named Riggs, millwrights, they being local preachers, organized that first class. They boarded at Baxter's, on the present farm of Ira Butler. This was then in the Baltimore Conference, and in the Blairsville circuit. He spoke of the early church movements at Parkison's Ferry; said that when Judge Gordon first came here, he was the only church member in the place. He related the incident which lead the Methodists to rent a room for their own use. When the church on the hill was built by general subscription, it was provided that the Presbyterians were to occupy it every third Sabbath, and on other Sabbaths the pulpit could be occupied by any regularly ordained evangelical preacher. One day Mr. White announced that "Lorenzo Dow would preach next Thursday evening." Dr. Ralston said "No." "Why not," asked White. "Because he is not a regularly ordained minister," answered the Doctor. However, it was insisted that he was, and on Thursday, Dow, with a large crowd, assembled, but no fire, no light, the doors closed. The evening was bitter cold, and by the time the door was opened, fire and light procured, the shivering Methodists had fully made up their minds to have a house of their own. Mr. Underwood joined Ira Butler's class, and he wound up his very interesting sketch by reviewing the past, and concluded by saying, "As I look over these past years, so full of precious memories, so filled with mercies and blessings, and know that I am still with you to see the infant church grown to vigorous manhood, firmly planted in the hearts of this people, I can only lift my heart in prayer and thankfulness, and say, "How good the Lord hath been."

Miss Carrie E. Coulter then read a paper entitled,

Ministers Who Have Served.

The beginning of Methodism at Parkison's Ferry has already been traced to the two brothers Riggs, local preachers, who took up the appointment and visited it for an indefinite period every three weeks. From their time until 1833, a period of twenty years, the appointment formed a part of the Beallsville circuit, and was served by such well known men as Revs. Thos. M. Hudson, Joshua Monroe, James G. Sansom, William Stevens and Samuel P. Brockunier. In 1833, Williamsport, then the name of the place, was erected into a station, and Rev. Chas. Cooke was sent by the Pittsburgh Conference as the first stationed preacher. His successors in the pastorate down to the present time are as follows : Matthew Simpson, Christopher Hodgson, William Hunter, Alcinus Young, Nathaniel Callendar, Wm. Lemon, Ebenezer Hays, E. P. Jacob, L. H. Costin,

Charles Thorn, Wesley Smith, Caleb Foster, Geo. S. Holmes. Josiah Mansell, Peter F. Jones, A. G. Williams, S. F. Minor, L. R. Beacom, J. C. Brown, A. J. Endsley, Ezra Hingely, A. W. Butts, H. Miller, S. M. Sickman, Ed. Williams, T. N. Boyle, W. Lynch, R. L. Miller, J. S. Bracken, I. A. Pearce and S. H. Nesbit. This makes thirty-two in all who have served the appointment in its fifty years as a station. The ministers who served the appointment before it became a station have all passed on to their reward. Twelve of the thirty-two who have served it as a station have also ended their labors and entered into rest. These are Chas. Cooke, Christopher Hodgson, William Hunter, Alcinus Young, Nathaniel Callender, Wm. Lemon, Ebenezer Hays, L. H. Costin, Charles Thorn, Caleb Foster, Geo. S. Holmes and Peter F. Jones (who died while pastor here, and Rev. Cyrus Black filled out his time). Whether E. P. Jacobs and A. C. Williams be living or dead is not now known. But the remaining eighteen are still living and, with one exception, in the active work of the ministry. This paper would be incomplete if it should end without a personal notice of some of the eminent men who first served the appointment as a station. Charles Cooke, tender, loving and beloved, transferred to the Philadelphia Conference, served several of the best churches in Philadelphia, and at last ended his days and labors in that city. Matthew Simpson is now Senior Bishop of the Methodist E. Church, a place of loftier eminence than any earthly throne.

Christopher Hodgson, earnest and convincing in argument, married a daughter of the early society, and his descendant, Rev. Thomas S. Hodgson, is perpetuating his name and his ability in the ministry, and William Hunter, eminent as a theologian, as editor, as educator, is still more eminent as poet. His hymns and songs are a rich legacy to the church. Time will not permit to further name and characterize the ministers that have served this charge. It must suffice to say that they did their work well, and made for us to-day a rich and beautiful heritage. Of the fathers we may all be proud. May their sons in the gospel do as well in their day. Mr. Joseph Warne was prevented by sickness from being present and R. M. Clark made the concluding address. Mr. Clark said that John Wesley once said that we must not do our duty just when we *feel* like it. We must do our duty when the occasion comes. He did not feel like speaking, but Dr. Nesbitt had put him on the program and made it his duty to say something. An old Quaker had once told him "Robert, when thee has nothing to say, say it." He had a few words to say, and looking back forty years so many blessings crowded to his memory that he must speak a word for the Master. He thought the class meeting a peculiar means of grace; he enjoyed them. His disposition was to look on the sunny side of life, and in the class he never told a doleful story; if he had nothing cheerful to say he said nothing. He believed in saying encouraging things, and this morning was full of promise and bright with hope. He was born in Lycoming county, of Presbyterian parentage; he had learned the teachings of that church, and its traditions too; he had been led to look upon the Methodists as "bad people" in a certain sense, and went from home with that idea. He boarded at Williamsport with a good Methodist family, and found out that they were real Christians. One evening he happened to pass a room where class meeting was being held. At that time a "word" or ticket from the class leader was required and the door-keeper refused me admittance. A good lady just inside the door said "Will you pray if you come in?" I told her I did not know much about that kind of business, but I would behave myself anyhow. I went in and heard a brother tell what the Lord had done for him; and a good woman came and laid her hand on my head, and said in her sweet persuasive voice "Don't you want to be a Christian?" I thank God to-day for the warm heart and sweet voice of that good woman. And that is why I love the class meeting. Some people say Methodism is not what it was fifty years ago. I think it is broader, deeper, wider than ever before. Mr. Clark concluded his very interesting talk by expressing a fervent wish that he would live his life out and die here among the people he loved. The services were of exceeding interest throughout.

A still larger audience assembled for the evening services. Rev. Dr. Nesbitt, after the singing, asked Miss Millie G. Bentley to read a paper, which she did as follows, entitled

OFFICIAL MEMBERS.

The earliest Methodists in this place held their meetings in private houses or in rented buildings. This continued for thirteen years, or from the origin of the movement, in 1813, to the year 1826. In the beginning of that period, Æneas Graham, as already seen, was class leader, and John P. Shugart class steward. At the end of that period, as nearly as can be ascertained, there were three classes, led respectively by Æneas Graham, Asher Vankirk and James Mills. In 1826 William Jones, Æneas Graham and Robert Beebe, appointed a committee by the Quarterly Conference of the Beallsville Circuit, for the purchase of a three-story building standing on the river bank, and had it remodeled and made into a two-story church. It seems fairly certain that during the nine years of worship David Sherbondy was added to the list of class leaders, making in all probability a fourth class. It is impossible at this day to tell who were stewards during the period when the appointment remained a part of Beallsville circuit. Some of the Trustees holding the property on the river bank were Wm. Jones, Æneas Graham, Robert Beebe, Asher Vankirk, Joseph Alexander and William and John Herron. James Mills was a local preacher. The removal of the society from the church on the river bank to the new church on the corner of Race and Chess streets took place in May, 1835. The Trustees that then existed and that have since been elected, are as follows: Æneas Graham, A. Vankirk, J. Alexander, James Mills, Cyrus Underwood, John Herron, James Williams, David Williams, H. M. Bentley, Charles Rose, James Officer, Wm. Cott, R. M. Clark, Robert Coulter, Hiram Filson, J. F. Ferree, O. C. House, James

Allen, R. F. Cooper, Abram Van Voorhis, S. P. Keller, Daniel Pierce, C. R. Stuckslager, Isaac Jones, William Coulter, Joseph Warne, John Blythe, Geo. T. Scott, M. Borland, J. D. Hammond, R. E. Byers and E. Downer. Of these thirty-four that held office during the half century just passed, seventeen have passed to their reward and seventeen are still on these mortal shores.

It has been found impossible, because of defective records, to give the names of local preachers, the exhorters, the stewards and the class leaders, that have served the society in the past fifty years. Revs. James Mills and John White, father of Judge White of Allegheny county, stand on the fragmentary records as class leaders at different times. They were located here and in business. In 1834 the class leaders were Ira Butler, Wm. Ihmsen, Asher Vankirk, David Sherbondy and Joseph Warne. Rev. Charles Cooke also had charge of two classes, making a total number of seven classes at that time.

It is a question of serious and practical import—have we been wise in allowing the class meetings to fall into a state of comparative decay? We have but three classes to-day. Ought we not to have ten? And if ten, and well attended, would there not come upon *us a new* aggressive life and force?

A. V Graham said the services had revived memories of his childhood. He knew most of the men named, and was proud that his own family name had borne such a part among those who had helped to lay the cornerstone and worked all these years at the edifice. He referred especially to the Sunday school, and said he could say he had spent his life in the Sunday school. It had kept pace with the sentiment of the day and had grown to be a part of the church, nursery, a recruiting station. He remembered when one person filled the offices of superintendent, secretary, treasurer, librarian, and taught a class besides. Now we have four librarians. He remembered back to Hunter, third in the list of preachers; remembered Holmes, who interested the young folks of the town, lectured to them during the week on scientific and literary subjects. He had peculiarities. One warm day, when some of the members dozed, he sat down, and said he would give the sleepers a chance to have their nap out. He was annoyed by members putting their hats on within the church, after the benediction, and broke it up by saying that he would "name out" those who did it again. Mr. Graham concluded by an apostrophe to the fathers, and asked that the seed they planted should be assiduously cultivated by those into whose keeping the garden of the Lord had been bequeathed—a priceless legacy.

His reminiscence of Holmes recalled to Dr. Nesbitt an incident at Morgantown where Holmes was sent by the old midsummer conference. He found that the leading men, like Senator Willie, Dr. McLean the vermifuge man, and others, regularly went to sleep during service. They were not only pillars of the church but sleepers, too. One day when the nap was on, he quietly said to the congregation, "I will take a moment's rest; please sing Days of Absence, and remain seated while you sing." It was the custom to "rise and sing," but the congregation joined in, remaining seated. Awakened by the singing, the sleepers suddenly rose up, thinking it the concluding hymn. They looked sort of sheep like, seeing no one else up, and presently sank into their seats abashed. That cured the nap business. Prof. J. P. Taylor, who has been seven years Superintendent of the Sabbath school, read a statistical paper full of facts of much interest. We have room for a few of them.

The Sunday School.

The school was organized and Thomas Collins, Esq., deceased, its first superintendent, served from 1827 to 1833, then Abraham Hull in 1833, David Sherbundy in 1834, William Mills in 1836, William Herron in 1838, John Herron in 1840, Joel T. Ferree in 1843, Cyrus Underwood in 1844, Robert McLardy in 1845-47, brother-in-law of Raphael Coulter; William Cott in 1848, Cyrus Underwood in 1854-57, R. M. Clark in 1852, Cyrus Black in 1855-56, Joel T. Ferree in 1857-58, S. B. Bentley in 1859-60, O. C. House in 1861,

S. B. Bentley and F. F. Kernan in 1862, F. F. Kernan in 1863, O. C. House in 1864, Dr. E. L. King in 1865, F. F. Kernan in 1866, Dr. J. W. L. Rabe in 1867, S. B. Bentley in 1868, R. H. Young in 1870-71, J. D. Hammond in 1872, R. H. Young in 1873, S. B. Bentley in 1874, R. H. Young in 1875-76, J. P. Taylor in 1877-83. Owing to the records of the Sabbath school prior to the year 1862 being lost, we can give no positive history of the number of officers, teachers or scholars of the school. The first we get is April 13, 1862, when the attendance was 208; at that time there were 9 officers, 27 teachers, and a total membership of 312.

June 15th of this year Emma Norfolk, Mary Gibbs. Josephine Shepler, Anna Young, Emma Clark, Amanda Filson, Fanny Cott, Emory Graham, Eva Graham, Mattie Heyser and Ella Heyser were presented with a music book for committing the Lord's prayer. The whole number of books in the library at this time was 883; 60 of these books were spelling books. The average attendance, 155 during the quarter ending July 1st. September 21st S. B. Bentley resigned and entered the army, joining the 140th regiment. Teachers John Blythe, O. C. House, S. Applegate, J. C. Brown, M. W. Mitchener and F. F. Kernan entered the military service of the state guards, but were all home in two weeks and at work. Perhaps they were back in one week but were too tired to be at Sabbath school.

January 12, 1868, the Sabbath school met for the first time in the present building, S. B. Bentley, superintendent; the infant department in the hands of sister Mary Scott. Up to this time, while there has been an increase in membership, the daily attendance scarcely ever exceeds 200, ranging from 125 to 185. The collections heretofore less than one dollar are about four dollars. March 1st, 1868, the Sabbath school room was dedicated, sermon by Rev. W. A. Davidson. April 25th, 1868, Mary Scott resigned as teacher of the infant department, numbering about 55, and Miss Nan Scott was installed in her stead.

August, 1870, sometime during the month, D. C. Valentine

died, date not given; he presents as good if not the best daily minutes of the Sabbath school found in any of the books. During the year one grand revolution and advance was made in the Sabbath school work—the bureau system was invented. February 5th, 1871, 275 volumes of books were donated to Dry Run and Leechburg schools; 1872, the daily attendance now runs from 165 to 250; 1873, international lesson leaf; January 2d, 1876, the school reached its highest attendance, 315. The speaker referred in passing to faithful teachers, to the triumphant deaths of those who had gone before, and closed with an earnest appeal for more workers and more earnestness in the work.

Miss Sallie Graham then read a paper, entitled, the Society and its growth.

Two brothers by the name of Riggs began preaching and organized a class about 1812 at the home of Samuel Baxter, in Carroll township, on the farm now owned by Ira Butler. About these two brothers but little has been preserved, except that they were batchelors, followed the occupation of millwrights, and lived up and across the river, most likely in the neighborhood of Fell's church. Though their memories are not perpetuated in monumental marble, they gave birth to influences that will be imperishable. So far as can now be ascertained they were the first Methodist preachers that ever preached in this neighborhood. Their visits to Parkison's Ferry began in 1813. They preached every third Sabbath, organized a class and led it on each of their visits. The first members of that class are pretty satisfactorily determined as John R. Shugart and wife, Letitia, Mrs. Vandever and her two daughters, Robert Beebe, Mrs McNary and Polly Baxter. Such was the seed planted seventy years ago. The class led every third Sabbath by the preachers was otherwise without a leader till Æneas Graham and his wife united with it, and he in a short time was made leader. This was in the latter part of 1813 or early in 1814. Thereafter the growth of the young society was rapid, and among its earlier additions were Elias Watkins and wife, Mrs. Mary Black, Mrs. Verner, mother-in-law of Bishop Simpson, Mrs. McNary and Nancy Roberts and William Jones, and the Padens, the Philipses and David Sherbondy and wife. Later along the society was further enlarged by such names as the Wickerhams, the Woodwards, the Warnes, the Alexanders, the Herrons, the Youngs, the Swartzs, the Mills, the Cotts, the Bentleys, the Coulters, the Hulls, the Collinses and the Williams. The eight members in 1813 had reached 300 in 1833, and now, fifty years later, are in excess of 400. Such is some of the fruitage of the seed planted here by the Riggs brothers seventy years since. It has grown into a tree of beauty and casts on every side a grateful shade. For the living of to-day the fathers have made this wilderness to bloom as a garden of the Lord. They, themselves, having finished their work, have, the most of them, passed to their rest. We hail and recall to-day those faithful men and women who filled up the measure of their days in serving God and doing good, and then entered into the gloryland. And we invoke blessings upon their co-workers who have come down to our times as so many relics of the heroic age of Methodism.

>Green be the path beneath them,
>And beautiful the sunset at evening.

The society has had a growth at once substantial and encouraging, but certainly more rapid and vigorous in the earlier than in the later times. In the first twenty years it grew from eight members to 300, and in its fifty years as a station it has only grown from 300 to 420 members. Is it not fitting that we ask ourselves to-day, are we doing in our place as well as did our fathers?

J. C. Swickard, one of the most earnest class workers in the society, spoke on that subject which was near to heart, he was a warm lover of the class. In the grand history of our local Methodism, running back 70 years, it began with a class organized, and in the days of its greatest prosperity there were eight or ten classes. At a class meeting near Bentleysville, he went in, just why he didn't know, but while there he heard that good man Richard Richardson give his experience, saying that he knew, he felt in his heart that he "had found his Saviour." I could not say that, and was then and there I resolved, and I never was satisfied till I had found that Saviour so precious to him, so dear to me. That is why I love the class. I was put in brother Clark's class, then Dr. Rabe's and finally Dr. Bracken asked me to take charge of the class. I felt my unworthiness, but I thank God now for the privilege it gives me to mingle my joys with those of my brethren. The preached word is a solace and a comfort, but religion gathers strength in the class room. God help us all to do our duty.

Dr. Nesbit announced that he would endeavor to place on record succint history of the church up to the time when the regular record began. In his introduction of the several speakers the Doctor was peculiarly happy, and in all the services there was a warm, generous feeling which showed how happily united were pastor and people in the celebration now drawn to a close. Sunday was a half mile stone on the journey toward the Promised Land, and the 23d of September, 1883, will long remain written with a gilt star on the date in the annals of local church history.

Mr. S. B. Bentley said this was a proud day to him, as he heard his family name so long and so intimately interwoven in words and works for the advancement of the Methodist Church. He wondered how old he really was when he heard all this back history repeated, and when he thought over how many of the old people he had personally known. The history of his family was a part of the town as well as of the church. His grandfather came in 1794; his mother was born here in 1795, in the old house which stood on the river bank below where Mr. Bearer lives. He seemed to have been always in the church; among his earliest recollections were being stood up on the broad altar-board, singing the old-time hymns as he learned them from his grandmother. My brethren, the singing now is more artistic, but the hymns of those days *converted* people. (A voice: Please sing one). To this request Bentley sang

"Saw ye my Savior and God," and the good old song must have awakened memories, for here and there a "treble" voice piped up in the chorus, showing that age had not forgotten the tunes of long ago—childhood. Some one asked him "Where will we be fifty years hence, when our centennial is celebrated?" He answered, "We will be *gone*." And oh! my brethren, what record will we make that the speaker on that occasion can refer to *something* we have done or said that will be worth remembering; worth repeating. He had been singing with the choir for thirty-five years, and at many a funeral, at merry makings and at meetings. Is there any one here who dare say that Christians may not be united in the great choir which will gather to sing the grand song—when our King shall be crowned —and the saved shall sing Hozannas forever.

Cyrus Underwood

Died at his home, corner Coal and Sixth streets, Monongahela City, Wednesday evening, November 11, 1885. The *Daily Republican* in noticing his death, remarks: Cyrus Underwood was born in Baltimore, Md., August 28, 1807. He was married in 1826 to Miss Rebecca Shriver. Eleven children blessed their union, five of whom are dead—three died in infancy. Wilbur was drowned from the steamer Bunton; Abraham died September 8, 1885. Six children yet live. Jane, wife of Hiram Filson; Amanda, wife of A. V Graham; Mary, widow of S. V Miller; James, married; Charles and Hannah, unmarried and still at home. He had twenty-one grandchildren and ten great-grandchildren. He came to this city from Brownsville in 1834. He was one of the earliest and oldest Methodists of this community, having been connected with the church for over 57 years. He was always greatly interested in education. The following paragraph is quoted from the historical address of Dr. J. S. VanVoorhis, delivered at the dedication of our new school house, July 1, 1881: "The rapid growth of the borough soon necessitated the erection of a new school building. In the year 1852 the Board of Directors, consisting of our venerable friend Cyrus Underwood as President and the late Alex. Wilson as Secretary, with Joseph Alexander, H. H. Finley, Wilson Thompson and Alex. Scott as members, resolved to build a new school house, which gave the town the brick house across the street from this house.

The lot was purchased from Henry Fulton. The house cost $7,000. Johnson Baird and William Wilson did the stone and brick work, whilst the veteran contractor, William Coulter, with us to-night, did the carpenter work. It was opened for school in the fall of 1853. Andrew Brown, now of the "Forks," and T. R. Hazzard, just returned from West Newton, were the first teachers, the former having been the last to teach in the old building.

Too much credit cannot be given president Underwood for his untiring industry and foresight in moulding public opinion and carrying the enterprise to successful issue. He first settled in this place in 1834, where he has resided ever since, excepting three years he served as recorder of the county. He and H. H. Finley are the only surviving members of that board of directors. We are glad to see them both here to-night. Kind friends, faithful Christians, human benefactors, we bid you God speed!"

Mr. Underwood took an active part in the establishment of our new cemetery and was very earnest in the advancement of its interests, and especially delighted in its adornment, making frequent visits to the city of the dead, never tired in admiring its trees and avenues. On Friday he will be laid to rest amid the graves and paths which shall know his footsteps no more, forever. He was a warm whig and a strong republican, and his public services were recognized by an election to be recorder, in which office he served during 1855-56-57, and left at the county seat a good record of fidelity to public duty, and upright walks in the social life. It does not evoke much pain to write the words *he is dead*. He waited the coming, his soul yearned for the rest, he was a ripe sheaf heavy for the harvest. Believing in Christ as his personal Saviour he has completed

the work of life and gone to his eternal home. Therefore it is
not sad to write the words "he is dead," for all these words
mean, when said of him, is that good, old "uncle Cyrus" has
gone to his eternal home, and linked with his memory is only
the fragrance of a pure life.

IRA. R. BUTLER.

Among the early and active class leaders in this church was
Ira R. Butler. We insert an interview the author had with
him a few years before his death.

His grandfather was born in Bristol, England. His name
was Noble Butler, and came to this country in 1716, about
two years before the death of Wm. Penn. He landed at Philadelphia and entered under the rules and regulations of Wm.
Penn, one thousand acres of land at a very small price in Yeoch-
land township, Chester county. His wife's name was Rachel
Jones, of Welsh descent. Noble was a single man when he
settled on this large farm, but not long after his arrival he was
married. They had twelve children, the youngest of whom
was Benjamin, the father of Ira. Noble died on this farm in
1804. Benjamin Butler had as sons and daughters, David,
Jonathan, Elizabeth, Abner, Eunice, Noble, Isaac, Benjamin,
Joel, Joseph and Ira R. His large family growing rapidly toward maturity, Benjamin Butler, although surrounded by every
comfort that wealth and opportunity could afford, began about
the beginning of the present century to show a disposition to
try his fortunes in the wilds of the Ohio. This increased after
the death of his father. To carry out his desires in a satisfactory way, he sent two of his sons on horseback to spy out the
new country, with instructions to purchase one well improved
farm, and to secure enough in the neighborhood to furnish the
family a farm each. They in due time returned with glowing
accounts of the Ohio valley, and reported in favor of a section
near North Bend on the Ohio river, some distance below Cincinnati. In a short time Father Butler sent the same sons
back to secure the property by absolute purchase. On their

return to the homestead in the spring of 1805, the old gentleman sold all he had except such things as were determined to be taken along. After harvest they all bid adieu to the old homestead with its magnificent stone mansion, and with a six-horse wagon, a five-horse wagon, a two-horse carriage and two extra horses the family set out on their journey to Ohio. They traveled by the way of Lancaster, Harrisburg and Bedford, and crossed the Monongahela river at Parkison's Ferry on Sabbath evening the 6th of October, 1805; put up at the tavern of George Trout, long known as the Caldwell stand, on Main street. Next morning the father arose from bed; went to feed the horses so as to be ready for an early start; returned to the house, laid down to await breakfast; when called he was speechless; died before midnight of palsy. Doctors at that time were not convenient, none nearer than Greensburg or the Upper Forks. In the midst of this sudden affliction to the newcomers, it was suggested to send up the country a a short distance for a man the name of Miller, who made pretentions to be a general doctor in all things, especially in cows and other animals. He arrived in due time, and with no little degree of pomp and self assurance, pronounced the old gentleman's disease to be yellow fever, supplementing his decisions with the remark that he had powders "for fifty cents each, which, if taken promptly, would prevent the rest of the family, and citizens generally, from taking the disease." Many powders were no doubt disposed of to the credulous. Most of the family were in a short time taken unwell, and within two weeks Isaac died. In the meantime Dr. Marchand, of Greensburg, was called. The history of the case of the old gentleman was related, and he declared it to be a stroke of the palsy; that the rest of the family, from exposure on the journey, had malarial fever. He denounced the cow doctor in severest terms, and on examination found his powders to be made of brick dust and some other as inert substance. He declared he would not hesitate to *cow*hide such a man.

Isaac was buried with his father in the Wickerham graveyard, now in the third ward. In the midst of this sorrow Captain Daniel VanVoorhis called to see and comfort the family. He said, "Boys, if you are not going to use your horses send them up to my farm and turn them into the fort field where the grass is knee deep, and leave them there as long as you deem proper." Ira and one of his brothers salted them regularly, and there Ira saw a bear for the first time, which was a pet of Abraham VanVoorhis, then about 20 years old. Some of the shoes that came off these horses were found a few years since in plowing the field. They are in the possession of John VanVoorhis, the present owner of the field. The death of the father of this family created no little stir in the town; the citizens generally were frightened, and some were so lost to shame as to insist on the Butlers leaving town even in their distress. The father's death necessitated the taking of an inventory of his goods. As this was being done the goods were to be removed to the Red house, now gone, at the mouth of First street, on the river, which had been rented from Samuel Black. Some of the citizens, more nervous than humane, persuaded Mr. Black not to allow the family to occupy the house, though part of the goods had been loaded on the wagons and in the way to the house. He yielded to their demands, leaving them in such a strait as they knew not what to do. At this critical moment appeared among them the good samaritan, Nathan W. Chalfant, saying, "Strangers, I have a house rented down on Race street which I will not need till spring. Drive your wagons to it and unload your goods, and let me see the man who will dare to disturb you." Thus the Butlers became citizens of the town, and their prospects for North Bend blighted. This man Chalfant lived in Brownsville, but was building keel boats in the town, being its first boat builder. His name and that of Capt. VanVoorhis were cherished in fond remembrance by the Butler family, and the Esquire at this day says, "I hardly know anybody else than the VanVoorhis name." Afterwards some time the family moved into the frame house, then unfinished, opposite the City Hotel, occupied by Keller & Co. The members of the family generally were short lived. One of the boys was thrown from a stage three miles this side of Washington, from the effects of which he died September, 1822. Rachel died 13th of October, 1822. Joel married Betsy, daughter of William Irwin, of whom we have written. Eunice married the late David Woodward, father of Noble and Joseph. She died a few years since, an account of whose death was written by Lewis Bollman and printed in the *Republican*. At this date Ira alone remains. He was born at the old homestead in Chester county, November 15th, 1792. He was married by George Bentley, Esq., to Mary Boyd, June 14th, 1822. She was born October 23d, 1801, at New London Cross Roads, Chester county. She died September 7th, 1874. Ira and his wife first set up housekeeping in what was long known as the Peggy Speers house, in Catsburg. In 1812 he kept store with his brother Benjamin in the house now occupied by T. H. Baird, Esq., on Main street, known as the Stewart property. He sold eggs for three to four cents per dozen, butter six to ten cents per pound, home made sugar $6\frac{1}{4}$ cents per pound, there was no other kind of sugar sold; used tallow candles for light in candlesticks of tin with brass mountings and about ten inches high. As people generally made their own wearing material from flax and tow, there was not much finery sold in the stores.

The mercantile business did not agree with his health. He sold out, went to Lake Erie, where he secured employment as super-cargo on the sailing vessel "Union of the Grand River," Captain Martin, Master. The boat was chartered by the North American Fur Company, of which John J. Astor was president, to bring furs and other goods from Fort Mackinaw, after its surrender to the British forces by Captain Darragh, brother of the late Daniel Darragh, of Mingo. One of the terms of the surrender permitted private citizens to take away their property. He was on the same vessel three years, during two of which he was captain of the craft, and hence he acquired the title of Captain Butler. In the winter of 1815 he returned to Williamsport and followed boat building. He moved from the Peggy Speers house to the Woodward place. where John Lamb first had his tan yard. He subsequently bought the property opposite the paper mill, and in 1837 built the brick house in which he lived until in 1841 he moved to his present residence. He sold his property opposite the paper mill to Douglas McFarland, father of Campbell McFarland, Esq., and Rev. John McFarland, who died some years ago in Greenfield, Dade county, Missouri. He bought his present residence from a man the name of Stockdale, who, we think, purchased it from the Baxters.

On the 12th day of May, 1880, we called on Esq. Butler. He was not at home, but was informed that he would be home shortly, as he only walked down to the blacksmith's at Victory coal works, and as he was a good walker would soon be back. I thought to myself, a pretty good walk for a man 88 years old. In a short time I heard him on the porch, met him with an extended hand ; looking me in the eyes, says : "I believe I do not know you." Giving him a gentle hint who I was, he exclaimed, "Why, John, I hav'n't seen you for thirty years. Set down, I am very glad to see you."

I soon discovered that he was a perfect encyclopædia of the past ; his recollection clear ; his conversational powers unimpaired ; his body erect ; in fact a man extraordinarily well preserved. He has preserved all his papers bearing on his history, business and travels. Still has his copy books used when at school in 1807 ; a memorandum of miscellany during his life ; a detailed description of a journey in a flatboat from Williamsport to Orleans ; his experience on Lake Erie, in fact the sum total of a long, active life on paper. After giving me a sketch of his family as above, only at length, I gathered from him much in a desultory way.

Well, Esq., which house do you think was first built in town ? Ans. The log part of the old Parkison mansion. Who was the first cabinet maker ? Joseph McClure, who made my father's coffin, and under whom the late John Eckles learned his trade. His shop was across the alley from the City Hotel, in which Joseph Hamilton afterwards had his cabinet shop. By whom and when was the City Hotel built? Washington Palmer, in 1811, just before he went out in Capt. James Warne's company to the war of 1812, this company being a part of Pennsylvania's first quota. Who built the old Glass Works, now gone? Parkison, Warne & Co., in 1816. The company consisted of William Parkison, James Warne, Joel and Benjamin Butler. Haywood did the job at a cost of $27,000 before it was ready to start. At the first blast the cap fell in and in fact the whole was a failure. It was sold at sheriff's sale to Samuel Black and J. and R. McGrew, who rented it to Wm. Ihmsen. How about Catsburg? When Esq. James Mitchell laid out East Williamsport in 1811, the widow Biddie Caldwell and her daughter were the only inhabitants on the site, and their cabin was the only dwelling except the old log house in which Daniel DePue had resided, on the point at the mouth of the creek. Biddie's cabin was situated in the orchard on the slope of the hill above the residence of the widow Collins. Biddie and her daughter were constantly quarrelling, squealing, pulling hair and crying like cats. So prominent a feature were these qualities that the household was called the "cat and kittens," and the people on the other side of the creek very soon took hold of the idea of calling the new town Catsburg, despite of the Esq.'s name. Who gave the old graveyard lot? William Parkison. The new addition was purchased by a general subscription under the supervision of the late Joseph Wilson. Who was Thomas Wells? The first saddle and harness maker in town. Who built the first saw mill? William Johnson, the father-in-law of William Layman. It stood not far from Neel, Blythe & Co.'s mills. In building boats before this time the creek mills sawed the timber into plank, but the whipsaw made it into shape. "Well, Esq., I must go." "If you must go," says he. "I want you to call again and I will give you a detail of the building of the town, and how I used to work for my old friend, Abram Van Voorhis, and others for 62½ cents per day."

Ira Butler died at his home in Carroll township, July 18, 1884. The *Daily Republican* in a notice of his death says, "His funeral took place on Sunday, July 20, from his old homestead, and was followed to Monongahela cemetery by the largest concourse of people that has ever been seen at the obsequies of any citizen in this part of the country. His death occurred at ten o'clock on Friday night, and the funeral was announced for two o'clock on Sabbath. Long before the hour appointed for the interment hundreds of people in scores of vehicles had collected at the venerated old man's residence to do honor to the memory of one who had lived among them a monument of honesty, uprightness and purity. The pall bearers were Wm. Galbraith, Wm. Coulter, David Rabe and Joseph Warne. The funeral was under the direction of Capt. A. D. O'Donovan. The casket furnished was of oak, draped with black cloth. On the plate was the following inscription :

CAPT. IRA REESE BUTLER,
AGED 91 YEARS, 8 MONTHS AND 3 DAYS.

Dr. Nesbitt, pastor of the Methodist Church of this city, officiated on the occasion, and in his discourse alluded feelingly and appropriately to the long life and Christian example of the deceased. The emblem of the sheaf of wheat placed upon the casket fitly illustrated that the harvest had been gathered and his many years of usefulness was to be well rewarded by the enjoyment of a bright and glorious beyond. He had been a consistent member of the Methodist Church of this city for over seventy years, having connected himself with it in its infancy, when about twenty-two years of age. Captain Butler was truly one of the pioneers of Washington county, and the many scraps of local history connected with his life would be of great interest to the general reader. About 1815 he was captain of a sailing vessel on the lakes, where he was accustomed to put in his time in the business season, returning to Monongahela City to spend the winter with his friends and family. In June,

1880, we published from the pen of our valued correspondent, Dr. Van Voorhis, reminiscences of Mr. Butler and family from which we to-day reprint a few extracts." These extracts were inserted in a former part of this article. Ira R. Butler was the last of seven sons, all of whom are now dead. The Captain left behind him eight children—Benjamin F., now deceased (1889), Ira William and Mrs. Dr. Keys, Mrs. James Blythe, Mrs. Pratt, Mrs. Keechline and Miss Sarah, all residing in or about Monongahela City.

ELIAS WATSON.

Among the early and devoted members of this church was Elias Watkins. His father, Joseph Watkins, came from Baskin Ridge, N. J, in 1801, and settled near Williamsport, on what farm we are not informed. He died within two years after his arrival. He seems to have been married twice. By his second marriage he had three sons, Jeremiah, John and Elias, and one daughter, Ann, who married the late Abram Van Voorhis. Jeremiah married Nancy Pugh, born in New Jersey. Her father and mother, it may be said, were both Revolutionary soldiers, he being in the American army during the entire war, and she living amidst many of its most stirring scenes; was frequently involved in the perils and hardships incident to a country occupied by contending armies. Jeremiah was a farmer of Fallowfield, living fourteen years on a tract of land belonging to the Grable estate on Pigeon creek, and from which, in 1839, he moved to Southeastern Indiana, where he owned a large body of land on which he died in 1845. His wife died about the year 1870, surviving her husband 25 years. They left three sons; two of whom are successful farmers in Kansas. The oldest son was named Joseph Finley, after Mr. Finley, who died years ago in Rostraver township, Westmoreland county. Joseph F. was 19 years old when his father took him with him to Indiana. He remained on his father's farm assisting in making improvements and caring for the family for ten years, during which time he represented his county for two terms in the Legislature. His differing with a majority of his constituents by advocating the passage of a stringent temperance law, caused his defeat afterwards for an important county office. He then abandoned politics, shook the dust of that county from his feet, moved to the western part of the State, where he successfully engaged in the mercantile business up to 1872, when he sold out with a view of partially retiring from business. His active disposition and business turn of mind would not allow him a life of retirement. He bought a half interest in the extensive Brown mills, in the city of Crawfordsville, in connection with which is a large grain elevator. The firm of Brown & Watkins is now largely engaged in shipping and manufacturing flour.

John Watkins was well known in this community for many years. He was a carpenter by trade and did much of the fine work in the older houses in this vicinity. His first wife was a daughter of Alexander McCaslin, who resided years ago near Ginger Hill. He moved from the farm to Williamsport about the year 1828, purchased the lot on which Dr. Linn erected his new house. On this lot in 1829 he built a dwelling house and store room, now being torn down. William Mills in 1839 had a store in this room, and also the firm of Mills & Storer occupied it for a time. He left town, in what year we can not tell, to reside on a farm on Mingo, not far from Kammerer's Mills, where he died about 20 years ago. We have no information as to his children.

Elias, the remaining brother, was a man of marked religious character, of deep and fervent piety. In connection with James Mills he built the old steam mill on the other side of the river from the mouth of First street. This mill was burned many years ago whilst owned and run by a man the name of Joseph Coulson. The cause of the fire remains a mystery to this day. Elias lived a long time at the mills, long since gone, belonging to Abram VanVoorhis, which stood on Pigeon creek. He died about the year 1834, leaving a widow and a large family of children. His wife was a half-sister of Robert

Phillips, the late Nancy Wickerham and Mrs. Jane VanVoorhis, and a full sister, we think, of Margaret Paden—Mrs. Hull, deceased. His son John was a glassblower by trade. He quit his trade on account of health; lived in and owned the house just above the Episcopal church on Main street. He married Miss Eliza Jane, daughter of the late James Warne. He with his family moved in 1857 to the vicinity of Parkersburg, W. Va., to engage in farming. Of his present whereabouts we are not able to say, further than that he some years ago moved to the west, and was accidentally killed. William, another son of Elias, was also a glassblower. He moved many years ago from this county to Indiana. Thornton F. died on the plains on his journey to California. One of the daughters married William Hugus, a glassblower, resided a short time in Belle Vernon, and at last accounts near Alliance, Ohio, where he was a successful farmer. As to the remaining members of the family we have not any tidings.

RICHARD STOCKDALE.

This old and well known gentleman died at his residence in Monongahela City January 20th, 1889, in his 74th year, of dropsy, superinduced by rheumatism.

RICHARD STOCKDALE, son of William Stockdale, was born October 15th, 1815, on the Curry farm, Forward township. Allegheny county. His father moved to the farm on the pike, where James Stockdale lived, while Richard was yet a lad. The family consisted of five brothers: John; James, who lived on the home place; William and Robert, who were in the furniture and lumber business for many years, both now dead. There were five sisters: Sarah, widow of the late Captain Samuel Morgan, of Gastonville; Rachel, wife of James Porter, of Bloomington, Ill.; Margaret, wife of James Kerr, of this city; Eliza, widow of Robert Patton; and Forbes, wife of William Coulter, both of this city.

Richard Stockdale learned the trade of tanner with Alexander Williams, and after his majority worked at his trade in Circleville and Zanesville, Ohio. Returning in 1843 he leased the ground and opened a tan yard on the site now occupied by the residence and grounds of James P. Shepler on Pike avenue. In 1850 he bought from James Gordon, Esq., the tannery on Main street, where he had worked as an apprentice, he also purchased the dwellings thereon, which now form part of his estate and where for many years he lived. Henry Fulton's lease had just expired and Mr. Stockdale succeeded him in the business. He operated this tannery until 1877, when the growth of city environments made it undesirable for that purpose. He relinquished the tanning business in 1878, having successfully followed the business for 35 years. He then engaged in the coal trade, operating the works known as "Stockdale's," in Carroll township. He retired from active business in 1881, since which time he had suffered from rheumatic trouble more or less.

Mr. Stockdale was married in 1845 to Miss Levina Hoffman, of Somerset township, six sons blessed the union, one of whom, Charles, died in infancy, the others are providentially able to be present at the funeral, except Richard, who is in Montana. Mrs. Stockdale died November 3d, 1880.

Mr. and Mrs. Stockdale were both active, earnest and hardworking members of the Methodist Episcopal Church. He was a trustee and a class leader, was one of the building committee and a liberal contributor to the present edifice on Main street. Mrs. Stockdale was a leader in woman's work for the church, her monument is established in the hearts of many hundreds. Together they walked hand in hand; a few years of separation; now again united beyond the river. Peace to their memory.

MARK BORLAND.

[From Monongahela *Republican* of July 14, 1893.]

Mark Borland, Esq., died suddenly at his home on Main street in this city on Thursday night about 11 o'clock, July 13,

1893. He had been unusually well, for him, all day, and had his trunk packed to go to-day with the grandchildren for a visit. He was suddenly stricken down, and attending physicians, hastily summoned, found that an internal hemorrhage had reached and filled his lungs.

Mark Borland was born Dec. 16, 1827, in Pittsburgh, son of Moses and Sallie Taggart Borland. He went to school to Master Meads in the Second ward school house on the bank where the Monongahela House now stands. At the age of 14 he went with Phillip Ross to learn the dry good trade, and for some years clerked in Pittsburgh stores, gaining the business experience so useful to him in later life. He clerked for Zebulon Kinstry, who did a general store and jewelry business; next with Stacy Lloyd, then with George F. Deihl. He went into the dry goods store of Perry Baker, of McKeesport, and finally at Port Perry hung out his own shingle upon which for the first time appeared the name of "Mark Borland, General Merchandise." He hadn't a dollar when he started but soon paid for his goods and had $8,000 in bank as his first earnings. He thought he saw in Limetown the coming centre for trade in the middle pool, and moved there. He also went into the coal trade with his brother-in-law, John Peterson, now dead, and J. B. Corey, now a coal king.

The tight times of just before the war came on, he sold out at Limetown and came to Monongahela, in 1857, forming partnership with John Young, and occupying a room on the present location.

The business has grown with the passing years, guided by his excellent judgment. In 1833 he joined Swickard and McCurdy in the erection of the city block, and the store now occupies five large rooms, the most extensive dry goods and shoe house in the valley. His sons were taken into the firm as they reached majority.

Mr. Borland was married to Miss Elizabeth Peterson, at Port Perry, in 1852, by Rev. Sparks. This dear wife survives him, together with his children, John, Howard, Ida, Sallie, Charles,

Bess, James and Hunter. No family was ever bound together by stronger ties, no parents ever strove more earnestly to make home the dearest spot on earth.

He was one of our most widely known citizens. He has served in City Councils, and was seven years town Treasurer. He was not active in politics, but held faith in the Republican party and the American tariff. In his moral relationship he was a Methodist, having joined that church during a revival, and became much attached to its services. He was an earnest member of the Masonic fraternity, and belonged to the Royal Arcanum, United Workmen, Odd Fellows, Good Templars. In his business life Mr. Borland was conservative, by nature companionable and social, enjoying a quiet joke and fond of company. Yet by the evening lamp, after business, surrounded by his family, or on the play ground enjoying a romp with his grandchildren, our friend found his chiefest joy. And when his coffin is carried forth, those who will be his chiefest mourners will be the ones who knew him best in his beloved home.

Hon. Alexander Hervey Houston.

Who was Mayor of this city in 1890 and 1892, died at his residence on Sixth street, at four o'clock on Sunday, July 16th, 1893, of typhoid fever, in the 34th year of his age.

The family always abbreviated his name Alexander to "Sandy" and as such he preferred to be called, so that he signed his name and is known as S. H. Houston. He was born in Washington, Pa., May 3rd, 1860, son of James Houston. His mother is dead, his father is in the city, and was at his bedside when he died. Sandy graduated at the Union School, Washington, studied Latin with a tutor, entered W. & J. College in 1878, and graduated in 1882. He also graduated at Philadelphia Dental College and took a post graduate course at Ann Arbor; held both diplomas, and was recognized as a skilled professional. He came to Monongahela City in October, 1886; married Miss Margaret Power, September 29, 1887, who remains his widow with three children, James, Rebecca and Florence.

Dr. Houston was a member of the Junior Order American Mechanics and the Royal Arcanum, both of which orders will attend his funeral.

The Doctor was a young man full of vigor; he had a fine professional reputation and was a valuable member of our community. Under his administration good order prevailed, and he did not hesitate to promote peace by his presence with the police when required. His form was commanding and his resolution so well known that evil doers respected the law in his person as Mayor. He favored improvements, and was public spirited. He was a young man who promised to develop strong points as a good citizen; his influence was on the right side, and his actions were prompt to good purposes.

Interment in Monongahela cemetery July 18, 1893.

AUNT MARGARET PHILLIPS.

By this endearing title Mrs. Phillips was known to nearly all our people. She was daughter of Benjamin Parkison, born at the old homestead, which stood near the present site of Mongah Mines, July 16th, 1807. She died in Monongahela City, in the brick corner house on Main street, where she has lived since 1848, on Saturday evening, July 15th, 1893.

She was married to John M. Phillips, March 11, 1830, and has had four children: Benjamin, William, James and Elizabeth, all dead.

Her husband died April 17th, 1838. She was a member of the Methodist church, and had been for so many years that the records do not seem to reach back to the date of her joining.

The funeral takes place at three o'clock to-day (Monday), interment at Monongahela cemetery. Mrs. Phillips was a quiet home-body, she lived peacefully the life of a devoted christian, and has simply gone home—it hardly seems as if she has died.

THE BLACK–BENTLEY–KING FAMILIES.

Samuel Black was one of the earlier business men of the valley. He was born in Down county, Ireland, in 1776; emigrated from his native country to the United States in 1794. He was married in Fort Pitt in 1795 to Mary Bealer. In the same year he located at Parkison's Ferry, now Monongahela City, Penn'a. He purchased from Joseph Parkison and lived in the well known Red house at the mouth of Ford, now Second street, where he carried on the mercantile business for many years. Owing to the falling in of the river bank from the washing away of 150 feet of the lot, there is at this time not a trace of the house remaining. Samuel Black died in 1846 at the homestead on the pike, where, also, his wife died in 1847. For many decades Samuel Black was considered the most wealthy man in Washington county. He owned the old Parkison farm on which Bellevidere now stands. He owned the farm now owned by Resin Frye, and also the farm on which Bellewood is now located. He owned a large tract of land on the river opposite Bellewood and adjoining the old Parkison mill property, now known as Elkhorn. He had quite a number of houses and lots in Monongahela City, besides valuable blocks in the city of Pittsburgh.

He was a man of large physical frame, always wore his hair in a cue, and in general appearance was austere, with the usual dignity of the primitive landholder. We presume that few of his cotemporaries are now living. Mr. and Mrs. Black had a large family of children, of whom were born in the red house, Elizabeth, Harry and Maria. In 1801 they moved to the homestead on the pike, where were born Samuel, Caroline, Cyrus, Marcus, Jane, Ross, Wilson, Mary and Hester, all of whom lived to womanhood and manhood. Elizabeth married William Bentley in 1825, who lived in the house near the present wharf, which for years had been used as the Methodist Episcopal Church. In this house his son Samuel B. Bentley was born in 1826, being the same year in which his father died.

Mrs. Elizabeth Bentley died October 10, 1878. S. B. Bentley now lives in the house built by Samuel Black in 1815, but it has been subject to many changes and remodelings since that time. Samuel B. Bentley's first wife was Sarah, daughter of Æneas Graham, and his second wife was Minerva, daughter of Henry and Elizabeth Swartz Rabe, thus uniting two of the oldest families about Monongahela City. They have four children living at this date, Millie G., Charles R., Harry K., and Mary M. Samuel B. Bentley joined the Methodist E. Church of his native city in 1847, under the pastorate of Rev. Nathaniel Calendar. His grandmother Black was one of the pioneer women of Methodism in Western Pennsylvania, and his mother was a member of the same church in its primitive days. He was the choirister of the church over forty years. His first school teacher was Miss Jane Hepburn, whose father was Principal and sister Eliza was assistant. They taught in a house now owned by Silas Haley, four doors above the People's Bank, on Main street. This school was in 1830 and 1831.

Samuel Black's son, Harry, married Miss Cotts, of Cincinnati, Ohio, both of whom are dead. They left two children who are still living: Samuel, a lawyer of Cincinnati, and Sarah, who married a Mr. Cox of the same city.

Maria Black, who died December 29th, 1889, in her 90th year, married Dr. S. M. King, a noted and highly esteemed physician of Monongahela City. He settled in that city about the year 1815, and died at his home on Chess street, September 7th, 1877. The Monongahela *Republican* in giving an account of his death, says, "Dr. King was born at Uniontown, Pa., October 8th, 1794. He received a thorough education at Canonsburg, Pa. He studied medicine at Greensburg, Pa., with Drs. Marchand and Postlewaite, and graduated at the University of Pennsylvania. He settled in Williamsport, now Monongahela City, in 1815 and commenced the practice of his profession. In 1817 he married Maria Black, daughter of the late Samuel Black. With the exception of a few months' residence in Madison, Indiana, about the year 1840, he has been continuously identified with the business and society of his adopted city for 62 years. Dr. King retired from the active practice of medicine only about 10 years ago, transferring his business to his son, the late Dr. William H. King."

Dr. S. M. King died a Christian as he had lived one, and those who visited him in his invalid chamber, expecting to find it shrouded under the shadow of gloom, found, instead, a house of rejoicing, a cheerful making ready for the Bridegroom, a chamber lit up with flashes of light from the Gates Ajar. A few days before his death, calling for his favorite walking stick, the dying man caught the staff firmly by its handle and exclaimed. "Farewell vain world. I am on my journey home." With rejoicing and not with trembling he went down into the valley, leaving behind as a legacy for us all, the record Christian life, and the triumph of a Believer's death. They had quite a large family of children. John L., who died September 12, 1881; Samuel K. married Harriet Woodburn, of Madison, Indiana, and died in 185-, leaving two children, Culver and Clarence. Wm. H. King studied medicine with his father, graduated at the Jefferson Medical College in 1853, resided all his life in Monongahela City, where he was regarded as one of the most prominent physicians and surgeons in Western Pennsylvania. He married Sarah, daughter of Rev. S. M. Sparks, one of the pioneers of the Cumberland Church in Western Pa. Dr. William H. King was noted not only as a thorough and learned physician and surgeon, but for his kind disposition and great benevolence. No poor man or woman was ever turned from his house, either in a professional or charitable way. He died in 1871, being just 50 years old the day he died. He had three children, all living at this date, Ida, Maria and Alvin.

Richard C., another son of Dr. S. M. King, never married and still remains as a household god in the old home. Dr. Cyrus B. was the youngest son of the older Dr. King. He graduated from Jefferson Medical College in 1862, and is now numbered among the most distinguished medical men in Allegheny City, where he has always pursued his profession, and is a Professor in the Western Pennsylvania Medical College. He married Euphemia, daughter of the Rev. John Kerr, who for many years was pastor of the Presbyterian Church of Monongabela City. Mrs. Euphemia King was a lady of more than ordinary Christian character. She was noted for her work of love and charity in the Third Presbyterian Church of Pittsburgh. Hers was a model Christian life, in all its phases, as wife, mother, church member and friend to the poor. Pollock's description of the dying mother is peculiarly applicable to her.

> "Her eyes, they set as sets the Morning Star,
> That goes not down behind the darkened west,
> Nor hides amid the tempest of the sky,
> But melts away into the light of Heaven."

She died July 26, 1881, in Allegheny City, Pa., honored and beloved by all who knew her, leaving three children, Annie, now Mrs. Bakewell, Nina and Victor, to mourn their loss.

Samuel Black, son of Samuel Black the older, died in the old stone house at the mouth of Dry Run, about the year 1833. He left two children, Samuel R. and Caroline.

Caroline, daughter of the older Black, married Robert Smith, a successful farmer, near Elizabeth, Allegheny county, Pa. She died July 24, 1885.

Cyrus Black, son of Samuel Black, once a noted revivalist of the M. E. Church, married Bellevidere McGahan, both are deceased, leaving two daughters, Mary and Cornelia, residents of New York.

Marcus, another son, married Matilda Morton. Both are dead, leaving two children: Morton, of the banking house of Alexander & Co., and Mary, wife of William M. Boggs.

Jane Black married W. S. Millinger, a well known military man, and postmaster of Monongahela City during the Tyler administration. He kept the postoffice in the house now occupied by S. B. Bentley. They had three sons, George V. L., Marcus and Robert F., and one daughter, Alice, the wife of Norman Wylie of Allegheny City.

Ross Black was educated at Jefferson College, and studied law with Hon. E. M. Stanton, under the tuition of Judge Stokeley of Steubenville, Ohio. He was admitted to the Washington, Pa., bar in 1841, and died in Monongahela City in 1857.

Wilson S., the remaining son, died on his way home from the Mexican war.

The remaining daughters were Mary, married to George S. Clark, who died in Chattanooga, Tenn., where his widow and children still live. Hester married Colvin Bissell and died long ago. They had two daughters, Mary and Ida, both of whom are living.

Mrs. Maria King.

Died December 29, 1889.

The Monongahela *Republican* of December 30, 1889, thus speaks of the death of Mrs. King :

The death of this lady removes from Monongahela its oldest resident, one who began life with the century, born in May, 1800, and who has lived as its years rolled by, till now she sees the light of its last decade, but before the dawn of the New Year she passed into eternity where years are not counted. The baby Maria, child of Samuel and Mary Black, was born in what afterward was known as the "old red house," which stood near the river bank, back from Mr. Beaver's, on First street. The family soon afterwards moved to their mansion house on the hill, where the girl spent her childhood, and where she was married to Dr. Samuel M. King, who has preceded her to the silent land. Of thirteen children Richard and Dr. Cyrus remain of the sons ; Mrs. Baird and Mrs. Mosely of the daughters. Mrs. King, like most old people, lived much in the past, and was familiar with the early history of the city which she had seen grow up about her. She was a pupil in the first Sunday school taught by Judge Gordon in 1811. She stood at her father's door step and saw the "Williamsport Rangers" march away under Captain James Warne to the war of 1812 ; she watched the builders put up the first glass factory near the place where Elijah Harrison's sons now live, by

Parkison and Warne; and subsequently saw the smoke curl from a factory owned and controlled by her father. She heard the new county question discussed for nearly a hundred years. She saw her father active in the erection of the "first house of worship" initiative steps for which were taken July 7, 1814, when Joseph Parkison for the sum of $45 conveyed to Samuel Black, James Gordon, James Hair, David Hamilton, William Irwin and others, trustees for building a Presbyterian meeting house on "lot No. 72, on the hill." She saw the first river bridge built, her father having "released the bridge company from all danger to any lands of his taken in the erection of a bridge." And so on.

Within her lifetime is a history of this town; when she was born Jefferson was the third President, and Aaron Burr Vice President of the United States; when she was seven years old Robert Fulton made his first steamboat trip. Slaves were then brought to this country from Africa and sold, and Ohio was not yet in the Union.

What a long life to live, and how many memories must have clustered about her as she sank peacefully to rest on the dawn of a Sabbath day.

WILLIAM JONES' FAMILY.

William Jones was born at Ellicott's Mills, Maryland, in May, 1763, and died in the latter part of March, 1862. He located in the neighborhood of Ginger Hill, in Washington county, a few years before the Whiskey Insurrection, on the farm still owned by his son William. He was a blacksmith by trade. When the U. S. troops were sent out to disperse the insurgents they halted near his farm, from whence they were ordered to return, as the insurrection was over. While in camp he shod some of the Government horses. He was loyal to the Government and took no part in the insurrection. By his first wife he had eleven children, five sons and six daughters, viz., John, Elijah, Jesse, Samuel and William, Rebecca, Delilah, Polly, Ruth, Rose and Ann. At an advanced age he married Mrs. Jane Philips as his second wife, by whom he had no children. John was the founder of Jonestown, in Fallowfield, where he lived most of his life, during which he was generally engaged in farming, merchandising and in keeping entertainment. His peculiar sign, "Entertainment," will be remembered by many of the older citizens. Here he died in 1874, at an advanced age. Elijah lived and died in the brick house on the hill above Jonestown. Among his children were Isaac W., who built the McGregor row on Main street in Monongahela City, and who is now a successful wool dealer in Washington, Pa. His son James married Caroline, daughter of the late Abram Van Voorhis. James died some years ago and his widow, with his children, are living near Ginger Hill. Jesse, another son of Wm. Jones, lived and died on a part of the old Homestead. William still owns the greater part of the original homestead, but lives in Monongahela City.

Samuel Jones, the remaining son of William Jones the older, was born on the homestead in 1800. He went to the "Forks of Yough" in 1824 and settled on the farm purchased by his father for him from Peter Shepler. Samuel resided on this farm until his death in June, 1867. He was killed by a log rolling over him. In 1826 he married Jane Fell, daughter of Benjamin Fell, in Rostraver township, Westmoreland county. The wedding took place at the Fell mansion, which consisted of a log cabin of primitive style. Mr. Fell was very positive that at this cabin was organized the first Methodist class west of the mountains. Through his influence was erected the old log church which formerly stood where the present stone church, known as Fell's church, is situated, about two miles from Webster. Samuel Jones had by his first wife four children. Mary married Dr. J. P. Watson, and are both dead, leaving no children. William, on the 8th day of February, 1850, married Sarah, daughter of the well known Captain Joseph Shepler. They have three children. Their son, Joseph S., is a member of the banking firm of S. F. Jones & Co., of Bellevernon, Pa., and married Miss Lizzie Mustard and resides in Bellevernon. Samuel married Miss Ann Murphy and resides in North Bellevernon. He is a member of the Bellevernon Saw and Planing Mill Co. The only daughter of William and Sarah Jones is Ella, who married Mr. Sears of Florida and resides in North Bellevernon. His father gave William the old Fell farm which was purchased at Orphans' court sale. On this farm he lived until he moved to North Bellevernon, where he is at this time a member of the banking house of S. F. Jones & Co. His son, S. F. Jones, married Sallie Thomas in 1861. They have no children. His father gave him the farm near Bellevernon known in olden times as the farm on which Rev. David Smith resided while he was pastor of Rehoboth church, and where he died in 1803. He was the father of Rev. Joseph Smith, author of the book "Old Redstone." The old house has given place to a fine brick, erected by S. F. Jones.

He sold this farm to Michael F. Cook, grandson of Col. Edward Cook, and removed to Bellevernon in 1872, where he became a member of the banking house of S. F. Jones & Co., formed in 1872. At this date, 1893, he has an interest in the Bellevernon Heat and Light Company, of which he is Superintendent.

James S., the remaining son of Samuel Jones by his first wife, married Miss Ann Finley, daughter of the late Wm. Finley, and grand daughter of Rev. James Finley, who was the first pastor of Rehoboth Church. They have no children. James served through the late war and died in Washington, D. C., in about 1891.

Samuel Jones' second wife was Miss Mary, daughter of the late Benjamin Thomas, of Rostraver, in the vicinity of the town of Webster, Pa. By her he had eight children. Elizabeth married John M. Bake as her first husband, now deceased. Her second husband is Thomas Hagerty, who now lives on Cook's run, near Fayette City, Pa. Malissa married Lowry Venable, and resides in the west. Rettie married Jonathan Rhodes. She died years ago, in Ohio. Amanda married

Thomas C. Douglass, and resides in Pittsburgh. Homer married Jennie McAlpin, of Gibsonton Mills. They reside in Bellevernon, Pa. Luther married Sallie Venable, and resides near Bellevernon. John married a daughter of D. P. Housman, and still resides on part of the homestead. Celia, the remaining daughter, is unmarried and lives with her aged mother in the homestead in Rostraver.

Samuel Jones, at his death, was the largest landholder in Rostraver township, and the distribution of his estate gave each of his children a fair patrimony. He was a man of warm feeling and ardent sympathies. Energetic in business, he was no less so in his church. He was long a member of the Methodist E. Church, held his membership at Fells, in the graveyard of which his remains are interred. He gave largely of his means and labor in erecting the church building in Webster.

Rosa, daughter of William Jones the older, married Hull Williams, who lived for many years in the neighborhood of the Dutch meeting house near Ginger hill, in Washington county, Pa. They are both dead. Rebecca married Andrew Mills. Both are dead many years. Ann married John Hess, who lived near what is called Edward's chapel, on the pike, above Ginger hill. They are both dead—John died some years ago, and his wife June 30th, 1889. Ruth never married, and died at an advanced age in Monongahela City. Delilah married James Mills. Both are dead. James Mills was a well known local preacher in the M. E. church, and a business man generally. He lived in the town of Williamsport early as 1828, in Washington, Pa., on a farm near lock No. 4, lately owned by Mrs. John Ryan, and on which he laid a prospective town called Lockport, which proved a failure. For years prior to his death he carried on business in Pittsburgh, where he died. He was a man of more than ordinary ability. His sermons were Scriptural and delivered in a plain though fervent manner. His wife died not many years since in Pittsburgh. They had quite a number of children. A. B. Mills, the oldest son, graduated at Washington college in 1846.

After many years in business he died in Philadelphia in 1888. James R., another son, is now one of the shining lights in the Methodist Episcopal Church. Some years ago he was the recipient of the degree of D. D., which he deservedly bears with his accustomed modesty. Mary, daughter of James Mills, married a Mr. Dolby, and resides on Craig street, Pittsburgh. Mary, the remaining daughter of William Jones, married Joseph Alexander, of whom we will write in another place.

The Alexander Family.

Joseph Alexander was born on Ten Mile Creek, in Washington county, Pa., on the first day of April, 1795, and died in Monongahela City June 20, 1871. When Joseph was quite young his father immigrated to Barnesville, Ohio, where he grew up to manhood. His father, Joseph Alexander, was born July 9, 1765, and died June 9, 1847, at his residence in Ohio. He was the son of Isaac Alexander, who was born December 16, 1716 ; he was the son of Elias Alexander, who was born in 1680, and died in 1780. Joseph, the subject of this sketch, was one of a large family. His brother James resided in Monongahela City some fifty years ago, and will be recollected by many of the older citizens as having kept a store in the McGrew room just above the present Odd Fellows building. He died in 1860, at Fort Gibson, Louisiana. A sister Hannah married Benjamin Thomas, of Rostraver township, Westmoreland county ; both are deceased. The children of Benjamin and Hannah Thomas were Elijah, Rosa Ann, Mary, Joseph B., Thomas Hudson, Harriet, Westley Ford, Van R., and James. Rosa Ann married James Davidson and died in Bellevernon August 20, 1887.

Mrs. Rosanna Davidson.

The Bellevernon *Enterprise* of August 27, 1887, contains the following articles on her death:

Died, on Saturday evening, August 20, 1887, at her late residence in Bellevernon, Mrs. Rosanna, wife of Rev. James Davidson. The deceased was the daughter of the late Benjamin Thomas, of Rostraver township. Her mother was an Alexander, sister of the late Joseph Alexander, of Monongahela City, who was the father of W. J. and Jas. S. Alexander, of the same city. The deceased was born September 17, 1816, on the old Thomas homestead, in the above named township, now owned by John Rankin. She was married to James Davidson Oct. 27, 1836, at the old homestead, by the Rev. Geo. McCasky. She joined the Methodist E. Church at Fells, in 1828, being in her twelfth year, under the ministry of the Rev. John Watterman. She, with her husband, united with the church of Bellevernon in 1850, whilst in charge of Rev. J. F. Nessly. She leaves a husband, two sons and nine daughters; one daughter, Mary, passed into the beyond on the 24th day of the same month just 46 years ago. Her nine loving daughters were all with her in her last days. The sons, on account of the sickness of the one and the great distance from his home of the other, were not able to be present during her last illness, but Robert, her youngest son, was present at the funeral. The deceased was truly one of God's own children; the community will bear witness to this fact. Her walk and conversation gave rich fruits of a life of over sixty years devoted to Christ. Only on account of sickness was her seat vacant in the house of God. She will be missed by her husband, with whom she had for over fifty years shared the troubles and pleasures of life; she will be missed in the home circle, where so long by example and precept she exemplified the truth of the Christian religion; she will be missed in the church of which she had been a devoted member for nearly sixty years; she will be missed by the community to which she was ever ready to grant acts of charity and kind sympathy; but she has not missed the crown which was laid up for her in glory.

> Servant of God, well done!
> Thy glorious warfare's past.
> The battle's fought, the race is won,
> And thou art crowned at last.

MOTHER DEAD.

Is she really dead? Has her spirit winged its flight to the glorious land? And what is death! Are some of the many thoughts that passed in quick succession through our mind as we stood at the death bed of our beloved mother-in-law on last Saturday afternoon, and gazed for the last time on her face while living. For 22 hours she had not changed her position, and as her life ebbed away she just fell asleep on the bosom of the Saviour, whom she had for 59 years loved and served.

On July 4th she sat at the table for the last time. She had to be helped, but she wanted to be where her children were. During her sickness she suffered much, yet there was no complaining, no murmuring, and when she realized that the master had called her to come home, she was prepared. Death had no terrors, as she had communed constantly with her maker she was ready to say,

> "My home, henceforth, is in the skies;
> Earth, sea, and sun, adieu.
> All heaven's enfolded to my eyes,
> I have no sight for you."

All realized that death would come, but we were not prepared to meet it. When the last silent breath had been drawn, and we knew she had gone, then, and not till then did the shock come. All her children were present but one, who having gone to Los Angeles, Cal., could not come. Before death came she could not speak or recognize any one. Loving hands administered to her wants and wishes as long as they could, and on Monday morning she was laid to rest in the cemetery. She leaves eleven children and an aged husband to mourn her loss.

> O! where shall human grief be stilled
> And joy for pain be given,
> Where dwells the sunshine of a love
> In which the soul may always rove?
> A sweet voice answered—Heaven.

The Pittsburgh *Christian Advocate* has the following notice of Mother Davidson's death, written by her pastor

She began very early in life to follow Christ, the result of which was that she became rooted and grounded in the Christian faith. Her steadfastness in the Apostles' doctrine grew with increasing years. She could say with Paul, "This one thing I do." She allowed nothing of a worldly character to interpose between her and Christian duty. Her seat in the house of God was seldom vacant. The word of Christ came to her not in word only, but in transforming power. The service of God was her chief joy. A little less than a year ago we met at the home of brother and sister Davidson to celebrate their golden wedding, little thinking that the bride of the occasion would so soon be enfolded in the embrace of death. She reared a large family of children, and had the satisfaction of knowing ere she passed away that they were in the fold of Christ. Her funeral was largely attended. Her last hours were spent in peaceful sleep ; and when the supreme moment came her spirit gently took its flight to the regions of the immortals. She was not, for God had taken her. Signed G. A. SHEETS.

Mary, another daughter of Benjamin Thomas, married Samuel Jones, as we have already stated. Harriet is the widow of Wm. Bealer and lives in West Newton. Thomas Hudson is a resident of Braddock, his wife having died some years ago. James married a Miss Winters, served in the army in the late war, and died soon after his discharge. Joseph resides in Evansville, Indiana ; Elijah lives in Iowa ; Van R. was in the late war and now resides in Webster ; Westley Ford has long been a resident of San Francisco, California. Hannah married Dr. J. C. Gamble, had long resided in Kansas, and whilst on a visit to Pennsylvania, died at the house of Rev. James Davidson in Bellevernon, August 4, 1885.

Rose, another sister of Jos. Alexander, married John Mosely —these were the parents of Westley B. Mosely, who died in 1876, and was a well known business man of the valley. Mrs. Mosely, the widow, is a daughter of the late Dr. S. M. King, of whom we have already written. She resides in Allegheny.

Joseph Alexander was married to Mary Jones, daughter of William Jones the older, March 8th, 1819, by the Rev. John White, father of Judge J. W. F. White, now on the bench in Pittsburgh. Mrs. Alexander died at her home in Monongahela City, August 15th, 1856. Immediately after his marriage Joseph Alexander with his bride moved to a farm in Rostraver township, Westmoreland county, adjoining the farms of Samuel Jones and Benjamin Thomas. The farm is now owned by D. P. Housman. The old log house has given place to a beautiful frame. The old barn still remains. Father Jones was on a visit to Joseph Alexander on the Sabbath morning during which the Marquis de Lafayette passed through the Forks, May 29th, 1825. Father Jones was very strict in his observance of the Sabbath, but in this instance yielded to the pressure and walked over the hill to take a look at the Marquis. Mr. Alexander, in the spring of 1828, sold his farm to Samuel Jones and removed to Williamsport, now Monongahela City, and entered into partnership with James Mills in the mercantile business. His son, William J., was born on the farm April 16th, 1820; Rose Ann, now Mrs. Adams, and Eliza, now Mrs. Herron, were also born on the same farm.

The three-storied brick house on Main street, above Church alley, owned by W. J. Markell, stands now on the site of the house in which Mills & Alexander did business. In the spring of 1829, the partnership with Mills being dissolved, Alexander removed to Cookstown, now Fayette City, and there carried on a successful mercantile business until the spring of 1831, when he returned to Williamsport, and entered into a partnership with James McCauley to conduct a general mercantile business. The building occupied by them was destroyed by fire in 1855, and the site is now covered by the three-story brick building near the corner of Main and Second streets. The last partnership proving disastrous to Mr. Alexander, it was dissolved in about one year, and the business carried on by Mr. Alexander. Not long after this date McCauley removed to Jacksonville, Illinois, where he soon afterwards died. He was a gunsmith by trade. He built and occupied until his removal west the house lately owned by Hon. G. V. Lawrence, on the corner of Main and Fifth streets. During this last partnership Alexander occupied the house on Second street, where now the brick building of Henry Sutman stands. In 1828-29 he lived in the old brick house near the old Presbyterian church on Coal street, owned and occupied for many years by the late Michael Johe. In this house his son James S. was born. In 1832 he purchased from John W. Hailman the property on Main street, below Second street, on which the McGregor block now stands. On this property his storerooms and dwelling were erected, and in which he died June 20, 1871, after having occupied it nearly forty years. He continued the business alone from 1832 to 1843, when the firm of Alexander & Son was organized by taking into the business his son William J. Alexander. This firm continued until September, 1850 when it was reorganized with the same partners under the style of Alexander & Co., which still exists. Subsequently James S. Alexander was taken into the firm, and at a later date Joseph A. Herron was added. This has long been considered one of the most solid banking houses in Western Pennsylvania, enjoying the confidence of every class of people. After the death of Joseph Alexander the real estate referred to was sold to Isaac W. Jones. During his ownership the buildings erected by Alexander were burned. but shortly afterwards re-built by Jones, and subsequently sold to Will McGregor, who is the present owner.

Death of William Wickerham, in 1879.

[From Daily *Republican*.]

William Wickerham, Esq., died in Carroll township in 1879 of general decline of age. His interment took place on Sunday, and assembled one of the largest funerals ever known in the valley.

The ancestry of the family runs back to Germany, from which country Peter Wickerham came to Pennsylvania colony and settled in Chester county. The second son, Adam, came to this place, took up a farm, the boundary being from the City Hotel out as far as Kearney's and down to the line of Dry run. The old Wickerham mansion was situated on the river bank, but the site has long ago crumbled into the river. Some of the timbers of the old house were used in building the Talbot cottage. Adam Wickerham laid out his farm into a town called Georgetown, the upper part of the place, owned by the Parkison's, being called Parkison's ferry. The two were merged by act of Assembly, in 1833, and called Williamsport.

Adam Wickerham had four children: a son George, who was drowned at the age of 22 in the Monongahela; Mary, who married Andrew B. Chess, who died in 1857; William, the subject of this notice, who was born in 1809; and Sarah, relict of John Bausman, Esq., late of Washington, Pa., and one of the most accomplished journalists of the state.

Mr. Wickerham moved to his farm in Carroll about 40 years before his death, where he had continuously lived ever since. Before he went to the farm he kept store for awhile in a building which stood near the pike, above alderman William's office. He was married three times: to Nancy, sister of Captain Robert Phillips; to Mrs. Mary L. Jones, of Ohio, in 1862, who died in 1876; and to Mrs. Elizabeth Radcliffe, of Washington, who yet survives him.

Mr. Wickerham's family consisted of Adam, who is married and now lives in Carroll; David H., who died in 1838; James S., married and now living near Beallsville; Eliza Jane, wife of Noah Grant, Esq.; William Henry Harrison, married and living in Carroll; Emeline Allen, who died in 1856; Maggie, now the wife of Clinton Teeple; Mary Chess, wife of Lemon Williams, now dead; Albert Gallatin, living on the home farm; Alexander Wilson, married and living in East Bethlehem; and John Dewitt, married and living on the home place. All honorable men and women, who bear the family name with credit to themselves.

The deceased was long a consistent member of the Methodist

Episcopal Church of this city. In this community, to his general character as a man, we need hardly refer. We sincerely believe no man lives whom he ever wronged out of a penny; no man lives who ever knew him to do a mean thing, or an act to stain a long record of honesty, probity and truth. He was careful in business and gave each one of his sons and daughters a home. He was hospitable, and there be few people in this neighborhood, young or old, who have not enjoyed the hospitality of his hearthstone. No person in all this valley has been kinder to the poor. To sum it up, William Wickerham lived the life of a good man, an honest man and a Christian.

His public spirit was unbounded. No matter what society or occasion asked for contribution, his basket and purse were both ready; he loved to attend public demonstrations. The Fourth of July his patriotism made him regard as sacred; Thanksgiving day his religion taught him to venerate; Decoration day his devotion to country made one of the holiest days of all the year.

The military spirit was strong in this family from its landing on our shores. The grandfather and uncle as young men went to Kentucky and volunteered in the Indian wars. He used to relate stories of that war as told him by his father. The boys had taken up 1,200 acres of land in Kentucky, and planted it to corn and pumpkins, when the Indians drove them back. Adam and Peter went over one day for some pumpkins, and having gathered a sackful, were about to return, when Peter saw an Indian; he gave the alarm and ran to the river, but Adam, thinking it only a joke, was soon confronted by Mr. Injun, and no chance of escape. Being a very strong man, he slung the sack of squash at the red man and squashed him.

During the Whiskey Insurrection, the grandfather, Adam, was arrested by one of the deputy marshals, and escaped being "sent over" as a prisoner by playing idiot. To every question asked, he answered: "Ah-ha-a," so that the officer said, "Let this man go, he is a fool. The archives of the Wickerham family are full of incidents of frontier life.

When the rebellion broke out Mr. Wickerham gave three of his boys to the right side; and when the rebels advanced to Antietam, he, himself, sixty years of age, shouldered his musket and went, under Capt. Wm. J. Alexander, to the front as a soldier of the 18th Pennsylvania Militia. In early life he was a member of Jackson Guards, under Capt. Sam. Morgan.

Rev. Dr. Bracken delivered a very excellent address at the funeral; and as the long cortage followed to his grave all that was left of this venerable man, the universal sentiment of the occasion was:—" He was a good man—may his soul abide in peace."

DEATH OF MR. JOHN KING, IN 1881.

Mr. King was born in 1791 in New Jersey. His father, Courtland King, moved to a farm near Library, in Allegheny county, crossing the Monongahela river at Elizabeth when John was one year old, and on his birthday in 1792. The father lived upon and died on that farm in his 62d year. Of the older family, all died some time ago, but John, the subject of this sketch, a brother named Elijah who lives in Indianapolis, and Isaac, who lives near Library.

John King lived with his parents till he was 28 years of age, when he married Miss Jane Stewart, and went to house keeping near his father's, in Jefferson township. The Stewart family was one of the most influential in that neighborhood. Mrs. King's father was active in the whiskey insurrection, and was siezed and taken to Little York, then the seat of government, for trial, but was included in the compromise pardon and returned to his home rejoicing that the disturbance was settled, and a better basis of taxation secured to his people. Mr. King removed with his family to Forward township, having bought the farm which he still owned at his death from Mr. John Storer, May, 1836. He lived there until 1873, when he moved to the house in Central Block, where the family now lives. This family consisted of Dr. James Stewart, now of Pittsburgh; Mary L., who died in 1877; Dr. William H., of this city; John, of Spring Valley, Minn.; Dr. Courtland, of Pittsburgh; Jane, wife of James Moore, who died in 1854; Dr. Calvin, of Pittsburgh; Samuel J., of Forward township; Robert, Harvey and an infant child, all dead; Dr. Milton S., of Pittsburgh; and Allie M., who married Mr. Devore. Of these sons, one is a farmer, one a merchant, and five are surgeon dentists of acknowledged ability and reputation.

Mr. King was a reader and a thinker; in early life a Whig, he left that party when it yielded its homage to a solid south on the slavery question; then an abolitionist. He was one of three voters in his district who ballotted for Birney, and since then a Republican. He was a Baptist, and in his opinion was rigid and unyielding, and he clung to his faith with a justifiable denominational pride, having at the same time a large measure of Christian love and charity which knew no boundary save the brotherhood of mankind.

Ninety years—almost the life of the nation! He has lived under every President of the United States, and has voted at every Presidential election since Madison. There have been 18 Governors of Pennsylvania elected since he was born, all now dead but two. When he was born Frederick the Great had just died; Benjamin Franklin's grave was not yet green; the Whiskey Insurrection was aflame; Napoleon was born and was entombed, all within Mr. King's recollection. He was 46 years of age when Victoria ascended the throne of England; He was 24 when Jackson fought Packenham at New Orleans; he has read in the papers the black-lined columns which announced the death of Washington, Adams, Jefferson, Madison, Monroe, Adams (John Quincy), Jackson, VanBuren, Harrison, Tyler, Polk, Taylor, Fillmore, Pierce, Buchanan, Lincoln and Johnson. He has lived to see the successful issue of our three wars. When he was born neither steamboat, nor telegraph, nor railroad, nor photograph had been invented, and a daily paper, an envelope, a postage stamp, a steel pen, were unknown. He has been counted in every census of the United States, and has seen his country grow from three (3,929,217) to nearly fifty millions of people.—*Monongahela Republican.*

Death of Dr. William H. King.

[From the Monongahela *Republican*.]

About 10 o'clock on Saturday evening, July 16th, 1892, Dr. William H. King, the well known dental surgeon of this city, died at his home in his 70th year. He had been ill but a few days. William H. King was born on the farm in Jefferson township, Allegheny county, Pa., April 17th, 1823, in what is now the centre of the West Elizabeth gas and oil field. He spent the first 14 years of his life there, and was playmate and schoolmate with the late James P. Shepler. He was the third child of John and Jane King, there being ten sons and three daughters. Six of the family yet live: Mrs. A. K. Devore, Williamson, Kansas; Dr. Courtland King, Uniontown; Dr. J. S. Calvin, and Dr. M. S., of Pittsburgh, and John King, of Spring Valley, Minn.

The family moved from Jefferson to Forward township, over the river, where the boys and girls mingled with Monongahela young folks, and grew up part and parcel of our local society. William stayed on the farm till he was 21 years of age, when he attended lectures at the Ohio College of Dentistry, Cincinnati, where he took an honorary degree. He practised dentistry in Lancaster, Ohio, for a number of years, then came to the home place, where he was living when the war broke out.

He enlisted in Co. F, 155th Pa. vols., under Captain John Markell, August 22d, 1862, in which regiment he served with distinction, being twice promoted for bravery, once from the ranks at the request of General Allebaugh, and once by General Pearson. He was mustered out as first lieutenant at the close of the war.

Dr. King, as officer of the skirmish line, had advanced with the troops opposite to Appomattox Court House when the flag of truce came in, and so he saw the end of the war, and received one of the surrender flags. His record as a soldier is a rich legacy left to his family, and as he rests in his coffin with the bronze brown badge of the Grand Army on his pulseless breast, it covers a heart that never faltered in war or in peace, in devotion to the flag, to country, to citizenship. His regard for loyalty could brook no excuse. Recently when the Homestead trouble began, his sympathy with the mill men was pronounced, but as soon as they overstepped the law he was instantly changed to the other side. When some suggested that the militia would run before a Winchester rifle, his indignation broke forth, saying, "What! would they run with the blue on? No, no! If they did I would be willing to help shoot them down myself." He was loyal to the blue.

In politics Dr. King was republican, in religious inclinations he favored the Baptist belief; as a citizen progressive, public spirited and modern. His ideas as to advanced education found expression in the new school building and the excellent schools then established. He was once in councils, and was assistant Burgess of the town in 1872. After the war he located in this city in the practice of dentistry, being quite successful always. He was married in Pittsburgh to Miss Jane Carpenter, May 4th, 1871, to whom, and to his only daughter, Jane, the sympathy of many warm friends go out in sincerity in this hour of shadow.

Dr. King was a genial, pleasant man; fond of humor, cheerful and contented: he hated sham, despised bigotry, and as a general thing was for the under dog in a fight—ready to help a man up, willing to befriend the weak, anxious to see justice done; and in a quiet way, without ostentation or parade, to do his own duty as he understood it.

We extract from the Elizabeth *Herald* of June 7, 1889, the following sketch of

JOHN E. SHAFFER, M. D.

John Eckert Shaffer was born at Washington, Pa., February 22, 1821, and died May 31, 1889, at his home in Elizabeth, Pa. He was a son of John and Charlotte Shaffer, two worthy people, and was one of a family of ten children, they being:

William, deceased ; Anna Charlotte Weirich, deceased ; Alexander Swaney, deceased ; Susan E. McCaskey, of Washington, Pa.; Rev. Jacob S. Shaffer, of Allegheny, Pa.; Mrs. Mary McElhinney, of Fairfield, Iowa; Mrs. Elizabeth Coffin, of Fairfield, Iowa ; Christian S. Shaffer, of Des Moines, Iowa ; Dr. J. M. Shaffer, of Keokuk, Iowa.

Dr. Shaffer was a self-made man. His parents, who were in moderate circumstances, aided him in getting through Washington College, at which institution he was graduated in 1840. He began the study of law, and soon after his graduation went to Preston county, Va., where he was admitted to the bar in 1842. This profession does not seem to have been congenial, for we find him soon reading medicine, and meanwhile teaching school at Kingwood, Va., for a livelihood. He was graduated from the medical department of the University of Pennsylvania, at Philadelphia, April 4, 1845. His preceptor in his medical studies was Dr. F. Julius LeMoyne, of Washington, Pa., of national fame as an Abolition leader, and of worldwide repute as the builder of the first crematory for disposing of the dead in the United States.

Dr. Shaffer came to Elizabeth December 10, 1845, and began the practice of medicine. His residence here has been continuous ever since that, and at his death he was the oldest practitioner of medicine in the Monongahela valley, his mantle now falling on the shoulders of Dr. J. S. VanVoorhis, of Bellevernon. His practice in the early days took him over a large extent of country, and from this fact added to his prominence in every public movement, he was one of the most widely known men, not only in his own community, but in the Monongahela valley.

He was married March 26, 1846, to Miss Elizabeth S. Holmes, daughter of Rev. George S. Holmes, and sister of Dr. C. A. Holmes, the well known Methodist Episcopal divine. His wife passed on before him to the other world July 2, 1880. They had eight children, and it is a remarkable fact that these have all lived to grow to maturity, and all now have families of their own save one. They are: Mary H. Kerbey, of Homestead, Pa.; John S. Shaffer, of Homestead; Dr. P. T. B. Shaffer, of Elizabeth; Mrs. Jennie Linn Jack, of Pittsburgh; Mrs. Annie Le Moyne Bower, of Homestead; Mrs. Susan E. Plummer, of Emsworth, Pa.; Dr. Charles Holmes Shaffer, of Elizabeth; Miss Elizabeth L. Shaffer, of Elizabeth. There are eighteen grandchildren and one great-grandchild living, and have never been any deaths among the Doctor's descendants.

Dr. Shaffer will be greatly missed in this community. He has been prominently identified with every public movement in the community for many years. He was a man of most positive convictions, and had the courage of his convictions at all times. He was not afraid of being on the unpopular side of any question, and if he thought he was right, would manfully uphold his opinions in the face of any amount of opposition. He was intensely fond of controversy, and his intimate friends knew that he would often take the contrary side of a question for the sake of argument. But in matters right and of principle, as he saw them, he was firm as a rock.

He was one of the most methodical of men, and ordered his daily walk by a system which was accuracy itself. During all the many years that he lived in Elizabeth he kept a daily record of conditions and events which has grown to be of almost incalculable value. This included a record of the state of the weather, temperature taken three times each day and the highest and lowest noted, rainfall and snow, any important events transpiring in the community, a record of all deaths in the town and vicinity, the ages of all inhabitants of advanced years, and a host of other things. The *Herald* acknowledges a great debt of gratitude for constant access to these records, and the aid they have been in making up the weekly record of this publication. Requests for information were reaching the Doctor almost constantly from various sources. and they always met a courteous, ready response with the information desired, if it was in his power to give it. It is to be hoped that this valuable record will not be allowed to stop with his death.

The Doctor was a frequent contributor to the local press, and his trenchant style and entertaining descriptive powers are familiar to readers of the *Herald*. His "Reminiscences of Forty Years in Elizabeth," published in installments in this paper a few years ago, attracted particular attention. He left an interesting autobiography in manuscript, which will probably be published. He was a great reader of the papers, and kept fully posted on events of the day. He was a great admirer of the New York *Tribune*, having read it daily from the time of Horace Greeley, whom he regarded as one of the greatest men this country ever produced. It is illustrative of his methodical habits to state that he had every daily issue of the paper above named carefully filed away where it could be had immediately if wanted. His file runs back to a period before the war. He likewise never destroyed a letter, and in his long and active career accumulated a vast collection of letters, all of which are carefully filed away.

For nearly a quarter of a century the Doctor was postmaster of Elizabeth, having been appointed first by President Lincoln. He held the office as long as he desired, and then resigned voluntarily. During the war he was in the front for a time as a volunteer surgeon. He filled at various times positions of honor and trust in the borough, among them, burgess, councilman and school director, and he took a deep interest in all public matters, being an earnest and active republican from the foundation of the party. He was a warm personal friend of Hon. James G. Blaine from boyhood, and when in Elizabeth, Mr. Blaine has always made Dr. Shaffer's house his stopping place, since the breaking up of Mr. Blaine's mother's home here. The family received a telegram of condolence from the secretary of state, who was unable to attend the funeral.

The following practitioners of medicine were students in Dr. Shaffer's office while pursuing their studies: Samuel W. McCune, M. D., of Winchester, Va.; George S. Holmes, M.

D., deceased; John S. Woods, M. D., of Kansas City, Mo.; J. A. Craighead, M. D., of Pittsburgh, Pa.; John N. McCune, M. D., of Suterville, Pa.; P. T. B. Shaffer, M. D., and Charles H. Shaffer, M. D., of Elizabeth.

In his religious life the Doctor was undemonstrative, but earnest and faithful. He became a member of the Methodist Episcopal Church under the ministry of Rev. McCready, about the year 1858, and continued in that relation up to the time of his death, partaking of the Lord's Supper at its altar the Sabbath before he was called from earth. He was almost constantly an office bearer in the church, and was always a liberal supporter of it. He was in a marked degree faithful in his attendance at the preaching of the word, and all the meetings which his official relation to the church entailed, though this was often at a personal sacrifice of the time of a very busy man. He was warmly devoted to the denomination of his his choice, but had nothing of narrowness or sectarian bigotry about him, having contributed to the erection of every church edifice erected since his settlement in Elizabeth. He was a Bible scholar of rare attainments, and read the sacred volume through scores of times, having made it his custom for many years to read it through at least once each year. He read his testament both in our authorized version and in the original Greek, and was seldom at fault in a scripture quotation or reference. He said to a friend a few days before his death that he believed every word of the Bible, that Jesus Christ came into the world, the Son of God, to save sinners, and he accepted him as his Saviour.

The Doctor was always a ready and liberal giver to all worthy objects, though much of his giving was unobtrusive, and never came to the light of publicity. He was a genial man, and even in his last days, when he knew that death was sure to come soon, and almost certain to come suddenly, he never lost his cheerfulness, but had a pleasant word or joke for every friend. He was peculiarly fond of children, and was never too busy to bestow some attention on the little ones. Was there one in town, old enough to know anything, who was not personally acquainted with the good old doctor? Was there one to whom he had not at some time given a bite of the ever present stick of licorice? We doubt it, for it was one of the commonest sights in our streets to see him surrounded by a group of little folks, and seemingly to enter fully into their youthful joys.

He was thrown from his gig July 28th, 1878, and received injuries from which he never fully recovered, his heart and bladder trouble being readily traceable to this injury. He suffered severely for some years before his death, his chief affliction was a bladder affection, the irritation and nervousness growing from which induced a heart trouble, manifesting itself by sudden failure of the organ. He fully expected to die just as he did, suddenly, and awaited the event with a calmness which was heroic. His funeral on Monday, with services in the M. E. Church, was one of the largest ever known here, the large auditorium of the church being wholly inadequte to contain the large crowd which, notwithstanding the downpour of rain, assembled from all the country around, to pay their last tribute of respect. The impressive services were conducted by Rev. J. J. Hill, pastor of the church, assisted by Rev. D. H. Pollock, pastor of the U. P. Church, and Rev. C. A. Holmes of Pittsburgh. In accordance with the Doctor's wish, his remains were carried to the cemetery, and the whole concourse walked. He was laid to rest in Elizabeth cemetery, his brethren of the Odd Fellows, of which order he was for many years a member, bearing his body to the tomb.

The Walker Family.

In the year 1785 Samuel Walker, with his wife Elizabeth and a family of children, emigrated from Wilmington, Delaware to Virginia Court House, situate on the west side of the Monongahela river, at McFarland's Ferry, about two miles above Elizabeth. Court had been held at this place from 1777 to 1781, while this region was still under the jurisdiction of Virginia.

Walker was of Irish extraction, but was born in Delaware, where he had served a number of terms in the Legislature before moving to the west. In 1768 he married Elizabeth Springer, the granddaughter of Carl Christopher Springer, a Swedish nobleman of prominence in the history of Wilmington, Delaware. In his new home Walker became a farmer and also operated the ferry at that place, where, in November, 1794, he ferried Gen. Morgan's army, which had been sent to suppress the whiskey insurrection, across the river. Shortly after this date his son, Major John Walker, came to Elizabeth, which had been laid out in 1787, by Stephen Bayard, where he, John Walker, married in 1797, Diana, daughter of Robert and Mary (Davidson) Craighead, and engaged in boatbuilding, which was then in its infancy, but was destined in a few years to make the town famous. In 1801 Major John Walker, with a company of farmers, built the schooner "Monongahela Farmer," a vessel of 200 tons. It was loaded with flour, whiskey, &c., and floated to New Orleans, where the vessel and cargo were sold. This was the first sea-going vessel built west of the Allegheny mountains.

In 1802 the brig Ann Jane of 450 tons was built here for the Messrs. McFarlane, merchants. Major Walker loaded her with flour and whiskey and sailed her via New Orleans to New York, where he disposed of both brig and cargo. The quadrant used by him on this voyage is still in the possession of the family at Elizabeth. In 1803 Major John Walker built the boats used in Lewis & Clark's exploration of the Missouri river and the Northwestern part of the United States. He also kept the Mansion House, the only hotel in Elizabeth, where he entertained General La Fayette on the occasion of the latter's visit to this region in 1825. He died in Elizabeth at the age of 86, having raised a family of eight children.

His second son, John Walker, Jr., married Nancy, daughter of Solomon and Nancy (Speers) Krepps, of Brownsville, Pa. He was extensively engaged in the mercantile business in Elizabeth for many years, but has retired, and now resides with his wife in Denver, Colorado. They have three children, John Brisben, Bolivar Krepps, and Mary Krepps. John Brisben Walker is the well known owner and editor of the *Cosmopolitan*.

His third son, Major Robert C. Walker, married Eliza, daughter of Ephriam and Maria, (Gillespie) Blaine, sister of the late Hon. James G. Blaine. He was engaged in various pursuits until the war of the Rebellion. He was at one time a member of the Pennsylvania Legislature. When the war broke out he entered the Union army and there attained the rank of major. After the war he continued in the regular army, stationed at St. Paul, Minnesota, and Helena, Montana, until he was retired by reason of his age. He still lives in Helena, and has four children living, viz: James Blaine Walker (City Treasurer of Helena); William G. Walker. of Washington, D. C.; Julia, (Mrs. Daniel Fiske), of Helena, and Margaret, (Mrs. O. J. Salisbury), of Salt Lake City, Utah.

Mary, the oldest daughter of Major John Walker, was married in 1819 to Solomon Speers, of Bellevernon, Pa. They moved to Peoria, Illinois, where they died. Five children survive them, viz: Diana, (Mrs. Joseph Gallagher), of Jefferson City, Iowa; Noah Speers, of Illinois; Solomon P. Speers, of Baltimore, Md.; Robert Speers, of Jefferson City, Iowa, and Mary Evaline (Mrs. Fred Gilbert), of Peoria, Illinois. Matilda, the second daughter of Major John Walker, was married to William K. Vankirk, of Elizabeth. They lived fourteen years in Millsboro, Pa., after their marriage, and then returned to Elizabeth, where they both died. Two children survive them, viz., Samuel W. Vankirk, a merchant of Elizabeth, and Angeline G. Walker, (widow of John S. Walker, of Minneapolis, Minnesota.) Diana, the third daughter of Major John Walker, was married to Samuel Frew, the first lawyer and editor of Elizabeth. They both spent their lives in Elizabeth. An only child survives them, viz., Eugene B. Frew, of Bolden, Colorado. Their daughter, Antonette, married Jacob H. Miller, Esq., of Pittsburgh. She died in 1890, leaving two children, Horace J. and Adelaide. Sarah, fourth daughter of Major John Walker, married Dr. W. A. Penniman, of Elizabeth. They lived from 1856 to 1871 in Minneapolis, Minnesota. They had no children.

Julia, fifth daughter of Major John Walker, was married to John McDonough, merchant, of Elizabeth, where they both spent their lives. Three children survive them, viz., Mary, (Mrs. I. N. Large), of Denver, Col.; Annie, (Mrs. Caleb McCune), of Hazelwood, Pittsburgh, and Corinne McDonough, of Denver, Col.

Samuel, the oldest son of Major John Walker, (born in 1798), succeeded his father in the boat building business, and it was during his administration that it attained its greatest proportions. For many years he kept three boat yards in constant operation, and built many famous boats, among them the renowned "J. M. White," the fastest steamboat that ever turned a wheel on the Mississippi river. Prior to 1857, 312 boats had been built at the Walker boat yards in Elizabeth. He was also extensively engaged in the mercantile business, and was the first postmaster of Elizabeth. In 1819 he married Nancy, daughter of Noah and Nancy (Frey) Speers, of Bellevernon, and in 1869 they celebrated their golden wedding. They raised a family of ten children, six of whom are living (1893), viz.; Wm. B. Walker, of Madison, Mo.; Lucinda, (Mrs. R. P. Voorhies), of San Jose, Cal.; Noah S. Walker, of Colorado, Texas; Samuel Walker, merchant, of Elizabeth; Nannie, (Mrs. A. R. Pope), of Macon, Mo., and Mary, (Mrs. T. B. Barnes), of Pittsburgh, E. E. The deceased are Thomas P. Walker, who left a widow and two children, of Elizabeth; James S. Walker, who left a widow and four children, now of McKeesport; John S. Walker, of Minneapolis, Minn., who left a widow (Mrs. Angeline G. Walker) and one son by adoption, Albert J. Walker, (a son of Noah S.), who now resides (1893) in Elizabeth. He is one of the rising attorneys at the Pittsburgh bar. His office is 129 Fifth avenue. Diana, (Mrs. General James A. Ekin), of Louisville, Ky., who left two children, Wm. M. Ekin, and Mary, (Mrs. A. E. Willson), of Louisville, Ky.

General James A. Eken was engaged in boat building business in Elizabeth at the outbreak of the Rebellion, having succeeded his father-in-law, Samuel Walker. He entered the U. S. army and in a short time was made assistant Quartermaster, and in time attained the rank of Colonel and Brevet Brigadier General. He continued in the service after the war was over, stationed at San Antonio, Texas, and later at Louisville, Ky., where he died in March, 1891.

SAMUEL FREW.

Samuel Frew, son of Andrew Frew, was born in Elizabeth in 1810, and studied law under Hon. Walter Forward, and became the first lawyer of Elizabeth. At the early age of 18 he was editor and proprietor of the *Pennsylvanian*, a campaign paper, and later of the Monongahela *Messenger*, one of the early newspapers of the valley. He served a term in the State Legislature, and was appointed by Gov. Ritner, Prothonotary of the Supreme Court. He was a brilliant and talented writer and lawyer, and was eminently *sui generis* in his make up. He was naturally endowed with wonderful abilities, was quick of comprehension and probably one of the finest conversationalists in his own or any other community. He was always revolving some vast scheme in his mind, and always intended to put them in execution but never succeeded. No doubt one trouble was his being ahead of the times in which he lived. One of his pet schemes was located at Tygart Valley Falls, West Va. This was laid out on a grand scale and work commenced, Mr. Frew asserting that it would not be long before a railroad would be located and put in operation in this apparently inaccessible region, which has since been accomplished. He married Diana, daughter of Major John Walker, and died in 1861.

A TRIBUTE—DEATH OF MRS. SARAH WILSON.

[From Daily Monongahela *Republican*.]

The death of this well known person, which occurred December 18th, 1889, at the residence of her brother, Rev. Dr.

Hamilton, in Washington, Pa., removes from among us one of our oldest native residents. She was born in this place October 24th, 1813, being the eldest child of Joseph and Margaret (Ferguson) Hamilton. With the exception of a few occasional absences her whole life was spent here. In 1837 she was married to Mr. Henry Wilson who died many years ago.

Since that time she has lived a comparatively secluded life. Last August she went on a visit to her friends in Washington. Her health seemed to be quite good for one of her age, but being suddenly attacked with acute pain in her breast she sank rapidly, and within 24 hours her life ended.

After brief religious services at Washington, conducted by Rev. Drs. Brownson, Woods and Stevenson, her body was brought to this place on the 19th, and the day following was interred from the house of her relative, C. W. Hazzard. Of her three surviving children, all residing in Illinois, two were present, Mrs. Smith F. Wilson, of Bloomington, and Mr. R. F. Wilson, of Chicago (accompanied by his wife). On account of the casual illness of her pastor, Rev. Dr. Maxwell, the services of a former pastor, Rev. Dr. Campbell, of Sewickley, were solicited and kindly tendered. Dr. C. spoke with much feeling of her christian character and of her sudden departure. She had feared the Lord from her youth, had been a member of the Presbyterian church here for more than 50 years, had been in some important respects an example for others to imitate,

Though the sphere in which Mrs. Wilson moved in the latter years of her life was a retired one, she will be not a little missed out of our community. She had lived here so long, she had in earlier life taken such an active interest in all current events, and possessed naturally such an unusually retentive memory that her mind seemed to be a storehouse of local information, and she was constantly being made the arbiter of doubtful points in local history. In personal ministry to the sick and afflicted she was a model of self-sacrificing kindness.

During the memorable period of the civil war, her two sons being in the army, she gave her time and thought almost incessantly to those ministries of kindness for the relief of the sick and wounded soldiers which were then so largely and constantly required, and which here as elsewhere throughout the country, were so freely rendered.

If the question were asked why it was that Mrs. Wilson, "Aunt Sarah" as she was familiarly called by so many, had such a warm place in the hearts of those who best knew her, the reply would doubtless embrace at least two points. One of these is that already alluded to, her sacrificing kind heartedness. The other, a certain cheerfulness and equinimity which she owed partly to nature and partly to grace, and which no adversity was able to extinguish. In youth she was remarkably vivacious, and with strong social tastes and attachments, enjoyed life fully. In later years, though overtaken with many and specially severe trials, she did not fall into a murmuring and repining spirit, but was patient, submissive, hopeful. She could always see a bright side to everything. She did not torment herself with fears and distrust of the future. Her faith in Providence was not a theory simply, it was thoroughly and habitually practical. She had nothing to complain of. She envied no one. She lived less for herself than for others. She was cheerful, contented, happy; and found her greatest delight in ministering to the happiness of others. Dear, kind Aunt Sarah! How much more she did for us all than any of us could ever do for her.—Monongahela City, January 5th, 1890.

Scott Family.

William Scott, Sr., with his wife, Rebecca, emigrated from Ireland with their family, consisting of Fannie, John, Thomas, Jane, Mary Joseph, Alexander, Angel and Rebecca. They sailed on the ship Dolphin and landed at New Castle, below Philadelphia, September 6, 1796. April 6, 1800, Thomas Scott, son of William and Rebecca, purchased the tract of land on Mingo Creek in Washington county, Penn'a, now (1888) owned by Cowan, Lofink and Crookham, upon which, near the bank of the creek, stood at that time a large log mill, and near by a log house, the latter of which was erected in 1790, and still stands firm. At what time or by whom the mill was built we have no information. Thomas Scott, with his sister Mary, took possession of this house on date of purchase and attended the mill, which was an undershot wheel mill. Thomas Scott married Margaret Turner, March 14, 1802. His father Wm. Scott, was, in the 26th year of his age, with most of his family, settled about the same time on the head waters of Mingo creek, near what is now known as Dunningsville.

William Turner, father-in-law of Thomas Scott, with his family, emigrated from Ireland at an earlier day, when the wife of Thomas was only two years old. William Turner also settled in the east end of Washington county. The Turners were nearly related to the Rogers family, one of whose girls married Benjamin Parkison, Sr., who was the grandfather of A. R. Parkison of this day. The Rogers were also Scotch-Irish, and in Ireland were considered of the highest class of citizens, fond of style and fine dress. In the log house above mentioned Thomas Scott and his wife had to them born eleven children, under the medical ministrations of the good old midwife, Granny McCord, at the cost price of two dollars for each birth. She made it the business of her life and was very successful.

In 1812 Thomas Scott erected the mill on Mingo, now or recently owned by R. Cowan. This mill had undershot wheels. In 1831 he applied a steam engine to this mill. In 1835 he sold the mill and farm to Samuel Morgan, and bought what was known as the Bentley mill and farm, now known as the Harrison Distillery, and is situated a short distance up from the mouth of Mingo creek. The wife and son John died here, the former December 24, 1849, and the latter at the date as above stated. In August, 1851, the mill, house and 16 acres of land was sold to T. Mitchell. The family then removed to Monongahela City. In 1852 Thomas Scott built the brick house in that city in which Mark Borland now resides. In this house Thomas Scott died February 19, 1856. Thomas Scott's brother Alexander inherited a large fortune on the death of his uncle Joseph Orr, a rich batchelor who died on the Jamaica Islands.

Mary, a sister of Thomas Scott, who was his housekeeper, on his settling in 1802, was married to John Friar, a merchant; who owned the farm three-quarters of a mile on the pike east of Ginger Hill. He, there for a time kept a valuable store. He died possessing what in those days was called great wealth. Their only child, a daughter, Jane, married Major John S. Clokey. He also run the mercantile business at this place, but being extravagant in his way of living, and unsuccessful in his dealings, he soon exhausted his wife's fortune, and both died poor.

William Scott died in Stubenville, Ohio, January 24th, 1876. The older citizens will call to mind William when he lived in the old log house over the mill-race, opposite the present residence of the late Nathan Wylie, on Pigeon creek, and attended the mill for Isaac VanVoorhis. They will no doubt recollect his little boy Winfield, who is now one of the most prominent mercantile men in Steubenville, Ohio, and president of several large business associations in that city.

Matilda had two sons, James and Oliver, who are now (1888) extensive business men in Toledo, Ohio. James owning one-half of a wholesale store doing yearly one million of sales.

Alexander raised a very large family, and nearly all his life lived in Monongahela City, and for the most part in the house still standing on Railroad, near Fourth street.

Moses, the survivor for many years of the family of Thomas Scott, being childless, was long a resident of Monongahela, where he lived with his wife in ease and comfort. He owned at his death, which occurred March 5th, 1891, a part of the old homestead on Mingo, not far from the spot where he first saw the light of day. He was one of the substantial elements in the make-up of his adopted city, where he was held in high esteem as a citizen and christian gentleman.

The Monongahela *Republican* of March 6, 1891, says:

MOSES SCOTT,

An aged and respected citizen of this city, died at his residence, Third ward, Thursday evening, March 5, 1891, at 7 o'clock, after a long illness.

Mr. Scott was born in the old Scott farm house on Mingo creek, October 12, 1809, where he lived until 1850, when he moved to Monongahela City. During the year '55 he was married to Rosanna McFarland, daughter of Colonel Joseph McFarland, of Franklin county. This branch of the Scott family are intimately connected with the early history of Washington county, and are well known in this part of Western Pennsylvania.

In '62 Moses Scott moved to Beaver, Ohio, but returned to Monongahela City soon after the war was over. Early in life he was converted and became a member of the Mingo Presbyterian Church, and remained a steadfast Christian during all his long life of 82 years. He was a member of the First Baptist Church, this city, and died in that faith.

For five years Mr. Scott was Justice of the Peace for Third ward. In politics he was formerly a strong Republican, but of late years has been a Prohibitionist. He carried on a mercantile business during one portion of his life in the store now occupied by Keller Bros. but has lived a retired life during his last days.

Moses Scott was known to all our people. He was raised in the strictest Covenanter Presbyterianism; his lessons of frugality came to him from Ireland, and were his by birth and training. This sometimes led him to a close economy, bordering on illiberality, and often misunderstood.

When one comes to sum up his rounded character as it stands finished, the verdict will be that Moses Scott lived up to the Christian life as it was given him to see it, and that much of the good that he did was hidden from the world by his own peculiar way of looking at duty. To illustrate: years ago he lifted a debt from the Baptist church, saying, you pay the interest, and at my death I will provide for the principal.

His funeral will take place on Saturday morning from the Baptist church. And when he is laid to rest his epitaph can well be written, "An honest, virtuous, God-fearing, intelligent Bible reading, correct living man has gone to his reward."

HON. JAMES SCOTT.

He died at his home in Lebanon, Ohio, December 16, 1888. His biography will be found among the proceedings of the Centennial at Monongahela City, November 15, 1892.

VAN VOORHIS FAMILY.

To Hon. T. G. Bergen we are indebted for the signification of the Van Voorhis, formerly written Van Voorhies and Van Voorhees, as we find it in his work, entitled "The history of the Bergen family, with notes upon some of the branches of the Voorhies and other Long Island families." "Steven Coerte Voorhies, who emigrated to this country from Holland in 1630, was a son of Coert Alberts Voorhies, who resided in front of the village of Hees, or Hies, in the Netherlands, the word " Voor" meaning in English "in front of." E. W. Van Voorhis in his ancestry of W. R. Van Voorhis, after a search by the St. James Heraldry office in London in 1872, obtained a certificate, under seal of the office, containing a description of the coat of arms, which states "That the armorial bearings of the family consisted in a golden tower on a red shield, quartered with a tree torn up by the roots, on a silver field. The motto being "Virtus Casteltum Meum."

Our knowledge biographical of the Van Voorhis family dates back only to Cornelis Coerte Van Voorhees, of Flatlands, L. I., who was baptised January 23, 1678, and left, among other children, his son Daniel Van Voorhees, who was born at Oyster Bay, L. I., December, 1701, and married Femmyte

Bennett November 27, 1724. She was born April 24, 1706.
Their children were : Elizabeth, born July 24, 1725 ; Cornelius, October 6, 1729 ; Femmyte, born January 16, 173– ;
John, born June, 1735 ; DANIEL, born July 8, 1738 ; Antyte,
born October 14, 1741 ; Jerome, born April 8, 1743 ; and
Abraham, November 6, 1751. Daniel, born as above stated,
July 8, 1738, was the ancestor of the family in Western
Pennsylvania. He was a seafaring man, following navigation
most of his life ; he was master of several merchant ships of
which he was part owner. During the revolution he was taken
prisoner three different times by the British, and each time
suffering a total loss of his vessel. During an engagement one
time a stanchion of the vessel against which he was leaning
was carried away by a cannon ball. With two other captains
as prisoners, he was taken to some Spanish island for safe
keeping, from the dangers of which they escaped only to be
recaptured. In 1764 Daniel was married to Mrs. Sarah Britt,
who was a daughter of Coerte Van Voorhees, of Fishkill, N. Y.
She died September 15, 1777. By this wife he had two
children, Samuel Newton and Sarah. He married as his
second wife Mary Newton, July 12, 1780. We are not informed just when Daniel left Long Island and settled in Rancocas Creek, New Jersey, twelve miles from Philadelphia, but
it was somewhere about 1780. By this second marriage were
born John, Daniel, Abraham and Mary. We have on a fly
leaf of a little history of New York, printed in London in
1757, these words in his own handwriting :

" Moved my family out into the backwoods in the month of
October, in the year of our Lord 1786."

DANIEL VAN VOORHIS.

In 1785 he had been out himself and selected his new home.
He brought with him in 1786 his second wife and his children
born to her as above mentioned.

He located on the farm now owned by John VanVoorhis,
in Carroll township, Washington county, Pa., where his wife,

Mary N., died October 31, 1789, and hers was the first burial in the VanVoorhis cemetery, his daughter, Mary, being the second. She was born at the new home January 30th, 1788, and died August 11th, 1789. Daniel first lived in the log cabin east of the well known spring, where yet may be seen traces of it. He occupied this cabin when he married, May 3d, 1791, his third wife, in the person of Nancy Myers, and in it were born their two children, Elizabeth and Isaac. Whilst Isaac was a mere youth the hewed log house was built that stood above the cabin nearly on the spot where is now the brick house of John VanVoorhis. Daniel died February 21st, 1819, in the homestead, and his wife, Nancy, died February 17th, 1840, at the home of her daughter, Mrs. Samuel Frye.

Samuel N., son of Daniel, was born July 12th, 1774, on Long Island, and was married to Sarah Myers June 22, 1800. Their children were:

Daniel, born April 13th, 1801, in Duchess county, N. Y.

William R. was born May 25th, 1803, in Duchess county, N.Y.

Charles E. was born October 11th, 1809, in Duchess county, N. Y.

Susan R. was born January 7th, 1812, in Washington county, Pa.

Sarah Ann was born May, 1816, in Washington county, Pa.

Isaac was born March 1, 1821, in Crawford county, Ohio.

Harriett was born February 20th, 1826, in Crawford county, Ohio.

Somewhere between the years 1809 and 1812, Samuel N. left New York state with his family to seek a new home in western Pennsylvania. They traveled in a two-horse wagon, rigged with yankee harness and other accoutrements, after the style of that day. They came direct to his father's, and in a short time were domiciled in the old log house that stood near the present entrance to VanVoorhis cemetery. He for a while taught school in what was then known as Hair's school house. After a not very long time he moved into a log house on the Joel Butler farm, near the present Black Diamond Railroad

Station, above Monongahela City. Sometime prior to 1820 he moved to Crawford county, Ohio, and located near where now stands the city of Bucyrus, which was then considered on the frontier of settlement. They moved in a two-horse wagon drawn by a stout yoke of oxen and one horse in the lead; took with them one cow and calf. Here Samuel N. and his wife, Sallie, spent the remnant of their days, and now lay side by side in Whetstone cemetery, Samuel having died February 24th, 1857, and his wife September 20th, 1848.

Charles Edward, son of Samuel N., has long been a resident of Knox county, Ohio, near the town of Bladensburg. He is a farmer to some extent but has been mainly engaged in the ministry connected with the Christian church. He was married July 9, 1832, in Crawford county, Ohio, to Miss Susan Jones, who was born January 28, 1813, and died September 17, 1870. They had eleven children.

On June, 1884, nine were living, all married, and had children more or less in number, but in the aggregate the total is forty-one. His children are all farmers and doing well. Charles E. married as a second wife Miss Ellen Fergeson, of Columbiana county, Ohio, April 27, 1871. Of the remaining children of Samuel N. VanVoorhis we know little, excepting that Isaac was a prominent politicion in Crawford county, Ohio, being County Commissioner for at least one term, and was held in high esteem by his fellow citizens.

Sarah, daughter of Daniel VanVoorhis, by his first wife, was born August, 1777, and married her cousin, John VanVoorhis, November 23, 1797, who was born August 2, 1768. He died near Goshen, N. Y., May 2, 1848, and his wife November 17, 1859. Their children were:

Phœbe, born June 19, 1798, and died September 2, 1830.

Daniel, born January 15, 1800, died July 12, 1812.

Susan, born November 18, 1802, married Thomas Faulkner, April 9, 1829.

Samuel N., born October 31, 1804, died August 3, 1826.

Sallie Ann, born October 14, 1806, died September 13, 1826.

William, born June 1, 1809, died July 10, 1834.

Mary R., born July 7, 1811, married William B. Vail May 29, 1833.

Emaline, born September 7, 1813, married Jeremiah R. Williamson February 11, 1847.

Elizabeth, born July 31, 1815, died September 9, 1873. She had married Albert Rockfellow December 30, 1835.

Jane, born April 11, 1818, married Charles S. Puff January 6, 1841.

This was the condition of the family in 1881. Samuel R. Williamson at that date had long been a resident of the vicinity of New Brunswick, New Jersey, where, as far as we know, the family still resides.

John, the oldest son of Daniel VanVoorhis by his second wife, was born in Burlington county, New Jersey, March 3d, 1781. He was married to Sarah Frye about the year 1805. He lived in a cabin near the VanVoorhis cemetery gate on the Brownsville road, the spring alone from which he used water remains to locate the spot. He moved with his family to Muskingum county, Ohio, in April, 1812. He located on a farm near the present town of Nashport, where he died June 28, 1874. He and a man the name of Trout built a keel boat at the mouth of Pigeon creek. In it he moved the heavier articles, among which were five barrels of whiskey, seven barrels of flour, two iron kettles, and a box filled with earth in which were placed scions of current bushes, apple and other fruit trees in embryo, together with a barrel of dried apples, and farming implements. The family went overland with the team. The men pushed and floated the boat down the Ohio to the mouth of the Muskingum, and thence up that river to Zanesville, from which point the goods were taken by wagon to Nashport, twelve miles distant. That region was then a wilderness of woodland, but John lived to see it blossom as the rose. John was a Baptist of the strictest kind in religion, and of the old political school a federal, and of the new a republican.

To John and Sarah were born as children:

Daniel, born in the log cabin above mentioned, November 25, 1806, and died June 3, 1893. The dates of the remaining children we have not obtained, but their names are as follows: Mary, Elizabeth, Theresa, Samuel, Sarah and Nancy. Daniel was married to Jane Roberts, of Muskingum county, January 24, 1834. She died April 11, 1871. He was not only a pioneer farmer but a successful merchant in the early days of that region. His thousands of acres and other sources of wealth attest his energy and capacity for gaining a competency. Against his own inclinations he was twice elected to the Ohio Legislature and in that body was reckoned as one of the most safe and useful members. In later years he was elected a member of the Constitutional Convention, where he did good service in aiding to mould many of the wisest provisions in the new Constitution. He (1892) still lives, and for years has sojourned in the city of Zanesville, while he holds his voting residence in Nashport, near his home.

Daniel and Jane had born to them seven children:

John, born July 23, 1836, and died from an accident in the summer of 1882. Of the dates of the birth of Victoria, Samuel, Sarah A., Mary I., Zenas F. and Henry C., we have no knowledge. Henry Clay is President of the Citizens' National Bank of Zanesville, Ohio, and elected to Congress in 1892.

Zenas F. remains unmarried.

HON. DANIEL VAN VOORHIS.

We insert the following extract from the Zanesville *Times-Recorder* relative to the death of Hon. Daniel Van Voorhis:

He died June 3, 1893, at the residence of his son, Hon. H. Clay Van Voorhis, in Zanesville, Ohio. He was born on the original Van Voorhis homestead, in then Fallowfield but now Carroll township, Washington county, Penn'a, November 25, 1806, and was moved by his father and mother, John and Sarah Van Voorhis, to Muskingum county, Ohio, locating in a log cabin near Nashport, Licking county, in April, 1812. His father at the time of his death was the oldest inhabitant of Licking township, and one of the oldest in the county. He was born in Burlington county, N. J., during the revolutionary war and when five years of age moved with his parents to Washington county, Pa., locating three miles west of Monongahela City. In 1805, having two large crops of wheat for which there was no home market, he had it ground, and building a flatboat, he started on April 5 for New Orleans with a cargo of flour. He disposed of part of it enroute for $8 a barrel and finally arrived at his destination May 22, when he disposed of the remainder of his flour and his boat, and after celebrating the Fourth of July in the metropolis of the Louisiana Purchase, he sailed to New York, reaching home August 28. He was married to Sarah Fry December 12, 1805, and continued to reside near the parental home until he came to Muskingum county with his family in 1812.

Daniel Van Voorhis was the oldest son, and soon after the family's arrival at Nashport was started to school in a log school house. The children sat on seats made by splitting round logs in two pieces, shaving the flat sides with a drawing knife, and driving pins into auger holes for legs. The house had a puncheon floor and a large fire place in the end of the building. It was a subscription school, at $2.50 a scholar, the attendance numbering about twenty-five. After taking advantage of these limited educational facilities, he worked on his father's farm until he was about twenty-five years of age. The Ohio canal had then been finished, and he boated on the canal part of the summer of 1831.

He was not pleased with the canal business, and in the fall of 1831 he concluded to open a general store at Nashport. His father agreed that if he would hew the framing timber, haul the logs and have the necessary lumber sawed, and quarry the stone for the cellar wall, he would furnish the necessary money for the erection of the building and would lend him all the money he had—about $800. The building was completed on the 14th of the next April, and with $200 dollars of his own and $800 borrowed from his father, he started on horseback the next morning for Washington county, Pa., where he borrowed $500 more of an uncle, and went to Pittsburgh and purchased a stock of goods. They were shipped to this city by water, and he had his store opened in May. In April, 1838, he associated with himself in the store at Nashport Mr. Abel Randall. They continued their partnership until November, 1843, when they sold out to John W. Thompson.

Mr. Van Voorhis then went back to farming, purchasing a large farm and managing it very successfully until April, 1877, when he rented it and retired from its active management. Since his retirement he has resided in this city, boarding at the Kirk House for a number of years and for the past two years making his home with his son, Congressman Van Voorhis. In October, 1859, he was elected to the Ohio Legislature from Muskingum county, as a Republican, and served during the sessions of 1860 and 1861. He was a strong supporter of the measures proposed in aid of the Government and voted for the two million dollar bill to aid in putting down the rebellion. In April, 1873, he was elected a member of the convention to frame a new constitution for the State of Ohio, but the constitution framed by it failed of adoption by the people.

He was married to Miss Jane Roberts, daughter of John and Barbara Roberts, of Falls township, January 24, 1834. Seven children were born to them, all of whom grew to manhood and womanhood. Six are still living, John having been accidently killed at Nashport several years ago. Those still living are, Mrs. T. M. Taylor and S. F. Van Voorhis, of Newark; Mrs. J. G. Stump, of Dresden; Mrs. N. C. Fleming, of Hanover, and Hon. H. C. and Fuller Van Voorhis, of this city. His wife, Mrs. Jane Roberts Van Voorhis, died April 11, 1871. Two sisters are all of his father's family that survive him. They are Mrs. Littleton Adams, of Madison township, and Mrs. D. R. Cook, of Macon, Ga.

He was a consistent member of the Methodist church at Nashport. During his residence here he attended divine services at the Market Street Baptist Church. He was a liberal contributor to institutions for the dissemination of knowledge and Christianity, among those aided very substantially by him being the American Bible Society, Kenyon College, Ohio Wesleyan University and Denison University.

Mr. Van Voorhis was an example of the noblest work of God, an honest man. He was honest in all the word implies.. He was true to every trust and sincere in everything he did. He was a thorough business man, which, coupled with his tireless energy and indomitable will power, resulted in bringing him a competence for his old age. He was a model husband and father and had the confidence and esteem of every one who knew him. He was a splendid example of the pioneer, who had not only witnessed the transformation from the wilderness to the heighth of civilization, but has had a share in it all.

Mary, daughter of John Van Voorhis, married Abel Randal, of the vicinity of Nashport. They are both dead.

Theresa married John A. Blair, a prominent merchant and politician of Zanesville. Both are deceased. Elizabeth married Samuel Adams, of Dresden, Ohio, and are deceased. Samuel died in 1840, by the fall from a horse. Nancy married Littleton Adams of Dresden, and both are living. Sarah A. married a man named Cook, and both are living and residents of Georgia.

Daniel, another son of Daniel Van Voorhis by his second wife, was born in Burlington county, New Jersey, December 22d, 1783, and died at his home in Carroll township, Washington county, Pa., August 6th, 1852. He married Mary Frye November 19th, 1807, who was born February 9th, 1788, and died May 4th, 1881. They lived during all of their married lives on the farm now owned by James Sansom in Carroll township. Daniel was one of those red-blooded persons that generally are long lived, yet he died the earliest of any of his brothers. He was one of the pioneer cattle dealers of Western Pennsylvania, and a man of distinguished integrity and moral worth. Uncle Danny, as he was familiarly called, had a large family of children, six of whom are living (1892).

Newton, who died April 2d, 1890, was named after his grandmother. Newton married Nancy Cooper, daughter of the late Valentine Cooper and grand daughter of Frederick Cooper, the older, who settled at the mouth of Maple creek, on the Monongahela river, in very early day. Newton's oldest daughter, Mary, married John Hill, both of whom are dead.

John Hill was the father of Joseph and Clinton Hill, now residents of Florida. Newton's daughter, Norcissa, married Harvey Yant of Horseshoe, he died not long ago. Julia married Clinton Van Voorhis, one of the most successful farmers in Carroll township. Elgy married Belle Frye, and lives in Kansas City, Mo. Josiah was drowned many years since in the Monongahela river, at Bellevernon ferry. Samuel married a Miss Adams, of Dresden, Ohio, whose mother was a daughter of John Van Voorhis, as above stated. Samuel died December 12, 1888, at Kansas City, Mo., and left a wife and two boys. Jerome remains on the homestead near the Witherow blacksmith shop in Fallowfield township. The daughter, Kate, married and moved west; and Nancy died near Spearville, Kas., a few years since. Elgy, another son of Uncle Danny's, was born in 1810, and married Hester Frye, daughter of Luke Frye. After living for a time in the stone house near the present distillery of W. J. Markell on Taylor's run, near Monongahela City, they removed to Greene county, where he still lives in comfort and affluence. His wife is deceased.

Abraham was born February 1, 1812; married Mary Carson, now deceased. They lived for many years on the farm now owned by Robert Coulter, in Carroll township. He removed many years ago to Illinois, where he again married, and where he died June 14, 1886.

Isaac, John F., Jerome, Daniel and Harvey B. are the remaining sons of Daniel.

Isaac, in 1846, married a daughter of the late Thomas Hopkins, of Pike run township, and now lives near Hillsborough, on the National Pike. He is, perhaps, the largest cattle dealer in Washington county. John F. married a Miss McBeth, whose parents resided near the old log house close by the present brick house of William Devore, near Monongahela City. He resided for several years in the old part of the house now owned by Robert McKean, near Lock No. 4. After changing bases at different times he finally settled at Spearsville, Kansas. Jerome married a daughter of the late Washington Cooper, and lived for a few years on the Uncle Danny homestead, then moved to Iowa, where his wife died. He still lives, having married a second wife. Daniel, after wandering to California on horseback among the early golden emigrants, and prospecting in different other places, settled in Illinois or Indiana, we are not sure in what State or what part, and there died. Harvey B. married a daughter of the late John Hopkins, of Brownsville, Pa. He farmed for a time on the "Rogally" farm, near the present town of Finleyville; then carried on the liquor business in Bridgeport, Pa.; then leased for some years the Oakland Park, out Fifth avenue, Pittsburgh. In the late war he was a major in the cavalry service in which he was severely wounded. After the war he went west and located in Speareville, Kansas, where he still resides.

Daniel had three daughters, Sarah, Christena and Mary. Sarah married Samuel Cooper, of Mingo creek. They are both dead. Christena married West Frye, whose death is noted elsewhere. His wife is also dead. Mary married B. F. Bentley, and are residents of Monongahela City.

Abraham, the remaining son of Daniel Van Voorhis, the older, by his second wife, was born in Burlington county, New Jersey, December 28, 1785, and died on the primitive old homestead December 4th, 1871. He married Ann Watkins May 11th, 1818, who died November 2d, 1828. He married as his second wife Jane Phillips November 27th, 1829, who lives on the old homestead.

Abraham by his first wife had as children Garrett T., born February 18th, 1819, married first time to Hester Frye, who died March 20th, 1864. He has always been a farmer and stock dealer, and now resides on Pigeon creek not far from the home of his youth. His second wife was Mary Jane Baxter, and still lives. Joseph was born August 27th, 1820; died November 17th, 1822, and was buried in the Van Voorhis cemetery.

Robert was born July 21st, 1822, and married Caroline Frye March 2d, 1848. She died December 18, 1885, and her husband, Robert Van Voorhis, died January 26th, 1892, at Fort Collins, Col. The remains of both are in the Van Voorhis cemetery. Their only daughter, Clara, married the Rev. R. B. Mansell, D. D. She died at McKeesport, Pa. January 12th, 1890. In 1887 Robert married as his second wife Miss Jane Hoffman. Having sold his farm to Captain M. Coulson he moved to Colorado.

Mary, the only daughter of Abraham by his first wife, was born May 5th, 1826, and died of diptheria January 31, 1863. She married Vincent Colvin April 6th, 1848, who died March 31st, 1876. Vincent was a soldier in the late war, and was in the service when his wife died. Shortly after her death he was honorably discharged from the army by order of the secretary of war. By his second wife Abraham had children as follows:

Eliza, born September 1st, 1830, married Thornton F. Watkins April 12th, 1849, and died February 28th, 1850. Thornton died January 2d, 1852, whilst on his way overland to California. They left their little boy, "Jimmy," who died whilst a youth, in the home of his grand parents, Van Voorhis.

Lucinda was born August 7th, 1832, and died of scarlet fever June 24th, 1840.

John was born September 6th, 1835, married Josephine H. Teeple September 15th, 1859, and lived until a few years ago (1892) on the original Van Voorhis homestead, since that time he has resided in Monongahela City, where he is a prominent business man, but still owns the homestead where his son Charles resides.

Emaline, born February 28th, 1838, married to Joseph Brown. They lived for many years on the Cunningham farm, a short distance from Fayette City, Pa. He now (1892) lives in ease and comfort on a farm in Marion county, Kas.

Caroline, born November 1st, 1840, married May 29th, 1862, to James Jones, who died June 25th, 1877. She now resides with her children in a comfortable home near Ginger Hill.

Serenia Ann, born July 2d, 1843, died March 23d, 1861.

The last of the children born to Abraham and Jane Van Voorhis was Cynthia, who was born January 16th, 1848, married October 15th, 1868, Cooper Bentley, who died July 12th, 1880. Cynthia married a man the name of Snyder as her second husband. They live in their nice residence on the pike, near Valley Inn, about two miles from Monongahela City.

Aunt Jane, as she is familiarly called, relict of Abraham Van Voorhis, still lives and resides on the old homestead in a house not far below where stood the primitive cabin. She is hale and hearty, full of vivacity, and wonderfully devoted to her children. She has for a long life time been a member of the Methodist Episcopal Church, and has listened to the preaching of the Gospel in the "church on the river bank" before many now in active duty were born. Long may she live to enjoy the love of her children, and to reap in her declining years much of the sweets of that religion she professed in early life.

By his third wife Daniel Van Voorhis had a daughter, Elizabeth, and a son, Isaac. Elizabeth was born in the primitive log cabin on the old homestead December 19th, 1792, and died August 18th, 1875. She married the late Samuel Frye, who died many years prior to the death of his wife, in the old log house that stood near the present brick house on the farm now owned by William Rogers in Fallowfield township.

Isaac Van Voorhis

Was born in the log cabin already spoken of, on the old homestead, March 15, 1794. He attended his first school in an old log house that stood near Witherow's blacksmith shop, in Fallowfield. The school was taught by an Irishman whose name we have forgotten. His common mode of punishment consisted in putting the unruly scholars up the huge chimney and giving them thereby a good smoking. The older Colvins, McComases, Witherows, Blythes,, Powers, Moodys were scholars in this primitive school. Isaac was married to Mary Hair by Rev. Samuel Ralston, May 13, 1819. They were married in the old log house, parts of which are still standing on the Hair farm, now owned by Williams brothers. He took his bride on horseback the next day to his home, where the plays and romping took place in good old style beneath the shade of the wide spreading sugar tree that stood below the house. They lived in this home until April 1, 1834, when they removed to the McFarland farm, now owned by his sons, Dr. J. S. and Clinton Van Voorhis, where he died June 4, 1875, and his wife died April 14, 1876. She was born March 10, 1797, near Gerardstown, West Va., and came to Washington county with her father and other members of the family in 1806.

Isaac Van Voorhis was ordained an elder in the Presbyterian church of Williamsport, now Monongahela City, February 12, 1836. He was a Presbyterian in the truest sense of the word, believing that the doctrines and usages of that church were founded upon the rock, Christ, as taught in the scriptures. He was among the first flatboat builders at the mouth of Pigeon creek. By means of these crafts hay and other farm products were taken to the Pittsburgh market. In one instance he hauled his produce to the river and had it shipped in a keelboat belonging to some other party, whilst he rode on horseback overland to the city, and returned the same day, the net proceeds of the sale aggregating six dollars and seventy-five cents, not much more than a coal miner now earns in a day. He often remarked in his latter days that people "now-a-days hardly had an idea what labor it required to earn a living in early days." He was a great friend of education, having aided, outside of his own family, at least two young men through college, one of whom was during his day on earth a distinguished minister of the gospel. He was one of the first Board of School Directors in his native township after the adoption of the Public School law in 1834. He was one of the original stockholders and for many years a member of the Board of Managers of the Washington and Williamsport Turnpike Company, serving in that capacity with Col. Joseph Barr, Samuel Hill and James Manown. He was born amidst the scenes of the Whiskey Insurrection and was about six months old at the time the great mass meeting was held at Parkison's Ferry, now Monongahela City, over which Col. Edward Cook presided, and Albert Gallatin acted as secretary.

His father had been a resident of Pigeon Creek for nine years, and on the 29th day of November, 1794, took the oath of allegiance, with many others, before Samuel De Pue, and the old gentleman being frequently waited on by the insurgents to ascertain his views, was always prompt to give the same reply: "If a few of you want to resist the power of the government, go ahead, for my part I have seen enough of that in my past life." Isaac Van Voorhis in politics was a Federalist, and as such cast his first vote for President in 1816 for Rufus King; in 1820-24-28 for John Q. Adams; in 1832 he voted for Henry Clay, who was the National Republican candidate. In 1836 and 1840 he voted for Gen. W. H. Harrison, the Whig candidate. In 1844 he voted for Henry Clay, and in 1848 for Gen. Taylor; in 1852 for Gen. Scott. In 1856, and up to his death, he voted for the Republican candidates.

He never belonged to any secret orders or other society than the church, which he considered amply sufficient for purposes intended for man's welfare on earth, or his spiritual preparation for the great hereafter. The Pittsburgh *Gazette* of June

5, 1875, in speaking of the death of Isaac Van Voorhis, said "Mr. Isaac Van Voorhis, an old, well known and respected citizen of Carroll township, Washington county, near Monongahela City, died on Friday morning, June 4, 1875, in the 82nd year of his age. From particulars furnished by a correspondent we learn that he was born on the 15th day of March, 1794, within two miles of the place where he died. He resided for forty years on the old homestead bequeathed to him by his father, and forty-one years on the farm where the declining years of his life were spent. His grandfather was one of three brothers, one of whom was killed by a poisoned arrow shot by an Indian. From Cornelius, the name of one of these brothers, the deceased was a lineal descendent. Daniel, the son of Cornelius, was the grandfather of the deceased. He was born at Oyster Bay, Long Island, December 17th, 1708, where also Daniel, father of the deceased, was born July 8th, 1738. Daniel for a time lived in New Jersey, but in October, 1786, he removed to the farm on which the subject of this sketch was born.

Mr. Van Voorhis was a subscriber to the Weekly *Gazette* for over sixty years, and during his life read over 3,000 copies of it, always depending on it for its political and general news and market reports. His father had taken the *Gazette* from its foundation in 1786. The deceased had always been identified with the whig and republican parties. He, with Robert McFarland, were the only persons in what was then Fallowfield township, Washington county, who voted for John Q. Adams, in 1824, for president. He never had any faith in, or trusted the democratic party, and during his long life of over four-score years he never sought an office. For over fifty years he had been a member of the Presbyterian church, and a ruling elder for more than forty years. He was an exemplary christian, and his early training in the teachings and doctrines of the Bible enabled him in his last illness to draw from it that spiritual consolation which, in the hour of death, the Christian alone can value.

In a notice of his death in the Presbyterian *Banner*, Rev. Dr. W. O. Campbell, pastor of the Presbyterian church of Monongahela City, says: "The deceased was perhaps the oldest inhabitant in Carroll township, having lived in it all his life. He was married the 13th of May, 1819, to Mary Hair, daughter of James hair, one of the first ruling elders of the church in Monongahela City. He leaves his wife and seven children to mourn his loss. He was admitted to the church in early life under the ministry of Dr. Ralston; since that time he has been a faithful and consistent Christian. He was ordained elder in the church of Monongahela City February 12th, 1836, and held that office 39 years. Officially he was the sole surviving representative of the early history of that church. He was a devout man of God, full of faith and the Holy Ghost, ripe in Christian experience and character. He was a steadfast believer in the Bible doctrines, as in our standards. He was not only beloved in his family but honored for his Christian consistency; his children leaned upon his prayers. He was not only honored in the community but beloved for his Christian charity. He was loved honored and trusted by the church as a member and officer. As a ruler he was prudent; in council cautious, but decided in action, charitable and conciliatory—a man of peace, yet true and firm in maintaining the interests of Zion. He was one of the worthy band of elders whom God pleased to give to this church in its early history, and was peculiarly respected because their worthy representative. For some years past he was seldom permitted to meet with the session; and was often, on account of his increasing infirmities, necessarily absent from public worship. He greatly regretted the deprivation, and had a constant interest in the affairs of God's house.

About one year previous to his death he had a severe illness which he, as well as others, thought would be his last. He was most happy in the prospect of death. His great desire was to depart and be with Christ. The writer has not seen a more happy Christian experience than this was at that time.

But God had something more for him to do. He was spared another year. During his last sickness he suffered great pain but had constant peace of mind. His faith did not for a moment forsake him. He knew by experience that God would not forsake him. At this time he did not forget the spiritual interests of his family or the church. He still preferred Jerusalem above his chief joy. His advice to his children was, "Trust in the Lord, he has not forsaken me, he will not forsake you." When he was told that all would soon be over, he said, "Bless the Lord, Oh my soul."

On Sabbath, June 6, 1875, attended by a large concourse of people, from the house where he had lived forty years, we bore his remains to the tomb. "Blessed are the dead which die in the Lord, from henceforth: yea, saith the spirit, that they may rest from their labors, and their works do follow them."

The Monongahela *Republican* in speaking of his death, says:

Mr. Isaac Van Voorhis, whose death we noticed two weeks since, was born on the farm now owned by John Van Voorhis, on the 15th day of March, 1794. He was the son of Captain Daniel Van Voorhis, who was born on Long Island, July 7, 1738, and was in the prime of life during the days of the Revolution. He was an accomplished scholar, and especially versed in the science of navigation, as his books now in existence at the old homestead fully show. Captain Van Voorhis followed the sea as captain of a merchant vessel for many years, and during the Revolution was taken prisoner three times by the British—twice having lost his vessel and cargo. At one time, being hard chased by a man-of-war, he raised the signal of surrender, but before it was recognized by the enemy, a cannon ball carried away the post against which he was leaning.

At one time he, with several others, were banished to an island, from which they escaped only to be re-captured, though shortly afterwards released. He was married three times. His first wife was originally a Van Voorhis, but was the widow Brett when he married her; they had two children. Samuel for a time was a merchant in New York State, but in the beginning of this century removed to this country, and for a short time lived in a cabin near the present Black Diamond Coal Works He afterwards immigrated to Crawford county, Ohio, where he died a few years since. Samuel's sister, Sarah, lived and died near Goshen, N. Y., in the 82nd year of her age. Captain Van Voorhis, prior to his coming to this country, resided some years on Rancocas creek, New Jersey, and in October, 1786, came with his family and purchased from a man named Decker 600 acres of land, now owned by John Van Voorhis and James Sampson. It was then a wilderness but now the garden spot in Carroll. He, with his two wives and three sons, sleep in the beautiful burying ground, selected by himself, overlooking Pigeon creek, for his remains and his kindred long before his death. Four generations of that name are now in that cemetery, incorporated and made perpetual by the laws of the land. Mr. Isaac Van Voorhis was the oldest resident in Carroll, having resided in it all his life. Cotemporary with him in the early history of this neighborhood were the Colvins, the Powers, McCombs, Hairs, Randolphs, Fryes, Depews, McGrews, Parkisons, Irwins, Rices, Beckets, &c. He was married to Mary Hair by the Rev. Dr. Ralston on the 13th day of May, 1819. They lived together a little over 56 years.

He always took a deep interest in our town. He, with his brothers, built the first keelboats at the mouth of the creek, just at the close of the war of 1812. He built the first coalboat, loaded with coal at Williamsport wharf, which was then at the old red house at the mouth of what is now called First street. The boat was twelve feet wide and forty feet long. It was filled with coal by the late Edward Kearney by hauling it with a one-horse cart from the old coal bank in Catsburg. It was sold to a returned horse drover for cash received from the sale of horses, and after his departure was never heard from. In those days it was necessary to have such crafts in order to get the produce of the farm to market, and even then the price of grain scarcely justified transportation.

He was in early times a federalist; in the days of Ritner, a strong anti-Mason; afterwards a whig; and finally a republican. He, with Robert McFarland, were the only persons in Fallowfield township who voted for John Q. Adams at the time he was elected president. He was a subscriber to the Weekly *Gazette* for over 60 years, and was said to be the oldest continuous subscriber the *Gazette* ever had. He was a Presbyterian by birth and profession for over 50 years, and was a ruling elder for 40 years. Ordained in 1836, he served in the session with Jesse Martin, James Gordon, James McGrew, Aaron Kerr, James Dickey, Henry Fulton, Joseph Kiddoo and John Power, all of whom had preceded him to the church on high, except John Power. He first attended Presbyterian church at the old horseshoe building, situate on the farm now owned by John Wilson, and in that old church yard are still to be seen evidences of the resting place of nearly all the first settlers of this country for many miles around. On the removal of the place of preaching to this city, he worshipped with his father-in-law, elder James Hair, and a few others in the old log school house near the old Presbyterian church on Coal street and Church alley. He contributed liberally toward the erection of the old brick church on the hill, also for the church building at the foot of the hill, and more recently aided in building the present beautiful church on Main below Sixth street. Thus in his life he gave of his substance for three church buildings of the same congregation, a no common affair in one life time. He lived on the farm on which he was born 40 years, and 41 years on the farm where he died.

He leaves behind his wife, seven children, 25 grand children and three great grand children. All his children survive him except Daniel, who died in 1848.

We need not say he died a christian, the world knew he was a christian, for it was as an humble follower of Christ his character shown the brightest. As the end drew nigh his faith and trust in a crucified Redeemer grew stronger and his hold on the merits and righteousness of Christ more firm. Although suffering intense pain, he never murmured, and with a halo of glory on his countenance he entered within the portals of the celestial city.

Mary H., wife of Isaac Van Voorhis, died at the homestead near Monongahela City April 14th, 1876. The Monongahela *Republican*, in a notice of her death, says:

"The deceased was born in Berkely county, Virginia, now West Virginia, on the 10th day of March, 1797. She came to this county with her parents, James and Rebecca Hair, in the year 1806. Her parents, not long after their arrival, settled on what was known then as the Platter farm, but afterwards was well known as the Hair farm, on Pigeon creek. Her father was the first ruling elder elected in the Presbyterian church in this city, which election occurred soon after the removal of the church organization from Horseshoe, in what year we are not able to say. The deceased had six brothers, John, James, Samuel, Gilbert M., Uriah, and B. W. Hair. John died in 1856 or thereabout, in Mount Union, Ohio. She had four sisters, Mrs. Martha Crouch, who died a few years since in the west; Mrs. Kela Baker, who died on the old Hair farm many years ago; Mrs. Eliza Potter, deceased in Allegheny City many years since; and Mrs. Louisa Brinton, who died years ago near Brownsville, Pa. She with her husband united with the Presbyterian church under the ministry of Rev. Dr. Ralston, and each were members of that church over fifty years. Being in full possession of her mental faculties to the last, she freely conversed on her prospects of Heaven; and, relying entirely on the blood of Christ, she was enabled to declare that death had no terrors. Thus in less than a year have passed within the portals of Heaven—two Christian parents, leaving behind a large circle of friends to mourn their loss. 'Blessed are the dead who die in the Lord.'"

Another paper, in speaking of her death, remarks: "She was a woman of true piety, conscious of her union with Christ, steadfast in her faith, not afraid to die, her trust was in Jesus. A faithful wife and mother, a true friend, a devoted Christian disciple; they who mourn for her mourn not as those who have no hope."

Isaac and Mary had eight children, all born on the old Van Voorhis homestead. Daniel was born March 15th, 1820. He was for awhile a student in Washington College; made a special study of surveying, which he practiced as a part of his business. He was a large full-blooded specimen of the Holland race, and possessed a mind of no ordinary caste. He was said to be more the image of his grandfather, Captain Van Voorhis, than any of the name in this country. He was a member of the original Ringold Cavalry and had rather a taste for military life. In August, 1844, he married Martha Houlsworth, of the vicinity of Jefferson, Green county, Pa. He lived and died in the house now owned by Nathan Wylie's heirs, near the homestead. He died March 12th, 1848. His daughter, Mary Ruth, married a Mr. Smalley, formerly of Waynesburg, Pa., but now a successful farmer in the west. His daughter, Theresa Jane, born shortly after his death, died when a small child. His widow married Elijah Adams, at one time sheriff of Greene county, Pa. He died a few years since, leaving Martha once more a widow, who made her home in the west with her children in Kansas, where she died in 1888. Daniel was an active member of the Presbyterian church, being converted under the ministry of Rev. John Kerr after hearing a sermon based on the "Barren Fig Tree." His remains are in the Van Voorhis cemetery. Nancy and James were the twin children of Isaac Van Voorhis. Nancy was born on the 19th and James on the 21st day of August, 1821.

Nancy was married to John Pollock by the Rev. W. F. Hamilton, January 1st, 1857. They lived in Monongahela City during the time he was connected with his uncle, Joseph Kiddoo, in the planing mill, which was burned in the latter part of 1856. Whilst residing here the little girl, Mary Jane, died. He operated for a time the flouring mill on Pigeon creek, now torn away, but for many years has resided on the Pollock homestead in Union township. Of their children,

Mary Jane, Coralinn, Belle and James preceded their mother to the better land. Isaac and Willie alone remain. Nancy died July 9th, 1884, at the Pollock homestead. Her pastor, Rev. J. F. Patterson, in a communication to the Presbyterian *Banner*, speaks thus of her death: "Mrs. Pollock was born August 19th, 1821. She was the eldest daughter of Isaac and Mary H. Van Voorhis. Her early life was spent near the place of her birth. In January, 1843, in a precious work of grace under the ministry of Rev. John Kerr, she gave her heart to the Lord and united with the Presbyterian church of Monongahela City. A few years after her marriage she moved into the bounds of the church of Mingo, with the membership of which she connected herself, remaining here a devoted follower of the Master until she joined the church above. Her conversion was a thorough one. In that good time when the spirit came to her the door of her heart was thrown wide open, and the Savior who came in was given entire possession. There in that first unreserved consecration to Christ was the basis of her consecrated life. She loved her Savior, and loving him she lived to do his will—He was the *alpha* and the *omega* of her life; her all in all." And so it was always the chiefest joy of her life just to follow him.

Her Bible was her daily companion. She seemed to live in the atmosphere of prayer and meditation upon God's word. She loved the courts of God's house, and her place in the sanctuary was seldom vacant, though living several miles away. In the darkest trials of her life, when her heart was almost broken, and in the severe sufferings of her last sickness, her religion was her solace and her support. She lived and died leaning on the bosom of her Savior, and death to her was only life. Yes, she is gone, and we feel her loss. In the home, in the church, and in the community where she lived, she is missed. But we sorrow not as those who have no hope, knowing that our loss is only her eternal gain.

James Hair Van Voorhis, twin brother of Nancy Pollock, was given by his father, in his earlier days, the farm now owned by William Devore, in Carroll township. August, 1846, he married Polly Smith, granddaughter of the late Dr. B. B. Smith, of the Forks, and also on the mother's side granddaughter of the Hon. George Plumer, long a member of Congress from Westmoreland county. After the death of Amzi Smith, her first husband, Polly's mother married Henry Fulton, at whose residence—the stone house in which Greer McElvain now lives, in Carroll—James and Polly were married by the Rev. John Kerr. Polly died July 29, 1848, leaving no children. James' second wife was Martha Dawson, of the vicinity of Springfield, Illinois. She died in the early fifties and was buried aside of the first wife in the Van Voorhis cemetery. She left no children.

James' third wife was a daughter of the late David Wilson, of Elizabeth, now Forward township, Allegheny county. He had by this wife several children, of whom Mary Lucinda, R. Finley, Grace and Anna are living, whilst Ellen, Marcie and Willie died within a few days of each other, and are buried in the Van Voorhis cemetery. James H. sold his farm to Wm. Devore and moved into Monongahela City about the year 1870 or '71. He built the fine brick house on Main street, now owned by Mrs. Nathan Cleaver. In April, 1876, James, with his family, moved to Colorado Springs, in the state of Colorado, where he engaged in wool growing and silver mining. He now is a resident of North Dakota, near Cooperstown, Griggs county, where he is engaged in farming. His daughter Mary Lucinda married James A. Loughrey, of Indiana, Pa., March 22, 1887. They reside in Indiana, Pa. Grace married Beecher Cox, of Sanburn, North Dakota, where they now reside. James was for many years connected with the Presbyterian Church of Monongahela City, of which he was ordained an Elder January 21, 1872.

Rebecca, another daughter of Isaac Van Voorhis, was born Jan. 28, 1825, and married T. B. Stewart, as his second wife, and is at this time a resident of Speareville, Kansas. Martha Jane remained at the homestead until the death of her parents. She never married and now resides in Monongahela City. Theresa married Thomas B. Stewart, of West Virginia, in 1854, and died February 16, 1876, in Union township, Washington county, Pa., only a short distance from the place of her birth. She was a devoted christian, having been a member of the Presbyterian Church from her early youth. She left a large family of children, all of whom are residents of Kansas, except James T., who married Vivia, Patterson, and died in Monongahela City, March 19, 1885, and was buried in the Van Voorhis cemetery. The *Daily Republican* thus speaks of his death: "The news of the death of the junior partner of Patterson & Stewart, which met our citizens this morning at the breakfast table, was sad news indeed. He was in health till Monday, the 9th, when he was attacked with typhoid fever. Reports of his condition from time to time, and especially in the last few days, had been discouraging, but it was hoped his constitution would enable him to pass the critical point at the turn of the fever. He died at fifteen minutes past one on Wednesday night. James T. Stewart was a young man of fine promise, active in business, and in social intercourse one of the most genial companions. He was a member of the Presbyterian Church and Librarian of the Sabbath school.

David, her oldest son, graduated at Washington-Jefferson College, and at the Western Theological Seminary, and is now a successful minister of the Gospel in Kansas. He is married and has several children. Clinton, the youngest son of Isaac and Mary H. Van Voorhis, married September 26, 1854, Julia Ann, daughter of Newton Van Voorhis, of Fallowfield. They reside on part of the old home farm, where he is regarded as one of the most successful farmers and cattle dealers in the eastern end of Washington county. His son Newton is married and now (1892) in business in Monongahela City, Pa. Albert has his home with his father. Willie and Nannie, darling children, passed away in childhood. His six girls are all at home at this date, 1892.

The remaining son of Isaac Van Voorhis, John S., was

born in the old hewed log house that stood where now is the residence of John Van Voorhis, on the 8th day of May, 1823. John was a pupil in the old Colhoun school, but always declared that he got his first ideas of education from the late R. F. Cooper, Esq., who for several years was his teacher in the school near the toll-gate on the pike. He was always an admirer of Cooper's talents, and expressed strong regrets at his early removal by death.

John began his college education in November, 1840, with Prof. J P. Thompson in the old carriage factory on Main street, Monongahela City. The recitations were held in the eastern room, upstairs, in which the Carroll *Gazette* was first printed, giving thus the place its first literary caste.

After the death of Prof. Thompson, John recited to John McFarland in the Ira Butler house, opposite the paper mill in Catsburg. He entered the sophomore class in Washington College in November, 1841, and graduated in 1844, dividing the first honor of the class with B. W. Allen and D. C. Reed. He entered the office of the late Dr. R. F. Biddle, of Monongahela City, October 9th, 1844. N. A. Adams, J. H. Connelly and A. B. Hill were fellow students in the office. They have all passed away. He graduated at the Jefferson Medical College March 25th, 1847, and settled in Bellevernon, Fayette county, May 25th, 1847. He was married by the Rev. John Kerr to Miss Betsy Plumer Smith September 7th, 1847, at the residence of her step father, Henry Fulton, in the house in Monongahela City now owned by the heirs of Richard Stockdale, deceased. On the 22nd of the same month and year the doctor and his wife set up house-keeping in the brick house on the corner of Main and Second street, in Bellevernon, Pa. They had two children, Lizzie and Isaac S. Lizzie graduated at Washington Female Seminary in the class of 1866, and during her seminary career she united with the Presbyterian church under the ministrations of the Rev. James I. Brownson, D. D. She was married to J. C. Cunningham by the Rev. L. Y. Graham, March 30th, 1871. She was born June 30th, 1848, and died November 26th, 1877, in Bellevernon, the town of her birth. She left her husband and little Bettie, a darling child, to mourn her death. Bettie is now (1892) a graduate of the Pennsylvania College for Women, of Pittsburgh, Pa. Her mother was a devoted christian and worker in the church. At her death she was a member of Rehoboth, the church of her parents, grand parents and great grand parents on her mother's side of the family. In the graveyard of that old church can be seen, near the main entrance, a beautiful marble slab, standing on a double marble base, surrounded with flowers of almost endless variety, bearing the inscription "Lizzie Van Voorhis, wife of J. C. Cunningham, born June 30th, 1848, died November 26th, 1877."

"But if around my place of sleep,
The friends I love should come to weep;
Soft airs and song and light and bloom,
Should keep them lingering by my tomb."

And on the marble base of the slab is inscribed:

I will behold thy face in righteousness.
I shall be satisfied, when I awake, with thy likeness."

DEATH OF MRS. JAMES H. VAN VOORHIS.

[From the Griggs *Courier*.]

Died at her late residence, near Cooperstown, Griggs county, North Dakota, August 29th, 1893, Martha J., wife of James H. Van Voorhis, aged 59 years and three days.

Weary and worn with long and painful battling with disease, the common foe of mankind, Mrs. Martha Van Voorhis "fell asleep" Tuesday at mid-day in her home west of town. For a number of days she has been unconscious, and apparently making her way slowly but surely through the "Shadow of the Valley of Death." When at length the end came, the spirit stole out of its clay house as silently as a mother from her babe's crib when he falls asleep. Mrs. Van Voorhis had been suffering from a complication of trouble since last spring, and especially from a stomach difficulty which has been before a source of perplexity. Some two months and a half ago she met with a stroke of paralysis which affected her entire left side. It was thought then that she would not live but a few days, but she has lingered along all these weeks, a great trial to herself and those about her.

Mrs. Van Voorhis was born in Allegheny county, Pa., 59 years ago last Saturday. For the past 11 years she has lived in North Dakota. She came into this state, together with her family, from Colorado, and was well established in a pleasant home when this last sickness came upon her. When a young woman she confessed her faith in Christ, and at the time of her death was a member in the Congregational Church of this city. Mrs. Van Voorhis and her husband have always been highly esteemed by the community which is pained to hear of her death. She leaves, together with her husband, four children, two married daughters, Mrs. J. A. Loughry, of Indiana, Pa., and Mrs. A. B. Cox, of Sanborn, and an unmarried son and daughter at home. Mrs. McCord, a sister from Zanesville, Ohio, was with her when she died, having come here a short time ago.

The funeral was conducted by the Rev. O. P. Champlin, from her late residence, on Thursday afternoon, and the remains were interred in the Cooperstown cemetery. The family has the sympathy of the entire community.

MRS. LIZZIE VAN VOORHIS CUNNINGHAM.

[We insert the following tribute to her memory from the *Presbyterian Banner*.]

IN MEMORIAM.—In Bellevernon, Pa., om Monday morning, November 26th, 1877, Mrs. Lizzie Van Voorhis Cunningham fell asleep in Jesus.

She was the only daughter of Doctor J. S. and Elizabeth P. Van Voorhis, and wife of J. C. Cunningham. She was born in Bellevernon, June 30th, 1848; united with the Presbyterian church of Washington, Pa., under the ministrations of Rev. J. I. Brownson, D. D., in 1866, whilst a pupil in the Female

Seminary of that place, from which institution she graduated in the same year. Upon leaving school she transferred her connection to Rehoboth church in which connection she died. To those who knew her best, her life from the time of her Christian profession gave evidence that she was a true member of the great Church Invisible, one of those whose names are written in heaven.

But it was when the Great Refiner cast her into the furnace that the pure gold of her Christian character shown with surpassing luster. Few persons have more to bind them to life. She was eminently happy in her family ties—with a devoted husband, a sweet child, father, mother and an only brother, to all of whom she was devotedly attached. Gifted by nature, cultured and accomplished, endowed with great executive ability, she longed to be one of Christ's workers in the world and Church. She was deeply interested in Sabbath school work, and but a few days before her death she expressed, in broken whispers, her joy that all the class for which she had labored and prayed had professed faith in Christ and united with his Church.

For years she made a brave struggle with disease, but when it became clear that God would have her suffer his will, rather than do it, she cheerfully laid down the work she loved, and through months of protracted and often fearful suffering, she glorified the grace of God by a faith and patience which never failed. God's word was the manna which sustained her, the rod and staff upon which she leaned during that long and fearful passage of the Jordan when the waters overflowed all its banks. "Out of the depths" she praised God in the language of the 103d and 23d Psalms.

In the days of her health she was passionately fond of and proficient in music, and often in those last days of feverish restlessness she would ask those about her to sing, herself selecting the old hymns of the church which she had learned and loved when a child. She longed to depart—to be with Christ; often exclaiming, "I long to go; come quickly, Lord

Jesus." Her clear mind was never for a moment dimmed by the power of disease. At the last moment she gave mute assent to the question, "is Jesus yet with you?" And the bright smile with which she departed told that she saw the glory and was entering upon it.

> " Death hath made no breach
> In love and sympathy, in hope and trust;
> No outward sign or sound our ears can reach;
> But there's an inward spiritual speech
> That greets us still, though mortal tongue be dust.
> It bids us do the work that she laid down,
> Take up the song where she broke off the strain,
> So journeying till we reach the heavenly town,
> Where are laid up our treasures and our crown,
> And our lost loved ones will be found again.

The Pittsburgh *Evening Telegraph* of November 26, 1877, in a notice of her death, says:

"Mrs. Lizzie Cunningham, wife of J. C. Cunningham and daughter of Dr. J. S. Van Voorhis, of Bellevernon, died this morning, after a long and painful illness. Mrs. Cunningham by her amiable disposition and generous nature, won many friends who will sympathise with the family in this their sad bereavement. The church too, of which she was a member, will lose an earnest an enthusiastic worker."

The Washington *Reporter* concludes a notice with the remark that "Mrs. Cunningham was a former pupil of the Washington Female Seminary and has many warm friends in this community." Col. Chill Hazzard in an editorial notice says:

ONLY GONE BEFORE.—We note with sincere sympathy for her friends and relatives, the death of Mrs. Lizzie Cunningham, at her late residence in Bellevernon, Pa., on Monday morning, November 26, 1877, at five o'clock. She was the wife of J. C. Cunningham and only daughter of John S. Van Voorhis, M. D. The funeral took place this morning at ten o'clock. Her days have been happy and full of gladness. Her life was a song—a prayer—a kiss—a ministry of peace. Unselfish, she acknowledged no duty but to do good to others. Forgetful of self she never forgot those about her. Unusually gifted with musical power, she gave way to its inspiration, and knew no greater delight than to sit down with the greatest masters, whose most intricate problems she loved to overcome. Above all her purest devotion and affection were given to her Savior, and in the interest of his church her zeal was only bounded by the limit of possibility. Truly she hath done what she could. And it is a sweet consolation to wounded hearts to know that in the hour of suffering and pain His arms were about her.

Dr. Van Voorhis removed with his family to Monongahela City April 1, 1855. Returned to Bellevernon August 3, 1858, where he remains to (1893) this day. Whilst a resident of Washington county he represented it in the lower house of the Legislature in the sessions of 1857. In the summer of 1885, in company of his son, he traveled through Europe.

Isaac S., the only son of Dr. J. S. Van Voorhis, was born in Bellevernon, June 5, 1851. He was a student in Washington and Jefferson College for nearly four years; in the fall of 1871 he entered the College of New Jersey at Princeton, from which he graduated in the class of 1873. He studied law with the late Hon. Theodore Cuyler, of Philadelphia; was admitted to the bar in that city in September of 1875, and in October of the same year to the Pittsburgh bar, where he has secured a lucrative practice. He was married by the Rev. L. Y. Graham in Philadelphia April 9, 1878, to Miss Genevieve Geib of the same city. They have two children: John S., born April 24, 1880, and Lavinia, born January 10th, 1885. They reside in Pittsburgh.

THE SMITH FAMILY.

Dr. Bela Smith

Was born in Connecticut in 1762, and came to the "Forks of Yough" between the years 1785 and 1789, and died October 17th, 1841, in the house recently torn down by Harry Markle to make place for his present beautiful residence. This old house was near the end of the West Newton bridge in Rostraver township, in Westmoreland county. The Doctor was highly educated, especially in polite literature and general science, and in manner was an accomplished gentleman. He studied medicine before leaving his native state. He immigrated to the Forks ostensibly as a yankee school teacher, and as such obtained a school in the lower Forks in the neighborhood where he first tarried over night. During the progress of his school a little child became very sick in the family with whom he boarded. A doctor from the region of Brownsville was called who visited the child every third day. One night the patient grew worse to the alarm of the household. The school teacher was aroused from his sleep. On looking at the little sufferer, he remarked that (if it was agreeable) "he had in his saddle bags a preparation which he thought would help it." He gave the medicine, under which it so rapidly improved as not to require any longer the physician who had been attending it. During the recovery of the patient the mother remarked to her benefactor, "you are no school teacher, but a doctor, and I want you to put out your shingle, and I will board you until you earn money enough to pay me." He took her advice, and in a short time acquired an extensive and lucrative practice. He married Elizabeth Patterson, who died May 23, 1844, in the same house in which the Doctor died. This property to which we have alluded, called "Allison Delight," was deeded to him in 1791, and has always been known as the Dr. Smith homestead. He left a very large landed estate to his children. Representatives of four generations lie burried in the Rehoboth graveyard, and one of the fifth in the West Newton cemetery. His son, Ebenezer, died in early life; Amanda died September 16, 1819, in her 19th year; Alvira died September 12, 1832; she was the first wife of John Niccolls, who at one time owned the farm in Carroll now owned by Grier McElvain, also the farm on which the Gibsonton mills now stand, below Bellevernon, he is still living, as far as we know, in Bloomington, Ills. Elizabeth, or as she was familiarly called, Betsy, married John

Housman, and died May 27, 1834. She was the mother of Bela S. Housman, still a resident of Rostraver, and of E. F. Housman, now a resident of Greensburg, Pa. Samuel Stanhope, son of Dr. Smith, died unmarried January 29, 1859. Talitha Cumi died unmarried April 13, 1846. Polly married Hugh Wright. She died March 20, 1822, and her husband November 20, 1826. Both remains are in Rehoboth church yard. Ezra, one of the sons of Hugh and Polly Wright, removed west in early life and resided many years near the town of Nashville, in Illinois, where he died, just at what date we are not informed. The Rensselaer *Gazette*, of Indiana, in noticing his death pays a glowing tribute to his memory.

Ezra was the grandson of John Wright, who lived in the "Forks of Yough" on the farm lately owned by the heirs of James S. Power. John Wright died May 1, 1833, aged 87 years, and was buried in Rehoboth graveyard. He left as sons James, Phillip, Joseph, John and Hugh, the latter of whom was the father of Ezra. Hugh Wright and Polly lived in the house long known as the Hassler mansion, on the Wright farm where Ezra was born. Ezra was a cousin on the father's side of Judge Wright who so long resided in Washington, D. C., during the winter and at Berkeley springs during the summer. Ezra on the mother's side was a cousin of E. F. Housman, of Greensburg, Bela B. Smith, of Rostraver, and Mrs. Dr. Van Voorhis, of Bellevernon. He was a brother of Mrs. Hiram Patton and John Wright, of Fayette county, Pa. Ezra removed to Jasper county, Indiana, in 1844, when that county was new and undeveloped. He settled near Rensselaer, where he carried on the tannery business. He was elected county treasurer in 1857 and re-elected in 1859; in 1861 was elected to the state senate, and in 1865 to the lower house. In his career as a public officer he was always conscientious and energetic, and acted up to highest conceptions of truth, and justice. In private life he was a zealous christian and loyal to his convictions of right. In 1871 he removed to southern Illinois where he engaged in fruit culture until he died.

Bela B. Smith, son of the Doctor's, died April 27, 1859, in the house now occupied by his grandson, Joseph H. Smith. His wife was Nancy Plumer, a daughter of the Hon. George Plumer. He died March 12, 1870. Esq. Bela B. Smith was for many years a prominent and useful man in his native township of Rostraver. He was elected Justice of the Peace for many years, and was by all parties looked upon as a just and upright judge, and as such his place was hard to fill.

Bela B. Smith left a son and two daughters, one daughter having preceded him to the better world. His daughter Elizabeth married James Todd, who died at Beaver Falls, Pa., not many years since. His wife still resides in that place. The daughter, Margaret L., married J. Westley Douglass, for many years a prominent educator in Westmoreland county, but recently a merchant of West Newton, in the same county. Bela B. Smith, Jr., son of Bela B. Smith, Esq., married Elizabeth Housman and resides on the old home place in Rostraver, where he was born. He has long been an active and useful Elder in Rehoboth church. Ami Ruhami, another son of Dr. Smith, was born in Rostraver, October 29, 1803, died October 27, 1883. His remains are in Rehoboth graveyard. His first wife was a Miss Clark, from Connellsville, Pa. She died October 27, 1854. They had several children, among whom were John, Elizabeth, Ross, Sarah Ann, married to John Flannegan, and Maggie, who is the sole survivor of the children and parents. She now resides in West Newton, Pa. Sarah Ann Flannegan died February 2, 1888. The second wife of Ami Ruhami was Mary Jane Power, sister of John Power, of Monongahela City, and mother of Mary Jane Power Smith, who died at the house of John Power, in that place, March 11, 1883. From the *Daily Republican* we extract the following notice of her death:

"Mary Jennie Power-Smith, adopted daughter of Mr. John Power, of this city, died at her home on Sabbath morning, at 10:30 o'clock, in her 25th year, of neuralgia. Funeral on Tuesday at one o'clock, Monongahela cemetery. She was the daughter of Ami R. Smith, of Rostraver, and came to Mr. and Mrs. Power's to live when but three weeks old, and has lived with them as their own child (the daughter of Mr. Power's sister,) growing up a lovely girl and charming woman. Jennie was more than ordinarily lovely in her disposition. She seemed to have the especial faculty of being happy, and her home was filled with the light of everything that her love could brighten.

She united with Pigeon Creek Church at the age of fourteen, and recently by certificate with the Presbyterian Church of Monongahela City.

Jennie has gone, for so it happened that 'Two angels went out the doorway where but one went in.'"

Ami Ruhami's third wife was Mary Beezel, daughter of the late Luke Beezel, of Rostraver. The issue of this marriage was their only daughter Lizzie, who died at Webster, Pa., August 12, 1884.

Ami Ruhami joined Rehoboth church in 1829, under the ministration of Rev. Robert Johnson, never having severed his connection. Whilst in health he not often failed to be in his seat. In all his dealings with men and the church he was prompt and upright. He passed to the grave not only old and full of years, but carrying with him the universal love of his fellow men, and with the brightest prospects of a glorious immortality. Harriet, daughter of Dr. Smith Fuller, late of Connellsville, Pa. She was the mother of Dr. Smith Fuller and Amzi S. Fuller, both of Uniontown, Pa.

Micajah P., another son of Dr. Bela Smith, died at his late residence in the village of Laurel, near Washington, D. C., May 14, 1884. His remains arrived by railroad at West Newton, Pa., May 16, and at 11 o'clock a. m. the funeral took place from the residence of his son-in-law, Harry Markle. The remains were followed to the cemetery by a large concourse of his former fellow citizens and others that had grown up around his old home. The services were conducted by the Rev. James Nicols, pastor of the Presbyterian church of

Laurel, of which the deceased was a member, and by the Rev. J. C. Meloy, of West Newton. The remains were deposited in the family lot in the cemetery of which he was the originator—there let them repose until the resurrection. He was born May 12, 1814, in the old Smith mansion in Rostraver township, Westmoreland county, Pa., now owned by his nephew, Bela B. Smith, and in which his grand nephew, Joseph H. Smith, resides. His first wife was Maria Markle, who died January 17, 1851. They had as children Harmar D., late postmaster at West Newton, but now a resident of Kansas. Ebenezer was born February 25, 1840, and was killed in the battle of Fredericksburg, December 13, 1862. His remains repose in the cemetery where now lay those of his father. Amzi has long been connected with the United States Senate as superintendent of the document room where he is regarded by all parties as an honest and upright man, and as an officer whose services are so highly appreciated as to command the continued support of every senator. Markle, the youngest, returned from the west recently and is now a resident of West Newton. Lizzie is the wife of John Krepps, of Allegheny City, who enjoys his summer residence at the old home of Ami Ruhami Smith in Rostraver. Amanda is not married, and has her home at this time in Washington, D. C. Allie married Harry Markle, and are now living in their new home, erected on the site of the former home of her father near the Rostraver end of the West Newton bridge. Micajah's second wife was Mrs. Brown, of Jamestown, N. Y. They had two children: Hattie E., who died October 14, 1860, and Eva, the wife of Mr. Fay, residing in Washington, D. C. Micajah was the youngest of twelve children of Dr. Bela Smith, the "pioneer" physician of the "Forks." He was the last born and the last to die. He left his home in the old house erected by his father a few months after the first inauguration of President Lincoln and became an attache of the census bureau, and subsequently was transferred to the Indian department. For many years of his early life he was identified with

West Newton's social, financial, religious and political interests. He was always in the front in originating and executing any new enterprise. He was an active co-worker with General Larimer, the Plumers, the Markles and others, in the old Youghiogheny slack water enterprise, and many will yet call to mind his beautiful speech at the reception given on the occasion of the arrival of the first steamboat at West Newton. Before his removal to Washington, D. C., he had been an elder in the Presbyterian church, and among his latest good deeds in the town of his youth was the giving life to the cemetery in which his remains are now interred. Peace to his memory. "The old oaks are falling."

Amzi, the remaining son of Dr. Bela Smith, died January 7, 1831, in the 31st year of his age, in West Newton, Pa. He left a wife and four daughters. His wife was Elizabeth Plumer, daughter of Hon. George Plumer. Polly was the wife of James H. Van Voorhis, now of Cooperstown, Dakota. She died near Monongahela City, July 29, 1848, leaving no children. Amanda was the wife of a man the name of John C. Carr. She died in Montecello, Ill., March, 1859. Margaret L. was the oldest of Amzi's children. She died in Rehoboth Valley, July 29, 1849. She was the wife of J. Crawford Cook, who died September 3, 1858, near Fayette City, Pa. They left one child, a daughter who married J. B. Speer, now of Marshalltown, Iowa. We extract from the Presbyterian *Advocate* the following notice of the death of Mrs. Margaret L. Cook:

Died, on the 29th day of July, 1849, at her residence in Rehoboth Valley, Fayette county, Pa., Mrs. Margaret L., wife of J. C. Cook, in the 26th year of her age.

In recording the virtues of the dead, we are too apt to overlook all faults, and extol and even over-rate the higher qualities; but if truth should ever be our untiring guide it should be in such cases. Though we may deceive and flatter the friends of the dead by obituary notices, we cannot influence Him who stands as the judge of the quick and the dead. The subject of the present notice was an object of very prolonged affliction. It was her lot to be sorely afflicted for months ere she departed, and she bore all with humble submission and Christian fortitude. She never was known to murmur against the will of the Lord; but often said, "the will of the Lord be done, blessed be His holy name." During her long suffering she seemed lost to the affairs of this world, and appeared wholly absorbed in the contemplation of and preparation for eternity.

She had a longing desire to be with Christ, and seemed anxious for the arrival of the hour when her spirit would take its flight to the bosom of God. When she would recover from a state of partial delirium she would often inquire whether she had said anything that would tend to dishonor Christ or erect stumbling blocks in the way of his enemies.

She had been a member of the Presbyterian church for many years, and lived a life devoted to the service of her Master, and fully maintained, at her closing hour, her ardent attachment to the cause of Christ.

Of Amzi Smith's four daughters, none of whom are now (1893) living except Betsy, wife of Dr. J. S. Van Voorhis, of Bellevernon, Mrs. Smith married as her second husband Henry Fulton, of West Newton. He moved to the farm in Carroll township, Washington county, now owned by Greer McElvain, in the spring of 1841. He moved to Monongahela City in 1847. He died at the house of John Power in Nottingham township, in the same county, April 13, 1869; his wife having died October 5, 1868. Abram Fulton, the father of Henry, came from Ireland, bringing his son, Abram, with him. Henry Fulton's first wife was Rebecca Jack. By this wife Henry had four children, viz: Abram, John, Jane and Ellen. Abram died years ago at Columbus City, Iowa. John has long been a resident of San Francisco, California. Jane married John Power September 13, 1836; they were long residents of Monongahela City, Pa. Ellen married Dr. Isett, and after his death she married a man the name of Nichols; at last account they were residing in Iowa.

Henry Fulton's second wife was Elizabeth Taylor. They had two children, Elizabeth and Rebecca. Elizabeth died in Washington, Pa., in 1866, unmarried. Rebecca married William J. Power; both died in the Pigeon creek Presbyterian congregation. They had a large family of children, among whom are Henry F. and William, elders in the Presbyterian church at Pigeon creek.

Henry Fulton's third wife was Mary Chapin. They had three children, James P., Margaret and Hannah. James P. graduated at Washington College in the class of 1846, and also graduated at the Western Theological Seminary. He married Miss Fannie Shouse of Monongahela City. After preaching successfully at different churches in Pennsylvania, he finally settled in Harper, Kansas, where he was the pioneer minister of the Presbyterian church in that region, and where his labors have been blessed especially in organizing churches and in erecting church buildings. By judicious investments he has acquired considerable wealth, which enables him to live comfortably and arms him with still greater power to do good. His son, William S., graduated at Lafayette College, and is now one of the most prominent ministers of the Presbyterian church in Kentucky. He has been located for many years at Lexington in that state. Henry C., another son, studied medicine with Dr. J. S. Van Voorhis of Bellevernon, graduated at the Jefferson Medical College, and is now located at Asotin, in the state of Washington. Two other brothers are located in business in the same vicinity. Margaret, daughter of Henry Fulton married September 5th, 1855, James Means, of Mifflin township, Allegheny county, Pa., where they have lived ever since their marriage. Their son, Henry F., graduated at Washington and Jefferson College and at the Western Theological Seminary, and is now pastor of a church in Centre county, Pa. Their son, Nathan, also is a graduate of Washington and Jefferson College, studied law in the office of Moreland & Kerr, and is now a member of the Pittsburgh bar.

Hannah, daughter of Henry Fulton by his third wife, was

married to Jonas Munson, of Connellsville, Pa. They lived for a time in a house on the river bank at what was known at that time as Fulton's landing, on the farm now owned by Greer McElvain, in Carroll. Whilst living in this house their little children, Mary, Elizabeth and Isaac Fulton, died of scarlet fever, the former June 3 and the latter July 12, 1849. Their remains are still in the old graveyard on the hill, surrounded by a neat iron fence. Shortly after the death of these little ones, Jonas Munson went to California to try his fortune in the new Eldorado on the Pacific coast. In a few years his wife and little Jennie joined him. They settled near Cold Springs where he carried on business in its different branches. He was attacked one time by some prospecting tramps and so severely beaten with picks and other tools as to be left on the ground as dead; his skull was so injured as to require the taking out of a part of the table of the skull two inches wide and four inches long; the piece so removed the writer has in his possession. He lived many years after this occurrence, but died in his new home, never having returned to this country. He left his wife and four children. His wife paid a visit to her native home some time before his death. She died not long after her return to California.

Henry Fulton, by his fourth wife (Mrs. Smith), had five children living at the time of his death, viz: Sarah, Nancy, George P., Almira and Robert H. Sarah married, May 24, 1864, Rev. J. H. Stevenson, now pastor of the Presbyterian church at Mount Carmel, Illinois. Sarah graduated at Washington Female Seminary in the class of 1857. Their daughters Judith Mary, and Sallie are graduates of the same Institution. Nancy graduated at the Steubenville Seminary, but in what class we cannot state. She is the wife of Rev. R. T. Price, pastor of the church of Scio, Harrison county, Ohio. Their oldest daughter Bessie married a Mr. Robinson, and now lives in Louisiana.

Almira married Rev. E. P. Lewis, who is at this time pastor of a Presbyterian church in St. Paul, Minnesota. Their oldest child, Eddie, in his eleventh year died, whilst they resided in Rochester, Penn'a. He was a bright boy and of fair promise.

Robert H., youngest son of Henry Fulton, graduated at Washington and Jefferson College in the class of 1866. He also graduated at Western Theological Seminary. Shortly after he was licensed to preach he was called to the pastorate of a Presbyterian church in Baltimore, Md. He is now and has been for some years pastor of the Northminster church in Philadelphia, where he ranks among the most talented and successful ministers in that city. At the annual commencement in 1887 he had the honorary degree of D. D. conferred on him by his Alma Mater.

George P. Fulton

The remaining son of Henry Fulton, was born in West Newton, Pa., November 1, 1833, and died October 4, 1887, and was buried at Rehoboth, Westmoreland county. The Monongahela *Republican*, printed in the place of his early life, in a notice of his death, says: "He was the son of Henry and Elizabeth Plumer Fulton, well known former citizens of this city. The deceased was a grandson of the Hon. Geo. Plumer, who represented Westmoreland county in Congress from 1821 to 1829. His grandmother on his mother's side was a daughter of Alex. Lowrey, a member of the convention which framed the Pennsylvania State Constitution of 1776. His father and mother were residents of this city for many years. The deceased was educated in the common schools of West Newton and this city, and took a partial course in Washington College. His life was devoted to teaching in the common schools. At seventeen years of age he taught his first school at the Cross Roads in Rostraver township, Westmoreland county; his next teaching was in Bellevernon, Pa., during the years of 1852 and '53.

He was teaching in the vicinity of Fayette City, Pa., when in 1862 he entered the Federal army, enlisting in the 155th Regiment Pennsylvania Volunteers. At the close of the war he was engaged in the Quartermaster's department at Washington, D. C. In 1870 he was elected Principal of the Hiland public school in the city of Pittsburgh, with which he has been connected ever since, and in June last he was unanimously re-elected for a term of three years. His success in teaching was unmeasured, and his personal popularity was well attested in the sympathy and condolence expressed in every community in which he ever resided. His loss as a teacher will be only fully estimated in the hearts of those who have for over one-third of a century shared the wisdom of his rich mind, and the kindness of his heart overflowing with tender feeling for those around him. His mission was to enrich the young mind with not only knowledge, but to cultivate the inner and more heavenly emotions that reign in the immortal spirit. Blessed be God, the world's loss is his gain. He went down to the grave with the bright hopes of awakening in the morning with the full realization of that everlasting rest which he often said could alone be secured through the blood of Christ. His remains, at his own request, were interred in the Rehoboth graveyard, along side of his father and mother, beneath the trees which he had ordered to be planted years ago.

Prof. Fulton married, when a young man, Miss Frazer, a relative of the Hon. R. S. Frazer, of the Allegheny county bar. He has four children living—Dr. Henry Fulton, who at present supplies his father's place as principal; W E. Fulton, a well known attorney; and Robert and Nannie, who are both children under 16 years of age. His family relations have ever been of the most admirable character.

Another paper, in giving an account of the funeral services, remarks; "Last night Rev. J. P. E. Kumler, of the East End Presbyterian church, conducted the funeral services over the remains of Prof. George P. Fulton, at the latter's late home in the East End. The services were simple in character, consisting only of prayer and an eloquent address. Among Rev. Kumler's remarks were the following: 'We have gathered to pay tribute to the friend now cold in death. The expressions of sorrow at his departure are not confined to his own household. They fall from lips of every one in the community in which he performed his trying labors, and are uttered also by those with whom he came in public contact. We all know how trying are the duties of those engaged in his profession. His Christian character, his even temperament, and an unusual affability charmed away their burdensomness. The yoke of duty was to him a yoke of pleasantness. He is not dead. It is simply the crumbling about him of a house in which he was the august tenant. His belief in Christ, and the knowledge that Christ would dissolve all earthly doubts and mysteries in the ineffable light of heaven limned the fall of the awful shadow with effulgent light. He has passed away, and naught remains now but to say that he is in an abode of blissful rest, and to commend to the care of the loving Savior the widow, now in lamentation, the children he so nobly reared to the manifold duties of life, and the tenderer ones who have yet to fathom its perplexities.' At the conclusion of the services the remains were viewed by several hundred."

PROF. GEO. P. FULTON'S MOTHER.

She was Elizabeth, daughter of the Hon. Geo. Plumer, for many years a member of Congress of Westmoreland county, Pa. She was born near West Newton, Pa., in 1803. After her marriage to Amzi Smith they lived in that place and in Rostraver until Amzi's death, January 7, 1831. After her marriage to Henry Fulton they lived in West Newton until the spring of 1841, when the family moved to the Cooper-Lynn farm above Monongahela City, now owned by Greer McElvain. In the spring of 1847 they moved to Monongahela City, occupying the house now owned by the heirs of Richard Stockdale. There Mr. Fulton carried on the tannery located in the rear of the same lot on which the house stood. He afterwards bought the old Cooper tannery, which occupied part of the lot on which Jas. P. Shepler's residence now stands, on the pike above Chess street. Fulton built the house on Third street, above

Chess street, on part of the tannery lot, where he resided until he moved to Washington, Pa., in the early sixties. In 1867 Fulton removed to Brownsville, where Mrs. Fulton, October 5, 1868, died. The Rev. W. S. Plumer, D. D., in an article published a short time after her death, states: "Died, in Brownsville, Fayette county, Pa., on the 5th of October, 1868, Mrs. Elizabeth Plumer Fulton, daughter of the late Hon. George Plumer, of Westmoreland county, Pa., and wife of Henry Fulton, Esq., in the 65th year of her age.

This excellent lady had at various times seen great trials and afflictions; but if she lost a child she seemed determined not to lose the benefit of such bereavement. She had a very good mind well stored with Bible knowledge, and well established in the doctrines of grace. Her last end was peace. She was in full possession of her faculties till her eyes closed in death. During her last illness she spoke freely of her own decease, gave her blessing to those around her, and a charge concerning her burial. The light of the Redeemer's countenance was abundantly shed upon her soul. From her birth she had been well cared for and early instructed in the great truths of religion. By one still living it is remembered that her grandfather, Jonathan Plumer, "the Indian's friend," and the zealous Elder, spent the night of her birth in prayer, devoting her to God with many prayers and tears. Her excellent parents always set before her an example of serious piety, and often prayed with her, and for her. Dear, gentle, faithful, loving one, we shall see thy meek and pleasant face no more on earth. But christians have no final partings with each other. Thou hast wept thy last tear, heaved thy last sigh, suffered thy last pang! Blessed be God for all his grace and mercy to thee! If we are faithful we shall soon join in thy worship around the throne of God and the Lamb.

A writer in the same paper, in a notice of her death, says: "Mrs. Fulton was descended from a line of godly ancestors, dating back to the settlement of America, when the Huguenot fathers left possessions and country for freedom to worship

God. She was the daughter of Hon. George Plumer of pious memory. Carefully trained in the doctrines of the Presbyterian church, parental faithfulness was awarded in her early conversion. To the close of her life she was a consistent and devoted member of the church whose doctrines and privileges she loved with no ordinary affection. Ever ready to do good as she had opportunity, the care of a large family and feeble health confined her efforts, in a measure, to her own family circle. But here she was eminently faithful—careful to teach her children by both precept and example; she prayed much with and for them. She often said with much feeling, "I have never sought earthly honors or riches for my children; but Oh! I have sought the riches of the Kingdom. She was called to pass through many afflictions. Sad change, sore bereavements and great bodily sufferings were in turn permitted to try her faith; but to one who by her death bed was alluding to her trials, she replied, "Goodness and mercy have followed me all the days of my life."

Although for some months her health had been failing, no immediate danger was apprehended by the family, yet she set her house in order, and when at last the messenger came suddenly, she was ready.

God's grace was very abundant to her in her last hours, enabling her fearlessly, even joyfully, to meet the last enemy, of whom all her life she had been greatly afraid. Her intellect was unclouded to the last moment of her life, and amid great bodily anguish she was enabled "to rejoice in the hope of the glory of God," and thus passed away "to be forever with the Lord." "Thanks be to God, who giveth us the victory through our Lord Jesus Christ."

The Monongahela *Republican*, in reference to her death, says:

DIED.—October 5, 1868, at her late residence in Brownsville, Pa., in the 65th year of her age, Mrs. Elizabeth Plumer Fulton, wife of Henry Fulton, formerly of this city. Mrs. Fulton was well known in this community as an eminently pious and devoted christian. She was a member of the Presbyterian church for more than forty years, and the walk and conversasation of her life gave ample evidence of the heavenly inheritance which awaited her at death. She lived for Christ, and died rejoicing in the full hope of that immortality which is in reserve for the people of God.

After the death of his wife Mr. Henry Fulton became a member of the family of Mr. John Power, in Bellevernon, Pa., and on their removal to the Rankin farm, on Mingo, in Washington county, he went with them, where he died April 13, 1869, and his remains were interred at Rehoboth beside his wife.

Death of Mrs. Mary Finley.

This estimable and christian lady died at the residence of her daughter, Mrs. Eberhart, in Winona, Minnesota, January 29, 1864, in the seventy-third year of her age. She was the eldest daughter of George and Margaret Lowrey Plumer. George Plumer was born December 5, 1762, on a farm of 200 acres, which his father, Jonathan Plumer, bought of Col. George Croghan, in February, 1759, now in the 17th ward of the city of Pittsburgh, Pa. The treaty of peace between England and France was signed in Paris on the 8th of November preceding, by which all of the region westward of the Alleghenies to the Mississippi was ceded to the English forever.

George Plumer and wife first lived in Puckety, seventeen miles above Pittsburgh, on the Allegheny river. In 1788 or 9, George Plumer and his wife were given by Col. Lowrey, Mrs. Plumer's father, the land at the junction of Sewickley creek and the Youghiogheny river, where were born the children of a happy union, whose memory is cherished by their descendants. In 1814 Mary Plumer married James Smith, who, with John C. Plumer, had been a year in Captain Markles' troop of horse in the war of 1812.

James Smith was an extensive business man in Robbstown, now West Newton, for many years. In 1825 he removed to

Pittsburgh, where for a time he was in business. From Pittsburgh he removed to Blairsville, where he had acquired a growing trade, but his health failed, and in August, 1829, he died.

After the death of Mr. Smith the family returned to their old home in Robbstown. Their oldest son, George P., at an early age, after the death of his father, through the kindness of Thomas Plumer, obtained in May, 1830, a position with an English firm, "Simpson & Smith," on Wood street, Pittsburgh. After the dissolution of this firm in 1831, he went to McClurg & Denniston, with whom he was a boy and man, for five years, after which time he became a member of the firm of Hampton, Smith & Co., in the wholesale and retail dry goods business. He retired from mercantile life in 1855. He resides now, 1893, in Philadelphia. J. C. P. Smith, another son, studied law in Pittsburgh, and with his brother, A. O. P. Smith, are residents of the west. Finley died many years ago in Iowa. The only daughter, Margaret L., married William Eberhart, and died, as stated elsewhere, in Chicago.

In 1835 Mrs. Mary Smith, the subject of this sketch, married Michael Finley, and in their new home near Rehoboth church, in Westmoreland county, Pa., passed 15 years most happily, he dying in 1850. About six or seven years after the decease of Mr. Finley, Mrs. Finley removed to Ohio, and finally settled in Winona, Minnesota, where she died. Wherever she lived, in whatever sphere she acted, her part was well done. Her company was sought after socially, and her influence for good was unbounded. We close this sketch by quoting from a western paper part of a notice of her death: "Her father, George Plumer, was said to have been the first white male child born under the British dominion west of the Allegheny mountains. Familiar from childhood with the history of the noble men and women who, in perils of Indian warfare, had made their homes in that beautiful region, and laid deep the foundations of the Presbyterian church in western Pennsylvania. She loved to dwell on their trials, and contrast present privileges with the narrations she had heard of early days. A mother indeed in Israel—beloved by all, revered and cherished by her children. She was sustained in her last hours by the everlasting arms of the Savior she had loved and served through life and trusted in death."

THE HAIR FAMILY.

JAMES HAIR.

Was born in Maryland, but his earlier days were passed on a farm near Girardstown, Berkeley county, Virginia, now West Virginia. He married Rebecca McKown of the same county. He moved his family from Virginia in 1806, and tarried for a time in the vicinity of Canonsburg, Washington county, Pa. He, in 1807, purchased from a man named Messenger the mill on Pigeon creek, well known in after years as Hair's mill. In connection with this property, he also bought the adjoining farm, known in those days as the Platter farm, on which he resided to the day of his death, which occurred September 12th, 1826. The family at first lived in one end of the mill. He was a member of the Presbyterian church before he settled on Pigeon creek.

James Hair served as an elder with Michael Powers and others in the old Horseshoe bottom meeting house, which stood on what was then the Crawford but now John Wilson farm, in Fallowfield. He was so completely identified with the Presbyterian church in its early day in Washington county that its history is that of James Hair to a very great extent. When the question was asked of Dr. Ralston, the pastor of Horseshoe meeting house, ho wa church could be organized in the town of Williamsport, now Monongahela City, he replied: "Elect James Hair, Esq., an elder, now already ordained, and go to work." Thus, at one ecclesiastical *coup de grace*, the old Horseshoe bottom congregation was swallowed up. He did perhaps, more for the Presbyterian church in his day than any of his cotemporaries. His remains, together with that of his wife, were interred in the old Presbyterian graveyard in Monongahela City but a few years ago—the kind hearts of his sons, Rev. G. M. Hair and Dr. B. W. Hair, had them removed to the Monongahela City Cemetery.

James Hair was appointed justice of the peace by Governor Snyder in 1811, and served as such to the day of his death. He kept his docket in copy-book form of foolscap paper, most of which docket is now in possession of the writer, and it is of interest to note its many and peculiar features.

Mrs. Hair died August 18th, 1840, on the old Hair farm. They had a large family of children, all of whom lived to manhood and womanhood. All were married and were members of the Presbyterian church. Mary, as we already have stated, was the wife of Isaac Van Voorhis. John was the oldest of the children; he married Harriet Brenton.

John was a miller by trade. He lived at and carried on the old Hair's mill until about the year 1836, when he moved to Stark county, Ohio, where he was one of the company which laid out the town of Mount Union. He died in 1855 or 56. His wife still (1892) survives him. Martha married John Crouch. Both are dead. Louisa married Joseph Brenton, of the vicinity of Brownsville, Pa. They are both dead, leaving a large family of children. Eliza, January 1, 1828, married John Potter, who was born December 15, 1803, and died August 28, 1878. His wife died in 1869.

He had arrived at four-score years of age. His remains were interred in the cemetery of the church of Pine Creek, Allegheny Presbytery, where those of his wife were laid some nine years since. He was married to Eliza, daughter of the late James Hair, Esq., and sister of Mary H., wife of the late Isaac Van Voorhis. Of the family connection present at that marriage, Mary, Martha, Eliza, Ibela, Louisa, John, James, Uriah, and Samuel, have gone to their rest, with the father and mother, sons-in-law Brenton, Van Voorhis, Crouch, and now Potter. Mr. Potter had four sons, all in the ministry. John died some years ago. James H., of Florida, Gilbert M., pastor of the Church at Pine Creek, and Henry N., pastor of the church of Darlington, Beaver county, Pa. He was born and brought up in the congregation of Mingo, under the pastoral care of Rev. Dr. Ralston, D. D., by whom he was married, and under whose ministrations he was taken into the church in his youth, and was elected a Ruling Elder at the age of twenty-two years.

Ibela, the youngest daughter of Esq. Hair, married James Baker. He was the son of Nicholas Baker, a prominent elder in the old Maple Creek church. His remains at last account were still in the graveyard of that now abandoned church. Ibela died January 13, 1843. Her remains are in the Monongahela cemetery.

Samuel, son of James Hair, was born on the old Hair farm on Pigeon creek, in Washington county, Pa., April 1st, 1808, and died May 11th, 1876, in Chicago. He graduated at Jefferson College in 1832; he also graduated from the Western Theological Seminary. He was licensed to preach by the Monroe Presbytery, of Michigan, in 1835, and continued in active service for Christ until a short time before his death. He was a finished scholar, and above all a true champion in the cause of Christ. At a meeting of the Chicago Presbytery held May 15th, 1876, suitable resolutions were passed in respect to his memory, and of condolence and sympathy for the family. A memorial sermon by his pastor, Rev. A. E. Kithredge has been printed and distributed among his friends, in which his character as a Christian is fully set forth, and the result of his labors in different fields are summed up. His great work seemed to be that of organizing churches, for which he had peculiar qualifications. Besides numerous churches which he was instrumental in organizing, he was the real founder of the Michigan University, of Ann Arbor, now one of the most flourishing institutions of the west. This institution sprang from what was known as the Michigan Manual Labor School, of which he was the first teacher, having twelve young men under his charge.

Samuel Hair was married April 22nd, 1834, to Miss Eliza E. Sample of Canonsburg, Pa., who survives him and resides in Chicago, Ill. Mrs. Hair was born in Philadelphia, but spent most of her days, prior to marriage, in Pittsburgh, Pa.

Mr. and Mrs. Hair had seven children, one died in early life and one daughter, Annie, died in 1887. A Chicago paper prints the following beautiful tribute to her memory:

"Mrs. Annie Hair Elphicke died at her home in Lawndale, Chicago, July 20th, 1887. She leaves a loving husband and three children, one an infant. Her death was sudden and unexpected. The home was a happy, loving home until death entered. She united with the church when young, was a conscientious, exemplary Christian, a loving, kind, affectionate wife and mother. Six months ago death came and claimed a beautiful boy. She bore this affliction with Christian fortitude. Now they know as they were known; now the victory is hers, and they are ascribing glory, honor and praise to him who bought them and washed them in the blood of the lamb.

> Dearest loved one, we must lay thee
> In the peaceful grave's embrace,
> But thy memory will be cherished
> 'Till we see thee face to face.

Mary J. V. another daughter, died November 21st, 1891. The remaining of the children living are all residents of Chicago.

James G., another son of 'Squire Hair, was born on the old Hair farm; was married to Phœbe Kerr, daughter of Aaron Kerr, of whom we have written in another place. James G. Hair died in Claysville, Pa., August 10, 1885, aged 80 years. His wife and one or two children survive him.

B. W. Hair, the youngest son of James Hair, Esq., read medicine with the late Dr. R. F. Biddle in the old office which stood where George A. Hoffman's store now is, on the corner of Main street and Church alley in Monongahela City. He obtained his early education in the common schools at the Dutch meeting house and in the old Colhoon school, and his college training at Washington, Pa. He married Margaretta L. Hamilton, of Frankfort, Pa., who died at Hamilton, Ohio, March 4, 1882. Dr. B. W. Hair has been married a second time. He now resides in Hamilton, Ohio, but carries on his extensive chemical works in Cincinnati. He is the inventor of Hair's Asthma Cure, which holds a large share of public confidence and from which he has realized a handsome competence.

Uriah was another son. He married Miss Thomas. daughter of James Thomas, of near Dunningsville, Washington county, Pa. They lived for a time in the stone house at Hair's old mill on Pigeon creek; moved West many years since; resided in Galesburg, Ill., for a term of years. Their home now (1891) is at 120 South Ashland avenue, Chicago. On the 14th of March, 1888, they celebrated their golden wedding, Uriah being 76 and his wife 75 years old at that time.

They have had several children, but we have not any notes in reference to their progress in life, excepting an account of the death of the wife of their eldest son James T. Hair, to which we give place. Mrs. Josephine Estelle Hair (nee Butler) died February 20, 1887, and was buried from the family residence, No. 3337 Michigan avenue, Chicago, on Friday, the funeral services being conducted by the Rev. S. J. McPherson, of the Second Presbyterian church. The deceased was the grand-niece of the late William O. Butler, of Kentucky, candidate for Vice President on the Democratic ticket, with Lewis Cass, in 1848, and was related also to Daniel Pierce Butler and Senator M. C. Butler, of South Carolina. She was married in 1875, in the 16th year of her age, to James T. Hair, the well known publisher, and a resident of Chicago since 1863. Five children were born to them, of whom three survive. Mrs. Hair was an accomplished lady, in the prime of womanhood, being only twenty-seven years of age, and in the enjoyment, a few weeks since, of perfect health. She was possessed of many rare qualities of mind and heart, having a remarkably quick perception that grasped almost intuitively matters which to most minds are made clear only by study and effort. She was of a sunny disposition, vivacious and winsome. She had traveled extensively with her husband, and had a large circle of friends in Cincinnati, New Orleans, St. Louis, Denver, and other cities, as well as in Chicago, who lament her loss and sympathise with the bereaved husband and his three motherless children.

[From Monongahela *Republican*, February 19, 1890.]

Death of Uriah Hair.

Clinton Van Voorhis hands us the following item, clipped from the Chicago *Daily News*, February 1st, 1890, noting the death of his uncle :

Uriah Hair, a well known citizen of Chicago, died yesterday at his residence, 120 Ashland avenue. Mr. Hair was nearly 78 years old. He was born in Washington county, Pennsylvania, and came to Illinois in 1856, locating on a farm in McDonough county. Appreciating the advantages of education, he removed to Galesburg in 1886 to give his children the benefits of schooling. They speak of the sacrifices he made to give them instruction, with the deepest sense of gratitude. Mr. Hair came to Chicago in 1876, but was not engaged in active business during his residence here. His wife and six of his children survive him—James T., William F., Lydia R., Josiah T., Samuel F., and John V Hair. He was a brother of the late Rev. Samuel Hair. His only living brother is Dr. B. W. Hair, a practicing physician of Cincinnati, the youngest of twelve children.

The Late Rev. G. M. Hair.

He was born September 4, 1815, in the old log house still standing on what was long known as the Hair farm, now owned by the heirs of the late John Hill, and situated in Carroll township, Washington county, Pa. He attended common schools in the neighborhood of his birth, was at first inclined to enter mercantile life, but in answer to the prayers of pious parents he entered upon a course of preparation for the ministry and graduated at Washington college, Pa., in 1838.

In the fall of the same year he married Miss Jane Sample, of Steubenville, Ohio, and immediately began to teach at Martinsburg, Ohio, where he built up a flourishing academy. While there he studied theology with the late Dr. Hervey, and was licensed to preach the gospel in the spring of 1840. His first charge was the church of Nottingham. While serving it he was elected president of Franklin college, Athens, Ohio, but declined the appointment. He then preached for a time at Wellsburg, W. Va..; started to New Orleans to accept an invitation to the First Presbyterian church of that city, but stopped at Covington, Ky.; was for five years pastor of the churches of Montgomery and Somerset in Hamilton county, Ohio, where his wife died in 1849; in 1850 was married to Miss Eliza Naylor, who survives him; in 1853 was called to the church of Franklin, Ohio, and afterwards labored two years at Carlisle, Ohio; and at the outbreak of the war was engaged in building up a female seminary near Lexington, Ky., but owing to his Union sentiments was compelled to leave at great personal sacrifice. After this he preached two years at Cambridge City, Ind.

Some time prior to 1864 he entered the Christian Commission, where in his term of twelve weeks he received into the church at the army chapel 600 soldiers. In 1864 he was called to the First church of Alexandria, Va., where he labored until the close of the war. In 1865 he preached nine months to the church at Gerardstown, W. Va., during which time 101 were added to the church—this was the church of his father, from which he brought his certificate to the old Horseshoe church in 1807. His next charge was Eaton, Preble county, Ohio, during the first year of which he was invited to and occupied the pastorate of the South church in Baltimore, Md. In 1869 he accepted a call to the First church of McKeesport, Pa. In 1872 he took charge of the Rehoboth church, Presbytery of Redstone. He resigned June 1, 1874, and removed to Chicago, Ill.; while in that city he organized a church at Lawndale. The care of his wife's aged parents was his next duty. Whilst with them he preached at New Carlisle, in the vicinity of Franklin, Ohio. In May, 1877, he took charge of the Westminster church, East End, Pittsburgh. His health failing, he retired from active service after forty years in the ministry. Partially recovering his health, he labored in the Knoxville church, near Pittsburgh, for a short time, during which the church increased in number three times as many as when he began to serve it.

In September, 1883, he removed to Florida in search of health, where he preached almost every Sabbath, and organized the church at Ravenswood, as a New Year's gift to the Lord. His health appeared to improve until February last; from that time he gradually declined. With his wife he started for his native state, and May 31 he reached the home of his daughter, Mrs. Spurgeon, at West Point, N. Y., where on Tuesday, June 3, 1884, he died. His remains were brought to Pittsburgh, and his funeral took place June 5 from the residence of his son-in-law, H. D. Gamble. He leaves three daughters and one son.

Mr. Hair's great delight was to do the work of an evangelist. This was the principal cause of his frequent removals. Unless he could see some visible fruit in the conversion of souls, he was not satisfied. He was a man of prayer and of earnest devotion to the cause of his Master.

THE SAMPLE FAMILY.

John Sample had three brothers and one sister: their names were William, Alexander, Samuel and Mary. Mary married Admiral Graves, a resident of north of Ireland, and was connected with the royal family. John Sample was second cousin to George the third. Admiral Graves was commander-in-chief of the marine forces of England, being appointed by the king on account of his connection with the crown through his wife. Admiral Graves was sent from England with a large fleet in the time of the revolution to relieve Cornwallis at the battle of Yorktown, but he arrived one day too late, as Cornwallis had been taken by General Washington. Admiral Graves returned with his fleet to England. He was owner of old Castle-Dawson with its elegant parks and hunting grounds.

John Sample's wife's maiden name was Margaret Whiteside, a resident of Belfast, Ireland. Her brother, James Whiteside, was Lord Chief Justice of Ireland, the highest gift of the queen. He was a nobleman. At the age of 16 Margaret Whiteside married a young man named William Thompson, also a resident of Belfast. They had three children, John T., William T. and Mary. Mr. and Mrs. Thompson immigrated to America while their children were quite young and settled in Philadelphia, where Mr. Thompson died not long after his arrival. In a few years after his death his widow married John Sample, of the same city. He was a merchant. The issue of this marriage was seven children, viz: Ann, Margaret, Sarah, Eliza, Alexander, Jane and Martha. John Sample died in Pittsburgh, Pa., in 1829; his wife died in 1850, in Kentucky, whilst on a visit to her daughter, Mrs. Martha Wheeler. Jane married Rev. G. M. Hair, both of whom are deceased. Eliza married Rev. Samuel Hair, whose death is noted elsewhere. His wife, at this date (1893) is still alive, and resides at No. 4417 Lake avenue, Chicago. Martha married John T. Wheeler, now deceased; his wife survives him and resides in Chicago. Alexander was long a resident of Steubenville, Ohio, where he was regarded as one of the most distinguished dentists in that profession.

ALEXANDER WILSON.

He was born near Roxbury, Franklin county, Pa., July 7, 1807; died at Heyworth, Illinois, June 14, 1862. He was the son and eldest child of Col. Stephen Wilson, a prominent citizen of Franklin county, who had taken an active part in the war of 1812, and three times represented his district in the Legislature of this state; born in the same county in 1789, and died there in 1823, in his 45th year, leaving his son Alexander, 16 years old, in charge of the farm, and his mother, with eight children, now all deceased, excepting Mrs. Margaret Herron, now residing in the 17th ward, Pittsburgh. Alexander received a common school education, principal part of which was prior to the death of his father.

He was married to Agnes Herron, of Franklin county, June 11th, 1828, who died in Pittsburgh, November 21st, 1832. He remained on the farm until about 1830, when he removed to Pittsburgh and engaged in the wholesale grocery business on Liberty street, where he did an active and extensive business for ten or twelve years.

He was married to Mary C. McFarland (his second wife), daughter of Robert and Ann St. Clair McFarland, at Monongahela City, February 3d, 1835, who died at her home in Allegheny City, February 1st, 1881, in her 78th year, and whose remains are interred, with that of her husband's in the cemetery at Monongahela City.

Alexander Wilson removed to Monongahela City in the spring of 1845, where he engaged in merchandising, and gradually extended his business until he became the largest dealer in the county in wool, grain, flour and produce generally. The farmers will still recollect that he was always ready to give them the highest prices, and sometimes even when the state of the trade did hardly justify it.

He also opened and operated the then extensive coal mines at the mouth of Mingo creek, and had, in connection with a boat yard, some 100 to 150 men in his employ. He was among the first that undertook to tow coal to Cincinnati by steam, having built the side-wheel steamer, Alexander Wilson, for that express purpose. She was run in that trade for some time, when her machinery was taken out and placed on the steamer Mingo, a stern-wheel boat.

His residence and business house was the one which Mark Borland has occupied for many years. This house was commenced to be built by the late Matthew Porter (grandfather of the Morrison Brothers) in 1833, but was in the spring of 1834 purchased by Robert McFarland, father-in-law of the deceased, and by him finished as a storeroom and dwelling, and in which he shortly died.

In the fall of 1856 he located at Heyworth, Illinois, and in December, 1857, removed his family to that place. There he built and operated with others one of the largest flouring mills in the state, which was afterwards destroyed by fire. He then engaged in the grain business in which he continued to the time of his death. Under the pious instructions of a Christian mother, he united with Rocky Spring Presbyterian church as early as his 20th year. On removing to Pittsburgh he united with the first Presbyterian church during the ministrations of Dr. Francis Herron., and at once engaged in active Sabbath school work. He afterwards became connected with the Minersville Presbyterian church, now known as the seventh Presbyterian church of Pittsburgh, and in it became a ruling elder about the year 1838, in which capacity he served almost continually during the remainder of his life, wherever he resided, including the church in Monongahela City and ending with the church at Heyworth, Illinois. He was especially interested in the Sabbath school cause, to which work he gave more than 30 years of his life, most of which time in the position of superintendent, and frequently had several Sabbath schools in active operation at the same time under his control.

He had two children by his first wife, both now living— Mary E. Wilson is the wife of Dr. J. M. Todd, of Bridgeport, Ohio, and William H. Wilson, of Pittsburgh, who has been cashier of the West End Savings bank since its organization, over twelve years ago. He had six children by his second wife —Eliza C., Robert M., Stephen, Ann St. Clair, M. Virginia and Susan E. Robert, Eliza and Susan are deceased, the rest still living. Robert M. went out with the 94th Illinois Regiment Volunteers in the late war. He participated in all the engagements in which his regiment was called to take part. He was promoted to lieutenant in Company B, and after nearly three years of active service, ending with the capture of Mobile and its defenses, was on board the steamer *St. Charles* with a portion of his regiment on their return to Spanish Fort from Ship Island, whither they had guarded an installment of prisoners. The night was dark, and being called suddenly on deck, he walked overboard and was drowned; all efforts to recover his body being unavailing. Stephen is married and lives in Minneapolis, Minn.; Ann St. Clair is the widow of Isaac N. Coursin, and is living in McKeesport, Pa., where she has two married daughters; M. Virginia resides with her brother, W. H. Wilson in Pittsburgh; Dorcas E. Wilson, widow of Robert, lives at Leechburg, Pa., and has a son and daughter now grown.

Alexander Wilson, the older readers will call to mind, was a man of robust constitution, active and energetic, with remarkble business qualifications, prompt to decide and quick to act, he pressed forward to the consummation of all he undertook. He was pleasing and affable in his every day walk and conversation, and ever ready to do a kind act for a neighbor. He was full of enterprise and always in the advance to constitute and work for the interests of the community in which he resided. He was generous and charitable, with a kind word for all; but, more than all, he was an earnest, active and faithful Christian.

After a busy and useful life, his strong constitution finally gave way, and he died comparatively a young man. As his soul passed within the pearly gates he uttered as his last words on earth, "Happy, happy, happy!"

He was interred at Heyworth, Ill., but after the death of his second wife, his remains were removed and laid by her side in the cemetery at Monongahela City, where a beautiful monument, erected by kind hands, perpetuate their memory. In this beautiful city of the dead, overlooking her native home and the scenes of his early life,

> Rest here, blest saints, till from His throne
> The morning break and pierce the shade.

THE GORDON FAMILY.

Thomas Gordon and his wife came from Franklin county, Pa., to Williamsport in the year 1810. The former died September 29, 1823, aged 74 years, and the latter March 27, 1821. Their remains were interred in the old graveyard on the hill, in their adopted town. These were the parents of the well known James Gordon, who figured so largely and so long in the affairs of Monongahela City. On his arrival in 1810, there was not a house below the pike, or now called Fourth street. For years he was the only Presbyterian in the town. From the first he took an active part in church matters, and was the first collector of stipends for the Presbyterian congregation after its removal from Horse Shoe Bottom. He aided both by his means and labor in the building of the church on the hill, in which he held a pew from the first to the last day it was occupied by the congregation. He organized the first Sabbath Scool in the town, in the face of much opposition on the part of the citizens, who claimed that children should have at least one day to themselves. He was elected and ordained an elder in the church October 15, 1835, and remained an elder in the same church until his death, covering a period of over forty years. Prior to the adoption of the constitution of 1838, Justices of the Peace held a life-time term in the office, and James Gordon being appointed Justice of the Peace by Governor Snyder, held the office until deposed by the operation of the new constitution of 1838, by the provisions of which this officer was elected by the people for a term of five years. James Gordon was elected to this office in 1850, serving five years, making in all a period of thirty-five years during which he acted as Justice. He was elected Associate Judge, and sworn into office March 8, 1845, and served five years. He was appointed by Governor Porter Register of Washington county, and served in that office from March 3, 1839, to October 14, 1839, when George Morrison, Register-elect, took his place. On the resignation of Walter Craig in 1819, as County

Commissioner, James Gordon was appointed to serve until the next October. He was a member of the Electoral College which placed Andrew Jackson in the Presidential chair for one of his two terms. He was always a Democrat; in the darkest hours of that party he stood firm to its principles, believing to the day of his death that they formed the basis on which alone the country could prosper. He was married in 1810 by the Rev. Mathew Brown, to Miss Mary Ann Officer, of Washington, Pa., by whom he had nine children. He first lived in a log house that stood on the site where now stands the McGregor row, on Main street, in Monongahela City. He lived and carried on the tanyard now owned by the heirs of Richard Stockdale, on Main street, and had his office in a little frame building adjoining the house. He was also in the mercantile business for a time. In later days he lived in the brick house on Fourth and Main streets, opposite what is now called (1889) the Hotel Wilgus. He had his office in the frame building now occupied by Alderman Williams. James Gordon was a trustee in Jefferson College from 1825 to 1863. He acted as deputy under Sheriff Officer and during his term conveyed on horseback thirty-three convicts to Philadelphia at an expense of nearly $400 for each trip. Physically Mr. Gordon was a remarkable man, tall and erect, and after he was eighty years old he would not hesitate to walk eight or ten miles. He was a man of strong feelings, and when his prejudices were aroused he was very apt to show his Scotch blood. He was a man of sterling integrity, and died at the age of eighty-five years full of faith and bright prospects of a glorious immortality. Of his nine children, all are dead excepting Martha and Elizabeth. Thomas P., his oldest son, graduated at Jefferson college in 1833, studied for the ministry, had the degree of D. D. conferred upon him by his *alma mater* in 1859, and died at Terre Haute, Ind., in 1865. James M. H., the remaining son, studied medicine with the late Dr. S. M. King, and practiced most of his professional life in Fayette City, Pa., where he died August 24, 1883. We quote from the *Daily Republican* of August 29, 1883, the article on Dr. Gordon's death:

Dr. James Martin Hunter Gordon died at his late residence in Fayette City, Pa., Friday, August 24th, 1883; his remains were interred in Mt. Auburn cemetery. His funeral was largely attended by relatives and friends. Drs. M. P. Morrison and George A. Linn, of Monongahela City, Dr. O. P. McKay, of Perryopolis, Dr. J. S. Van Voorhis, of Bellevernon, Dr. Mitchell, of Allenport, and Dr. Porter, of Fayette City, acted as pall bearers. The remains were dressed in a black suit and encased in a beautiful silver mounted octagon casket furnished by undertaker Curtis Reppert, of Bellevernon.

The deceased was born April 25th, 1825, in the house now owned by heirs of Richard Stockdale, on Main street, Monongahela City, then known as Williamsport. His father was the late Hon. James Gordon. The deceased was one of nine children, of whom only Martha and Lizzie are living, and were at the funeral. * * *

Dr. Gordon was educated in boyhood in the public schools of his native town; received his collegiate course at Jefferson and Washington Colleges, leaving the latter college in 1843. * * * As far as the writer can ascertain, he commenced the practice of his profession in Temperanceville, Allegheny county, and subsequently in Perryopolis, California, Brownsville, and finally settled in Fayette City, where for over 30 years he had been a prominent and successful practitioner. On 16th of May, 1850, he married Miss Margaret K. Church, who, with four children, survive him. His son, John W., a graduate of Jefferson Medical College, was his associate in business and will continue to occupy his father's office. A few months after his marriage, with his brother-in-law, Solomon Alter, Esq., Shesh Bentley, T. F. Watkins, and other Washington county adventurers, he crossed the plains to California. The rough living and hard work incident to the new El Dorado did not suit either his taste or health. He returned to Fayette City and found a host of friends to greet him, and in a very short time had gathered up a lucrative practice. At the outbreak of the rebellion he went into the army with the first regiment of West Virginia volunteers. Being transferred to Washington, D. C., he was appointed to hospital service on Fourteenth street. After leaving the united service he gave his whole attention to the practice of medicine. Naturally of a vigorous and robust constitution, he was able to undergo a vast amount of exposure. Whilst in health he never refused to respond to the wants of the sick, whether rich or poor. His uncollected accounts attest the amount of service rendered the afflicted without compensation. The writer knew the deceased from early boyhood and knew him well. As medical men we met each other often in consultation and otherwise—he was a safe counsellor and a wise practitioner. In his profession, Dr. Gordon was well read; in practice, was more than ordinarily successful. His manners were pleasing, and to the sick kind and sympathizing. In general intelligence he was well posted. In combatting disease he had an unbounded store of therapeutical knowledge, from which he drew in every emergency. He was a fine Bible scholar, so much so that a few years since he was able, in public debate, to defend its truths successfully against one of the champion infidels. For his success on that occasion his fellow citizens presented him with a beautiful copy of the Bible, from which Rev. Hollister read during the funeral services, and which, no doubt, will long be cherished as a sacred memento of the deceased.

In his professional career he was associated more or less with his friends, Drs. A. M and W. H. King, Biddle, Adams, Connelly, Hill, Lank and Castner, who either studied or practiced medicine in this city, all of whom have preceded him to the spirit land. He has run his race; his voyage of life is ended; his usefulness has ceased; he has gone, and may we not hope that in the unconscious hours, before dissolution, a lucid moment may have flashed upon his soul in which he was enabled to look upward and whisper, "My father," and to hear the blessed response from within, "My son."

Mary, daughter of James Gordon, married Rev. W. P. Harshe, and died many years ago. Elizabeth married P. H.

Rhinehard, of Lebanon, Pa., who for a short time printed the *Sentinel* in the old room which stood where is now the Peoples Bank, in Monongahela City. He is now located at Lebanon, Pa., where he has grown into a large and lucrative law practice. Martha married Solomon Alter, who established the Monongahela *Republican*. He died many years ago, and she still survives him, making her home generally in Washington, D. C. Sarah never married, and has been dead for many years. Margaret, the oldest daughter, married Rev. James Sloan. He was a brother of the Hon. J. C. Sloan, of Hopewell township, Washington county, Pa., who was a member of the Legislature during the session of 1857. The Daily Monongahela *Republican* publishes the following notice of her death :

About 10 minutes before 10 o'clock, Monday morning, (December 12th, 1881,) Dr. James G. Sloan entered his office and found his mother dusting the table. She stopped as he came in and said she felt a pain in her breast. The doctor asked her if it were in the neighborhood of her heart. She said "yes" and at once appeared to grow faint. He assisted her to lie down upon the lounge, and seeing evidences from the absence of pulse at the wrist that the attack was serious, went at once for Dr. Linn, who arrived almost immediately. The attack was at her heart, and failing to rally, Mrs. Sloan died at 10.30 a. m., some 15 or 20 minutes after her first mention of the sharp pain to her son. Mrs. Margaret Sloan was the widow of the late Rev. Dr. Sloan, a Presbyterian clergyman, for long years pastor of the Pigeon creek church, who died in March, 1871. She was in her 67th year, and was an eminently pious mother in Israel. She has gone to her rest covered with the mantle of the sweetest and purest Christian faith. Mrs. Sloan was conscious up to her death; gave messages of love to her family who stood beside her. To Maggie, her favorite, she said, "Live near to Jesus, Maggie;" and when the end was near, she folded her hands and said, "Lord Jesus prepare me for the end." She has gone home— she was ready and waiting—the tears that will come are forced back by the thought that God hath taken her; and he doeth all things well. If ever a good woman lived and died, that woman was Aunt Margaret Sloan—the term of endearment by which she was called by so many who knew her and loved her with the highest esteem, and the greatest respect.

JESSE MARTIN.

The remains of Jesse Martin lay in the old graveyard. He died May 27, 1848. He was elected an elder in the old church on the hill in 1816, just after the first communion was held, at which elder Hair, assisted by elder Benjamin Williams, of Mingo, officiated. He was one of the committee appointed to select a site for a new church, which resulted in the choice of the lot on which the church at the foot of the hill was erected, and which is now used as a tenement house, on Coal street and Church alley, Monongahela City. He served as an elder to the day of his death. Jesse Martin married Miss Abba Gordon, sister of Hon. James Gordon, by whom he had seven children. His son Thomas lived the greater part of his life in St. Louis, Mo., where he died. James C. always resided in Monongahela City, his native town, where he died some ten years ago. His wife was Hannah Smith, a niece of Rev. John Kerr. James C. was elected State Librarian in 1849, by the joint committee of the Senate and House of Representatives at Harrisburg. Mary married Samuel Scott and was the mother of James C. Scott, the druggist, now deceased. Margaret died about the year 1855. Cynthia married James Smith; both have passed away. Belle married a Mr. McBride, near Washington, Pa., now deceased. She alone survives of all the children of Jesse Martin. Eliza married Jesse Teeple, both of whom are now dead. They lived all their married life on part of the old Teeple homestead, in Carroll township. Jesse Martin was Postmaster at Parkison's Ferry, now Monongahela City, for many years, being the successor of George Wythe, and was succeeded by W. S. Mellinger in 1841. Jesse Martin erected and lived in the old brick house on Main, below Second street, which has given way to the beautiful edifice built by his grandson, the late James C. Scott. He always carried on the boot and shoe business, in connection with the postoffice; the office itself at that time was not worth the labor it cost. The old market house stood on Main street, in front of Martin's residence, where, much to his annoyance, it attracted the boys, especially in the early spring of the year, when playing "knucks" was on the surface.

Beneath the shelter of this aniquated structure such youths as Wash Spence, Samuel King, John King, Robert McGrew, Sam Guthrie, Dick Roberts, Thomas Martin, John Chess, William and Moses Devore and a host of other bloods were wont to spend many an hour in playing marbles. Through the influence of Jesse Martin, more than any one else, no doubt, this unsightly and useless market house was removed to a site on Second above Main street, in front of what is now the People's bank, where it could only annoy Constable Gabriel Silverthorn on the one side and the semi-occasional occupants of the old red house on the other. Here it remained until the next generation with wisdom and forethought for the good of humanity, so far mutilated the pillars as to render it so dangerous that the authorities were compelled to have it taken away, and to this day no other market house has ever existed in the town. Even whilst the old one stood, such butchers as Daniel Cort, Sammy Roberts, John Clemens, John McFeely et al, had scruples against offering their beef for sale within its walls.

Hon. Jesse Martin, with Wallace McWilliams and James McFarren as colleagues, represented Washington county in the Legislature of 1842. He died in St. Louis at the date above stated; his remains were brought home by steamboat, and interred in the old graveyard on the hill where Elders Hair, McFarland, Gordon and McGrew were also buried. Absence from home or sickness alone prevented his attendance at church and at the prayer meetings, where his plain petitions were regarded as the outpouring of a heart filled with love and gratitude to God. His peculiar voice, when leading in singing, will no doubt be called to mind by many of the older citizens.

THE McFARLAND FAMILY.

Robert McFarland and Anna, his wife, were well-known personages in the Pigeon creek valley. He lived from his youth on the farm originally called Bath Mills, but now well known as the Van Voorhis homestead, lately the residence of Isaac Van Voorhis, deceased, and now owned by his son, Dr. J. S. Van Voorhis. Robert McFarland was a man of fine feeling, and of more than ordinary modest deportment. His attire was always neat and of black cloth. He and his wife were not often absent from church, and in consideration of his excellent Christian character he was at one time elected an elder in the Presbyterian church, but he never felt satisfied to take the ordination vows, prefering to do his part as a private member. His house was a resort for the young and old, and his hospitality knew no bounds. He manufactured salt in the works now gone which stood just below the spring house. The well was of the artesian nature, and to this day water constantly flows from it. With one exception, these were the only salt works in the county. He sold the farm to Isaac Van Voorhis, who took possession April 1, 1834. Although his goods had all gone, Mr. McFarland never left the house until Mr. Van Voorhis arrived, to whom he gave the keys in person. McFarland purchased the house, then unfinished, now occupied by M. Borland and others as store rooms, on Main street, Monongahela City, from Mathew Porter, grandfather of Dr. M. P., Joseph and A. P. Morrison, Esqs. Having completed his dwelling and store room, he purchased a fine stock of new goods in the Eastern cities, where he traveled in the old stage coach and from the fatigue and exposure of which journey he never recovered.

He died in 1835, and his remains were interred in the old graveyard on the hill, where also those of his wife were afterwards laid to rest. His wife was also a McFarland—Ann St. Clair McFarland. She had several brothers, of whom were Thomas and John. The former lived for many years in the old mansion still standing on the bank of the Monongahela, near lock No. 3. He moved to the west and died many years since. This house was in early days well known to the pioneers, being a kind of headquarters for the leading spirits of the day. In this house Major McFarland died, after being wounded at the attack on General Neville's house during the whiskey insurrection of 1794. His remains were interred in Mingo graveyard, and the circumstances attending his death are almost forgotten, save by those who cherish the record of the past.

John, or Uncle Jack, as he was familiarly called, was a man of peculiar traits of character; in demeanor a perfect gentleman, a fine talker, a good philanthrophist, a bachelor of considerable wealth, popular among all classes of the people. He was a merchant by inclination as well as in fact. He passed many of his latter days in what was then called the far west, in trading among the Indian tribes. In more than one instance he had to abandon his post, barely escaping with his life. At one time he made good his flight by skating on the ice over 20 miles. At another time he was overtaken in his flight by the Indians, and was scalped by them, as they supposed; but to his delight the Indians discovered to their chagrin that it was a false scalp in the form of a wig which Uncle Jack had been accustomed to wear.

He enjoyed *that* joke (on the Indians) as well as many others of which he was very fond. His many Indian stories seemed to the masses as much exaggerated, but subsequent development of the true Indian character, since his day, give warrant to their truth. At his death the late Isaac Van Voorhis and Elijah Teeple were appointed administrators of his estate, which consisted chiefly in a large amount which he claimed from the government as losses incurred by the depredations of the Indians. After a long delay the claim was collected and distributed among the heirs. He and a man named Lyons had a coal works on the river just above the mouth of Wolf Harbor run, not far below Lock No. 4. They were among the first to load coal in flat-boats by means of an incline from the pit to the river. They soon found that the enterprise would not pay and so abandoned the work.

Robert McFarland left two daughters, Eliza and Mary. Eliza married Rev. S. M. Sparks, one of the early pioneers in the Cumberland Presbyterian Church. She died long ago and was buried in the old graveyard where are the remains of her father and mother. She died in Pittsburgh, and her body was transported over land, as steamboating was an uncertain matter in those days. She left one daughter, wife of the late Dr. Wm. H. King. Mary, the remaining daughter of McFarland, married Alex. Wilson, of whom we have written in another place. Robert McFarland was no politician, but never failed to vote, even when he had to go almost half way to Brownsville to do so. He and his friend Isaac Van Voorhis cast the only votes in old Fallowfield township for Adams in 1824, when he was elected President over Jackson. The result in the township created no little merriment at the expense of the two lone voters, but the general outcome changed the tune of the other good old boys, who had shouted so loudly for the "Hero of New Orleans."

THE McGREW FAMILY.

The names of J. and R. McGrew were long familiar to the older citizens of Williamsport, now Monongahela City. They were citizens of the town prior to 1816, but from whence they came, and in what year, we have failed to discover. The firm of J. & R. McGrew for long years carried on the hatter business on the corner now occupied by the Odd Fellows' building. This firm made the wool and fur hats for the whole surrounding country, and to the wear and lasting of their wool hats there seemed to be no end, and such a quality of the article was not always valued by the chaps who never got a new hat until the old one was worn out. It was the wear, not the style, the purchaser looked at. It was to this firm the country boys took their rabbit skins to exchange them for hats, and were rejoiced when each would bring the value of eight cents. The rabbits were skinned from heel to head, and the skin inverted and drawn carefully over a forked stick so as to have it dried in a perfect state. Hats both fur and wool were often taken to this firm to be ironed over and their shape remodeled after each one's own fancy or some stray idea of style.

James was the older of the two brothers. Though intimately associated all their lives, it is said they never had any difficulties, one with the other. James McGrew had, by his first wife, one daughter, Matilda, who married Rev. Samuel Hudson, a distinguished minister in the Cumberland Presbyterian Church. His second wife was the widow of Thomas Gordon, a brother of the late Hon. James Gordon, who had two daughters by her first husband: Margaret, now deceased, wife of Captain Samuel Reynolds; and Maria, widow of Robert, the junior member of the firm of J. & R. McGrew; she also is deceased, having died in Monongahela City, September 1st, 1884. By his second wife, James McGrew had one daughter, who married John Gilfillan, of West Alexander, Pa., but resided most of their lives in Parkersburg, W. Va., where Alvira, his wife, died about 1886 or 87. Robert, son of James McGrew, was a well known merchant, and died many years ago in the prime of manhood.

James McGrew was elected and installed as an elder in the old church on the hill in April, 1816, and served during his lifetime. He was a member of the building committee of the old church at the foot of the hill. He was appointed a justice of the peace by Governor Wolfe, but never took out his commission, yet he was always called Esquire McGrew.

THE BEAZELL FAMILY.

Benjamin F. Beazell

Died August 27, 1886. He was born in Rostraver township, Westmoreland county, Pa., January 2, 1796. His grandfather and grandmother came from Bazil-on-the-Rhine, in Germany, and located in Berkeley county, Va., in 1760. Mathew and Catherine made acquaintance on board the ship during the voyage to this country, and were married at Georgetown, now in the District of Columbia, before settling in the town now known as Martinsburg, W. Va. While residing here, William and Eliza (twins), Mathew, Christian, John and Luke were born to them. In 1774 Mathew Beazell and family left Virginia and settled first in a cabin on land now owned by James Moore, known at this day as Moore's woolen factory, and now owned by a man named Kelly, who bought it from the heirs of Samuel W. Power. The farm is on the West Newton road between Bellevernon and that town in Rostraver township, Westmoreland county, Pa. The old factory has long since been converted into other uses. In 1775 Beazell moved to a cabin on the land recently sold to Andrew Graham by Wm. Jones, in the same township. Here he purchased what was then known as a "location site," containing 290 acres. On this farm the remainder of his children were born, viz.: Catherine, Barbara and Joseph, the latter died when a mere lad. Here Mathew died, but in what year we have overlooked. His tombstone will tell; it was placed over his grave, which was near the West Newton road on what was then known as the Pentecost farm, now owned by either John Rankin or Joseph Power. For many years this stone was the wonder of the stranger. Some years since it was removed by kind friends to the graveyard at Fell's church. His wife died in 1815, at the house of Robert Stevens, on Redstone creek in Fayette county. The wife of Stevens was her daughter. Mathew's son Mathew died on the farm now owned by David Finley, near the town of Webster. His remains were buried at Fell's church. His wife was a Miss Neal, whose second husband was William Sampson, the father of the venerable James Sampson, of Horseshoe, in Carroll township, Washington county.

The late Mrs. Belar, of Monongahela City, was a daughter of Mathew Beazell. John Beazell married Mary Sutherland, moved to the neighborhood of Warren, Ohio, where he died, and all of his family except one. Luke married Elizabeth English, lived in different parts of the "Forks of Yough," and died on the farm now owned by a man named McGogney, adjoining the well known Hassler farm in Rostraver township. His remains were interred at Fell's Church. He had sons Mathew, Joseph, John, James, Lemuel and William, all of whom are dead except William. His daughters were Margaret, married to Van Reeves, and died not many years ago at Coal Centre, Catherine, widow of James Ailes, Mary, widow of A. R. Smith, and Eliza, who never married. Mrs. Ailes resides in California, Pa. Mrs. Smith and Eliza are residents of West Newton, Pa. Joseph married a Miss Spharr, sister of John Spharr, of Allen township, Washington county, Pa. Joseph died a few years since in the old McCrory house, on Maple creek, in the same county, where his widow still has her home. James married a Miss Springer, whose grandfather emigrated from Stockholm, in Sweden, and settled on the farm called "Springersburgh," near Bellevernon, in very early days. James and his wife both died at their home on part of the original Springer homestead. Their remains are in the Bellevernon cemetery.

Mathew died not long since in Rostraver. Lemuel died in Webster not long ago. John was married to Jane Patterson, at the residence of the late George Houshold, in Rostraver, by the Rev. Hiram Miller, November 25, 1853, and died in Bellevernon, Pa., January 13, 1879. His wife still lives. William alone remains, and has long lived in Fallowfield, Washington county, near John Witherow's blacksmith shop. He still looks hale and hearty. Elizabeth, one of the daughters of Mathew Beazell the older, married John Sturgess, removed to Kentucky and then to Missouri. Christina married John Fell. She died in the house occupied lately by John Coughenour, and owned by the heirs of Wm. Flannegan, in Rostraver. William, the remaining son of Mathew Beazell the older, was the father of Benjamin F. Beazell, the subject of this sketch. William married Rebecca Fell in a part of the house in which Benjamin F. lived so long and in which he died. William also died in the Coughenour house. He had twelve children, four of whom were boys, viz Mathew, William, John F. and Benjamin F., of whom we are writing. Mathew died many years ago. He was the father of H. B. Beazell. John F. lived for a while in Webster, but the latter part of his days was passed in Uniontown, Pa., where he was for years editor of the *Pennsylvania Democrat*, published in that place.

Benjamin F. was married to Sarah Sampson November 17th, 1820, by the Rev. John White. She was a daughter of William and Dorcas Sampson—Dorcas was a Neal, sister of James Sampson's mother. Her father settled on Long run and was killed by the Indians. At the date of this marriage Sampson lived at the old "Black Horse Tavern," now owned by Lew Weaver, and situate in Rostraver. This and the Red Lion Hotel in Redstone, were the two celebrated stopping places between Pittsburgh and Uniontown in old times. The issue of this marriage was a large family of boys and girls, among whom was Dorcas, married to John Darr, of Rostraver; William married Elizabeth Biggs, of Sewickley township, Westmoreland county; Thomas died, aged 14 years; James married Jessie Woodruff; Mary I. and Rebecca remained at home; Benjamin F. married Mary D. Welling, of Ohio, and is now a prominent minister in the Methodist Episcopal church of the Pittsburgh conference; Sarah Emma is the wife of Dr. J. A. Mink, of Topeka, Kansas; Samuel is a farmer and John a lawyer, of Chillicothe, Mo.; James and William live in Rostraver.

Benjamin F. joined the Methodist church in 1828, in the old church which stood on the site of the present stone building known as Fell's church, not far from the town of Webster. Rev. John Watterman was the minister at the time of his joining. His wife joined the same church in a short time after Benjamin did. Benjamin F.'s grandfather Fell donated a part and his father the remainder of the lot which now belongs to the church. The Beazells and Fells hewed the logs for the old church; they whip-sawed the material for the stairs and pulpit. The floor was made of split logs and so were the seats; the building presented an unfinished appearance. This was so plain to the stranger that at the first time Lorenzo Dow preached in it he used the following expression in his prayer: "Oh, Lord! here is a house from all appearances has been building for 40 years, and not yet finished;" and he prayed the Lord to put it in the hearts of the people to finish it and revive his work. Richard Ferguson did the *clerking* for him on this occasion, singing St. Martin's fast as he could. This was in 1818. B. Bascom, the celebrated divine, preached in this old church on more than one occasion. The present stone church was built in 1834. The board of trustees under whose supervision it was built consisted of Hugh C. Ford, Samuel Jones, Manassah Reeves, Benjamin Thomas, Luke Beazell, Nathaniel Lender, Benjamin Stewart, Randall Johnson and Benjamin F. Beazell, all of whom have passed away. The carpenter work was done by Townsend for $400; the plastering by Michael Dravo.

The dedication sermon was preached by Rev. Charles Elliot. Among the many distinguished divines who preached in the old and new churches we may mention Bishops McKendry and Morris and Revs. Charles Cook, J. G. Sansom, Jamison, Smith, the Millers, and Rev. B. F. Beazell, son of Benjamin F. Beazell. William, father of Benjamin F. Beazell, laid out the town of Webster in 1835, the late Joseph Van Kirk doing the surveying. Benjamin F. Beazell built the first house in the town of Webster, being known as the Rev. J. G. Sansom mansion, on the lot lately occupied by the residence of Dr. J. T. Krepps. During the first five years of his married life Benjamin lived on the Fell farm. In 1825 he rented what was known at that time as the "Daly" farm, on which he lived two years. He then moved to the Black Horse Tavern and kept store for Samuel Walker for a time; then bought out Walker and ran the store himself until in 1835. In the spring of 1836 he moved to his house in Webster, where he carried on merchandising and boat-building until 1841, excepting two years that he moved back to the Black Horse Tavern. In 1844 he purchased the old Fell homestead, in which he lived to the day of his death. In 1835 he built for Captain Shrodes the steamboat *Moravian*. He built keelboats and flatboats for the lower trade, as it was then called. For himself he built a trade boat — loaded it with a variety of goods, as flour, cherry bounce and boiled cider. For the latter he paid $3 per barrel and sold it for $5, making a nice profit. He sold his whole cargo on the way and at Cincinnati, and walked home, carrying the proceeds.

Father Beazell, by his example and precepts, was a power for good in whatever community he resided. He was a walking encyclopædia of religious experience. His interest in the church was only exceeded by his zeal in the cause of Christ. "Blessed are the dead that die in the Lord."

JAMES K. MARSHALL.

On a plain marble slab standing on the brow of the hill in the old graveyard can be seen the name of James K. Marshall, who died March 24th, 1856, aged 81 years. He lived most of his life on the farm now owned by his son-in-law, William Blyth's heirs on Pigeon creek, in Carroll township. His florid complection, white hair, robust form and pleasant manners will be called to mind by many of the present day. His farm in early day was known as the Joseph Hall farm, and was secured by Virginia entry about the time the Deckers took possession of their large tracts. The old house still standing was erected by Joseph Hall—it being a hewed log house with clapboard gable ends shows that it was the successor of the primitive house built of round logs with clapboard roof. His wife was one of the Hall family. He had several children. James settled in Beaver county, but in after life we learn he moved to the west. He was a man of fine natural ability, and had only a limited education, yet in debate he was able to hold his own with the late talented R. F. Cooper, Esq., Dr. James

Scott and Dr. Frank Shugart, with whom he had many an intellectual contest in school house debating societies. Whilst the others exhibited a flow of Rhetoric, he was content to present his views in a plain, logical, common sense manner. He died March 19th, 1892, at Lyndon, Kansas. The other son was a soldier in the late war of the rebellion, and is still a fixture on Pigeon creek. Their daughter, Susannah, in 1835, married a man named John H. Marshall, who died at Hazel Dell, Lawrence county, Pa., August 10th, 1887, in the 77th year of his age. He was born in November, 1810, on what is known as the David Quail farm, near Washington, Pa. His wife died in April, 1886. They left eight children. The other daughter, Nancy, married Enoch Hays, and died at her home near Steubenville, Ohio, in March, 1892, at an advanced age.

THE TEEPLE FAMILY.

Christopher Teeple was born in New Jersey. He came to this country in 1775, and remained only a short time. Leaving his son Isaac, the old gentleman removed to Canada, where he died. Isaac purchased a hundred acres of land, known now as the Teeple homestead, in Horseshoe, in Carroll township. He bought it from Massah or Maish Case, who was the father of Leonard Case, Sr., who was the father of Leonard Case, of Cleveland, Ohio. Isaac Teeple had five brothers and two sisters, but none of them, excepting one sister, settled in the neighborhood. Isaac married Catherine Castner on the farm owned by the Castner heirs in Horseshoe, on the 22nd day of November, 1788. Isaac was born near New Brunswick, New Jersey, August 28, 1760. His wife was born in Greensburg, Pa., or near that place, January 24, 1772. She was a daughter of Peter and Mary Magdaline Castner.

Peter was the father of Michael and John Castner, the latter of whom was the father of the late Daniel Castner, and grandfather of B. W Castner, Esq., now residing on the Castner homestead in Horseshoe. Isaac lived from his first coming to to this country on the Teeple farm, where he died December 7, 1828. His wife died January 9, 1849, and was buried with the remains of her husband in the Columbia graveyard, but in later years both remains were removed to the Monongahela cemetery. Isaac had a large family of girls and boys. Jemima was born October 26, 1790. Peter and Christopher—twins—were born August 6, 1792; Mary, September 4, 1794; Joseph, December 13, 1797; Elijah, January 7, 1799; Elizabeth, February 27, 1801; Isaac, February 11, 1803; Michæl, May 9, 1805; Catharine, March 29, 1807; Christena, April 9, 1809; Sarah Ann, October 29, 1812; Theresa, April 4, 1814.

Christopher and Peter were twins and named after their grandfathers. They died in the state of Indiana. Joseph married a Miss Lash, February 7, 1820, near Bentleysville, attended mill on Pigeon creek for a short time, kept store in Beallsville, then removed to Stark county, Ohio, within eight miles of Massilon. He had two sons and five daughters.

Jemima, March 11, 1819, married Andrew Burgett, of Burgettstown, Washington county. Both are dead, leaving one son, now living on the home place, adjoining the town.

Mary, March 11, 1819, married Samuel Rutan, who lived for many years on the farm now owned by W. J. Manown, situated on the Monongahela river just above the old Brown ferry in Rostraver township, Westmoreland county. After the death of Rutan she married Samuel Davis, a brother of General John M. Davis, United States marshal for Western Pennsylvania under Jackson. Samuel Davis was the father of Samuel Davis, of the town of California, on the Monongahela, and of Mrs. Eliza Allen, wife of the late George W. Allen. The late Fortner Davis was a half brother of Samuel and Eliza. Mrs. Samuel Davis *neé* Teeple died some years ago on the Newkirk farm, near Bentleysville.

Elizabeth Teeple, March 30, 1819, married Peter Smock. They are both dead. Their sons, Thomas and Leroy, reside in Wisconsin. They had five daughters of whom we have not any information. From what we can learn Peter Smock was the son of Abraham Smock, who married Polly Teeple, a sister of Isaac Teeple, the older, she having remained with him after the father removed to Canada. This Abraham Smock and Polly, his wife, had four pairs of twins in succession, viz.: Peter and Sallie, John and Barnett, Nettie aud Jennie, William and Jacob. This said Abraham Smock's father was Leonard Smock, and he had several sons, viz.: Abraham, Barnett, John, Leonard and Cornelius. Barnett was the father of Mrs. Mary Corwin, lately deceased in Bellevernon, Pa., and father of the late Henry Smock, whose wife was Betsy, daughter of the older Peter Shepler, of Rostraver.

Christena Teeple married Casper Castner, brother of the late Daniel Castner. They had two children, Lewis Cass and Kate E. Lewis is in the drug business and Katie has long been one of the corps of teachers in the Hiland public school of Pittsburgh.

Sarah Ann Teeple died in her 26th year, and Theresa in her seventh. Isaac Teeple married Margaret Williams December 9th, 1839. Isaac at first settled on a farm in Richland county, Ohio. He traded this farm for the one on which he died, situated in Carroll township. Philip Crabb owned this farm at the time of the trade, but the late Edward Sprowls, the shoemaker, resided on it for many years, Mr. Crabb never having resided on it. He lived for long years in Fallowfield, where he died. Edward Sprowls was the father of Obediah and Isaiah Sprowls, of Bentleysville. Isaiah was a scholar in the old Calhoon school; his father living at that time in the old house on the farm formerly owned by Abe Hull, but now by one of the Shannon boys. Isaac Teeple, soon after his marriage, moved to the farm where he died. He first occupied the old house, but afterwards built the present brick house. His wife died in 1868. They had 10 children. One boy and two girls are dead. Kate C. married Clark Preston, near Ginger hill. Emma S. married Alcinus J. Hess, near the same place. Of Ada, Theresa, Sarah Ann and Josephine, we have no knowledge as to marriage. Thomas W. resides in Neosho county, Kansas, and Theodore resides on the old home.

Michael Teeple, named after Michael Castner, was born on the homestead in Carroll, and lived all his life on part of it. He married Eliza, daughter of the good Jesse Martin, so long connected with "the old church on the hill." They had four children. Jesse M. is dead; he was in the 22nd Regiment Pennsylvania Cavalry, in the late war, under Capt. James Chessrown. Clinton married Margaret, daughter of Wm. Wickerham, a granddaughter of Adam Wickerham, proprietor of the lower end of Williamsport, that part of the town known originally as Georgetown. Thomas B. married a Miss Giles. Kate B. married Robert, son of West Frye, of Finleyville.

Elijah, son of Isaac Teeple, the older was born on the homestead January 7, 1799, and died February 5, 1873. His first wife was Louisa Reagan, of Westmoreland county, Pa. They had several children. Cynthia married John Yohe, and died many years ago. John M. died in childhood. Ulysses R. resides in Monroe county, Iowa. Isophine married John Van Voorhis September 15, 1859, and resides in Monongahela City. John, her husband, was born September 6, 1835, on the old Van Voorhis homestead.

John owns the old homestead farm called "Sicily" in the patent, where the Captain located his family in October, 1786. The patent, signed by Benjamin Franklin, was granted to him, bearing date March 17, 1787, under a survey granted Joseph Decker August 26, 1769, and deeded to Daniel Van Voorhis February 7, 1785. In those days deeds were often executed before a patent was issued. This deed demonstrates beyond all doubt that the Captain came to this country in 1785. John and Isophine have six childen, viz: Charles E., Lulu J., Carrie E. Cynthia Serena, William T. and Eva I.

Elijah Teeple's second wife was Dorcas, sister of James Sampson, of Carroll township. Their only child by this marriage was James Harvey. His third wife was Elizabeth Thomas. Elijah first lived after marriage and kept store in the frame house now owned by Mr. Robert Nelson, on Main street, above Dr. Linn's dwelling, in Monongahela City. He moved from this house to a brick house on Railroad street, a short distance below the planing mill of Neel & Blythe. He removed from this house to a frame house on the Pike, above Chess street, now owned by William Hanna. He finally moved to the stone house about one mile up the Pike, where the late Alexander Campbell resided for many years, and afterwards owned by a man the name of Beazell. In this house Elijah died.

GENERAL JOHN M. DAVIS.

Catherine, daughter of Isaac Teeple the older, was born on the Teeple homestead, March 29th, 1807. Married General John M. Davis by the Rev. Boyd Mercer, May 17th, 1825. Made "their appearance" at church in Centreville, Washington county, Pa., after a wedding trip to Ohio on a visit to her sister and brother Joseph. General Davis was born in Lancaster, Pa., January 10th, 1783, and died November 28th, 1853, in Pittsburgh, in that part known now as the East End. General Davis was a military man by nature, and cultivated the military spirit throughout his life. He was appointed by Governor Thomas McKean a captain in the militia of the district of Franklin and Cumberland counties, his commission bearing date of May 3d, 1804. He was commissioned as 2d lieutenant in the 2d regiment United States infantry by President Jefferson May 3d, 1803. He was appointed 1st Lieutenant in the same regiment by President Madison, January 1st, 1810, and was commissioned captain in the same regiment by Madison May 30th, 1813; and for gallant conduct during the siege and battle of New Orleans he was appointed major by brevet December 23d, 1814. He enlisted while a resident of Lancaster, went to New Orleans part of the way on foot and part in a barge. He served during the war under General Jackson; was wounded by a ball in the foot, and in the face by a bayonet, at the famous battle of New Orleans, and was personally complimented by Jackson for his brave behavior in that battle. At the close of the war he went to the state of Georgia, where his excellency, John Clark, commissioned him captain of the Independent Blues, attached to the 46th regiment, June 7th, 1823. Altogether he was in United States service 14 years, having also been in the Seminole war. His wife, to the day of her death, retained in her possession all of his commissions, and many autograph letters from General Jackson to her husband. After his return from Georgia, Davis settled in Washington county, Pa.

On the election of General Jackson as President, he was appointed Marshal of the Western District of Pennsylvania, over David Lynch, of Allegheny. In January, 1839, Jackson, with A. J. Donaldson and wife, attended by servants, started to take his seat, traveling in his own conveyance. They came to Washington, Pa. via Wheeling, and were persuaded there to go east via Pittsburgh. General Davis having heard that he had gone out of his way, started from Beallsville, where he had resided since his marriage to Catherine Teeple, and overtook the President-elect at a hotel formerly known as the Merchant's Hotel, on Wood street, Pittsburgh. He found at the door a large crowd eager to get a sight of the new President, and among them was David Lynch, Davis' competitor for the Marshalship. Davis was informed by those having charge of the door that he could not be admitted, which announcement seemed to please Lynch very much. Davis, not discouraged, wrote his name on a slip of paper and asked one of the doorkeepers if he would please hand that to the President-elect. He said yes, and the moment the name met the eye of Jackson he exclaimed, "Certainly, admit my old friend." He greeted him with a hearty shake of the hand, saying, "How are you, Major, my old friend and fellow soldier, with whom I have fought many a battle, and how is little 'Andy,'" (Davis' son A. J.) As Davis entered the door amidst the crowd, some one cried out, "Lynch, that is too old a soldier for you." Although a committee from Pittsburgh had met Jackson at Washington and escorted him to the city, yet he, through the advice of his friend Davis, retraced his steps to

Washington, accompanied by Davis. He stopped with Davis for dinner at his residence in Beallsville, where over five hundred people were assembled, most of whom partook of the hospitality of Davis. Three kinds of wine, made by Mrs. Davis, were on the table, and Jackson declared the wine to be the best he ever tasted. He was dressed in a plain black suit, with a hat *a la mode* stove pipe. Davis accompanied him to Uniontown, promising his wife to return that evening, but enjoying the company of Jackson so well, he hesitated about going home that day, but the President said, "Friend Davis, you promised your wife to be at home this evening and you must return."

Shortly after taking his seat Jackson appointed Davis marshal of the district, which he held during both terms of his administration, and on his retirement from office Davis was retained one year under the administration of Van Buren at the special request of his friend Jackson. Davis was appointed by Governor Shultze justice of the peace in Washington county April 3, 1828, which office, as well as postmaster at Beallsville, he held when he removed to Allegheny City to enter upon his duties as marshal. He had been for some time in the mercantile and tannery business before his removal from Beallsville. In 1834 he removed to the beautiful residence near East Liberty, now on Penn avenue, and owned at this time by his son, Dr. A. J. Davis. At this place he died November 28, 1853, and here also his wife Catherine died February 28, 1886.

Davis received his title as general from the position of major-general of the Allegheny County Militia, in which office he served for many years. His first wife was Nancy McGirk. They had no children. By his second wife, Catherine, he had two boys and two girls. John, Minor and Theresa Maria died in early life. Ann Elizabeth was born July 1, 1827, in Beallsville, and died at the homestead in East Liberty July 10, 1853. A. Jackson was also born at Beallsville, and is now one of the most prominent physicians in Allegheny county. He never married, and still (1893) resides at the homestead in the full enjoyment of health and wealth.

THE FRYE FAMILY.

The Speers and Frye names were introduced into the wilds of Western Pennsylvania about the year 1772. Henry Speers, the older, with Regena Froman, his wife, settled on the farm now known as the Gibsonton Mills, on the Monongahela river below Bellevernon. Abraham Frye and family located on the opposite side of the river. He owned and afterwards gave to his children, among others, the farms now owned by John Conrad at Lock No. 4, by Joseph Ryan, William McMehan, Smith Frye, James Sampson and William Rogers. The Speers and Fryes were intimately associated in everything that pertained to each other's comfort, and this fact, in those days of trial and danger, was no small affair. In going from place to place or in the field these settlers were compelled, for personal safety, to carry fire-arms so as to meet the attacks of the Indians. At one time the girls and boys of the Frye family having gone across the river to milk their cows, were overtaken by a storm. They sought shelter under a tree, and whilst there one of their number was killed by lightning. In the midst of this sore trouble the Indian's whoop was heard in the distance, warning them of a new danger. Leaving the dead one, the others sought security beneath the floor of an old cabin. They were hardly quiet in their new retreat before the Indians entered the cabin, in which they remained all night, dancing and whooping, unconscious of the prize within their grasp. It was a long night to the prisoners beneath the floor, but when morning came the Indians departed and the milkers escaped to their dwelling, where the sad story was told. The bones of this dead one no doubt was the first of the Frye family to bleach on the banks of the Monongahela. We are able to trace the history of two sons and one daughter of Abraham Frye, Sr. Their names were Abraham, Nancy and Samuel. We cannot determine whether Benjamin Frye, one of the executors of the older Henry Speers, was a brother of the last named or not, but his wife being a daughter of Henry Speers leads us to infer that he was a brother of Abraham Frye, Sr.

Abraham Frye, Jr., son of Abraham Frye, Sr., married a daughter of Henry Speers, and had a large family. In this way we make it out that he and Benjamin were brothers and married sisters—daughters of Henry Speers. Their sons were Thomas, Benjamin, Abraham, Smith, Luke, Johnson, Noah, James and Elijah. He lived and died on the farm now owned by the late Mrs. Joseph Ryan, near lock No. 4, on the Monongahela river. He built the old house which was torn down by James S. Jones, to give place for the present building. We think his remains are in the old Frye graveyard on the hill, above the upper end of Charleroi.

His son, Benjamin, resided for many years on the farm now owned by the heirs of John Carson, lately deceased. Benjamin also ran an old-fashioned water grist and saw mill, in what is now known as Scott's hollow, which lead from his farm to Pigeon creek, in Carroll. The entire mill at one time was washed into Pigeon creek by an imaginary water spout; the very millstones were taken into the creek, a mile distant. He removed west very many years ago.

Abraham's son, Abraham, known in his day as West's Abe. lived on the Jacob Crabb farm, in Fallowfield, now owned by the heirs of Washington Cooper. He kept an Inn where travelers were entertained and musters of the militia were held on the first Monday of May in each year until the good old law was repealed. After the building of the state road from Pittsburgh to Brownsville, in about 1832, the traveling on this route was very large for that day. Four-horse coaches were at times on regular days run on this road, but the principal travel was by horseback. Frye's Inn was a famous stopping place on this road. The mail was never carried on this road—It was carried from Beallsville via Bentleysville, Williamsport, Rogally, &c., to Pittsburgh. Even after the building of the Pike the Williamsport people depended on the cross mail via Rogally for their principal mail. Benjamin Frye removed many years ago to Sandusky, Ohio, where he died at an advanced age.

About 60 years ago Smith Frye moved to Illinois; was one of the first settlers of Peoria city; was Sheriff of Peoria county; was a fine talker; and was regarded as a shrewd, popular and successful business man and politician. He was killed in a personal encounter with some individual at the same place where his son, Jacob, was killed in after time.

Luke lived near the old Baptist church in Horseshoe. His wife was a West. Luke was the father of West Frye, Esq., who had long been a resident of Finleyville, in Washington county, where he died March 12, 1891. He was also the father of the wife, Elgy Van Voorhis, who many years ago lived at the old distillery, which is now owned by W. J. Markell, in Carroll, on what is known as Yerty's run. Elgy is still living, but his wife is dead; he has long been one of Greene county's most wealthy cattle dealers. West Frye married Christina, daughter of the late Daniel Van Voorhis. She was a sister of Mrs. Sallie Cooper, of Mingo, and Mrs. B. F. Bentley, of Monongahela City.

Johnson, another son of Abraham Frye, died at Ringland's old mill on Maple creek, now known as the Twilight mill. He was the father of A. P. Frye, who died on the old Cooper farm, at the mouth of Maple creek, a few years since. His remains, along with those of his wife, who died afterwards, were interred in the Monongahela cemetery. A. P. Fry was the father of Johnson, of whose whereabouts we do not know; also the father of Hester, wife of B. Parsons, of Maple creek, and H. B. Frye, a well known business man at this time in Allegheny City. The oldest son, Noah, died many years ago in Bellevernon. Noah, son of Abraham Frye, married Lucy Colvin; he lived in East Williamsport, better known as Catsburg, in the first ward of Monongahela City. Noah was killed in a coal bank near Dagg's ferry. Thomas, another son, married a West and lived all his life on the farm at Lock No. 4, now owned by John Conrad. The old house in 1889 was torn down and in its stead John Conrad has erected a beautiful mansard roof frame building. It is one of the most attractive residences in the valley, and its design and finish reflects great credit on the owner, architect and builder.

Thomas' son Resin now resides in the town of Bellewood below Monongahela City, although his large landed estate is situated in Fallowfield and Carroll townships. He is one of Washington county's most successful farmers. His wife is a daughter of the late John Eckles, a well-known mechanic in early days. She is a sister of Hamilton Eckles, a well-known river man, whose wife was Lucinda, daughter of the late Samuel Reeves, of Rostraver township, Westmoreland county, who lived and died on the farm now owned by his son Samuel.

One of Thomas Frye's daughters married John Wilson, who resided near the site of the old Horseshoe meeting house and was a wealthy and successful farmer. He is deceased. Another daughter married Noah Jones, of Bentleysville. Rev. O. P. Hargrave's wife is also a daughter; her former husband was Stephen Thomas, long known in his connection with Lock No. 4. Another daughter married Andrew Hazelbaker, now deceased. The remaining members of the family of Thomas Frye we cannot trace.

Nancy, daughter of Abraham Frye, was the wife of the late Noah Speers, who laid out Bellevernon, and whose history in detail will be given in another place.

Samuel, brother of Abraham Frye, occupied the high lands of the Frye family. He built and died in the old frame house that stood near the new one erected by Jackson Frye, and now owned by James Sampson. Samuel married Christina, daughter of Henry Speers, the older. They had several sons and daughters. Isaac moved to Illinois, where he died many years ago. Samuel married Elizabeth, better known as "Aunt Betty," daughter of the late Captain Daniel Van Voorhis by his third wife, and only sister of the late Isaac Van Voorhis. They lived in the old log house which stood near the brick house built by their son Solomon, and on the farm now owned by William Rogers, it being a part of the original Frye homestead.

Samuel and wife had a large family of boys and girls. Solomon married a daughter of Parker Scott, Esq. She died a few years since in the town of California, on the Monongahela river. Her husband was one of the old fashioned mechanics who work to the scribe. He acquired considerable reputation by the publication of a volume of miscellaneous poems. He is dead. Nancy married Samuel McCrory, whose mother was a daughter of the well known elder, Henry Speers, and grand daughter of the older Henry Speers, and sister of the late Apollus Speers, of Speers' Ferry. Nancy's husband died in 1852, leaving her with a large family. She is deceased. Lewis, another son of Samuel and Elizabeth Frye, married a sister of John Shanton, of Carroll township, and has been dead many years. Henry is a wealthy farmer in the vicinity of Bentleysville. His wife has been dead some years. Samuel resides in or about Bentleysville.

Louisa, one of the daughters, married John Shanton, Esq., Ursula was Jefferson Redd's first wife, and Sallie was his second wife, all of whom are dead.

Bettie married E. T. Cooper, son of F. K. Cooper, of the Dutch settlement in Carroll. He built the stone distillery just below the upper wharf in Monongahela City. Shortly after it was in operation it was destroyed by fire. Of late years it has been converted into a knitting factory. The Doctor and wife are now residents of Beaver county.

The father, Samuel Frye, of these children, died some 60 years ago; but "Aunt Betty" lived until August 18th, 1875. Rebecca, sister of Samuel Frye, married Henry Shepler, who lived and died in the old house that stood where the new residence of William Rogers was erected, near what is known as Cooper's mill, on Maple creek.

Katie married William Croskey, of the vicinity of Cadiz, Ohio. Sarah married John Van Voorhis. In 1812 he moved to Muskingum. The history of John and Sarah is given more in detail elsewhere. Mary Frye married Daniel Van Voorhis, whose history is given in the Van Voorhis Family.

Abraham Frye, better known as Ringland's Abe, was born in the old house before mentioned, on the old Frye tract of land, on the 12th day of January, 1793. He married Isabella Ringland September 13th, 1813, in the old house that stood above the present residence of his son-in-law, Abram Colvin, on the Brownsville road, in Fallowfield. In the same house was born his wife, on the 5th day of April, 1796. Her father, John Ringland, was in his day regarded as the largest land holder in Washington county. His children all died early, excepting Mrs. Frye, who, at his death, inherited his large estate.

Abraham was one of the best of men. Naturally good-hearted, was generous to a fault. He never learned any trade, yet he was skilled beyond his day in almost every trade. He made of iron or wood whatever he needed. In the absence of an anvil he used his ax driven into a piece of wood, and with this improvised anvil before the kitchen fire he made many a useful article, even at the expense of annoying the cooks. He was general pewter-spoon moulder for the neighborhood, and his moulds, then so convenient, are still in existence. He shod his own horses, made his own grain cradles and sickles, his own files; made and operated the first threshing machines in the county, or anywhere else, a part of which can still be seen; he cut the stone for and built his model spring house; cut and put in place the stone in the house in which he and his wife lived and died, and in which his son Smith now resides. In a word, he was a man of extraordinary genius. He always lived on the farm where he was born. The remains of both are interred in the family burying-ground on the farm. Soon after his marriage he went to Tennessee to see if he could find a better location, but returned in a very short time and told his wife: "No better place than home; we will build a new house," and the sequel speaks for itself. His sons Samuel and John both married daughters of Parker Scott, Esq., and both of them have nearly always since marriage lived on the old Ringland mill farm on Maple creek. Their wives are deceased. Christina, daughter of Abraham Frye, married Abram Colvin. They reside in the new brick house near the old Ringland mansion on the Brownsville and Pittsburgh state road. Smith lives on the homestead where his parents died. Jackson recently sold to James Sampson his part of the home farm, and removed to Southern Kansas. His first wife was a daughter of Garret Wall, Esq., of Allegheny county, and his present wife is a daughter of the late Moses Colvin. Henry, Abraham and Noah live in Tennessee. Noah is dead. Sarah Ann is the wife of Thomas McGowan, of Lock No. 4, who has been identified since his youth with the Monongahela Navigation Company. Clarissa married Alexander Allman, and is dead. Isabella is the wife of E. T. Van Voorhis, of the vicinity of Kansas City, Mo.

Dr. Matthew Porter Morrison.

At five o'clock on Tuesday evening, November 10th, 1885, this excellent man passed peacefully away, at his home in Monongahela City, Pa. He was aged 58 years, 10 months and 27 days.

Doctor Morrison was born on the farm situated on the Monongahela river, near lock No. 3, in Elizabeth township, Allegheny county, December 14th, 1826. In April, 1837, his father having sold his farm removed to Monongahela City with his family, and occupied the house owned by the Doctor and occupied by the family ever since. His father died a few months after he settled here, on October the 16th, 1837.

He received his first academic training at the academy of the late T. R. Hazzard, Esq., and E. S. Blake. He entered Washington College, where he graduated in the class of 1847. Hon. James G. Blaine, Hon. John H. Hampton, Esq., of Pittsburgh, Alexander Wilson, Esq., of Washington, were members of the same class.

After reading a course of medicine with the late Dr. Samuel M. King, he graduated at Jefferson Medical College in the year 1851. He subsequently attended and held a diploma from a Boston institution, where he took a special course on diseases of women and children. Soon after his graduation as a physician he was associated in practice and as a partner with Dr. R. F. Biddle, in this city, where he has practiced continuously till within a few weeks, except during his four years' service in the Union army during the war for the suppression of the rebellion. His practice of medicine covers about 34 years, being at the time of his death the senior physician of the place, and of course with a very large clientage.

He joined the army August 6th, 1861, as assistant surgeon of (the old 13th) Col. Rowley's 102nd Penn'a Vols.; was promoted to surgeon with the rank of major, September 12th, 1862, and was mustered out June 28th, 1865, being at that time surgeon of the second division of the sixth corps. He was a member of Post 60, G. A. R.

Of his worth as a friend, his judgment and sagacity as a physician, his learning as a scholar, his integrity and nobility of character in the walks of civil life, and of his devotion to his country as a soldier, his warm hearted friendship, his stern adherence to right living and thinking, of the warm place he held in the hearts of the families which he visited both as physician and friend—of these things we need not speak—they are the choicest memories of this sad hour in a thousand hearts.

Dr. M. P. Morrison brought to his profession a mind thoroughly familiar with the principles and practice of medicine. He honored the profession in which he was eminently successful.

His death brings a genuine sorrow, brightened only by the words which his lips framed, almost with his last breath, "Not my will but Thine."

THE DEATH OF JOSEPH S. MORRISON, ESQ.

Died in Pittsburgh, Pa., April 20th, 1886, in the 62nd year of his age. He was buried in the Monongahela cemetery April 22nd, at 2.30 o'clock. The *Daily Republican* says:

The death of this estimable gentleman, following so soon that of his brother, the doctor, comes with peculiar sadness to his many friends. He was one of us—he never wearied of Monongahela, his happiest moments were spent on the hills of his birth, and he loved the trees whose history he knew and whose companionship he sought as if they were his elder brother. The river never lost its charm to him; and coming up on the train, his chosen seat was on the shore side, watching the sun-lit sparkle of its waters and the ripple of its waves. A botanist of reading and much lore, each pleasant day at home found him among the flowers and leaves; but in the special work of arbor culture he found chiefest delight, and a tree to him was a book, a picture, a poem—with Thompson he sang:

> Welcome ye shades, ye bowery thickets hail!
> Ye lofty pines, ye venerable oaks;
> Delicious is your shelter to the soul.

His College Life.

Joseph Scott Morrison was a graduate of Washington College of the class of 1844, having for his classmates Rev. J. T. Brownlee, D. D., Dr. J. S. Van Voorhis, Rev. W. F. Hamilton, D. D., Hon. M. B. Hagans, Hon. J. H. Wallace, and others, during the Professorship of Dr. McConaughey, Profs. Alrich, Lee, Milligan, Ferguson. From the "class history" we quote the following sketch:

Morrison was more distinguished at college for proficiency in the exercises of the literary society than the class-room. The treasures of English literature were treasures over which he gloated with delight. When the names of McCauley, Carlisle, Tennyson, Bancroft, Motley and Longfellow were names less familiar to the public ear than now, it was his pleasure and pride to cultivate familiar acquaintance with their works. As an essayist, he was perhaps unexcelled by any of his fellow-students during the later part of his collegiate course. On two occasions he represented his literary society on contest—once as an essayist and once as a debator. On the former occasion he was successful, and on the latter represented his society with distinguished credit. In person, Morrison was tall and slender.

When poised in the balance many of his class-mates could weigh him down, but none of them looked down from so lofty a height as he. It was a conceit with which he was wont to please himself, that in future years he would grow out in largeness as he had already grown up in height; but the latest reports do not bring to view as yet any marked symptoms of the anticipated physical development. After graduation he studied law in the office of the Hon. T. M. T. McKennan in Washington, Pa., and from the time of his admission to the bar till the present has been engaged in the practice of his profession in the city of Pittsburgh. To Morrison, thus far, belongs the sole distinction among his class-mates of having remained proof against the captivating power of the sex. He is the bachelor of the class. Of this there were no special premonatory symtoms while he was a student. The arrows of the little winged archer, which fly as thickly through a college atmosphere as elsewhere, seemed quite as likely in him as in others to find their mark.

On commencement day, when the time was drawing near for the announcement of his name, he whispered in the ear of his class mate, who sat hard by, his determination to draw inspiration for the effort before him from the pair of large bright eyes that were sparkling near one of the columns back in the audience. Other evidences were not wanting of his liability during student life as readily as any of the "lords of creation" to be under "woman's control." But his independence is still maintained. His class mates are no doubt ready to extend unto him their congratulations or sympathy, from whichever fund he may choose to draw.

The daily papers of Pittsburgh, noting his death, speak of the deceased in the highest terms as a gentleman, a scholar, and a wise counsellor at law.

A TENDER MEMORY.

Joseph S. Morrison, Esq., while home on Sabbath day last, paid his usual afternoon visit to the cemetery, and on his return remarked to his sister, Mrs. Alexander, "It is very beautiful in the cemetery, Eliza, very beautiful, and the birds seem so happy; I felt as if I would like to stay up there all the time." How prophetic! To-day he is laid there, amid the flowers and the birds and the trees—to stay all the time.

[From Monongahela *Republican*.]

DEATH OF MAJOR A. P. MORRISON.

Major Andrew Porter Morrison died at his office, No. 155 Fourth street, Pittsburgh at 12:40, Wednesday noon, November 5th, 1890, in his 61st year, of myocarditis, or weakening of the muscles controlling the heart action.

The details of his death are thus told by Attorney C. E. McIlvain: "The Major and myself were accustomed to sit in my office, which is on the floor below his, and together read the morning papers, possibly to chat a bit over the news, then he would go up to his office. Wednesday we both went down on the train together, and when I got to my office he was standing at the door waiting, and we both went in together; about nine he remarked, 'this election is a surprise in many respects,' and passed on up stairs. Soon after a number of young attorneys gathered in, and we were talking over the election when I heard a rapping on the floor above, coming from Major Morrison's room, and knowing that it was certainly done for a purpose, I stepped into the hall and there met the letter carrier, who said, 'that gentleman up stairs is quite sick.'

"I went at once, and found Mr. Morrison on the floor in front of the fire, a large book under his head and his heavy cape coat drawn over his shoulders. He was unconscious; his spectacle case was on his table, the paper folded and laid beside it, and to all appearance feeling sick and chilly, he had lain down by the fire, too weak to do more, and while there he had made the alarm I heard. Summoning some friends from below, I at once dispatched for his relatives, and for physicians, calling Dr.

Fleming, who was, with Dr. Patten, his consulting physician. The major recovered consciousness, was placed on a cot, and seemed easier. He calmly announced. however, that he was dying. He said to me, 'Tell Eliza and William, and all my friends that I am thinking of them now.' When Dr. Fleming arrived he was recognized, and said, 'This is the end, doctor, of which you spoke; I am dying now, and he said this as calmly as if he had said, I am going to sleep. He died at twenty minutes to one o'clock, his last words being ' My sister Eliza.' "

Mr. McIlvaine was with him all those last hours, and we have given these datails because it is well for the world to know how peacefully a good man dies.

Andrew P. Morrison, the fourth child of John and Margaret Morrison, was born November 2nd, 1829, on their farm, then known as Leechburg, on the Allegheny county side, just south of lock No. 3. The family came to this city in 1837. After graduating from Washington College he read law with his brother and with Judge McKennan in 1852-4. He practiced law in Pittsburgh with Joseph from 1854 till 1861, when he entered the Union army. He enlisted May 1st, 1861, in Company A, Ninth Reserves; was made a corporal, and promoted July, 1862, to be sergeant major; was wounded badly at South Mountain; was mustered out with his regiment May 12th, 1864.

He was a member of Duquesne Post, No. 259, G. A. R., Pittsburgh, and that post to-day attends the funeral services of two members, Major Morrison and Dr. Benham, both graduates of the same college and both Union veterans. Comrade Morrison, it will be remembered, was the installing officer of Post 60, in our Opera house last winter, when Colonel Tom Stewart was here. He was historian of the Ninth Regiment at the dedication of the Gettysburg monuments, and his address on that occasion will be published by the state. It is a careful, conscientious and accurate historical paper.

Major Morrison was married September 11, 1866, to Rebecca S. H. Davis, of Pittsburgh, who died in September of 1877. More than a year ago, being warned of the approach of this heart trouble, he relinquished his law practice, refused all new business, and was rapidly closing up his docket.

A. P. Morrison was a man of the highest type; the moral atmosphere which surrounded him was pure, the example which he set was helpful. He was an elder in the Presbyterian church, upright, honorable, courteous. His instincts were all gentle, his manner urbane, his friendship true as gold; his career was that of honorable manhood, respected citizenship, unquestioned morality and professional integrity.

Mrs. Eliza Morrison Alexander,

The beloved wife of William J. Alexander, died suddenly at her home, on Wednesday morning, June 28th, 1893, in her 73rd year. She had been suffering from the weakness of advancing age for the past few years, and on Thursday evening fell to the floor from an attack of cerebral hemorrhage, and died very much as her brothers had died. "Aunt Eliza," as she was known to her nearest friends, and as she chose to be called, has lived evenly and quietly a life of love, walking in a pathway made as smooth for her as affection could suggest, in a thousand ways, and giving in return the unaffected devotion of an unselfish heart. This is the whole story of her life—she was gentle and good and considerate of others—she illustrated her Christian faith by fidelity to its teachings. Her's was a kindly soul, and her's a home-loving heart—home-loving in a marked degree.

Eliza Morrison Alexander was born January 11th, 1821; married to William J. Alexander November 14th, 1844, by Rev. John Kerr.

THE MORRISON FAMILY.

Eliza is the last of the family, and when she is laid to rest its annals will be closed. John Morrison was born in Ireland, near Londonderry, in 1789; emigrated to the United States in 1812, and settled in the neighborhood of Mingo creek church on February 29th, 1820. He was married to Margaret Porter, daughter of Mathew and Elizabeth Porter, residing on a farm about three miles from this town. About the time of his marriage he purchased a farm to which he and his young wife moved.

The farm was situated on the Monongahela river, $2\frac{1}{2}$ miles from Elizabeth, in Forward township. On this farm all their children, Eliza, Joseph, Porter, Andrew, Jane and James, were born. In the spring of 1837, having received a satisfactory offer, the farm was sold and he removed to this town with his family. He purchased the real estate for a home which now becomes the decedent estate of his oldest daughter, Mrs. Eliza Alexander. John Morrison died October 16th, 1837, leaving his widow with five children. She died September, 1882.

Hon. T. R. Hazzard.

Died on Monday morning, September 3, 1877, at his late residence in Monongahela City, Pa., Hon. T. R. Hazzard. He was taken ill while at church Sabbath evening. He died of disease of the heart. The deceased was born on the 25th day of October, 1814, at Oxford, in Shenango county, N. Y. He emigrated from Jamestown, N. Y., to Williamsport, now Monongahela City, Pa., in the year 1836. After teaching a classical academy for a time he returned to Allegheny College at Meadville, Pa., and completed his collegiate course. Among his classmates were ex-Governor F. H. Pierpoint, of West Virginia, and ex-Governor Reuben E. Fenton, of New York. He studied law with Judge Marvin, and on his return to Washington county, Pa., was admitted to the Washington bar at November term, 1840. At the time of his death he was the oldest member of the Washington bar, excepting A. W. Acheson. He was married by Rev. Dr. Ralston to Miss Harriet Hamilton, daughter of the late Joseph Hamilton. His wife and four sons survived him, but his wife passed away March 10,

1887, in her 64th year. His little Willie, Nettie and Martha had preceded them to the spirit land. He lived, with the exception of a few years, all the time in this city since his first arrival in Monongahela City, where he was the first academic teacher, and to him his adopted city owes the largest measure of that educational spirit which is so characteristic of its citizens. He was especially versed in polite and classical literature, and as a teacher he had few superiors. To him are indebted for their taste for learning many who are now active and prominent participants in the great field of literature and science. He was a finished musical scholar, and was for many years a leading musician in the Presbyterian church of Monongahela City. He was principal of the Bellevernon academy from 1842 to 1845.

Dr. J. S. Van Voorhis, of Bellevernon, Pa., in his centennial address in 1876, said: "This academy was started in the spring of 1842. T. R. Hazzard, Esq., an experienced teacher formerly of New York state, was the principal. The institution closed in 1845. At the institution, among Hazzard's students, were Chief Justice G. W. McElvain, of Ohio; Hon. D. M. Letterman, of Pennsylvania; Dr. J. H. Storer, of West Virginia; Dr. J. C. Cooper, of Philadelphia; James L. Finley, of Westmoreland county; Neal G. Blaine, brother of the distinguished prime minister of Maine; William Fuller, of Fayette county, and now a distinguished business man of Philadelphia; Dr. Robert Niccolls, of Bloomington, Ill.; William G. Johnson, of Pittsburgh; Major R. C. Walker, of Helena, Mont., and others whose names we cannot recall. Hon. T. R. Hazzard long resided in Monongahela City, where, as counsellor and citizen, he enjoyed the confidence of his fellow-men."

T. R. Hazzard, Esq., was for many years editor and proprietor of the *Republican*. In it he always fearlessly defended and advocated the right. He was a chaste, intelligent and forcible writer, expressing his ideas in short but well finished sentences. He was a great friend of literary institutions, and was always in the front when the good of literature was in question. He was devotedly wedded to his adopted city—ever ready to aid whatever might redound to its progress. He was a democrat when he came to Washington county, but in the hard cider and log cabin campaign of 1840, he was converted to the doctrines of the great whig party at a mass meeting at Wall's, near the old William Penn school, in Elizabeth (now Forward) township, at which meeting W. W. Irwin—Pony Irwin, and Frances C. Flannegan were the principal speakers. He held on to this faith until the dissolution of the party in 1852, when he became thoroughly engulfed in the unparalelled flood of knownothingism which swept all old political organizations out of existence. After that party had worked out its mission, he became identified in 1856 with the republican party and adhered to it to the day of his death.

His son, Chill W., is the accomplished editor of the Monongahela *Republican*, and as an editor he holds position in the highest rank. For over 30 years that paper has been under his management, and to its influence Monongahela City owes its greatest measure of progress. He passed through the late war with a conduct that not only elicited the commendation of his superior officers, but of the government, as shown in his being breveted major for meritorious service. He served as postmaster for 12 years in his native town, and retired from the position without a blemish on his integrity as a man or ability as an officer. His name has often been mentioned in connection with high civil office, but he has never been a candidate otherwise than in the Grand Army of the Republic, where he has held the highest position. Joseph DeVernon, another son of T. R. Hazzard, passed through the late war with the loss of an arm. He is now an orange grower in Forida.

Thomas L., the youngest son, is a prominent physician in Allegheny City, and a member of the Medical Faculty in the Western Pennsylvania Medical College, located in Pittsburgh. John J., the remainining son, was connected with the banking business for many years in Pittsburgh, but where he is now engaged in business we are unable to state.

T. R. Hazzard, Esq., was long a member of the Presbyterian Church, and cherished its precious doctrines as an epitome of that Holy Bible, of which he was a devoted student. He always took an active part in the prayer meetings and Sabbath school, of which he was many years Superintendent. On the last Sabbath of his life he attended church in the morning, sat at the communion table at noon, attended his Bible class in the afternoon, went to church in the evening, was taken ill while there; when the morning came he was in Heaven. The smile that graced his countenance at death tells the story "that he heard the music within," and as he passed from earth, heard the voice of the Savior saying, "Come ye blessed of my Father, inherit the kingdom prepared for you." He was buried in the beautiful cemetery overlooking his adopted city. The deceased was often called to stations of honor and trust by his fellow citizens, who never regretted their choice, for, when his work was done, he surrendered these trusts and received the plaudit "Well done thou good and faithful servant." Our friend has gone to the grave with true nobility stamped on his brow. He was a member of the Constitutional Convention of 1873-4, in the proceedings of which he took an active and prominent part. His speeches, delivered in his usual calm and dignified manner, grace many pages of its Journal, and to his learning and sound judgment we are indebted for many of the valuable ideas incorporated in the new Constitution. His domestic virtues cannot be more beautifully portrayed than by quoting his own words as uttered by himself on the occasion of the death of his colleague, Col. Wm. Hopkins, a member of the same convention: "He (Col. Hopkins) was an affectionate and true husband, a kind parent, a considerate neighbor, a faithful friend, a sound and wise counsellor, and an exemplary christian gentleman. He was charitable to the poor, and foremost in all benevolent and christian enterprises. By his death his immediate neighborhood will lose the inspiration of his public spirit, his interesting, highly respectable and intellectual family his kind words of wisdom and advice, and the rich gifts of his social nature."—J. S. V.

Socrates died like a hero, but friend Hazzard like a Christian. In the full consciousness of his condition, with his characteristic coolness, he declared "This is the end," and passed away, "like one who wraps the drapery of his couch about him, and lies down to pleasant dreams."

Dr. Wilson Dead.

Dr. William Lowrie Sparks Wilson, agent for the Pennsylvania railroad at Monongahela City, superintendent of the telegraph office and agent for Adams Express Company, died at his residence, Third ward, Monday morning, September 6, 1886, at 10:30.

Dr. Wilson was born at Merrittstown, Pa., June 26, 1834. He read medicine with his uncle, Dr. Wilson, an old practitioner then located at Beallsville, and entered on the practice of his profession at Youngstown, Ohio, removing after a year to East Liverpool, Ohio. He engaged there also in the drug business, but came to Monongahela City in 1859, where he opened a drug store and soon became widely known as a popular pharmacist.

He was married to Miss Allicia Mitchell, at Beallsville, December 27, 1853, by Rev. Hiram Winnett, and was blessed by twelve children, James Allen, George Reed, William Park, A. C. Sampson, Mary, John Robert, Ida King, Dora Bell, Emma, Nellie, Frank and Wannita.

The doctor was made superintendent of the first telegraph built to this place, and in 1863 sent over the wire the first message from O. C. House, now dead. When the P., V. & C. railroad was finished to make connections here in 1873 the doctor was made its agent, and sold the first ticket to Major P. A. Foster, now in Florida.

He was a notary public, and served four terms, declining reappointment. He served several terms as school director, two terms as burgess and served in the council of the old borough. He was connected with the Presbyterian church, and was two years superintendent of its Sabbath school. His death was the result of degeneration of the kidneys, which had crept upon him slowly for nearly a year. He died suddenly while sitting on the porch at his residence, having walked out there a few minutes before to "get air and be quiet," as he expressed it. He had taken an early Sunday morning walk to the station the day before.

Dr. Wilson was a man of kindly, cheerful manner. He had a flow of good humor. The best portion of his life was made up of those little nameless acts of kindness which every person whom he met will now recall. A cheerful salute sprang to his lips when he met you, and in his cordial greeting there was honest warmth. Monongahela City had few men more respected, more loved, more useful; none more obliging, and no one will be more universally missed. Rest in peace, good doctor —

——Your friends will feel the woe,
Your's be the touch of joy.

Dr. R. F. Biddle.

Dr. Robert F. Biddle, a well-known educated physician hailing from Washington, Pa., where he obtained a collegiate education and where he studied medicine under Dr. Stevens, commenced practice in Monongahela City. He was a man fully six feet high, of rather heavy build, slow in motion when taking a walk or mounted on horseback he leaned forward. He appeared mostly to be absorbed in thought, or deep study. Large eyes and a prominent forehead. He was a man of robust constitution, capable of great endurance, and of strong, vigorous intellectual qualities. He very soon obtained the largest practice of any physician ever known in the Monongahela Valley, which he maintained until his health and physical strength gave way. His charges for medical services were notedly moderate, and it was said by persons who knew that he was so negligent in making entry of his visits to sick chambers that one-third or more of such visits were never charged at all. Nor was the waste of the doctor's hard earning confined to his very low bills, or negligence of making entry, but, added to this, he was wonderfully loath to make out bills against any parties who were ready and willing to pay such bills when rendered. One man who, it is said, was indebted to the doctor for medical service and who had demanded of him right along for three years his account without success, brought him for settlement before one of our old-time 'squires. On hearing day the doctor declared that he didn't owe the plaintiff one cent. "All right," said the plaintiff, "my object in bringing the suit against you is to put matters in such a shape that I will know how much I owe you.". The doctor's bill was at once rendered and payment made, and both left the 'squire's office well pleased that things were no worse.

The popularity of Doctor Biddle as a man and a physician became so great that he was kept on the go mostly day and night, for many years. One of the Doctor's two favorite horses called Ned had considerable sagacity—became so well acquainted with the roads and by-roads and lanes of the country for eight or ten miles round and many stopping places, knowing the Doctor's habits of occasionally taking a snooze in the late hours of night whilst astraddle of his back, was careful as to how he carried the Doctor when in such condition. One night at a late hour having alighted at a sick house on Mingo creek, after seeing his patient he remounted Ned and in a few moments afterwards fell asleep. The next stopping place, as the faithful horse well knew, would be at Valley Inn on the Pike, to which place the animal gently posted its way up a long hill and from the creek. In coming to the front of the residence where the sick lay, the sagacious horse made a halt without the pulling of the rein, and loudly neighed with its head towards the patient's house, as much as to say to the inmates, "here we are, but the Boss you wish to see is enjoying a snooze upon my back." The weary Doctor was soon waked up and dismounted and the sick seen to. The Doctor was opposed to all kinds of display and pomposity.

Plain in his dress, economical in his expenditures, a man of excellently well-balanced mind. Shrewd and quick in detecting the plots or connivances of designing men. He was strictly conscientious and honest in all his dealings. He took the grounds that every person should render a full consideration for the amount of bill charged—a man of sterling integrity, of mild temper and disposition. He would not jangle or quarrel with persons disposed to be abusive, but would get away. A profound thinker, he wrote several sensible articles for the local press upon the transpiring matters of his day.

Although no office seeker he took a deep interest in the affairs of the country. When he took the stump, as betimes he did in the most exciting political campaigns, his speeches were delivered with force and telling effect. He was a warm, reliable friend and good neighbor, fond of a cigar, also of hearing or telling of a joke having a good point, which, without fail, would extort from him a hearty laugh. He was a close observer of the sagacity and acuteness of some of the animals; was disposed to think that such of them thus acute were endowed with reasoning powers. Sometimes in the Doctor's leisure moments he would close his eyes and take a hearty laugh preparatory to relating a good one in regard to some funny occurrence which had come under his notice, which he could always tell with such a grace as to bring a spontaneous burst of laughter from the whole company present.

It was a matter of wonder to many why a man possessing such an excellent mind and good sense as Dr. Biddle would be so careless in keeping his accounts, and manifest so much dislike to rendering bills for service. For some 35 years he practiced early and late through every part of this town, and over the hills and dales of the surrounding country for eight or ten miles distant, for which arduous labors he nor his intelligent widow has never been half paid.

Worn out in the service of the people, he died May 12th, 1864, at his home in Monongahela City, and sweetly slumbers in the Monongahela cemetery, where a snug monument is erected to his memory.

MOSES SCOTT.

Mrs. M. J. Biddle.

Died, at her home on Fourth street, in Monongahela, Monday, July 17, 1893, Mrs. Mary Jane Cooper, relict of the late Dr. R. F. Biddle, to whom she was married in 1848. At her death she was perhaps the oldest continuous resident of this city. She was born October 10, 1818, in this town, the daughter of John and Charity Cooper. Cooper removed from West Newton in 1810. His wife's maiden name was Charity Sparks, daughter of Colonel Richard Sparks, who was a colonel in the United States army at the close of the revolution, and who owned in early days the well-known Garret Wall farm in Forward township, in Allegheny county, Pa., on which the mother of our deceased friend was born.

John Cooper and Charity Sparks were married March 2, 1809, and Cooper died March 1, 1820, leaving a widow and four sons, Richard Sparks, Hezekiah D., John S. and Robert F., and one daughter, Mary Jane, the deceased.

With the decease of Jane, John Cooper's children have all passed away. Mrs. Cooper, mother of Jane, married John Shouse, March 28, 1828, who died at the Valley Inn, now Baidland, August 13, 1834, leaving one son, W. H. Shouse, now of Cincinnati, Ohio, and one daughter, Fannie C., wife of Rev. J. P. Fulton, of Harper, Kas. When the father of Mrs. Jane Biddle settled in this city, then called Williamsport, there were only four resident Presbyterians in the place, namely: John Lamb and wife, and James Gordon and wife, the arrival of John Cooper and wife making up the faithful eight who, with James Hair and wife, formed the nucleus of that blessed church which has stood for a century gathering in the generations of the past. In this church Jane was born and lived all of her years, doing service in untold ways and means to aid the cause of her Master.

She was intellectually bright, which added much to her usefulness as a member of the church and of society in general. Many of the older citizens will call to mind her success as a teacher in private and public schools.

When the deceased joined the Presbyterian church the congregation worshipped in the brick church building on the hill, where now only can be seen the remains of the resting places of those who once made up the number who listened to the instructions of the good old minister, Dr. Ralston, and the younger Chambers and Porter. Mrs. Biddle's associates in early church work have about all gone home.

Her race was long, but she reached the goal and won the prize of eternal life, through Jesus Christ.

SAMUEL POLLOCK DEAD.

Samuel Pollock, of Pollock's hill, an old resident of Union township, died Tuesday, July 18th, 1893, of heart failure, in his 77th year. Interment at Mingo.

J. SUTTON WALL.

Mr. Wall's ancestry dates from an early period in the history of America; he being a lineal descendant of Walter Wall, who emigrated from England to St. Christopher's Island (one of the British West Indies) in 1635. (Vide N. E. Geneological and Antiquarian Register for 1860, p. 355). From thence he removed to Gravesend, Long Island, in 1640; and subsequently became an influential member of the so called English Colony, which the celebrated Lady Moody and her followers joined at that place in 1643. She having left Salem, Massachusetts, to escape the religious persecutions of the rulers at that place. Walter Wall owned considerable quantities of land in and about Gravesend, (Vide Thompson's History of Long Island, Vol. II, p. 177, &c.) but owing to the unsettled condition of governmental affairs in that region, he, together with a number of intimate friends and their families, removed to East Jersey (now New Jersey) in 1657, where they purchased lands from the Indians, and made a more permanent settlement. He purchased a large tract of land in the neighborhood of Middletown, where he resided during the remaining portion of his life. This is where his grandson, General Garret D. Wall, was born, who subsequently took a prominent part in the public affairs of New Jersey, and was one of its representatives in the United States Senate for a number of years. (Vide Whitehead's History of Eminent Jerseymen.) The family remained together in this region during the succeeding hundred years, and mainly throughout the Colonial troubles that led to, and included the separation from the mother country. The Wall family were zealous supporters of the Revolutionary cause, giving their services and lives freely in the behalf of the new country, as many of them more recently have done.

James Wall (great grandfather of the subject of this sketch), together with his brother Walter, in 1766, emigrated from "Jersey" to the "Forks of Yough," as they then called it, afterwards known as the "Jersey Settlement," now comprised within the portion of the county of Allegheny lying between the Youghiogheny and Monongahela rivers, in Pennsylvania, where they settled and subsequently purchased large tracts of land from the state. James Wall took a leading part in the public affairs of the new settlement during his life. (Vide. Crumrine's History of Washington county and other local histories of the region).

Garrett Wall (son of James and grandfather of J. Sutton Wall) married a daughter of Colonel Richard Sparks, of the United States army. He served in the war of 1812-13, as quartermaster of Colonel Ferree's regiment of volunteer infantry in the campaign of the northwest, under General William Henry Harrison.

Colonel Richard Sparks served as captain in Clark's battalion under Major General St. Clair, in 1791, and in 1792 was appointed captain third United States infantry, and subsequently promoted to colonel of the second United States infantry. He was also engaged in the campaign of the northwest under General Harrison, and remained in the army until the time of his death in 1815 (see Records of War Department), at Port Gibson, Mississippi.

Colonel Richard Sparks had five children, all daughters, viz:

Mary, married to Garret Wall; Catherine, married to Richard McClure, of Clermont county, Ohio; Charity, married to John Cooper, he died and she afterward married John Shouse; Elizabeth, married to —— Braezeale; and Elenor, who married John Printy, of Clermont county, Ohio.

Captain Brisben Wall, late deceased, (son of Garret and father of J. Sutton Wall) a civil engineer by profession, and widely known for his ability in that profession throughout south-western Pennsylvania, entered the Union service, in the war of the late Rebellion, as First Lieutenant in Company D, 79th Regiment P. V., September 21st, 1861, and served under General James S. Negley, in the Army of the Tennessee, until disabled for further duty during the following year.

Major William Wall, (brother of Captain Brisben Wall) graduated from the U. S. Military Academy in 1832, commissioned Second Lieutenant Third U. S. Artillery, and subsequently Captain and Assistant Quartermaster. He served in the campaign against the Seminole Indians in Florida, and continued in the army until the time of his death at Pueblo, August 13, 1847, while engaged in the war with Mexico.

J. Sutton Wall (son of Captain Brisben Wall) was born March 21, 1849, at the old "homestead," in the "Jersey Settlement." He received early training in mathematics and the natural sciences under the tutelage of his father, and in the public and private schools of that region. His rapid progress in these studies enabled him to commence the practice of civil engineering at the early age of eighteen, and he has continued in the active practice of the various branches of that profession to the present time. He was elected city engineer of Monongahela City in 1871, and held that office almost continuously from that time to June, 1887, when he resigned to accept the office of chief draftsman in the Department of Internal Affairs of Pennsylvania, under the administration of Colonel Thomas J. Stewart, which he still retains.

He served as a mining engineer on the board of examiners for the bituminous coal regions of Pennsylvania, under the administrations of Governors Hartranft and Hoyt, from 1877 to 1885, and was reappointed to the same office by Governor Beaver.

He was appointed in 1881 to make a special survey and report on the coal mines and mining operations of the Monongahela Valley and the Pittsburgh coal regions, under the auspices of the Second Geological Survey of Pennsylvania, which work has been published as Volume K 4, of the reports of that survey.

He has been engaged on numerous other public and private surveys where considerable professional skill and knowledge were essential to a proper execution of the work.

ONE HUNDRED YEARS.

Mrs. Nancy Quinby Larwill celebrated her 100th birthday at her home in Wooster, Ohio, May 9th, 1893. She was born in Fallowfield township, or what may now be Carroll, Washington county, Pa., three miles from Parkison's Ferry, which she tells me is as familiar to her as Wooster. Her father, Ephraim Quinby, Jr., married Miss Ammie Blackamore, in Brownsville, Pa., and three children were born when he founded the colony in Warren, Ohio. Their names were Nancy, Samuel and William. The latter has often been heard to say that his mother rode on horseback behind him when he came to Ohio. As he was a babe six months old, it is altogether probable he was right. Samuel and William are deceased, as are Elizabeth Heaton, Arabrilla Potter, Mary Girling Spelman, Charles, James and Ephraim III. Warren and George Quinby live at Wooster—Warren at the age of 85 and George at 78. The family are and ever have been singularly and happily united, and maintain the fondest affection for each other. Ephraim Quinby's father, Ephraim, never emigrated. Ephraim, Jr., came west with his uncle, Joseph Hall, and family while a lad. His brother, Samuel Quinby, lived at the Horse Shoe Bend, on the farm now owned by James Sampson, and did not leave Washington county until some years after Ephraim, Jr., formed his settlement of twenty families at Warren, Ohio, in 1799, nearly all former residents of Washington county, Pa. Joseph H. Larwill, a surveyor, was employed by Col. Beaver to draught plans and survey his lands. Beaver was the starting point of emigration either by land or water. My father remembers no sugar, tea, coffee or calico could be had on the western reserve nearer than Beaver, and the produce was there exchanged for these then, as now, necessaries of life.

May 22nd, 1817, Joseph H. Larwill and Nancy Quinby were married at her father's, in Warren, by Rev. Adamson Bentley. The home overlooks the town, on the banks of Mahoning river, and is known as Quinby hill—a beautiful place—now occupied by George B. Quinby, grandson of Ephraim, Jr. The wedding party went to Wooster on horseback, and on July 4th, 1817, Mrs. Larwill cooked her first dinner in a house which stood where now stands the Frick Memorial Block.

Early in life Mrs. Larwill united with the Baptist church of Warren, and has been a member of the Bethany Baptist Congregation of Wooster since it was organized, and the Quinby family in Warren has always been among the staunch supporters of the Baptist faith. Samuel Quinby, Sarah Quinby Reeves, and Mr. and Mrs. James Campbell, were the only remaining members to charter a new church when Adamson Bentley and his whole church membership were converted to Disciple belief by the eloquent evangelistic sermons of Alexander Campbell, in 1832. It was then the Quinby element held to the Baptist faith, and began anew to build the present outlook for Baptists in Warren.

Descended from Quaker stock, born and reared on the neutral grounds of the revolutionary days, faith in God, and great goodness of heart, had secured to them the confidence and love of their fellow men.

Joseph H. Larwill honored his employer, Mr. Beaver, by naming the streets in Wooster, Beaver, Henry for the son, Martilla for the daughter, and Larwill street for his own family, where he resided the greater part of his life, dying November 20th, 1867. No children blessed the union, but nieces and nephews call them blessed. One, Mrs. Nannie Laubach, of Pittsburgh, was presented by her centenarian aunt with the gold watch and chain she had carried, which had been purchased for her by Mr. Larwill in Philadelphia, in 1857.

A hundred rosebuds arranged in an immense bowl, from her two brothers and the nieces and nephews, a hundred navel oranges, from a niece, Mrs. Estep, of San Francisco; a book entitled "100 Birthdays," from nieces in Washington, D. C., and many evidences of love and affection were noticed. The room, which is in her own home, and where she has lived since her husband's death, to be near her brothers, was most handsomely decorated with flowers in profusion from loving friends. On waking in the morning she remarked, "If Mr. Larwill were living, we'd have a feast to-day;" and though Mr. Larwill looked down from his portrait, draped in flowers and evergreens, there was a feast of reason and a flow of soul, for she was able to receive over a hundred friends, who each said a few congratulory sentences, to all of whom she replied fittingly and presented them with a card on which were printed these lines, arranged and suggested by a deceased but loving niece, Lizzie Quinby Stiles :

> A hundred years, a hundred years,
>   To walk the grand old earth,
> And see a nation rise and grow
>   To greatness from its birth.
>
> A hundred years, a hundred years,
>   To drink the air and light ;
> But happy when the shadows fall
>   To bid the world " good-night."
>
> A hundred years of tranquil life,
>   And nearer God each day ;
> The years, like roses, when they die,
>   In fragrance pass away.

That any one could enjoy life at 100 years is evidence of care for youth and latter-day attendance most complete. Mrs. Kate Potter Petit, a niece, has guarded her the past seven years from every possible care, and Frederika Link has performed for thirty-eight years a loving service in the Larwill household. Mrs. Larwill cannot be said to suffer from the weight of years. Her hearing has been defective, but time has not dimmed her sight or repressed for her the voice of friends. She sits up all day and observes everything about her, and in the funeral of her life-long friend, Rev. Dr. David Kammerer, which took place the same day, was heard to express sorrow and sympathy. She made inquiry for absent friends and sent messages of love to those who feared to weary her by coming. En route I made the acquaintance of Mrs. Parkison, of Beaver Falls, who informed me her husband is a descendant of Joseph Parkison, and on telling Mrs. Larwill of the incident, she replied: "I was seven years old when my father moved to Warren; I rode on horseback, and had often in his company been to Parkison's Ferry, where Mr. Parkison had his three mills, and was entertained by Mrs. Parkison while the grist was being ground." She particularly remembers the flowers and fruit, and was impressed that the surroundings were superior.

Ephraim and Samuel Quinby were the only sons of Ephraim Quinby, Sr., and Elizabeth Hall Halliday, who emigrated to Washington county and are the progenitors of the name in this vicinity, excepting William H. Quinby, of Cleveland, who is descended from Moses Quinby, a brother of Ephraim, Sr., and William E. Quinby, president of the Detroit Free Press company, of Detroit, whose father emigrated to that city from Brewer, Me., in 1845, and can in all probability trace his lineage to previous Huguenot emigration. In connection with this sketch it is of interest to note that Mrs. Teresa Quinby Carver, of Sharon, Pa., is a daughter of Samuel Quinby, and for a number of years made her home with her aunt, Mrs. Larwill, in Wooster. Her father, Samuel Quinby, was a soldier in the revolutionary war and was honored by military obsequies September 10, 1840. She is one of the exceptional daughters of the revolution, in that she is entitled to a pension, among but few others left in the Union, and enjoys length of days in the home of her youth amid pleasant associations.

E. R. BEEBE.

BELLEVERNON.

The territory embraced within the limits of the borough of Bellevernon was prior to the formation of Fayette county, in 1783, a part of Rostraver township, Westmoreland county, Pa. Rostraver at that time was bounded by the Youghiogheny and Monongahela rivers, and a straight line from the mouth of Big Redstone, on the Monongahela, to a point on the Youghiogheny, opposite the mouth of Jacobs creek. When Fayette was formed the line was changed so as to run due east and west from Jacob's creek to the mouth of what is now known as Speer's run, on the Monongahela. This line was so changed by the Act of Assembly of April 15, 1863, as to run from the mouth of Speer's run to the middle of the stone bridge, thence in a straight line to the corner of the school house lot now owned by R. J. Linton, along the upper side of said lot to Long Alley, thence to the county line, and thence along said line east to to the Youghiogheny river. This line as it runs from the stone bridge is better defined by making the next point at the corner of State Road street and Short street and thence along said Short street to Long alley. At the first court held in Fayette county December, 1783, the county was divided into twelve (12) townships, one of which was named Washington, in honor of General Washington. The township of Washington originally embraced a part of Perry and all of Jefferson township. The primitive settlers in the vicinity of what is now called Bellevernon first voted July 8, 1776, at Spark's Fort, near Burns' Ford, on the Youghiogheny. By the Act of March 3, 1790, Fayette county was divided into four election districts. The citizens of Washington township voted at Fort Burd, now Brownsville. After some time the place of holding the elections was removed to the Red Lion, kept by Thomas Patterson. When Jefferson township was formed in 1840, the election place was removed to Cookstown, by consent of the voters, without the usual process of law.

The site on which the town of Bellevernon is built lies within 40 degrees 35 minutes north latitude and 3 degrees of longitude west of Washington, D. C.—two hundred feet below Uniontown, seven hundred and sixty feet above the sea, one hundred and seventy-two feet above Lake Erie. In the Washington, Pa., *Reporter* of July 12, 1812, was first advertised the sale of lots in Bellevernon, by Noah Speers, the proprietor of the ground, and founder of the town. According to this notice the lots were laid out 75 by 100 feet, and main streets 50 and cross streets 40 feet wide. There seems to have been no sales under this notice. Subsequently, for some cause, the size of the lots was reduced to 60 by 100 feet. The first sale was made by public outcry on the 18th day of April, 1814. A premium of $10 was offered for the first house erected, which prize was won by Thomas Ward, who built the house that until recently stood on the corner of Main and Second streets. During 1890 this house was moved to the corner of Second and Solomon streets to give place to the stately building of Howard McClure, erected in the autumn of 1890.

The next house erected was the Hornbeck tavern, which stood for many years on the corner of Main street and Cherry alley, which gave place to the large building erected by Amon Bronson and sold by him to J. S. Henry, Sr., and now, 1893, occupied by J. S. Henry, Jr., as a storeroom.

The title to the land on which Noah Speers founded Bellevernon was possessed by him through his father, Henry Speers the older, who obtained it by purchase from John Cockey Owens, to whom the state granted a patent bearing date of May 17, 1791. The ground originally was thickly grown with sugar trees. That part of the ground between First street and Speer's Run was not in the original plot of the town. This tract included the ferry and was called "Summer House" in the patent granted Regina Speers, widow of Henry Speers the older, and to Benjamin Frye, a son-in-law, both of whom were the executors of the estate of Henry Speers. The patent was dated June 1, 1784, and included the ferry and three acres of ground. This tract was conveyed to Noah Speers by Regina Speers, acting executrix of Henry Speers, by deed bearing date of January 16, 1797. Noah Speers, by will dated June 2, 1832, conveyed it to Solomon Speers. Noah Speers between 1816 and 1820 erected the brick house still standing, and now, 1893, occupied as a hotel and ticket office for the Bellevernon and & McKeesport Railroad Company. In the corner room of this house was kept the first store in the town, although David Furnier had a store below Speer's run as early as 1790. The late Uriah Ward often said "that the first money he ever earned was for hauling water and carrying brick for that house, at six cents per day and boarded himself." The oldest house in the town is the one on Main street below Fourth, owned and occupied so long by the late Mrs. Mary Corwin. It was the original house erected by Michael Springer, on the well known Springer farm in Rostraver township, Westmoreland county, and now owned by heirs of James Ward and the heirs of James H. Springer, deceased. It was removed to its site in the summer of 1815, and was from that date to the day of her death occupied by Mrs. Corwin.

The first attempt to incorporate the town was made in 1850. On the petition of sundry citizens, Hon. J. D. Leet, a member of the House of Representatives from Washington county, read a bill in place March 19, 1850, to incorporate Bellevernon, in Fayette county, into a borough. It was reported favorably from the committee on corporations promptly, and passed through both houses and signed by Governor W. F. Johnson. The proposed borough was to be bounded and limited as follows: Beginning at the mouth of Speer's Run, following the county line to the coal pit on the State road in front of the present dwelling owned by John Gray in North Bellevernon; thence in a direct line to Gould's Run; thence to the graveyard, including it; thence to the river, including the house of J. B. Gould; thence following the river to the place of beginning. The bill was bitterly opposed by Solomon Speers, through his brother-in-law, R. C. Walker, a member from Allegheny county, but now a major on the retired list in the United States army, residing in Helena, Mont. Mr. Leet succeeded.

By tradition more than otherwise, the county line was supposed in its course east to take in the mouth of the old coal pit in front of the lot now owned by John Gray on State street in North Bellevernon. After the building of the brick school house, which stood on the lot owned by R. J. Linton, on the corner of State and Short streets, it became a question to determine the exact and true location of the county line. The primitive act of incorporation failed to go into operation. It was passed in what was called an "omnibus" bill, and in order for any one of the different acts to have effect of law the enrollment tax had to be paid on all the "omnibus" bill contained. Through neglect and indifference on the part of the friends of the Bellevernon act the tax was not paid, and at the next session that part of the "omnibus" bill was repealed, and Bellevernon remained a part of Washington township.

The voters in the town becoming wearied at the inconvenience of traveling to Cookstown, determined to have the privilege of casting their votes at home, petitioned the Legislature, during the session of 1854, to have created a new election district. Hon. W. Y. Roberts took charge of the bill, which he speedily had passed through both houses and approved by Governor Bigler April 13th, 1854. The new district was bounded as follows, viz: Beginning at the mouth of Speer's run, running the county line three-quarters of a mile, thence in a straight line to the dwelling house of Joseph Springer, including the same, thence to the upper coal way of Samuel Clark, thence by the river to the place of beginning. The Act named Adolph Eberhart as Judge, A. P. Frye and Thomas Taggart as Inspectors, to hold the first election, which was held on the second Tuesday of October, 1854. Solomon Speers and John B. Gould were appointed Clerks. Gould's school house was fixed by the Act as the place for holding the elections. The prospective increase of the town and the building of the new school house in 1857 created a new interest in determining the exact locality of the dividing line between Westmoreland and Fayette counties, as it related to the town. To settle the question an Act of Assembly was obtained, approved March 30th, 1860, creating a commission "to survey, ascertain and establish" this line between Jacob's creek and Speer's run. The commission under this Act were E. F. Housman, of Westmoreland county; J. S. Van Voorhis and H. F. Blythe, of Fayette. They appointed the late Samuel C. Griffith surveyor, and Alexander Wilson and Jacob B. Speers ax men. They run over the line three different times in order to have it correct beyond doubt. The true line was due east and west between the above named points. It was thus discovered that the line at Bellevernon end put the dwellings now occupied by Mrs. Jane Beazell, the dwellings owned now by L. J. Jeffries, Esq., part of the property of Henry Coughenour, and that owned by the heirs of William Jacobs, and school house lot now owned by R. J. Linton, into Westmoreland county. During the investigation of this line, Hon. David Kaine, now deceased, found in the prothonotary's office in Uniontown the original draught of the county line as run at the formation of the county. In running the first line it was commenced at Jacob's creek, and when the surveyor's corps arrived at the Monongahela river the terminus was 30 rods below the mouth of Speer's run, with $\frac{1}{4}$ degree north of a due east and west line. In a foot note the surveyor remarked that if any one wants to know the true line it is a due east and west line, $\frac{1}{4}$ degree above this line. As that was the only line surveyed, it was held by tradition to be the true line, and hence an error was continually being made until the commission of March 30th, 1860, fixed, by actual survey, the true location of the line which was sanctioned by the courts of both counties.

The discovery of the true county line had more to do than anything else toward the incorporation of the Borough by the Act of April 15th, 1863.

The town of Bellevernon was formed into a borough with territory taken partly from Fayette and partly from Westmoreland counties. By this act the place of holding the elections was changed from Gould's school house to the public school house on the hill, within the borough limits. The voters in the remaining part of the old district were replaced into Washington township. The last election in the old district was held March 20, 1863, the election officers being: Judge, J. M. Springer; inspectors, O. D. Johnson and John Reeves. At this election James Corwin was elected judge and C. Amalong and Jacob Brendel inspectors. By the act of incorporation the officers elected last in the old district were authorized to hold the first election in the new borough. The act fixed May 16, 1863, as the time for the first election. The board consisted of James Corwin, judge; Jacob Brindel and S. W. Watson, inspectors. Mr. C. Amalong having failed to qualify, S. W. Watson was appointed in his place. This election perfected the organization. By an act of Assembly approved March 31, 1864, the borough was placed for all purposes under the jurisdictiom of Fayette county, and the proceedings of the burgess and town council were legalized. This act of Assembly was supposed to be necessary, owing to a difference of opinion in the construction of the act of incorporation. By an act of the Legislature approved March 1, 1866, the citizens of the borough were authorized to elect six councilmen—two for one year, two for two years and two for three years. During the session of 1868 the Legislature passed an act prohibiting the sale of intoxicating liquors as a beverage within the borough. As far as we are advised, this was the last act relating to the borough, except the one giving power to the school board to issue bonds bearing interest not exceeding eight per cent. The churches, cemetery association, loan associations and Odd Fellows' Hall association obtained their charters through the courts. At the first election, held May 16, 1863, Amon Bronson was elected burgess; J. R. Powell, Bazil Brightwell, Wm. Sutton, Ed. Martin, James Corwin and Ed. Jordan, councilmen; James French, John W. Wright, Robert Boyle, J. S. Van Voorhis, N. Q. Speer and James Davidson, school directors; auditors, Robert Boyle, J. M. Springer and O. D. Johnson; John Watson, Justice of the Peace; assessor, J. W. Lindsay. J. M. Springer, under a commission dated April 10th, 1860, for Washington township, served as first Justice of the Peace in the borough. He was elected in the borough in 1865, and at this time (1893) he is serving his eighth term of five years.

The name of Speers has figured in the history of this town in a variety of transactions for over a century. Appearing at first from German descent the name remains among us to-day. Henry Speers, the older, settled about the year 1770 on what is now known as the Gibsonton farm, and to insure protection from the Indians he located his domicil near the fort, which stood just befow Gibsonton Mills of this day. A more extensive notice of the family will be given in another place in this work. He was not only a large landholder, but an extensive slaveholder. He was undoubtedly among the first business men on the river in this region. The Coopers and Fryes on the opposite side of the river began their settlements cotemporary with Speers, and in their after history formed important alliances. From what we can learn the ferry had its primitive existence just below the mouth of Maple creek, under the joint ownership of Speers and the older Cooper. The machinery of the ferry consisted in a primitive canoe dugout, somewhat after the fashion of an old timed horse trough. Horses had either to ford the river when the water was low enough, or swim in higher stages of the river. The ferry now existing was established by Henry Speers the older, and the title vested subsequent to his death for that part of the ferry on the Belle Vernon side of the river, but the Washington county side was patented to his son, Henry Speers, January 12th, 1789, on a survey entered by

Henry Reef, May 23rd, 1769, and conveyed to Henry Speers by deed dated September 14th, 1784. The ferry was carried on by means of the primitive canoe, and in progress of time the flat was invented, and its power to cross the river consisted in the broad-bladed oars and pike pole, so long used in after years to push the keel boat. The rope ferry is a modern invention. Of the earlier persons who plied the oar we have no information.

Noah Speers, by will dated June 2, 1832, conveyed the Fayette side of the ferry to his son Solomon, who sold it to Louis M. Speers, the date thereof we do not know. At the death of Henry Speers, the younger, his son Apollos, came into possession of the Washington side of the ferry, and at his death his son Noah inherited it. The ferry is now working under a charter granted April 1, 1870, by the Legislature to Noah, L. M. Speers and W. F. Speers. At the assignee's sale in bankruptcy of L. M. and W. F. Speers, about 1880, Noah Speers became sole owner of the ferry, and is at this date (1893) its owner. At a very early date a man named Pennywell lived in a house where now stands the Presbyterian church. He carried on shoemaking, and his wife attended the ferry. In those days shoemaking was a laborious and not very profitable trade. He had to make his own wax, the thread, the pegs, and the polish was a compound of soot and white of an egg. The paste was home-made and kept for use in an ox horn hung on a peg in the wall by means of a tow string. The shoes were generally made of what was then called upper leather, with calf-skin strings. The shoes intended to be worn with buckles and breeches were not often made by common shoemakers. The leather was furnished by those wanting shoes. Andrew Brice was another ferryman, and also a shoemaker. A mar named Joseph Cloud was also a ferryman. He was jack of al trades, but seemed especially inclined to be a stone-mason an(blacksmith. He built the huge chimney in the late Aunt Poll Corwin's house in 1815, which still stands as a monument to hi want of skill. Cloud lived and had his shop on the river ban near the ferry. The land on which it stood has long since been washed away by the river. Four generations of ferrymen have plied the oar, and, excepting the rope, it remains the same as one hundred years ago. For a century this ferry was sought by the drovers in their route from West to East, and as ferrymen the names of Speers, Ward, Cooper, Wells, French, Husher, *et id. omne genus*, were household gods from the Mississippi to the Delaware. The "Swan," built in 1845 at Fredericktown for Apollos Speers, by Charles Bowers, was the first horse-boat at this ferry. The idea of a horse-boat was suggested by the completion of dam No. 4 of the Slackwater. Charles Bowers was an uncle of Morgan Bowers, for many years a resident of Bellevernon. Capt. S. C. Speers recollects very well the fact of his going on horseback with his father, Apollos Speers, to bring down the boat. The horses on which they rode were placed on the boat and worked it down to the Bellevernon landing, were it was greeted with applause by the citizens. Samuel St. Clair was the pilot on her trip down.

The Belle Vernon horse boat was built by L. M. Speers at the boat yard then carried on at the mouth of Third street, Belle Vernon, in 1852 or 53. The mouse colored Davy and sorrel Barney long did duty on this boat, and won quite a reputation among the stockmen of the west. The horse boat gave way to the steam ferry boat, "Polly South," built at Belle Vernon in 1858. This boat was run in charge of Captain James French as master, and his sons, Willie and Sylvester, as engineers. The boat becoming more or less unfit for duty and always an expense to the owner, gave way to the rope ferry. The engine is now doing duty for the Speer White Sand Company at the "Juniata works," Mapleton, on the Pennsylvania railroad, 159 miles east of Pittsburgh. After the dismantling of the Polly South the engine also did service in digging the old oil well up Speers run. W. A. Coughenour, now a wealthy citizen of Idaho, was the engineer. The well was originally drilled to a depth of 250 feet by hand in the days of Noah Speers, the older, in search of salt water, which in those days was a great desideratum. In the latter drilling, oil was the object, but at 1010 feet the effort was abandoned, having not found any oil, though plenty of salt water and some gas. Now (1893) this old well is found to be in the midst of a great gas field.

The store given Solomon Speers by his father in the brick house was no doubt the first one within the limits of the town, but not in the vicinity. The first store in the "Forks" was the one Col. Edward Cook brought with him from eastern Pennsylvania about 1768, and located it in his primitive cabin, near the present spring house of his great grandson, Joseph Cook, in Rehoboth Valley. The next store was in the old log house which stood on the river bank where now is the saw and planing mill of the Jones'. This house and store, with the "barter" mill, of which we will speak hereafter, was conveyed to David Furnier by Elliot & Williams about the year 1790. This was the first store about Bellevernon. Storekeepers then as now were often obliged to trust their neighbors for goods; but it was the rule in old times that if a bill was not paid at the promised time, the case was at once made known and the debtor was drummed out of the neighborhood as an unworthy citizen. The second store in Bellevernon was kept by William Reeves, whose wife was a daughter of Noah Speers. He occupied at first the room in what is now known as the Sutton house, on Water street, and afterwards moved it to the corner of Water street and Cherry alley, long known as the Methodist church; it now stands in the rear of the former brick store of R. C. Schmertz & Co., on the corner of Cherry alley and Long alley. Barnes Reeves had a store in the house recently owned by Dr. I. C. Hazlett, corner of Main street and Cherry alley. Some time between 1835 and 1837, Barnes Reeves erected the brick building on the corner of Main and Second streets, now owned by L. Z. Birmingham, and occupied as a hotel and Brown's pharmacy. The late Thomas Taggart did the carpenter work. Into the corner room Barnes Reeves moved his store, and carried on business there until he sold out to his brother-in-law, Rev. John Strickler, who had married Rhoda, daughter of Manassah Reeves. Mr. Strickler sold to John S. Markle, now a resident of Monongahela City, but in what year we are not informed, it was, however, in the early forties. How long he did business on this corner we do not know; but when the writer, in May, 1847, settled in the town, the store room was vacant. On the building of the glass works, of which we have said more in another place, William Eberheart had a store in the house on the corner of Main street and Cherry alley, known then as the Hornbeck tavern, but the corner is now occupied by J. S. Henry, Jr., with a store. The tavern house was moved to the lot below, and is now (1893) owned and occupied by A. L. Brown, the druggist, as a residence. Some years afterwards Eberheart moved his store to the corner now owned by R. C. Schmertz & Co., and occupied as dwellings.

Ford McKee in 1847 had a store in the basement of the house now owned and occupied by Andrew Guiler, on the lower end of Main street.

Boat building was an early element in the business and industry of the town. Solomon Speers and Morgan Gaskill were the first boat-builders. The original yard was in front of the present residence of Lario, on Water street. The wide-spreading elm which passed into the river during the flood of 1844, the stump of which can yet be seen, afforded shade for lookers-on in the yard. The yard was started a short time prior to 1830. The whip-saw and the old water mill across the creek, relics of which are still visible, furnished the sawing of this timber. The long timber was all sawed by the whip-saw. The log was placed on a kind of a platform, and under the log one man worked the lower end of the saw and another did the same duty on the top. The whip-saw was peculiarly constructed, and would be a curiosity nowadays. It had a handle at each end, with the one at the lower end moveable, so that it could be taken off at will. As far as we can ascertain, the first boat built was a kind of horse-boat for a party down the river. To launch the boat it was necessary to haul it to the wharf at the ferry. Keelboats and steamboats were the product generally of this yard. The "Lancaster" was the first steamboat hull built at this yard. The hull was contracted for Captain James May, and was intended for the New Orleans trade. The hull was contracted for by Samuel Walker, of Elizabeth, who sub-let it to Speers & Gaskill. The late General Isaac Hammett, whose remains lay in the Bellevernon cemetery, drafted the boat on paper in Elizabeth and laid it down on the floor of the old stable which stood until recently on the rear of the lot of the residence of Lario, on Water street. It is said that keelboats had been built in this yard as early as 1822 by William Reeves. The date of the change of the boatyard to the mouth of Third street is contemporary with the building of the saw mill by Solomon Speers, which stood on the lot where the beautiful residence of L. Z. Birmingham is now located at the corner of Water and Third streets. The mill was burned on the morning of February 29, 1880, together with nearly all the buildings on the square. In 1875 a disastrous fire had occurred on the same square, on Main street. Solomon Speers sold the mill to L. M. Speers; L. M. Speers sold it to Daniel Springer and Edward Jordan; Daniel Springer bought out Jordan and became its sole owner. At the death of Daniel Springer it was bought by his son Manoah at the administrator's sale. Manoah Springer sold it to O. D. Johnson, who took in W. J. Anderson as a partner in the business, but not in the ownership of the mill.

In 1875 James M. Springer become sole owner and took in as a business partner, W. J. Anderson, forming the firm of Springer & Anderson. In 1878 the mill was sold to C. B. Wiley by the Assignee of Springer & Anderson. C. B. Wiley was the owner at the time of the fire. The date of the building of this saw mill is well fixed by the fact that it occurred the fall of the year in what happened the wonderful falling of the stars and that event was in 1833. The late Daniel Springer did the carpenter work and Samuel Sisley the stonework. Robt. Patterson, lately deceased, called to mind the date from the fact that Sisley was doing the mason work and was almost fatally frightened at the "falling of the stars." Captain French, now deceased, a well-known citizen was engineer, sawyer, fireman, etc., for many years in the early history of this mill. He related a story in connection with this mill well worth recording. John Brunthoover, well-known in the town as John Bunty, about to be arrested for debt, sought in haste the saw mill as a place of safety. The Captain took in the situation at once and kindly concealed him in the cistern. By and by either on purpose or thoughtlessly, he started the pump. When the water had gotten to about his neck, Bunty became alarmed at the prospect, and cried out in his usual emphatic tones, "Hallo, Jim; I'd rather go to jail than be drowned."

Among the boats built at the Third Street Yard were the Ontario, Protector, Monongahela, Dolphin and Pittsburgh, together with many others whose names we have not obtained. Among these were the Minstrel, which in April, 1842, fell from the blocks, killing Robert Winters, and very seriously injuring John Baldwin by fracturing his leg and breaking the jaws of John Corwin. Daniel and Joseph Springer, James Housman, Samuel Massey, and others were under the boat but escaped with but very slight injury. Speers & Gaskell suspended operations at this yard a short time prior to 1847. About the year of 1851 or '52, L. M. Speers and Wm. Latta resumed active operations in the same yard, L. M. Speers having purchased the saw mill. Some very fine boats were built by this firm and among the last was the well-known tug Clipper for S. Clark & Son. During the years 1853-54, L. M. Speers erected the large saw mill below Speers Run and the firm in due time moved the boat-building to it. In 1857 or '58 the firm was dissolved and the business was carried on by L. M. Speers alone, until the close of the war of the rebellion, when W. F. Speers became a partner, and thereafter the firm was L. M. & W. F. Speers. On the morning of October 7, 1876, the mill was burned by fire. The saw mill was rebuilt in 1877, and the yard was carried on until the firm went into bankruptcy in November of the same year. In the building of the first mill at this yard the late Daniel Springer was the contractor for the carpenter work and David Furnier for the mill-wright work. John Herbertson, of Brownsville, furnished the engine. Captain James French was the first sawyer after re-building of the mill. During the proceedings in bankruptcy Wm. Jones and and S. F. Jones obtained permission from the U. S. Court to foreclose a mortgage, in pursuance of which the Sheriff of Westmoreland county sold the mill to William and S. F. Jones, February 7, 1880, and they sold it to the Bellevernon Saw and Planing Mill Company, May 12, 1880, the firm being composed of Wm. Jones, S. F. Jones, Samuel Jones, and Isaac Shepler. The mill as now constructed has an extensive planing apparatus connected with it.

From a diary now in possession of Nelson Johnson, son of the late Levi Johnson, kept by David Furnier in 1790, we learn that the old Barter mills, which stood near the present residence of Samuel McKain on Speers' run, were erected prior to 1790, and was the first flouring mill about Bellevernon. It was conveyed before 1790 to David Furnier, together with the log house and store located on the bank of the river, where now is the boat-yard just below Speers' run.

The well is there yet from which the early settlers drew, with sweep and moss-covered bucket, water to quench their thirst; and to make it more palatable the grog of the old-time stillhouse near by was mingled generally with it. This mill, in its crude state, having had its day, was torn down, and in 1803 the well-known brick mill was built by David Furnier. This mill was situated not far from the north end of the present stone bridge near the mouth of Speers' run. The only known remnants of this mill are the bricks in the old house, called for over half a century "Gould's school house," at the upper end of Main street in Bellevernon. This mill was torn down in 1836.

William Hornbake in his day attempted to start a carding machine in his building, corner of Main street and Cherry alley, but failed. In the same building, in its back part, Apollos Speers, the cabinet-maker, in 1854 put an engine to drive his turning lathe; and in 1855, in this shop, occurred among the first fires ever in the town.

William Walker was the first tailor in the town. He located in 1834 in the house known as the ferry house, on Water street and owned (1893) now by D. W. Owens. James Hagerty arrived in 1837, and set up in the tailor business in 1838, in the house recently owned (1890) by Alex. Brown, on Water above First street. He has been ever since that date a resident of the town—to his death—except for a short season when he lived on the opposite side of the river from the town. John Merrick, the tailor, in the same year Hagerty commenced business, settled in the town. John L. Dehn, now of Mansfield (1890), Ohio, carried on the tailoring business first in the Sutton and afterwards in the Wise house. He came to town in about 1859; but can not say in what year he removed to Mansfield, Ohio. J. B. Zeh was his successor, who, with Samuel Bedsworth and J. H. Treasure, constitute the tailor fraternity in town. A German named Blair built the house now owned by Andrew Guiler, on lower Main street, and in it carried on the tailoring business. And just before the war of the rebellion, William McWilliams, now deceased, had his residence and tailor shop in this same building.

Father Thomas Ward was the first cabinet maker; he at first had his shop near the present residence of William Kyle on Grant and State streets, in North Bellevernon, but removed in 1815 to the house he built on the corner of Main and Second streets, in town. He was also the first and only wheel-wright ever lived in the place. He died many years since in Ohio, whither he had gone to pass the remnant of his days among children who had generally preceded him. He was a very skillful mechanic, and had peculiar traits of character which many of the older citizens still relate to the amusement of the younger. Apollos Speers succeeded him as undertaker and cabinet maker on the corner of Cherry alley and Main street.

He was regarded as one of the most skillful mechanics in the valley. In 1848 he took in as partner Thomas Taggart. The firm carried on the business until Speers sold the house to Robert Patterson in the early fifties. Speers moved to Peoria, Illinois, where he was connected with a coffin manufactory, and where he died suddenly and was buried in a coffin of his own making.

James M. Springer first entered into the furniture business and undertaking in the summer of 1847. He purchased from Mrs. Nancy Reeves, his mother-in-law, the house and lot long afterwards known as the Hutton dwelling on Main street above Strawberry alley. In the same year he built the shop still standing between the residence and the M. E. church. Solomon Speers had sold this lot to Barnet Corwin, May 13, 1830, and he, in 1839, built the house. Barnet Corwin sold the same to Nancy Reeves November 4, 1845. Nancy Reeves sold it to J. M. Springer February, 1848. Springer sold it to John Hutton April 2, 1848, and purchased from Solomon Speers the lots just below Strawberry alley on Main street, and built a shop on the corner, lately the store-room occupied by Clarke Corwin. He also built the dwelling burned in 1880. The first coffin made by Springer was for the father of A. J. Taylor, who built and lived for many years in the house now owned by Mrs. Isaac Hammett, on the corner of Wood and Third streets. The coffin was of the old style, made of black walnut and polished with beeswax. In 1872 Springer retired from the business, having sold out to F. M. Myers. Myers, May 20, 1880, sold the business to Curtiss Reppert & Sons, who still carry on the business on the corner of Main and Third streets.

Henry Speers, the older, was perhaps the first person who died in this vicinity. His death occurred in 1772, from the kick of a horse, and it is generally believed that his remains were interred in the Gibsonton graveyard on the original Speers farm just below Bellevernon. This old graveyard is now incorporated as a cemetery and is enclosed by a substantial fence This was the first burial place in the neighborhood, the Rehoboth's first interment being in 1790.

The older Coopers were interred in the private grounds on the farm recently owned by Thomas Redd at the mouth of Maple creek, but now (1893) a part of the flourishing town of Charleroi. The older Fryes were buried on what is called Smith Frye's farm, being a part of the original Frye farm on the hill above Lock No. 4.

The Fryes, Speers and Coopers were intimately connected, both by marriage and association, in their early life, and at death their remains occupied the same burial grounds, the four graveyards being in sight, one from the other. The first burial ground intended for Bellevernon was on the well-known Gould hill, situated now in the village of "Seldom Seen." During Wylie's ownership of the land, permission for burial was granted and J. B. Gould, who succeeded Wylie, gave the same privilege. The remains of Louis Cisly were the first to be interred in this ground, but in what year we cannot ascertain. Then followed the burial of Casper Ebner, Joseph Billiter and his two sons, James and Lewis.

The next burial place was in the one which the old Free Will Baptist Church still stands on Wood Street near Flint Alley. Mrs William Hutchison, who lived in the house now owned by James Housman on the State road beyond La Grange School-House, was the first person buried in this grave-yard. She was buried in 1843. The increased population of the town and vicinity demanded better facilities for the burial of the dead. Hence the organization and incorporation of the Bellevernon Cemetery Association, Bellevernon, Pa., November 1st, 1866, Denton Lynn, Noah Q. Speers, J. M. Springer; J. S. Van Voorhis, Daniel Springer and Bazil Brightwell purchased a lot of ground of James H. Springer for burial purposes and organized themselves into Bellevernon Cemetery Association. The above named purchasers were elected managers, of whom Dr. J. S. Van Voorhis was chosen President and James M. Springer, Secretary and Treasurer.

A charter for said Association was granted by the Westmoreland County Court, May 13th, 1867. The first meeting of the lot holders under the charter was held September 27th, 1867, and Denton Lynn, Noah Speers, J. S. Van Voorhis, Bazil Brightwell, and Daniel Springer were elected managers. On the same day the managers met and elected J. S. Van Voorhis, President, N. Q. Speers, Secretary and J. M. Springer, Treasurer.

The first person buried in these grounds after its purchase was Abram Smock, who died in the house now occupied by his widow in Bellevernon, September 24, 1866. Prior to this date, however, the ground in a limited space had been known as the burial place of the Springer family.

The slaves of the Speers family were buried on the point above the property now owned by James Carnes' heirs, a short distance above the mouth of Speers' run. Some of the older citizens used to speak of a few burials on the high ground not far from the public school house in North Bellevernon.

In laying out the lots in Bellevernon, the space between Water street and the river was reserved by the original proprietor, no street but the state road reaching to the river, thus cutting off the town from all wharf privileges, even remaining in the ownership of the Speers' descendants to this day, either by inheritance or purchase. There is no doubt but the intention originally was to have this river front set apart for wharf purposes, in the interest of the town.

From the time of the establishment of the ferry its wharf was used as a landing for trade boats, keel boats and steamboats until 1850 or thereabouts, when conflicting rights and privileges forced the boats to go to the glass factory, where Wm. Eberheart had landing rights, and to which for his own convenience, he gave free wharfage to all craft. Goods and produce shipped to and from all points on the river were received and taken from the ferry wharf by the early merchants and business men of the town. The keel boats of Captain Bob Ray—Caleb, Harvey, Creekbaum, Anger, Danks, etc., were objects of great interest to the populace along the river, and their arrival was watched for eagerly. Sometimes parties, especially military companies, were carried on these boats. A few of our older citizens still call to mind one unfortunate excursion. A keel boat in charge of Captain Rogers, loaded with soldiers, enroute to attend a celebration of some kind in Pittsburgh, in 1826; in passing the town the swivel on deck was to be fired as a salute, and as the boat seemed to be midway of the town without the firing, the captain concluded he would go above to see what was the trouble; just as he raised his head above the deck, off went the cannon. Samuel Dougherty, a colored man, well known in the community, having excitedly taken the job of putting off the gun from the regular gunner on duty for that purpose, shot away the back of the head of the captain, scattered blood, bones and flesh in all directions. His body was taken to the front parlor in the residence of Solomon Speers, now the Roley house, where to-day can be seen traces of the blood on the floor.

Aunt Polly Corwin, in the absence of a doctor, washed and dressed the dead man's wounds and had the remains in good condition for burial by the time the friends arrived from Brownsville overland with the hearse and carriages.

Steamers Louis McLane and Consul, the former commanded by Captain Adam Jacobs and the latter by Captain Samuel Clarke, were among the first to land at the ferry wharf. The Baltic and Atlantic for a time also landed here, but shortly after going to the glass-factory wharf, they gave place in 1852 to the Jefferson and Luzerne. After the removal of the boat yard over Speers' run in 1853 the steamboat landing was changed to the mouth of Third street, where it remained until the new wharf was graded at the mouth of Second street in 1857. The new wharf was the work of L. M. Speer, who prior to that date had purchased the space outside of Water street from Solomon Speers, who had obtained it by will from his father, Noah Speers. The wharf in a short time became an affair of profit. For some years there had been growing disposition on the part of the citizens and town council to obtain the wharf privileges.

To carry out the project a petition was presented to the Fayette County Court, June 23d, 1874, asking for a jury to appraise the value of said privileges. The Court appointed James French, W. H. Jones, S. F. Jones, Henry C. Coughenour, J. T. Roley, James Corwin and John Hixenbaugh as the jury of good and true men, who placed such a value on the privilege as to render it impracticable to take any further action. During the proceeding in bankruptcy of L. M. & W. F. Speers, the wharf rights were sold to J. W. Carothers, of West Virginia, who sold it to Noah Speers; with the exception of the made wharf at Second street there scarcely remains any space of that ground reserved in the original plot of the town, it all being washed away by the encroachments of high water. The two lots now owned by the heirs of George Lang only run to low water mark and this wise idea gives the heirs full right to use the river shore as a landing for 120 feet. The wharf-boat for the use of the packets is moved to the front of these lots.

At this date 1893, Water street only extends north to First street, between First street and Speers' run there never has been any street opened, the ground now being principally occupied by the railroad. At the ferry wharf and along the river shore quite a number of persons have been drowned, even within the recollection of citizens now living.

Isaac Boles, who lived on Water street just above Strawberry alley long ago, was drowned on his return from a corn husking over the river at Henry Speers' farm. In company of others he attended the husking, but having imbibed a little too freely of spirits, which was so generally used at that time, he tarried behind his companions. On arriving at the river he found by the absence of the skiff that they had gone over. He took off his clothes and shoes, and in attempting to swim across was drowned in front of his home. The finding of his clothes told the story. The discovery of a skeleton buried in the river bank opposite the glass works induced the belief that some one had been drowned before Boles. In 1856 or 1857 a little daughter of Peter Corwin was drowned at the ferry wharf. She was attending the school of Miss Tower, who taught in the store room of now the Roley house. In about 1862 John Speers, of Dunbar; Harvey Bryner, of this town, and Josiah Van Voorhis, of Washington county, in attempting to cross the river in the night in a small flat, at the ferry were thrown out by its upsetting, and although only a few feet from the shore Van Voorhis was drowned. The other two in some way reached the shore, although neither of them could swim. Speers and Bryner have since died. Whilst playing at the same wharf August 25, 1881, little Fannie, daughter of M. H. Arters, was drowned. Her body was recovered by Thomas W. Dean. In 1877, Van, son of the late Samuel Hammett, was drowned from a raft of logs above Third street. His body was recovered by John Raum. In 1880 a stranger, a laborer on the railroad, was drowned just above Speers' landing, opposite town.

In the fall of 1883 Resin Fox was drowned at the ferry wharf by jumping from the flat as it was about to go down with a load of cattle. His body was recovered by Curtis Reppert. This was the first person ever drowned who worked about the ferry. On the 9th of November, 1876, Capt. O. D. Johnson was drowned off the steamer Athletic, near Gibsonton wharf. His body was recovered the next day by Capt. W. W. Williams. In 1885 a son of Henry King was drowned at Third street wharf by going through the ice. In 1846 a boy named Dunlevy, a nephew of the late Andrew Dunlevy, was drowned at Lock No. 4. He was learning the tailor trade with James Hagerty, of Bellevernon. Hagerty, Dr. Johnson, Dunlevy and some others were fishing. Dunlevy had gone above for some purpose and the remaining party was apprised of something being wrong by the empty skiff floating over the dam. After a search of many hours his body was recovered. Just above this dam and a short distance below the Rostraver coal works a child of John Foulkes was drowned not long since. A stranger from Pittsburgh was drowned a few years since in front of the present town of Charleroi. The venerable Joseph

Crow committed suicide by drowning just above Maple creek, many years ago. A little child of James Huttenhour, of Bellevernon, was drowned some twenty-seven years ago near the present residence of Wm. Spharr, and not far from the Gibsonton wharf a man was drowned from one of the packets, some twenty years ago. His body was recovered by James Carns.

Long ago in keelboat times a Captain of one of these crafts was drowned near the glass works and near the same place in after years an intoxicated man fell into the river from one of the keelboats and though the water was very shoal he drowned, having fallen face downward and was unable to extricate himself. In April 1866, Thomas W. Dean discovered the body of James H. Housman floating in the river just above the glass works cinder pile. He was a citizen of Fayette City, was killed by one Thairwell, who was hanged for the crime. A stranger and Joseph Archibald were drowned about the same year near Tremont Coal Works, over twenty years ago. In later years, Mary, daughter of David Davis, and her little child were drowned just above town by the upsetting of a skiff, in which were also her father and mother, the latter two reaching the shore in safety.

A man named House was drowned in June, 1845, at the mouth of Maple Creek, by getting entangled in a fish seine. He lived in a log house that stood above the old Peter W. Shepler farm, now owned by heirs of Esquire Swabb. July 4th, 1868, a Mr. O'Neal was drowned by falling in the river whilst pushing a flat through Lock No. 4. A little son of George Tabron was drowned June 29th, 1885, by falling from a board raft above the glass works. Many years ago the oldest child of William Reeves—a little girl—was drowned in a vat in the tan yard, now property of the heirs of George Lang, deceased.

THE PRESBYTERIAN CHURCH.

The Presbyterian church had its first introduction into the "Forks of Yough" on the arrival of Rev. James Finley from the east in 1765, although he did not permanently reside in his new home until 1783. The result of his initiative labors was the organization of Round Hill and Rehoboth churches, in the year 1778. He died January 6th, 1795, when the site on which Bellevernon now is situated was an unbroken forest. We have no data on which to base any belief that he ever preached to the pioneers on the river. About sixty years ago Rehoboth congregation appointed elders Michael Finley and William Bigham to visit the village of Bellevernon and inquire into the expediency and propriety of erecting a church building, so as to have a point for stated preaching. After looking over the matter fully the committee reported against the enterprise, but recommended occasional preaching at private houses in the town and neighborhood. Rev. Robert Johnson, pastor of Rehoboth, preached at long intervals in the house of Abner Reeves, whose wife was a member of his church. The house stood almost on the space now occupied by the new residence of Leonard Luce in Rostraver township, about one mile and a half from town. Rev. N. H. Gillette, who succeeded Rev. Johnson as pastor in 1834, preached frequently in the old Methodist church on corner of Water street and Cherry alley, now used as a dwelling on the corner of Cherry and Long alleys.

Rev. J. R. Hughes and his successor, Rev. L. Y. Graham, as pastors of Rehoboth, oftentimes held services in the frame Methodist Episcopal church building on Water street, above Strawberry alley; it is now owned and occupied by the Disciples. In the summer of 1868, John B. Cook, E. F. Housman and L. M. Speer were appointed by Rehoboth to go on the ground and inquire into the propriety of erecting a house of worship in Bellevernon. The committee considered the matter with favor, but the effort only resulted in the renting of the old Methodist building, and for a time services were held in it. Among the Presbyterian ministers who preached in this old church at different times in its history were Dr. Gillette, Dr. N. West, Dr. Brownson, Dr. Sloan, Dr. Allison, Dr. M'Laren, Revs. J. R. Hughes, L. Y. Graham, J. H. Stevenson, James P. Fulton, and others whose names we cannot recall. The venerable Dr. David McConnaughy, president of Washington College, preached one sermon in 1848 in the old church corner of Water street and Cherry alley.

In July, 1869, the members of the Presbyterian church in Bellevernon and vicinity determined to have a church building. Dr. J. S. Van Voorhis undertook to raise the money, and how he succeeded the sequel told the fact of a neat little church complete and paid for. A lot on the corner of First and Main streets, 60x50 feet, was presented by L. M. Speer. After receiving bids for the construction of the building, the contract was awarded L. M. Speer for $2,000, and at his own expense he added to the edifice the spire and weather-vane complete. Dr. J. S. Van Voorhis, as chairman of the building committee, superintended the work. The foundation excavation for the stonework was commenced on the 7th day of August, 1869, and the whole building was completed and furnished before the 19th day of December of the same year, on which day it was dedicated free of debt. The masonwork was done by Thomas Hagerty and brothers, and the carpenter work under the contractor by J. R. Powell, of California, and Sansom B. Miller, Bellevernon. The glass for the windows was presented by R. C. Schmertz & Co., of their own manufacture.

The painting was the work of John Hatfield, of Brownsville, now of Columbus, Ohio. The funds for the furnishing of the church were raised by Mary Speer, Lizzie Van Voorhis, Mrs. Margaret Kyle and Mattie Miller, amounting in all to $297.70. The ladies had remaining on hand after buying all needed furniture $6.44, which they transferred to the building fund.

The bell and furnace were purchased with the building funds. A. Fulton & Son sold to the committee the bell; it was moulded for a church in Williamsport, Md., which accounts for the name on it. The clock was presented by Mrs. Wm. Scott. The Bible and hymn-book by Mrs. Eliza Hair, wife of Rev. G. M. Hair, of McKeesport, but shortly afterwards pastor of Rehoboth.

This church building was constructed by the voluntary act of the members of the Presbyterian church in Bellevernon and vicinity, independent of any organization. It was intended for a place of worship as preaching might be given by Rehoboth congregation, which had been and was proposed to continue the custom of services one Sabbath afternoon out of three. Rev. L. Y. Graham was now pastor. The 19th day of December, 1869, was appointed for the dedication of the new church, and Rev. Graham invited Rev. G. M. Hair to aid in the service. That Sabbath day at the hour of 11 o'clock, A. M. found the house crowded. The invocation and dedicatory prayer was pronounced by the Rev. L. Y. Graham and the sermon by Rev. G. M. Hair. Miss Lizzie Van Voorhis had formed a choir consisting of Misses Kate Barkman, Olivia Barkman, Mirtilda Brown, Galena Bunting, Josie Sills, and Messrs. A. S. Woodrow, L. H. Reeves, W. A. Coughanour, and others perhaps, whose names we cannot recall, over which she presided as organist. The organ was loaned by Mrs. L. M. Speer until a new one could be purchased. Under arrangement Rev. Graham preached each alternate Sabbath afternoon, until Septembar 24th, 1871, when he preached his last sermon in the Bellevernon church, having resigned the pastorate of Rehoboth. Under his ministry a large number of persons in the town and vicinity united with the church. Candidates for Rehoboth now occasionally preached as circumstances would arise. Rev. G. M. Hair having accepted a call to Rehoboth entered upon his duties as pastor September 1st, 1872, and on the 8th of the same month preached in Bellevernon church for the first time since he became pastor, and continued to preach at stated intervals during his pastorate.

August, 1872, Rev. L. Y. Graham, formerly pastor, preached

to a crowded house. He baptized Bettie P. Cunningham, daughter of J. C. and Lizzie Van Voorhis Cunningham. This was the first child ever baptized in the church. Among the ministers, besides the pastors, who preached in this church during its connection with Rehoboth, we call to mind Revs. Wm. Wilson, Wood, of the Cumberland church, Robert H. Fulton, Eben Caldwell, J. F. Boyd, W. G. Nevin, Mitchell, E. P. Lewis, Dickey, J. H. Flannigan, W. H. Gill, W. Campbell, W. V. Kean, Andrews, R. R. Gaily and Rev. Morton. The first funeral services in the church were those of little Noah Bright Abel, March 9, 1873.

The continued prosperity of the church enterprise and the bright future predicted by some of the more enthusiastic, induced a determination to ask the proper authorities to organize a separate church in Bellevernon. Some of the older members were very unwilling to sever their connection with the mother church, but in the end yielded to the majority, with grave doubts as to the propriety of the change.

For many years Wm. Hasson, the father of John C. Hasson, was the only member of the Presbyterian church residing in Bellevernon. In April, 1848, Dr. J. S. Van Voorhis and wife were taken into the church at Rehoboth under the ministry of Rev. N. H. Gillet. These three composed the Presbyterian family in the town for many years. The town and vicinity at the change was represented by about sixty members, which increase was the great reason for a separate organization. On Tuesday, December 2nd, 1873, the Presbytery of Redstone met in Bellevernon, being its first meeting in the town. At this meeting the question of the organization of a church in Bellevernon was presented, and after some little discussion a committee consisting of Rev. G. M. Hair, of Rehoboth, Rev. R. R. Gaily, of Redstone, and elder Alexander Rankin, of Rehoboth, was appointed to organize said church if the way be clear. This committee met on Thursday evening, December 11th, 1873, and in due form constituted the First Presbyterian Church, of Bellevernon. Dr. I. C. Hazlett, R. J. Linton and

S. F. Jones were elected elders. The two former were ordained and installed, Mr. Jones being only installed, as he had served as an elder in Rehoboth. The following persons were received by certificate from Rehoboth, viz: D. B. Johnson, Mrs. E. S. Van Voorhis, James French, Dr. J. S. Van Voorhis, Sarah Johnson, L. M. Speers, Fannie S. Speers, Celia G. Speers, S. F. Jones, S. E. Jones, R. J. Linton, Caroline S. Linton, Nancy Smock, Ellen McFall, Margaret Garrison, Harriet Patterson, Lizzie V Cunningham, I. C. Hazlett, Samuel Clarke, Anna Clarke, Maria E. Hughes, Jennie French, W. F. Speers, Mary P. Speers, W. P. Mackey, Samuel McKain, S. McKain, Agnes McAlpin, Mary Smock, Elizabeth Lucas, Nancy Sheets, Maggie McFall, Jane Hopkins, Alvira M. Furnier, Mary E. Cook, Susan C. Wise, James McAlpin, John McAlpin, Jennie Jones, Sarah Barkman, Philip Smock, W. B. McAlpin, Olive Barkman, Lavinia Smock, W. McFall, Robert McFall and Charlotte Hammett. From other churches: W. F. Morgan and wife and Mary C. Alter; in all, fifty-one. Of this number, at this date, December, 1890, fourteen are deceased.

Rev. G. M. Hair, of Rehoboth, continued to preach for the new church organization until June 1, 1874, at which time he ceased to be pastor of Rehoboth. The Bellevernon church called Rev. A. B. Lowes, who was installed as the first pastor October 28, 1874. He remained connected with the church until Sept. 1, 1882. The present pastor (1893) Rev. Perrin Baker was called Jan. 10, 1883, and installed May 3, 1883. From the day he entered upon his duty Rev. Baker infused new life into the church, and through his ministry a large number have been added to the membership His wife died at the parsonage in North Bellevernon November 27, 1885. December 21, 1881, W. F. Morgan was added to the session, and in April, 1886, Dr. I. C. Hazlett, one of the original elders, was dismissed at his own request to the church at Uniontown, to which place he had moved his residence. This congregation was chartered by the courts of Fayette county March 11, 1876. Of the two families who took the most active part in the erection of the church building, not one at this time (1893) is a member. L. M. Speers has passed away, and his family removed to other parts. Dr. Van Voorhis and family, at their own request, were dismissed to Rehoboth December, 1875.

To L. M. Speers more than any one else the Presbyterians are indebted for this church building, and we trust his memory will ever occupy a green spot in the hearts of those who worship within its doors.

THE CUNNINGHAM FAMILY.

James Cunningham was born in Merrittstown, Fayette county, Pa., July 26, 1812, and died on his farm near that place April 5, 1888.

In 1835 he married Rosanna Muir, who was born March 28, 1811, and died September 8, 1885. During his early days James Cunningham taught school; then learned the blacksmith trade, and finally abandoned it and turned his attention to farming, in which occupation he was engaged until his death. He was an elder in the Cumberland Presbyterian church near Merrittstown until 1880, when he withdrew to become a member of the Dunlaps Creek Presbyterian church, in which he was elected a ruling elder. He served his county prominently during his life, holding many offices, the last being commissioner for two terms. He had six children. Mary Jane, born November 2, 1836, married Isaiah N. Craft. Of their two children, Harry Clyde was born March 7, 1862, and died September 28, 1865. Ewing O. was born October 17, 1859, and married Emma Krepps October 17, 1883. They have two children, Clara Pauline, born April 19, 1887, and Edgar W., born July 30, 1891.

John C., oldest son of James Cunningham, was born September 27, 1838; married March 30, 1871, M. Lizzie, daughter of Dr. J. S. and E. S. Van Voorhis, of Bellevernon, Pa. She was born in Bellevernon, Pa., June 30, 1848, and died November 26, 1877. Their daughter, Bettie Plumer, was the only child. Bettie Plumer was born January 24, 1872. She graduated from the Pennsylvania College for Women, Pittsburgh, in June, 1891, and was married to David Stewart June 22, 1893. John C. has been for nearly thirty years a prominent and successful merchant in Bellevernon.

Alfred, son of James Cunningham, married Laura Springer, daughter of James M. Springer, of Bellevernon. They have three children, Clyde, Lillian and Mary.

Martha Acklin, Sara Margaret and Anna Eliza, daughters of James Cunningham, are unmarried. The former resides in the family of I. N. Craft, and the others own and live on the home farm near Hopewell church.

Thomas Cunningham the great-grandfather of James Cunningham, emigrated from Ireland before the war of the revolution. He settled in that part of Chester county which was included within the limits of Lancaster county on its formation in 1729. His son James, in whom we are especially interested in this sketch, was born in Lancaster county, Pennsylvania, in December, 1747. Before the outbreak of the Revolution, James Cunningham came from Lancaster county to what is now Washington county, where he toma-hawked a claim near the site of the present town of Washington. After building a house and doing a little clearing he returned to Lancaster to make ready for a return trip to his proposed new settlement. On his return in the fall of that year, he found his claim already occupied. He abandoned the idea of settlement in the western part of the state and bought a farm in Lancaster county where he remained until the war. He entered the U. S. Army in June, 1776, in Captain Calhoun's company which served under Colonel Clautz. In 1792 he joined his brother John in Fayette county. He built the stone house near Merrittstown, owned by Armstrong Porter, now deceased.

James died in 1832, leaving two sons and two daughters, John and William, Jane and Isabel. Jane married William Gallagher and Isabel married David Porter. John boated on the Monongahela river for his father and uncle and died at an early age. William was born in 1783, and September 3, 1811, married Mary Gallagher, who was born July 3, 1788, and died October 23, 1822.

In 1810 he opened a store in Merrittstown. He also built the house known as the Baird residence. His establishment was known as the "Centennial Store," and as he had other business interests to look after he employed John Gallagher and Benjamin Barton as clerks. He also owned the grist mill property, to which he attached a fulling mill. He served as County Commissioner, U. S. District Marshall, and was an excise officer for some years. In 1817 he moved to his farm near Merrittstown, on which he died June 2, 1819. He had four children, John, Ann, Eliza and James, whose history we have given in the beginning of this article. Eliza died unmarried. Ann married James Work and died July 12, 1885. They had eight children. George, Belle, Clara and Sallie are dead; Jane is unmarried; Margaret, Martha and Alexander are married. John married Mary Muer. Of their six children William, Emma and Robert are dead. Eliza never married. Jane and Elizabeth are married.

John, the other son of Thomas Cunningham, of whom we have record, after enduring for many years hardships in the war, among them being captured by the enemy and carried on a prison ship to a distant fort, settled in Luzerne township, Fayette county, Pa., and carried on a successful business in that township until 1820. He died in the old stone house built by James Cunningham, in 1830, at the age of 87 years, remaining always a bachelor, and bearing wherever known the title of "Uncle John." He was a member of the Pennsylvania Legislature, with Albert Gallatin, from 1793 to 1805, and from 1805 to 1807, and declined to appear any more as a candidate.

BELLEVERNON SABBATH SCHOOL.

The first meeting for the purpose of establishing a Sabbath school in the First Presbyterian Church of Bellevernon, was held December 26th, 1869. The organization was completed by the election of Dr. J. S. Van Voorhis, superintendent; N. Q. Speers, assistant superintendent; William A. Coughanour, secretary; W. P. Mackey, librarian and treasurer; Mrs. J. S. Van Voorhis, Mrs. L. M. Speers, Mrs. R. C. Byers, Misses Celia Speers, Lizzie Van Voorhis, Mary Speers, Angeline Hasson, Kate Barkman, Mary Bradman and Mattie Miller were elected teachers. Of the number Miss Lizzie Van Voorhis, married to J. C. Cunningham, is deceased, having died November 26th, 1877; and Miss Mary Bradman, the date of whose death we do not know; and Mrs. Kate Barkman also. Messrs. R. J. Linton, Alexander Brown, N. Q. Speers, W. F. Speers and J. W. Morgan were elected teachers; and of these Mr. Linton alone is now (1893) connected with the school. January 9th, 1870, the school was in full operation, with 100 scholars present. January 16th the secretary reported 126 scholars in attendance, and says in his remarks: "Very good attendance of both scholars and teachers, but a lack of a number of teachers. There appears to be such an interest manifested by the citizens as will crown the school with success." January 23rd additional teachers were elected. March 20th, 1870, William A. Coughanour resigned the secretaryship, and W. C. Byers was elected in his place. Mr. Coughanour, in a day or two afterwards, left for his new home in Idaho.

The necessity for a library was very apparent, and in order to obtain funds for the purpose, Alex. Brown, W. P. Mackey and W A. Coughanour were, January 23, 1870, appointed a committee to solicit subscriptions and the result was the start made in the direction of books. April 17 a committee consisting of J. T. Shepler, Virgil Miller and W. C. Byers with Misses Celia G. Speers, Kate Barkman and Lizzie Van Voorhis, was appointed to canvas for funds to add to the library, who reported May 1st that $190.00 had been raised. The committee was authorized to purchase more books which, with those already on hands, formed a good sized library; and the fact is that at no time since the organization of this missionary Sabbath School had there been any difficulty in raising funds for its benefit. June 19th, the secretary reported 153 scholars in attendance and not a teacher absent, with increasing interest in the school. The organ loaned by Mrs. L. M. Speers being returned to her on November 20th, the music was carried on without an instrument.—Miss Lizzie Van Voorhis by individual subscriptions and musical concerts determined to raise funds for a new organ. The friends of the school responded nobly and the organ was purchased by her from C. C. Mellor, of Pittsburgh, at a cost of $290, of which she contributed $90. The new organ was used for the first time in the Sabbath School December 4, 1870, in the hymn "Sabbath School Battle Song."

The first year of the school closed December 25th, 1870, with flattering prospects. The greatest daily attendance of scholars during the year was 153, and the lowest 36. The average daily attendance was 100.46. January 1st, 1871, being the day of election of officers, Dr. J. S. Van Voorhis was elected superintendent; N. Q. Speers, assistant; W. P. Mackey, librarian; A. L. Brown, secretary. April 2nd, 1871, Miss Olivia Barkman acted as assistant organist for the first time. In the progress of the school, James French, J. C. Cunningham, J. C. Hasson, H. Patterson, W. F. Morgan, L. Z. Birmingham, A. S. Woodrow, William Scott, and others whose names we can not recall, were added as teachers. At the beginning of this year prizes of a Bible were offered to the scholars who should attend every day during the year. On January 28th, 1872, 32 Bibles were awarded to different scholars for attendance during the past year, the class of James French receiving the largest number. The year 1871 closed with an average daily attendance of 99.1; the greatest attendance being 136, and the least 54. The superintendent presented teacher French with a copy of Cruden's Concordance for the largest average class for the year. January 7th, 1872, the old officers re-elected, excepting R. J. Linton was elected assistant superintendent. January 12th, 1873, old officers re-elected, excepting S. F. Jones was elected assistant superintendent. February 2nd, another addition to the library, which gave it a very interesting size, and the new books were of more than ordinary interest. The record of 1873 is not very full, and hence much of interest no doubt is lost.

December 7, 1873, was the last day of this missionary Sabbath school, which was organized January 2, 1870; it was on the 14th taken under the general supervision of the First Presbyterian church of Bellevernon and became a Presbyterian Sabbath school. Mr. S. F. Jones was elected superintendent, and continues as such to this day, 1893. The superintendent of the missionary school in his closing remarks December 7, 1873, said: "May the Lord bless the infant church and infuse new life into the Sabbath school under the new organization, and may it indeed become the nursery of the church in which may grow up many precious souls for Christ."

The history of those who were connected with the first organization of this school is of interest no doubt to many of their friends. Mrs. L. M. Speers and her three boys are now living in Wooster, Ohio; Celia G. Speers married Rev. R. B. Porter, and is residing in the presbytery of Allegheny; Mary Speers married Rev. T. S. Parks, and lives in Illinois; Lizzie Van Voorhis married J. C. Cunningham, and died November 26, 1877; Mary Bradman is deceased; Olivia Barkman married L. H. Reeves, and is a resident of Coal Center, Pa.; Harriet Patterson married W. H. Noble, and resides in Pittsburgh, Pa.; W. F. Speers, deceased in 1893, and his family reside in Pittsburgh; N. Q. Speers and family at Benvenue, near Pittsburgh; Mattie Miller is residing in Missouri; Kate Barkman married L. R. Boyle, who died in 1890, and she died in 1893. Angeline Hasson is a resident of North Bellevernon; Mrs. R. C.

Byers is a citizen of Monongahela City; Virgil Miller died before his father's family left for the West, and his remains are buried at Rehoboth; Dr. W. C. Byers is practicing his profession in Pittsbuigh; A. S. Woodrow is in Warren, Ohio.

METHODIST EPISCOPAL CHURCH OF BELLEVERNON.

The Methodist Episcopal was the pioneer church organization in Bellevernon, and to it we owe the largest share of our early religious character. We have no definite date fixing when or who preached the first sermon in the town, but it is known on reliable authority, that the Rev. J. G. Sansom did preach as early as 1830, in the house now owned by W. P. Mackey, on Main Street. In 1834 the village was taken into the Redstone circuit which at that time extended from Elizabeth, in Allegheny, to Upper Middletown, in Fayette county. Rev. Robert Hopkins was the presiding elder and John H. Ebbert, Warner Long and Isaac Macabee were the ministers. On the 5th day of October, 1834, Rev. J. H. Ebbert organized the first class in the town, composed of Barnet Corwin, John Corwin, Rebecca Jacobs, Eleanor Corwin, Sabina Gaskill, Katherine Ward, Jane Corwin, and Grace McFall. November 14th, 1834, William Hutchinson joined the class which increased the membership to nine. Rev. Ebbert was the first leader. He was succeeded by Robert Dumain. Preaching was supplied by the above named preachers every three weeks in the house owned then by Samuel Reeves, but recently by James Davidson, on Main Street; in Morgan Gaskill's house, now owned by R. C. Schmertz, on Water Street above Locust Alley; in John Corwin's house now owned by the heirs of Thompson Patterson; in the house now owned by heirs of John Hutton, and sometimes they held services in Rostraver, at the house of the late Samuel Reeves, now owned by W. J. Manown, and occupied by Elliott Minney.

Grace McFall is the only member living, 1893, of the original class. After the erection of the brick school house, in 1836, which stood for so long a time on the lot on which Thomas D.

Lehew's house now is, the appointment was moved to this house, where preaching was often held. During the time the class was held in that house, Jesse Fell was the leader. He lived in the old log house which stood near the present brick house in Rostraver township, owned by the heirs of Fairman, of Allegheny City. He moved long ago to Ohio, and died near Cleveland. He was a brother of the mother of William Jones, now a prominent member of this church. In 1840 Peter Swearer and his brother John, both of whom are now deceased, became residents of the town and joined the class, and very shortly aferwards the appointment was changed to the house of John Swearer, but in which house he lived in at that time we are not informed. We do know that in 1847 he occupied one of the houses in the long row, upper end of Main street, and subsequently he resided in the house first now above Fourth, on Main street. In about the year 1841 the brick church building, now owned by Harrison Husher, on the corner of Main and First streets, was erected. Hugh Ford, Benjamin Thomas and Solomon Speers were the building committee. This was only used as a church for a short time, owing to its unsafe condition.

It was sold and bid in by Thomas Taggart, the contractor. Many ridiculous incidents are related of the last meeting held in this building. During the time meetings were held here, Rev. D. L. Dempsy, Josiah Adams and Samuel Dunlap were the principal preachers. In 1842 the frame building, corner of Water street and Cherry alley, was purchased from William Reeves, who had kept store in it. This, after its purchase, was speedily converted into a church; to whom the deed was made in trust for the church we are not able to discover. In 1850 Cookstown and Bellevernon were stricken from the Redstone circuit, and made into a station with Rev. J. F. Nessly as preacher. Rev. Nessly resided in the house in Bellevernon standing now on the corner of Long and Cherry alleys, but at that time was on Main street, where the store of Abe Lewis is now, 1893.

The first quarterly conference of Cookstown and Bellevernon Station was held in Cookstown, September 7th, 1850. Members present were Rev. Z. H. Costen, P. E.; Rev. J. F. Nessly, preacher in charge; Samuel Hassler, local preacher; exhorter, James Davidson, class leaders, Jesse Jackman, Michael Slotterbeck, William Winters and James Davidson. At this meeting Dr. C. H. Connally, S. McCrory, M. Slotterbeck, John Mullin and Adam Shunk were elected stewards for the circuit; and on the recommendation of the charge at Bellevernon, Mr. James Davidson was licensed to preach the Gospel.

The Second Quarterly Conference of this station was held in Bellevernon, December 21st, 1850, present Rev. Z. H. Coston, P. E.; Rev. J. F. Nessly, preacher in charge; James Davidson, local preacher; John Swearer, exhorter; class-leaders, Thomas Fields, Jesse Jackman, Geo. B. Cook, Anthony Hazelbaker and William Winters. At this meeting in addition to Frederick Shively and Anthony Hazelbaker already acting Van Reeves, Adam Shunk, John Mullin, William Lewis and John Swearer were elected trustees to the new church in Bellevernon. The trustees purchased the lot on Water Street above Strawberry Alley from Wm. Eberheart for $125, and sold to him the old church for $300. On the first day of March 1852, Wm. Eberheart, the contractor for the new church, rendered to the trustees his account, viz:—Wm. Eberheart in account with the M. E. Church, of Bellevernon, Dr.—To cash as subscription, $69; U. Ward amount subscribed, $10; Hartranft subscription, $5; Phillip Smock, $2; cash as per subscription, $80.50; L. M. Speers, $15; L. M. Speers for J. Beazell, $5; cash as per subscription, $13; Thomas Fields' subscription, $5; Ziba Whiting's reduction on stone, $4; Methodist Church per bill, $300; Wm. Eberheart his amount as subscription for self and hands, $228; Ziba Whiting's order for amount, $42; cash as per subscription receipts, $156; total, $934.50. Cr. —By one lot, $125; Ziba Whiting building church per contract of Wm. Eberheart, $775; Uriah Ward amount assumed by Wm. Eberheart, as payment, $150; total, $1,050; leaving a balance due Wm. Eberheart of $115.50. August 31st, 1852. Received payment in full. W. Eberheart.

To William Eberheart the church was very much indebted for this building, and his liberality was highly appreciated. At the time the deed of this church was reported to the Quarterly Conference, there were present Z. H. Coston, P. E.; Peter F. Jones preacher in charge; James Davidson, local preacher; class leaders and stewards, M. G. Ebbert, Johnson Noble, Alex Fleming, M. Sloterbeck, Geo. B. Cook, Adam Shunk, O. H. P. Scott and Wm. Winters. Of these are dead all except one and of the trustees not one are living at this date, June 20th, 1887.

Of the stewards elected September 7th, 1850, only one is living out of the five. We can find no special record of the services first held in this new church, other than that Rev. Peter F. Jones was the preacher in charge, and Rev. Z. H. Coston was presiding elder. No formal dedication took place as we are informed. We are indebted to Rev. James Davidson for the list of preachers, not heretofore named, who were on the circuit up to 1847, and from that date to this day, 1893. They are as follows, viz: Rev. Alcinus Young, B. F. Sawhill, Thomas Baker, Moses Hill, Moses Jamison, David Hess, Josiah Mansell, George W. Cranage, Thomas Jamison, Richard Armstrong, Westley Smith, David Sharp, Henry Kern, Martin Ruter and John J. Moffit. We have but two of the presiding elders during that time, viz: Revs. Samuel Wakefield and J. J. Swayzie. The preachers from 1847 to the present time, 1893, are as follows, viz:

1847–48. Revs. J. G. Sansom, Josiah Mansell and George W. Cranage.

1849–50. Revs. J. F. Nessly and John Coil.

1851–52. Rev. Peter F. Jones. Z. H. Coston, P. E.

1853. Rev. J. Borbridge.

1854. Rev. D. Rhodes. Franklin Moore, P. E.

1855–56. Rev. John Williams.

1857.   Rev. Joseph Horner.   J. G. Sansom, P. E.
1858–59.   Rev. John C. Brown.
1860–61.   Rev. George Crook.   R. Hopkins, P. E.
1862–63.   Rev. James Hollingshead.
1864–65.   Rev. M. L. Weekly.
1866.   Rev. J. F. Jones.
1867.   Revs. C. H. Edwards, C. A. Holmes.   A. J. Endsley, P. E.
1868–69.   Rev. E. Williams.
1870–71–72.   Rev. E. B. Griffin.
1873–74–75.   Rev. M. McK. Garret.   L. R. Beacom, P. E.
1876–77.   Rev. N. P. Kerr.   This was called the short term, owing to changing of the meeting of conference from March to September.
1878–79.   Rev. S. W. Davis.
1880–81–82.   Rev. A. P. Leonard.
1883–84–85.   Rev. J. B. Uber.
1886.   Rev. George A. Sheets.
1889–91.   Rev. Robert Cartwright.
1891–93.   Rev. I. H. Pershing.

Rev. J. G. Sansom died in Brownsville May 4th, 1861, after 43 years of active work in the ministry.   Rev. B. F. Sawhill has been 20 years at work.   Thomas Baker died in Ohio county, W. Va., in 1845.   George W. Cranage died in 1882 in Pittsburgh.   Josiah Mansell is still living, and now stationed at Upper Middletown, Fayette county, and has been in the ministry 41 years.   Thomas Jamison died at Senecaville, Ohio, November 3rd, 1851.   Richard Armstrong died aged 84 at Freeport, Pa., August 19th, 1859.   Westley Smith is dead. David Hess died at Pittsburgh in 1873, after an effective career of 36 years in the service.   Henry Kern died at Mt. Pleasant, Iowa, in 1872.   Martin Ruter died at Washington, Texas, in 1838.   John J. Moffit died in Uniontown, from an injury, in 1881, after a service of 40 years.

Samuel Wakefield resides in West Newton, Pa., and although he has been in active work for over seventy-five years, he is still vigorous and bids fair for some years yet of physical before he enters upon the spiritual life. He preached his first sermon in Mt. Pleasant in 1820. J. J. Swayze left this world in 1853, in Allegheny City. Peter F. Jones died in Brooke county, W. Va., in 1856. Z. H. Coston died in Lawrence, Kas., in 1874. Joseph Horner is in Pittsburgh. R. Hopkins resides in Sewickly, Pa.; was received on trial in 1823, came to Pittsburgh conference in 1825, has been effective forty years, presiding elder nineteen years. W. L. Weekly died very aged and had a career of fifty years of effective work. J. F. Jones is stationed at Washington in full vigor of active service. E. B. Griffin died at Canton, Ohio. Frank Moore graduated at Washington college in the class of 1842, attended for a time the sessions of the Western Theological seminary, entered the ministry in the Methodist Episcopal church, and while quite young in years had the honorary degree of D. D. conferred on him. At his death, which occurred in the state of California some years since, he was considered one of the most learned and distinguished ministers in the Methodist denomination. The writer knew him well and watched with great interest his career in life.

John C. Brown lived in Iowa. After having filled many important stations in the church, his latter days have become over-shadowed with a cloud that the many friends of his early life still hope and pray may be removed ere he passes away. C. H. Edwards is a member of the East Ohio Conference. M. McK. Garrett died in Forest City, Iowa, in 1883. L. R. Beacom is in Pittsburgh, having already had 38 years of effective service with 8 years as presiding elder. Rev. A. J. Endsley after many years in the service, has been retired under not favorable surroundings. Charles A. Holmes is in Allegheny, has been 45 years in active service, and is looked upon as one of the strongest pillars in the church. N. P. Kerr, Waynesburg. S. W. Davis, Washington, Pa.; A. P. Leonard, Jeannette; J. B. Uber, Canonsburg. Rev. J. H. Ebbert, the leader of the original class, is now a resident of Philadelphia, he has been an effective minister only five years, he entered the ministry in 1831, was supernumerary one, and superannuated 50 years. For many years he was connected with the banking business in Pittsburgh. We have a letter written by him to Rev. James Davidson in 1876, in reference to the original class, but cannot find it. Of the original class and its formation, Mrs. Grace McFall yet speaks very distinctly. Her maiden name was Call; she is a sister of the late Nicholas Call, whose wife was a sister of Rev. Jas. Davidson; also of Daniel and John Call, a sister of Mrs. Alexander Frazer, near this place, and also of the first wife of Barnet Corwin who was a member of the class. Mrs. McFall was born August 25, 1813, in an old log house that stood on the George Fisher farm near Lenity school house; she was married to Thomas McFall July 28, 1831, by Rev. J. G. Sansom, assisted by Rev. John Irwin, in a house on the farm long owned by Benjamin Thomas in Rostraver; she has lived in the house in which she now resides ever since 1833, in which year her husband built it. She joined the M. E. church in March, 1828, under the ministry of Father Stevenson at Fell's old log church; Benjamin Beazel was her first class-leader; in 1834 as we have already stated, she became a member of Rev. Ebbert's class in Bellevernon.

Barnet Corwin, now dead, resided near town and had long been a member of the Free-Will Baptist church. At what time he dissolved his connection with the M. E. church we are not informed. His wife Eleanor died in February, 1839, in the house now owned by the Hutton heirs on Main street. John Corwin died many years ago in Morgan county, Ohio; Jane, his wife, was a daughter of Mathew Patterson, of Washington county; she died in Greene county, Ind., in 1886. Her second husband's name was Davis. Mrs. Katy Ward, another of the class, died in the house occupied recently by James Hagerty, the postmaster. Sabina Gaskill's maiden name was Lane; she died about the year 1885, in Ohio. Rebecca Jacobs was a member of the M. E. church for nearly half a century, lived much of her life in this town and vicinity; she died January 17, 1879, at the residence of her grandson, H. H. Elliot, in Pittsburgh, Pa. She was a sister of Mrs. Katy Ward.

Robert Demain succeeded Rev. Ebbert as leader of the class. He came from Norfolk, England, in 1832, to Brownsville. In 1838 he came to Bellevernon and lived for one year in the house now owned by Mrs. Eliza Smock, and then moved into the house occupied by Captain J. M. Bowell and Morgan Bowers, on Water street (which he purchased from the late William Eberheart), where he lived to the day of his death. He was killed January 13, 1843, in a coal bank above town near the stone house now owned by R. C. Schmertz. He was a man of great piety and Christian influence. In 1840 Peter Swearer was added to the old class. He joined the M. E. church in 1832, and was an active and devoted member to the day of his death, which occurred at Brownsville, Pa., February 15, 1877, aged seventy-two years. He was a class-leader forty years. In 1876 Rev. James Davidson wrote to him making some inquiries relating to the early history of the church in this place, and in reply his son writes as follows:

"My father often speaks of the church in Bellevernon; of its struggles for success, and of the glorious success attending the prayers and efforts of the few who were found on the Lord's side. He speaks of the glorious meetings—the sweet counsel taken with many who since that have finished their course and gone to their heavenly home. Father is now an old man, waiting by the river, his race nearly run, and sometimes bursts forth in shouts of praise to the God who has kept him all the journey through up to the present, and fully believes the promise, "I will never leave nor forsake thee."

JAMES R. SWEARER.

John Swearer, brother of Peter, was a zealous Christian of the early days of this church. He died many years since with the brightest hopes of a blessed immortality. He too was a class leader of long standing.

Among the early reminiscences of the church the name of Noah W. Speers looms up with as much prominence for active work as any one of those days. It affords us very great pleasure to be able at this time, over his own signature, to give many historical facts and incidents relative to the early struggles of the Methodist Episcopal Church, of Bellevernon.

MEMPHIS, June 26th, 1887.

J. S. VAN VOORHIS, M.D.

DEAR SIR:—In compliance with your request, I send the following.

My father, Noah Speers, born March 27, 1769, was founder of Bellevernon. I remember distinctly of helping to plant corn where the glass works now stand down to the hollow where the steamboat yard was. My father died June 9th, 1832. One or two years before or perhaps prior to above date, James G. Sansom, an eloquent holy Methodist minister, who travelled Red Stone Circuit including a considerable portion of Washington county, making a four weeks circuit, then crossing the river at Bellevernon, stopping at father's house, he would arrange to give an evening service on his return home, which was near Fell's Church, in the forks of the two rivers, Youghiogheny and Monongahela. Preaching was then held in the school-house (owned by father,) which was about three doors south of the old Ward Mansion, opposite Jones' bank, on Main Street. My father gave Rev. Mr. Sansom the use of a fine horse during his time on that circuit.

Luke Beazell, his wife and sons Lemuel and John, also daughters Susie and Mary, were living on the Miller farm, opposite Lock and dam No. 4. Manassah Reeves, Esq., Samuel and Jesse Reeves, brothers, were living on farms adjoining my fathers. The above named persons (except my father) were members of Fells Church. Class meeting and monthly preaching was held at Samuel Reeves' till his death, then for an indefinite time at Manassah Reeves' Andrew C. Ford was class-leader. Some time during the year, after father's death, sister Clara and I joined the church at Williamsport, under the preaching of the Rev. S. R. Brocknour. I don't remember dates as all my books and memoranda were burned at Cincinnati, at the time of my great loss by fire. I think in 34, or 35, maybe 36, Revs. Alcinus Young and John Irwin were on Redstone circuit and occasionally preached at private houses in Bellevernon.

It was not until Mr. William Eberheart established the glass works, in '36 or '37, that Robert Demain, coal miner; Peter and John Swearer and Nelson Goslin, glass blowers, and prominent Methodists, established class and weekly prayer meetings; also Barnes C. Reeves and David Parkhill, builder and carpenter, took part in these meetings. During this period I was away at Meadville College, and on my return in the spring of '37 these meetings were kept up in the private residences. About this period we organized a church with Hugh Ford, Barnes C. Reeves, Solomon Speers, Peter Swearer, David Parkhill, Goslin, Manassah Reeves, I think, and myself, as trustees and stewards, and built the brick church on the side of the hill, a little south of where the Presbyterian church now stands. The foundation proved bad, and the people were fearful and did not occupy it. During a suit for damages we lost title to the building.

I rented this church for the commencement exercises of the Bellevernon Academy, and it was packed to its utmost capacity, which gained the confidence of most of the members. Still it was not used; the meetings continuing in private houses till the glass works went out of blast in July and August, when the glass blowers (principally from Albany, near Brownsville), as was their custom during the session of the annual conference, held protracted prayer meeting till the new minister arrived. The meetings were kept up for a week or two without any perceptible feeling except the fervent faithfulness of the dozen or less which attended.

A meeting was held in Father Demain's residence. My niece, Diana Speers, daughter of brother Solomon Speers, said to me as I passed, "I will go to prayer meeting with you." As was our custom the invitation was given, "All who desire prayer to signify by remaining on their knees while a verse would be sung." While no one knelt the effect of the invitation was as if the Holy Spirit was present. Friday and Saturday evenings my niece was not present, but the house was filled on both evenings, and the deepest feeling of religious interest was felt throughout the village and surrounding neighborhood. Without further notice than being asked by Brother Demain to hold the Sunday evening service in his house, with the special request by him that the members make a special prayer for the sinners of Bellevernon, and the new pastors, not knowing who they would be. If they would make this the burden of their hearts and come to the meeting a great work could be accomplished. An hour before candle lighting people from the country and village arrived, and before the hour for service from 150 to 200 collected in and around the house as if by magic. I proposed renting the brick church for our meetings. Gaining consent, I sent out runners with candles to light the church, and when the hour arrived the house was literally packed.

Brothers Demain, Peter and John Swearer were the principal leaders, but when we entered the alter they refused to lead, saying to me, "you brought us here, you are the man to lead." Not knowing why, only by the power of compulsion, I opened to and read the good old hymn:—"Alas! and did my Savior bleed!" with a trembling voice. Sobs and sighs were heard all over the house. After the hymn read from Ephesians 2nd chapter, not knowing why. Fifteen mourners without invitation knelt at the altar. These meetings were kept up for several days, the brothers Peter and John Swearer and Father Demain leading alternately. When the new pastors came, brothers Dempsey and Adams, from Conference, we handed them 27 names as the result of the protracted prayer meeting. We occupied the church during the fall and winter, then the old building known as Reeves' store house, was used till March '47, I think, when I moved to Cincinnati.

There are doubtless many things I might say of interest after more mature deliberation. There is one circumstance which I remember very forcibly. During a service in the brick church in the early spring, a deep snow had fallen and a thaw and a freeze had made the ground very slippery. The church had two entrances, one in front with high steps, the other at the side next the hill with a wall five or six feet high. On the hillside by the church a number of sugar trees were growing, some of which had been tapped. While Brother Adams was preaching, giving a terrible description of the Judgment Day, and about 8 p. m., two boys were getting sugar water with a couple of lanterns just as the preacher came to a climax of fire and brimstone, the boys started to see which could go fastest down the hill swinging lanterns in hand. One or two sympathetic sisters sang out in a very high key, "The fire is coming indeed." This attracted the entire congregation to the two balls of fire, as the lanterns appeared to be. The people made for the doors down the slippery walks toward Main street and home. In an instant the boys put out the lantern and quietly slipped home, keeping the secret. One of the boys, my nephew, came quietly to me and begged me to keep the secret, which I did, until a full description had been given by all who witnessed the scene, and in their own way. In listening to the various descriptions of the scene, I believe the lanterns were described as being large as hay stacks, etc., the smallest mentioned was the size of a barrel. Don't you think had you witnessed that scene it would have made you git?

Brothers Moses Jamison, Cornelius Battell and Gallehew were on the circuit, but I forget in what years.

Yours,

N. W. SPEERS.

STEWARDS IN BELLEVERNON M. E. CHURCH.

Among the many persons who have been class-leaders and stewards in this church besides those we have already mentioned, we have gathered the names of the following up to

February, 1866:—Samuel Reeves, Van Reeves, James Davidson, Robert Davidson, John Watson, Wm. Winters, Milton G. Ebbert, Anthony Hazelbaker, Fred Shibler, John Mullin, Thomas Edwards, J. T. Roley, Chas. Bolse, Davis Shepler, O. H. P. Scott, Adam Shunk, Samuel Sutton, Benjamin Hughes, C. B. Chalfant, Wm. Gaskill, W. H. Jones, W. H. Johnson, John R. Powell, John N. Beazell, Wm. Kyle, J. J. Zimmerman, D. P. Housman, Church Porter, Curtiss Reppert, Amon Bronson. James Davidson has been recording Steward since March 10th, 1865, with the exception of one year. The Rev. James Davidson with John Watson, Davis Shepler, David Fetz and Howard M. Fish, have been in this church as local preachers. The organ was first introduced into the church music in the fall of 1866. From contributions and the proceeds of a concert held by Miss Lizzie Van Voorhis and others, in the old frame Church, sufficient funds were raised to purchase the small organ still in use in the Sabbath School. Lizzie Van Voorhis was the organist until the new organ was placed in the brick church.

In a former article we said that the lot on which the new frame church on Water street was erected had been purchased from William Eberheart. The title we find, however, came through L. M. Speer and Jane, his wife, by deed of conveyance to Van Reeves and others, the then trustees of the Methodist Episcopal church of Bellevernon, dated November 20, 1852. and by deed from Noah Speers and others, the then trustees of said church, dated October 2, 1867, to Robert C. Schmertz. Robert C. Schmertz and Mary Elizabeth, his wife conveyed the same lot and church building, by deed dated December 10, 1868, to John B. Gould and James H. Springer, trustees of the Church of Christ by the name of Christians or Disciples of Christ of Bellevernon. The old Disciple church and lot, corner of Water and Fourth streets, was sold to R. C. Schmertz, and is now numbered among the glass factory buildings. The rapidly increasing population of the town, and a corresponding prosperity of the church, necessitated larger accommodations, for the comfort of the congregation. During the conference year of 1866, when Rev. J. F. Jones was preacher in charge, the preliminaries were entered into for the raising of the funds. As we have stated the old church was sold. The board of trustees appointed at the last quarterly conference of the year 1866, held in Bellevernon February 19, 1866, consisted of James Davidson, A. Bronson, J. R. Powell, William Kyle, C. Reppert, Noah Speers, Jasper Haught, Samuel Sutton and Jacob Haught, for Bellevernon, and Jabez Nutt, Thomas Page, John Mullin, James Billiter, J. H. Weaver, G. R. Thirkield, W. H. Faulkner, J. J. Zimmerman and Church T. Porter, for Fayette City.

As far as we can discover, most of these brethren were in the board during the building of the brick church on Main street. The lot on Main street, 50 x 100 feet, No. 53, was purchased for $442 from William H. Jones and wife, by deed of conveyance to the Methodist Episcopal Church, of Bellevernon, dated 19th day of October, 1867, it being a piece of ground which John Tiernan, administrator of Thos. Taggart, deceased, deeded to said William H. Jones, December 18th, 1863. Rev. C. H. Edwards was pastor during these proceedings in the year 1867. The corner stone was laid June 10th, 1867, by Mrs. Eliza Weaver, Misses Emma, Maggie and Lydia Davidson. The stone work was done by Robert Hagerty, the carpenter work by J. R. Powell, the brick work by Solomon Meridith, and the painting by John Hatfield. The fine bell which graces the tower was presented by John Gibson, of Philadelphia.

October 27, 1867, was the day appointed for the dedication of the chapel or lecture room of the new church. The opening sermon was preached by Rev. I. C. Pershing, D.D., President of the Pittsburgh Female College to a large and attentive audience. In the afternoon a deeply interesting sacramental service was held. In the evening Rev. A. J. Endsley, Presiding Elder, preached a very excellent sermon. The entire length of the building is seventy feet, by forty-two in width. The main audience room is forty by fifty-eight feet exclusive of the gallery over the vestibule. The lecture room is thirty-nine by forty-four feet, with two class rooms at the entrance. A well proportioned tower rises twenty-three feet above the roof and is surmounted with a spire fifty-two feet in height; making a total of one hundred and thirty-seven feet from the ground. During the ministry of Ed. Williams, in the year 1869, the audience room and other unfinished parts were completed, and on the 25th of July, 1869, the house entire was dedicated to the service of God, according to the form prescribed in the Book of Discipline. In the dedication services the pastor, Rev. Ed. Williams was assisted by Revs. M. L. Weekly, J. Horner, J. H. Conkle, S. H. Nesbit and E. Dudley. The entire cost of the building is estimated at $15,000. To the untiring industry and perserverance of the Pastors Rev. Edwards and Williams, and the board of trustees, whose names will appear in the charter, the church is indebted for this beautiful and substantial building. To facilitate the financial and legal operations of the church matters it was deemed prudent and wise to have the church incorporated, thereupon an application for a charter of incorporation was presented to the Court of Common Pleas, of Fayette county, June 7, 1867.

The court having examined the Articles of Association June 7th, 1867, ordered the application to be filed in the office of the prothonotary of said court, and the court also directed notice to be inserted in the *Genius of Liberty* of said application. In the court of common pleas, of Fayette county, Pennsylvania. And now, to wit, September 2nd, 1867, having satisfactory evidence that the proper notice was given pursuant to the former order of this court, and no sufficient reason having been shown why the foregoing charter should not be granted, we do hereby decree and declare that the members of the Methodist Episcopal Church, of Bellevernon, and their successors, shall, according to the articles and conditions in the within instrument set forth and contained, become and be a corporation and body politic, and direct that this, their charter of incorporation, shall be recorded in the office for the recording of deeds in this county. By the court.

At a meeting of the members of the church November 12, 1867, the charter was accepted and at the same time the trustees organized by electing Jasper Haught, president; Noah Speers, secretary, and Curtiss Reppert, treasurer. During the year 1870 the Bellevernon charge was separated from Fayette City, Rev. E. B. Griffin being the preacher, and resided in the house on the corner of Water and Fourth streets. In the year 1881 the church purchased from Amon Bronson, for a parsonage, the house situated corner of Wood street and Locust alley. The trustees for 1887 were Noah Speers, C. Reppert, Amon Bronson, James Davidson, W. C. Kittle, J. B. Zeh, L. Steen, Wm. Jones and J. B. Thompson. Wm. Jones, president; L. Steen, secretary, and W. C. Kittle, treasurer. The present class leaders (July 14, 1887) are Noah Speers, James Davidson and J. B. Thompson. The stewards are James Davidson, J. B. Zeh, J. B. Thompson, C. Reppert, W. C. Kittle, Amon Bronson, Wm. Jones, John Durst, Leightty Steen and Noah Speers. We again acknowledge our indebtedness to Rev. James Davidson for his aid in furnishing much material for this historical sketch of the Methodist Episcopal church. He has been so long identified with this church that his work is everywhere, for nearly half a century, mingled with its progress. He was converted in May, 1838, in the old stone church in Elizabeth, under the preaching of Rev. John Coil, but first joined the church at Fell's not long afterwards. He connected himself with the Bellevernon church in 1850, while Rev. J. F. Nessly was in charge. Mrs. Margaret Lewis, Grace McFall, Samuel Reeves and wife, Levi Harris, are the only persons he can recollect as members now, who were such at the time he came to this church.

FREE WILL BAPTIST CHURCH.

In April, 1843, certain brethren living in Bellevernon and vicinity made a request in the form of a petition to Elder Joshua Newbold, for the organization of a Free Will Baptist Church in that village. The request was presented to the

Jacobs Creek Church at the monthly meeting held on the second Saturday (8th) of April, of the same year. At this same quarterly meeting, Elder Joshua Newbold, S. G. Smutz, David Smith, Jr., Robert Armstrong and Alexander Armstrong were appointed a council to organize such a church, April 22, 1843; if they considered it proper so to do. The council met in the old brick school house on the hill, and all being present except Alexander Armstrong, they proceeded to business by choosing Elder Joshua Newbold, president, and S. G. Smutz, secretary. after examining the matter solemnly and truly as required, the council duly organized and constituted the petitioners into a church.

The names of the twelve persons which constituted the church are as follows: Thomas C. Jordan, Daniel Springer, Roger Jordon, Isaac Ferree, Jas. M. Springer, Hannah Jordon, Rachel Springer, Lydia Springer, Eliza Jordon, Elizabeth Elder, Catharine Shocky, Sarah Ann Jordon ; Elder Joshua Newbold was elected pastor for one year. Daniel Springer and Isaac Ferree were chosen Deacons and Roger Jordon clerk. At a meeting of the members, April 22, 1843, it was resolved that we will agree to form ourselves as Free Will Baptists into a church, to be called the Bellevernon church, and we agree to take the Scriptures for our only rule of faith and practice, and to walk according to the order of the Free Will Baptists as laid down in the Treatise of the General Conference in 1834, and that we agree that the majority shall rule in all cases except in receiving members and excluding them, it will be expected to be a unanimous vote of the church so far as practicable, and that we agree to support a preacher, so far as we are able. Signed by all the 12 members.

The first meeting of the church in conference was held on the 4th Saturday of May, 1843, being the 27th day. June 3rd, 1843, at this second quarterly conference meeting, Daniel Springer was appointed delegate to the Jacobs Creek quarterly conference, being the first of the kind appointed. At the conference held July 1st, Dr. Charles B. Egan delivered his first exhortation. September 12th, 1843, it was resolved to make an effort to build a church by subscriptions of money. March 26th, 1844, the effort to raise money being successful to such an extent as to warrant the building of a church, it was resolved to appoint Daniel Springer, Roger Jordon and William Wayts trustees for the funds already raised, and the same persons were named as a building committee, and authorized to erect a church building 26 x 36 feet. It was built on the lot on Wood street near Flint alley, now owned by D. W. Owens; Thomas Taggart was the contractor. The church was dedicated September 8th, 1844; elder Joshua Newbold preached the dedicatory sermon.

December 16, 1856, Roger Jordon resigned his position as clerk and trustee, which he held since the organization of the church. James M. Springer was elected in his place, and served until May 25th, 1869. Pierson B. Luce was elected clerk April 23d, 1870, Mrs. Allie Cooper, February 2nd, 1877, Mrs. Erzanna Browneller, January 6th, 1879, and John C. Lynn, was elected January 5, 1885. The deacons are P. B. Luce, James Phillips; and treasurer, Dr. A. N. Marston. The old church becoming too small for the growing congregation, it was determined to erect a new building. A lot on Short street, North Bellevernon, was purchased from L. M. Speers for $350; on it the present beautiful structure was erected in in 1871-72. The total cost was $2800. The contractor for the frame work was the late O. D. Johnson. The plastering was done by Thomas Cooper and the painting by Robert McClure.

The church was dedicated April 21, 1872, Rev. James Calder, of Harrisburg, preaching the dedication sermon. The spire was blown down by a storm in the fall of 1876, and was replaced by the present cupalo. The lot, No. 71, on which the church is erected, was deeded by L. M. Speers and wife, Fannie, June 1, 1871, to J. Wesley Corwin, Joseph B. Courtney and John Hixenbaugh, trustees of the Free-Will Baptist church of Bellevernon borough. To the untiring efforts of the late J. W. Corwin the church is indebted for this building more than any one other individual. From the day the idea of building it was conceived until the last dollar was paid he never let up in his labor to have the work accomplished, and he had before his death not only the comforts of a beautiful church edifice but the consolation of having done his duty well. He had been a member of this church since 1854.

On the 4th day of April, 1846, elders Joshua Newbold, Edward Jordon and David Smutz were elected to preach alternately every two weeks for the next year. These preachers were succeeded in their time by Drs. Egan, Newbold, Reardon, Winton, Plannet, Cook, Blakely, Jordon, Bryant, Springer, Lacock, Joy, Nye, Rogers, Fish, Smutz, Knap, Hills, and the present pastor, Joel Baker, who took charge May 6th, 1883. Rev. Joel Baker was born in Connecticut, studied theology at New Hampton Theological School, was licensed to preach at the quarterly meeting held at Meredith, New Hampshire, May 27th, 1856, and was ordained at Alton, N. H., November 19th, 1857. Like most of other churches, this one has no regular record of the origin and early workings of its Sabbath school.

The Free Will Baptist Sabbath School was organized in 1844, after the occupancy of the church building on Wood street; Daniel Springer was the first superintendent, and continued as such until he removed to Brownsville sometime in the early fifties, where he only remained two months. He afterwards was superintendent at different times. The school at this date, July 27, 1887, is in a flourishing condition. Its present officers are: Superintendent, Dr. A. N. Marston; Assistant, Ed. J. Corwin; Teachers, the pastor, Joel Baker, Mrs. Katty Marston, Mrs. Luther Corwin, Mrs. Barnet Corwin, Mrs. D. W. Jones, Mrs. John Dowling, Misses Jennie Worrell, Ella Fuester, Mintie Clegg, Lizzie Scott; Secretary and Librarian, Thomas Scott, Jr.; Treasurer, Mintie Clegg.

Disciple Church of Bellevernon.

The exact date at which the Disciples first held meetings in Bellevernon cannot be fixed, but from all the information we can gather, in 1838 two elders named Landfier, of Ohio, preached in the house on Water street below Cherry alley, lately occupied by Alexander Brown. A lady whose name has been forgotten, was immersed by them, being the first baptism by the Disciples in the town. After these gentlemen, Elder Pool came into the neighborhood and preached in private houses and the brick school house on the hill. In conversation with Elder L. P. Streator, we learned that he preached in 1841 in the Brown house on Water street, then occupied by Bowman Furnier; after the discourse Miss Sallie Gould was baptized at the ferry wharf. During the religious excitement in this vicinity in 1843, among the different churches, a number of Disciple preachers visited the town and began preaching in private dwellings. Among these were Elders Pool, Pyatt, Benedict, McKenzie and some others whose names are lost. They held meetings in the houses of J. B. Gould, James Corwin, A. P. Frye, Nathaniel Everson, and the school house on the hill. The result of these meetings was the gathering into the Disciple faith of quite a number, among whom we may mention John B. Gould and wife, James Corwin, Sr., and wife, Joseph Springer and wife, James H. Springer and wife, Mary Corwin, Hester and Mary, daughters of James Corwin, Sr., Ackey and Sallie Gould whom we have already named. The brethren in 1844 determined to build a meeting house, and the result was the building corner of Fourth and Water streets.

In 1869 this house was sold, as we have stated in a former article, to R. C. Schmertz, and the old Methodist church purchased. Elder Pool preached for a year or perhaps two after the completion of the new house. He lived in the house corner First and Water streets. As yet there was no congregation regularly organized in the town. Meetings were held on every alternate Lord's day with Fayette City congregation. Meetings were held at different times by such elders as Benedict, Hughes, Walk, Southmaid, Delmont and Rowe, until 1869, when Elder Rowe, having held a successful meeting, it was thought best to organize a separate organization in Bellevernon. A written request being sent to Fayette City congregation and granted, in May, 1870, an organization was effected. John B. Gould, D. B. H. Allen and James M. Springer were chosen elders, and James H. Springer and Thomas Fawcet, deacons; D. B. H. Allen, treasurer, and James M. Springer, clerk. In the Disciple church the pastors are elected by the individual congregation at pleasure. The first regular pastor after the organization was Elder J. B. Cox, who remained a year or two, and was succeeded by Southmaid, Delmont, Pyatt, Streator, Rowe, Chase, Vogel, and Jobes, the present pastor is Elder Brice L. Kershner. In the absence of a pastor the meetings are conducted by the elders, who have the oversight of the church, and preaching is had as the congregation may desire by employing preachers to hold meetings.

THE FIRST SCHOOL IN BELLEVERNON.

The first school in the village of Bellevernon was taught by John Hazelbaker in the kitchen part of the house of the venerable Mary Corwin. This house originally stood on the farm now owned by James Ward, in Rostraver, and was the primitive dwelling of Michael Springer, who emigrated to this country from Stockholm, in Sweden. John Hazelbaker was a brother of the late Jacob Hazelbaker, who lived for many years in the stone house just above town; also of the late George Hazelbaker, of Allen township, Washington county. Schools were also taught by John B. Gould and others in the house now occupied by W. P. Mackey, and in the house owned now by Mrs. Eliza Smock, and in several other houses.

After the common school system was adopted in 1834, the old brick school house on the hill was erected with brick taken from the old Rehoboth church which had been built in 1803. The money to build this school house was raised by subscription, and erected under the supervision of Solomon Speers and A. P. Frye. This house being in the woods and on the hill, was soon considered so inconvenient that the school board of Washington township determined to build a new one in Gould's hollow. It was built of brick taken from the old mill near the mouth of Speers' run, owned in the long ago by David Furnier. This old school building is still standing, a monument of the past. The only remnant extant of the old brick church of Rehoboth may be seen in the pavement in front of the residence of W. P. Mackey. Whilst he owned the house Dr. Van Voorhis had the pavement made of brick taken from the old school house on the hill.

After the erection of the school house in Gould's hollow the one on the hill was abandoned, but in after years, when two schools became necessary, it was again occupied under the auspices of the Washington township school board. Among the teachers in the brick school house on the hill we can mention William, or Billy Bolt, as he was called. He lived in the house recently owned by John H. Shepperd, in Rostraver. Robert T. Galloway was another teacher. He afterwards became a lawyer; resided in Uniontown; was elected to the Legislature in 1844, was elected prothonotary in 1854, and died in Connellsville not many years since ripe in honors and esteem of his fellow-citizens. David Longnecker also taught in this house. Nancy J. Gould, John C. Hasson, John B. Gould, John Wilson, a Mr. Martin, Henry Fulton, now of California; Prof. George P. Fulton, of Pittsburgh, and Sallie Gould, were among those who taught in this old house.

John C. Hasson taught his first school in 1852 in the old Tremont House, over the river nearly opposite the glass works. He was the first teacher in Fayette county examined by Joshua V Gibbons, who was the first County Superintendent. The examination was in 1854 in Gould's school house. Mr. Hasson is still among us, being one of the most substantial citizens of

North Bellevernon. Geo. P. Fulton had been a teacher of common schools since he was seventeen years old. Was three years in the army, and had been for seventeen years principal of the Hiland Public School, in Pittsburgh before his death. He very kindly undertook to give the writer a paper on his early career as a teacher in Bellevernon, but before completing it, as he desired, he was overtaken with disease, disabling him from giving a full history. We subjoin his letter. Prof. Geo. P. Fulton says:

"In April, 1852, I commenced teaching in Bellevernon, in the old brick school house on the hill. It was a subscription school. The glassmen of the works of W. Eberheart, Sr., composed the controlling element in all the affairs of the town and neighborhood. Old man Eberheart was '*rex absolutus*' of the glass trade from New Geneva to New Orleans. Then there were no strikes. If a workman was not satisfied with his wages he threw up his 'pot,' vacated the tenement of his employer on summary notice, received his pay and left the town. Adam and George Shunk, Oliver Scott, Christ Welzer, Oliver Town, John Hutton, Charley Coll, George Bunting and William H. Faulkner, were glass-house men whose names are still fresh in my memory. The farmers of Allen and Fallowfield over the river, brought their butter and eggs to Eberheart's store, whilst the Finley's, the Smocks, Robinsons and Springers, from the farms in the forks and Rehoboth valley, furnished from their herds grass-fed beeves and swine for the glass-works families.

"Side by side the glass making industry, were the boat yards of L. M. Speers whose sterling character for probity and generous dealings in all this great enterprise, will be remembered as long as the name of the town shall stand, or hearts can beat in the breasts of those who then enjoyed his friendship, his confidence and his princely hospitality.

"Clarke's coal works above town were then in operation, but the custom of the miners in the stores generally went to Cookstown, so that the glass works and boat yards alone kept the community in thrift and industry.

"The first of July, when the fires were out was a carnival season for Bellevernon creditors from the highest to the lowest in the ranks of the year's workers. Dr. Van Voorhis gathered in his yearly harvest of dues for healing offices; the preachers and school teachers were then paid; old Dr. Jacob Hazelbaker ran down delinquents for his cobling services, on the hob-nailed shoes of the teazers, rendered in the intervals of his veterinary practice; old man Jones who kept the ale-house on the corner of First and Water streets, rubbed out the chalked scores for the nut brown draughts dealt to the toilers during the year, and laid in fresh supplies of refreshment for the summer solstice.

"I taught but two terms in the town. The second school was held in a hall fitted up by Division No. 286, Sons of Temperance, converted long since into a dwelling, and now owned and occupied by Allen K. and Curtiss Reppert, on Main below Third street. William Eberheart and L. M. Speers jointly paid my salary, and they sent as pupils the children of their families and such of their employes as could be admitted with the prescribed limit of attendance. This was truly a mixed school. Boys were reciting Virgil preparatory to admission to Washington college; one bright girl was studying botany, whilst some were in the alphabet. To hear talk about work in the school room now makes me sigh, when I think of those jubilant days of yore. 'Hope in the prow and pleasure at the helm,' when the hours of the longest summer day were never tiresome or irksome amid the cheerful group that were always in step with the longest stride of my enthusiasm.

"I had a large school of young ladies older than their teacher, and big boys of equal ages filled the seats around the walls, while scores of six year olds held down the little benches in front of the master's desk. Professors were unknown in those days. It would have been Professor John Wilson of the Lagrange and Professor John B. Gould of Gould's Hollow, and Professor Fred Cooper, who used to come on Saturday's from his school on Maple Creek and drown his school "sorrows in the flowin bole," as Artemus Ward would say. Cooper was a fine scholarly fellow, six feet in height, erect and had the air and manners of a well-bred gentleman.

Our school work was carried on without the help of the many valuable appliances which now abound in the hands of the skillful teachers of to-day; yet with only primers I had my six year old tads reading in the first reader in six weeks.

"Captain Jim French, the jolly skipper of the Swan and Bellevernon, and afterward of the Polly South, had his first-born in this class, and could attest the correctness of this statement.

"I was in the height of sympathy with my work—my whole soul was in it, and I fairly got up early to see these young scions unfold the leaves of their mental growth, and note their progress from night until the next morning roll-call, and herein lies the whole secret of the teacher's success—to love his charge with all his heart and soul and strength, letting his neighbor in other pursuits attend to his own business, and drive his school along to success when he gets it a-going, as Sheridan did his soldiers, not giving them time to halt, lie down or skulk."

SCHOOL TEACHERS AND SCHOOL HOUSES.

Among the many persons who taught school in Gould's Hollow were John Wilson, deceased for many years, John B. Gould, dead only a few years, John Q. Robinson, who is at this time one of the most prominent medical men in Westmoreland county; has always resided in West Newton since commencing to practice his profession. J. H. Wilson whilst teaching here in 1856, was a resident of Washington county, but now resides near Chatsworth, Illinois. After teaching over thirty years retired from the profession. His mother was a sister of the late Nancy P. Davidson, whose maiden name was Palmer, and whose first husband was Samuel Reeves, the father of our fellow citizens Samuel and John Reeves and the late Mrs. J. M. Springer.

Levi J. Jefries is now a citizen of Bellevernon. He was originally a glasshouse boy. His fellow boys taught him the alphabet by means of letters made on the foot-benches with chalk. Within three years afterwards his chalk-mark teachers were among his scholars during the time he taught in the old Gould's Hollow school house. Sallie Gould married a man by the name of Morrison, and has been dead many years. She was the mother of Elmer Morrison, now a resident of Seldom Seen, adjoining the borough. Sarah Fulton graduated at Washington Female Seminary in 1857. She was the wife of Rev. J. H. Stevenson, of Mt. Carmel, Ill. She is deceased. George W. Nichols, after leaving this town, was long a resident of Lawrenceville, Pa. He has been dead a number of years. A part of the house owned by the late J. W. Corwin used to stand on the corner of Main and Second streets, and it was utilized for a time as a school house. A man by the name of Adly taught here for awhile, and also A. J. Colvin, about the year 1848. Miss Vashti Budd, about 1849, had also a school in this building. She was a cousin of John C. Hasson. Miss Florilla Tower had a select school in 1856 and a year or more subsequent, perhaps, in the room for a long time known as the store room of Solomon Speers, but more recently it has been used as sitting room in the hotel known as the Roley house near the ferry.

In 1857 the old school house on the hill and also the one at Gould's were abandoned and sold, and the new brick building was erected on the lot now occupied by the beautiful residence of R. J. Linton, corner State and Short streets. It was a two-story building with two rooms on the first and one room on the second floor. It was built under the supervision of James Davidson and J. M. Springer as building committee of the school board of Washington township. Solomon Meredith did the brick and Peter Snyder the carpenter work. The brick were made in and shipped from California, in Washington county. The entire cost of the building was $1327.18. It was first occupied in January, 1858, by John Wright and Miss Florilla Tower as teachers. In the fall of 1858, Mr. Ross W. Phillips and Miss Sallie Vanhook were elected teachers. In 1859 the same Mr. Ross was elected principal, but during the night after the first days school he mysteriously disappeared, leaving nothing to tell the reason for such conduct. Mr. E. C. Griffith was elected in his place. Having no record from this year until the incorporation of the borough, we cannot give in full the names of all the teachers, but we can recall the names of C. C. Baugh, John Hasson, Miss Mary Beazell, Miss Myra Fulton. Miss Beazell was the wife of J. P. Cunningham, of Rostraver; she is now dead. Miss Fulton is the wife of Rev. E. P. Lewis, of St. Paul, Minn. Mr. Baugh has been in the mercantile business in Perrypolis and some other places. In the *Enterprise* some time ago was published a full official list of all the teachers in the public schools of Bellevernon from the time of the incorporation in 1863 to the present, to which we refer our reader.

The records of Washington township have been lost or mislaid prior to 1841. In 1841 William Eberheart was elected school director, being the first from the village of Bellevernon. James Davidson, J. S. Van Voorhis, J. M. Springer, and perhaps others whose names we cannot remember, have served as directors in the township. Below we give a list of the persons who have been directors of the borough since its organization: Robert Boyle, James Davidson, J. S. Van Voorhis, James French, John W. Wright, N. Q. Speers, James M. Springer, J. A. Piersol, Curtiss Reppert, O. D. Johnson, John Power, Jesse P. Sill, W. F. Speers, John Reeves, Henry Haler, Alex. Brown, J. W. Corwin, Amon Bronson, S. F. Jones, Church Porter, R. J. Linton, A. P. Lewis, A. A. Taggart, W. P. Mackey, J. H. Lewis, W. E. McCrory, Eli W. Martin, L. Z. Birmingham, Ephraim Lewis, J. B. Enos, E. M. Kyle, J. M. Bowell, John A. Acklin, W. H. Noble, S. M. Graham, Dr. A. N. Marston, Isaac Coldron, John Durst.

The corps of teachers for 1892–93 consisted of Ira R. Smith, principal; Miss Carrie Greathead, Miss Ida Hug, Miss Clara Lang and Miss Sphar.

The New Brick School Houses in Bellevernon.

The growth of the town and increase of scholars, seemed to demand greater accommodations in the building. June 17th, 1869, resolutions were offered in the Board looking to the erection of an additional building in the rear of the main building twenty-four by thirty feet, two stories, to cost about $1800. The resolutions were referred to a committee consisting of O. D. Johnson, J. A. Piersol and James French, who reported on the 22nd of June the resolutions with very little modification, and on motion they were adopted with one negative vote, James M. Springer. At a called meeting of the Board on June 25, the resolutions were re-considered and negatived. The failure of the project arose from opposition on the part of the citizens. The opposition was owing to the assessment of eighteen mills to pay for the additional rooms, and little did the grumblers think that in a very few years a massive structure would go up requiring that amount of money to be levied for generations yet unborn. At a meeting January 22nd, 1872, at which were present James French, Henry Haler, J. A. Piersol, Amon Bronson and W. F. Speers, committee on legislation were appointed.

June 14, 1872, J. W. Corwin was added as a new member to the board.

The bill reported in its passage was so amended and changed as to only authorize a per capita tax, confining it to three years, and allowing the use for building purposes of the excess of school tax not used in carrying on the schools.

In 1873 an act was passed authorizing the school board to borrow money at a rate not exceeding 8 per cent, after having exhausted the powers of the court in such cases provided. Of the 8 per cent bonds issued running fifteen years under this act, $5,500 at this date (August 29, 1887) remaining not due and unpaid. These will be due in 1888–89.

In July, 1872, J. M. Springer and Captain W. F. Speer

were appointed a committee to ascertain a plan of building for a new school house, cost, specifications, etc., Haler, Springer, Bronson, Speers and Brown voting yea.

August 5.—On motion Amon Bronson and Henry Haler were appointed to make arrangements with Samuel Bedsworth to burn brick for school house at $6 per 1,000. Committee on plan of school house reported a three-story building, two feet larger than the one at Fayette City. On motion W. F. Speer, Henry Haler and J. W. Corwin were appointed to offer for sale the old school house, and negotiate with J. A. Piersol for the purchase of his house and lots, subject to the approval of board.

August 6.—Committee to see Piersoll reported in favor of purchasing his property at $3,000. The board unanimously received the report.

August 16.—Committee on brick reported that they had bought 200,000 at six dollars per 1000 at the kiln. By a unanimous vote it was resolved to instruct the committee on purchase of school property, to negotiate for the Hasson heirs property. On motion it was agreed that if the school house be sold on Saturday the 17th inst., that the conditions should be as recorded but fails to specify to whom it was sold and for what price. In another part of the record we discover it was sold to R. J. Linton, not naming the price in the minutes.

December 12.—It was resolved to build the new school house sixty by seventy feet. On motion Brown, Speers and Corwin were appointed a committee to draw up specifications for both a two and three story building, and to receive bids for both plans. On motion it was resolved to sell the Piersol property. December 26th, the specifications for school building as written out and presented were unanimously adopted, not stating whether for two or three stories or for both. January 30th, 1873, the bids were opened and read as follows :—Wm. Coulter and A. A. Taggert, $13,990; Ziba Whiting, $14,000; Samuel Daugherty and Larimerl, $15,650.

February 14.—On motion the contract was awarded Wm. Coulter and A. A. Taggart at their bid, yeas Springer, Corwin,

Speers, Bronson, Brown and Haler. The committee made sale of the old house on Hasson lots and the Piersoll property to Amon Bronson, the former for $150 and the latter for $2810.

March 31st an order was issued in favor of Hasson's heirs for $1450, which seems to be the price paid for the two lots corner of Wood and Third streets on which the new building was erected.

June 2, 1873, S. F. Jones was elected instead of Haler, and W. F. Speers re-elected members of the board. June 25, S. F. Jones and J. M. Springer were appointed to superintend the building of the new school house, and July 19 Amon Bronson was added to the committee. August 25 J. M. Springer resigned his seat in the board, and August 30 Church Porter was appointed in his place. We have not been able to find in the record the exact cost of the new school house, including the fixtures and furniture, but from all the information we can gather the total cost was not far from $30,000.

September 17, 1873, J. W. Gibbons was elected principal of the first school in the new building at a salary of $80 per month; H. T. Baily was elected to room No. 2 at a salary of $60 per month; Theo. J. Allen to No. 3, wages $45, and Miss Hattie Davidson to room No. 4, wages $45. This school house has been subject to much severe criticism. The plan, the size and cost, have all undergone an ordeal of complaint. In many particulars the building has faults, but perhaps the board did all for the best, as things were seen at that time. Then everything was carried on under a high pressure.

THE BELLEVERNON ACADEMY.

The Bellevernon Academy was founded in 1842 by Noah W. Speers. The Academy occupied the stone house then owned by said Speers, and now by John Gibson's Son & Co. William Eberheart in his day remodeled and improved it for his dwelling, and more recently it, under the above firm, has been still more modernized, and now is the beautiful residence of Captain T. L. Daly, superintendent of the Gibsonton mills, located in the vicinity. The late T. R. Hazzard, a native of New York, was the principal; he was an accomplished scholar, and stood in the front rank as a teacher. At the founding of this school he was considered the most successful classical educator in the Monongahela Valley, and did more perhaps than any other one man to foster in the youth of the valley a desire for a thorough academical course of education. Whilst principal of this academy he lived in the house now owned by Conrad Metz, on the corner of Main street and Cherry alley. In this house was born his son Joseph de Vernon, named in honor of this town. He was a soldier in the late war, coming out of it minus an arm.

He is now a prominent orange grower in the state of Florida. T. R. Hazzard had for his assistants in the academy, Wm. F. Hamilton, now a distinguished Doctor of Divinity in the Presbyterian church. He now resides in Washington, Pa. Among the students of this school are some very prominent public actors. Dr. J. C. Cooper, a prominent physician of Philadelphia, the late Hon. Demas M. Letherman an ex-member of the Pennsylvania Legislature, who was the father of Dr. J. A. Letherman, of California, Dr. John H. Storer, of Triadelphia, West Virginia, who ranks in the front of the medical men of the State, Dr. R. Nicolls, now retired among the wealthy men of Bloomington, Ill., the late Hon. George W. McIlvain, ex-chief Justice of Ohio, who was looked upon as one of the most distinguished jurists in that or any other state of the Union, the Fuller boys, now the largest cattle dealers in Philadelphia, N. G. and Ephraim Blaine, brothers of ex-Secretary Blaine of the state of Maine, were students at this Academy.

T. R. Hazzard, Esq., was a member of the Washington bar for nearly forty years; was more than once elected Burgess and Justice of the Peace in his adopted City of Monongahela, and was a very active and influential member of the late Constitutional Convention. He died September 3, 1877, his wife followed him on March 10th, 1887. They left to mourn their loss four sons, Chill W., the accomplished and talented editor of the Monongahela *Republican;* J. De Vernon, of whom we have spoken above; John J., connected with one the banks of Pittsburgh, and Thos. L., one of Allegeny City's prominent physicians and a professor in the Western Pennsylvania Medical College, located in Pittsburgh. Owing to circumstances of which we have no special knowledge, the proprietor closed the Academy a few years after its founding, and removed to Cincinnati, where he had been for many years an active business man. N. W. Speers is now a resident of Memphis, Tenn. He and Jacob are the only surviving members of the family of Noah Speers, the founder of Bellevernon.

POST OFFICE AND TELEGRAPH.

We wrote to the Department to ascertain at what time the Bellevernon post office was established, but failed to get a reply to the request. It seems to have been established about 1830, or perhaps a few years prior to this date. Solomon Speers was the first postmaster, and kept the office on the corner of Water and First street, in the well known brick house now used as a hotel. The same case of alphabetical boxes then obtained is still in use. Uriah Ward, who had been in the employ of Speers as a clerk, succeeded him in 1836 as post master. Ward was succeeded by Wm. Eberheart, the well-known glass manufacturer, who kept the office in the brick store room, corner of Water street and Cherry alley. John Mullin was next in office. He had the office in his store room on the corner of Main street and Cherry alley, where now stands the beautiful three story building of A. A. Taggart. It was during his term that the office was broken into and the letters carried into a corn field on the hill and destroyed. Stephen Whetsel was arrested for the robbery and tried in the U. S. Court at Pittsburgh, but the evidence was not sufficient to convict him. It remains a mystery to this day who committed the deed.

John Mullin was succeeded by James R. Davidson, somewhere about the year 1855-56. He had the office in the brick store room corner of Main and Second streets now occupied by

Browns' Pharmacy. James R. Davidson is now a prominent lawyer of Hillsboro, Henry county, Iowa, was succeeded in time by J. B. McKennan, Robert Boyle, L. R. Boyle, James Davidson, Jas. Haggerty, and the present postmaster, L. M. Kyle. Jas. Davidson was in office from 1869 to 1885. Even within the recollection of the writer postage was rated according to the number of sheets of paper and the distance carried. There were no stamps in early days. The postage on letters run up from $6\frac{1}{4}$ cents or a fip, $12\frac{1}{2}$ cents or a levie, $18\frac{3}{4}$ cents and 25 cents to be prepaid or not, as people determined. It was considered a breach of etiquette to prepay a letter. Prior to the establishment of the post office the Bellevernon people received their mail at Cookstown which office had been erected in 1813. The mail was carried on horseback and it was considered a big thing to get it twice a week. We cannot find out who first carried the mail on this route but we do know that Richard Everson and James Kerr were two of the contractors, and that in 1847 the late Joseph Hassler, of Rostraver, in person brought the mail to Bellevernon on every Tuesday and Saturday. The mail pouch resembled the old-time saddle-bags, and was thrown across the horse, the carrier riding on it. Even in 1847 only a small mail was received at this office. Wm. Eberheart got most of the letters; a few copies of the *Genius of Liberty*, the *Pennsylvania Democrat*, now the *American Standard*, the *Presbyterian Advocate*, now the *Banner*, the *Christian Advocate* and *Morning Star*, were received weekly. The Greensburg *Herald* was carried to the subscribers in Rostraver by Samuel Douglass who was employed as private carrier. Outside of the cities daily papers were not often taken. Along in the early fifties Wm. Eberheart took one daily paper, the first in the town, now 1893; the newsman sells 200 copies of the Pittsburgh dailies.

In the early spring of 1865, James L. Shaw, through his individual exertions, had formed the Monongahela Valley Telegraph company, which erected the first line of telegraph along the Monongahela river. The office in Bellevernon was first placed in the store room of Harvey B. Frye, well known as Speers' corner. The first operator was Miss May Johnston and the present operator is Mrs. J. F. Frye. The office was opened on the 14th day of April, 1865, the day of the assassination of President Lincoln. The first message sent was as follows:

"BELLEVERNON, PA., April 14, 1865.
"*To Harvey Fleming, Cookstown, Pa.:*
"What is Jane Hunter selling eggs at? Answer.
"8 D. H. H. B. FRYE."

NEWSPAPERS.

The first effort at starting a newspaper in town was made by the youthful E. A. Hastings. In the winter of 1873-74 he printed a small sheet called the *Young Patriot*. The outgrowth of this effort was the establishing of the Bellevernon *Patriot*. E. A. Hastings was the editor and J. T. McAlpin associate. The first number was issued April 24, 1874. May 7, 1874, McAlpin retiring, E. A. Hastings assumed full control of the *Patriot*. The paper was published by McAlpin and Hastings in kind of alternate way until July 29, 1875, the date of the last issue. January 4, 1877, J. T. McAlpin obtained control of the Valley Leader press and issued No. 1, Vol. 1, of the Bellevernon *Courier*. He published this paper until June 13, 1878, when it ceased to live. The press was sold to a firm in Uniontown, and is now doing service in some office in Ohio. The writer has the *Patriot* and *Courier* complete, bound in one volume, which is an epitome of the local history of the town of that day.

The Bellevernon *Enterprise* was first issued on the 3rd day of April, 1886, by L. M. Truxal, and is now one of the fixtures of the town.

The first persons married in the town were Miss Fannie Billiter and John Thompson, the ceremony being performed by William D. Mullin, Esq., in 1824.

Glass Works and Business Men in Bellevernon.

The glass works have always been the prominent business of the town. The factory long known as the "old house," was commenced by Kendall & Patton, in 1834, but was completed and put in operation by William Eberheart in 1836. The venerable John S. Carns, now deceased, remembered very well of being present at the first blowing. Persons in large number from the surrounding country were in the factory to witness the operation of blowing glass. The cylinders or rollers were only large enough to make from six to nine lights of eight by ten. Mr. Carns lived at that time in the old log school house on the farm, then belonging to the late Samuel Jones, but now the lot owned by Henry Lang, near the colored church in Rostraver. Mr. Carnes could not recall to mind any of the blowers unless it be that of Chas. M. Coll, who he thought was among the number, and perhaps Gabler, Burk, Sedgwick, Benedict, Kimber, Goslin, Berry, Reddick, Downs and Denny. Griffith Wells, a well-known former citizen, now dead, was the first glass-cutter who worked at these works. Eberheart inherited his glass-making propensities from his father Adolph Eberheart, who carried on for many years in New Geneva, the works erected by the late Hon. Albert Gallatin.

Each blower flattened his own glass in what was called shove-down ovens. There were no snappers and second-handers— only the tending boys who were generally apprentices to the trade. They made six melts in a week and flattened the glass. At what time the upper house was built we cannot say positively, but think it was about 1841. Financial troubles compelled Eberheart in 1853 to close up the business. The works were purchased by Geo. A. Berry, of Pittsburgh, and the business was revived under the firm of Geo. A. Berry & Co., which was in a few years merged into Geo. A. Berry, J. B. McKennan and Samuel Vanhook retiring, but remained agents for Mr. Berry, until he sold to Robert C. Schmertz & Co., in 1865. This firm is still carrying on the works, which have been enlarged and so improved as to hold the highest rank in the United States. It is now a thirty-pot establishment, employing near 200 men and boys. In the future (1887) natural gas will be used throughout the whole plant. The gas will be furnished by the Bellevernon Light and Heat Company from its five wells in which R. C. Schmertz & Co. is the largest stockholder. The firm employs the most skillful workmen in every department, and the glass turned out commands a ready market in every part of the United States. Rollers or cylinders are now made which cut forty-eight lights eight by ten inches.

Hotel-keeper—A. C. Houseman, State road and Main street. In 1847, Tanner—A. P. Frye, Water and Second streets. The tan-yard was established by William Reeves in 1830. It was owned in succession by William Reeves, Alex. and John Bigham, John Niccolls, A. P. Frye, J. W. Wright and W. C. Drum, during whose ownership it was abandoned as a tan-yard about the year 1866. It is now owned by the heirs of George Lang, deceased. Morgan Reeves was the first tanner.

There was no justice of the peace, but 'Squire J. B. Gould in 1847 did "all the law business," as he resided adjoining the the town.

The first tailor in town was Billy Walker, who in 1836 had his shop in the house on the corner of Water and First streets.

Milton Sloppy, the first harness-maker, had his shop in 1857–58 in store room corner of Main and Second street, and he was succeeded in March, 1859, by W. P. Mackey, who had his shop in a room near Second on Main, where now Dr. Van Voorhis has his office.

Budd Gaskill was the first gunsmith. He had his shop in the rear part of the present Lang residence, Water street. He was succeeded by Wash. Everson, in the middle room of the old Taggart row on Main street below Strawberry alley.

J. S. Van Voorhis, M. D., became a resident of Bellevernon May 25, 1847, and in 1893 is still in the town, having long since become one of its fixtures.

The Odd Fellows' Hall Association of Belle Vernon was chartered by a decree of the Fayette county court, December 1, 1879, with a capital stock of four thousand dollars, divided into shares of ten dollars each. The original stockholders were John Hackett, Samuel McKean, John S. Neil, John W. Wilkinson, W. B. McAlpin, John S. Sharpnack, J. S. Van-Voorhis, R. C. Guffy, Ephraim Lewis, A. L. Brown, L. R. Boyle. The first officers were, Trustees John Hackett, Samuel McKean and Ephraim Lewis; President, Samuel McKean; Treasurer, John W. Wilkinson, and Secretary, J. S. Van Voorhis. At a meeting of the stockholders October 21, 1879, the trustees were authorized to purchase lot 38 with the building thereon well known as Speer's corner, in Bellevernon, from John W. Wilkinson, for the sum of $1,333.33½, the Association assuming the mortgages on said property. John W. Wilkinson had purchased it at the sale of the assignee of L. M. & W. F. Speer. This purchase by the Association was made prior to its incorporation, but became the legal property of the incorporated Association.

This property in 1889 was sold to Wm. Jones and Lyia M. Graham, and the Association in the same year purchased from W. K. Wise 30 by 100 feet of the lot on corner of Main and Second streets, and in January, 1890, bought an additional five by 100 feet, making the lot 100 by 36 feet. On this lot during the summer of 1890, the Association erected a frame three story building. A. A. Taggart was the contractor. It is one of the most complete buildings in the town.

THE GRAND ARMY POST.

We are indebted to Joseph E. Nutt for the following sketch of General George D. Bayard Post, No. 178, of the G. A. R.

June 24, 1880, was the red-letter day in the history of Bellevernon, for military display and for the number thronging the streets of the old town who had carried the musket in defense of the Union in the dark days of 1861 to 1865. The early morn was ushered in by the booming of cannon and the enthusing and stirring martial music of the fife and drum. Why all this excitement in our staid old town? Why this hurrying to and fro, completing preparations as though to withstand a besieging enemy momentarily expected to appear and demand the surrender of the fortress? Is grim-visaged war again abroad in our loved land, as twenty years ago demanding each patriotic father and mother to bring forth their most cherished treasures, their eldest and perhaps their only dependent for support on the sun set side of the hill of life?

Thanks to that kind Providence that led our heroes in blue through a series of splendid victories to a permanent peace, the answer comes, "We are not preparing for war" but are about to muster a Post of the Grand Army of the Republic, an organization composed exclusively of surviving Union soldiers who took part in the war of the rebellion, were honorably discharged and on whom rests no stain of treason. The questions may be, and often are asked, why this organization? Are not its objects calculated to retard the healing of the breach between north and south, and to perpetuate the sectional feelings which in the past led to such terrible consequences in the enormous sacrifices of blood and treasures? Again the answer comes, bearing the assurance that its mission is peaceful, and to any careful observer of the day, this fact is apparent that there is no class that stood opposite each other across Mason and Dixon's line, that entertain a higher regard for or estimate at nearer the true value of each other as the ex-Union and ex-Confederate soldier class. The merits and soldiery qualities recognized and acknowledged by either side only tends to give additional lustre to their own achievements, hence there can be no motive for the men led by Grant, Sherman, Sheridan and Meade, to withhold from the men led by Lee, the Johnsons, Jackson and Longstreet, the credit due their military daring and wonderful endurance, and vice versa.

But there is in the heart of every old soldier an undefined feeling that binds him to every other one who shared like dangers and endured privations that cannot be appreciated by those inexperienced in such things, and though the person maybe despised in almost every other respect, the fact substantiated that he did noble duty, and was a "good soldier," generally admits him to the honor and benefits of the order. Mutual interests make it necessary to organize, that the pledges of the country to those who sacrificed all their dearest idols, their hopes of distinction in their chosen professions, the best years of their bright young manhood may not stand a meaningless verbage on the nation's statute books.

The old adage that "Republics are always ungrateful" would have still held good in this case, had it not been for the influence brought to bear through the G. A. R., as nearly all the relief thus far obtained has been secured directly or indirectly through this agency, and even in local affairs to accomplish anything in the way of relieving cases of distress and want of soldiers or their families, we could not, without organization bring the matter so intelligently before the public and obtain the needed help, and right here be it said the appeal for such purposes, has never been in vain in this community.

The people have always given enough and more than enough to accomplish the object on hand, and the balance was religiously placed in the fund reserved for similar future drafts which were sure to come.

There was on the 24th of June, 1880, three hundred old soldiers in Bellevernon, and thanks to the liberality and patriotic sympathy of our town and vicinity, an elegant and substantial dinner was spread for the immense crowd of visitors from other places and the surrounding country. The occasion was graced by the presence of (now Past Department Commander) Chill. W. Hazzard, F. H. Dyer, Capt. Tom. Gist, Capt. N. W. Truxal, Hon. J. K. Billingsby, and other distinguished Grand Army men whose names cannot now be recalled, and a full turn out of Henry Billingsby Post 168, and J. W. Stephens Post 168. The exercises and entertainments of the day passed very pleasantly, and in the evening the Post was duly mustered by the visiting comrades, Com. C. W. Hazzard, then Department Commander, acting as mustering officer, and Com. Tom. Gist as officer of the day. During the evening Comrade F. H. Dyer gave a grand series of sciopticon views, which were explained by C. W. Hazzard, some of which were grandly instructive, others very fun provoking.

The records of the first meetings of the Post are too much abridged to give a satisfactory account of the first year's work, even the roster of officers is not recorded. The charter members were as follows, viz: J. B. Thompson, John Dowlin, James W. Morgan, W. C. Johnson, Joseph T. Bell, W. S. Harvey, Jas. H. Acklin, W. H. Noble, John Fell, Thos. Scott, S. B. Miller, Geo. R. Waters, Pierson B. Luce, John W. Dean, Nathan Worrel, Wm. F. Boothe, Robt. Fields, Wm. Bunting, Isaac Coldren, J. E. Nutt, A. B. Lowes, John S. Reeves, W. F. Morgan, John H. Weaver, Stewart Patterson. Comrade John B. Thompson was elected Post commander, and hence is the Sr. Post P. C. He chose for his Adjutant Comrade W. H. Noble. Rev. A. B. Lowes was elected Chaplain, which important office he ably filled as long as he remained in the community. The Post adopted for its name that of Brigadier Gen. Geo. D. Bayard, who was the Colonel of the First Pennsylvania Reserve Calvary when it first took the field, was afterwards about the 1st of May, 1862, commissioned Brigadier General, and ably in camp and in field led a brigade of calvary until on the 12th day of December, 1862, on the disastrous and ill-fated field of Fredericsburg, he poured out his rich young life blood on his country's alter. Being only 22 years of age he gave promise of a bright future, as a calvary leader, and had he lived it might not have been necessary to call Sheridan from the west to lead the calvary of the Army of the Potomac on those memorial campaigns which covered alike the leader and those led, with such a halo of glory that their deeds of valor are imperishably fixed on the pages of the country's history.

The term ending December 31, 1880, was a fairly prosperous one, some seven or eight recruits having been added to the body of charter members. The roster of officers for 1881 was as follows: W. S. Harvey, Post Commander; L. R. Boyle, Sr., Vice Commander; Wm. Boothe, Jr., Commander; W. H. Noble, Quarter-Master; J. W. Morgan, Adjutant; J. B. Thompson, officer of the day; Joseph Bell, officer of the guard; Rev. A. B. Lowes, Chaplin. During this term the Post procured the necessary order for the admission of, and sent a comrade with the orphan children of Comrades Isaac Hammitt and Chas. Hixenbaugh, to the Soldiers Orphan School near Uniontown at Jummonville. The Post was not very successful in recruiting new members during the year 1881, but three were mustered during this year, events transpired which stirred to their depths the hearts of every member of the patriotic fraternity. In the midst of the enthusiasm of celebrating our great national holiday, the news reached us that our most distinguished comrade and honored President, James A. Garfield, was stricken down by the hand of the assassin. Words cannot picture the chill of horror or determination to have full justice meted out to the miserable wretch who committed the foul deed. As soon as it could be attended to a committee was appointed and resolutions of sympathy and condolence drafted and forwarded to the wounded President, of which the following is a copy:

WHEREAS, our comrade, his excellency, the President of the United States, has been stricken down by the hand of a cowardly assassin, which act has secured and merited universal condemnation throughout the civilized world; therefore,

Resolved, That we, the members of General G. D. Bayard Post, No. 178, of Bellevernon, Fayette county, Pa., do deplore this terrible national calamity, and we do hereby extend to our wounded comrade our heartfelt sympathy, and we do most earnestly hope for his speedy recovery. Signed,

              W. S. HARVEY, P. C.

W H. NOBLE, Adjutant *pro tem*.

The following is the reply secured from the private secretary of President Garfield:

'EXECUTIVE CHAMBER,
WASHINGTON, D. C., August 1, 1881.

Dear Sirs—The resolutions adopted by your association, expressive of the sympathy and condolence which its members feel with the President and his family in the great calamity which has befallen them, have been received. In acknowledging their receipt, permit me to assure you that it will afford me great pleasure at the most favorable and opportune time, to invite the attention of the President to this gratifying action on the part of your organization. In the meantime, expressing the thanks of the President for this courtesy, I am, yours very respectfully,   I. STANLEY BROWN,
Private Secretary.

I. O. O. F.

Belle Vernon Lodge No. 656, I. O. O. F., was instituted at Belle Vernon, Fayette county, Pennsylvania, on the afternoon of March 26, 1869, by Special D. D. G. M., U. L. Clemmer, of Triumph Lodge No. 613, assisted by P. G. Master Alfred Slack, of Pittsburgh, then a candidate for G. W. of the Grand Lodge of Pennsylvania; P. G. Patriarch Sholes, of the same city, then Grand Patriarch of the Grand Encampment of Pennsylvania; D. D. G. M., J. Mullin, of Allegheny county, and a large number of visiting brothers from Lodges Nos. 51, 377, 491, 511 and 613. The meeting was called to order by D. G. M. Clemmer, and the names of the charter members being called were as follows: P. G. M. Alter, P. G. Samuel McKean, Bros. A. P. Lewis, R. C. Byers, Noah Speers, J. M. Springer, John T. Steiner, J. H. Lewis, T. F. Lewis, Milton Lanehart, G. V Abel, J. S. Van Voorhis, J. B. Thompson, J. W. Dean, W. French, C. A. Patterson, J. Gould, W. Bright, R. J. Patton, R. K. Feuster, J. S. Bolsinger and E. L. Hyatt.

After the usual ceremonies the charter was read and the Belle Vernon Lodge No. 656, was duly constituted. The election for officers resulted in the choice of R. C. Byers, N. G.; J. S. Van Voorhis, V G.; Samuel McKean, Secretary; A. P.

Lewis, Assistant Secretary, and J. M. Springer, Treasurer. In the evening J. H. Weaver, J. E. Hixenbaugh, E. E. Stickel, J. F. Reed, J. H. Hixenbaugh and O. D. Johnson were initiated, being the first under the charter. J. B. Foulk was the first admitted by card. During the year 1869, twenty-three were initiated and twenty-five admitted by card, including charter members; withdrawn by card, four; leaving January 1, 1870, a membership of forty-four.

January 1, 1875, the lodge had a membership of 101, and in 1893 the same number. January 31 of this year the building in which the meetings were held was burned, destroying nearly everything belonging to the lodge, including the charter, the whole loss being estimated at $1,200. The following persons have filled the office of Noble Grand since its institution, viz.: R. C. Byers, J. S. Van Voorhis, A. P. Lewis, J. B. Thompson, J. M. Springer, J. E. Hixenbaugh, J. F. Reed, J. H. Weaver, F. Hixenbaugh. A. G. Beazell, George Treasure, John Wilkinson, N. Speers, J. Hackett, W. C. Kittle, G. Amalong, M. Lanehart, J. F. Young, R. C. Guffy, G. V Abel, W. S. Harvey, E. S. Young, William Vaughan, L. R. Boyle, W. B. McAlpin, J. W. Morgan, J. H. Eller, Hugh Price, Ad. Young, Samuel Houseman, L. Thompson, Leightty Steen, J. A. Neil, George F. Culp, W. H. Neil, Charles Clegg, C. C. Hammett, Wm. Corwin, John Gray, W. H. Hammett, Oliver Hixenbaugh, S. M. Warrensford, Anthony Hugg, J. R. Bovard, C. M. Jones, M. F. Packer, Wm. Eller and J. B. Shawman. We can recall the names of the following P. G.s who have served as representatives to the Grand Lodge, viz.: M. Alter, Samuel McKean, A. P. Lewis, J. B. Thompson, J. M Springer, J. W. Morgan, Leightty Steen, E. S. Young, L. Thompson and I. N. Neil. Samuel McKean and J. M. Springer have each served one year as district deputy grand master. With the exception of one year, Samuel McKean had served as secretary from the institution of the lodge until April, 1890, when E. S. Young was elected. The lodge held its first meetings in a hall in Kittle's building, in the second story ; then occupied a room over Springer's store room on Main street, below Strawberry alley. The meetings were held here when the fire occurred. For years after the fire the lodge used the hall in the third story of Kittle's building, and in 1886 the lodge rented Corwin's hall on Main street. The lodge is now made up of seventy-one members. Its financial standing has always been good. It holds $2,900 stock in the Odd Fellows Hall Association; the paraphernalia and furniture is estimated at $1,500, and a respectable balance in the treasury October 1, 1893. The lodge had paid out for the relief of the sick and widow and orphan funds from January, 1874, to October 1, 1887, the sum of $3,712. Owing to the loss of the records by the fire we are not able to give the amount from 1869 to 1874, but no doubt the same proportion held good.

Maple Grove is the name of the Encampment instituted shortly after the lodge was and is made up of third degree members of the lodge, or rather such of them as may apply for membership and be accepted. The Encampment holds $400 of stock in the Hall Association above named.

Other Lodges.

Monongahela Lodge No. 362, Knights of Pythias, was organized June 13, 1872.

The first Division of the sons of Temperance in the town was Belle Vernon Division No. 286, instituted by D. G. W. P., James Piper, September 22, 1847. It ceased to exist about 1852. The present Division, No. 147, was organized Sept; 24, 1885, and meets in Odd Fellows' Hall every Tuesday evening. In addition to those organizations already named, we have a variety of other societies and institutions such as Accomac Tribe of Red Men, Knights of Labor, Council 531 of the Royal Arcanum, U. S. Benevolent Fraternity, Ethan Allen Council 355, O. U. A. M., Western Council No. 79, Junior O. U. A. M., Equitable Aid Union, W. C. T. U., L. and O. Society, M. E. Lyceum, Presbyterian Mite

Society, Presbyterian Happy Band, the Baptist Social, Foreign Missionary Societies of the different churches, Conamore Club, Cornet Band, Drum Corps. As place of amusement we have the opera house, skating rink, and the public halls are Taggart's, Bronson's and the school hall.

NATURAL GAS HISTORY, 1887.

R. C. Schmertz during the past three years has drilled three gas wells. Two of these are located on the low land just above the town outside the borough limits; the other one on Speer's run, near the old Johnson mill site, on the farm formerly owned by L. M. Speer, but now by S. F. Jones & Co. R. C. Schmertz also purchased from the Belle Vernon Light and Heat Company the well on the high land above the green house of Samuel McKean, about a half mile from town in Rostraver township. All of these four wells have been piped to the glass works, and at this date, October 15, 1887, all of the ten pot furnaces are run with natural gas.

The Bellevernon Heat and Light Company was organized under a charter granted by the Governor of this Commonwealth bearing date March 15th, 1886. The corporators were R. C. Schmertz and one of his sons, S. F. Jones, R. J. Linton and T. L. Daly. The company during the year 1886 drilled the well sold to R. C. Schmertz above mentioned, and drilled a well of very great pressure on the farm of J. B. Carson, in Washington county, one mile from the Monongahela river at Maple Creek. The company laid pipe from this latter well to Bellevernon and Gibsonton Mills, crossing the river a short distance above the mouth of Maple Creek. The pipe is laid along the river shore on the east side to the upper end of the town. The object of the company was to supply Gibsonton, Bellevernon and the vicinity with natural gas as fuel for manufacturing and domestic use to take the place of coal. The right of way for the pipe was granted to the company by the Borough authorities on certain conditions of which we are not informed.

On the 7th day of October, 1887, R. J. Linton introduced the use of natural gas into his dwelling, being the first to use it in the town as fuel.

BELLEVERNON ELECTRIC HEAT AND LIGHT COMPANY.

This company was chartered by the Governor May 27, 1892. The corporators were J. C. Cunningham, Thomas G. Brown, A. L. Brown, Isaac S. Van Voorhis and J. S. Van Voorhis. Directors for 1893: A. L. Brown, Thomas G. Brown, J. S. Van Voorhis and Isaac S. Van Voorhis. Treasurer, J. C. Cunningham.

BELLEVERNON WATER COMPANY.

This company was chartered by the Governor May 27, 1892, for the purpose of furnishing water for Bellevernon and territory adjacent thereto. The incorporators and officers for 1893 are same as the Electric Heat and Light Company.

BELLEVERNON BRIDGE COMPANY.

The design of this company is to construct a wagon and foot bridge across the Monongahela river at Bellevernon. The company was incorporated February 11th, 1891. The Act of Congress authorizing the construction was passed in February, 1893. The corporators were S. F. Jones, J. S. Jones, S. C. Speers, Charles P. Speers, Thomas P. Grant, J. S. Van Voorhis, J. C. Cunningham, Isaac S. Van Voorhis, A. L. Brown, T. L. Daly, R. J. Linton and W. J. Manown.

Directors for the year 1893: J. S. Van Voorhis, T. L. Daly, Isaac S. Van Voorhis and Thomas P. Grant. Treasurer, S. F. Jones. Secretary, J. S. Jones.

FIRST NATIONAL BANK OF BELLEVERNON.

OFFICE OF THE COMPTROLLER OF THE CURRENCY,
WASHINGTON, February 7th, 1893.

Whereas, by satisfactory evidence presented to the undersigned, it has been made to appear that the First National

Bank of Bellevernon, in the town of Bellevernon, in the county of Fayette, and state of Pennsylvania, has complied with all the provisions of the Statutes of the United States required to be complied with before an association shall be authorized to commence the business of banking.

Now, therefore, I, Alonzo Barton Hepburn, Comptroller of the Treasury, do hereby certify that the First National Bank of Bellevernon, in the town of Bellevernon, in the county of Fayette, and state of Pennsylvania, is authorized to commence the business of banking, as provided in section fifty-one hundred and sixty-nine of the revised Statutes of the United States.

In testimony whereof, witnessed my hand and seal of office, this 7th day of February, 1893.

A. B. HEPBURN,
[SEAL.] Comptroller of Currency.

The officers for the current year are as follows: Directors, S. M. Graham, J. S. Henry, M. G. Finley, R. G. Patton, Samuel Thompson, S. E. Taylor, W. J. Manown, Joseph A. Cook and R. J. Linton. President, W. J. Manown; Vice President, R. J. Linton; Cashier, Joseph A. Cook; Assistant Cashier, Frank Z. Taylor. Capital, $50,000.

CLEVELAND COAL COMPANY.

The Cleveland Coal Company has its works a short distance above Bellevernon and is largely engaged in shipping coal by railroad. Large tracts of coal land have been purchased by different parties along Speer's Run and the "Middle Forks," which will be operated through a lateral railroad along said run, a survey of which has already been made. This lateral railroad is supposed to have in view a connection with a bridge connecting Charleroi, and thus the coal company will have the advantages of shipment by either the Pittsburgh & Lake Erie Railroad or the Pennsylvania.

Romana Land Company.

This company was incorporated in 1892. It holds in fee simple the farm owned for many years by the late Samuel Clarke, a short distance above Bellevernon, on the opposite side of the river. Among the prominent stockholders are S. M. Graham and Joseph S. Jones, of Bellevernon. It is the intention of the company to lay out the bottom land in town lots, and they have already had inducements which almost guarantee the location of large manufacturing establishments. There is no doubt but these beautiful bottom lands will in the near future furnish the location of very important business interests, as few places offer more eligible situations or more favorable terms. Romana is destined to be a great hive of industry.

The main street in Bellevernon was paved with brick during the summer of 1893.

Washington and Westmoreland Ferry Company.

This company was incorporated in 1893 to conduct a ferry between Charleroi in Washington county, and Rostraver township in Westmoreland county. Under the supervision of John W. Irons it has already become a successful convenience to the public, and will be in a short time a source of revenue to its stockholders.

The Militia, Fourth of July, Temperance, Centennial and Railroads.

The old militia system came to an end in this state in 1846, about the time of the breaking out of the Mexican war. The last company of militia to which citizens of Bellevernon belonged was commanded by John R. Wilson, now of Uniontown. The law required every able-bodied male citizen to be enrolled between the ages of 18 and 45 years, and subject to duty under a penalty of one dollar for each day absent from muster. In the last days of the law the fine was reduced to fifty cents. On the first Monday of May each company had to muster, and about the first of June the general or regimental parade took place. The little muster was held for this neighborhood at Cookstown and the general muster at Col. Billy Patterson's, some distance above that place, in Jefferson township. The militia was made up of companies commanded by a Captain, with a First and Second Lieutenant; of regiments with their Colonel, Lieutenant Colonel, Major and Adjutant; of brigades made up of regiments and commanded by Brigadier Generals; of divisions in command of Major Generals. There was also a Brigade Inspector in each county. These officers were generally well uniformed and presented a very fine appearance. Uniformed volunteer companies were not uncommon in early days. Any person serving seven years in one of such companies was exempt from military duty unless in time of war.

In the early forties the Washington Cavalry was in the pride of existence. It was made up of the best men in the community. John Ong was its captain until he removed west, then Jacob Wolf, still living on Redstone, succeeded in the office. James Cope, now a dentist, was first lieutenant; Richard Latta, orderly sergeant. Among the members of the company were Pierson Cope, Samuel Galloway, Joseph Galloway, Jacob Housman, the bugler, the Ellet boys, Jacob McLain, Lewis Krepps, Bazil Brightwell, James McCrory, Edward, William and Crawford Cook. The company had caps with the ostrich feathers; blue coats trimmed with red.

The Monongahela Blues was a company of footmen composed of citizens of Cookstown, Bellevernon and the surrounding country. James Hagerty and others from this vicinity belonged to the company. William Krepps was the first captain and Joseph Shepler was the last. The company was disbanded before the breaking out of the Mexican war. The uniform of this company was white pants, blue coats trimmed with white, a heavy bell crowned leather cap with a white plume tipped with red. Each one carried an old fashioned flint lock musket, well polished, a cartridge box on one side and a bayonet sheath on the other, suspended to huge straps on each shoulder. Somewhere about 1840 these companies named above, with the Jackson Guards from Monongahela City, and others whose names have been forgotten, had a grand celebration on the 4th of July in a grove near the residence of the late Robert Patterson.

The dinner was served on the lot now owned by Geo. Vernon, corner of Wood street and Strawberry alley. The Declaration of Independence was read by the late Dr. O. D. Todd. David Smith, a revolution soldier, was present. He was the grandfather of Mrs. Robert Patterson. His remains repose in Rehoboth graveyard. On the breaking out of the late rebellion the town was well represented in the army. Hillery Miller was the first to enlist. He enlisted in Capt. R. F. Cooper's company of three months men, and within two weeks after the call of the President for troops, April 15, 1861, the company was in active service. Jeremiah Huttenhour, killed at Petersburg, June 18, 1864, was the only one from the town killed in battle, others were wounded and some died in hospitals and at home from the effects of service. Among many who volunteered early in the war we recall the names of Michael Dolan, John Young, Wm. Bunting, Geo. W. Beam, John Fell, Joseph Wiltsie, Joseph T. Beall, J. W. Dean, Chas. Hixenbaugh, Jesse Strickland, S. B. Miller.

Among the many large meetings held in the town in its history none perhaps were greater than on the 29th day of May, 1848, at which there was a Bible presented by the ladies to Division No. 286, Sons of Temperance. The book was given in the name of the ladies by the late Rev. J. G. Sanson, and was received on the part of the Division by Dr. J. S. Van Voorhis. An original ode on the Bible written by Miss Rebecca Van Voorhis, now of Spearville, Kansas, was sung by the ladies. The speech of the day was delivered by J. Robinson Elder, at that time editor of the *Temperance Banner*, and one of the most eloquent orators of his day.

The centennial of the signing of the Declaration of Independence was celebrated jointly July 4, 1876, by the citizens of Bellevernon, Fayette City and surrounding neighborhoods. The meeting was held in Springer's grove, midway between the two towns on the hill road. It was estimated to be the largest assembly of people ever held in the For'ks. Old and young of both sexes were congregated to do honor to the day. Rev. Marcus W. Wishart, then pastor of Rehoboth, presided over the meeting. Samuel McKean, as grand marshall of the day, with his aids, had charge of the procession. Dr. J. S. Van Voorhis delivered the historical address which was listened to with very great attention by the immense crowd. In the afternoon the pleasure was very much interfered with by a severe rain storm.

In 1852 there was a prospect of the Hempfield railroad crossing the river at this place in its route from Greensburg to Wheeling. Hon. T. M. T. McKennan, president of the road from the steps of the residence of Solomon Speers delivered an address on the subject, and regarded the route with favor. The Mingo route, via Monongahela City, was adopted, and after a very large sum of money had been lavishly expended, the portion east of Washington was abandoned. In 1873, the Baltimore and Ohio Railroad Company having purchased the Hempfield, changed its route from Washington to a point near Layton's station, on its Connellsville branch.

A vast deal of work was done on the route including the deep cut on the other side of the river from Bellevernon, and a magnificent bridge located to pass from hill to hill over the lower end of Main street and in the midst of apparent prospect of an early completion, the work was in May, 1874, abandoned. Sometime subsequent to this date last mentioned, a charter was obtained for a railroad to be run from Bellevernon to a point on the Connellsville railroad, near Amieville below West Newton. After sufficient stock had been subscribed and a survey made, the project was given up and court dissolved the company. At this date, 1883, a charter has been obtained for a railroad from McKeesport to this place, and the prospect for its early completion is favorable. The town is shut out from the transportation facilities which its business deserves. The glass works products and raw material are taken across the river by a private ferry in charge of the firm, also the transportation to and from the Gibsonton distillery is carried on by a rope ferry in charge of S. C. Speer. The public ferry owned by Noah Speers is now worked by a wire rope and is the best conducted and safest ferry on the Monongahela river.

NORTH BELLEVERNON.

It is situated in Westmoreland county, adjoining the borough of Bellevernon, in Fayette county. It was laid out by the late L. M. Speers. On the original plan of lots we find the following note, viz: Diagram or plan of lots laid off by L. M. Speers, situated on Bellevernon hill, second addition partly in Westmoreland and partly in Fayette counties, April 9th, 1872, D. B. H. Allen, Surveyor. On the 23rd day of October, A. D. 1875, a petition was presented to the Westmoreland county court for the incorporation into a borough of that part of North Bellevernon, within said Westmoreland county, bounded and limited as set forth in said charter. February 26th, 1876, the court issued a decree incorporating said borough, and ordered that the first election be held at the school house in said borough on the 6th day of May, 1876, between the hours of one and six o'clock p. m. To hold said election, the court appointed Samuel Dougherty, Judge; Frank Morgan and Thomas Hunt, Inspectors. In the absence of a school house, this election was held in S. Dougherty's carpenter shop, which was used for a school house. The election board appointed A. G. Vanhook and W. R. Springer, clerks.

This, the first election, resulted in the choice of the following persons for the different offices: Burgess, W. R. Springer; Justice of the Peace, Samuel Dougherty; Council, Peter Corwin and Thomas Hunt for two years; John S. Henry and J. C.

Hasson for three years; Francis Keistler and Samuel Dougherty for one year; School Directors: for one year, Thos. Hunt and Wm. Jones; two years, Samuel Dougherty and Francis Keistler; three years, J. A. Piersoll and John S. Henry; Judge of Election, Samuel Dougherty; Assessor, J. S. Henry; Assistant Assessors, J. C. Hasson and Thos. Hunt. The first meeting of the council was held in Dougherty's carpenter shop, June 2, 1876. John S. Henry was elected President; J. C. Hasson, Secretary; Thos. Hunt, Treasurer, and Peter Corwin, Street Commissioner.

The first borough tax was one and one half mills, and was levied July 27, 1876. The first code of ordinances was adopted August 18 and September 12. J. C. Hasson was elected Collector. Among the many persons elected to the more important offices we note from the record the names of W. R. Springer, Samuel Dougherty, A. C. Dougherty, Thos. Hunt and Wm. Jones for Burgess. For Justice, Samuel Dougherty, J. A. Piersoll, J. E. Nutt, Thos. Hunt, Wm. Jones, R. L. Weller and J. S. Reeves. Several of these did not take out their commissions. W. R. Springer, under a commission bearing date of March 13, 1875, was the first acting Justice, being elected in the township of Rostraver prior to the incorporation of the borough.

For Council we note the names of Peter Corwin, J. S. Henry, F. M. Keistler,, Samuel Dougherty, J. C. Hasson, Wm. Jones, J. E. Nutt, C. A. Patterson, R. L. Weller, John L. Housman, Leroy Bedsworth, Isaac H. Shepler, E. M. Kyle, John T. Gould. The present Council, 1887, consists of J. S. Henry, John T. Gould, F. M. Keistler, J. C. Hasson, E. M. Kyle and R. L. Weller. The School Directors named above held their first meeting June 6, 1876, but the record does not state where. The Board was organized by electing Wm. Jones, President; J. S. Piersoll, Secretary; Wm. Jones, Treasurer; and Thos. Hunt Collector. The first assessment for the borough as returned by the assessor amounted to $48,369. The rate for 1876 was fixed at 5 mills each for school and building purposes.

The lot corner Grant and Henry streets was purchased from L. M. Speers for a school house. The office of president and treasurer being incompatible, Wm. Jones, July 17, 1876, resigned the office of treasurer and S. F. Jones was elected in his place, and at the same date Homer Hunt was awarded the contract for building the new school house, for the sum of $854.81. August 3, 1876, J. C. Hasson was elected teacher for the fall and winter term. September 29, 1876, school house reported completed according to contract. The term of school was fixed to begin on the second Monday of October, and the salary $45 per month.

November 30th, a joint meeting of the directors and those of Lagrange was held at Lagrange, to which district this town belonged before the formation of the borough, and resulted in arranging matters so that the funds on hand should be equally divided between the two districts, the whole amount being $680.75, one-half going into the treasury of each district. May 4th, 1877, on first settlement in the district, whole amount of money received during the year was $1,333.65, amount paid out $1,224.51, Balance in treasury $109.14.

John S. Henry, J. A. Piersoll, Thomas Hunt, Samuel Dougherty, F. M. Keistler, William Jones, J. E. Nutt, Peter Corwin, R. C. Guffy, John W. Goslin, L. H. Reeves, Isaac H. Shepler, James Ferguson, W. R. Springer, R. L. Weller, William Jones, have been directors. As teachers, John C. Hasson, F. R. Hall, Leightty Steen, W. V Barnum, Miss Bowman, Clara Lang, Miss Lizzie Morgan, L. M. Axtel, Miss Stockdale, J. R. Bovard and Miss Alton have served.

In 1884 the school house was enlarged by an additional story, and thereafter two schools were carried on to acommodate the increasing population, and in 1892 one other room was added. In 1892-93 Alva Chalfant, Miss McAlpin and Miss Wylie were teachers. In 1893, Prof. S. C. Kelley, Miss Agness McAlpin and Miss Charlotte Harr are the teachers.

Prior to the organization of the borough the citizens belonged to the Lagrange independent school district. In 1876 Eli W.

Martin taught a school under the Lagrange authorities in Dougherty's carpenter shop, situated on the southwest corner of Spring and Hunt alleys. This was the first school in the town. Samuel Dougherty, now a resident of Rostraver, claims to have built the first dwelling on the site of the town, not taking into account the primitive log house which stood in the rear of the present residence of William Kyle, corner of State road, and Grant street. Thomas Ward occupied this primitive house when he erected his new house in Bellevernon in 1815, on the corner of Main and Second streets. Richard Wells, the father of Mrs. William Jacobs, afterwards lived in the old house, and was perhaps the last who occupied it. The occupants of this house used the water from the well-known spring that gushed forth in such abundance for many long years on the State road near Grant street. This spring has disappeared since the coal has been taken out underneath it. Samuel Dougherty, for his new house on State road near Spring alley, hauled the lumber to the site on the 4th day of July, 1870, and moved into it September 10 of the same year. The property is now owned and occupied by John Gray.

The old coal mine was opened just in front of the house, but during the building of the house it was nicely covered over with earth. Much of the ground on which the town is situated is undermined by the coal being taken out, though enough was reserved to render perfectly secure the surface. The cavity is filled with water which has been utilized through pipes leading from the mouth of the mine to the surface along State Road to Short street. The house now owned and occupied by S. Reeves, northwest corner of State Road and Short street, and also the one owned and occupied by E. M. Kyle, north-east corner of the same streets, were erected about the same year as Dougherty's house: the former was built by Wm. P. Mackey and the latter by Thos. Hunt, who purchased this, the first lot in the town. These houses were built whilst the surrounding ground was planted in corn. The flouring mill at the corner of Speer street and Long alley was erected by John McLain and Thos. Hunt in 1874, but now is owned and operated exclusively by the former. Recently the roller process of making flour has been introduced, and now the mill has all the machinery necessary to compete with city manufacturers.

The foundry on north side of State road above Spring alley was built in 1873 by Daniel Johnson, now a resident of one the western states. It was purchased by Mackey and Linton in 1875. The foundry has been torn down and the beautiful residence of John Smith stands now on its site.

Since 1875 the houses on the north-east corner of Graham and Grant streets has been occupied as a parsonage for the Presbyterian ministers of Bellevernon. Rev. Perrin Baker, the present pastor, occupies it at this date. The Springer house, north-west corner of Speer and Grant streets, was erected by W. R. Springer in October, 1871. It is now the property of Everil T. Springer. He put a drug store in a part of it in 1884, and remains as such to this date. James Webb had a blacksmith shop in 1872 on Grant and Speer streets, being the first shop in the town. In 1877 A. C. Dougherty and a man named Kinney started a marble works on the corner of State road and Spring alley. This firm sold out to Steen and Baird, and in a short time, about 1884, Alonzo Baird, one of the partners, became sole proprietor, and carries on the business at this date. W S. Garret about 1876-77 had a marble shop on Long alley, near Third street, in Bellevernon. S. A. Piersoll built a store room in 1880 on the south-east corner of State road and Spring alley, and established the first store in town. He enlarged the store room to its present size in 1882.

Officers in 1892: Burgess, vacant; Council, John Gray, President, John H. Eller, S. Brogan, S. McKean, Jr., Joseph Robinson, C. M. Jones; Borough Treasurer, E. M. Kyle; Clerk of Council, J. R. Bovard; Justice, Wm. Lehew; Constable, J. L. Housman; School Directors, John Gray, H. M. Fish, J. H. Eller, Pressly Jones, Joseph Williams, Edward Jordon. At this date, 1893, John S. Reeves is an acting justice.

GIBSONTON.

This village is situated on the Monongahela river, in Westmoreland county, about one quarter of a mile below Bellevernon. In 1771, Henry Speers the older and Regina Froman, his wife, from Germany, settled near the site of this place and became the owner of it, as well as a large tract of land surrounding it. The farm at that time was within the limits of Bedford county, from which Westmoreland was formed February 26th, 1773. Richard Penn was then Governor. The old log house, the primitive part of which he built, stood across the ravine from the present stone mansion, where yet may be seen some old fruit trees. This was in time improved until it was sixty feet long, most of the timber being hewn logs. The house now occupied by Jacob Irons was built partly with logs taken from this house. Henry Speers the older died from the kick of a horse in 1773, not having long enjoyed the comforts of his new home. His remains are supposed to be interred in the graveyard near the present school house on the same farm. We have no data on which to fix the date of the death of his wife. By his will, Henry Speers, May 14th, 1773, conveyed the present Gibsonton farm to his son, Noah Speers, who, by his will, bearing date of June 2nd, 1832, conveyed it to his son, Noah W. Speers, now a resident of Memphis, Tennessee. Noah Speers was born March 27th, 1769, being only about two years old when his father, Henry Speers settled on the farm. He, that is, Noah, died June 9th, 1832, also from a kick of a horse, having lived on this farm ever since his father settled on it. The addition to the primitive house was built by Noah Speers, this part being of hewn logs whilst the original cabin was of round logs, as were all the first houses.

It was the second generation of settlers who in Western Pennsylvania began to erect houses with hewn logs. So far as we can ascertain, the round logs in the primitive house formed the blacksmith shop which once stood near the old residence, but most of which shop now constitute the old Jane

Goe house on Bellevernon hill, to which place it had been moved in 1843. The late Jas. Beazell for a time worked at his trade in this shop whilst it stood on the Speers farm, of which we are now writing. The old log barns which stood one in the meadow just below the present road before reaching the row of houses of Gibsonton, and the other on the site of the present large frame barn in front of the residence of Jacob Irons, were both burned about 1850 or 1851. Noah Speers was in his early days a large slaveholder, and to accommodate his slaves he erected the main part of the stone mansion. His slaves were manumitted under the gradual emancipation laws and were all free before his death. The mansion house was enlarged and fitted up by Noah W. Speers for an academy in 1842, as we have already mentioned in a former part of this history. He also resided in it after the school closed until the farm was sold to John Niccolls in about the year of 1846. In 1848 it was sold to Wm. Eberheart, who remodelled and improved the stone mansion, putting on the cornice around the roof and adding other changes which gave it a neat and desirable appearance. The present large frame barn on the public road was built for Eberheart by the late Geo. Whiting, of Fayette city. During his ownership Eberheart also had erected the stable now standing near the mansion on the site of the former one which was burned. After the financial embarrassment of Wm. Eberheart in 1853, the farm was sold to J. K. Moorhead by the Sheriff of Westmoreland county. The farm was sold by Moorhead to John Gibson, of Philadelphia. At the death of John Gibson, his son Henry C. became sole owner. The extensive distillery known the world over as Gibsonton Mills, was erected on this farm in 1856-57 by the firm of John Gibson Son & Co. The firm subsequently took in Charles Gibson, and then it was changed to John Gibson, Sons & Co. On the death of Charles the firm became John Gibson Son & Co.

After the death of John Gibson the firm was changed to John Gibson's Son & Co. This firm was succeeded in January,

1884, by Messrs. Moore & Sinnott, who at this time carry on the mammoth establishment. These mills as originally erected were superintended by Westley Ballinger, of Philadelphia, who took charge in 1856 and remained until April, 1858, a short time after the distillery went into operation. The main building was built of hewn sandstone taken from a quarry on the farm. Westley Ballinger was succeeded by Harrison Mason, of Brownsville. In November, 1858, L. C. Baldwin was placed in charge as superintendent. He remained until July, 1873. In the same month he was succeeded by Thomas L. Daly, the present efficient superintendent.

The distillery was put in operation in April, 1858. Thomas Daily, father of Thomas L., superintended the placing in position the distillery apparatus, but April 7, 1858, a few days before the starting of the mills, he by some misstep fell through one of the hatchways and was killed. He was a man of extraordinary genius, beloved by all with whom he associated, and his death was a loss not easily to be replaced in the establishment.

Harrison Mason was the first miller. The first distiller was Thomas Donaway, who took charge in April, 1858. He remained until the fall of 1869. He is now a resident of Virginia City, Cass county, Ill. John D. Yerty succeeded him. He left in 1872, and in a few years afterwards died near Monongahela City. The present distiller is James Frost, who took charge in 1880.

Joseph Abell was the first foreman in the cooper shop, and made the first barrel in this shop for the firm. He took charge in 1858 and left in 1868. He died in Monongahela City. John W. Wilkinson since February, 1866, has been engineer and general machinist. Edward Hendrickson, now deceased, had been miller for twenty years, and had also been grain inspector. Among the first coopers, we recall the names of Andrew Graham, William Gall, Samuel Alloways, William McFall, Ben Bayless, William Garten.

On the morning of December 11, 1882, the main building

with warehouse No. 1 were consumed by fire, occasioned by the explosion of the copper still. Wm. Lucas, a soldier of the late war, was so badly injured by the explosion as to die in a short time. He was attending to his duties about the still when the accident occurred.

Three thousand barrels of whiskey were lost by the fire. The main building and warehouse were rebuilt and ready for starting in October, 1883. June 2, 1883, warehouse No. 2 and 3 were consumed by fire through an accident happening inside one of the buildings. Quite a number of persons were more or less injured but none fatally. The loss in this case was 7,000 barrels of whiskey. The present capacity of these mills is 1,000 bushels daily and warehouses for 100,000 barrels.

The telegraph office at these mills was established in 1877, with Allen Wilson the first operator. The present operator is W. H. Lewis, (1893.)

The postoffice of Gibsonton was established in July, 1884, with T. L. Daly postmaster. L. R. Boyle had been bookkeeper for the firm since April, 1869, and to his death. The late John F. Beazell was night watchman for many years and was succeeded by the present incumbent, Fred. Mounser. Thos. L. Daly, the present superintendent, grew to manhood with his father around the mills, and was whilst quite young an employee. He after leaving these mills was for many years proprietor of the well known Boyle distillery in Washington county, Pa., and was in business in Monongahela City when he was tendered his present position.

The products of the "Gibsonton Mills" are sought after in every state and territory in the United States. The firm export to many foreign countries including China. No article is turned out but the pure whiskey manufactured from rye by the most modern chemical process.

The establishment in all its departments is most complete. The machinery includes all the latest improvements. The grain is ground by the recently invented roller process. At this date, November 15, 1893, natural gas is introduced and used instead of coal, the mills and dwellings all being heated by gas. In connection with the mills is a complete water works distributing water from the Monongahela river all through the establishment and dwellings.

From Bellevernon *Enterprise*, July 19, (1890.)

GIBSONTON.

A history or sketch of Bellevernon would be incomplete without reference to this valuable suburb. In the bend of the beautiful Monongahela river, in Westmoreland county, about one-fourth mile below Bellevernon, nestled among the lovely shade trees, is the works.

The introduction of the excise law was the death-blow of the small distiller. It was a case of the survival of the fittest, and from that time forth instead of small establishments run in connection with other interests, large mills succeeded them, which supply thousands of barrels annually to all parts of the world. The most widely known and greatest of these manufactories is situated at Gibsonton, on the east bank of the Monongahela, about forty-two miles from Pittsburgh.

To subdue the whiskey rebellion it cost the government of the United States $669,992.34. In the year 1885, and nearly every year since, the same government received in taxes alone from the great Gibson Distillery at Gibsonton, the sum of $675,000, or more than the cost of the entire rebellion

In 1854 the late John Gibson, of Philadelphia, who had been in the habit of making large purchases of Monongahela whiskies in the valley, found himself unable to secure the quantities that his growing business demanded. The local distillers objected to selling in large quantities—they were content with a certain annual production, and would not listen to any suggestion as to its increase. Mr. Gibson, with a view to the future, thereupon determined to erect a distillery of his own and on a grander scale than had yet been seen in western Pennsylvania. In 1856 the corner stone of the present works was laid, and in April, 1858, the first whiskey was made at the distillery. When Mr. Gibson began building, his neighbors strongly advised him against committing what they termed an act of the greatest folly. The idea was termed extravagant, and a speedy failure was predicted by those who were considered among the farseeing ones in the neighborhood. Mr. Gibson, however, still persevered in his building. He saw the advantages of the situation and its undoubted future. When completed the capacity of the work was 250 bushels of rye per day. At various times down to the year 1882 it rose to 750 bushels. In December, 1882, the works were destroyed by fire, and in their rebuilding, the capacity was further increased to 1000 bushels a day, which amount they have retained to the present time.

Upon the death of Mr. John Gibson in 1865, he was succeeded by his son, Mr. Henry C. Gibson, who, together with Mr. Andrew M. Moore and Mr. Joseph F. Sinnott, formed the firm of John Gibson's Son & Co. In 1884, Mr. Henry C. Gibson retired from business, and the firm's name was again changed to that of Moore & Sinnott, the present proprietors of the Gibsonton distillery.

Gibsonton is a model manufacturing town. The settlement consists of thirty-two comfortable dwelling houses for the employes of the works; twelve great warehouses, which contain at times as high as 100,000 barrels of whiskey; three principal mills, stave and barrel shops scattered here and there, and the numerous lesser offices which are necessary in a large manufacturing center. In addition to this there are six live stock barns on the premises which cover from ten to fifteen acres of land. In these 12,000 hogs are annually fed with the refuse from the distillery, occupying the pens in four relays of 3,000 each every year.

The employes of the firm live in comfortable cottages, which are leased to them at a nominal rent. They are a prosperous, thriving set of artisans, and are seldom known to change their employment. Each cottage has its little garden alongside, and nearly every tenant posesses a cow or two and is interested in the improvement of his individual holding as well as the larger work in the mills. They are usually men of family and children of all ages may be seen at all times crowding the streets or coming to and from the little school which has been built upon the estate. Counting the manufactories, wood land and farm land, the settlement of Gibsonton covers about 400 acres. The land is fertile and full of promise. From two-thirds or three-fourths of it is underlaid with a fine vein of bituminous coal, and the Gibsonton quarries, situated on the property, produce sufficient limestone for all the building purposes that can ever be needed.

Under the present rules there can be no collusion by which whiskey can be abstracted in the manufactory. The workmen cannot have access to the spirits they are making and consequently a great source of temptation—that of drinking—is entirely removed. In Gibsonton to-day, although the greatest whiskey center of this country, there is not a single workman on the premises who could procure without permission a pint of whiskey for himself, no matter how much he might try to do so. The consequence of this is that there are none of those scenes which the ill-informed commonly associate with the localities in which alcoholic liquors are manufactured in great quantities. The general manager of the works, Mr. T. L. Daly, is a thorough disciplinarian in this respect. He holds that it would not be just to pass over the Gibsonton distilleries without mention of some of the associate industries which cluster around the institution. Of these the most important as well as the most interesting, is the coopering department. All the barrels used for storing the whiskey are made upon the premises. The staves of which they are made are of solid oak. They are secured from Kentucky and Indiana, and a stock of about one million is continually carried in order that they may be well seasoned.

Each stave is kept exposed to the atmosphere for three years before it is considered sufficiently well seasoned to be used in the manufacture of barrels. And here it may be remarked that one of the chief points in the distilling trade is the provisions for the future. The grain market must be closely studied, and favorable opportunities for buying can never be allowed to escape. The probable consumption for years ahead must be considered with prophetic eye. The supply must be equal to a future demand and must not exceed it. The possible effect of legislation must be taken into account and a policy shaped suitably to its provisions. In every way the distiller must be far seeing, and must consider the future as of equal importance with the present.

The case of the manufacture of barrels in one respect furnishes a problem that may be of interest to American inventors. Up to the present time no machine has been invented that will make a perfect whiskey barrel. They are all made by hand. No nails are used in their construction. The workmen, wonderfully skilled to their trade, put them together with almost incredible speed. An expert can, without aid, put together and make three complete barrels a day—a wonderful performance, considering the solidity and difficulty of their construction. In the barrel factory at Gibsonton, however, each man has a certain assigned task to perform, and thus by combining the whole force is enabled to work in a quicker as well as a more systematic manner. One man shapes the staves, another with his compass and adze, traces out the headings, another puts the barrel in shape, and still another tightens the rivets which hold the parts together. No barrel is used twice. They are all new and, when they leave the store houses at Gibsonton they never return. One hundred thousand, however, filled with whiskey of different ages, are resting in the warehouses at present. These will be removed a batch at a time as future consumption may demand.

Another department of the Gibsonton works, and one scarcely less interesting than the cooper shop, is the malt house. The works malt all their barley required in the process of whiskey manufacture. The amount of malt used averages from thirty to fifty thousand bushels a year. It is obtained mostly from Canada and shipped directly to the mills. Here it is cleaned, steeped and spread on stone floors until used. All the barley malt is kiln dried like the rye.

The magnitude of the business transacted by the firm of Moore & Sinnott is exceedingly great. Although their distillery is situated at Gibsonton, their principal office is at 232 and 234 South Front street, Philadelphia. They have branch offices in New York, Boston, New Orleans, San Francisco, Charleston, Savannah and Augusta, Georgia. Each year their taxes to the government exceeds half a million of dollars, and their freight carried by the railroads reaches as high as five thousand carloads. The whiskey from Gibsonton supplies the majority of the wholesale dealers throughout the United States, but the reputation of their whiskies is not confined to this country alone. At the present time Gibson whiskies are being shipped to Mexico, the West Indies, France, England, and even China, in large quantities. Over $50,000 is paid out annually in wages at Gibsonton, and the company own no stores; hence Bellevernon reaps a large benefit therefrom.

The large plant lies on the line of the McKeesport & Bellevernon Railroad, which is operated by the P. & L. E. Company. The shipments are made also by P. R. R. and boats.

This place, like Bellevernon, is a natural gas town. The Bellevernon Light and Heat Company piped the place, and for some years have been furnishing the plant as well as the homes with gas. Mr. Daly having faith in the farm being on the line of the great gas belt, secured Mr. Stewart, who has drilled two wells, the capacity of either being sufficient to furnish twice as much gas as is needed for all purposes. Daly & Co. purchased the pipe line of the Light and Heat Company and furnish gas now for themselves.

That this is the section for any one contemplating locating in a rapidly growing and popular place, no one doubts. This is a healthy boom and no mistake.

(From Bellevernon *Enterprise*.)

NATURAL GAS.

The stranger visiting Bellevernon for the first time cannot fail to be impressed with the clearness of the atmosphere. Great establishments covering acres of ground, and with stacks pointing high into the sky, front on the river. There is ample evidence that they are in full operation, but no smoke rolls from their stacks and there is no grim anywhere to mar the beauty of the surroundings. Ask the reason for this and the average intelligent citizen of Bellevernon will say "It is because we have natural gas." And then the visitor may expect to be entertained with an enthusiastic description of the richness of the natural gas territory surrounding Bellevernon; the wonder of natural gas as a fuel; the comfort and luxury it has brought to the people of Bellevernon, and the great aid it will be in working out the destiny of what every true Bellevernonite believes will be a great city.

The boasts may seem overdrawn, but only until the visitor has some knowledge of their foundation. Then it must appear that eloquent statement is necessary to convey an idea of the wonders of Bellevernon's natural gas field. And it must appear too, that when all has been told, words have fallen far short of adequately paying tribute to the beneficient work of Dame Nature, who has supplied right at the doors of our people a fuel whose quality for light and heat are unexcelled, and that in quantities that justify the claim that the supply is inexhaustible, and whose measurement places the Bellevernon gas field in the lead of all others in point of richness. Some idea of the facts may be obtained when it is stated that the production of two of the wells of the Bellevernon Light and Heat Company is 45,000,000 cubic feet of gas every twenty-four hours. The figures are almost too great for comprehension, but they are most eloquent testimony to the magnitude of the Bellevernon natural gas interests, and the most cogent reason for the confidence of our people in the future of our town.

It is fair to presume that natural gas has been with us as long as the hills and rivers, and everything else that surrounds us, but it did not proclaim its presence. It was found only after a long search, in which the people of Bellevernon displayed that patience and perseverance that is one of the most important elements in the success of any community, and whose possession and exercise is always a subject for congratulation. It was about the year 1865 that the presence of natural gas was first discovered at Bellevernon. Mr. L. M. Speer while drilling a well for oil struck a flow of gas at a depth of 1,000 feet. The value of the discovery was not apprehended at that time, and it was not until eighteen years later, in 1883, that the first real efforts to find gas with the idea of utilizing it as a fuel were made. In the fall of that year a well was put down on the river bottom by R. C. Schmertz & Co. At a depth of 2,800 feet enough gas was found to justify the belief that Bellevernon was either directly on the natural gas belt, or so near to it as to leave no doubt that if the search were continued gas sufficient for all purposes would be found. This conviction was all that was necessary to furnish the leading spirits of Bellevernon with the incentive to exertion, which should be continued until the end was reached. R. C. Schmertz & Co. drilled three more wells, testing the territory along the river for a mile north of their factory. In one of the wells the bit was lost at a depth of 1,000 feet, and work was abandoned. The other wells showed gas in small quantities, but proved that the true gas belt had not been found. The Schmertz and other developments had involved the outlay of a small fortune without securing important results, save to deepen the conviction in the minds of Bellevernon's progressive men that natural gas in great quantities could be found if the search for it was continued.

It was decided to work systematically, and the Bellevernon Light and Heat Company, with a capital stock of $10,000, divided into 200 shares of $50 each, was formed, and a charter was obtained March 5th, 1886. The incorporators were R. C.

Schmertz, W. E. Schmertz, Jr., S. F. Jones, T. L. Daly and R. J. Linton. The first officers were R. C. Schmertz, President; S. F. Jones, Vice President; R. J. Linton, Secretary.

The first move of the company was to secure the services of J. C. White, State Geologist, and Professor of Geology in the University of West Virginia, to survey the field and point out a suitable location for a well. Professor White designated a spot north of Bellevernon, on which was drilled a well known as the Carnes well. This well when completed showed a pressure of thirty pounds to the minute. It was the largest flow so far discovered, and while the pressure as compared with that of what are now known as Bellevernon's great gas wells was small, the Carnes well was regarded as of great importance. The well was sold to Mr. Schmertz, who laid a pipe line to his glass factory, and the gas has been used there ever since.

More important than this, however, was the determination of the company to prosecute in a new direction the search for gas. That four wells should have been completed and another partially drilled without striking gas in great quantity, might have been considered good reason to believe that rich strikes could not be made in the vicinity of Bellevernon. But the people of Bellevernon were not made of that kind of stuff—their faith was not exhausted. While they had faith they were willing to spend money, and they decided to drill another well and in a new direction.

While Professor White was prospecting for the company, S. F. Jones made himself familiar with the anticlinal and other theories. This knowledge Mr. Jones utilized at this juncture. With a pocket compass and an atmospheric barometer he ran a line across the Monongahela river below Gibsonton. The line struck the west shore of the river near the mouth of Maple creek, and then ran through John Redd's farm to a point one mile beyond B. L. Parson's farm. The company decided to drill a well on J. B. Carson's farm, one mile from the river, in Washington county. This well was completed September 15th, 1887. It showed a pressure of 125 pounds to the minute.

At last Bellevernon had natural gas in sufficient quantities to enable its people to not only supply themselves with light at nominal cost, but to hold out inducements to capitalists in other quarters to cast their lot with them and share their good fortune.

The company at once contracted for pipe and proceeded to lay a six-inch line from the well to the river at a point opposite Gibsonton Mills. There the river was crossed, and then the line ran up the east shore to the glass factory, a distance of two miles from the well. The work was completed and gas delivered to the distillery and factory about November 15th, 1887. Ten days later the fuel was turned into the dwellings of the people of Gibsonton and Bellevernon, and they have since had a steady and cheap supply of light and fuel.

On January 12, 1888, a resolution was passed by the gas company to increase its capital stock from $10,000 to $100,000. This action was proposed because more than double the original capital had been expended on the plant, and because it was considered wise to make further developments. The increase was properly authorized February 26, 1888. The additional stock was taken by the stockholders in the same proportion as their former holdings, and paid up stock certificates to the amount of $50,000 were issued.

With abundant capital and a firm faith in the richness of the territory, the Bellevernon Light and Heat Company secured valuable leases and concluded to drill two additional wells, one each on the Parsons and Rider farms. That on the Parson's farm was begun on April 4, 1888, and completed May 21st, the gas sand having been reached on the 16th. The Rider farm well was completed soon after. The two wells rank among the wonders of the natural gas development of the country. Their combined daily production is not less than 45,000,000 cubic feet of gas. Natural gas strikes were becoming common when these wells were brought in, but so great was the volume of the gas put out that they attracted widespread attention from all parts of the country. The roar of the gas escaping from them could be heard for miles. It sounded a proclamation to the world that the enterprise and energy of Bellevernon's people had been rewarded; that gas in quantities beyond the wildest expectations of the people had been found, and that the quiet trip of S. F. Jones, with his pocket compass and barometer, had resulted in defining the lines of a natural gas field, whose existence had not only not been suspected, but whose richness was beyond compare. The sound was music to the ears of the people of Bellevernon, and they had a right to so regard it. It was a clarion note of invitation to the whole country to come and see and be convinced that to Bellevernon's manifest advantages of long standing had been added another and the greatest of all the advantages, one which in a day placed Bellevernon in the front rank of suitable locations for great enterprises.

R. C. Schmertz, the President of the Bellevernon Light and Heat Company, died just a few days before the first of the great wells in the Maple creek field was brought in. Mr. Schmertz was one of the most indefatigable spirits in the prosecution of the search for natural gas, and one of the most firm believers in the possibility of Bellevernon's future if the new fuel could be found in large quantities. It was his sturdy faith that was proof against the repeated discouragements that attended the first year's experiments. And rarely has faith been more richly justified. Rarely, too, it must be said, has any man earned a greater amount of gratitude than that which the people of Bellevernon owe to R. C. Schmertz.

Mr. Schmertz was succeeded as president of the Bellevernon Light and Heat Company by S. F. Jones, who was also made general superintendent with large powers. T. L. Daly became vice president; R. J. Linton, secretary; and J. S. Jones, treasurer. During the year 1888 contracts were entered into with the Brownsville, Fayette City and Lock No. 4 Gas Company to supply them with gas. Since that time, these companies, as well as Bellevernon and Gibsonton, have been amply supplied from two wells through a system of high pressure pipe lines aggregating about 20 miles in length. Eight miles of this line belongs to the Bellevernon Light and Heat Company, and is supplied with improved appliances for safety and economy. Recently the company assigned a portion of its territory to the Monongahela Natural Gas Company, of Pittsburgh, on advantageous terms. The Philadelphia Company has also some territory and some good wells in the Bellevernon and Maple Creek fields. The Bellevernon Light and Heat Company, however, has reserved enough territory of approved quality to guarantee an inexhaustible supply of natural gas for all time.

There is another important fact in connection with the Bellevernon gas field, however, which deserves extended mention. Within the past few months two wells have been drilled on the east side of the river, about a quarter mile north of Gibsonton. One of these wells is directly on the anticlinal line defined by the Carson, Parson and other good wells in the Maple Creek field, and the other is a short distance east of the line. These wells are known as the Daly wells, in honor of T. L. Daly, who is responsible for the experiment in this direction. They are both good wells and are of the highest importance, as proving that the gas belt which is so wonderfully rich in the Maple Creek field crosses the Monongahela river in a northerly direction and runs into Westmoreland county, no person yet knows how far. The territory will be thoroughly tested, however, and it will not be strange if the field in which the Daly wells are located proves as rich as that which has produced the wonderful wells on the western side of the river.

There is no doubt of the staying qualities of the wells on both sides of the river. They may fail in time, but the people of Bellevernon have secured enough territory to make sure of a plentiful supply of gas at nominal rates to all who come for generations.

Thus the people of Bellevernon have every right to proclaim their advantages over other towns to the world. They ask for nothing better than that capitalists who are seeking for advantageous locations shall come and see what Bellevernon has to offer. Here is natural gas in quantities too great for measurement; here are facilities for the transportation of freight, either by rail or river, that are unsurpassed anywhere; here are great beds of coal and limestone and sand; here are free sites for any responsible parties who will locate with us, and here are a people who have shown themselves progressive, public spirited and ready to help along any enterprise that will aid in the development of their town and its surroundings.

Glass Works of R. C. Schmertz & Co.

Spread over five acres of level ground at the south end of the town is one of Bellevernon's proudest monuments. It is not a shapely shaft surrounded by beautiful gardens, but a collection of substantial brick buildings, the glass works of R. C. Schmertz & Co., Limited, whose product has done more to make the name of Bellevernon known to the outside world than anything else that has gone out of the town, and at the same time has added year after year to the prosperity of its people.

Glass making is among the oldest of the important industries of Bellevernon. Far back in the thirties its advantages as a site for a glass factory were recognized, and in 1836 or 1837 a factory was established by William Eberheart. Not much information of its size or capacity is in existence, but it is known that it was a small affair, and it is fair to presume that its owner never dreamed that fifty-three years later one of the largest manufactories in the country would be located on the ground where he made his beginning.

After some years the property passed into the hands of Geo. A. Berry, now president of the Citizens National Bank, of Pittsburgh, and was operated by him until the year 1865, when it was purchased by the late R. C. Schmertz, who united with careful business training amount of indomitable energy that was certain to cause to grow to its fullest capacity any enterprise in which he was interested.

Mr. Schmertz formed the firm of R. C. Schmertz & Co., consisting of himself, William Loeffler and R. J. Linton. In the hands of this firm the plant has grown to its present proud dimensions and has attained, in many important particulars, a position far in advance of any concern of the kind in the country. Mr. Schmertz died in 1888. The members of the firm now are the Schmertz heirs, William Loeffler and Robert J. Linton, and the corporate name, R. C. Schmertz & Co., limited. The manager of the factory is Lawrence Morrison.

The establishment consists of ten four-pot furnaces, five flattening ovens, a large three-story pot room, immense cutting rooms, two large ware rooms, batch room, clay house, grinding room, pot room for working flattening stones and furnaces, saw mill and box shop, pot shell room, lime and sand houses, etc., all closely connected and conveniently arranged. The last warehouse to be erected is 60x300 feet, and it is certain that the end of the growth is not yet. When to this statement is added the fact that the capacity of the establishment is 4,000 boxes of glass each week, those who have any knowledge of glass industry will appreciate the important position in the manufacturing world held by the firm of R. C. Schmertz & Co., limited.

But this importance is as largely due to excellence in special lines as to the mere capacity of the establishment. At the Schmertz factories glass making has always been conducted on the most scientific principles and the best results have therefore been secured. The factory is famous for its ability in twenty-four hours to transform the raw materials from which glass is made into highly polished sheets of double-thick glass of the largest size made in the country, ready for shipment. In the cutting rooms may be seen sheets 36x96 inches, 42x88 inches, 44x80 inches, 46x98 inches, 48x80 inches, 50x74 inches. Many of these sheets contain nearly 4,000 square inches of glass.

The aim of the firm for years has been to make the quality of the glass manufactured by them equal to the product of the famous Belgian factories. How well they have succeeded may be understood when it is stated that the Schmertz glass is to a great extent used for pictures, show cases and large store fronts, taking in each of these particulars the place of imported glass and giving in every case equal, if not better, satisfaction.

Another important particular in which the firm of R. C. Schmertz & Co., Limited, excels is in the manufacture of ground and frosted glass, which is now so largely used for office partitions and windows. This firm was the first in the United States to add this department to the manufacture of window glass, and in doing so again proved the ability of American glass manufacturers to compete with those of Europe in a field that was considered most firmly held by them.

Not the least interesting or important of the features of this great glass establishment is the saw mill and box factory. The firm buys lumber in large quantities in the river, piles it up in the yard and drys it, and then seasons it and cuts the boards up into the thousands of boxes that are required every week to ship the finished product. The Schmertz firm is the only glass concern that does this, and it is an important advantage. Another advantage is the fact that the railroad runs into the factory yard and that the rates for freight are those ruling at Pittsburgh.

The firm employs over 200 men, and these enjoy the proud distinction of receiving higher wages than those employed in any other glass factory in the country. Some men make from $300 to $500 in four weeks, and all are well paid, many having been in the employ of the firm for many years and are among the most respected citizens of the town.

In September, 1893, the R. C. Schmertz & Co., limited, was merged into the R. C. Schmertz Glass Company, incorporated with a capital of $250,000, of which Wm. Loeffler is President, A. L. Swift is Secretary, and Wm. E. Schmertz, Jr., Treasurer. Principal office at Pittsburgh. The company has just completed a tank of 48 pots capacity, with a ten pot furnace, making an increased capacity of 50 per cent.

EXTRACTS FROM THE BELLEVERNON ENTERPRISE.

Any history of the town of Bellevernon would be incomplete and unsatisfactory without reference to the gentlemen who are and who have been for years untiring in their efforts to bring the advantages of our town before the world. In doing this they have, unconsciously perhaps, performed a great service to all our people, in that they have kept awake in the heart of every man the spirit of "push" which is so essential to the well-being of every community. Their example in enterprise and public spirit has always been earnest and effective, and the people of Bellevernon are largely in their debt.

S. F. JONES.

One of the most familiar figures on the streets of Bellevernon, and one of the leaders in everything calculated to advance its interests, is S. F. Jones. Mr. Jones is manager of the firm of S. F. Jones & Co., bankers, and also president of the Bellevernon Light and Heat Company. He was born in Rostraver township, Westmoreland county, Pa.; was educated in the common schools; followed the life of a farmer nntil 1872, when he and his brother, William, formed the banking house of S. F. Jones & Co., meeting a want long felt at Bellevernon. Notwithstanding it was a new experience for him, and the great panic of 1873 coming so soon after, this firm stemmed the tide, and to-day is one of the firm financial fixtures of Bellevernon. He is also one of the firm of the Bellevernon Saw and Planing Mill Company, doing an extensive business.

Mr. Jones is largely interested in the development of the Maple Creek gas fields, and it was in a great measure due to his efforts that the late R. C. Schmertz was induced to join with a few capitalists in the organization of the Light and Heat Company, of which Mr. Jones is president and general superintendent. This company was the pioneer in the Bellevernon and Maple Creek field which has attracted so much attention. He is also vice-president of the Fayette City Natural Gas Co.

He was one of the chief promoters and devoted much time securing rights of way and encouraging the building of the McKeesport and Bellevernon R. R. Mr. Jones combines thorough painstaking with great enterprise and executive ability. He is always active for the public good and is prominent in all of Bellevernon's most important affairs. His manner is quiet and unostentatious, but the most casual observer cannot fail to be impressed, even after a short conversation, that Mr. Jones is a man with a great reserve force and that he is a safe adviser for any community.

ROBERT J. LINTON.

The first impression of the average man who may be introduced to Robert J. Linton is that he is a man of fixed purpose, large ability, a safe adviser and a gentleman whose word in every respect is equal to his bond. First impressions are often erroneous, but the people of Bellevernon unite in the agreement that Mr. Linton is just what he appears to be—a straight forward man of affairs who can always be relied upon to do anything that will aid in furthering the best interests of the town. For over twenty years he has been in their midst, and this testimony is the result of long experience and the intimate knowledge that comes from close acquaintance.

Mr. Linton is a member of the firm of R. C. Schmertz & Co., limited, glass manufacturers, and resides in one of the most pleasant homes in the town. No man in the country has more thoroughly mastered than he every detail of the mysteries of glass making. He knows every foot of the great factories covering acres of ground, and no space is wasted. Quick to appreciate the real value of any new device, and prompt to grasp all its benefits, and to improve on them if improvement is possible, it is not strange that he should rank among the most advanced manufacturers in the country, and one whose counsel is always sought in important matters. This being the case, the declaration of Mr. Linton that he considers Bellevernon one of the best towns in which manufacturers can locate must have great weight. He is of the Scotch-Irish race and one of its most sturdy representations. In the prime of life and full of vigor and kindliness, it is not presumptious to say that he may reasonably expect to see the fulfillment of his hopes for the town in which he takes so much pride.

THOMAS L. DALY.

A thorough and accomplished gentleman, and a man who enjoys the respect of all citizens is Captain Thomas L. Daly, the general manager of the Gibsonton distillery. Mr. Daly was born in Philadelphia, September 19th, 1839, the sixth in a family of eight children of Thomas and Mary (Marr) Daly. His father and mother were natives of Dublin, Ireland, and after coming to this country settled in Philadelphia, and in April, 1857, was employed to come to Gibsonton to superintend the erection of the Gibsonton mills. Here he was joined by the subject of this sketch, who came from Indianapolis, Ind., where he had been engaged in the extensive flouring mills of William Winpenny & Co. At Gibsonton mills he has filled one position after another since April, 1857, in these extensive works. In July, 1873, he was appointed general manager, which position he still holds. He is a large stockholder in the Light and Heat Company, and thoroughly in earnest in anything he undertakes. As the manager of great enterprises, Mr. Daly is the equal of any man in the country. Modest and unassuming in his manner, his character is of the positive order that always wins for its possessor a place in the front ranks. His executive ability is unquestioned, and the ease with which he controls the details of a business whose ramifications extend to all parts of the world commands general admiration.

JOHN S. VAN VOORHIS, M. D.

A finished scholar, a cultured gentleman, a man of wide experience in the affairs of the world, and one of the most pronounced believers in the future of Bellevernon—that is John S. Van Voorhis, M. D. Dr. Van Voorhis in a sense was "to the manor born," having first seen the light May 8, 1823, near Monongahela City, which is just a few miles distant from Bellevernon, and having spent his whole life among our people. He graduated from Washington College September 25, 1844, and on March 25, 1847, took his degree at the Jefferson Medical College. Locating in Bellevernon in May of the same year, he has practiced his profession in this town almost continuously ever since, the longest exception being a residence of three years in Monongahela City. Shortly after locating in Bellevernon Dr. Van Voorhis was married to Miss E. P. Smith, an estimable lady, and his home has always been one of the pleasantest in the town.

While devoted to his profession and ranking as one of its most skillful members, Dr. Van Voorhis has found time to engage in many other important projects, all of which have advanced the best interests of the Monongahela valley. He was one of the earliest to advocate the construction of railroads in the Monongahela valley, and with voice and pen labored diligently in that direction. The efforts of few men have been crowned with greater success. He was the organizer of the Pittsburgh, Virginia & Charleston Railroad Company, whose road he has seen grow to be one of the most important branches of the Pennsylvania system. He also worked early and late in the interests of the McKeesport & Bellevernon road; and in recognition of his services and standing in the community, was made chairman of the general committee on celebration, and delivered the address of welcome when the road was opened to Bellevernon. In 1857 he represented Washington county in the Legislature, and he has been an honored member of the American Medical Association since 1872. In 1885 he made an extended tour through Europe. His latest work, in addition to the practice of his profession, is the preparation of a volume that will be devoted to the history and biography of the Monongahela valley. He enjoys the respect and esteem of all classes, and has abounding faith in Bellevernon's future.

BELLEVERNON.

"All things come to him who waits."
"Patience and perseverance overcometh all things."
The two sayings that times without number have revived hope in the hearts of hosts of earnest men and women, striving under apparently insurmountable obstacles to accomplish great objects, have been proven true once more. The sturdy people of Bellevernon, after generations of waiting, and after long years of intelligent exercise of patience and perseverance, are on the eve of the realization of their fondly cherished hopes for the future of the town. On every hand signs are abundant that the quiet which has been the characteristic of the town, and which underthinking observers have mistaken for indifference and lethargy, is to be shaken off, that the well directed bustle that proclaims prosperity, is to fill its streets; that the enterprising spirit of its people is to spread far and wide; in a word, that Bellevernon is to have a boom.

That this is not idle speculation can easily be demonstrated. To begin with, no locality in the country has been more highly favored by Dame Nature. Much wilder exaggeration passes current as good sense than the statement that in the construction of things material extra pains must have been exercised to make perfect the territory of which Bellevernon is the centre. The beautiful Monongahela river, running in a straight line, for miles along a bottom high enough for health, and wide enough for the needs of a busy people, was the first element of nature's kindness. Picturesque hills rising in a gentle slope from what has become the site of a busy town, and supporting in their turn level fields of such an extent as to be equal to the requirements of a great city, are another natural advantage. When it is added that under everything, and easy of access, are inexhaustible deposits of coal of the finest quality, sand for manufacturing and building purposes, and stone enough to lay the foundations of a state, there might be reason for saying: "Nature has done enough; nothing is left for man but to rest and be happy!"

Something of this spirit may have animated the people of the Bellevernon of one day. But that was long ago. Man's enterprise and ingenuity have added so much to Bellevernon's advantages as a place for residence, and a site for great business operations, that if there were no other inducements these would weigh for much.

During all time the energy that demonstrated the eligibility of Bellevernon as a site for great enterprises must be given one of the first places in the record of the notable accomplishments in its history. The first move was the establishment of a factory for the manufacture of glass. It was at the time an experiment, whose success was in doubt, but that success has been so great that it has carried the name of Bellevernon to nearly every civilized country on the face of the globe. Not less important in its bearing on the future of the town was the establishment of a distillery, which has grown to be the largest of its class in the world.

The success of these enterprises proved that Bellevernon had as good a right to look for greatness as any other locality. But there was a long time to wait, and much patience and perseverance was called into play before the people were in condition, as they are to-day, to strike out for the realization of their hopes.

First of all it became evident that the river, while an important factor in the prosperity of any community, did not afford the rapid and certain means of communication with the balance of the world that are necessary to keep up with the hurry of the last quarter of the nineteenth century. A railroad was stretched along the opposite side of the river, due to the efforts of Dr. J. S. Van Voorhis and others of our town. It was an aid to the growth of the town, but it failed to meet all requirements. It was evident that Bellevernon must have a railroad of its own. The town could not be moved to any point already traversed by tracks, so the railroad had to be brought to Bellevernon. What this task involved—how often hope was deferred, and how gloriously it was finally realized, are subjects not to be discussed here. Suffice it to say that the railroad came to the town, and every day its good effects are felt by all classes.

Before the railroad, though not before it was discussed, the people of Bellevernon had natural gas. With an abundance of coal under every foot of ground, it would not have been surprising if the people of Bellevernon had left the discovery of natural gas in their neighborhood to persons from other localities who needed it more. But by the time it was generally understood that natural gas was far superior to coal as a fuel, and long before many shrewd minds realized that fact, the active men of Bellevernon concluded that what they needed was natural gas. They went to work with the spirit that has characterized all their acts. Discouragement and large and apparently useless expenditure came first. But perseverance seemed to be the motto of the town. The search was continued, and to-day Bellevernon is the center of the richest gas producing territory in the world. The wells are so near the doors of the people that the best fuel ever given to man is supplied at nominal cost. Natural gas was the last discovery needed to make complete the preparations for the future of Bellevernon. It brought the railroad; it has stimulated energy in every direction.

Without detail the reasons have been given for the faith of the people of Bellevernon, in proclaiming to the world the belief that they offer better advantages than any other locality to capitalists of all classes, to come to them and help make Bellevernon a great manufacturing center. Summarized these advantages are:

Natural gas.

Railroad and river outlets.

Coal of the best quality.

Sand and limestone in abundance.

A locality whose eligibility has been demonstrated by successful capitalists.

A community whose members can be relied upon to

actively aid any enterprise calculated to promote the general prosperity.

Added to all these, and reserved to the last because it is one of the greatest, is the offer made of free sites for manufactories to capitalists who will locate in Bellevernon.

"Bellevernon *may* be a city some day," was the remark we were accustomed to hear from enthusiasts in the old days.

"Bellevernon shall be a city," is the expression and intention of its people to-day.

The two greatest events in the recent history of Bellevernon were the discovery and introduction of natural gas and the construction of the McKeesport and Bellevernon railroad. The story of the long search for and final location of the richest natural gas field in the world is given on another page. It is proper that the advent of the railroad should be recorded here.

A direct railroad connection with the outside world was the dream of the people of Bellevernon for forty years. That it was not realized until the 10th of October, 1889, was no fault of the people of Bellevernon and other towns along the east shore of the Monongahela. Thirty years before an attempt was made to secure a railroad, and at various times after that the effort was renewed. Hopes ran high when in 1881 the East Shore Railroad Company was incorporated under the auspices of the Pittsburgh and Lake Erie Railroad Company, but the charter expired without any work being done.

In 1886 the McKeesport and Bellevernon Railroad Company was chartered, and in December, 1887, the work of building a line from Reynoldton, opposite McKeesport, to Bellevernon was begun. Owing to successive troubles over rights of way, but eleven miles of the road was completed up to April, 1889. Between that date and the 7th of October, 1889, seventeen miles were added, and on the memorable Monday, the 7th of October, the last spike was driven. The road was formally opened on the 10th of October with a celebration at Bellevernon that will be remembered as long as the youngest person present that day lives, and long afterward. Hundreds were present from points in the neighborhood, and distinguished guests came from a distance. Dr. J. S. Van Voorhis was master of ceremonies for the day, and the exercises consisted of speeches by residents of the town, officials of the railroad company and other distinguised visitors, and a grand banquet. The people thought they had occasion to rejoice and everybody joined in. There was particular reason for joy, because three of the foremost promoters of the railroad were Bellevernon men—Messrs. S. F. Jones, T. L. Daly and R. J. Linton— and all of the leading men of the town had given their time, energy and money to the successful prosecution of the work.

Five passenger trains and a large number of freight trains are running over the road daily now, thus affording rapid, direct and cheap communications with east and west through Pittsburgh. The ability of Bellevernon and the east shore of the Monongahela generally to support a railroad has been demonstrated, and it is only a question of a short time until the road is extended to Brownsville or some point more distant. The capital stock of the company was $600,000, and over $1,000,000 was expended in the construction of the road. The officials at the date of the opening were: President, Jacob Wainwright; Secretary and Treasurer, W. T. Wallace; Directors, S. F. Jones, R. J. Linton, J. M. Guffey, C. H. Sackrader, P. H. Green, B. L. Wood, Jr., and J. Chamberlain. The road is now operated by the P. & L. E. R. R. Co.

The Bellevernon of to-day, to state the case briefly, is one of the most prosperous towns and pleasantest places to live or do business in the United States. With a river that is always navigable by reason of the improvements of the Monongahela Navigation Company flowing past its doors; with two railroads affording direct communication with all parts of the country; with an inexhaustible supply of natural gas; with coal of the finest quality underlying every foot of ground; with sand and limestone to be had for the quarrying—with all these advantages, what community could be more richly endowed, and what town has a better right to raise its voice and stretch out its hand and invite men with money to come and help build a city. This can be done with better grace, than by the residents of many other towns for a reason not given alone. The foresight of such citizens as R. J. Linton, S. F. Jones and Thomas L. Daly has secured to the business men of Bellevernon, a boon which every business man will appreciate, and which entitles the gentlemen named to the gratitude of all the people of Bellevernon.

By the terms under which the McKeesport & Bellevernon Railroad obtained admittance to the town, shippers are guaranteed a freight rate even to that charged shippers in Pittsburgh and other terminal points. The same condition prevails with regard to freight received into the town. The advantage of this will be apparent to everybody when it is stated that the growth of hundreds of towns throughout the country is retarded by freight discrimination—that is, the charging of excessive rates on freight from the time it leaves the main system of the railroad. In more than one case within the knowledge of the writer, the freight rates imposed on the shippers in towns situated as Bellevernon is, have been greater for less than 20 miles than those charged shippers in the main line for a distance of 150 miles. What this means any business man can calculate for himself. It answers the one argument that foreign capitalists might urge against investing in this town. When they verify the statements concerning freight rates, as they can easily upon application to the proper officials, they will ascertain that with plants located at Bellevernon they will have the same advantages with regard to freight rates as are enjoyed by the largest shippers at the most important terminals.

Enterprise seems to be the chief characteristics of the people of Bellevernon.

The Gibsonton distillery from the small beginning of 1854 has grown to be the largest pure rye whiskey distillery in the world. The plant covers ten acres of ground, and the daily capacity of the concern is from 4,000 to 4,200 gallons. From

48,000 to 50,000 barrels of whiskey are permanently stored in the great bonded warehouse of the firm, and from 2,000 to 3,000 barrels are stored in the free warehouses subject to the order of customers. The keeping up of this great stock is necessary because the average yearly demand for the product of the distillery is from 15,000 to 16,000 barrels, and the proprietors adhere rigorously to the old idea that whiskey is not fit for consumption before it is at least three years old. That, perhaps more largely than any other circumstance, is responsible for the fact that Gibson's whiskey is a prime favorite everywhere. In addition to being the largest distillery of its class, the Gibsonton concern is one of the most perfectly appointed. The barrels in which the product of the still are stored are made on the ground; all the grain grown in the surrounding country is utilized, and the employes, many of them in the service of the proprietors for more than twenty years, are sober, intelligent men of family and good citizens in every respect. This high standard of excellence in all departments is very largely due to Captain Thomas L. Daly.

The Glass Works, which many years ago became the property of R. C. Schmertz & Co., have also a distinction that is claimed by no other factory in the country. It has produced the largest sheets of window glass manufactured in the United States. The establishment, which is in every respect a model, is under the management of Robert J. Linton, than whom no man is more deeply interested in everything that concerns Bellevernon's welfare and prosperity.

Next most prominent in the industrial field is the plant of the Bellevernon Saw and Planing Mill Company, which operates an extensive planing mill and boat yard. Under the energetic management of Samuel Jones this concern has achieved an excellent reputation and is doing a large business.

The banking house of S. F. Jones & Co. is another of the prominent features of the town. Mr. S. F. Jones is president and gives his personal attention to the management of its business. This is the best guarantee that could be given of the solidity of the concern, and it is a matter of common consent that the bank is as stable as the United States Treasury.

Another institution of which the people of Bellevernon are proud is the foundry. This concern manufactures stoves and ranges in large numbers. Those known as the "Torchlight" and "Coal Valley" stoves and the "Braddock" ranges are unexcelled by the product of any other stove foundry in the country. The proprietor, Mr. Amon Bronson, is a self-made man, and is one of the "fixtures" of the town.

The people of Bellevernon never have occasion to go away from home for good flour. John McClain has a large mill and has a reputation as a miller that is second to none.

As a contractor and builder, C. R. Corwin ranks among the first in any locality.

It is impossible within the limits prescribed for this article to go into details concerning all the business enterprises of the town. It must suffice to say that they embrace every class; that Bellevernon has as good stores as any town of its size anywhere; that its merchants are wide awake and accommodating; and that there is nothing that is necessary for the comfort or happiness of any person that cannot be found in the town.

One more feature of the enterprise of our people deserves especial mention however. That is that the go-ahead spirit is not confined to any class. This will be evident to any person who spends a day in the town, from the bustle in the stores; the thrifty appearance of everybody met on the streets; the number of new buildings in course of erection, and the improvements on old buildings that have been made and are in progress. In a word, everybody is awake and they want the outside world to know it.

Independent of its facilities as a business location, Bellevernon is one of the best places in the country in which a man can live with his family. Its beautiful location has been described. When to this is added the fact that rents are low, that lots can be purchased for little money, and that fuel costs almost nothing, there is little to be desired. But these are not half the advantages Bellevernon offers. It has excellent schools and a fine school building; four churches, representing the Presbyterian, Methodist, Baptist and Disciples' denominations; the people are sociable and refined, and have fewer vices than are usual among a population made up of so many diverse elements. Another matter that counts for a great deal is the fact that very generally the workmen of the town own the homes in which they live. As a consequence, the poor man is equally alive with the rich man to the necessity of doing everything possible to advance the best interests of the town and all its people.

Our people know all this, and much more which their modesty deters them from exploiting, to be true. They invite outsiders to come and see for themselves, satisfied that the town and its inhabitants will be benefited by the closest inspection.

An Address.

An Address of Welcome Delivered by J. S. Van Voorhis, October 10, 1889, at the Opening of the McKeesport and Bellevernon Railroad to Bellevernon, Pa.

Messrs. President, Board of Directors of the McKeesport and Bellevernon Railroad Company, Citizens and Strangers Within Our Gates :

The spirits of four generations look down upon the event of this day and beckon us to give you a hearty welcome.

To-day we realize a forty years' dream overshadowed by your presence in celebrating the crowned efforts of science and labor. This is the dawn of the day when our valley will take a proud position in the great railroad highway from the rising to the setting sun. In the name of the fathers who sleep beneath the sod, and in the spirit of all that is dear to the present, we bid you partake of our hospitality. The importance of a full development of the resources of the Monongahela valley has at last been appreciated. Skill, capital, wisdom, foresight and individual energy has completed a railroad to this point on the east shore of our beautiful river. For long years we have been using our efforts, in divers ways, to induce the opening up of the valley by means of railroads. The river has long been an efficient agent in giving life and wealth to the valley, but the demands of progress are such that water transportation cannot satisfy the increasing trade. The spirit of the age requires rapid transit and quick returns. Our side of the river to-day can boast of such facilities as we have been dreaming of for nearly three score years; and perhaps but for the industry, energy and business shrewdness of Wainwright, to-day might have found us " waiting still for something to turn up." God bless such a man and may his shadow never grow less.

Sixty years ago the building of railroads was a mere experiment in this country, with a population of 12,000,000. To-day 156,000 miles of railroad traverse our country from ocean to ocean and from the lakes to the Gulf of Mexico, with a population of 60,000,000. Sixty years ago the wealth of our country was $1,000,000,000; to-day it over reaches $56,000,000,000. The railroads of this country, in 1888, carried 475,000,000 of passengers and 600,000,000 tons of freight. The railroads of the United States employ 1,000,000 workmen. They have 30,000 locomotives, 21,000 passenger cars, 7,000 baggage cars and 1,000,000 freight cars. The capital invested exceeds $8,000,000,000 and over $600,000,000 are paid annually for labor and supplies.

The first attempt at building a railroad from any point in the valley of the Monongahela was made by the Baltimore & Ohio Company in 1829. The surveys were made under the supervision of Jonathan Knight, at that time chief engineer of the company. He ranked among the most distinguished civil engineers of this or any other country. This survey was principally made with the view of a direct line to Wheeling with the contingency of a branch to Pittsburgh. On the completion of the B. & O. railroad to Cumberland in 1844 the citizens of Pittsburgh and the valley generally were opposed to the project and the Pennsylvania Legislature refused to grant the right of way for the company to pass along the valley, and the result was the building of their road through the mountains of West Va. The opposition in Pittsburgh arose from a visionary fear of a foreign company interfering with the projected Pennsylvania R. R., and the farmers of Fayette and Washington counties opposed it because it would destroy the trade of the national pike. The national pike to-day is, in many places, overgrown with weeds and grass, but the farms are worth four times as much. Such is progress. The first survey of a railroad along the river from Brownsville to Pittsburgh was made in 1835, on the west side, under the direction of the Hon. B. H. Latrobe. He estimated at that time the cost at $27,662.22 per mile. Pittsburgh long since repented of her unwise action, and in after years made herculean efforts to secure competing lines to and from the city. Railroads have made that city what she is to-day and what we expect to make our valley— what she ought to be.

The Hempfield railroad was another abortive effort to aid in the developement of the valley. It was incorporated by an act of the Legislature May 15th, 1850. Its original intention was to construct a railroad from Greensburg, in Westmoreland county, to Wheeling, in West Virginia. After being completed to Washington, the remaining portion was abandoned, although an immense amount of money had been expended. Its franchises are the property of the B. & O. Company. Its chief engineer, Charles Ellet, Jr., was an extravagant, though in the main a successful builder of railroads, but in this scheme he failed for want of funds, in addition to a strong outside pressure of opposing elements. About the time the Hempfield was being constructed at the western end, the Central Ohio, from Wheeling to Newark, Ohio, was under contract, and it was the intention of the Hempfield Company to obtain a controlling interest in this road so as to have a continuous line from Philadelphia westward; but by a sharp manouvre, the Baltimore & Ohio purchased the Ohio Central so as to give

The Old and New Monongahela. 421

their main railroad a western connection. The Pennsylvania Railroad Company, thus foiled in the attempt to push their westward idea by way of the Hempfield, abandoned its interest in this latter project and purchased the bankrupt Pittsburgh & Steubenville Company's franchise, which gave it in the end by what is now called the "Pan-Handle," a route to the west. The Hempfield was finally sold to the Baltimore & Ohio Company.

During the progress of the survey of the location of the Hempfield, a petition was presented by the citizens of Bellevernon, and others, to Hon. T. M. T. M'Kennan, President, asking an examination of the route by way of the north branch of Pigeon Creek and south branch of Maple Creek, in Washington County, crossing the Monongahela river at Bellevernon, and thence by way of Smith's mill, on the Youghiogheny river, to Greensburg. During the summer of 1852 Mr. M'Kennan visited Bellevernon and made a speech from the steps of the residence of Soloman Speers, now the Roley House, in which he portrayed the advantage of the proposed railroad and pledged himself to an examination of the route, which was done, though in a very hasty manner, and rejected on account of its greater distance. The Ohio and Baltimore Short line R. R. Co. was organized in February, 1872. This charter was obtained for the purpose of extending that part of the Hempfield completed by way of Bellevernon to Dawson station on the B. & O. R. R., formerly known as the Pittsburgh and Connellsville railroad. The object was to secure an outlet west to this latter road, which had been refused by way of Pittsburgh.

Work on this extension was commenced in December, 1873, and prosecuted with vigor at the heavy grading at Bellevernon and Bentleysville, but in May, 1874, work was suspended for reasons which were never satisfactorily explained to the outside world. This charter was allowed to lapse, but May 5, 1881, a new organization under the same name was effecte, with a change of route from Washington via Coal Centre to a point above Connellsville on the Baltimore & Ohio Railroad instead of Dawson station. Work was promptly commenced and pushed with vigor as though it was intended to be speedily finished. Heavy grading, tunnels, &c., were being worked with large forces of men; the stone work of the bridge at Greenfield, now Coal Centre, was ready for the superstructure, when lo! suspension all along the line was ordered and so remains to this day. Four attempts had thus been made to construct a railroad across the counties of Fayette and Washington. This last abandonment seems to have been occasioned by the fact that the B. & O. road had secured a western route from Pittsburgh via Streets Run and Washington. The first direct movement to construct a railroad up the valley on the east side of the river was during the session of the Legislature in 1864. A bill was prepared and sent to the late Hon. R. R. Reed, then a member of the House from Washington county. This bill was intended to give the Pittsburgh & Connellsville R. R. Co. authority to construct a branch road up the Monongahela river. In after years, however, the good policy of the project was duly appreciated by the B. & O. Railroad Company, but it was too late. It was one of the many mistakes of the officers of that company.

During the session of 1865 we sent a bill to the late Hon. T. J. Bingham, a senator from Allegheny county, incorporating the Monongahela Valley Railroad Company, which was allowed to have a peaceful rest among the archives of the Senate. In 1866 a bill was carefully prepared and sent to the late Joseph B. Welsh, a member of the House from Washington county. He seemed to take hold of the matter in the true spirit, and succeeded finally in having it passed through the House, just in time to have it die under the rules in the Senate. By request, on the 8th of January, 1867, Col. T. B. Searight, a senator from Fayette, read a bill in place which contained all the provisions desired by its friends, but merely read it in place without any further attention. It was carefully preserved from the Senate in the committee. In 1867, Mr. Day, of

Washington, had the bill of 1866 so remodeled as to satisfy its friends as well as enemies, and so had it passed, which was approved by the governor April 8th, 1867. During the summer of 1867 your speaker agitated the organization of the company. The first meeting of the corporators was held at the Monongahela House, in Pittsburgh, and adjourned to meet at Elizabeth, June 7th, 1867. This meeting was largely attended and a progressive spirit manifested. Many capitalists and other business men were present. Meetings were subsequently held in Monongahela City, Fayette City, Brownsville, West Brownsville, Carmichaels, Finleyville and Library.

The act of Assembly fixed the capital at $20,000 per mile, and 10 per cent. of said stock was required to be subscribed and 10 per cent. on the subscription to be paid in before Letters Patent could be granted. The distance was computed by the river from Pittsburgh to Waynesburg. In order to shorten the distance and thereby reduce the amount to be subscribed, it was suggested that a supplement to the act should be obtained, allowing the road to be located on any route from Pittsburgh to Monongahela City, and thence along either side of the river to a point at or near Rice's Landing. The bill was in charge of Mr. Day, of Washington, who forced it to its final passage against the eloquence of Mr. Playford, of Fayette. This act gave new life to the project and the survey was completed in the spring of 1869. By the act of February, 1870, the name of the Monongahela Valley Railway Company was changed to that of Pittsburgh, Virginia and Charleston Railway Company. In the spring of 1870, operations in the building were commenced, and in 1873 the railroad completed and in full operation to Monongahela City. In May, 1881, the railroad was completed to West Brownsville. In August, 1882, the Redstone branch from West Brownsville to Uniontown was finished. In May, 1879, the road and its franchises passed to the control of the Pennsylvania R. R. Co. and is now operated as one of its lines.

By the Act of Assembly approved April 14, 1870, the Pittsburgh & Virginia R. R, was incorporated and partially organized. Its object was another effort toward opening up the resources of the east side of the Monongahela river by a railroad. Like former similar attempts this proved a failure. It was expected that the B. & O. Co. would take hold of such an enterprise and insure its success.

The characteristic timidity and short-sightedness of that company again failed to realize what a bright future awaited such an enterprise.

In December, 1870, the Bellevernon branch of the Pittsburgh and Connellsville railroad was chartered by the courts of Westmoreland county. The object of this company was to build a railroad from the lower end of Main street in Bellevernon to a point on the Pittsburgh and Connellsville railroad at Amieville, not far below the mouth of Sewickley creek. L. C. Baldwin, superintendent of the Gibsonton mills was the president, and among the managers were S. F. Jones, John Rankin, N. Q. Speer and Hortensius Lowry. The prospects for its construction were, apparently, very bright; large subscriptions of stock were readily obtained and the right of way generally secured when, for some, not generally known, cause, the company went into court and obtained authority to dissolve the corporation, which was promptly done, the stockholders being refunded their ten per cent. minus expenses incurred. This was another mistake.

In August, 1881, the East Shore Railroad Company was organized under the auspices of the Pittsburgh & Lake Erie Company. Surveys were made and considerable of a stir made along the river, but the charter was allowed to expire by limitation. However, about this time a new spirit seemed to have taken hold, even of some of the minds connected with the East Shore enterprise. Mr. Wainwright, who had constructed the Pittsburgh, McKeesport & Youghiogheny Railroad along a route on the Youghiogheny river, where no ordinary genius would have dreamed of a road, had the boldness, the shrewdness and the talent to not only resuscitate the project, but to carry it out in so successful a manner as to elicit the applause and congratulations of not only the people of the valley, but business men both east and west.

Napoleon, when he proposed to march his army into Italy, was told that "the Alps were in his way." He replied, "I will show to the world that there are no Alps." He built the Simplon road. So Wainwright, when confronted with the heretofore almost hopeless task of building a railroad on the east shore of the Monongahela, was able to say that "railroads can be constructed where everything else fears to tread—save genius.,' The road, as it now stands, is a monument to his genius more enduring than marble, for it is written in the hearts of his fellow citizens; and when the great railroad system of which we have written, and whose birth to-day we celebrate, shall have extended from the great chain of lakes in the north to the burning sands of the Atlantic, his name, with that of Vanderbilt, will be applauded, and generations yet unborn will rise up and call him blessed.

To-day our valley puts on a new verdure; to-day the East Shore has its gates open to the outside world; to-day our village of seventy years growth will stand erect with her sister towns on the west side; to-day the unmeasured wealth of the West Virginia hills are within our grasp; to-day a new page is written in our history.

In a short time, no doubt, the McKeesport and Bellevernon railroad will be extended to connections in the south. This company was quietly organized solely for the purpose of building it, and we see it is a reality to-day. Wainwright is president of the company. Very recently Vanderbilt has purchased a large interest in the Chesapeake and Ohio railroad which foreshadows, at no distant day, connection with that road by Wainwright. The upper Monongahela Valley has long been neglected, but to-day the progress of this new railroad enterprise shows that it is reaching for something heretofore hidden. We long ago predicted that a railroad would be built on each shore of the Monongahela, and the realization of the prophecy is only a matter of a short time. For years we have been trying to convince the people that every mile of railroad along this valley would pay its own dividend. Already can be noted new life on the east shore.

New towns and new enterprises are bound to spring into existence on almost every mile of this road. The trade is here now and will continue to grow. The people along this new road have already cast aside their slow motion style and now bestir themselves in the true double quick. Already land along the line has quadrupled in many places in price, and inquiries are being almost daily made for sites favorable to manufacturing interests. Our great gas field is sufficient to furnish fuel for all who will invest their capital. On the extension of this new railroad to the sources of the Monongahela, a new coal field of three hundred square miles will be within the reach of the consumer, and within the present generation a thousand furnaces will light up our valley, furnishing to the laborer a never ending employment, and to capitalists a rich reward for their investment.

[From the Bellevernon *Enterprise.*]

AN OPENING OPENED, AND A BIG DAY OF CELEBRATION.

The marriage has taken place, the reception is over, and the 10th of October will long remain in the minds of the many who witnessed the celebration of Bellevernon being joined to the outer world by the bonds of the iron horse. The preparations for the occasion were ample and truly the union was celebrated appropriately.

Promptly at 7 A. M. the special left our depot for McKeesport to meet the guests coming from Pittsburgh and other points. The train was gaily decorated with the national colors, of which all are so grandly proud, and as she pulled out the whistle at the mill and gas regulator greeted her with extra toots. No wonder Sam Jones blowed the whistle so loud on her return, either. People came to town in almost every conceivable way and by the time the special train returned the staid old village was one tumultuous throng. Banners of "Welcome" were hung from the house tops and never in our time was there so much genuine enthusiasm. Everybody was happy and thus added to the enjoyment of "our guests."

Never in the history of this thriving settlement has such an important occasion enthused its citizens. The advent of natural gas was a cause for great rejoicings—it was the harbinger of great things—but now that the "iron horse" is here the place was wild with enthusiasm.

The gaily decorated train carrying the Pittsburgh visitors arrived at McKeesport at 9.30. At Reynoldton Junction the members of the Bellevernon committee with the Bellevernon cornet band and G. A. R. drum corps, met the visitors.

The train reached Gibsonton, a suburb of Bellevernon, at 11. Here the train was met by several hundred citizens, whose cheers and huzzas welcomed them to the region of king gas and coal. The conclusion of a lively selection by the band was the signal for a demonstration, and for a period of time, during which the train proceeded from Gibsonton to Bellevernon, the booming of cannon, the toot! toot of whistles, the escape of gas and the cheers of the people combined, was an excellent imitation of pandemonium.

At Bellevernon the visitors were received by Chief Marshal Samuel McKean and staff, and a procession was soon formed with the officers of the road and distinguished men in the van, which the band led to the speakers' stand on Main street.

Dr. J. S. Van Voorhis delivered the address of welcome.

President J. Wainright, of the McKeesport and Bellevernon railroad, responded to the address of welcome. Mr. Wainright said in substance: The manner of greeting by the people of Bellevernon is thankfully received by the directory of the road, and being no speaker himself, he would have to be excused from a formal address. He was reminded of an incident that occurred a few weeks' since between a farmer below our town and himself. The farmer required a good deal of persuasion before being convinced of the propriety of giving the right of way to the road passing over his farm, but finally consented.

The next day on meeting a neighbor he remarked that the man Wainwright last night had talked him into giving the right of way, and if he had stayed all night with me he would have gotten my whole farm. I am called sometimes the Right of Way Wainwright. From the tenor of the doctor's speech he would have been a good talking right of way man. We are doing the best we can to furnish the east with short railroad facilities, and we are glad to see that our efforts are appreciated by the citizens of the Valley. We again thank you for your greetings.

Hon. Geo. V. Lawrence, of Monongahela City; Judge Hunter, of Westmoreland county; Judge Ewing, of Fayette county, and State Senator Robbins, of Greensburg, all praised the man who had the head and heart to open the east shore railroad, as well as to thank the people of Bellevernon for their grand demonstration. Letters of regret were read from prominent men who were unable to be present.

The banquet prepared at the Roley House was one of the affairs of the day, and judging from the smiling visages of those who partook of the hospitality of Mr. Roley, it was a great success.

After dinner the visitors spent a few hours strolling around looking at our immense glass factory, gas system and wells, as well as taking in a short trip to Gibsonton distillery, which is one of the largest in the country.

When the time came for the departure of the special, many were loth to leave their late made friends, yet with promises of a return visit "some day," good byes were said and a day of pleasure was about closed.

Among the Pittsburgh visitors who attended the opening were: J. S. Scully, R. H. Smith, George B. Hill, John Swan, W. W. McCreary, Max K. Moorhead, W. W. Patrick, Capt. T. Fawcett, Alexander Dempster, Benjamin Elwood, T. E.

Umstaetter, Charles R. Meyran, Capt. Horner, Samuel Dilworth, W. R. Holmes and Dr. J. B. Murdock.

The railroad officials were: D. P. Corwin, secretary Pittsburgh, Virginia & Charleston; F. A. Dean, general freight agent Pittsburgh & Lake Erie; F. G. Bailey, W. G. Taggart, F. H. Kennedy, George McCague, of the Lake Shore & Michigan Southern, M. E. Valiant, T. W. Galleher, division freight agent of the Baltimore & Ohio, and J. W. Wainwright, J. H. Drake, O. A. Rogers and W. T. Wallace, of the McKeesport & Bellevernon Railroad.

From McKeesport: J. B. Shale, E. P. Douglass, attorney of the road; A. B. Campbell, J. L. Devenney, editor *News*; Dr. White and others.

Elizabeth: J. Speer, comptroller of Allegheny county; Wm. Walker, Attorney J. B. Patterson, Dr. Charles Shaffer, Dr. Van Kirk, Dick Wiley, editor *Herald*; Geo. Roberts, Jr., Gen. Pass. Agent J. C. Grooms.

Monongahela City: Capt. T. H. Williams, W. J. Alexander, C. G. McIlvaine, Jos. A. Herron, E. Downer, Postmaster James Moore, John S. Markle, John Van Voorhis, J. B. Finley, Isaac Yohe, Jr., James Yohe, Moses Scott, B. F. Bentley, Hon. G. V. Lawrence, W. H. Smith, John Swichard, Frank Hendrickson and others.

Uniontown was represented by Judge Ewing, Geo. D. Howell, R. F. Hopwood, Wm. G. Guiler. A. F. Cooper, O. G. Chick, Geo. A. McCormick, L. H. Frazier, Editor Cook, John D. Carr, R. P. Kennedy, Editor Scott, of the *News;* Doll Johns, and others whom we did not meet.

Personal mention cannot be made of all the reporters and editors who favored us with a call, because they invaded our sanctum and office in such numbers that we could not remember names or faces, but were glad that so many came, and are sure that our city friends will now know how Bellevernon is situated geographically.

The banquet in Taggert's hall wound up the appropriate celebration, and in the morning the trains carried away the last of our guests of a great day.

Letters of regret were received from Thos. M. Bayne. E. A. Montooth, John Dalzell, A. A. Wallace, S. D. Warmcastle, President Harrison, M. S. Quay, J. G. Blaine, John H. Hampton and Isaac S. Van Voorhis.

NATHANIEL EVERSON

AND MISCELLANEOUS MATTERS.

Nathaniel Everson, father of Mrs. Louisa Taggart, came from Chester county, was married in Baltimore, came to Pittsburgh first then to the old log house on Jesse Reeve's farm near Rostraver coal works above the house long occupied by Levi Harris. Old Joseph Johnson lived and died in the old house about forty years ago. Nathaniel Everson moved into the old house that stood on the site of the Presbyterian church, corner of Main and First streets, Bellevernon. In this house, in 1816, Mrs. L. Taggart was born. Nathaniel, some years subsequently, built and moved into the house which still stands on corner of Locust and Long alley, long known as the Granny Taggart house.

The first fire in the town happened in this house, and in this way: Henry Doyle had married Harriet Everson, October 29th, 1820, and in due course of time the first born appeared on the stage of life, and as was the custom, many of the female inhabitants were invited to give honor to the occasion, among whom were Aunt Rutan, Polly Corwin, Katy Ward, Hannah Gaskill and Mary Hornbeck; but to add further zest to the occasion, the father, Henry Doyle, in the evening invited as his guests Morris Corwin, Budd Gaskill, Billy Hornbeck and Thomas Ward. In the midst of the festivities, Doyle thought of the barrel of good old rye he had stored away in the loft. With the primitive lamp made of tin, a wick and grease in hand he hied away to the secret place for a pitcher full of the desired fluid. As the spirits flowed freely from the spigot, he thought it would be a good chance to taste it in advance of his guests. So he stooped to catch it as it ran, but in so doing the lamp came in contact with the gas from the liquor, and way went the barrel up and through the roof, setting fire to everything in the loft, and the spilled whiskey pouring on to the open floor passed down in a blaze to the room where the mother and new born babe were in bed. The bed with its living contents was hurriedly taken to the kitchen, and all hands got to work to put out the fire.

The next fire was in 1856, in the cabinet shop of Apollos Speers, where now is the rear part of J. S. Henry, Jr.'s store. The next fire was January 31, 1875, by which the house below Strawberry alley on Main street, occupied by Henry Haler, was consumed, together with the store room in which was the store of Cunningham & Craft, and the second story which was occupied by the Odd Fellows and other orders. The dwelling house in which Rev. A. B. Lowes resided and the dwelling of Jas. H. Lewis, made a narrow escape from being burned. The great fire of the town occurred February 28, 1880, by which was destroyed the saw mill and nearly every building on the square bounded by Main, Third, Water streets and Strawberry alley.

On the night of February 24, 1886, a fire consumed the dwelling and drug store room of Henry Lang, together with what was known as Kyle's row, all situated on State Road near Main street.

The first tavern in town was kept by Billy Hornbeck in the house now owned by A. L. Brown whilst it stood on the corner of Main street and Cherry alley. He was succeeded by Abe Bugher, after he married Mrs. Darr, who kept the first cake shop in town, in the old part of the Lanehart house as it was built by Geo. Hazelbaker, the hatter, who had his hat shop in it at first, but afterwards as the firm of Hazelbaker & Dunlevy, he carried on the making of hats in the house on Water street, near what is now known as the Bull Run bridge. This house was built for John Springer by his father, Daniel Springer, about the year 1830. Geo. Kintner built the house now owned by Mrs. Eliza Smock. Kintner's wife was Polly Everson, sister of Mrs. L. Taggart.

The first carpenter work done by Thomas Taggart in town was the long row on Main street below Strawberry alley. He built it for his father-in-law, Nathaniel Everson.

Richard Everson had erected the Wise House and kept in it the second tavern. It was built at three different dates with as many divisions. Among others who kept tavern in this house we call to mind, A. C. Housman, Griffith Wells, J. W. Wright and L. A. Eberheart. The house in which Mrs. Louisa Taggart now (1893) lives was built by Thomas Taggart himself having purchased the lot from Solomon Speers.

Budd Gaskill built the old log part of the Lang house on Water street. The late Samuel Winters had built the Bunting house on Main street. The house now owned and occupied on Main street by Jacob Haught was built by Joseph Pearson the bricklayer and Wm. Wayts the plasterer.

The first doctor in town of which we have any account was Dr. Horner, he boarded with Hornbeck; he was succeeded by Drs. Pool, Kirk, Johnson, Roberts, Egan, Van Voorhis, Creigh, Chalfant, Fetz, Rupp, Conklin. Hazlett, Enos, and at this date, 1893, the resident physicians are: J. S. Van Voorhis, A. N. Marston, Geo. E. Nickel, Andrew Guiler, N. B. Lowman and W. H. Lewis. Dr. Van Voorhis came to Bellevernon May 25th, 1847, and is now the oldest practitioner of medicine in the valley.

In 1829 the Caughenour house was built by James Corwin, who with Robert Patterson, did the carpenter work. During its building Corwin lived in the house now occupied and owned by Henry Haler and heirs on Main street, and Robert Patterson had a cooper shop in that part of the Lang house recently occupied as a drug store by Henry Lang. The house corner of Second and Water streets was built by A. P. Frye, where for a time he resided prior to his purchase of the tanyard now the property of the heirs of George Lang.

In 1834 Robert Patterson built the old house out of which has been made the fine residence now owned by Mrs. Neal on Main above Third street. Robert Patterson and Thos. Todd did the carpenter work, and Robert G. Mullin, lately deceased, of Fayette City, did the painting, and Thomas, brother of Henry Doyle, the plastering. In October, 1833, Robert was married to Keziah Winters. They boarded at different places until the house was finished, moved into it in 1834 and lived in it forty-four years.

The first regular packet boat that plied between Bellevernon and Brownsville was the Minnie Harris, commanded by Capt. McGinnis. It was a neat little screw propeller. It was succeeded by the W. Q. Shrodes, Capt. Brooks. It was a stern wheel boat of small size. These boats were in service in 1872–73. The next boat in the trade was the Athletic, Capt. O. D. Johnson, who was drowned November 9, 1876, whilst landing a barge at the Gibsonton wharf. At the administrator's sale of the estate of O. D. Johnson, the Athletic was sold to Bowell, Bowers & Loomis, J. M. Bowell and Morgan Bowers of this place, purchasing one-half and Stephen Loomis, of Lock No. 4, the other half. They commenced to run her January 17, 1877, and in 1878, Bowell and Bowers became sole owners. They sold it in 1881 to W. H. Moore, and built at Brownsville complete the J. M. Bowell, and in 1882 made the first trip. The J. M. Bowell on her trip on the 24th day of July, 1884, was capsized by a storm in the bend of the river below what is now called Coal Centre, and although over thirty passengers were aboard only one was drowned.

Alex Austin was the first barber. He had his shop about 1859 on Main street, where is now the office of Dr. Van Voorhis. It had, before Austin's time, been occupied by different persons, among whom was H. B. Frye, who kept in it the first confectionary in town. Austin entered the ministry of the African M. E. Church, and in about 1860 moved to Barnesville, Ohio. He died not long ago after having been rather a prominent man in the church.

The present resident barbers are George Bolden, Wilbur Minnie and Conrad Metz. George came to town in 1872, had his first shop and lived in a house not far below Second and Water streets. Minnie came to town a few years ago, and first worked in the rear of Jacob T. Roley's store on State Road. He is now located on Second street and Long alley, and Bolden on Main street above Locust alley.

The last licensed hotel in town was in the brick corner now owned by L. Z. Birmingham. It was kept by R. C. Byers, now a resident of Monongahela City.

Somewhere about 1859-60 R. L. Kenah had a drug store in part of the room recently occupied as a part of the laundry recently burned on Main street. In a short time moved it to the Wise store room, and finding the business would not pay, he removed to Beaver county, where he still carries on the business. The town now has four paying drug stores (1893.)

In the winter of 1853-54 existed the most successful literary society in town of which we have any account. Among the active members we recollect very distinctly the names of Rev. James Davidson, Rev. J. W. Planett, J. J. A. Reynolds, John C. Gabler, William Haney, J. S. Van Voorhis, James H. Speers, J. C. Hasson. During its existence the members had a very fine literary entertainment in the old Methodist Episcopal church above Strawberry alley, a program of which Rev. James Davidson has in his possession.

The first festival was held in 1862 by the Ladies' Soldiers' Aid Society, the proceeds of which purchased certain articles of clothing for the soldiers, whom the people had conceived were not sufficiently provided for by the government. The festival was held in the old school house on the hill, where now stands the residence of R. J. Linton. Provision beyond measure was sent in by the soldiers' friends until the house would scarcely contain it and leave room for the great gathering of the people; never before or since had the old building so many people within its walls. Music on the organ and vocal were features of the occasion. Among the music was "Twenty Years Ago," sung and played by the late Prof. Fulton, who was a soldier at home on furlough.

The election in 1872 was held in the bellfrey of this same

school house, it being fixed for the purpose on the torn down foundation. From that year to the present elections have been held in the old Speers brick house near the ferry.

SPEERS.

Henry Speers and Regina, his wife, were born in Germany, and in about the years 1771-'72 settled on what is now known as the Gibsonton farm. Henry Speers had four sons, Jacob, Solomon, Noah and Henry, and one daughter, as far as we can ascertain, who was the wife of Benjamin Frye, one of the executors of the estate. Henry died in 1773. His son Jacob emigrated to Kentucky in early days, where for many years he was a successful business man, and from whom the Kentucky Speers had their origin. Solomon was killed by the Indians, on Salt river, in Kentucky, where he had gone to engage in trapping and trading. Henry, born July 8th, 1756, was sixteen years old when his parents located near the present town of Bellevernon. He married Rebecca Frye, a daughter of Abraham Frye, Sr., September 24th, 1777. She died July 16th, 1835. This Henry Speers and wife were the parents of thirteen children, only a few of whom we have knowledge. Henry, all of his married life, resided on the farm called "Speers Intent," opposite Bellevernon. He was long a member of the Baptist church, was licensed to preach by the church of Enon, May 5th, 1793, and ordained by Rev. John Cobley, on the last Saturday of March, 1797, and he continued as pastor of Enon church to the day of his death, which was January 26th, 1840. Enon church was located in chief, opposite Bellevernon. He was the principle man in building up this church, the members of which at first worshiped in the old log building long since gone, but more recently in the brick house still standing on the hill near the ferry, and now owned by his grandson, S. C. Speers. The old log church is said to have been built prior to the old Horse Shoe Presbyterian church, which stood on the farm long known as the Simon Wilson, back of Lock No. 4, but owned by his son John Wilson. The brick mansion near the ferry owned and occupied now by his grandson, Noah Speers, was built by him, that is Henry Speers, in 1806. One of his sons was a soldier in the war of 1812, was in the battle of New Orleans with Gen. Jackson. He lived for many years in the log house on Maple creek, where the late Geo. Norris so long resided ; he died many years ago in the old log house on the south branch of the same stream where the widow of the late Joseph Beazell now lives.

Samuel, another son of Henry Speers, was also a soldier in the war of 1812, exposure in the army caused him to be a cripple in his last days, which were passed in the mansion near the ferry. Many of our older citizens will call to mind "Uncle Sam" with his many peculiarities of character. He was never married. John passed most of his life at Dunbar, in Fayette county. His heirs still own part of the farm above the original Speers farm, on the river. This tract of land was in early day owned by Col. Edward Cook, one of the most prominent public actors in the settlement of Western Pennsylvania. At Dunbar he had a mill and a farm which are yet property of his heirs, although the mill has ceased to grind. He had quite a large family, several of whom have passed away. One of the daughters of Henry Speers married Geo. Hill, of Ten Mile, in Washington county; another was the wife of William Ward, deceased, who lived many years in the brick house about one mile above Twilight, in Washington county. Kattie married John McCrory. Apollos, the remaining son, was born near the ferry September 8, 1801. After his marriage to Elizabeth Cooper, who died at Marshalltown, Iowa, September 13, 1874, he lived for a time at Fish Pot, on Ten Mile. With this exception he resided all his life in the ferry brick house where he died February 23, 1857, and was buried in the grave yard overlooking his residence, a site selected by his father as a burial place. Apollos had five sons and six daughters. Solomon C. resides on part of the "Speers Intent" tract, below the ferry. Noah still owns and occupies the brick homestead of his father and grandfather. Jasper died January 8, 1859. Jacob and Henry have been residents for many years of Marshalltown, Iowa. Margaret married Enoch Baker, of Ten Mile. Nancy, now deceased, married Samuel Frye. Mary married B. W. Johnson, and now resides at or near Marshalltown, Iowa. Clara married James Walker, and lived near the same place, so does Sarah. Noah, the remaining son of Henry Speers, the older, was not three years old when his father settled on the Gibsonton farm, where he, Noah, died June 9, 1832.

He not only owned the Gibsonton farm, including the tract now belonging to John W. Irons, but also the farm on which the late L. M. Speers so long resided, together with the ground on which Bellevernon is situated. He carried on farming very extensively, and had under him a large number of slaves. He was founder of Bellevernon. His wife, who was a daughter of Abraham Frye, Sr., died May 12th, 1845. The remains of Noah and his wife are buried in what is known as the Gibsonton graveyard, on the old Speers homestead. Noah left a large family to enjoy his estate as disposed of by his will, dated June 2nd, 1832, just seven days before his death, which was caused by the kick of a horse. Jacob married a daughter of the late Major John Power, of Rostraver, and resided for many years on that part of the Speers homestead now owned by John W. Irons. He built the brick house still standing above the public road. Thomas Taggart did the carpenter work and Joseph Pearson, we think, did the laying of the brick. In about 1846 Jacob moved to Illinois, where he still lives at a good age. Solomon, after living for nearly half a century in the brick house near the ferry, removed west in 1857, where he died in 1860. Noah W. inherited the old homestead; we have already written in detail his career.

Louis M. Speer.

For more than fifty years Louis M. Speer was the most prominent factor in the history of Bellevernon. Although dead, his many good qualities of head and heart will not soon be forgotten. He was nearly six feet in height, of a dark complexion, and in weight bordering on 180 pounds. His disposition was excitable, yet firm, though pliable to reason and a sense of right. He was born July 26, 1810, in the old log mansion on the Speer homestead, now the Gibsonton farm. He was tutored to the business of farming by his father, Noah Speers, and always more or less manifested much of his father's disposition and habits of life. He married Miss Jane Finley, daughter of the late Wm. Finley, who lived all his life near Rehoboth church, and died in the stone house still standing near that church. Mrs. Speer died March 13, 1857, in the brick house built and so long owned by her husband. After their marriage they went to housekeeping in the old log house which stood in front of the brick house. The old house was removed by Alexander Austin, the barber, in 1843, to Bellevernon hill, and was for many years the residence of Peter Lehew. It has given way to Lehew's present fine residence on Market street, near Strawberry alley. Louis was one of the most successful farmers of his day. He was the pioneer sand dealer in the valley, his acres of sand yielded him a very handsome revenue. At first it was washed and prepared for the glass manufacturer by hand power. The apparatus consisted of a square trough about two by ten feet long. The rude sand was taken from the field on his own farm by cart and horse to the wash, then shoveled into the trough, water turned on, stirred well and then the sand was settled to the bottom by clubs beating the sides, the dirty water running off in the meantime. After being washed it was stored in sand pens to await market. We call to mind the wash below the present Jones barn; the one near the present residence of Geo. Fisher, and another near the present residence of J. T. Roley. Then came the horse power over the river near the old Tremont school house where he washed sand taken from the land of Noah Speers. Finally he was connected with the steam washer opposite town, now owned by S. C. Speers. In addition, he dealt in stock, lumber, coal and merchandise. Early in the late war he was appointed inspector of horses in the Quartermaster Department at Indianapolis, to which place he repaired and entered upon the discharge of his duties. He soon discovered that his honest manner respecting the office was not compatible with the surroundings, so that rather than be annoyed by attempts to swerve him from a correct and open discharge of his duties, he resigned in a very short time.

His first wife was Jane Finley, daughter of William Finley, and grand daughter of the Rev. James Finley who was the first pastor of Rehoboth. She died March 13th, 1857. They had as children William F. who married Mary, daughter of the late James S. Power. At the beginning of the late war William raised a company of Cavalry, went into the service as second lieutenant, served during most of the time as captain, and at the close of the war was honored for meritorious services with the brevet rank of major of cavalry. With his father he carried on boat building and the coal business for many years. After their financial embarrassment in 1877, William moved to Sewickley on the Ohio river, where he was a member of the Pittsburgh Boat Building Company. He is now (1892) connected with a brick manufacturing company in Pittsburgh and resides on Atwood street.

Noah Q. has long been connected with the sand business, both with his father and more recently as a member of the Speer White Sand Company, which has extensive crushing and washing works on the Youghiogheny river, and at Mapleton on the Pennsylvania Railroad, in Huntingdon county. He built the residence in Bellevernon now owned and occupied by Levi J. Jeffries. He resides at this time in BenVenue, in Pittsburgh. His wife is a daughter of the late Hon. Aaron Bugher, of Fayette City, who represented Fayette county in the Legislature in 1841. The other sons of Louis M. Speer are by his first wife—J. R. Hughes and Eddie, now deceased. The daughters are Mary, Margaretta and Celia. Margaretta, more familiarly known by the name of Rettie, married her cousin, Solomon P. Speer. They reside in Baltimore, where he is an active and successful business man. Mary married Rev. T. S. Park; they live in Illinois. Celia married Rev. R. B. Porter; they reside on the border of Butler and Allegheny counties, the name of the town we can not recall.

In about the year 1859, Louis M. Speer married Miss Fannie Stewart, of Colerain Forge, in this state. The children by this marriage, who are now living are David S., Calhoun, and John S. V., little Frankie having died in infancy, his remains are in the Bellevernon cemetery marked by a beautiful monument. In 1878, Louis M. Speer and wife with their three boys by his second wife moved to Wooster, Ohio. From the day of his financial trouble Louis M. Speer seemed to fail in heart and body, and on the 15th day of September, 1883, he died whilst on a visit to his daughter Mary, near Cadiz Junction, Ohio. His remains were brought on the 18th to Bellevernon and interred at Rehoboth. The exercises attending the burial were graphically described in a communication in the Monongahela *Daily Republican* which we insert:

BELLEVERNON, PA., September 19th, 1883.

Dear Colonel:—Yesterday we laid to rest in Rehoboth grave yard along side the wife of his youth, the remains of my old friend L. M. Speer. As the body was borne by his sons from the depot, the four bells of Bellevernon sent forth their solemn echoes in memory of the dead proprietor. At the ferry wharf the people en masse in open ranks with uncovered heads met the cortege of sorrowing friends, and as it passed through to the Presbyterian church, a death stillness reigned and every heart seemed impressed with emotion. The large concourse of people in and around the church was made up of his former fellow citizens in every walk of life. The old and young all seemed to vie in attempts to honor his memory. In the church erected principally by his own liberality and of which he had been a member for many years, the services were conducted by Rev. D. K. Nesbit, of Hazelwood, assisted by Revs. Baker and Leonard of this place. The body in full dress was encased in a beautiful iron casket weighing over seven hundred pounds. The remains were followed to the grave yard by a long line of carriages and two spring wagons conveying the town councils of both boroughs, which had turned out in their corporate capacity to do honor to his memory.

As the solemn procession approached his old homestead every eye was turned and every heart filled with recollections of the past. Here he first located, here he passed his early and greater part of his active and useful life, here his children were all born ; and from this sacred temple he had borne the remains of his first love. Here he lived when he gave himself to that God in whom he trusted to the last. At Rehoboth an additional crowd had convened to honor the remains. On their return the friends in sorrow were entertained by kind hearts all over town.

For two generations he had furnished employment to a large proportion of the citizens of Bellevernon, whereby they were fed and clothed. As a farmer, boat builder, coal operator and merchant, he was generous and ever ready and willing to lend a helping hand to the needy. It could truly be said of him that he fed the hungry, clothed the naked, visited the sick. He joined in every enterprise that promoted local or general interest of the valley of which he had so high estimate. Thus has passed away one who in my early struggles with the world was ever ready to give a word of cheer ; in maturer age a companion in whom I could trust and in whose death is a loss I cannot estimate the value thereof.

Yours truly,   J. S. V.

Few men in this valley had rendered more service to his fellow men than Louis M. Speer. He was a good neighbor, a kind friend and a human benefactor. He was about the last of the cotemporaies who gave caste to the infant Bellevernon. His name will not soon be forgotten. It is written everywhere around his native place in deeds of charity and benefaction. The world is the loser by the death of such men.

Louis M. Speer had a brother James who died in early life, and Abram, who studied medicine but never practiced his profession very much. He lived and died in the old log house long known as the Rev. Dr. Smith house, which stood in Rostraver, near the brick house erected by S. F. Jones, and now owned by the heirs of Robert Fairman, on the road leading from town to Webster. He was the father of David P. Charles and Solomon Speers, of Elizabeth, Pa. Louis M. Speer had several sisters all of whom we think are dead. Clarissa married Andrew Ford, of Fayette county; Lucinda married Wm. Mills, one married Samuel Walker, long a boat builder at Elizabeth, and another was the wife of Robt. McFarland, of Lower St. Clair, in Allegheny county. Jacob and Noah W. are the only living ones of the family.

Death of Col. William F. Speer, Brick Manufacturer and Steamboat Builder.

Lieutenant Colonel William F. Speer died September 15, 1893, after a lingering illness at his residence, 321 Atwood street, Pittsburgh, Pa. Over a year ago he was getting in a car on the Central traction road when the car started and he was run over. His right arm was crushed and his back hurt. He was never well afterward, and Bright's disease developed. He was a very sick man for some months past, all hope of his recovery being given up weeks ago by his relatives.

Colonel Speers was the son of the late Louis M. Speers, a well known boat builder, and was born in Bellevernon, September 3d, 1835. He received his collegiate education at the college at Washington, Pa., and at the outbreak of the rebellion entered the service of his country, enlisting as a private. He was made a second lieutenant, and then promoted to lieutenant colonel in a general order from the war department for coolness and daring courage on the field. He was captured and served three months in Libby prison. After he was exchanged he served as provost marshal in the Shenandoah Valley, and there had the pleasure of administering the oath of allegiance to the United States to the man who had made him a prisoner a short time before. He was wounded at Winchester, and at the close of the war was mustered out after an active service of three years and three months. He was a member of the Grand Army of the Republic, and served as commander of Hays Post, No. 3, of Encampment No. 1 of the Union Veteran Legion and of Pennsylvania Commandery of the Loyal Union. After the war Colonel Speers engaged in boat building with his father at Bellevernon under the firm name of L. M. & W. F. Speer. In 1879 he moved to Sewickley, later to Freedom, following the same business. In 1885 he severed his connection with the firm and embarked in the manufacture of brick under the name of the Speer Brick Company. His wife, three sons and one daughter survive him, his oldest son having died last April. One of his sons, Captain L. M. Speer, is a member of the firm of John A. Wood & Co. the coal men, and another son, Harry, was engaged with him in the brick business. The third son is with the furniture firm of Jacobs & McGilvray. Colonel Speer had a large family connection. Noah Q. Speer, of the Speer Sand Company, and J. R. Speer, of Denver, are his brothers, and Mrs. Rev. Thomas S. Park, of Tower Hill, Ill, Mrs. S. P. Speers, of Baltimore, Md., and Mrs R. B. Porter, of Mars, Pa., are his sisters. Colonel Speer was well known by all the river and army men, and his genial disposition and social qualities made him a general favorite. He was buried in Homewood cemetery, Pittsburgh, Pa.

DAVID FURNIER.

David Furnier was born in France. He left France to escape the persecution of the Protestants by the Catholic church. He first settled near Hagerstown, Md. At what particular time he came to Western Pennsylvania we cannot ascertain. He must have settled on Speers run or in the vicinity about the years 1771-'72, as his dealings with Henry Speer the older will show. Among other lands Henry Speer held a right to a tract of land with a river front of 29 perches, at the mouth of Speers run, and in the aggregate on each side of said run including 94 acres, which was granted by letters patent to Regina Speers, widow and executrix of Henry Speers deceased, dated June 21st, 1774, and the said Regina Speers in order to fill a contract made by her husband in his life-time, by her deed dated March 31st, 1798, did convey a part of said tract to David Furnier to whom Noah Speers, one of the heirs of Henry Speers, by deed dated May 30th, 1798, did also convey an adjoining part. Near the Monongahela river and just where boats are now being built, the old log house was erected and stood for many years after it ceased to be occupied. Whether this house was built by Henry Speers or David Furnier we do not know, but as land was held pretty much by tomahawk right prior to the first issuing of patents by the state and as Speers had a mansion a short distance below this house, it is altogether likely that Furnier had this log house erected even before the tract was patented or deeded to him, under the contract spoken of above. A verbal contract was sacredly held inviolate in early days.

Besides this tract, Furnier owned additional land up the said run, most of which is now the property of the heirs of Levi Johnson. The title of much of this land was in dispute and has been the source of much litigation. The original tract of land on the river was deeded by the heirs of Furnier to Solomon Speers in 1823, and in after years Solomon sold it to L. M. Speer, and is now the property of S. F. & Wm. Jones. On this river tract was built in a very early day a flouring mill, which stood just below the present stone house owned by Samuel McKean. It was a log mill run by water power. From all we can learn the firm of Elliott & Williams erected this old mill and had a store in connection therewith, but sometime prior to 1790, David Furnier became sole proprietor of both mill and store, yet there is no record to show that Elliot & Williams ever owned by deed the mill. The probability is that they erected this mill on a lease for a term of years, which was no uncommon custom in those days. On Furnier assuming the control of the mill and store with his distillery attached thereto, the whole concern was carried on under the name of "The Barter Mills," as is shown by the day book, running through the years 1790-91, in the possession of the writer at this time, the said book being kept by Jacob Bowman, David Furnier's clerk. Jacob Bowman was a poor boy when he entered first into the employ of David Furnier, in time he became one of the most wealthy and influential men of Brownsville, Pa.

The term "Barter Mills" arose from the fact that in the change of the owner of the mills, there was some kind of a trade or barter. The mill, distillery, store and farm made up a large business. The books were kept in the money denomination of pounds, shillings and pence. This was the first store in this vicinity, and at the same time he had one at what was known as Devore's ferry, opposite Monongahela City. Furnier's books show considerable trading with this last store, as well as one in Pittsburgh, known in the day book as the Pittsburgh store. He also traded with the store at Beckets, now known as Dagg's ferry. Grain from all the surrounding country was brought to Furnier. The rye was made into whiskey, and the wheat into flour, and sold in Pittsburgh to which place it was taken by trade boats and over land in wagons.

July 2, 1791, store at Pittsburgh, Dr. to sundries, including 142 barrels of fine flour, 84 do of superfine, 5 quarts of whiskey for the boatmen, 10 pounds bacon, 1 tin cup, 16 pounds bread, 1 blanket, all shipped on board the Enterprise under the direction of Mr. John Bartlett, the whole amounting to £323 or $1,615 in federal money. We can thus see what an extensive business this "Barter Mills" carried on.

Among the customers in the day book we may name Reasoner, Reeves, McLaughlin, Shepler, McCoy, Cummings, Cissley, Speers, Corwin, Kerr, Ellis, Stewart, Hall, Patterson, Cook, Hilleryhand, Leard, Spharr, Bonchom, Hill, Albin, Barkhammer, Lippincott, Fulton, Springer, Fell, Housman,

Frye, Robinson, Burgan, Bigham, West, Cunningham, Rutan, Crawford, Quimby, Cooper, Beazell and many other of the early settlers. This was perhaps the largest business firm in the valley at that time. The distillery was situated some distance up the run above the log mill. It gave way to the stone still house that stood near the present green house of Samuel McKean. We have no information of what disposition Furnier made of the store before his death, which occurred in the fall of 1807. His will dated September 15th, 1807, does not mention particularly any disposition of property only in a general way. The old log mill gave way to the large brick mill erected in 1803. This mill stood near the present stone bridge across Speers run, and not far from the residence now occupied by Mr. Curl. This mill was torn down in the years 1836-'37, and a part of the brick remain to this day in the old school house in Gould's hollow. The saw mill which stood near the site of the brick mill, was no doubt erected by Solomon Speers after he became owner of the land.

David Furnier had brothers, Henry, John and James. James was unmarried, lived with Henry in Washington county, and died of sunstroke.

John, too, never married. He had a tannery on the farm now owned by John Irons, below town, then belonging to one of the early Reeves. He had a store at Becket's, now known as Dagg's ferry. He boarded with Becket while running the store, and rode on horseback between his two places of business. He sold out his business and went west, where he died long ago. This man, Joseph Becket, Jacob Bowman and Polly Furnier were the executors and executrix named in Furnier's will, which was witnessed by Dr. Bela Smith, Daniel Burgan and Manasseh Reeves, all well known in early days.

The remaining brother of David Furnier, Henry, built the stone part of the house near the river, in Allen township, Washington county, in which his son, Simeon, died in 1848, and now owned by Philip Johnson. Henry had quite a large family, among whom the best known in this neighborhood were Simon and David. Simeon married Jane Stout: his children were Henry, Jesse, John W., William, Simeon and Mary.

Henry's oldest son, David, married a Dunlevy, sister to the late Andrew Dunlevy. Her mother was a Crawford, and sister to the wife of the distinguished Colonel Edward Cook, of the Rehoboth valley. This David Furnier had also a large family, among whom we call to mind Andrew, of Allenport, David, deceased in 1893, of the vicinity of lock No. 4, and Matilda, wife of the the late Apollos Speers, who for years was a cabinet maker in Bellevernon.

David Furnier, the older, had two sons and two daughters. Bella died when quite young; Matilda never married, and lived and died on the old Homestead; Lucinda married Judge James Fuller, of Perryopolis in Fayette county, both are dead. They were the parents of the well known Fuller boys, who have been for years extensive cattle dealers in Philadelphia. They own the old Fuller homestead near Perryopolis, together with an additional large tract adjoining it. It has the reputation of being the best improved farm in the county.

Furnier's son Bowman, named after Jacob Bowman, lived on part of the Furnier homestead. He is deceased. He married a Miss Ebbert, who has been dead a number of years. Bowman had three daughters and six sons. Mary married the late M. F. Cook. Priscilla never married and remains at home. Matilda, the wife of James French, who was a fixture in Bellevernon for nearly half a century; both are dead. Thornton entered the army in the late war and never returned home. David is a mill-wright and resides near Dawson, Pennsylvania. Levi remains a part of his father's home. Volney is in California. John was a resident of Bellevernon, now dead, and Hugheson died when twelve years old of congestion of the brain. Polly, widow of David Furnier, married Robt. Johnson. The only issue of said marriage being Levi Johnson, deceased, a few years since. Mrs. Johnson died May 24, 1851, many years after the death of her second husband, and forty-four years after the decease of David Furnier, her first husband. Furnier, Johnson, Polly, their wife, and Levi and his wife, are buried at Rehoboth.

CORWIN.

Aunt Polly has passed away, was on the lips of almost every one on Friday evening as her death was announced. Mrs. Mary Smock Corwin was ninety-seven years old on Wednesday prior to her death, which occurred Friday, January 6, 1888. She was born January 4, 1791, on the farm now owned by Capt. Joseph Shepler, in Rostraver township, Westmoreland county, Pa. The farm at that time was owned by one Joseph Becket—a name well known in the early history of Western Pennsylvania. She was a daughter of Barnet Smock, who emigrated from New Jersey in 1789. Her father lived on this farm twenty-one years. The maiden name of the mother of the deceased was Jane Berdine. She was married to Peter Wene, by whom she had three children, named Sarah, Anna and Jane. Barnet Smock was her second husband. The deceased was married to Morris Corwin at Brownsville by Esq., Elias Baillins, on the 18th day of June, 1807. Morris Corwin died in Bellevernon, September 20, 1835, in the same house in which his wife died. Aunt Polly Corwin, as she was familiarly called, and her husband came to Bellevernon April 1, 1816, and occupied the house in which she died. She lived in this same house for seventy-two years, with the exception of three months. She lived to know that the sugar camp of three-quarters of a century ago had become a thriving town of two thousand souls. She outlived three generations of citizens. She was born in the early days of Washington's first term as President. She was born amid the struggles and trials of the new Government, and lived to the time when that Government had extended its limits from ocean to ocean, and its population increased from 4,000,000 to 60,000,000.

Since her birth new territory has been added sufficient to make forty states, each in size equal to all the original thirteen if combined in one. She lived to see the pack horse give way to the common wagon, Conestoga wagon, stage coach, canal boat and finally to the locomotive with its sixty miles an hour.

The telegraph and telephone had not yet been in the dreams of invention. At her birth the Monongahela valley was known only as the hunting ground of the Indian, with here and there a settlement of the sturdy pioneer, for it is a remarkable fact that the upland out from the river was first occupied by the white man. Shepler's hill, on which the deceased was born, attracted very early the attention of immigrants. She lived to see the rise, progress and final doom on a desert isle, of Napoleon, the man of fortune and of destiny. She outlived three American wars, and had realized in her day that the western wilds had become fields of ever blooming flowers, and that the glad tidings of the Gospel of the Son of God had been proclaimed in every tongue and nation of the globe. There were but three families in Bellevernon when she moved into it.

The deceased was a member of the Christian church since about 1843, and always a faithful attendant at public worship whilst her health permitted, and above all her walk and conversation gave fruit of a true Christian woman. Although for years deprived of seeing the outer world, owing to a loss of sight, and being confined to bed for many years, yet she never murmured against the Almighty, but earnestly longed and prayed for the time to come when she could see her Savior face to face, and just before her departure she repeated clearly and earnestly these words of a familiar hymn:

> How long, dear Savior, Oh! how long
> Will these bright hours delay!
> Fly swift around ye wheels of time
> And bring the welcome day.

Except during the last months of her life, her recollections of the past were very vivid, and to her memory the writer is indebted for very much of the early history of Bellevernon and vicinity. She recalled an incident which happened to her personally on the day of the funeral of Rev. James Finley, which occurred in 1795, she being only four years old. She remembers very well of being present at the birth of our citizen, Robert Patterson, who will be 80 years old next St. Patrick's day (17th of March). Whilst her health permitted, she was ever ready to extend a helping hand to the sick and needy, and she was present at the birth of more children than any other woman who ever lived in the valley. Not one of her early kindred or associates are living. She was the mother of Barnet, James, John and William Corwin. John and William are dead and Barnet is dead also. His first wife was a Miss Coll, sister of Mrs. Thomas McFall and Mrs. Alex. Frazier. By his first wife Barnet had two children, John W., the Main street grocer, and Mary. Mary was taken into her grandmother's family—Aunt Polly—when she was 11 years old, and remained with her until death separated them—a period of 41 years. In joy or sorrow, in sickness or health, Mary was ever alert in that household, and when her kind old grandmother was worn out by age and affliction, she was the ministering angel that soothed her pains and made soft her pillows until God took her dear one home. Barnet's second wife was a daughter of the late Joseph Springer, the issue of which marriage was several sons and daughters, most of whom are still living. His third wife was a Mrs. Cooper.

James, the remaining son living of Aunt Polly, resides on Main street, Bellevernon. His first wife was Eleanor Walker, long since deceased. She left two daughters—Georgiana and Eva; the latter is dead. His second wife also is deceased. Her name was Indiana Jacobs. Her aged mother, Jane Jacobs, survives her and has been a resident of this town over 55 years. James by his second wife has living William, Clarke, George, Elma, Alice and Lizzie.

The funeral services of Aunt Polly were held Sunday at 2 o'clock, January 8, and were conducted by Rev. Joel Baker, of the Free Will Baptist church, and Elder James M. Springer, of the Christian church. Her remains were interred in Bellevernon cemetery, in full view of the place of her birth. One grandson and three great-grandsons acted as pall-bearers.

Barnet Corwin, son of Aunt Polly, died July 20, 1889. He was taken sick with something like a sunstroke and paralysis, and did not think much of it until taken to his bed, which he never left. He was born near Bellevernon, April 27, 1814, and grew up to manhood's estate. At the age of twenty he married a neighbor's daughter, Miss Nellie Call. To this union came three children, J. W., Mary and Baker, the latter dying quite young. Mrs. C. only lived six years, and then went to join her child in the realms of glory.

Mr. Corwin married Miss Margaret Springer, and quite a family of children were born to them, those living being: Sarah A., Charles R., Joseph F., Luther C., Rowland W., and A. Odell. The second Mrs. C. followed her children, and her name is sacred to the children left. Mr. Corwin did not like to be left alone, and about seven years ago he married the widow of Thomas Cooper, who survives him. He was always a highly respected citizen and his loss was a blow. He in early years was a member of the Methodist Episcopal church, but later joined the Free Will Baptist church, of which he was a member at his death. He had not attended church in his last days on account of his hearing being defective. His funeral took place Monday morning at 10 o'clock, and the remains placed in the Bellevernon cemetery. The pallbearers were all grandchildren of the deceased. The last sad rites had been performed, when words similar to the following came to the minds of the mourners and brought relief.

> "Weep not for him who dieth,
> For he sleeps and is at rest,
> And the couch whereon he lieth
> Is the green earth's quiet breast.

J. WESLEY CORWIN,

Died on Saturday, November 8, 1890, at his late residence on Main street, Bellevernon, Pa. of paralysis of the heart. He was born in the house adjoining his late residence, well known as the "Aunt Polly Corwin house," July 6, 1834. He was the only son of his father, Barnet Corwin, by his wife, Eleanor Call Corwin. He was married to Miss Margaret Jane Jacobs, June 21, 1866, by the Rev. Jordon C. Nye. He joined the Methodist Episcopal Church of his native place in 1850, under the ministration of the Rev. John Coil, by whom he was baptized. In 1853 he transferred his church membership to the Free Will Baptist Church, during the ministration of Rev. David Winton. This church then worshipped in the old building near the corner of Wood street and Flint alley on the hill. In his new church relation the deceased assumed an active and influential position, and continued faithful to its interests and the cause of his Master to the end. He was among the first to agitate the project of erecting a new church edifice. To this end he devoted his untiring energy, and to him more than any one individual is that church indebted for the new building, now standing on the corner of Short and Speer streets. As a deacon in the church he was faithful and ever on the watch for its interests and the welfare of souls. As a citizen he was honest and upright in all his dealings, and was so regarded universally by the community in which he always lived. In the municipal affairs of his native borough he was often called to take part, and always performed his office satisfactory to his fellow citizens. At the time of his death he was a member of the school board of which he was treasurer. He leaves a wife, one son and sister, with several half brothers and one half sister, to mourn over his sudden departure. On Monday, October 10th, his remains were interred in Bellevernon cemetery, where three generations of his kindred await the resurrection morn. Blessed be his memory. His transition from earth to eternity was sudden, and without a struggle his eyes were closed in death and opened to behold the Son of Righteousness in all his glory.

DEATH OF MRS. SARAH A. SPRINGER.

Mrs. Sarah A. Springer, wife of J. M. Springer, Esq., died on July 25th, 1893, and was interred in the Bellevernon cemetery at 3 o'clock July 27th. She was born December 5th,

1825, in Rostraver township, and was in her 68th year. Her maiden name was Reeves, daughter of Samuel and Nancy Reeves, and she was united in marriage to J. M. Springer May 15th, 1847, and was the mother of nine children, all of whom survive her and who were present at the time of her death and burial. A true devoted Christian mother, it was her happy lot to see all her children grow to manhood and womanhood, and her's was the first death in the family. In this union was cemented, though existing, social ties between two of the oldest and best known families in this part of the state. Each of these families dating their settlement among the first in the wilderness of the Monongahela valley.

Her disease was an acute affection of the stomach, from which she suffered deep and painful affliction for about five months. Her end was peace, and was marked by the quiet resignation of a long life earnestly spent in the service of the Master on high, and her bereaved husband and family have the heart-felt sympathy of a large portion of the community who knew her but to love her. The thought is, however, a consoling one—that their loss is her gain, as she has gone to reap the reward deservingly won. The funeral was attended by a large assemblage of relatives and friends, and the service was conducted by Rev. B. L. Kershner, pastor of the Christian church, assisted by Rev. Charles Clark, pastor of the Presbyterian charge at Rehoboth.

J. B. GOULD.

John B. Gould was born in Hillsborough county, New Hampshire, June 6, 1795. He left the paternal roof at an early age to try his fortune amid the hills of the coast bound State of Maine, but in 1810 he emigrated from that State and came to the neighborhood of what is now known as the Red Lion, above Fayette City, Pennsylvania. In 1811, in company with the families of a man named McCalla and Ziba Whiting, father of the late Geo. Whiting, of Fayette City, in all fifteen persons, immigrated to the territory of Louisiana.

Two of the men died there together with four of their children. Gould returned in 1812, and was the last to die of the company. Shortly after his return to the Red Lion he became an apprentice to a Mr. Coldron to learn the scythe and sickle trade, and remained with him over four years. Miss Jane Trainer, an inmate of the household of the widow Whiting, early attracted the attentions of the young Gould, and after an engagement of five years, he concluded one day whilst "hoeing corn," that if Jane was willing and the next 4th of July came on Thursday and in the light of the moon, they would get married. He hastily consulted the never failing almanac, and to his great joy he found all right in accord with his wishes. They were married on the 4th day of July, A. D. 1824, and to use his own words, "in the year that Jackson first ran for President." They located on the farm just above Bellevernon, a part of which he owned to the day of his death.

They commenced housekeeping in the old log house that stood on the bank of the river, but what has long since passed away. He did not work much at his trade, but devoted his time generally to farming, and in the winter taught school. For many years Gould and John Wilson seemed to have a mortgage on the "art of teaching" in the town and vicinity. Gould "kept school" in the house now owned by W. P. Mackey on Main street, and in other houses about the town prior to the building of the brick school house on the hill and in the hollow. Many of our older citizens owe their early education to the influence of Gould's ferule and birch. He informed the writer when speaking on the subject of education, that for a long time he regarded himself as one of the educators of the land, but found in reality that progress had so far outstripped his Yankee notions as to force him to acknowledge to having scarcely learned his A. B. C.'s half way.

Gould was always held in high esteem by his fellow citizens. He held many offices in his adopted township of Washington. He was elected Justice of the Peace in 1845–50–55. He served as Assessor in 1840–51–54–62–65–68. He was Auditor in 1858–63–66. He was School Director in 1849. He served many years as Constable when that office was considered one of the most important in the township. His career as Justice marked well his effort to do right between man and man, and he spared no pains in settling petty cases without the process of law suits. Gould was one of the pioneers in the Disciple church of the town; and to him, more than any one individual, is that people indebted for its success in the town. His wife died some years prior to his death, at the old homestead. Gould died September 9th, 1884, while on a visit to his daughter, Mrs. John Coldron, near Fayette City, in the 90th year of his age. His remains were interred beside those of his wife in the Bellevernon cemetery. They had several children, some of whom preceded the parents to the grave.

Malissa married William Beam, and is now deceased. Lorena is the wife of John Coldron, above Fayette City. John resides in North Bellevernon. Ephraim is in Colorado. Elmer Morrison, a grandson, resides in Seldom Seen, a village being built on part of the old farm. He lives in his own home alone, and seems to enjoy life and the good will of his fellow citizens. Nancy Jane married Thomas Richards, now deceased. She lives in Zanesville, Ohio. One daughter married a Mr. McKinney, but where she resides we are not informed. Another daughter married a Mr. Stout, and have their home in Kentucky. James has long been a resident of Illinois.

John B. Gould, in politics, was always a democrat, having voted for every democratic candidate for president since the days of Madison, having voted the first time 1816. During the great know-nothing excitement in 1854, he was one of the ten democrats in Bellevernon district who stood up for William Bigler, the democratic candidate for governor. He always had a poor opinion of the know-nothing organization.

WM. EBERHEART.

The first glass manufacturer in Bellevernon died at the residence of his son-in-law, Leonard Laneheart, in Redstone township, Fayette county, Feb. 23, 1882. He was born in New Geneva on the Monongahela, in the year 1800. He was the son of Adolph Eberheart, who emigrated from Germany and settled in New Geneva, soon after that place was founded by Albert Gallatin, a native of the city of Geneva in Switzerland. Gallatin had erected in his new Geneva home the first glass works in the west, and the older Eberheart was in his employ until Gallatin was called by President Jefferson in 1802 to a seat in his cabinet as Secretary of the Treasury. At the time Gallatin entered Jefferson's cabinet, Adolph Eberheart became proprietor of the Geneva glass works, and in due time his son learned the glass blowing trade. William married Rachel Hutton, a sister of the late John James and Nathan Hutton, all well known in this community in their day. Not long after his marriage, in about 1828, he moved to Williamsport, now Monongahela City, where for several years he followed his trade in the works of Wm. Ihmsen, at that time the most extensive window glass manufacturer in the west. One of his children died at that place, and its remains are now among the unknown relics of the old grave yard on the hill. Eberheart subsequently carried on the glass business at Albany, below Brownsville. In 1832 he started in the same business in what was then called Freeport, afterwards Cookstown, and now known as Fayette City. In 1836 he removed to Bellevernon, where he purchased of Patton and Kendall the unfinished glass factory, ever since known as the old glass house. He first resided in the Demain house on Water street, now owned by the heirs of the late Capt. J. M. Bowell. From this house he moved to the house on Water street, near Third street, known as the Morgan Gaskill house. About 1849 he purchased from John Niccolls the Noah W. Speer farm, now known as the Gibsonton farm. In 1852 he became financially embarrassed. In 1855 he closed up the glass business in Bellevernon and removed to Fayette City, where for a time he aided one of his sons in the business. His daughter Elizabeth married Noah W. Speers. She died of yellow fever a few years ago in Memphis, Tennesse.

His son, William, married Margaret L. Smith, grand daughter of the late Hon. George Plumer. Adolph married a daughter of the late William D. Mullin, Esq., of Fayette City. Rebecca married A. C. Housman, who, in 1847, kept the hotel now known as the Wise house, in Bellevernon. They left that house for Baltimore, Md., where they still reside. Allen K., another son, is perhaps the best known shoe man in Pennsylvania. His first wife was a Reed, and present wife was of the name of Brick. He has for many years resided in Philadelphia, and is now connected with the shoe firm of Graff, Son & Co., No. 512 Market street, Philadelphia. Thomas Niccolls married William Eberheart's daughter, Elma, in 1845. He died many years ago in Cincinnati. Her present husband is Leonard Lanehart. They live in ease and comfort in a beautiful home on the National pike, between Brownsville and Uniontown. Charles D., the remaining son, married a Miss Mason, daughter of Morgan Mason, a well known river man of Brownsville, but of later day a resident of Missouri. We are not able to say when Eberheart erected the second or new glass house, but it must have been in the early forties. The long and short rows, well known as the factory tenements, at the upper end of town, were built by him for his workmen. He also built the storeroom lately occupied by R. C. Schmertz & Co. Eberheart was very liberal in his views and treatment of men. In his day there were no butchers, so called, so that his men were supplied with eatables and meat at his well filled store. In the fall of the year he bought hogs by the score and distributed them ready dressed among his men. So with beef, he sold to his men a quarter at a time. His cellar and warehouse were frequently replenished. The writer has known fifty five barrels of molasses to go into the store cellar at one time, together with barrels and hogsheads of sugar. He generally purchased his stock of dry goods, &c., in Baltimore, and it was a common affair to see 12 W boxes of dry goods hauled from the wharf, now the ferry, with notions, hats, caps and hardware, in proportion. For convenience and as a labor saving machine it was the custom for many years to use his own script as money. This currency was charged on the books in sums as drawn by the employes, and taken back in return for goods. The script was issued in the denominations of $6\frac{1}{4}$ cents, $12\frac{1}{2}$ cents, quarter and half and one dollar pieces. Specimens of this script is still preserved by some of the curious.

Eberheart was proverbally generous to the poorer class of his employes, in many instances would forgive a long extravagant account rather than oppress. Whilst a resident of the town he was not connected with any church, but had a high regard for all denominations. Whilst holding a pew for many years in Rehoboth, under the ministrations of Revs. Gillett and J. R. Hughes, he was a liberal contributor to the support of the Gospel in the Methodist Episcopal Church, of Bellevernon.

In his day glass making was principally confined on this side of the mountains to Pittsburgh and the Monongahela valley. The Gallatin factory at New Geneva, the Albany, the Bellevernon, the Williamsport, the Elizabeth, the Cookstown, and the Perryopolis glass works were in early day in the valley, all of which, save those in Bellevernon, have long since passed away. They have been supplanted by one at Brownsville, one at Fayette City and one at Monongahela City.

Eberheart sold his glass chiefly in Pittsburgh and Cincinnati, his son-in-law, N. W. Speers, being for many years his agent in the latter city. In his works he generally made two qualities of glass. The first quality was branded Bellevernon, and the second W. Eberheart. The sizes were principally 8 by 10 and 12 by 14, but in his latter days the size began to increase. It was the custom in his day to agree with the blowers for the fire early as February preceding the end of the current year ending July 1. Strikes and other troubles as now a days were unknown, harmony and good feeling prevailing between the employer and employes. Dr. David Porter was the next physician after Dr. Smith, who located in the Forks. He was born in Wheeling, West Virginia, March 17, 1794. His father, Wm. Porter, was a neighbor of Capt. Wm. Woolsey, who in early days owned the lands in Rostraver township, recently owned by Dr. Porter and now belonging to the heirs of Mrs. Levi Johnson, deceased. Wm. Porter took a lively interest in the whiskey insurrrection of 1794. On account of his open opposition to the enforcement of the whiskey law, he was compelled to flee from the "Forks." With his young wife he went to Wheeling where his son David was born. After the excitement of the insurrection was over, Wm. Porter returned to Rostraver, where he taught school until his thirst for travel induced him to accompany Wm. Darby to New Orleans. The yellow fever was prevalent at that time in the south, on account of which Darby refused to complete the journey. Darby returned, but Porter, not daunted, pushed forward to the city and was never heard from afterwards. Capt. Woolsey mourned over the loss of his friend. Being childless he adopted David as his own son, under whose care he was educated, and at his death, in 1834, David inherited his large estate. For more than half a century Dr. Porter was the leading physician of the "Forks." He was a man of good physical structure and very well adopted to endure the exposures of the pioneer doctor.

He was a man of fine literary culture and a writer of more than local reputation. He was not a graduate of any Medical College, but in 1825 the Trustees of Jefferson College conferred on him the honorary degree of Doctor of Medicine. The first wife of Dr. Porter was a daughter of the distinguished Dr. Obadiah Jennings. By this wife he had two sons and one daughter. The daughter married Levi Johnson both of whom are dead leaving Nelson and William as their only issue. Obadiah his son was a physician and died many years ago. William the surviving son died in Texas. The second wife of Dr. Porter was a sister of A. H. and J. B. Miller well known in their day. The only issue of this second marriage was their daughter Ada who died years ago: Mrs. Dr. Porter is now a resident of Uniontown. Dr. David Porter died in Uniontown September 22, 1875, the remains being interred in Rehoboth grave yard.

Capt. Woolsey

To whom Dr. Porter was so much indebted for his start in life was born in Ireland in 1748. He followed a sea faring life from early boyhood to the age of thirty years when he immigrated to this country and joined the continental army, in which he commanded a company, at the close of the war he settled on the farm on which Dr. Porter resided. He married Margaret Goe, who had immigrated to these parts co-temporary with Col. Edward Cook and many other well known early settlers. The common mode of traveling in those days was something different from that in use now a days. When the Goe family immigrated the children were carried in baskets suspended on each side of the horse—white and black mixed together, and on the way the races would occasionally kick up a fuss which would require the intervention of the parents and master to settle. The Captain though very eccentric in manner and customs had many good qualities of heart, and was very peculiar in his likes and dislikes. The few older citizens now living yet recall his peculiar traits of character.

SPRINGER FAMILY.

The name of Springer has long been identified with Bellevernon and vicinity. It was introduced by the arrival of Michael Springer, who was born in Stockholm, Sweden, about 1727, and came to this country somewhere in 1760. The exact date of his marriage is not known. His wife's surname was not known, but she was called Mary Ann. Michael Springer's father found Mary Ann asleep at the foot of a tree when she was supposed to be only about three years old. Her clothing was of fine quality, but nothing was found about her person or clothing to indicate who she was; all that she could remember was that she lived in a large house where there were lots of flowers and a big porch, and where one day she was when a man came riding along on a black horse and said, "Come, little lady, and take a ride." Michael Springer's father raised her, and his son (Michael) married her and emigrated from Germany to America about 1760. They first settled near Philadelphia, where Daniel was born September 15th, 1762. Michael Springer and family crossed the mountains about 1783 on pack horses or mules, his wife carrying her spinning wheel on her back. They took by tomahawk right the land now (1893) owned by the heirs of James Ward, deceased, and others in Rostraver township, Westmoreland county. The tract originally contained 355½ acres, and was called Springersburgh. The patent for this land was granted Daniel Springer dated May 18th, 1787, on a warrant issued to Michael Springer and signed by Benjamin Franklin, President of the Supreme Executive Council. Michael and Mary Ann had five children, John, Mathias, Michael, Mary and Daniel. The father died 1797, and was buried in the family burial ground, near a part of the Bellevernon cemetery grounds. Their sons, Michael and Mathias, settled in the west. Mary married John Worley and moved to the west.

The old homestead was given by will to Daniel. He married Rachel Higgins in 1790. He was born in Virginia in 1760 and came to this region about the time the Springer family located in Rostraver. Daniel had eight children, Michael, Mathias, John, Joseph, James H., Nancy, Daniel and Martha. John married Sallie Billiter. John was killed by a limb from a tree which he was felling, in 1833. John had four children, Nancy, who married Harrison Hornbake; Rachel, who married Thompson Carmichael, and after his death she married Jesse Sills, who for many years lived in Bellevernon, but at his death was a resident of Ohio. John R. married a Miss Jordon, of Monongahela City. They lived for a time in Shelbyville, Indiana, but at last accounts were in the State of Cali-

fornia. Mary married Joseph Culler, of Rostraver, where
they now reside. After the death of John Springer his widow
married Luke Hornbeck. They lived for many years in the old
log house that stood where is now the residence of George
Scribner on the State road leading from Bellevernon to West
Newton. Luke was a shoemaker by trade. He died July 22,
1866. Daniel, son of Daniel the older, was never married,
and has been dead many years. He lost the use of one leg
from white swelling. He spent most of his time in studying
music, though he had no voice for singing, but loved the
science.

Joseph, son of Daniel, married Margaret Driver. They
lived in the old log house on the county line near town. The
farm in part is owned by S. F. and Wm. Jones, and part now
divided into lots forming the town of East Bellevernon. The
ground was purchased from J. W. Carothers by Geo. C. Maxwell and J. T. Roley, who laid out the town. Joseph had
born to him twelve children. James and Newton died in
childhood. Daniel was the oldest and married Rachel Jordon,
who still survives her husband, who died October 21, 1870.
Daniel lived most of his days in Bellevernon where his widow
still resides.

Martha married Barnet Corwin, both of whom are dead.
John married Sarah A. Baily, and has been a resident of
Brownsville for many years. Rachel and Lydia were twins.
Rachel married James Carroll and died December, 1879.
Lydia married Asa Hastings, who died in Brownsville in 1882.
His widow lives in Findlay, Ohio. She was the mother of E.
A. Hastings who published the first newspaper in Bellevernon.
Nancy married Edward Cook, both of whom are dead. James
M. married Sarah Reeves, and has been a resident of the town
ever since their marriage in 1847, excepting a short time in
Mount Pleasant, Pa. He has long been an active citizen,
having been honored by his fellow citizens with many offices of
trust. With the expiration of his present term, 1893, he will
have served forty years as Justice of the Peace. Joseph

The Old and New Monongahela. 463

married Hannah J. Davidson. They reside in Circleville, Westmoreland county, Pa. William R. married Margaret Reed, and are residents of North Bellevernon. Margaret, the remaining daughter of Joseph Springer, married Frederick Browneller. They live in Findlay, Ohio.

Joseph Springer, the father of these children, died at Brownsville June 20, 1871, and the mother October 28, 1876. James Higgins Springer, another son of Daniel the older, inherited the old homestead. He married Sallie Smith, daughter of David Smith, a Revolutionary soldier, whose remains are in Rehoboth graveyard. He died in Webster, Pa., April 26, 1876, his wife having died January 17, 1864. Their remains are in the Bellevernon cemetery. They had seven children. Martina married D. B. H. Allen, who died February 22, 1881. Sophia married Dr. J. R. Nickel, who died July 17, 1874, in Connellsville, Pa. Mrs. Nickel resides in Bellevernon. Theodore is married and lives in the west. Ancelmo married Barbara Newcomer and is a resident of Clinton, Iowa. Everil F. married Ella Huffman, of Iowa, and now lives in North Bellevernon, where he is in the drug business. Caroline died December 12, 1885. Rebecca is also dead. Martha, daughter of Daniel Springer the older, married James Beazell, who so long carried on blacksmithing where now Mr. Cowan has his shop, near the Bellevernon cemetery. James Beazell died February 28, 1868, and his wife October 18, 1869. Their remains are in Bellevernon cemetery. They had a large family, some of whom have passed away. We recall Jasper, now living in Cincinnati. Elizabeth, widow of Wm. Ballou, resides in North Bellevernon. James, now dead, and Albert, resided in California, where many years ago, Thomas Benton died. Mortimer, after having been in California for some years, returned to his native heath. Malissa and Anna reside on the old homestead. Rachel married Samuel Bedsworth, who resides near the old home. Jane lives at Ruffsdale, Westmoreland county.

Andrew Dunlevy.

In the early days of Bellevernon Andrew Dunlevy and his brother-in-law Geo. Hazelbaker carried on the manufacture of hats in the house at that time known as the Billiter house on Water below Third street. It was truly a manufactory as all the work was done by hand power. They not only made the popular wool hat of that day but also the fine fur hat. The wool hat did a boy an undesirable long service. There seemed to be no wear out to it, as it was the custom at that day to iron over and shape anew the hat whenever it became discolored or presented an unseemly appearance. The fine fur hat was also subjected to a renovating process that made it good as new. This firm was the market for rabbit and mink skins, from which the fine fur hat was manufactured. Caps and mufflers, so called, were made from coon and fox skins with the tails as ornamental appendages.

Andrew Dunlevy was born July 24, 1795, on the farm now owned by his son Jehu in Allen Township, Washington County, Pa. He died July 24, 1879, in the house still standing a few rods distant from the spot where he was born. The farm is situated on the Monongahela river about one mile above Speer's ferry. This farm was the home of his parents. His mother was a Crawford, sister of the wife of Col. Edward Cook well known in the early days of the "Forks" neighborhood. The wife of Andrew Dunlevy was a daughter of the older Wm. Jackman who was father also of the late Jehu and Simeon Jackman well known citizens of Washington County.

Andrew had five sons and two daughters. Joseph died in his youth. Anthony was drowned many years ago in Galveston Bay. William married a Furnier and resides in the west. Crawford married a lady in Brownsville, and has resided for some years near the hot springs, in Arkansas. Barbara married S. T. Williams, well known in former years in this vicinity; they now live in Iowa. The remaining daughter was accidently burned to death. Jehu resides on the homestead, and is one of the solid farmers of Allen township. His first wife was a daughter of the late Hugh McKee; his present wife was a Smith from the Youghiogheny valley. Andrew Dunlevy's wife died in 1845.

Andrew by birth and profession was a Presbyterian in religion. At his birth Dr. Ralston had not commenced his ministry at Horseshoe Meeting House, now only known by the rough stones that mark the graves of the early settlers. Dr. James Finley had just closed his earthly labors as pastor of Rehoboth, where Dunlevy's parents were accustomed to worship with his uncle, Col. Cook. Dunlevy was one of the number who organized, about 1840, the Maple Creek Presbyterian Church, and during its existence was a member of the sessions.

In the eldership of that church he was associated with such men as Moss, Baker, McJunkin and Simeon Jackman, all of whom have passed to the beyond. In politics Dunlevy was always a Democrat of the Jeffersonian school, and even the Know Nothing allurements of 1854 could not entice him from his inborn Democracy. He always possessed the confidence of his fellow citizens as an upright Christian gentleman. Honest in habit, generous in heart, kind in disposition and devoted to his country and church, he was ranked among those whose place it would be hard to fill. His remains were buried along side those of his wife in the Speer's graveyard, opposite Bellevernon.

HAZELBAKER.

Peter Hazelbaker immigrated to this country from Anspach, in Germany, as an English soldier during the revolution. He was taken prisoner by the American forces, was never exchanged, and at the close of the war he settled in the United States. Shortly after the war Peter married Elizabeth Shively, daughter of Daniel Shively, of Berkely county, Va., now West Virginia.

After their marriage Peter and his wife immigrated to

Washington County, Pa., and settled in an old log house on the farm now owned by one of the heirs of S. A. Chester, in Allen Township. He died in 1800 and his remains are buried in the field just above the present residence of Major Henry Spharr. Peter had six sons, Peter, Daniel, John, Jacob, Abraham and George. John was an old time school teacher. He taught the first school in Bellevernon. The kitchen part of the residence of the late Aunt Polly Corwin on Main street was the schoolhouse. He and Daniel died in the West. Peter died six weeks after the death of his father and was buried in the same graveyard. Abraham died near Brush Creek in Ohio. Jacob was well known in the community. He was a shoemaker by trade and lived many years in the stone house just above Bellevernon now owned by R. C. Schmertz & Co. About 1848 he removed to a farm near Perryopolis where he died. George lived beyond all of his brothers. He was born in Berkely County, West Va., January 18, 1790. His wife was Matilda Dunlevy sister of Andrew Dunlevy. She died in 1853. After his marriage he erected the lower part of the old house on Main street in Bellevernon where now stands the house owned by A. L. Brown and occupied by Abe Lewis. In the old house George and his wife first set up housekeeping and there he carried on the hat business until he and Dunlevy started the shop in the Billiter house. He also resided for a time on the Gould farm, then on the Levi Johnson, then on the Rutan farm opposite Columbia owned now by W. J. Manown. He moved from this farm to the Cooper farm near the mouth of Maple Creek and finally in 1841 he purchased the farm on which he died, in Allen township, from Abia Allen and Robert Stockdale.

His son Andrew married a daughter of Thomas Frye and died about the year 1856 near Lock No. 4. Joseph died at the homestead unmarried. Anthony lived for many years in the house near the mouth of Maple Creek now owned by Charles Baltzee. He carried on the flouring mill which stood between the dwelling and the present bridge. The mill has passed away. Anthony over thirty years ago moved to Illinois where he died a few years since. Jacob married a Miss Crow and lives in Clarion County. George married a Miss Riggs and lives on part of the homestead and John resides in Allen township not far from Wood's Run.

Matilda married Joseph Wolf and resides in the west. Mary married John Cooper, now deceased. She lives in Illinois. Sarah Ann is the wife of Addison Cummings, of Allen township. Margaret married R. C. Guffey and died in North Bellevernon. George Hazelbaker, the father of this large family, died on the home farm, June 23, 1880. He united with Rehoboth church in his seventy-fifth year and remained in that membership until his death. He was a good citizen, a genial neighbor, and above all a Christian. His remains were interred in Howe Cemetery.

THOMAS WARD AND FREDERICK COOPER.

Thos. Ward built the first house in Bellevernon. In the summer of 1815 he purchased the lot on the corner of Main and Second streets, now owned by Howard McClure and Mrs. Kittle, and built thereon the well known house now moved to the upper end of the lot, and occupied now (1893) by James Haggerty's widow. Before moving into this house Ward resided in the old house that stood near the present home of Wm. Kyle in North Bellevernon.

He was a most skillful mechanic in every art of making in wood. He was born May 23, 1776, but where we cannot say, or just when he came to this vicinity. He lived to a good old age in Bellevernon, and when the decrepitude of age prevented his earning his own living he was kindly taken to the household of his children in Ohio, where some thirty years ago he died. His wife was a daughter of the old Frederick Cooper who settled about 1768 on the farm lately owned by Thomas Redd, and the farm of Robert McKain, both of which now form the site of the flourishing town of Charleroi. This settlement was made after the death of his first wife. On this farm (then embracing both the Redd and McKain land) he reared a shanty or cabin under the protection of the fort that was located near the present Gibsonton distillery on the opposite side of the river. Notwithstanding the fort, the depredations of the Indians were so frequent and dangerous that the new emigrant concluded to return for a time to the east, where he had left his son John and two daughters, Polly and Betsy. Whilst in the east he married Elizabeth Kyle as his second wife, and in a short time after the marriage he returned to his farm on the Monongahela, with his new wife and children, where he remained to the day of his death. His remains were no doubt interred in the family burying ground yet to be seen in the orchard above the present residence of Mrs. Thomas Redd. Frederick's son Valentine inherited the farm and lived at his death in the old house that stood not far from the present brick house. Jehu, son of Valentine, inherited the upper part of the land and in his day erected the brick house. He sold, before going west, to A. P. Frye, whose heirs sold to Thomas Redd, who in 1890 sold the farm, excepting the house and surroundings, to the Charleroi Land Company. The lower part of the original Cooper farm was sold at administrator's or executor's sale, Daniel Van Voorhis becoming purchaser, who in his day sold it to his son John F. John F. sold it to Elgy Van Voorhis, his nephew, now of Kansas City, Missouri. After a short residence on it Elgy sold the farm to Robert McKain, a greater part of which he sold in 1890 to the Charleroi Land Company, on which they are now building the flourishing town of Charleroi.

[From Bellevernon *Enterprise*, May 20th, 1892.]

CAPTAIN JOSEPH SHEPLER.

Died Sabbath, May 15th, 1892, at his late residence in Rostraver township, Westmoreland county, Pa. He was born March 6th, 1807, on the old home farm recently owned by his brother, Lewis, but now occupied by David Deaterly. He was the oldest of seven children of Isaac and Sarah H. Shepler. His ancestors on both sides of the family emigrated from Germany and settled in Virginia, near Winchester. The grandfather of the deceased, Mathias Shepler, with two brothers, Peter and Philip, moved from Virginia before the war of the revolution and settled in Rostraver, taking up farms on the Monongahela hill in that township, on part of which his descendant, Philip Shepler, now resides. Mathias married Margaret Houseman, whose family too was one of the early settlers in the township. Their children were John, Philip, Abraham, Isaac, Jacob, Mary, Margaret and Catherine. All were married and raised families, and all are deceased. Isaac, the father of Joseph, the subject of this sketch, married Sarah, daughter of Joseph and Mary Hill. Her father, at the age of eighteen, came to Rostraver township, before the Braddock expedition, and is supposed to have been the first white settler in the region included within the township. Isaac had as children Joseph, Lewis, Samuel, Margaret, Elizabeth, Sarah and Polly. Lewis died December, 1881, on the farm on which he was born, now owned by David Deaterly, above named. Polly married James Wright, and are both dead. Samuel, brother of Joseph, was born July 14th, 1814, and resided on and owned a farm adjoining Joseph, being a portion of the land taken up by his grandfather Hill. He is now deceased. He had been twice married. His first wife was Eveline Steele, whom he married December 12th, 1839. She died April 18th, 1850. Jan. 29th, 1852, he married Elizabeth Couldren. Elizabeth, now deceased, was the wife of Davis Shepler, now deceased. He lived on and owned the farm recently sold by his heirs to David W. Owens, in Rostraver. Sarah, another sister of Joseph, is the wife of Jehu Stephens, a farmer living in Washington township, Fayette county, Pa. Isaac Shepler, father of Joseph, died December 10th, 1837, and his wife survived him many years, dying July, 1869. The remains of both are interred in the graveyard at Fell's church.

Capt. Joseph Shepler passed his whole life in Rostraver

township; he was educated in the schools of the township, and always attended church within its limits. Until the age of 22 he lived on the homestead where he was born. He married April 16, 1829, Mary, daughter of Joseph and Nancy Blackburn, who lived on a farm not far from what is now known as Rostraver postoffice. Mary, wife of Joseph Shepler, was born March 28, 1807, being twenty-two days younger than her husband and she survives him. Her family was among the early settlers in Rostraver. For one year after marriage Joseph and wife lived in the house of his father, then went to housekeeping on one of his father's farms, where he resided and carried on farming for eight years. In 1838 he moved to the farm on which he died. Capt. Shepler had been a member of Fell's M. E. Church over sixty years, and one of its chief supporters. His wife joined the church at the same place and time and remains in its membership to this day. Joseph Shepler had four children, two sons and two daughters. Sarah born January 7, 1830, is the wife of William Jones, of the Bellevernon banking house of S. F. Jones & Co. They have three children, Ella Jane, Joseph Shepler and Samuel. Violet another daughter of Joseph Shepler, was born August 20, 1833 and is the wife of Capt. Martin Coulson, now residing on a farm near Monongahela City, Pa. They have as children Joseph S., Margaret E. and Alfred Kerr. John B., son of Capt. Shepler, was born February 18, 1835, married Josephine Claywell, of Jo Daviess County, Ill. Their children are Shedrack Claywell, and David Richey. Isaac Hill the remaining son was born March 20, 1840, married Eveline, daughter of Samuel Shepler, to them were born James Kerr, Mary Blackburn, William Jones and Elizabeth. The death of Capt. Joseph was the first in his family or in any of his descendants. He left 12 grandchildren, eight of whom acted as pall bearers at his funeral—two sons from each of his children's families. In the church Joseph Shepler had acted well his part in the offices of Trustee, Steward and class-leader and in all other church work to which he was called. In his native township, to which he was so devoted, he held every office and performed his duties with fidelity. He was a man of undoubted and well known integrity.

He was a military man by nature and disposition. He received the sobriquet of Captain by serving at the age of twenty-one in that capacity in the first company Eighty-eighth regiment of State Volunteers. He held the position of Captain for seven years in this company; was afterwards Captain for five years of the Monongahela Blues and First Lieutenant of the Rostraver Cavalry for seven years. His voice and commanding appearance, together with his knowledge of military tactics, gave him a first rank as an officer. He had a wonderful memory, especially for the things of long ago. He seemed to have never forgotten the incidents of the neighborhood from boyhood to the day of his death. He was firm in his convictions of right, yet gentle and hospitable in the inner man. He was a Jackson Democrat, having voted for him twice, and always voted for the Democratic candidate for President since he cast his first vote in 1828. He believed the hope of the country was in the carrying out of the principles of Democracy as first enunciated by Jefferson and confirmed by Jackson in his two administrations. He recalled to mind very vividly the incidents of the Sabbath day in 1825, when Gen. LaFayette passed through the Forks by way of Rehoboth valley.

His funeral took place on Tuesday, May 17, from his late residence. His remains were interred in Bellevernon Cemetery. His pastor, Rev. Hildebrand, and his old friend, Rev. McIlyar, officiated at the last rites.

[From Bellevernon *Enterprise*.]

CROSSED OVER THE RIVER.—MRS. ROBERT J. LINTON.

On Wednesday morning, September 21, 1887, at 4.40 o'clock, Mrs. Robert J. Linton quietly and peacefully ended her days on earth and went to join the countless army who have gone before into the land from whence no traveler returns. She was in her 51st year, and during all her life she was an earnest and zealous Christian woman. There seemed no task that her Master desired her to do, that she would not do. She was a member of the First Presbyterian Church of this place, and when her health would permit she was always found among the worshippers. During the past eight months she knew she could not get well, but there was no complaining or fretting. Her thoughts seemed to be "Thy will, not mine, be done," and when the time came she losed her hold on earthly things and went to join the host where sorrow and parting are never known. She was married to Mr. Linton on August 30, 1864, and leaves a husband and three children to mourn her loss. The funeral services took place on Friday at 2 p. m. from the Presbyterian Church, and the remains were interred in the Bellevernon cemetery.

Mrs. Caroline S. Linton was born at Hudson, Ohio, 1836. She was the third child of Rev. Giles and Mrs. Electa Doolittle. Her father was a man prevalent in prayer and unshaken faith in a covenant keeping God. He died in the prime of his days, committing his children in the hand of his God, saying, though I had a bag of gold to leave them, I could not be as sure of their being provided for. Mrs. Linton ever felt that her father's prayers followed her. At eight years of age she was placed in the primary department of the Hudson Female Seminary, receiving most of her education in that institution, under the charge of the most accomplished New England teachers, but later was sent to the Western Female Seminary at Oxford, Ohio, where she graduated in '58, and taught successfully for a few years. In '64 she was married to Robert J. Linton, and they moved to this place in 1870. Three children were given them, and it was her unspeakable joy to see them all brought into the visible church.

The tender kindnesses from friends and neighbors that flowed in a constant stream into Mrs. Linton's sick room, are known only to the Lord, and her sincere thanks and those of the family are returned to all with prayer that the Lord will abundantly reward all with his grace.

Rehoboth.

The Presbyterian Church of Rehoboth was organized in 1778, by Rev. James Finley.

In 1784 Mr. Finley became pastor of this church. He continued as its pastor until his death January 6th, 1795. His remains are in the church graveyard. Preaching was held in an old log house near the present (1893) residence of Joseph A. Cook, in Rostraver township, Westmoreland county, Pa., about one mile from the present church building. In Rev. Finley's time the old hewed log church was erected, which stood about where the public road is, in front of the present church. This log church gave way, in 1803, to the brick building known in all western Pennsylvania as the brick church, and even at this late day (1893) Rehoboth is called by many as the brick church. The present building was erected in 1836. Two years after the death of Finley, Rev. David Smith became pastor, and continued as such until his death, August 24th, 1803. Rev. Smith was succeeded by Rev. William Wylie, who was installed in 1805, and continued pastor until in the spring of 1817.

In June, 1817, Rev. Robert Johnson became pastor and continued as such until December, 1832. In December, 1834, Rev. N. H. Gillett was installed pastor. In 1848, at his own request, he was released from the pastoral charge of Rehoboth. In 1849 Rev. James R. Hughes became pastor. In 1865 he resigned to take charge of the Blairsville Seminary.

Rev. James R. Hughes was born in Beaver County, Pa., March 17, 1819. He is one of ten children of the late Rev. Thomas E. Hughes who was the first minister ordained north of the Ohio river. James R. Hughes is the only survivor of seven brothers, four of whom were ministers. Watson, John D. and William having served their Master here for many years, have gone to receive their reward. James R. Hughes received his education preparatory to College in the good old academies of Steubenville and Wellsville, Ohio. In 1843 he entered the Junior class of Washington, Pa., College and graduated in 1845. Soon after graduating he entered the Western Theological Seminary. In 1848 he was licensed to preach. He was called to Rehoboth church near Bellevernon, Pa., in 1849, and was installed November 8, in the same year, by a committee appointed by Redstone Presbytery, consisting of Revs. Samuel Wilson and John McClintock. In 1869 he was called to his present (1893) charge in Dayton, Ohio, where his ministrations have been successful in building up one of the largest churches in that city. His wife was a daughter of the late David Stewart of Huntingdon County, Pa. She died in 1868.

Rev. Hughes was succeeded by Rev. Loyal Young Graham, who was installed October 11, 1865, and dismissed at his request to accept a call to the Olivet Presbyterian Church, of Philadelphia, where he remains this day, October, 1893. Rev. Graham was succeeded by Rev. G. M. Hair, who was installed December 20, 1872. In June, 1874, Rev. Hair resigned, and was succeeded by Rev. Marcus Wishart, who was installed October 28, 1874, and resigned April 24, 1877. August 30, 1874, Rev. A. F. Boyd was installed as his successor. December 11, 1883, Rev. Boyd had, at his own request, the pastoral relation dissolved. October 24, 1884, Rev. W. G. Nevin was installed as pastor. February 1, 1887, he was, at his own request, released from the charge to accept a call to the Presbyterian church at Sharon, Pa. Rev. S. F. Farmer, D. D., was installed pastor April 30, 1887. In the autumn of 1891 he was released from Rehoboth to accept a call from the new church of Charleroi, in Washington county, Pa. In the latter part of 1892, Rev. Charles A. Clarke was installed pastor, and remains as such to this date, October, 1893.

DEATH OF MRS. ANNA M. BAKER.

Died at Bellevernon, Pa., November 27th, 1885, in the 40th year of her age, Mrs. Anna M. Baker.

Mrs. Baker was the daughter of Joseph and Salome Shoemaker, was born and grew up to womanhood on her father's farm near Apollo, Pa. At an early age she united with the Presbyterian church of Apollo, under the ministry of Rev. Robert McMillen. She was married October 12th, 1876, to Rev. Perrin Baker, then pastor of the churches of Boiling Spring and Appleby Manor. She was the mother of two children, viz: Theodore and Daniel.

She was naturally of a steadfast disposition and grace, built upon this foundation an inflexible devotion to divine truth, which she received with implicit faith and reverential fear. She was unusually gifted with womanly grace and tidiness, so that she made beautiful whatever she wrought with her hands. Her religion was rather practical than emotional, and though not without doubts and fears in her mental struggles, she approached her latter end with steadfast confidence and peace.

HON. GEORGE PLUMER.

We are indebted to the writings of the late Isaac Craig of Allegheny, Pa., for the following interesting biographical sketch of Hon. George Plumer.

George Plumer was of English descent. His ancestors were of an ancient and honorable family. Members of the Plumer family were among the earliest settlers in Massachusetts. From that State Jonathan Plumer immigrated to Pennsylvania in 1750. He was a commissary to General Braddock in 1755, and after Braddock's inglorious defeat he settled at Old Town, near Fort Cumberland. A tradition in the Plumer family has it that he was with Forbes when that "Head of Iron" took possession of Fort Duquesne in 1758, and named it Pittsburgh. He returned east with Forbes' army, and located at Fort Frederick. Here he met and married Miss Anna Farrel. In 1759 we have an account of Plumer at Fort Pitt, but not until 1761 did he bring his family to the west. In that year, by permission of Colonel Boquet, he built a cabin and "made valuable improvements" on a tract of 1,500 acres of land along the Allegheny river which he had become jointly interested in with Colonel Croghan, who had obtained it on a grant from the Indians. This land includes the location of the United States Arsenal and the Allegheny Cemetery.

The peace of Fontainebleau, "which secured to the British crown this long-disputed section," was signed on November 3, 1762. Immediately after British possession was assured emigrants began to flock in from Eastern Pennsylvania, Virginia, Scotland and the North of Ireland. Jonathan Plumer's cabin was one of the pioneer structures outside of Fort Pitt. It was located about 100 yards east of where the old Ewalt mansion now stands, which was built by Samuel Ewalt, who purchased the property when it was sold by the sheriff at the suit of Croghan's creditors. In that rude frontier cabin, whose blue wood smoke curling among the trees was a guide for the settlers on the 5th day of December, 1762, the first white child was born west of the Allegheny mountains under British dominion. He was christened George Plumer, and his after career was as notable as his birth.

The youthful Plumer became a noted hunter and scout, and occasionally accompanied parties of surveyors. Soon after the close of the revolution he met Miss Margaret Lowrey, the youngest daughter of Colonel Alexander Lowrey, of Lancaster county. Miss Margaret was visiting her sisters here, Mrs. Daniel Elliott and Mrs. John Hay, when she met the strapping young backwoodsman in buckskins. It was a case of love from the beginning, and shortly the young couple were engaged. When the engagement was announced to Mrs. Hay there was a storm. The Lowrey family were wealthy and proud. Mrs. Hay opposed the match and threatened to send Miss Margaret home. Before this could be done the youthful couple set an example which has been followed by many ardent lovers since. They eloped, and were married in August, 1784, but the girl henceforth was an outcast from home.

The first home of the newly wedded couple was on the right bank of Pucketos (now Puckety) creek, near Fort Crawford, within the present boundaries of Westmoreland county, where

Plumer had taken up 300 acres of land and built a log cabin. Here he conducted his aristocratic bride, and the two bravely began the struggle of life together without a hope of the father's forgiveness. Plumer cleaned the land and hunted the game that abounded in the woods. They were often annoyed by Indians, and were compelled to take refuge in the woods and occasionally in Fort Crawford. There is something pathetic in the situation of the high born girl who preferred to share the dangers and privations of such a life with the man she loved, rather than give him up for the luxuries of the Lowrey home and a share of the Lowrey fortune.

George Plumer and Robert Hays being called upon to perform a month's military duty as scouts, a Pittsburgh attorney took advantage of their absence to send a surveyor to survey their lands, and had a patent taken out before they knew anything about it. By this scoundrelly action they lost their all. Shortly after this Plumer met his father-in-law for the first time. Colonel Lowrey had a large body of land north of Hanna's town, near Greensburg, about which there was litigation, and preparatory to the trial of the case, he was there with a party of surveyors to fix the boundaries. Plumer was hunting in that direction and met the party. Being well acquainted with the surveyors, he shook hands all around, and then he was presented to his astonished father-in-law.

The unexpected meeting was a trifle embarrassing to Plumer. He invited his father-in-law to go home with him and see his daughter and grandchildren. But the Colonel declined, and bade him a cold farewell. But in a day or so who should appear at the little log cabin in the woods but the stately Colonel Lowrey, unannounced, but greeted with a tearful welcome. The Colonel fairly overwhelmed his long lost daughter and her little sons with embraces, and everything went well after that. That reconciliation between a disobedient daughter and an irate father was notable as the first event of its kind west of the Alleghenies.

Lowrey followed up the reconciliation by giving Plumer and

his wife their choice of three fine tracts of land near the mouth of Big Sewickley creek. The selection was made and Plumer erected a house at the mouth of the Sewickley, near West Newton. So attracted was Col. Lowrey with his son-in-law's enterprise and thrift that two years later he presented him £800 ($4,000) to erect mills on his property.

The next year the Colonel came again and found the saw mill running, and masons at work on the foundation of the grist mill. He was delighted and presented Plumer with £300 more and sent him burr stones for the mill. Plumer afterward sold his mill and built a large square log house on the upper portion of his farm, where he spent the remainder of his days. He went into the distilling and mercantile business in 1808 and carried them on with great success. Shortly after this his public career began. He was elected to the Legislature by his admiring constituents in 1812, and was re-elected in 1813, 1814, 1815 and 1817. In 1820 he was elected a representative to the seventeenth Congress from the Westmoreland district. He was then in the prime of his vigorous life, and performed efficient, though modest service, in the national legislature.

Mr. Plumer was re-elected to the eighteenth and nineteenth Congresses, and after that retired to private life. When urged to allow the use of his name as a candidate for Congress again in 1832 he positively declined. In 1818 he lost his wife, that gentle and steadfast companion of his joys and sorrows. He afterward remarried.

Mr. Plumer was a pillar of the early Presbyterian denomination here, and was one of the nine ruling elders elected to select a site and establish a theological seminary west of the mountains. He did not favor the site finally selected on Hogback Hill, Allegheny, but favored the purchase of Braddock's Fields for the purpose. He died January 8th, 1843, at the ripe age of eighty years, six months and three days.

This valiant pioneer left a numerous and vigorous line of descendants. Branches of the Plumer family are scattered throughout the state and in the western states. John Campbell Plumer, who distinguished himself in the war of 1812, at the seige of Fort Meigs and in other engagements, and who was a member of the Legislature and State Senate from the Westmoreland district, was his oldest son.

Gibsonton Cemetery.

The Gibsonton Cemetery Company was incorporated June 4, 1890. The grounds are located on the property of Gibsonton Mills in Rostraver township, Westmoreland county, Pa., and within one-half mile of the Borough of Bellevernon, Pa. The Board of Directors in 1893 are T. L. Daly, Hugh Price, John W. Wilkinson, H. C. Daly, John W. Irons, James Frost, Jacob Irons. President, James Frost. Hugh Price, Secretary, Treasurer and Superintendent. Already (1893) lots have been sold—enough to make the corporation self-sustaining.

Long Branch.

By the Court of Washington county, Pa., in 1893, a certain portion of Allen township was incorporated into a borough, under the name of Long Branch. This borough includes with its limits territory exclusively rural, no village belonging thereto. This is said to be the first instance of the kind in the state.

Speers.

Application will be made to the Court of Washington county on the 13th day of November, 1893, for the incorporation of the above village into a borough. It is situated opposite Bellevernon, in Allen township, Washington county, and is a fast growing town, with ample room for manufacturing sites.

Stockdale.

The application for the incorporation of this village into a borough will also be made on the 13th day of November, 1893. This village is situated above Allenport, in Washington county, on the Monongahela river, and is a rapidly growing town.

GLASSPORT.

This is a new town laid out by the United States Glass Company. It is located on the east bank of the Monongahela river, about three miles, above McKeesport, in Allegheny county, Pa. The McKeesport and Bellevernon Railroad runs through the town. It is one of the most desirable sites for a manufacturing town on the river. The United States Glass Company are at this time, November, 1893, erecting a mammoth brick glass works on this site, and other large plants are in contemplation.

[From the Monongahela *Republican.*]

COL. SAM. B. BENTLEY.

Samuel Black, the first of this family in Washington county of whom there is any record, was born in 1775 in County Down, Ireland. In 1791 he came to America, and in 1793 embarked in business as a trader at Parkison's Ferry. His oldest daughter was Elizabeth, who married William Bentley, and her son was Samuel Black Bentley, who died of appoplexy at his home in Monongahela City on Sabbath day morning, October 29th, 1893.

Col. S. B. Bentley was born in Monongahela City, April 29th, 1826, son of William and Elizabeth Bentley. He received a common school education.

He joined the Methodist Episcopal Church at the age of 17, and was a most devoted and a very loyal member. His fealty to the Methodist church was steadfast, it held first place always in his affections. He was a class leader, a Sunday school superintendent, a steward, and for nearly forty years a choir leader. No society ever had a more devoted member—no one a more industrious or self-sacrificing adherent—and in his long life the Christian idea pervaded, and Bible morality controlled him.

Mr. Bentley was twice married—to Miss Graham, February 22nd, 1847, and after her death to Miss Rabe, February 28th, 1856, who survives him. Their children are Charles, Harry,

Millie and Mary, who now mourn the loss of a father whose tenderness and watchful care are now a sacred memory.

Col. Bentley was a patriot—he loved his country and its flag—he was an honored member of the Grand Army of the Republic. That patriotism lead him in early life to join the military. He was a private in the old Monongahela Blues; was commissioned first lieutenant in the Monongahela Artillery by the governor in 1857; was commissioned colonel of the seventh regiment, Pennsylvania Militia, by Governor Packer in 1858. When the war broke out he was commissioned by Governor Curtin quartermaster of the 140th volunteers, and served throughout the war in that capacity, a trusted and honorable career. When the war was ended Col. Bentley came home and has lived here since.

The editor of this paper begs here to record an incident which mirrors the man. The story has been told before, but not printed. In one of the campaigns, I was sent by General Crawford on an afternoon to find his ammunition train and bring it up to the command. Going through the wood on that errand, a small party was observed, and riding over to where it was assembled I heard the voice of S. B. Bentley saying, "Hold on, men; this will not do; ——— was too good a man to be buried without some sort of Christian ceremony." I pushed my horse through the pines, and was an onlooker while our friend and comrade, Bentley, led in a hymn, and then kneeling offered a prayer. My seeing this was purely accidental—we were in different wings of the army—but I can never forget it: the shallow grave, the yellow clay, the dead soldier, the interested and upturned faces of the blue coated kneeling comrades, the sad song of requiem, and the short but earnest prayer. Unfortunately the name of the dead officer is not now remembered, although Col. Bentley has frequently named him, and I understand his body was subsequently recovered and removed from its bed under the soughing pines where I had witnessed its wierd and solemn funeral. This little story tells of our dead friend's tenderness, his piety and his respect for the dead. How often here at home we have all heard his voice at funerals, how willingly he responded to the sorrows of others.

Col. Bentley was a member of the Masonic Order; was made a Mason in Beallsville Lodge, and became a charter member of Henry M. Phillips Lodge, No. 337, this city, when it was instituted, May 5th, 1860, along with John Withrow, David Riddle, Shesh Bentley and A. J. Buffington.

He was elected to councils in 1856, when H. D. Cooper was burgess. He was an Odd Fellow and a member of the Equitable Aid Union, which order will pay $1,100 benefits to his family.

In his death our town loses a prominent figure, always full of public spirit, always ready to help, always efficient. The church will feel his loss more, and his family most. When he is laid to rest and the grave shall have covered him, Monongahela will be bereft of a man whose life is a part of its history. The suddenness of his death is a reminder once more that

> " ——There is a reaper, Death,
> And with his sickle keen,
> He reaps the bearded grain at a breath."

(From the *Daily Monongahela Republican*.)

MRS. JANE VAN VOORHIS.

At the home of her daughter Mrs. Snyder, Baidland, near Monongahela City, October 29, 1893, occurred the death of an aged lady, whose lovable traits and christian life endeared her to a host of friends, young and old. This lady was Mrs. Jane Van Voorhis, mother of John Van Voorhis, and sister of Capt. Robert Phillips of this city. Mrs. Van Voorhis for some weeks had been a sufferer from grippe, but within a few days past seemed to regain her usual health and spirits. Her granddaughters spent Friday with her and found the old lady cheerful and well, making merry their day by her lively ways and witty sayings. Saturday night she retired as usual; about one o'clock her daughter, Mrs. Snyder, was called to the bedside by a moan, and was horrified to find her mother dying. The physician pronounced it neuralgia of the heart. Jane Phillips was born in 1810, was married November 28, 1829, to Abram Van Voorhis. Seven children were born to them, Three of whom have been dead some years. Lucinda, Serena and Eliza, (Mrs. Thornton Watkins.)

The four living are John Van Voorhis, of this city ; Emaline, Mrs. Joseph Brown, of Peabody, Kansas, Mrs. Caroline Jones and Mrs. Cynthia Snyder, of Baidland.

Since her husband's death, some years ago, Mrs. Van Voorhis made her home near her son John on the old home place in Carrol township, but at his removal to town, went to live with her daughter Cynthia, from whose home in Baidland she will be laid to rest in the Van Voorhis cemetery.

Mrs. Van Voorhis was a frequent visitor with her son's family here and has made many Monongahela friends. Her erect figure and sweet face framed in a wealth of snow white hair were always admired, and it seemed as if time had but lightly touched the energetic, intelligent woman, whose 83 years have been weighted with loving thought and deed for those nearest and dearest to her. Almost all her life a consistent christian, she sleeps the sleep that the Master giveth his beloved.

BUILDING AND LOAN ASSOCIATION OF BELLEVERNON, PA.

The Southern Building and Loan Association, of Knoxville, Tennessee, was one among the first associations established here by J. P. Miller, Special Agent, and has now nearly four hundred shares of installment stock, besides some paid up stock that is drawing six per cent. interest. On February 20th, 1892, Mr. Miller organized this association with S. F. Jones, President; J. C. Cunningham, Vice President; J. S. Jones, Treasurer; and Leightty Steen as Secretary, with the following Board of Directors: S. M. Graham, Thomas G. Brown, John C. Lynn, J. S. Jones, J. C. Cunningham, S. F. Jones, Leightty Steen.

The next association to organize was the First United States Excelsior Building Association, with office at W. P. Mackey's store on Main street. The officers were R. J. Linton, President; Wm. P. Mackey, Vice President; Perry L. Byard, Secretary; J. S. Jones, Treasurer, with depository with S. F. Jones & Co., bankers. This association was short lived, as they were never able to make a loan; they closed up business in about a year from the time they were organized as an association, and failed for want of patronage.

Another thriving association that has gotten a foothold here is the First National Building and Loan Association, of Pittsburgh, Pa. Some stock is held here, but no local association has been organized, but in the near future they expect to have an organization.

October 7th, 1893, The German National Building and Loan Association, of Pittsburgh, organized an office here with the following officers: J. C. Cunningham, President; Samuel Brogan, Vice President; P. L. Byard, Secretary and Treasurer; Medical Examiner, N. Bert Lowman, M. D.; Appraisers, James R. Ferguson, M. H. Arters and S. M. Graham; Directors, J. C. Cunningham, Samuel Brogan, P. L. Byard, M. H. Arters, James R. Ferguson, J. O. Springer, John L. Nelson, S. C. Kelly, C. M. Jones, N. Bert Lowman and S. M. Graham; Attorney, Hon. Edward E. Robbins, Greensburg, Pa. This association started in with 350 shares of installment stock, and nearly 100 have been added since.

The Cooperative Savings and Loan Association, of Sioux Falls, South Dakota, was organized under the most favorable circumstances by Andrew Linn, Esq., November 5th, 1893, with the following officers: President, J. C. Cunningham; Vice President, S. M. Graham; Secretary, Wood Lang; Treasurer, Jos. A. Cook; depository, First National Bank, of Bellevernon, Pa.; Appraisers, William Lang, S. M. Graham and J. S. Jones; Directors, C. Reppirt, L. M. Kyle, J. O. Springer, E. M. Kyle and John C. Lynn.

CHARLEROI.

This town is situated on the Monongahela river, in Fallowfield township, Washington county, Pa. The land was purchased from Robert McKean by the Charleroi Land Company in 1890, and was laid out by that company in January, 1890, the first lot being sold March 4th, 1890. It is now, 1893, an incorporated borough of nearly 5,000 inhabitants. Its industries consist of one of the largest plate glass works in the United States, an extensive shovel factory, and Macbeth & Co. are now, in October, 1893, erecting a very extensive plant for the manufacture of lamp chimneys, etc. There are five churches, with another in course of being erected. It has also a large public school house with 400 scholars within its walls. It has also a mammoth coal works in full operation within its limits. It has also three first class licensed hotels. In a word—it is the magic city of the valley.

DEATH OF ROBERT McKEAN.

He died at his late residence in Charleroi, Washington county, Pa., October 24th, 1893.

He was born in Kirkcudbrightshire, Scotland, March 6th, 1826. In boyhood he attended the schools of his native parish, assisting also in the duties of the farm. January 1st, 1849, he married Janet Caird, who was born at New Abbey, Scotland, a daughter of James Caird, a native and merchant of the same place, and a member of the established church.

Mr. and Mrs. McKean resided on a farm near New Abbey for about one year after their marriage, then set sail for America. After a voyage of thirty days they landed in New York in July, 1850. They proceeded to Newburg, N. Y., where they spent about one year, going from that place to Johnstown and Allegheny City, Pa., traveling by railroad and canal. In 1851 he worked four months on the canal for seventy-five cents per day. He then moved to Chartiers creek, about six miles out from Pittsburgh, on the Steubenville turnpike, where he followed gardening for about six years. He then passed several years at Mansfield, Pa., in gardening and farming on a place near that town. In 1865 he purchased and moved on a farm of 220 acres near lock No. 4, in Fallowfield township, Washington county, Pa., on which in part is situated the town of Charleroi, where he died. He in 1890 sold 140 acres of this farm to the Charleroi Land Company which laid out the town. He was a successful business man and his place in the new town will be hard to fill. In religion he was a member of the United Presbyterian Church; and in politics a republican. He leaves a large estate. At his death he was a member of the town council. He leaves as children, James S., Postmaster at Pittsburgh; John C., Postmaster at Charleroi; William R., conducting the Charleroi greenhouse; Andrew C., dealer in real estate in Charleroi; Robert A., civil engineer, Pittsburgh; Agnes, wife of H. S. Stewart, Pittsburgh; and Mary, wife of Charles Thompson, of Charleroi.

The funeral exercises took place Thursday, October 26th, at his late residence, Revs. S. F. Farmer, D. D., H. S. Giles, of Charleroi, and Perrin Baker, of Bellevernon, officiating. Interment private in Monongahela cemetery.

The author knew S. B. Bentley from boyhood and owes much of the loved history of his native town to his kindness in furnishing data. Not many weeks before his death, he said to the author, "Doctor, hurry up your book, or some of us will be dead before seeing it." Blessed be his memory. The world has been bettered by his life.

INDEX

A

Abel, G.V., 373, 374
Abel, Noah Bright, 324
Abell, Joseph, 390
Abrams, R.B., 106
Abrams, R.R., 10
Acheson, A.W., 281
Acklin, Jas.H., 371
Acklin, John A., 358
Adams, _____, 106, 342, 343
Adams, B.W., 107
Adams, Doctor, 248
Adams, Elijah, 207
Adams, John Q., 200, 201, 205
Adams, Josiah, 333
Adams, Littleton, 194
Adams, Miss, 195
Adams, Mrs. Littleton, 193
Adams, N.A., 211
Adams, Samuel, 194
Ailes, James, 257
Albin, _____, 445
Alden, T.J.Fox, 99
Alexander, _____, 24
Alexander, Elias, 160
Alexander, Eliza, 164, 278, 280
Alexander, Hannah, 160
Alexander, Isaac, 160
Alexander, James S., 108, 114, 165
Alexander, James, 160
Alexander, Jas.S., 161
Alexander, Joseph, 22, 108, 120, 124, 128, 136, 160, 161, 163, 164, 165
Alexander, Rose, 163
Alexander, W.J., 17, 40, 108, 161, 429
Alexander, William J., 164, 165, 280

Alexander, Wm. J., 33, 64, 168
Allebaugh, General, 170
Allen, Abia, 466
Allen, B.W., 211
Allen, D.B.H., 352, 383, 463
Allen, Eliza, 262
Allen, George W., 262
Allen, James, 129
Allen, Theo. J., 361
Allison, Doctor, 322
Allman, Alexander, 274
Alloways, Samuel, 390
Alrich, Professor, 276
Alter, _____, 373
Alter, M., 374
Alter, Mary C., 325
Alter, Solomon, 111, 247, 249
Alton, Miss, 385
Amalong, C., 304
Amalong, G., 374
Anawalt, John, 104
Anderson, W.J., 310
Andrews, Rev., 324
Anger, _____, 316
Annan, Wm., 77
Applegate, Aaron, 108
Applegate, Abe, 76
Applegate, Jesse, 63, 70, 103
Applegate, Mrs. Susan, 74
Applegate, Mrs. Walter, 103
Applegate, S., 131
Archibald, Joseph, 320
Armstrong, Alexander, 348
Armstrong, Richard, 335, 336
Armstrong, Robert, 348
Arters, Fannie, 319
Arters, M.H., 319, 484,
Arthurs, Moses, 18, 25,
Arthurs, Mrs. Moses, 36
Astor, John J., 140
Austin, Alexander, 433, 438

Axtel, L.M., 385

B

Backhouse, Bob, 93
Backhouse, Mrs., 99
Bailey, F.G., 429
Bailey, Samuel G., 110
Baillins, Elias, 448
Baily, H.T., 361
Baird, Alonzo, 387
Baird, Johnson, 23, 136
Baird, Judge, 59
Baird, Mrs., 155
Baird, T.H., 36, 140
Baird, Thomas H., 57, 113
Baizor, Daniel, 107
Bake, John M., 158
Baker, _____, 465
Baker, Anna M., 474
Baker, Daniel, 475
Baker, Enoch, 437
Baker, James, 235
Baker, Joel, 350, 450
Baker, Mrs. Kela, 206
Baker, Nicholas, 235
Baker, Perrin, 325, 387, 475, 486
Baker, Perry, 148
Baker, Rev., 440
Baker, Theodore, 475
Baker, Thomas, 335, 336
Baldwin, John, 311
Baldwin, L.C., 390, 424
Ballinger, Westley, 390
Ballou, Wm., 463
Baltzee, Charles, 466
Barkhammer, _____, 445
Barkman, Kate, 323, 329, 331
Barkman, Olive, 325
Barkman, Olivia, 323, 330, 331
Barkman, Sarah, 325

Barnes, Mrs. T.B., 179
Barnes, Rev. W.H.H., 111
Barnum, W.V., 385
Barr, Col. Joseph, 200
Bartlett, John, 445
Barton, Benjamin, 328
Bascom, B., 259
Batch, Stephen B., 107
Battell, Cornelius, 343
Baugh, C.C., 358
Bausman, John, 75, 90, 110, 166
Bausman, Mrs. John, 96
Baxter, ____, 124
Baxter, Mary Jane, 197
Baxter, Polly, 118, 132,
Baxter, Samuel, 118, 132
Bayard, Geo. D., 371, 372
Bayard, George D., 368
Bayard, Stephen, 177
Bayless, Ben, 390
Bayne, Thos. M., 430
Beacom, L.R., 126, 336, 337
Bealer, Mary, 151
Bealer, Wm., 163
Beall, Joseph T., 381
Beam, Geo. W., 381
Beam, William, 455
Bean, Jane, 51
Beard, George P., 34
Bearer, Mr., 134
Beaver, ____, 24
Beaver, Colonel, 294
Beaver, Governor, 293
Beaver, Henry, 295
Beaver, Martina, 295
Beaver, Mr., 155, 295
Beazell, ____, 446
Beazell, A.G., 374
Beazell, Albert, 463
Beazell, Anna, 463
Beazell, Barbara, 256
Beazell, Benjamin F., 255
Beazell, Benjamin, 338
Beazell, Catherine, 256, 257
Beazell, Christian, 256
Beazell, Christina, 257
Beazell, Dorcas, 258
Beazell, Eliza, 257
Beazell, Elizabeth, 257, 463
Beazell, H.B., 258
Beazell, J., 334
Beazell, James, 257, 463

Beazell, Jane, 303, 463
Beazell, Jas., 389
Beazell, Jasper, 463
Beazell, John F., 258, 391
Beazell, John N., 344
Beazell, John, 256, 257, 258, 340
Beazell, Joseph, 256, 257, 436
Beazell, Lemuel, 257, 340
Beazell, Luke, 256, 257, 259, 340
Beazell, Malissa, 463
Beazell, Margaret, 257
Beazell, Mary I., 258
Beazell, Mary, 257, 340, 358
Beazell, Mathew, 256, 257, 258
Beazell, Mortimer, 463
Beazell, Rachel, 463
Beazell, Rebecca, 258
Beazell, Samuel, 258
Beazell, Sarah Emma, 258
Beazell, Susie, 340
Beazell, Thomas, 258
Beazell, William, 256, 257, 258
Beazell, Wm., 47
Bebee, Charles, 17
Bebee, Miss, 23
Bebee, Robert, 118, 119, 123
Becket, ____, 204
Becket, Joseph, 446, 448
Bedsworth, Leroy, 384
Bedsworth, Samuel, 313, 360, 463
Beebe, E.R., 297
Beebe, Robert, 105, 128, 132
Beebee, Robert, 97
Beezel, Luke, 220
Beezel, Mary, 220
Behanna, Charles, 46
Behanna, David, 46
Belar, Mrs., 256
Bell, Joseph T., 371
Bell, Joseph, 372
Benedict, ____, 351, 352
Benham, Dr., 279
Bennet, Elisha, 10
Bennett, Femmyte, 187
Bentley, Adamson, 294

Bentley, B.F. Mrs., 270
Bentley, B.F., 18, 196, 429
Bentley, Charles R., 152
Bentley, Charles, 480
Bentley, Cooper, 198
Bentley, Elizabeth, 152
Bentley, George, 140
Bentley, H.M., 128
Bentley, Harry K., 152
Bentley, Harry, 480
Bentley, Ianthus, 113
Bentley, Mary M., 152
Bentley, Mary, 481
Bentley, Millie G., 128, 152
Bentley, Millie, 481
Bentley, S.B., 71, 101, 103, 115, 122, 130, 131, 134, 154
Bentley, Samuel B., 151, 152
Bentley, Samuel Black, 480
Bentley, Shesh, 247, 482
Bentley, Sheshbazzar, 113
Bentley, W.W., 91
Bentley, William, 151, 480
Benton, Thomas, 463
Berdine, Jane, 448
Bergen, Hon. T. G. , 186
Berry, ____, 366
Berry, Geo. A., 366, 403,
Biddle, Dr. R.F., 211
Biddle, Dr., 27, 63, 76, 248
Biddle, Jane, 103, 115,
Biddle, Mary Jane, 289
Biddle, R.F., 22, 76, 100, 114, 211, 236, 275, 286, 289
Biggs, Elizabeth, 258
Bigham, ____, 446
Bigham, Alex, 367
Bigham, John, 50, 367
Bigham, William, 321
Bigler, Governor, 302
Bigler, William, 455
Biles, W.P., 87, 97, 108
Biles, William P., 118
Biles, Wm. P., 102
Billingsby, Henry, 370
Billingsby, J.K., 370
Billiter, Fannie, 365
Billiter, James, 315, 345
Billiter, Joseph, 315
Billiter, Lewis, 315
Billiter, Sallie, 461

Bingham, T.J., 422
Birmingham, L.Z., 308, 310, 330, 358, 434
Bissell, Colvin, 155
Bissell, Ida, 155
Bissell, Mary, 155
Black, Caroline, 151, 154
Black, Col. Sam., 32
Black, Cornelia, 154
Black, Cyrus, 120, 126, 130, 151, 154
Black, Elizabeth, 151, 480
Black, Harry, 151
Black, Hester, 151, 155
Black, Jane, 151, 154
Black, Marcus, 151, 154
Black, Maria, 151, 152, 155
Black, Mary, 133, 151, 154, 155
Black, Morton, 154
Black, Ross, 151, 155
Black, Samuel R., 154
Black, Samuel, 17, 95, 98, 139, 142, 151, 152, 154, 155, 156, 480
Black, Sarah, 152
Black, Wilson, 151, 155
Blackamore, Ammie, 293
Blackburn, Joseph, 470
Blackburn, Mary, 470
Blackburn, Nancy, 470
Blaine, E.L., 112
Blaine, Eliza, 178
Blaine, Ephraim, 178, 362
Blaine, J.G., 430
Blaine, James G., 112, 174, 178, 274
Blaine, Maria (Gillespie), 178
Blaine, N.C., 362
Blaine, Neal G., 282
Blair, _____, 313
Blair, John A., 194
Blair, John, 109
Blake, E.S., 26, 274
Blakely, _____, 350
Blythe, _____, 24, 103, 199
Blythe, H.F., 303
Blythe, Henry, 72
Blythe, John, 124, 129, 131
Blythe, Mrs. James, 144
Blythe, William, 260
Blythe, Wm., 19, 58, 110
Boggs, William H., 154

Boggs, Wm. M., 111
Bolden, George, 433
Boles, Isaac, 318
Bollman, Charles, 97, 108
Bollman, Lewis, 140
Bolse, Chas., 344
Bolsinger, J.S., 373
Bolt, William, 353
Bolton, David, 105
Bonchom, _____, 445
Booth, Wm., 71
Boothe, Wm. F., 371
Boothe, Wm., 372
Boquet, Colonel, 475
Borbridge, Rev. J., 335
Borland, Bess, 149
Borland, Charles, 148
Borland, Howard, 148
Borland, Hunter, 149
Borland, Ida, 148
Borland, James, 149
Borland, John, 148
Borland, M., 129
Borland, Mark, 102, 119, 147, 242
Borland, Moses, 148
Borland, Sallie Taggart, 147
Borland, Sallie, 148
Bovard, J.R., 374, 385, 387
Bowell, J.M., 339, 358, 433, 456
Bower, Annie LeMoyne, 173
Bowers, Charles, 307
Bowers, Morgan, 307, 339, 433
Bowman, Elijah, 97
Bowman, Ellen, 103
Bowman, Jacob, 445, 446, 447
Bowman, Miss, 385
Bowman, Thomas, 97
Boyd, A.F., 474
Boyd, J.F., 324
Boyd, John, 54
Boyd, Mary, 140
Boyer, J.B., 118
Boyle, Felix, 46
Boyle, J.S., 126
Boyle, L.R., 331, 364, 368, 372, 374, 391
Boyle, Philomen, 46
Boyle, Rev., 168

Boyle, Robert, 305, 358, 364
Boyle, T.N., 126
Bracken, Dr., 134
Braddock, General, 6
Bradman, Mary, 329, 331
Braezeale, _____, 292
Brant, _____, 124
Brawdy, Aaron, 64
Brendel or Brindel, Jacob, 304
Brenton, Harriet, 234
Brenton, Joseph, 234
Brett, _____, 203
Brett, Widow, 203
Brice, Andrew, 306
Brick, _____, 457
Bright, W., 373
Brightwell, Bazil, 305, 315, 316, 380
Brinton, Louisa, 206
Brinton, Mrs. Louisa, 206
Britt, Sarah, 187
Brocknour, S.R., 340
Brockunier, Samuel P., 125
Brogan, S., 387
Brogan, Samuel, 484
Bronson, A., 345
Bronson, Amon, 300, 305, 344, 347, 358, 359, 360, 361, 417
Brooks, Capt., 433
Brooks, Dr., 97
Brooks, James R., 107
Brooks, Joseph R., 107
Brown, A.L., 309, 330, 368, 377, 431, 466
Brown, Alex, 313, 329, 358
Brown, Alexander, 329, 351
Brown, Andrew, 23, 136
Brown, I. Stanley, 373
Brown, J.C., 126, 131,
Brown, John C., 336, 337
Brown, Joseph, 88, 106, 198, 483
Brown, Matthew, 62, 246
Brown, Mirtilda, 323
Brown, Mrs., 221
Brown, Thomas G., 377, 483
Brown, Wm., 106
Browneller, Erzanna, 349
Browneller, Frederick, 463
Brownlee, J.T., 276

Brownlee, John, 99
Brownson, Dr., 322
Brownson, J.I., 213
Brownson, Rev. James I., 211
Brownson, Rev., 181
Brunthoover, John, 311
Bryant, _____, 350
Bryant, C.W., 104
Bryant, Wm., 104
Bryner, Harvey, 319
Budd, Vashti, 357
Buffington, A.J., 482
Bugher, Aaron, 439
Bugher, Abe, 431
Bunting, Galena, 323
Bunting, George, 354
Bunting, Wm., 371, 381
Burgan, _____, 446
Burgan, Daniel, 446
Burgess, Samuel, 93
Burgett, Andrew, 262
Burk, _____, 366
Burke, Miss, 24
Burke, Patrick, 87
Butler, _____, 103
Butler, Abner, 137
Butler, Benjamin F., 144
Butler, Benjamin, 96, 97, 98, 137, 142
Butler, Daniel Pierce, 237
Butler, David, 137
Butler, Elizabeth, 137
Butler, Eunice, 137, 140
Butler, Ira R., 120, 137
Butler, Ira William, 144
Butler, Ira, 91, 118, 124, 125, 129, 132, 211
Butler, Isaac, 137
Butler, Joel, 97, 98, 108, 137, 140, 142, 188
Butler, Jonathan, 137
Butler, Joseph, 87, 137, 140
Butler, Josephine Estelle, 237
Butler, M.C., 237
Butler, Noble, 137
Butler, Rachel, 140
Butler, Sarah, 144
Butler, William O., 237
Butts, A.W., 126
Byard, Perry L., 484
Byers, R.C. Mrs., 329, 332
Byers, R.C., 373, 374, 434

Byers, R.E., 129
Byers, W.C., 329, 332

C

Caird, James, 485
Caird, Janet, 485
Calder, James, 349
Caldwell, Biddie, 24, 142
Caldwell, Eben, 324
Caldwell, John, 98
Caldwell, Joseph, 89, 96, 99, 107, 109, 112
Caldwell, Kitty, 87
Caleb, _____, 316
Calhoun, Capt., 327
Call, Daniel, 338
Call, Grace, 338
Call, John, 338
Call, Nellie, 451
Call, Nicholas, 338
Callendar, Nathaniel, 125, 126, 152
Campbell, A.B., 429
Campbell, Alexander, 100, 265, 294
Campbell, Allen D., 68
Campbell, Anne B., 68
Campbell, Dr. W.O., 202
Campbell, James, 294
Campbell, Miss, 26
Campbell, Rev., 181
Campbell, W., 324
Campbell, W.O., 60, 66, 202
Carmichael, Thompson, 461
Carne, James, 316
Carns, James, 320
Carns, John S., 366
Carothers, J.K., 318, 462
Carpenter, Jane, 171
Carr, Jane, 50
Carr, John C., 222
Carr, John D., 429
Carr, Moses, 72
Carroll, James, 462
Carson, J.B., 376, 399
Carson, John, 269
Carson, Mary, 195
Carson, Thomas, 107
Cartwright, Robert, 336
Carver, Teresa Quinby, 296
Case, Leonard, 261

Case, Maish, 261
Case, Massah, 261
Cass, G.W., 9
Castner, B.W., 261
Castner, Casper, 263
Castner, Catherine, 261
Castner, Daniel, 261, 263
Castner, Dr., 248
Castner, John, 261
Castner, Kate E., 263
Castner, Lewis Cass, 263
Castner, Mary Magdaline, 261
Castner, Michael, 261, 264
Castner, Peter, 261
Catlin, Alfred, 107
Catlin, Lizzie, 107
Catlin, Philip, 107
Catlin, Vachel, 107
Catlin, Wm., 107
Chalfant, Alva, 385
Chalfant, C.B., 344
Chalfant, Dr., 432
Chalfant, Nathan W., 139
Chalfant, Nathan, 96
Chamberlain, J., 414
Chambers, _____, 290
Chambers, Rev., 63
Champlin, Rev. O.P., 213
Chapin, Mary, 224
Charles, David P., 442
Chase, _____, 352
Chess, A.B., 96, 99
Chess, Andrew B., 166
Chess, John, 251
Chess, Mary, 96, 99, 166
Chessrown, James, 264
Chessrown, John, 99
Chester, Joe, 93
Chester, S.A., 466
Chick, O.G., 429
Church, Margaret K., 247
Cisly, Louis, 315
Cissley, _____, 445
Clark, Andrew, 121
Clark, Charles, 453
Clark, Emma, 131
Clark, G.W., 10
Clark, George S., 155
Clark, Hannah, 44
Clark, John, 44, 266
Clark, L.N., 10
Clark, Miss, 219

Clark, R.M., 82, 102, 124, 127, 128, 130
Clark, Robert, 43
Clark, Ruth, 44
Clark, Samuel, 9, 43, 302
Clarke, Anna, 325
Clarke, Charles A., 474
Clarke, Miss, 18, 19
Clarke, Samuel, 317, 325, 379
Clautz, Col., 327
Clay, Henry, 75, 200
Claywell, Josephine, 470
Cleaver, Mrs. Nathan, 209
Clegg, Charles, 374
Clegg, Mintie, 350
Clemens, John, 251
Clemmer, U.L., 373
Clingan, Joseph, 109
Clokey, John S., 184
Cloud, ____, 306
Cloud, Joseph, 306
Cobley, John, 435
Coil, John, 335, 347, 452
Coldron, Isaac, 358, 371
Coldron, John, 455
Coldron, Mr., 454
Colhoun, Andrew, 42, 50
Colhoun, Elizabeth, 50
Colhoun, Jane, 50
Colhoun, John, 50
Colhoun, Maria, 50
Colhoun, Rebecca, 50
Colhoun, Ruth, 50
Colhoun, William, 42, 50
Coll, Charley, 354
Coll, Chas. M., 366
Coll, Miss, 450
Collier, ____, 75
Collins, James, 104
Collins, Thomas, 92, 104, 120, 130
Collins, Thos., 20, 21, 59
Colvin, ____, 199, 204
Colvin, A.J., 357
Colvin, Abraham, 56
Colvin, Abram, 273, 274
Colvin, Betsy, 56
Colvin, Enoch, 46
Colvin, Jay, 46
Colvin, Lewis, 46
Colvin, Lucy, 270
Colvin, Mary, 56

Colvin, Moses, 40, 46, 56, 73, 274
Colvin, Sarah, 56
Colvin, Stephen, 46, 56
Colvin, Vincent, 56, 197
Conkle, J.H., 346
Conklin, Dr., 432
Connally, C.H., 334
Connelly, Dr., 248
Connelly, J.H., 211
Connelly, Mrs. J.H., 112
Conrad, John, 268, 270,
Cook, ____, 350, 429, 445
Cook, ____, 194
Cook, Charles, 259
Cook, Col. Edward, 200
Cook, Crawford, 380
Cook, D.R., 194
Cook, Edward, 158, 200, 308, 380, 436, 447, 460, 462, 464
Cook, Geo. B., 334, 335
Cook, J. Crawford, 222
Cook, John B., 321
Cook, Jos. A., 484
Cook, Joseph A., 378, 473
Cook, Joseph, 308
Cook, M.F., 447
Cook, Mary E., 325
Cook, Michael F., 158
Cook, Mrs. D.R., 193
Cook, William, 380
Cooke, Charles, 120, 123, 129
Cooke, Chas., 125, 126
Cooke, Rev., 124
Cooper, ____, 307, 446
Cooper, A.F., 429
Cooper, Allie, 349
Cooper, Betsy, 468
Cooper, Capt., 30
Cooper, E.T., 272
Cooper, Elizabeth, 436
Cooper, F.K., 272
Cooper, Fred, 355
Cooper, Frederick, 195, 467
Cooper, H.D., 98, 482
Cooper, Henry, 74
Cooper, Hezekiah D., 100, 289
Cooper, J.C., 26, 37, 113, 282, 362
Cooper, Jehu, 467, 468
Cooper, John S., 100, 289

Cooper, John, 87, 100, 108, 289, 292, 468
Cooper, Mary J., 26
Cooper, Mary Jane, 100, 289
Cooper, Mrs. H.D., 101
Cooper, Mrs., 450
Cooper, Nancy, 45, 195
Cooper, Polly, 468
Cooper, R.F., 22, 34, 36, 76, 101, 110, 114, 129, 211, 260, 381
Cooper, Richard Sparks, 100, 289
Cooper, Robert F., 100, 289
Cooper, Sallie, 270
Cooper, Samuel, 196
Cooper, Sarah, 196
Cooper, Sparks, 30
Cooper, Thomas, 349, 451
Cooper, Valentine, 48, 195, 468
Cooper, Washington, 47, 55, 91, 196, 269
Cope, J.B., 148
Cope, James, 380
Cope, Pierson, 380
Cort, Daniel, 251
Cort, Jacob, 104, 112
Corwin, ____, 445
Corwin, A. Odell, 451
Corwin, Alice, 450
Corwin, Baker, 451
Corwin, Barnet, 314, 332, 338, 450, 451, 462
Corwin, C.R., 417
Corwin, Charles R., 451
Corwin, Clarke, 314, 450,
Corwin, D.P., 429
Corwin, Ed. J., 350
Corwin, Eleanor, 332, 338, 451
Corwin, Elma, 450
Corwin, Eva, 450
Corwin, George, 450
Corwin, Georgiana, 450
Corwin, Hester, 351
Corwin, J. Wesley, 349, 451, 452
Corwin, J.W., 357, 358, 359, 360, 451
Corwin, James, 304, 305, 318, 351, 432, 450
Corwin, Jane, 332

Corwin, John W., 450
Corwin, John, 311, 0.332, 338, 450
Corwin, Joseph F., 451
Corwin, Lizzie, 450
Corwin, Luther C., 451
Corwin, Mary, 263, 301, 351, 352, 448, 450, 451
Corwin, Morris, 430, 448
Corwin, Mrs. Barnet, 350
Corwin, Mrs. Luther, 350
Corwin, Peter, 318, 383, 384, 385
Corwin, Polly, 306, 317, 430, 448, 466
Corwin, Rowland W., 451
Corwin, Sarah A., 451
Corwin, William, 450
Corwin, Wm., 374
Costen, Z.H., 334
Costin, L.H., 125, 126,
Coston, Z.H., 334, 335, 337
Cott, Fanny, 131
Cott, William, 130
Cott, Wm., 128
Cotts, Miss, 152
Coughenour, Henry C., 318
Coughenour, Henry, 303
Coughenour, John, 257
Coughenour, W.A., 307, 323,
Coughenour, William A., 329
Couldren, Elizabeth, 469
Coulson, _____, 110
Coulson, Alfred Kerr, 470
Coulson, Capt. M., 197
Coulson, Joseph S., 470
Coulson, Joseph, 145
Coulson, M., 197
Coulson, Margaret E., 470
Coulson, Martin, 470
Coulter, _____, 24, 103
Coulter, Carrie E., 125
Coulter, Raphael, 130
Coulter, Robert, 44, 124, 128, 195
Coulter, William, 115, 129, 136, 146,
Coulter, Wm., 23, 24, 25, 59, 103, 143, 360
Coursin, Isaac N., 244
Courtney, Joseph B., 349
Cowan, _____, 182

Cowan, Edgar, 76, 77
Cowan, Mr., 463
Cowan, R., 183
Cox, Beecher, 209
Cox, J.B., 352
Cox, M.A., 10
Cox, Mr., 152
Cox, Mrs. A.B., 213
Crabb, Henry, 47, 54
Crabb, Jacob, 269
Crabb, Philip, 47, 54, 263
Crabs, Jacob, 72
Craft, Clara Pauline, 326
Craft, Edgar W., 326
Craft, Ewing O., 326
Craft, Harry Clyde, 326
Craft, I.N., 327
Craft, Isiah, 326
Craig, Elizabeth, 74
Craig, Isaac, 475
Craig, Walter, 74
Craighead, Diana, 177
Craighead, J.A., 175
Craighead, Mary (Davidson), 177
Craighead, Robert, 177
Cranage, George W., 335, 336,
Crawford, _____, 233, 446, 464
Crawford, Gen., 481
Crawford, Miss, 42, 45,
Creekbaum, _____, 316
Creigh, Dr., 432
Crickbaum, Conrad, 93
Croghan, Col., 476
Croghan, George, 231
Crook, George, 336
Crookham, _____, 182
Croskey, William, 272
Crossan, Robert, 56
Crossan, Thomas, 56
Crouch, John, 234
Crouch, Mrs. Martha, 206
Crow, Joseph, 320
Crow, Miss, 467
Culbertson, Rev., 44
Culbertson, Samuel D., 106
Culler, Joseph, 462
Culp, George F., 374
Cummings, _____, 445
Cummings, Addison, 48, 467
Cunningham, _____, 446

Cunningham, Alfred, 327
Cunningham, Ann, 328
Cunningham, Anna Eliza, 327
Cunningham, Bettie P., 324
Cunningham, Bettie, 212
Cunningham, Betty Plumer, 326
Cunningham, Boyd, 124
Cunningham, Clyde, 327
Cunningham, Eliza, 328
Cunningham, Elizabeth, 328
Cunningham, Emma, 328
Cunningham, Isabel, 327
Cunningham, J.C., 211, 213, 324, 327, 329, 330, 331, 377, 483, 484
Cunningham, J.P., 358
Cunningham, James, 326
Cunningham, Jane, 327, 328
Cunningham, John C., 326
Cunningham, John, 80, 327, 328
Cunningham, Lillian, 327
Cunningham, Lizzie Van Voorhis, 213, 324, 325
Cunningham, Martha Acklin, 327
Cunningham, Mary Jane, 326
Cunningham, Mary, 327
Cunningham, Mr., 105
Cunningham, Mrs. Lizzie, 215
Cunningham, Robert, 328
Cunningham, Sara Margaret, 327
Cunningham, Thomas, 327, 328
Cunningham, William, 327, 328
Curl, Mr., 446
Curry, James, 64
Curtin, Governor, 481
Cuyler, Hon. Theodore, 216

D

Daily, Thomas, 390
Daly, Capt. Thomas L., 408, 415, 416

493

Daly, H.C., 479
Daly, Mary (Marr), 408
Daly, T.L., 376, 377, 391, 394, 396, 399, 401, 402, 414, 479
Daly, Thomas, 390
Dalzell, John, 430
Danks, ____, 316
Daragh, Cornelius, 76
Darby, Wm., 459
Darling, J.H., 34
Darr, John, 258
Darr, Mrs., 431
Darragh, Capt., 140
Darragh, Daniel, 140
Daugherty, Samuel, 360
Davidson, A.W., 22, 110
Davidson, Emma, 345
Davidson, Hannah J., 463
Davidson, Hattie 361
Davidson, James R., 363
Davidson, James, 160, 161, 163, 305, 332, 334, 335, 338, 344, 345, 347, 357, 358, 364, 434
Davidson, Lydia, 345
Davidson, Maggie, 345
Davidson, Mary, 161
Davidson, Nancy P., 356
Davidson, Robert, 161, 344
Davidson, W.A., 124, 131
Davis, A.J., 26, 37, 70, 266, 267
Davis, Ann Elizabeth, 267
Davis, David, 320
Davis, Fortner, 262
Davis, John M., 262, 265
Davis, Mary, 320
Davis, Rebecca S.H., 280
Davis, S.W., 336, 337
Davis, Samuel, 262
Davis, Theresa Maria, 267
Dawson, J.L., 9
Dawson, John L., 75
Dawson, Martha, 209
Day, Mr., 422, 423
De Pue, Samuel, 200
De Vernon, Joseph, 362
Dean, F.A., 429
Dean, J.W., 373, 381
Dean, John W., 371
Dean, Thomas W., 319, 320
Deaterly, David, 468, 469
Decker, ____, 204

Decker, Abraham, 83, 85
Decker, Joseph, 264
DeGarmo, H.C., 56
DeGarmo, Harrison, 55, 56
DeGarmo, Salathiel, 56
DeGarmo, W.H.H., 47
Dehn, John L., 313
Deihl, George F., 148
Delmont, ____, 352
Demain, Father, 342
Demain, Robert, 339, 341
Dempsey, ____, 342
Dempster, Alexander, 428
Dempsy, D.L., 333
Denny, ____, 366
Depew, ____, 86, 204
DePue, Daniel, 95, 101, 119, 142
DePue, Samuel, 200
Devenney, J.L., 429
Devore, ____, 84
Devore, A.K., 170
Devore, Moses, 251
Devore, Mr., 169
Devore, Samuel, 59, 102, 104, 121
Devore, William, 196, 209, 251
Devore, Wm., 17, 102, 209
Dewitt, John, 166
Dickey, Elizabeth, 47, 56
Dickey, James, 47, 56, 64, 103, 205
Dickey, Rev., 324
Dilworth, Samuel, 429
Dolan, Michael, 381
Dolby, Mr., 160
Donaldson, Peter, 10
Donaway, Thomas, 390
Dooley, Michael, 31
Doolittle, Caroline S., 472
Doolittle, Electa, 472
Doolittle, Giles, 472
Dougherty, A.C., 384, 387
Dougherty, Margaret, 82
Dougherty, Samuel, 317, 383, 384, 385, 386
Douglass, E.P., 429
Douglass, J. Westley, 219
Douglass, Samuel, 364
Douglass, Thomas C., 159
Douthett, Prof., 40
Dow, Lorenzo, 125, 259
Dowlin, John, 371

Dowling, Mrs. John, 350
Downer, E., 129, 429,
Downer, James W., 105
Downs, ____, 366
Doyle, Henry, 430, 433
Doyle, Thomas, 433
Drake, J.H., 429
Dravo, Michael, 259
Driver, Margaret, 462
Drum, W.C., 367
Dudley, E., 346
Duff, Geo. C., 51
Dumain, Robert, 332
Dunlap, S.G., 64
Dunlap, Samuel, 333
Dunlevy, Andrew, 319, 447, 465, 466
Dunlevy, Anthony, 464
Dunlevy, Barbara, 464
Dunlevy, Crawford, 464
Dunlevy, Jehu, 464
Dunlevy, Joseph, 464
Dunlevy, Matilda, 466
Dunlevy, William, 464
Dunn, Mr., 21
Dunning, John, 25
Durst, John, 347, 358
Dyer, F.H., 370, 371

E

Earnest, Stephen, 99
Ebbert, J.H., 332, 337
Ebbert, John H., 332
Ebbert, M.G., 335
Ebbert, Milton G., 344
Ebbert, Miss, 447
Ebbert, Rev., 332
Eberhart, Mrs., 231
Eberheart, Adolph, 302, 366, 456, 457
Eberheart, Allen K., 457
Eberheart, Charles D., 457
Eberheart, Elizabeth, 457
Eberheart, Elma, 457
Eberheart, L.A., 432
Eberheart, Rebecca, 457
Eberheart, William, 232, 309, 335, 339, 341, 344, 355, 358, 361, 366, 403
Eberheart, Wm., 316, 334, 363, 364, 389
Ebner, Casper, 315

Eckles, Hamilton, 271
Eckles, John, 97, 103, 142, 271
Eckles, Washington, 100
Edwards, C.H., 336, 337, 345
Edwards, Rev., 346
Edwards, Thomas, 344
Egan, ____, 350
Egan, Charles B., 348
Egan, Dr., 432
Eken, General James A., 180
Ekin, Mrs. General James A., 179
Ekin, Wm. M., 179
Elder, Elizabeth, 348
Elder, J. Robinson, 381
Eller, J.H., 374
Eller, John H., 387
Eller, Wm., 374
Ellet, ____, 380
Ellet, Charles, 420
Elliot, Abe, 99
Elliot, Charles, 120, 259
Elliot, H.H., 339
Elliot, Rev. Dr., 63
Elliott, Mrs. Daniel, 476
Ellis, ____, 445
Elphicke, Mrs. Annie Hair, 236
Elwood, Benjamin, 428
Endsley, A.J., 126, 336, 337, 345
English, Elizabeth, 257
Enos, Dr., 432
Enos, J.B., 358
Estep, Mrs., 295
Evans, Dan, 47
Evans, Daniel, 47, 53, 55, 57,
Evans, Nelson, 46, 53,
Evans, Oliver, 53
Evans, Sarah, 47, 53, 57
Evans, Simon, 53
Everhart, Margaret Lowrey, 79
Everson, Harriet, 430
Everson, Nathaniel, 351, 430, 432, 447, 464
Everson, Polly, 431
Everson, Richard, 364, 432
Everson, Wash., 367
Ewalt, Samuel, 476

Ewing, Judge, 428, 429,
Ewing, Rev, 77

F

Fairman, ____, 333
Fairman, Robert, 442
Farmer, S.F., 474, 486,
Farrel, Anna, 475
Faulkner, Thomas, 189
Faulkner, W.H., 345
Faulkner, William H., 354
Fawcet, T., 428
Fawcet, Thomas, 352
Fay, Mr., 221
Fell, ____, 445
Fell, Benjamin, 157
Fell, Jane, 157
Fell, Jesse, 333
Fell, John, 257, 371, 381
Fell, Rebecca, 257
Fenton, Reuben E., 281
Fenton, William, 72
Fergeson, Ellen, 189
Ferguson, Benjamin, 69, 103,
Ferguson, James R., 484
Ferguson, James, 385
Ferguson, Peggy, 109
Ferguson, Prof., 276
Ferguson, Richard, 259
Ferree, Col., 291
Ferree, Isaac, 348
Ferree, J.F., 128
Ferree, Joel T., 124, 130,
Ferree, Joel, 122
Fetz, David, 344
Fetz, Dr., 432
Feuster, R.K., 373
Fields, Robt., 371
Fields, Thomas, 334
Filson, Amanda, 131
Filson, Hiram, 128, 135,
Findlay, William, 108
Finley, Ann, 158
Finley, David, 256
Finley, H.H., 22, 23, 64, 136,
Finley, J.B., 109, 429, 112
Finley, James L., 282
Finley, James, 158, 321, 439, 449, 465, 473,
Finley, Jane, 438, 439,

Finley, M.G., 378
Finley, Mary, 231
Finley, Michael, 232, 321,
Finley, Mr., 144
Finley, Wm., 158, 438, 439
Fish, ____, 350
Fish, H.M., 387
Fish, Howard M., 344
Fisher, Geo., 438
Fisher, George, 338
Fiske, Mrs. Daniel, 178
Flannegan, Frances C., 283
Flannegan, John, 219
Flannegan, Wm., 257
Flannigan, F.C., 76
Flannigan, J.H., 324
Fleming, Alex., 335
Fleming, Dr., 279
Fleming, Mrs. N.C., 193
Frye, ____, 204
Frye, Bell, 195
Frye, Caroline, 197
Frye, Hester, 195, 196
Frye, Luke, 195
Frye, Mary, 194
Frye, Mrs. Samuel, 188
Frye, Orilla, 47
Frye, Rebecca, 272, 435
Frye, Resin, 151, 271
Frye, Rezin, 48
Frye, Robert, 264
Frye, Sallie, 272
Frye, Samuel, 47, 48, 55, 74, 198, 268, 271, 272, 273, 437
Frye, Sarah Ann, 274
Frye, Sarah, 190, 192, 272
Frye, Smith, 268, 269, 270, 273
Frye, Solomon, 48, 272
Frye, Thomas, 269, 270, 271, 466
Frye, Ursula, 272
Frye, West, 196, 264, 270
Fuester, Ella, 350
Fuller, ____, 362
Fuller, Amzi S., 220
Fuller, Dr. Smith, 220
Fuller, Harriet, 220
Fuller, James, 447
Fuller, William, 113, 282
Fulton, ____, 445
Fulton, Abram, 77, 99, 223
Fulton, Almira, 78, 225

Fulton, Elizabeth, 224, 226, 228
Fulton, Ellen, 223
Fulton, Geo. P., 15, 27
Fulton, George P., 29, 35, 40, 78, 226, 353, 354
Fulton, Hannah, 224
Fulton, Henry C., 224
Fulton, Henry, 23, 64, 66, 77, 80, 101, 136, 147, 205, 209, 211, 223, 224, 225, 226, 228, 231, 353
Fulton, J.P., 100, 289
Fulton, James P., 28, 66, 77, 114, 224, 322
Fulton, Jane, 77, 78, 223
Fulton, John, 223
Fulton, Margaret, 78, 224
Fulton, Myra, 358
Fulton, Nancy, 78, 225
Fulton, Nannie, 227
Fulton, Prof., 434
Fulton, Rebecca, 77, 224
Fulton, Robert H., 77, 114, 225, 226, 324
Fulton, Robert, 156, 227
Fulton, Sarah F., 80
Fulton, Sarah, 78, 225, 357
Fulton, W.E., 227
Fulton, William S., 224
Fulton, Wm. S., 77
Furguson, Benjamin, 97
Furnier, ____, 464
Furnier, Alvira M., 325
Furnier, Andrew, 447
Furnier, Bella, 447
Furnier, Bowman, 447, 351
Furnier, David L., 56
Furnier, David, 84, 301, 308, 312, 353, 443, 446, 447
Furnier, Henry, 446, 447
Furnier, Hugheson, 447
Furnier, James, 446
Furnier, Jesse, 447
Furnier, John W., 447
Furnier, John, 446, 447
Furnier, Levi, 447
Furrier, Lucinda, 447
Furrier, Mary, 447
Furrier, Matilda, 447
Furrier, Polly, 446, 447
Furrier, Priscilla, 447
Furrier, Simeon, 446, 447

Furrier, Susan, 56
Furrier, Volney, 447
Furrier, William, 447

G

Gabler, ____, 366
Gabler, John C., 434
Gaily, R.R., 324
Gaily, Robert, 48
Galbraith, Wm., 58, 143
Gall, William, 390
Gallagher, John, 328
Gallagher, Mary, 328
Gallagher, Mrs. Joseph, 178
Gallagher, William, 327
Gallaher, T.W., 429
Gallatin, Albert 166, 200, 328, 366, 456
Gallehew, ____, 343
Galloway, Joseph, 380
Galloway, Robert T., 353
Galloway, Samuel, 380
Gamble, H.D., 240
Gamble, J.C., 163
Gardner, Francis I., 64
Gardner, Francis, 27, 70
Garret, Rev. M. McK., 336, 337
Garret, W.S., 387
Garrison, Margaret, 325
Garten, William, 390
Gaskill, Budd, 367, 430, 432
Gaskill, Hannah, 430
Gaskill, Morgan, 309, 332
Gaskill, Sabina, 338
Gaskill, Wm., 344
Gaskin, Sabina, 332
Gebhart, ____, 94
Gee, R.M., 106
Geib, Genevieve, 216
Gibbons, J.W., 361
Gibbons, Joshua V., 353
Gibbs, Mary, 131
Gibson, Charles, 389
Gibson, Henry C., 389, 393
Gibson, John, 345, 389, 392
Gilbert, Mrs. Fred, 178
Giles, H.S., 486
Giles, Miss, 264
Gilfillan, John, 255
Gill, W.H., 324

Gillet, Celia, 26
Gillet, Rev. N.H., 26, 321, 322, 324, 473
Gillett, Rev., 458
Gist, Tom, 370, 371
Glass, Joseph, 72
Goe, Margaret, 460
Gold, Orlando H., 17
Gordan, James, 62, 63
Gordon, Abba, 250
Gordon, Elizabeth, 246, 248
Gordon, J.M.H., 28
Gordon, James M.H., 246, 247, 248
Gordon, James, 70, 97, 101, 113, 147, 156, 205, 245, 246, 248, 250, 255, 289
Gordon, Jas. M.H., 37
Gordon, John W., 247
Gordon, Judge, 27, 124, 155
Gordon, Margaret, 249
Gordon, Maria, 255
Gordon, Martha, 246, 249
Gordon, Mary, 248
Gordon, Sarah, 249
Gordon, Thomas P., 27, 114, 246
Gordon, Thomas, 87, 245, 255
Goslin, ____, 366
Goslin, John W., 385
Goslin, Nelson, 341
Goucher, John, 114
Gould, Ackey, 351
Gould, Ephraim, 455
Gould, J., 373
Gould, J.B., 302, 315, 351, 367
Gould, John B., 303, 344, 0.352, 353, 355, 356, 453
Gould, John T., 384
Gould, John, 455
Gould, Lorena, 455
Gould, Malissa, 455
Gould, Nancy J., 353
Gould, Nancy Jane, 455
Gould, Sallie, 351, 353, 357
Grable, Jerome, 49
Grable, John M., 108
Grable, John, 108
Graham, A.V., 129, 130, 135

Graham, Aeneas, 97, 101, 119, 120, 122, 128, 132, 152
Graham, Andrew, 256, 390
Graham, E.S., 68
Graham, E.V., 107
Graham, Emory, 131
Graham, Eva, 131
Graham, Grant, Jonathan, 56
Graham, L.Y., 211, 216, 321, 322, 323
Graham, Loyal Young, 474
Graham, Lyia N., 368
Graham, Miss, 480
Graham, Noah, 166
Graham, Rev. L.Y., 211, 216
Graham, Rev., 323
Graham, S.M., 358, 378, 379, 483, 484
Graham, Sallie, 132
Graham, Sarah, 122, 152
Graham, Thomas P., 377
Graves, Admiral, 240
Gray, John, 301, 302, 374, 386, 387
Grayson, _____, 76
Greathead, Carrie, 358
Green, P.H., 414
Gregg, A.T., 19, 21, 60, 99
Gregg, Nimrod, 21
Grieves, Joseph, 17
Griffin, E.B., 336, 337, 347
Griffith, E.C., 358
Griffith, Samuel C., 303
Grooms, J.C., 429
Grove, George, 106
Guffey, J.M., 414
Guffey, R.C., 467
Guffy, R.C., 368, 374, 385
Guiler, Andrew, 309, 313, 432
Guiler, Wm. G., 429
Guthrie, Margaret, 95
Guthrie, Mrs. S., 105
Guthrie, Sam, 251
Guthrie, Samuel, 17

H

Hackett, J., 374
Hackett, John, 368

Hagans, M.B., 276
Hagerty
Hagerty, James, 313, 319, 338, 380, 467
Hagerty, Robert, 345
Hagerty, Thomas, 158, 322
Haggerty, Jas., 364
Hailman, Adam, 91
Hailman, John W., 165
Haines, Miss, 26
Hair, _____, 73, 204
Hair, Annie, 235
Hair, B.W., 206, 234, 236, 237, 238
Hair, Eliza, 206, 234, 323
Hair, G.M., 114, 234, 238, 241, 323, 324, 325, 474
Hair, Gilbert M., 206
Hair, Ibela, 234, 235
Hair, James G., 70, 236
Hair, James T., 237, 238
Hair, James, 62, 72, 156, 202, 205, 206, 233, 289
Hair, John V., 238
Hair, John, 71, 206, 234
Hair, Josiah T., 238
Hair, Kela, 206
Hair, Louisa, 206, 234
Hair, Lydia R., 238
Hair, Martha, 206, 234
Hair, Mary J.V., 236
Hair, Mary, 199, 202, 204, 234
Hair, Phoebe, 74
Hair, Rebecca, 206
Hair, Samuel F., 238
Hair, Samuel, 114, 206, 234, 235, 236, 238, 241
Hair, Uriah, 206, 234, 237, 238
Hair, William F., 238
Haler, Henry, 358, 359, 360, 431, 432
Haley, Silas, 152
Hall, _____, 445
Hall, F.R., 385
Hall, Joseph, 260, 293
Halliday, Elizabeth Hall, 296
Hamilton, David, 156
Hamilton, Harriet, 281
Hamilton, Joseph, 19, 58, 87, 92, 94, 97, 99, 103, 109, 142, 181, 281

Hamilton, Margaret (Ferguson), 181
Hamilton, Margaretta L., 237
Hamilton, Rev. W.F., 207
Hamilton, Rev., 68, 181
Hamilton, Sarah, 181
Hamilton, W.F., 26, 66, 109, 114, 207, 276
Hamilton, William F., 113
Hamilton, Wm. F., 362
Hammett, C.C., 374
Hammett, Charlotte, 325
Hammett, Isaac, 310
Hammett, Mrs. Isaac, 314
Hammett, Samuel, 319
Hammett, Van, 319
Hammett, W.H., 374
Hammitt, Isaac, 372
Hammond, _____, 24
Hammond, J.D., 129, 131
Hammond, J.W., 114
Hammond, John W., 110
Hammond, W.A., 114
Hampton, John H., 274, 430
Haney, William, 434
Hanna, Amanda, 74
Hanna, Mr., 70
Hanna, William, 265
Hare, Samuel, 26
Hargrave, O.P., 271
Harmon, Mr., 44
Harr, Charlotte, 385
Harris, Levi, 347, 430
Harrison, Elijah, 82, 155
Harrison, Gen. W.H., 200
Harrison, William Henry, 166, 291
Harshe, W.P., 248
Hartranft, _____, 334
Hartranft, Governor, 293
Hartrick, _____, 24
Harvey, _____, 316
Harvey, Caleb, 99
Harvey, W.S., 371, 372, 374
Hassler, Joseph, 364
Hassler, Samuel, 334
Hasson, _____, 360, 361
Hasson, Angeline, 329, 331
Hasson, J.C., 330, 384, 385, 434
Hasson, John C., 324, 353, 357, 385

Hasson, John, 358
Hasson, Wm., 324
Hastings, Asa, 462
Hastings, E.A., 365, 462
Hatfield, John, 322, 345
Haught, Jacob, 345, 432
Haught, Jasper, 345, 347
Hay, Mrs. John, 476
Hays, Ebenezer, 125, 126
Hays, Enoch, 261
Hays, Robert, 477
Haywood, ____, 142
Hazelbaker, Abraham, 466
Hazelbaker, Andrew, 271, 466
Hazelbaker, Anthony, 334, 344, 466, 467
Hazelbaker, Daniel, 466
Hazelbaker, Geo., 431, 464
Hazelbaker, George, 352, 466, 467
Hazelbaker, Jacob, 352, 355, 466, 467
Hazelbaker, John, 352, 466, 467
Hazelbaker, Joseph, 466
Hazelbaker, Margaret, 467
Hazelbaker, Mary, 467
Hazelbaker, Matilda, 467
Hazelbaker, Peter, 465, 466
Hazelbaker, Sarah, Ann 467
Hazelbaker, Shively, 99
Hazlett, Dr., 432
Hazlett, I.C., 308, 324, 325
Hazzard, ____, 22, 26, 27, 28, 31, 37
Hazzard, C.W., 181
Hazzard, Chill W., 283, 362, 370, 371
Hazzard, Chill, 91, 39, 109, 111, 215
Hazzard, Col., 117
Hazzard, J. De Vernon, 362
Hazzard, John J., 283, 363
Hazzard, Joseph De Vernon, 283
Hazzard, Martha, 282
Hazzard, Nettie, 282
Hazzard, T.R., 21, 23, 64, 76, 112, 113, 136, 274, 281, 362
Hazzard, Thomas L., 283
Hazzard, Thos. L., 363
Hazzard, Willie, 282

Heaton, Elizabeth, 293
Hemphill, G.E., 34
Henderson, Sheriff, 88
Hendrickson, Edward, 390
Hendrickson, Frank, 429
Henry, J.S., 300, 309, 431
Henry, John S., 383, 384, 385
Hepburn, ____, 25
Hepburn, Alonzo Barton, 378
Hepburn, Eliza, 152
Hepburn, Jane, 152
Herbertson, John, 312
Herron, ____, 98
Herron, Agnes, 242
Herron, John, 128, 130
Herron, Jos. A., 429
Herron, Joseph A., 108, 165
Herron, Margaret, 242
Herron, William, 128, 130
Hervey, Dr., 239
Heslep, Thomas, 42, 45
Hess, Alcinus J., 263
Hess, David, 335, 336
Hess, John, 159
Heyser, Ella, 131
Heyser, Mattie, 131
Heyser, Shadrick, 106
Hickman, David, 109
Higbee, Rev. Dr., 33, 34, 40
Higenbotham, H., 116, 117
Higenbotham, Samuel, 117
Higenbotham, Theodore, 117
Higgins, Rachel, 461
Hildebrand, Rev., 471
Hill, ____, 445
Hill, A.B., 211
Hill, Clinton, 195
Hill, Dr., 248
Hill, Geo., 436
Hill, George B., 428
Hill, J.J., 176
Hill, John, 195, 238
Hill, Joseph, 195, 469
Hill, Judge, 24, 105
Hill, Mary, 469
Hill, Moses, 335
Hill, Norcissa, 195
Hill, Samuel, 63, 113, 200
Hill, Sarah, 469
Hilleryhand, ____, 445
Hills, ____, 350

Hindman, Miss, 26
Hindman, Mr., 65
Hindman, Samuel, 64, 105, 106
Hingely, Ezra, 123, 126
Hixenbaugh, Chas., 372, 381
Hixenbaugh, F., 374
Hixenbaugh, J.H., 374
Hixenbaugh, John, 318, 349
Hixenbaugh, Oliver, 374
Hodgeson, Thomas, 114
Hodgson, Christopher, 125, 126
Hodgson, Miss, 23
Hodgson, Thomas S., 126
Hodgson, Thomas, 27
Hoffman, George A., 114, 236
Hoffman, Jane, 197
Hoffman, Levina, 147
Holland, John, 92
Hollingshead, James, 336
Hollister, Rev., 248
Holmes, C.A., 172, 176, 336
Holmes, Charles A., 337
Holmes, Elizabeth S., 172
Holmes, Geo. S., 126
Holmes, George S., 172, 174
Holmes, W.R., 429
Hopkins, Jane, 325
Hopkins, John, 196
Hopkins, R., 336, 337
Hopkins, Robert, 332
Hopkins, Thomas, 195
Hopkins, Wm., 284
Hopwood, R.F., 429
Hornbake, Harrison, 461
Hornbake, William, 312
Hornbeck, Billy, 430, 431
Hornbeck, Luke, 462
Hornbeck, Mary, 430
Horner, Capt., 429
Horner, Dr., 432
Horner, J., 346
Horner, Joseph, 336, 337
Houlsworth, Martha, 207
House
House, ____, 320
House, O.C., 106, 124, 128, 130, 131, 285
Houseman, A.C., 367

Houseman, Margaret, 469
Houseman, Samuel, 374
Houshold, George, 257
Housman, ____, 445
Housman, A.C., 432, 457
Housman, Bela S., 218
Housman, D.P., 159, 164, 344
Housman, E.F., 218, 303, 321
Housman, Elizabeth, 219
Housman, J.L., 387
Housman, Jacob, 380
Housman, James H., 320
Housman, James, 311, 315
Housman, John L., 384
Housman, John, 218
Houston, Alexander Hervey, 149, 150
Houston, Florence, 149
Houston, James, 149
Houston, Rebecca, 149
Howard, Veronica, 303
Howell, Geo. D., 429
Hoyt, Gov., 293
Hudson, Samuel, 26, 255
Hudson, Thomas, 163
Hudson, Thos. M., 125
Huffman, Ella, 463
Hug, Ida, 358
Hugg, Anthony, 374
Hughes, ____, 352
Hughes, Benjamin, 344
Hughes, J.R., 321, 322, 458
Hughes, James R., 473
Hughes, John D., 473
Hughes, Maria E., 325
Hughes, Thomas E., 473
Hughes, Watson, 473
Hughes, William, 473
Hugus, William, 146
Hull, Abe, 24, 46, 53, 263
Hull, Abraham, 130
Hull, Abram, 71
Hull, James, 71
Hull, John, 121
Hunt, Homer, 385
Hunt, Thomas, 383, 384, 385
Hunt, Thos., 386, 387
Hunter, Jane, 365
Hunter, William, 125, 126
Hunter, Wm., 97
Hurd, S.T., 75

Husher, ____, 307
Husher, Harrison, 333
Huston, Cyrus, 99
Huston, S.H., 92
Hutchinson, Ann, 51
Hutchinson, John, 51
Hutchinson, William, 332
Hutchison, Mrs. William, 315
Huttenhour, James, 320
Huttenhour, Jeremiah, 381
Huttenour, Mother, 53
Hutton, John James, 456
Hutton, John, 314, 332, 354
Hutton, Nathan, 456
Hutton, Rachel, 456
Hyatt, E.L., 373

I

Ihmsen, Henry, 98
Ihmsen, William, 105
Ihmsen, Wm., 98, 120, 121, 123, 129, 142, 456
Irons, Jacob, 388, 389, 479
Irons, John W., 379, 437, 479
Irons, John, 446
Irwin, ____, 204
Irwin, Betsy, 140
Irwin, John, 95, 338, 341
Irwin, W.W., 76, 283
Irwin, William, 71, 95, 140, 156
Irwin, Wm., 73
Isett, Dr., 223

J

Jack, Mrs. Jennie Linn, 173
Jack, Rebecca, 223
Jackman, Jehu, 464
Jackman, Jesse, 334
Jackman, Simeon, 48, 464, 465
Jackman, William, 55
Jackman, Wm. H., 47
Jackman, Wm., 464
Jacobs, Adam, 9, 317
Jacobs, Captain Adam, 317
Jacobs, E.P., 125

Jacobs, Indiana, 450
Jacobs, Jane, 450
Jacobs, Margaret Jane, 452
Jacobs, Mrs. William, 386
Jacobs, Rebecca, 332, 338
Jacobs, William, 303
Jamison, Moses, 335, 343
Jamison, Rev., 259
Jamison, Thomas, 335, 336
Jeffries, L.J., 303
Jeffries, Levi J., 356, 439
Jennings, Obadiah, 459
Jennings, Prof., 23
Jobes, ____, 352
Johe, Michael, 165
Johns, Doll, 429
Johnson, O.D., 304, 305, 310, 319, 349, 358, 359, 374, 433
Johnson, B.W., 437
Johnson, C.C., 28, 112
Johnson, D.B., 325
Johnson, Daniel, 387
Johnson, David, 120
Johnson, Dr., 319, 432
Johnson, Joseph, 430
Johnson, Levi, 312, 444, 447, 459
Johnson, Nelson, 312, 459
Johnson, Philip, 446
Johnson, Randall, 259
Johnson, Robert, 220, 321
Johnson, Robt., 447
Johnson, Sarah, 112, 325
Johnson, W.C., 371
Johnson, W.F., 301
Johnson, W.G., 113
Johnson, W.H., 344
Johnson, William G., 282
Johnson, William, 105, 142, 459
Johnston, Mary, 365
Jones, ____, 308, 355
Jones, Amanda, 158
Jones, Ann, 156, 159
Jones, C.M., 374, 387, 484
Jones, Caroline, 483
Jones, Celia, 159
Jones, Delilah, 156, 159
Jones, Elijah, 156, 157
Jones, Elizabeth, 158
Jones, Ella Jane, 470
Jones, Ella, 158
Jones, Homer, 159

Jones, Isaac W., 157, 165
Jones, Isaac, 124, 129
Jones, J.F., 336, 337, 345
Jones, J.S., 377, 401, 483, 484
Jones, James S., 158, 269
Jones, James, 157, 198
Jones, Jennie, 325
Jones, Jesse, 156, 157
Jones, John, 156, 157, 159
Jones, Joseph A., 107
Jones, Joseph S., 157, 379
Jones, Joseph Shepler, 470
Jones, Luther, 159
Jones, Malissa, 158
Jones, Mary L., 166
Jones, Mary, 157, 160, 164
Jones, Mr., 325
Jones, Mrs. D.W., 350
Jones, Noah, 271
Jones, Peter F., 126, 335, 337
Jones, Polly, 156
Jones, Pressly, 387
Jones, Rachel, 137
Jones, Rebecca, 156, 159
Jones, Rettie, 158
Jones, Rosa, 159
Jones, Rose, 156
Jones, Ruth, 156, 159
Jones, S.E., 325
Jones, S.F., 158, 312, 318, 325, 331, 358, 361, 376, 377, 385, 399, 401, 406, 414, 415, 416, 424, 442, 444, 462, 483
Jones, Sam., 426
Jones, Samuel, 156, 157, 158, 159, 163, 164, 259, 312, 366, 416, 470
Jones, Sarah, 158
Jones, Susan, 189
Jones, W.H., 107, 318, 344
Jones, William H., 345
Jones, William, 44, 120, 128, 133, 156, 157, 158, 159, 160, 164, 333, 385, 406, 470
Jones, Wm., 256, 312, 347, 368, 384, 385, 444, 462
Jordan, Ed, 305
Jordan, Edward, 310
Jordan, Thomas C., 348
Jordon, _____, 350
Jordon, Edward, 350, 387
Jordon, Eliza, 348
Jordon, Hannah, 348
Jordon, Miss, 461
Jordon, Rachel, 462
Jordon, Roger, 348, 349
Jordon, Sarah Ann, 348
Joseph, M.P., 252
Joy, _____, 350

K

Kaine, _____, 76
Kaine, David, 303
Kammerer, David, 296
Kean, W.V., 324
Kearney, Edward, 204
Keechline, Mrs., 144
Keenan, F.F., 131
Keenan, Samuel, 59
Keistler, F.M., 384, 385
Keistler, Francis, 384
Keller, S.P., 124, 129
Kelley, S.C., 385
Kelly, _____, 256
Kelly, Mr., 25
Kelly, S.C., 484
Kenah, R.L., 434
Kendall, _____, 456
Kennedy, F.H., 429
Kennedy, R.P., 429
Kerbey, Mary H., 173
Kern, Henry, 335, 336
Kern, Mary, 83
Kerr, _____, 445
Kerr, A.H., 26, 71, 113, 0.114
Kerr, Aaron H., 70
Kerr, Aaron Harvey, 74
Kerr, Aaron, 63, 70, 74, 90, 97, 111, 205, 236
Kerr, Allen C., 68
Kerr, Amanda, 70
Kerr, B.B., 68
Kerr, David, 44
Kerr, Ella, 68
Kerr, Euphemia, 68, 154
Kerr, Hampton, 71, 74
Kerr, J.M., 68
Kerr, James, 67, 146, 364
Kerr, Jno., 63
Kerr, John, 66, 68, 69, 80, 102, 154, 207, 208, 209, 211, 250, 280
Kerr, Joseph, 71, 74, 114
Kerr, Mrs., 73, 95
Kerr, N.P., 336, 337
Kerr, Phoebe, 70, 236
Kerr, Rev. John, 207, 208, 209, 211
Kerr, Susan, 70
Kerr, Thomas, 68
Kershner, B.L., 453
Kershner, Brice L., 352
Ketcham, Curry, 31
Ketcham, William, 31
Keys, Mrs., 144
Kiddoo, Jos., 64
Kiddoo, Joseph, 205, 207
Kimber, _____, 366
King, _____, 24
King, A.M., 248
King, Allie M., 169
King, Alvin, 114, 153
King, Annie, 154
King, C.B., 68
King, Calvin, 169, 170
King, Clarence, 153
King, Courtland, 168, 169, 170
King, Culver, 153
King, Cyrus B., 27, 153
King, Cyrus, 37, 155
King, Dr., 97
King, E.L., 124, 131
King, Elijah, 168
King, Harvey, 169
King, Henry, 319
King, Ida, 153
King, Isaac, 168
King, James Stewart, 168
King, Jane, 169, 170, 171
King, John L., 153
King, John, 168, 169, 170, 251
King, Maria, 153, 155
King, Mary L., 168
King, Milton S., 169, 170
King, Nina, 154
King, R.C., 87, 88
King, Richard C., 153
King, Richard, 155
King, Robert, 169
King, Rufus, 200

King, S.M., 152, 153, 163, 246
King, Samuel C., 17
King, Samuel J., 169
King, Samuel K., 153
King, Samuel M., 155, 274
King, Samuel, 251
King, Victor, 154
King, W.H., 27, 37, 248
King, William H., 153, 168, 170, 171
King, William, 31
King, Wm. H., 254
Kinney, _____, 387
Kinstrey, Zebulon, 148
Kintner
Kintner
Kintner, Geo., 431
Kirk, Dr., 432
Kirk, Van, 429
Kirkpatrick, John M., 75
Kithredge, A.E., 235
Kittle, Mrs., 467
Kittle, W.C., 347, 374
Knap, _____, 350
Knight, Jonathan, 419
Krepps, Emma, 326
Krepps, J.T., 259
Krepps, John, 221
Krepps, Lewis, 380
Krepps, Nancy, 177
Krepps, Solomon, 177
Kumler, J.P.E., 227
Kyle, E.M., 358, 384, 386, 387, 484
Kyle, Elizabeth, 468
Kyle, L.M., 364, 484
Kyle, Margaret, 322
Kyle, William, 313, 345, 386
Kyle, Wm., 344, 467

L

Lackey, David, 105
Lacock, _____, 350
Lafferty, W.L., 68
Lamb, John, 100, 141, 289
Landefeld, _____, 119
Landfier, _____, 351
Lane, Sabina, 338
Lanehart, M., 374
Lanehart, Milton, 373

Laneheart, Leonard, 456
Lang, _____, 367
Lang, Clara, 358, 385
Lang, George, 318, 320, 367, 432
Lang, Henry, 366, 431, 432
Lang, William, 484
Lang, Wood, 484
Langhead, Benjamin, 109
Lank, Dr., 248
Large, Mrs. I.N., 179
Larimer, Gen., 222
Larimerl, _____, 360
Lario, _____, 310
Larwill, Joseph H., 294, 295
Larwill, Nancy Quinby, 293
Lash, Miss, 262
Latrobe, B.H., 94, 420
Latta, Richard, 380
Latta, Wm., 311
Laubach, Nannie, 295
Lawrence, G.V., 102, 165
Lawrence, Geo. V., 111, 112, 428, 429
Lawrence, Geo. W., 36
Lawrence, George V., 30
Lawrence, Joseph, 76, 77
Layman, Fred, 102
Layman, Frederick, 97, 101
Layman, William, 101, 142
Layman, Wilson, 102
Leard, _____, 445
Lee, Prof., 276
Leet, J.D., 301
Lehew, Peter, 438
Lehew, Thomas D., 333
Lehew, Wm., 387
Lemon, Wm., 125, 126
LeMoyne, F. Julius, 172
Lender, Nathaniel, 259
Leonard, A.B., 124
Leonard, A.P., 336, 337
Leonard, Rev., 440
Letherman, D.L., 113
Letherman, Demas M., 362
Letherman, Dr. J.A, 362
Letterman, D.M., 282
Levingston, Thomas, 67
Lewis, _____, 20, 0.58
Lewis, A.P., 358, 373, 374
Lewis, Abe, 333, 466
Lewis, E.P., 78, 225, 324, 358
Lewis, Eddie, 226

Lewis, Ephraim, 358, 368
Lewis, J.H., 358, 373
Lewis, Jas. H., 431
Lewis, Margaret, 347
Lewis, T.F., 373
Lewis, W.H., 106, 391, 432
Lewis, William, 334
Lindsay, J.W., 305
Link, Frederika, 296
Linn, _____, 24
Linn, Alonzo, 28, 77
Linn, Andrew, 484
Linn, Dr., 28, 145, 249, 264
Linn, George A., 78, 121, 247
Linn, George, 37
Linn, John J., 101
Linton, _____, 387
Linton, Caroline S., 325, 471, 472
Linton, R.J., 299, 302, 303, 324, 325, 329, 331, 357, 358, 360, 376, 377, 378, 399, 401, 404, 414, 415, 434, 484
Linton, Robert J., 404, 407, 416, 472
Lippincott, _____, 445
Liver, Michael, 262
Lloyd, Stacy, 148
Lockhart, Lizzie, 26
Loeffler, William, 404, 405
Lofink, _____, 182
Long, Warner, 332
Longnecker, David, 353
Loomis, A.W., 76
Loomis, Stephen, 433
Loughrey, James A., 209
Loughry, Mrs. J.A., 213
Lowes, A.B., 325, 371, 372, 431
Lowman, N.B., 432, 484
Lowrey, Alex., 226
Lowrey, Alexander, 476, 477, 478
Lowrey, Col., 231
Lowrey, Margaret, 476
Lowry, Hortensius, 424
Loyd, Leech, 46
Lucas, Elizabeth, 325
Lucas, Wm., 391
Luce, Leonard, 321
Luce, Pierson B., 349, 371
Lucky, George J., 34

501

Lucky, Prof., 40
Lynch, David, 266
Lynch, W., 126
Lynn, Cyrus, 106
Lynn, Denton, 315, 316
Lynn, George, 31
Lynn, John C., 349, 483, 484
Lyon, George M., 80
Lyons, _____, 253
Lytle, George Elmer, 78, 79
Lytle, Perry A., 78

M

Macabee, Isaac, 332
Mackey, _____, 387
Mackey, W.P., 325, 329, 330, 332, 352, 353, 358, 367, 454
Mackey, Wm. P., 386, 484
Manks, Dick, 97
Manown, Frank, 28, 93, 104
Manown, Franklin, 17
Manown, J.H., 70
Manown, James H., 26, 113
Manown, James, 59, 63, 87, 88, 122, 200
Manown, W.J., 262, 332, 377, 378, 466
Mansell, Josiah, 126, 335, 336
Mansell, Rev. R.B., 197
Marchand, Dr., 138, 152
Markell, Charles, 82
Markell, Edward, 82
Markell, Eliza, 81, 83
Markell, John S., 82, 98, 101
Markell, John, 170
Markell, Lewis, 82
Markell, Norman Keys, 83
Markell, W.J., 59, 91, 164, 195, 270
Markell, William J., 81, 82, 83
Markell, William, 81, 82
Markill, John S., 98
Markle, Capt., 231
Markle, Harry, 216, 220, 221
Markle, John S., 309, 429
Markle, Maria, 221

Marr, Mary, 408
Marshall, James K., 58, 260
Marshall, James, 59, 260
Marshall, John H., 261
Marshall, John, 59
Marshall, Mary, 110
Marshall, Nancy, 261
Marshall, Rev., 114
Marshall, Susannah, 261
Marston, A.N., 349, 350, 358, 432
Marston, Katty, 350
Martin, Belle, 250
Martin, Capt., 140
Martin, Cynthia, 250
Martin, Ed., 305
Martin, Eli W., 358, 386
Martin, Eliza, 250, 264
Martin, James C., 250
Martin, Jesse, 62, 63, 91, 97, 98, 112, 205, 250, 264
Martin, Margaret, 250
Martin, Mary, 250
Martin, Mr., 353
Martin, Thomas, 250, 251
Marvin, Judge, 281
Mason, Hannah, 67
Mason, Harrison, 390
Mason, J.D., 26, 70, 74
Mason, Miss, 457
Mason, Morgan, 10, 457
Massey, Samuel, 311
Maxwell, Geo. C., 462
Maxwell, Jas . M., 66
Maxwell, Rev., 181
May, James, 310
McAllister, _____, 105
McAllister, Alexander, 46
McAllister, William, 46
McAlpin, Agnes, 325
McAlpin, Agness, 385
McAlpin, J.T., 365
McAlpin, James, 325
McAlpin, Jennie, 159
McAlpin, John, 325
McAlpin, Miss, 385
McAlpin, W.B., 325, 368, 374
McBeth, Miss, 196
McBride, Mr., 250
McCague, George, 429
McCain, Grand-daddy, 71
McCain, Henry, 71
McCain, Hugh, 71

McCain, Margaret, 71
McCain, Robert, 467, 468
McCain, S., 325
McCain, Samuel, 312, 325
McCalla, _____, 453
McCalla, James, 102
McCalla, Nat, 98
McCasky, Rev. Geo., 161
McCaslin, Alexander, 145
McCauley, James, 164
McClain, John, 417
McClintock, John, 474
McClure, Howard, 300, 467
McClure, Joseph, 97, 141
McClure, Richard, 292
McClure, Robert, 349
McClure, W.B., 76
McComas, Daniel, 47
McComas, William, 47
McComase, _____, 199
McComb, _____, 204
McConaughey, Dr., 276
McConnaughy, David, 322
McCord, Granny, 183
McCord, Mrs., 213
McCormick, Geo. A., 429
McCoy, _____, 445
McCready, Rev., 175
McCreary, W.W., 428
McCrory, James, 380
McCrory, John, 436
McCrory, S., 334
McCrory, Samuel, 272
McCrory, W.E., 358
McCullough, James, 70
McCullough, John, 70
McCune, John N., 175
McCune, Mrs. Caleb, 179
McCune, Samuel W., 174
McCurdy, T.S., 92
McCutcheon, Jen, 72
McDaniel, William, 76
McDonough, Annie, 179
McDonough, Corinne, 179
McDonough, John, 179
McDonough, Mary, 179
McElvain, Chief Justice G.W., 113, 282
McElvain, Greer, 209, 217, 223, 225, 228
McFadden, O.B., 112
McFall, Ellen, 325
McFall, Grace, 332, 338, 347

McFall, Maggie, 325
McFall, Mrs. Thomas, 450
McFall, Robert, 325
McFall, Thomas, 338
McFall, W., 325
McFall, William, 390
McFarland, _____, 26
McFarland, Ann St. Clair, 242, 251
McFarland, Campbell, 141
McFarland, Douglas, 141
McFarland, Eliza, 254
McFarland, Jack, 76
McFarland, John, 26, 70, 114, 141, 211, 252, 253
McFarland, Joseph, 185
McFarland, Mary C., 242
McFarland, Mary, 254
McFarland, Robert, 62, 108, 201, 205, 242, 252, 254
McFarland, Robt., 442
McFarland, Rosanna, 185
McFarland, Thomas, 252
McFarren, James, 251
McFeeley, John, 251
McGinnis, Capt., 433
McGirk, Nancy, 267
McGogney, _____, 257
McGowan, Thomas, 274
McGraham, Bellevidere, 154
McGregor, Will., 165
McGrew, _____, 204
McGrew, Alvira, 255
McGrew, J., 97, 98, 102, 142
McGrew, James, 62, 63, 108, 205, 254, 255
McGrew, Matilda, 255
McGrew, R., 97, 98, i02, 142
McGrew, Robert, 17, 251, 254, 255
McJunkin, _____, 465
McKay, O.P., 247
McKean, Agnes, 486
McKean, Andrew C., 486
McKean, James S., 486
McKean, John C., 486
McKean, Mary, 486
McKean, Robert A., 486
McKean, Robert, 196, 485
McKean, S., 387

McKean, Samuel, 368, 373, 374, 376, 382, 427, 444, 446
McKean, Thomas, 265
McKean, William R., 486
McKee, Ford, 309
McKee, Hugh, 465
McKeever, Mrs., 17
McKelvey, John, 44
McKendry, Bishop, 259
McKennan, Hon. T. M. T., 76, 277, 279, 382, 421
McKennan, J.B., 364, 366
McKenzie, _____, 351
McKinney, Mr., 455
McKnight, James, 72
McKown, Rebecca, 233
McLain, Jacob, 380
McLain, Jefferson, 97, 103
McLain, John, 386
McLardy, Robert, 130
McLaren, Dr., 322
McLaughlin, _____, 445
McLean, Dr., 130
McIlvain, C.E., 278
McIlvain, George V., 362
McIlvaine, C.G., 429
McIlyar, Rev., 471
McMahon, Wm., 103
McMehan, William, 268
McMillen, Robert, 475
McNary, Elizabeth, 118
McNary, Mrs., 132, 133
McNeal, John, 110
McNulty, _____, 106
McPherson, S.J., 237
McWilliams, Wallace, 251
McWilliams, William, 313
Meads, Master, 148
Means, Henry F., 78, 224
Means, James, 78, 224
Means, Nathan, 224
Mellinger, W.S., 91, 250
Mellor, C.C., 330
Meloy, J.C., 221
Mercer, Boyd, 265
Mercer, James, 63, 99, 105
Mercer, Rev., 61, 109
Meredith, Solomon, 357
Meridith, Solomon, 345
Merrick, John, 313
Messenger, _____, 233
Metz, Conrad, 362, 433
Meyran, Charles R., 429

Mifflin, Thomas, 119
Miller, _____, 138
Miller, A.H., 459
Miller, Adelaide, 179
Miller, George T., 27
Miller, H., 126
Miller, Hattie, 322, 329, 331
Miller, Hillery, 381
Miller, Hiram, 257
Miller, Horace J., 179
Miller, J.B., 459
Miller, J.P., 483
Miller, Jacob H., 178
Miller, Michael, 87
Miller, R.L., 126
Miller, Rev., 27, 259
Miller, S.B., 371, 381
Miller, S.V., 135
Miller, Sansom B., 322
Miller, Virgil, 329, 332
Miller, W.H., 99
Milligan, Prof., 276
Millinger, Alice, 154
Millinger, George V.L., 154
Millinger, Marcus, 154
Millinger, Robert F., 154
Millinger, W.S., 154
Mills, A.B., 159
Mills, Andrew, 120, 159
Mills, James R., 160
Mills, James, 110, 120, 128, 129, 145, 159, 164
Mills, Mary, 160
Mills, William, 105, 130, 145
Mills, Wm., 76, 120, 121, 442
Mink, J.A., 258
Minney, Elliott, 332
Minnie, Wilbur, 433
Minor, S.F., 126
Mitchell, _____, 97
Mitchell, Allicia, 285
Mitchell, Dr., 247
Mitchell, James, 87, 108, 142
Mitchell, Miss, 47, 55
Mitchell, Rev., 324
Mitchell, T., 183
Mitchener, M.W., 131
Moffat, J.D., 40
Moffit, John J., 335, 336
Monroe, Joshua, 125

503

Monroe, Tillie L., 51
Montgomery, William, 111
Montgomery, Wm., 77
Montooth, E.A., 430
Moody, ____, 199
Moody, Lady, 290
Moody, Robert, 46, 53
Moody, Samuel, 53, 71, 72
Moore, ____, 390
Moore, Andrew M., 393
Moore, David, 64
Moore, Frank, 337
Moore, Franklin, 335
Moore, James H., 23
Moore, James, 169, 256, 429
Moore, Jas. H., 91
Moore, Rev., 63
Moore, W.H., 433
Moorhead, J.K., 9, 389
Moorhead, Max. K., 428
Morgan, Capt. Sam., 168
Morgan, Frank, 383
Morgan, Gen., 177
Morgan, George, 103
Morgan, J.W., 329, 372, 374
Morgan, James W., 371
Morgan, Lizzie, 385
Morgan, Samuel, 146, 183
Morgan, W.F., 325, 330, 371
Morris, A.P., 26, 113, 252, 278
Morris, Bishop, 259
Morris, Morrison, ____, 26, 36, 357
Morrison, Andrew P., 279
Morrison, Andrew, 281
Morrison, Eliza, 279, 281
Morrison, Elmer, 357
Morrison, Geo., 19
Morrison, George, 245
Morrison, H., 61
Morrison, J.S., 71, 113
Morrison, James, 281
Morrison, Jane, 281
Morrison, John, 279, 280, 455
Morrison, Joseph S., 22, 26, 30, 275
Morrison, Joseph, 281
Morrison, Lawrence, 404

Morrison, M.P., 28, 37, 113, 247
Morrison, Margaret, 279
Morrison, Matthew Porter, 274
Morrison, Porter, 281
Morrison, W.H., 105, 106
Morton, Matilda, 154
Morton, Rev., 324
Mosely, John, 163
Mosely, Mrs., 155
Mosely, Westley B., 163
Moss, ____, '465
Mouck, E.W., 34
Mounser, Fred., 391
Muer, Mary, 328
Muir, Rosanna, 326
Mulhollan, George, 80
Mullin, J., 373
Mullin, John, 334, 344, 345, 363
Mullin, Robert G., 433
Mullin, William D., 365, 457
Mumbower, George, 103
Munson, Elizabeth, 225
Munson, Isaac Fulton, 225
Munson, Jennie, 225
Munson, Jonas, 225
Munson, Mary, 225
Murdock, J.B., 429
Murphy, Ann, 158
Murry, Prof., 68
Mustard, Lizzie, 157
Myers, F.M., 314
Myers, Nancy, 188
Myers, Sarah, 188

N

Naylor, Eliza, 239
Neal, Miss, 256
Neal, Mrs., 432
Neblack, Thos., 47
Negley, James S., 292
Neil, I.N., 374
Neil, J.A., 374
Neil, John S., 368
Neil, W.H., 374
Nelson, Francis, 60
Nelson, John L., 484
Nelson, Robert, 264
Nesbit, D.K., 440

Nesbit, Dr., 134
Nesbit, S.H., 126, 346
Nesbitt, Dr., 127, 128, 143
Nesbitt, Pastor, 122
Nessly, J.F., 161, 333, 334, 335, 347
Neville, General, 253
Nevin, W.G., 324, 474
Newbold, ____, 350
Newbold, Joshua, 347, 348, 349, 350
Newcomer, Barbara, 463
Newton, Mary, 187, 188
Niccolls, John, 217, 367, 389, 456
Niccolls, Robert, 113, 282
Niccolls, Thomas, 457
Nichols, ____, 223
Nichols, George W., 357
Nickel, Geo. E., 432
Nickel, J.R., 463
Nicolls, R., 362
Nicols, James, 220
Nixon, J. Benton, 55
Nixon, J. Brinton, 47
Noble, Johnson, 335
Noble, Mrs., 30, 36
Noble, W.H., 331, 358, 371, 372
Norfolk, Emma, 131
Norris, Geo., 436
Nutt, J.E., 371, 384, 385
Nutt, Jabez, 345
Nutt, Joseph E., 368
Nye, ____, 350
Nye, Jordon C., 452

O

O'Donovan, A.D., 143
Oehle, George, 106
Officer, James, 128
Officer, Mary Ann, 246
Officer, Mrs. James, 105
Officer, Robert, 28, 71
Officer, Sherriff, 246
Officer, Thomas, 97
Ogle, Andrew Jackson, 75
Ogle, Charles, 75
Ogle, Jack, 75
O'Neal, Mr., 320
Ong, John, 380
Orr, Joseph, 184

Owens, D.W., 313, 349
Owens, David W., 469
Owens, John Cockey, 300

P

Packer, Gov., 481
Packer, M.F., 374
Paden, Margaret, 146
Page, Thomas, 345
Palmer, Nancy P., 356
Palmer, Washington, 97, 99, 142
Park, T.S., 440
Parkhill, David, 341
Parkinson, Benjamin, 44
Parkinson, James, 9
Parkison, ____, 116, 204
Parkison, A.R., 104, 183
Parkison, Benjamin, 83, 104, 150, 183
Parkison, David, 83
Parkison, James, 83, 96
Parkison, Joseph, 83, 96, 107, 151, 156, 296
Parkison, Margaret, 150
Parkison, Mary, 83, 96
Parkison, Mrs., 296
Parkison, Thomas, 83
Parkison, William, 83, 85, 92, 95, 96, 98, 108, 142
Parks, T.S., 331
Parson, B.L., 399
Parsons, B., 270
Patrick, W.W., 428
Patten, Dr., 279
Patterson, ____, 94
Patterson, A.O., 77
Patterson, C.A., 373, 384
Patterson, Elizabeth, 217
Patterson, H., 330
Patterson, Harriet, 325, 331
Patterson, J.B., 429
Patterson, J.F., 208
Patterson, Jane, 257, 338
Patterson, John, 64, 65
Patterson, Mathew, 338
Patterson, Robert, 314, 381, 432, 449
Patterson, Robt., 310
Patterson, Stewart, 371
Patterson, Thomas, 300
Patterson, Thompson, 332

Patterson, Vivia, 210
Patton, ____, 456
Patton, Mrs. Hiram, 218
Patton, R.G., 378
Patton, R.J., 373
Patton, Robert, 146
Paull, ____, 20
Pearce, I.A., 126
Pearson, General, 170
Pearson, Joseph, 432, 437
Penn, Richard, 388
Penniman, Dr. W.A., 179
Pennywell, ____, 306
Pershing, I.C., 345
Pershing, I.H., 336
Peterson, Elizabeth, 148
Peterson, John, 148
Petit, Kate Potter, 296
Philips, Jane, 157
Philips, Mrs. John, 103
Philips, Robert, 59
Phillips, Benjamin, 150
Phillips, David, 60
Phillips, Elizabeth, 150
Phillips, James, 150, 349
Phillips, Jane, 196, 482, 0.483
Phillips, John M., 150
Phillips, Margaret, 150
Phillips, Mrs., 101, 122
Phillips, Nancy, 166
Phillips, Robert, 19, 20, 60, 146, 166, 482
Phillips, Ross W., 357
Phillips, William, 150
Pierce, Daniel, 124, 129
Pierce, Enoch, 103
Pierce, Jonathan, 119
Pierce, Mrs. Frank, 78
Pierce, Will., 31
Pierpoint, F.H., 281
Piersol, ____, 360
Piersol, J.A., 358, 359, 360
Piersoll, ____, 361
Piersoll, J.A., 384, 385
Piersoll, J.S., 384
Piersoll, S.A., 387
Piper, James, 375
Plannet, ____, 350
Plannett, J.W., 434
Playford, Mr., 423
Plumer, Elizabeth, 80, 222, 228

Plumer, George, 79, 80, 219, 222, 226, 228, 231, 232, 457, 475
Plumer, Hon. George, 209
Plumer, John C., 231
Plumer, John Campbell, 479
Plumer, Jonathan, 229, 231, 475, 476
Plumer, Margaret Lowrey, 231
Plumer, Mary, 79, 231
Plumer, Miss Betsy, 211
Plumer, Nancy, 219
Plumer, Thomas, 232
Plumer, W.S., 229
Plummer, Susan E., 173
Pollack, Dr., 97
Pollack, ____, 154
Pollock, Belle, 208
Pollock, Coralinn, 208
Pollock, D.H., 176
Pollock, Isaac, 208
Pollock, James, 208
Pollock, John, 207
Pollock, Mary Jane, 207, 208
Pollock, Nancy, 208
Pollock, Samuel, 290
Pollock, Willie, 208
Pool, ____, 351
Pool, Dr., 432
Pope, Mrs. A.R., 179
Porter, ____, 290
Porter, O.J., 113
Porter, Ada, 460
Porter, Armstrong, 327
Porter, Church T., 345
Porter, Church, 344, 358, 361
Porter, David, 327, 459, 460
Porter, Dr., 247
Porter, Elizabeth, 281
Porter, Geo. D., 63
Porter, James, 146
Porter, Margaret, 281
Porter, Matthew, 242, 252, 281
Porter, Obadiah, 459
Porter, R.B., 331, 440
Porter, William, 459
Porter, Wm., 459
Postlewaite, Dr., 152
Potter, Abrilla, 293

Potter, Eliza, 206
Potter, Gilbert M., 234
Potter, Henry N., 235
Potter, James H., 234
Potter, John, 234
Powell, J.R., 305, 322, 0.345
Powell, John R., 344
Power, ____, 199, 204
Power, Hannah, 72
Power, Henry F., 224
Power, James S., 218, 439
Power, Jane Fulton, 77, 78
Power, John, 64, 72, 77, 205, 219, 223, 231, 358, 437
Power, Joseph, 256
Power, Margaret, 149
Power, Mary Jane, 219
Power, Mary, 439
Power, Michael, 71, 73
Power, Samuel W., 256
Power, William J., 224
Power, William, 224
Power, Wm. J., 77
Powers, Michael, 233
Power-Smith, Mary Jennie, 219, 220
Pratt, Mrs., 144
Prescott, Mr., 20
Preston, Clark, 263
Preston, Father, 118
Prian, William, 72
Price, Bessie, 225
Price, Hugh, 374, 479
Price, R.T., 78, 225
Prine, James, 72
Printy, John, 292
Puff, Charles S., 190
Pugh, Nancy, 144
Pyatt, ____, 351, 352

Q

Quail, David, 261
Quay, M.S., 430
Quimby, ____, 446
Quimby, Abrilla, 293
Quimby, Charles, 293
Quimby, Elizabeth, 293
Quimby, Ephraim, 293, 294, 296
Quimby, George B., 294

Quinby, George, 293
Quinby, James, 293
Quinby, Mary Girling, 293
Quinby, Moses, 296
Quinby, Nancy, 293
Quinby, Samuel, 293, 294, 296
Quinby, Sarah, 294
Quinby, Teresa, 296
Quinby, Warren, 293
Quinby, William E., 296
Quinby, William H., 296
Quinby, William, 293

R

Rabe, David, 143
Rabe, Dr., 134
Rabe, Elizabeth, 152
Rabe, Henry, 102, 152
Rabe, Hiram, 118
Rabe, J.W.L., 131
Rabe, Minerva, 152
Rabe, Miss, 480
Radcliffe, Elizabeth, 166
Ralph, Wm., 107
Ralston, Rev. Dr., 26, 53, 72, 73, 109, 125, 202, 204, 206, 233, 235, 281, 290, 465
Ralston, Rev. Samuel, 199
Ralston, Samuel, 16, 62, 63, 66, 199
Randall, Abel, 193, 194
Randolph, ____, 204
Rankin, Alexander, 324
Rankin, John, 161, 256, 424
Rathborne, E.E., 117
Raum, John, 319
Ray, Bob, 316
Reagan, Louisa, 264
Reardon, ____, 350
Reasoner, ____, 445
Redd, Jefferson, 272
Redd, John, 399
Redd, Thomas, 315, 467, 468
Redd, Thomas, 48
Reddick, ____, 366
Reding, Charles, 121
Reed, ____, 457
Reed, Alexander, 44
Reed, C.M., 44

Reed, D.C., 211
Reed, J.F., 374
Reed, Lizzie, 70
Reed, Margaret, 463
Reed, R.R., 422
Reed, Rev., 70
Reef, Henry, 306
Reeve, Jesse, 430
Reeves, ____, 445, 446
Reeves, Abner, 321
Reeves, Barnes C., 341
Reeves, Barnes, 308
Reeves, J.S., 384
Reeves, Jesse, 340
Reeves, John S., 371, 387
Reeves, John, 304, 356, 358
Reeves, L.H., 323, 331, 385
Reeves, Lucinda, 271
Reeves, Manassah, 259, 309, 340, 341, 446
Reeves, Morgan, 367
Reeves, Nancy, 314, 453
Reeves, Rhoda, 309
Reeves, S., 386
Reeves, Samuel, 271, 332, 340, 344, 347, 356, 453
Reeves, Sarah A., 453
Reeves, Sarah, 294, 462
Reeves, Van, 257, 334, 344
Reeves, William, 308, 310, 320, 333, 367
Register, Porter, 245
Reppert, Allen K., 355
Reppert, C., 345, 347
Reppert, Curtis, 247, 319
Reppert, Curtiss, 314, 344, 347, 355, 358
Reppirt, C., 484
Reynolds, Capt. Samuel, 255
Reynolds, J.J.A., 434
Rhinehard, P.H., 249
Rhodes, D., 335
Rhodes, Jonathan, 158
Rice, ____, 204
Richards, Thomas, 455
Richardson, Richard, 134
Riddle, David, 482
Riggs, ____, 118, 119, 124, 125, 132, 133
Riggs, Miss, 467
Ringland, Isabella, 273
Ringland, John, 273
Rippey, ____, 75

Ritner, _____, 204
Ritner, Gov., 180
Robbins, _____, 428
Robbins, Amos, 25
Robbins, Edward E., 484
Roberts, Barbara, 193
Roberts, Dick, 251
Roberts, Dr., 109, 432
Roberts, Geo., 429
Roberts, Jane, 191, 193
Roberts, John, 193
Roberts, Nancy, 133
Roberts, Sammy, 251
Roberts, W.Y., 302
Robinson, _____, 446
Robinson, J., 381
Robinson, John Q., 356
Robinson, Joseph, 387
Robinson, Mr., 225
Robinson, W.C., 91
Rockfellow, Albert, 190
Rogers, _____, 183, 350
Rogers, Captain, 317
Rogers, O.A., 429
Rogers, William, 198, 268, 271, 272
Rogers, Wm., 74
Roley, J.T., 318, 344, 438, 462
Roley, Jacob T., 434
Roley, Mr., 428
Rolinson, W.C., 98
Rose, Charles, 128
Rose, Chas., 98
Rose, Dr., 96
Rose, George, 99
Rose, Grand-Daddy, 53
Ross, Phillip, 148
Rowe, Elder, 352
Rowley, Col., 275
Rupp, Dr., 432
Rutan, _____, 262, 446, 466
Rutan, Aunt, 430
Rutan, Samuel, 262
Ruter, Martin, 335, 336
Ryan, Joseph, 268
Ryan, Mrs. John, 159
Ryan, Mrs. Joseph, 269

S

Sackrader, C.H., 414
Salisbury, Mrs. O.J., 178
Sample, Alexander, 240, 241
Sample, Ann, 241
Sample, Eliza E., 236
Sample, Eliza, 241
Sample, Jane, 239, 241
Sample, John, 240, 241
Sample, Margaret, 241
Sample, Martha, 241
Sample, Mary, 240
Sample, Samuel, 240
Sample, Sarah, 241
Sample, William, 240
Sampson, _____, 20, 58
Sampson, A.C., 109
Sampson, Dorcas, 258, 264
Sampson, James, 204, 256, 258, 264, 268, 271, 274, 294
Sampson, Sarah, 258
Sampson, William, 256, 258
Sansom, J.G., 259, 332, 335, 336, 338
Sansom, James G., 125, 340
Sansom, James, 194
Savage, Billy, 102
Sawhill, B.F., 335, 336
Schmertz, Mary Elizabeth, 344
Schmertz, R.C., 332, 339, 351, 376, 398, 399, 401, 403, 406
Schmertz, Robert C., 344
Schmertz, W.E., 399
Schmertz, Wm. E., 405
Scott, _____, 106, 429
Scott, O.H.P., 335, 344
Scott, Alex., 20, 23, 27, 136
Scott, Alexander, 124, 182, 184
Scott, Angel, 182
Scott, Colonel, 29
Scott, Fannie, 182
Scott, General, 200
Scott, Geo. T., 129
Scott, James C., 98, 250, 251
Scott, James, 27, 36, 114, 186, 261
Scott, Jane, 182
Scott, John, 182, 183
Scott, Joseph, 182
Scott, Lizzie, 350
Scott, Lucy, 48
Scott, Mary, 131, 182, 183, 184
Scott, Moses, 184, 185, 288, 429
Scott, Mrs. Wm., 323
Scott, Nan, 131
Scott, Oliver, 354
Scott, Parker, 272, 273
Scott, Rebecca, 182
Scott, Samuel, 250
Scott, Thomas, 182, 183, 184, 350
Scott, Thos., 371
Scott, William, 182, 183, 184, 330
Scott, Winfield, 184
Scribner, George, 462
Scully, J.S., 428
Searight, T.B., 422
Sears, Mr., 158
Sedgwick, _____, 366
Shaefer, Henry, 124
Shaefer, John, 124
Shaffer, Alexander Swaney, 172
Shaffer, Anna Charlotte Weirich, 172
Shaffer, Annie LeMoyne, 173
Shaffer, Charles H., 175
Shaffer, Charles Holmes, 173
Shaffer, Charles, 429
Shaffer, Charlotte, 171
Shaffer, Christian S., 172
Shaffer, Elizabeth L., 173
Shaffer, Elizabeth, 172
Shaffer, J.M., 172
Shaffer, Jacob S., 172
Shaffer, Jennie Linn, 173
Shaffer, John E., 171
Shaffer, John S., 173
Shaffer, John, 171
Shaffer, Mary H., 173
Shaffer, Mary, 172
Shaffer, P.T.B., 173, 175
Shaffer, Susan E., 172, 173
Shaffer, William, 172
Shale, J.B., 429
Shannon, _____, 263
Shannon, Dutton, 16, 57
Shannon, Van, 42, 44, 46, 47

Shannon, Wash., 56
Shanton, John, 272
Sharp, David, 335
Sharpnack, John S., 368
Shaw, J.L., 106
Shaw, James L., 364
Shaw, Wm. C., 64
Shawman, J.B., 374
Shearer, Henry, 106
Sheets, G.A., 163
Sheets, George A., 336
Sheets, Nancy, 325
Sheplar, Peter, 49
Shepler, ____, 24, 445
Shepler, Abraham, 469
Shepler, Betsy, 263
Shepler, Bowman, 74
Shepler, Catherine, 469
Shepler, David Richey, 470
Shepler, Davis, 344, 469
Shepler, Elizabeth, 469, 470
Shepler, Eveline, 470
Shepler, Henry, 72, 74, 272
Shepler, Isaac H., 384, 385
Shepler, Isaac Hill, 470
Shepler, Isaac, 312, 469
Shepler, J.T., 329
Shepler, Jacob, 469
Shepler, James Kerr, 470
Shepler, James P., 100, 147, 170
Shepler, Jas. P., 99, 228
Shepler, John B., 470
Shepler, John, 106, 469
Shepler, Joseph, 157, 380, 448, 468, 469
Shepler, Josephine, 131
Shepler, Lewis, 468, 469
Shepler, Margaret, 469
Shepler, Mary Blackburn, 470
Shepler, Mary, 469
Shepler, Mathias, 469
Shepler, Peter W., 54, 320
Shepler, Peter, 74, 157, 263, 469
Shepler, Philip, 469
Shepler, Polly, 469
Shepler, Samuel, 469, 470
Shepler, Sarah H., 469
Shepler, Sarah, 157, 469, 470
Shepler, Shedrack Claywell, 470

Shepler, Violet, 470
Shepler, William Jones, 470
Shepperd, John H., 353
Sherbondy, David, 120, 128, 129, 133
Sherbundy, David, 130
Sherrard, J.H., 77
Sherrard, Jennie, 77
Shibler, Fred, 344
Shively, Daniel, 465
Shively, Elizabeth, 465
Shively, Frederick, 334
Shockey, Catharine, 348
Shoemaker, Anna N., 474
Shoemaker, Joseph, 474
Shoemaker, Salome, 474
Sholes, ____, 373
Shouse, Fannie C., 100, 289
Shouse, Fannie, 224
Shouse, John, 87, 97, 98, 100, 289, 292
Shouse, Peter, 97, 87, 118
Shouse, W.H., 100, 289
Shriver, Rebecca, 135
Shrodes, Captain, 260
Shugart, Frank, 260
Shugart, J.R., 27, 102
Shugart, John P., 128
Shugart, John R., 87, 118, 121, 132
Shugart, Letitia, 132
Shultz, Governor, 267
Shunk, Adam, 334, 335, 344, 354
Shunk, George, 354
Shunk, Governor, 113
Sickman, S.M., 126
Sill, Jesse P., 358
Sills, Jesse, 461
Sills, Josie, 323
Silverthorn, Gabriel, 25, 251
Simmons, Mr., 34
Simpson, Bishop, 133
Simpson, Matthew, 125, 126
Sinnott, ____, 390
Sinnott, Joseph S., 393
Sisley, Samuel, 310
Slack, Alfred, 373
Sloan, Dr., 322
Sloan, J.C., 249
Sloan, James G., 249
Sloan, James, 249

Sloan, Maggie, 249
Sloan, Margaret, 25
Sloan, Mrs., 27
Sloppy, Milton, 367
Slotterbeck, Michael, 334, 335
Smalley, Mr., 207
Smith, ____, 98, 465
Smith, A.O.P., 232
Smith, A.R., 257
Smith, Allie, 221
Smith, Alvira, 217
Smith, Amanda, 217, 221, 222
Smith, Ami Ruhami, 219, 220, 221
Smith, Amzi, 209, 221, 222, 223, 228
Smith, Bela B., 218, 219, 221
Smith, Bela, 216, 446
Smith, Betsy Plumer, 211
Smith, Betsy, 223
Smith, David, 158, 348, 381, 463, 473
Smith, Dr. B.B., 209
Smith, Dr., 459
Smith, E.P., 409
Smith, Ebenezer, 217, 221
Smith, Elizabeth, 217, 219, 225
Smith, Eva, 221
Smith, Finley, 232
Smith, George P., 232
Smith, Hannah, 250
Smith, Harmar D., 221
Smith, Hattie E., 221
Smith, Ira R., 358
Smith, J.C.P., 232
Smith, J.W., 91
Smith, James, 79, 105, 231, 250
Smith, John, 219, 387
Smith, Joseph H., 219, 221
Smith, Joseph, 158
Smith, Lizzie, 220, 221
Smith, Maggie, 219
Smith, Margaret L., 222, 232, 457
Smith, Margaret, 79, 219
Smith, Markle, 221
Smith, Mary Jane Power, 219
Smith, Mary, 232

Smith, Micajah, 220, 221
Smith, Nancy, 103
Smith, Polly, 209, 218, 222
Smith, R.H., 428
Smith, Rev., 259, 442
Smith, Robert, 154
Smith, Ross, 219
Smith, Sallie, 463
Smith, Samuel Stanhope, 218
Smith, Sarah Ann, 219
Smith, Talitha Cumi, 218
Smith, W.H., 429
Smith, Wesley, 126
Smith, Westley, 335, 336
Smock, Abraham, 263
Smock, Abram, 316
Smock, Barnett, 263, 448
Smock, Cornelius, 263
Smock, Eliza, 339, 352, 431
Smock, Henry, 263
Smock, Jacob, 263
Smock, Jennie, 263
Smock, John, 263
Smock, Lavinia, 325
Smock, Leonard, 263
Smock, Leroy, 262
Smock, Mary, 325, 448
Smock, Nancy, 325
Smock, Nettie, 263
Smock, Peter, 262, 263
Smock, Philip, 325
Smock, Phillip, 334
Smock, Sallie, 263
Smock, Thomas, 262
Smock, William, 263
Smutz, ____, 350
Smutz, David, 350
Smutz, S.G., 348
Snyder, ____, 198
Snyder, Cynthia, 483
Snyder, Governor, 234, 245
Snyder, Mrs., 482
Snyder, Peter, 357
Southmaid, ____, 352
Spahr, John, 48
Spahr, Rachel, 48
Sparks, Catherine, 292
Sparks, Charity, 289, 292
Sparks, Elenor, 292
Sparks, Elizabeth, 292
Sparks, Mary, 292
Sparks, Miss, 100
Sparks, Rev., 148

Sparks, Richard, 289, 291
Sparks, S.M., 66, 153, 254
Sparks, Sarah, 153
Speer, Abram, 442
Speer, Calhoun, 440
Speer, Capt. L.M., 443
Speer, Celia, 439, 440
Speer, Clarissa, 442
Speer, David S., 440
Speer, Eddie, 439
Speer, Frankie, 440
Speer, Harry, 443
Speer, Henry, 443
Speer, J., 429
Speer, J.B., 222
Speer, J.R. Hughes, 439
Speer, J.R., 443
Speer, Jacob, 442
Speer, James, 442
Speer, John S.V., 440
Speer, L.M., 321, 322, 344, 368, 376, 398, 440, 443, 444
Speer, Louis M., 439, 440, 441, 442
Speer, Lt. Col. William F., 442
Speer, Lucinda, 442
Speer, Margaretta, 439
Speer, Mary, 322, 439, 440
Speer, Mrs. L.M., 323
Speer, Mrs., 438
Speer, N.Q., 305, 424
Speer, Noah Q., 439, 442, 443
Speer, Noah W. , 442, 456
Speer, S.C., 383
Speer, Solomon P., 439
Speer, W.F., 359, 368, 443
Speer, William F., 439, 442
Speers, ____, 445
Speers, Apollos, 47, 55, 306, 307, 313, 431, 436, 447
Speers, Apollus, 272
Speers, Capt. S.C., 10, 307
Speers, Celia G., 325, 329, 331
Speers, Charles P., 377
Speers, Clara, 340, 437
Speers, David P., 442
Speers, Diana, 178, 341
Speers, Fannie S., 325

Speers, Henry, 55, 268, 269, 271, 272, 300, 301, 305, 306, 314, 318, 388, 435, 436, 437, 444
Speers, Jacob B., 303
Speers, Jacob, 363, 435, 437
Speers, James H., 434
Speers, Jasper, 436
Speers, John, 319, 436
Speers, Kattie, 436
Speers, L.M., 306, 307, 310, 311, 317, 318, 325, 326, 329, 334, 349, 354, 355, 383, 385, 437
Speers, Louis M., 306, 437
Speers, Lucinda, 121
Speers, Margaret, 437
Speers, Mary Evaline, 178
Speers, Mary P., 325
Speers, Mary, 329, 331, 437
Speers, Mrs. L.M., 329, 330, 331
Speers, N., 374
Speers, N.Q., 316, 329, 330, 331, 358
Speers, N.W., 363, 458
Speers, Nancy (Frey), 179
Speers, Nancy, 47, 55, 177, 179, 437
Speers, Noah Q., 315, 316
Speers, Noah W., 339, 361, 388, 389, 437, 442, 457
Speers, Noah, 178, 179, 271, 300, 301, 306, 307, 308, 316, 317, 318, 340, 344, 345, 347, 363, 373, 383, 388, 389, 435, 436, 437, 438, 442, 444
Speers, Peggy, 140, 141
Speers, Regina, 301, 435, 444
Speers, Robert, 178
Speers, S.C., 377, 435, 438
Speers, Samuel, 436
Speers, Sarah, 437
Speers, Solomon C., 436
Speers, Solomon P., 178
Speers, Solomon, 178, 301, 302, 303, 308, 309, 310, 314, 317, 333, 341, 353, 357, 382, 421, 432, 435, 442, 444, 446

Speers, W.F., 306, 311, 318, 325, 329, 331, 358, 359, 360, 361
Springer, Daniel, 310, 311, 312, 315, 316, 348, 349, 350, 431, 461, 462, 463
Springer, Elizabeth, 177
Springer, Everil F., 463
Springer, Everil T., 387
Springer, J.M., 304, 305, 315, 316, 357, 358, 359, 361, 373, 374, 452
Springer, J.O., 484
Springer, James H. (Cont.), 352, 461, 463
Springer, James H., 301, 315, 344, 351
Springer, James M., 310, 314, 327, 349, 352, 359, 450, 462
Springer, James, 462
Springer, Jas. M., 348
Springer, John R., 461
Springer, John, 431, 461, 462
Springer, Joseph, 302, 311, 351, 450, 461, 462, 463
Springer, Laura, 327
Springer, Lydia, 348, 462
Springer, Manoah, 310
Springer, Margaret, 451, 463
Springer, Martha, 461, 462, 463
Springer, Martina, 463
Springer, Mary Ann, 460
Springer, Mary, 461, 462
Springer, Mathias, 461
Springer, Michael, 301, 352, 460, 461
Springer, Miss, 257
Springer, Mrs. J.M., 356
Springer, Nancy, 461, 462
Springer, Newton, 462
Springer, Rachel, 348, 461, 462
Springer, Rebecca, 463
Springer, Sarah A., 452, 453
Springer, Sophia, 463
Springer, Theodore, 463
Springer, W.R., 383, 384, 385, 387
Springer, William R., 463

Sprouls, Edward, 46, 57
Sprouls, Elwood, 46
Sprouls, Isiah, 46
Spurgeon, Mrs., 240
St. Clair, Major General, 291
St. Clair, Samuel, 307
Stanton, E.M., 155
Steele, Eveline, 469
Steen, L., 347
Steen, Leightty, 347, 374, 385, 483
Steiner, John T., 373
Stephens, J.W., 370
Stephens, Jehu, 469
Stevens, Dr., 286
Stevens, Robert, 256
Stevens, William, 125
Stevenson, Father, 338
Stevenson, J.H., 78, 225, 322, 357
Stevenson, Jos. H., 80
Stevenson, Judith Mary, 225
Stevenson, Rev., 181
Stevenson, Sallie, 225
Stevenson, Sarah F., 80
Stewart, ____, 445
Stewart, Andrew, 75
Stewart, Benjamin, 259
Stewart, Colonel Tom, 279
Stewart, David, 210, 327, 474
Stewart, Fannie, 440
Stewart, H.S., 486
Stewart, James P., 97
Stewart, James T., 210
Stewart, Jane, 168
Stewart, Mr., 396
Stewart, Mrs. A.J., 97
Stewart, Rebecca V., 109
Stewart, T.B., 209
Stewart, Thomas B., 210
Stewart, Thomas J., 292
Stickel, E.E., 374
Stiles, Lizzie Quinby, 295
Stockdale, ____, 104
Stockdale, Charles, 147
Stockdale, Eliza, 146
Stockdale, Forbes, 146
Stockdale, James, 19, 64, 146
Stockdale, John, 146
Stockdale, Margaret, 146

Stockdale, Miss, 385
Stockdale, R., 124
Stockdale, Rachel, 146
Stockdale, Richard, 18, 101, 146, 147, 211, 228, 246
Stockdale, Robert, 146, 466
Stockdale, Sarah, 146
Stockdale, William, 146
Stokeley, Judge, 155
Storer, ____, 36
Storer, J.H., 70, 113, 282
Storer, John H., 26, 112, 362
Storer, John, 168
Stout, Jane, 446
Stout, Mr., 455
Strange, ____, 107
Streator, ____, 352
Streator, L.P., 351
Strickland, Jesse, 381
Strickler, John, 309
Stuart, James P., 108
Stuart, Mrs., 74
Stuchell, J.S., 64, 65
Stuckslager, C.R., 124, 129
Stump, John, 257
Stump, Mrs. J.G., 193
Styles, Joseph, 57
Sutherland, Mary, 256
Sutman, Henry, 165
Sutton, Samuel, 344, 345
Sutton, Wm., 305
Swab, Wm., 74
Swabb, ____, 54, 320
Swabe, Esq., 49
Swan, John, 428
Swan, William, 61
Swartz, Catherine, 109
Swayze, J.J., 337
Swayzie, J.J., 335,
Swearer, James R., 339
Swearer, John, 333, 334, 339, 341
Swearer, Pete, 333, 339, 341, 342
Swichard, John, 429
Swickard, Daniel, 120
Swickard, J.C., 133
Swift, A.L., 405
Synder, ____, 198

T

510

Tabron, George, 320
Taggart, A.A., 358, 360, 363, 368
Taggart, Louisa, 430, 432
Taggart, Mrs. L., 431
Taggart, Thomas, 302, 308, 314, 333, 349, 432, 437
Taggart, Thos., 345
Taggart, W.G., 429
Talbot, E.A., 18, 20
Taylor, A.J., 314
Taylor, Elizabeth, 224
Taylor, Frank Z., 378
Taylor, General, 200
Taylor, J.P. 130, 131
Taylor, Joseph, 124
Taylor, Mrs. T.M., 193
Taylor, S.E., 378
Teal, Prof., 34
Teeple, Ada, 263
Teeple, Catherine, 262, 265, 267
Teeple, Christens, 262, 263
Teeple, Christopher, 261, 262
Teeple, Clinton, 166, 264
Teeple, Cynthia, 264
Teeple, Elijah Harvey, 264
Teeple, Elijah, 253, 262, 264
Teeple, Elizabeth, 262
Teeple, Emma S., 263
Teeple, Iosephine, 264
Teeple, Isaac, 54, 261, 262, 263, 264
Teeple, Jemima, 262
Teeple, Jesse M., 264
Teeple, Jesse, 250
Teeple, John M., 264
Teeple, Joseph, 262, 265
Teeple, Josephine H., 197
Teeple, Josephine, 263
Teeple, Kate B., 264
Teeple, Kate C., 263
Teeple, Mary, 262
Teeple, Michael, 262, 264
Teeple, Peter, 262
Teeple, Polly, 263
Teeple, Sarah Ann, 262, 263
Teeple, Theodore, 263
Teeple, Theresa, 262, 263
Teeple, Thomas B., 264
Teeple, Thomas W., 263

Teeple, Ulysses R., 264
Teeters, _____, 24
Teeters, Abram, 99
Teeters, Dan, 99
Tevis, John, 98
Thairwell, _____, 320
Thirkield, G.R., 345
Thomas, Benjamin, 158, 160, 161, 163, 164, 259, 333, 338
Thomas, Elijah, 160, 163
Thomas, Elizabeth, 264
Thomas, Hannah, 163
Thomas, Harriet, 160, 163
Thomas, James, 160, 163, 237
Thomas, Joseph B., 160
Thomas, Joseph, 163
Thomas, Mary, 158, 160, 163
Thomas, Miss, 237
Thomas, Rosa Ann, 160
Thomas, Rosanna, 160
Thomas, Sallie, 158
Thomas, Stephen, 271
Thomas, Thomas Hudson, 160
Thomas, Van R., 160, 163
Thomas, Westley Ford, 160, 163
Thompson, Charles, 486
Thompson, J.B., 347, 371, 372, 373, 374
Thompson, J.P., 26, 70
Thompson, Jimmy, 56
Thompson, John B., 371
Thompson, John T., 241
Thompson, John W., 193
Thompson, John, 365
Thompson, L., 374
Thompson, Mary, 241
Thompson, Prof. J.P., 211
Thompson, Samuel, 378
Thompson, William T., 241
Thompson, William, 241
Thompson, Wilson, 22, 136
Thomson, J.P., 74
Thorn, Charles, 126
Tiernan, John, 345
Todd, Dr., 70
Todd, J.M., 243
Todd, James, 219
Todd, O.D., 381
Todd, O.M., 114

Todd, Thos., 432
Tower, E.W., 64
Tower, Edward, 17
Tower, Florilla, 357
Tower, G.H., 17
Tower, Miss, 319
Tower, Theo., 17
Town, Oliver, 354
Townsend, _____, 259
Trainer, Jane, 454
Treasure, George, 374
Treasure, J.H., 313
Trout, _____, 190
Trout, George, 96, 99, 138
Truxal, L.M., 365
Truxal, N.W., 370
Tuman, Joseph, 106
Tuman, Mrs., 48
Turner, Margaret, 183
Turner, William, 183

U

Uber, J.B., 336, 337
Umstaetter, T.E., 429
Underwood, Abe, 28
Underwood, Abraham, 135
Underwood, Abram, 70
Underwood, Amanda, 135
Underwood, Charles, 135
Underwood, Cyrus, 22, 23, 114, 124, 125, 128, 130, 135, 136
Underwood, Father, 122
Underwood, Hannah, 135
Underwood, James, 135
Underwood, Jane, 135
Underwood, Mary, 135
Underwood, Mr., 18
Underwood, Wilbur, 135

V

Vail, William B., 190
Valentine, D.C., 131
Valiant, M.E., 429
Van Shannon, _____, 42, 44
Van Voorhees, Abraham, 187
Van Voorhees, Antyte, 187

Van Voorhees, Charles E., 188, 189
Van Voorhees, Coerte, 187
Van Voorhees, Cornelis Coerte, 186
Van Voorhees, Cornelius, 187
Van Voorhees, Daniel, 186, 187, 188
Van Voorhees, Elizabeth, 187, 188
Van Voorhees, Femmyte, 187
Van Voorhees, Harriett, 188
Van Voorhees, Isaac, 188
Van Voorhees, Jerome, 187
Van Voorhees, John, 187
Van Voorhees, Mary, 187, 188
Van Voorhees, Sallie, 189
Van Voorhees, Samuel Newton, 187, 188, 189
Van Voorhees, Sarah Ann, 188
Van Voorhees, Sarah, 187
Van Voorhees, Susan R., 188, 189
Van Voorhees, William R., 188
Van Voorhis, Abraham, 44, 59, 139, 195, 196
Van Voorhis, Abram, 59, 129, 143, 144, 145, 157, 483
Van Voorhis, Albert, 210
Van Voorhis, Anna, 209
Van Voorhis, Bettie, 212
Van Voorhis, Capt. Daniel, 203, 204
Van Voorhis, Captain, 207
Van Voorhis, Caroline, 157, 198, 483
Van Voorhis, Carrie E., 264
Van Voorhis, Charles E., 264
Van Voorhis, Charles, 197
Van Voorhis, Christena, 196
Van Voorhis, Christina, 270
Van Voorhis, Clara, 197
Van Voorhis, Clinton , 195, 199, 201, 238
Van Voorhis, Cornelius,, 201

Van Voorhis, Cynthia Serena, 264
Van Voorhis, Cynthia, 198, 483
Van Voorhis, Daniel, 42, 44, 45, 47, 110, 139, 189-196, 198, 201, 205, 207, 264, 270, 271, 468
Van Voorhis, Danny, 196
Van Voorhis, David, 210
Van Voorhis, Dr. J.S., 199, 213, 215, 216
Van Voorhis, Dr., 36, 124, 144, 355
Van Voorhis, E.T., 274
Van Voorhis, E.W., 186
Van Voorhis, Elgy, 60, 195, 270, 468
Van Voorhis, Eliza, 197, 483
Van Voorhis, Elizabeth P., 213
Van Voorhis, Elizabeth, 190, 191, 194, 198, 271
Van Voorhis, Ellen, 209
Van Voorhis, Emaline, 190, 198, 483
Van Voorhis, Eva I., 264
Van Voorhis, Fuller, 193
Van Voorhis, Garrett T., 196
Van Voorhis, Grace, 209
Van Voorhis, Harvey B., 195, 196
Van Voorhis, Henry C., 191
Van Voorhis, Isaac S., 216
Van Voorhis, Isaac S., 377, 430
Van Voorhis, Isaac, 19, 58, 59, 63, 70, 71, 184, 195, 198-201, 203, 204, 206-211, 234, 252-254, 271
Van Voorhis, J.S., 15, 40, 71, 83, 112, 135, 172, 223, 224, 247252, 276, 282, 303, 305, 315, 316, 322, 324, 325, 326, 329, 330, 340, 358, 367, 368, 373, 374, 377, 381, 382, 411, 414, 418, 427, 432, 434
Van Voorhis, James H., 209, 212, 222

Van Voorhis, James Hair, 208
Van Voorhis, James, 207
Van Voorhis, Jane, 190, 146, 482, 483
Van Voorhis, Jas. H., 64
Van Voorhis, Jas., 65
Van Voorhis, Jerome, 195, 196
Van Voorhis, John F., 195, 196, 468
Van Voorhis, John S., 210, 216, 408
Van Voorhis, John, 71, 139, 187, 188, 190, 191, 197, 203, 204, 211, 264, 272, 429, 482, 483
Van Voorhis, Joseph, 197
Van Voorhis, Josiah, 195, 319
Van Voorhis, Julia Ann, 210
Van Voorhis, Julia, 195
Van Voorhis, Kate, 195
Van Voorhis, Lavinia, 216
Van Voorhis, Lizzie, 211, 212, 322, 323, 326, 329, 330 331, 344
Van Voorhis, Lucinda, 197, 483
Van Voorhis, Lulu J., 264
Van Voorhis, Marcie, 209
Van Voorhis, Martha J., 212
Van Voorhis, Martha Jane, 209
Van Voorhis, Mary H., 208
Van Voorhis, Mary I., 191, 194
Van Voorhis, Mary Lucinda, 209
Van Voorhis, Mary R., 190
Van Voorhis, Mary Ruth, 207
Van Voorhis, Mary, 191, 195-197, 206, 207
Van Voorhis, Mary, 272
Van Voorhis, Mrs., 213
Van Voorhis, Mrs. E.S., 325
Van Voorhis, Mrs. James H., 212, 213
Van Voorhis, Nancy, 191, 194, 195, 207

Van Voorhis, Nannie, 210
Van Voorhis, Newton, 45, 46, 47, 53, 195, 210
Van Voorhis, Phoebe, 189
Van Voorhis, R. Finley, 209
Van Voorhis, Rebecca, 26, 209, 381
Van Voorhis, Robert, 20, 197
Van Voorhis, S.F., 193
Van Voorhis, Sallie Ann, 189
Van Voorhis, Samuel N., 189
Van Voorhis, Samuel, 191, 195, 204
Van Voorhis, Sarah A., 191, 194
Van Voorhis, Sarah, 191, 196, 204
Van Voorhis, Serena, 483
Van Voorhis, Serenia Ann, 198
Van Voorhis, Susan, 189
Van Voorhis, Theresa Jane, 207
Van Voorhis, Theresa, 191, 194, 210
Van Voorhis, Victoria, 191
Van Voorhis, W.R., 186
Van Voorhis, William T., 264
Van Voorhis, William, 189
Van Voorhis, Willie, 209, 210
Van Voorhis, Zenas F., 191
Vanderbilt, _____, 425
Vandever, Mrs., 118, 119, 123, 132
Vanhook, A.G., 383
Vanhook, Sallie, 357
Vanhook, Samuel, 366
Vankirk, _____, 105
Vankirk, Angeline G., 178
Vankirk, Asher, 59, 103, 120, 122, 128, 129
Vankirk, Joseph, 259
Vankirk, Samuel W., 178
Vankirk, William K., 178
Vaughan, William, 374
Venable, Lowry, 158
Venable, Sallie, 159
Verner, Mrs., 133
Vernon, Geo., 381

Victor, Mr., 17
Vogel, _____, 352
Voorhies, Coert Alberts, 186
Voorhies, Mrs. R.P., 179
Voorhies, Steven Coerte, 186
Vorehas, Daniel, 72

W

Waddell, Wm., 97
Wainwright, _____, 419, 424, 425
Wainwright, J., 427, 428
Wainwright, J.W., 429
Wainwright, Jacob, 414
Wakefield, Samuel, 335, 336
Walk, _____, 352
Walker, Albert J., 179
Walker, Angeline G., 179
Walker, Billy, 367
Walker, Bolivar Krepps, 178
Walker, Diana, 178, 179, 180
Walker, Eleanor, 450
Walker, Elizabeth, 176
Walker, James Blaine, 178
Walker, James S., 179
Walker, James, 437
Walker, John Brisben, 178
Walker, John S., 178, 179
Walker, John, 107, 177, 178, 179, 180
Walker, Julia, 178, 179
Walker, Lucinda, 179
Walker, Margaret, 178
Walker, Mary Krepps, 178
Walker, Mary, 178, 179
Walker, Matilda, 178
Walker, Nannie, 179
Walker, Noah S., 179
Walker, R.C., 113, 282
Walker, Robert C., 178
Walker, Robert, 105
Walker, Samuel, 176, 179, 180, 2S9, 310, 442
Walker, Sarah, 179
Walker, Thomas P., 179
Walker, William G., 178
Walker, William, 313

Walker, Wm. B., 179
Walker, Wm., 429
Wall, Brisben, 292
Wall, Garret D., 290
Wall, Garret, 107, 108, 274, 291, 292
Wall, J. Sutton, 290
Wall, James, 291
Wall, Walter, 290
Wall, William, 292
Wallace, A.A., 430
Wallace, J.H., 276
Wallace, W.T., 414, 429
Ward, _____, 307
Ward, Artemus, 355
Ward, James, 301, 352, 461
Ward, Katherine, 332
Ward, Katy, 338, 339, 430
Ward, Thomas, 300, 313, 386, 430, 467
Ward, Uriah, 301, 334, 363
Ward, William, 436
Warmcastle, S.D., 430
Warne, Eliza J., 26
Warne, Eliza Jane, 146
Warne, James, 17, 95, 96, 98, 99, 101, 108, 142, 146, 155
Warne, Joseph P., 96, 103, 115
Warne, Joseph, 17, 120, 127, 129, 143
Warrensford, S.M., 374
Washington, Captain, 30
Waters, Geo. R., 371
Watkins, Ann, 144, 196
Watkins, Elias, 20, 59, 110, 132, 144
Watkins, Jeremiah, 144
Watkins, Jimmy, 197
Watkins, John, 26, 97, 103, 144, 145, 146
Watkins, Joseph Finley, 144
Watkins, Joseph, 144
Watkins, T.F., 247
Watkins, Thornton F., 146, 197
Watkins, Thornton, 483
Watkins, William, 146
Watson, J.P., 157
Watson, John, 103, 305, 344
Watson, Mr., 18, 19
Watson, S.W., 304

Watterman, John, 161, 258
Waugh, ____, 94
Wayts, William, 349
Wayts, Wm., 432
Weaver, Eliza, 345
Weaver, J.H., 345, 374
Weaver, John H., 371
Weaver, Lew, 258
Weaver, Margaret, 83
Webb, James, 387
Webster, Miss, 23
Weekly, M.L., 336, 346
Weekly, W.L., 337
Weller, R.L., 384, 385
Welling, Mary D., 258
Wells, ____, 307
Wells, Griffith, 366, 432
Wells, Richard, 386
Wells, Thomas, 97, 142
Welsh, Joseph B., 422
Weltner, Jacob, 99
Welzer, Christ, 354
Wene, Anna, 448
Wene, Jane, 448
Wene, Peter, 448
Wene, Sarah, 448
West, ____, 446
West, Elizabeth, 47
West, N., 322
West, Samuel, 47
Wheeler, John T., 241
Whetsel, Stephen, 363
White, D.N., 75
White, Dr., 429
White, J.C., 399
White, J.W.F., 26, 36, 75, 91, 120, 164
White, John, 120, 129, 164, 258
White, Judge, 129
White, Mr., 91, 125
Whiteside, James, 241
Whiteside, Margaret, 241
Whiting, Geo., 389
Whiting, Ziba, 334, 360, 453
Wickerham, Adam, 165, 166, 167, 264
Wickerham, Albert Gallatin, 166
Wickerham, Alexander Wilson, 166
Wickerham, David H., 166
Wickerham, Eliza Jane, 166

Wickerham, Emeline Allen, 166
Wickerham, George, 166
Wickerham, James S., 166
Wickerham, John Dewitt, 166
Wickerham, Maggie, 166
Wickerham, Margaret, 264
Wickerham, Mary Chess, 166
Wickerham, Mary, 166
Wickerham, Nancy, 145
Wickerham, Peter, 165, 167
Wickerham, Sarah, 166
Wickerham, Vandella Fell, 122
Wickerham, William Henry Harrison, 166
Wickerham, William, 118, 165
Wickerham, Wm., 264
Wickerman, Adam, 87, 89, 96, 99, 100
Wickerman, William, 96
Wiley, C.B., 310
Wiley, Dick, 429
Wilgus, T.B., 99
Wilkinson, John W., 368, 390, 479
Wilkinson, John, 374
Williams, ____, 24, 31
Williams, A.G., 126
Williams, A.L., 98, 99, 108, 121
Williams, Aaron, 26
Williams, Alderman, 246
Williams, Alexander, 147
Williams, Benjamin, 62, 250
Williams, D.H., 25
Williams, David, 19, 58, 128
Williams, E., 336
Williams, Ed., 126, 346
Williams, Hull, 159
Williams, James, 124, 128
Williams, John, 335
Williams, Joseph, 387
Williams, Lemon, 166
Williams, Margaret, 263
Williams, McCarty, 19, 59
Williams, Rev., 346
Williams, Robert, 72
Williams, S.T., 464

Williams, Samuel, 26
Williams, T.H., 33, 429
Williams, Thomas T., 27, 37
Williams, Thomas, 59
Williams, W.W., 319
Williamson, Jeremiah R., 190
Williamson, Samuel R., 190
Willie, Senator, 130
Willson, Mrs. A.E., 179
Wilson, A. Park, 106
Wilson, A.C. Sampson, 285
Wilson, Alex., 103, 136
Wilson, Alexander, 22, 66, 119, 166, 241, 254, 274, 303
Wilson, Allen, 391
Wilson, Ann St. Clair, 243, 244
Wilson, Captain Clark, 31
Wilson, David, 209
Wilson, Dora Bell, 285
Wilson, Dorcas E., 244
Wilson, Dr., 106
Wilson, Eliza C., 243
Wilson, Emma, 285
Wilson, Frank, 285
Wilson, George Reed, 285
Wilson, Henry, 99, 181
Wilson, Ida King, 285
Wilson, Isabel, 56
Wilson, J.A., 106
Wilson, J.H., 356
Wilson, James Allen, 285
Wilson, John R., 379
Wilson, John Robert, 285
Wilson, John, 31, 46, 47, 56, 205, 233, 271, 353, 355, 356, 435, 454
Wilson, Joseph, 17, 63, 95, 96, 105, 121, 142
Wilson, M. Virginia, 243, 244
Wilson, Margaret, 242
Wilson, Mary E., 243
Wilson, Mary, 285
Wilson, Mrs. Smith F., 181
Wilson, Nellie, 285
Wilson, R.F., 181
Wilson, Robert M., 243
Wilson, Robert, 244
Wilson, S.C., 18
Wilson, Samuel, 474

513

Wilson, Sarah, 180
Wilson, Simon, 46, 56, 61, 435
Wilson, Stephen, 241, 243, 244
Wilson, Susan E., 243
Wilson, W.H., 18
Wilson, W.L.S., 94
Wilson, Wannita, 285
Wilson, William H., 243, 244
Wilson, William Lowrie Sparks, 285
Wilson, William Park, 285
Wilson, William, 136
Wilson, Wm., 23, 324
Wiltsie, Joseph, 381
Winnett, Hiram, 285
Winters, Keziah, 433
Winters, Miss, 163
Winters, Robert, 311
Winters, Samuel, 432
Winters, William, 334, 335
Winters, Wm., 344
Winton, ____, 350
Winton, David, 452
Wise, Susan C., 325
Wise, W.K., 368
Wishart, John, 77
Wishart, Marcus W., 382
Wishart, Marcus, 474
Witherow, ____, 199
Witherow, Alexander, 54
Witherow, Benjamin, 73
Witherow, David, 73
Witherow, James, 73
Witherow, John, 16, 44, 54, 73, 257
Witherow, Noah, 54
Witherow, Samuel Finley, 54
Witherow, Samuel, 44, 54, 73
Witherow, William, 54, 72, 73
Witherspoon, John, 61
Withrow, John, 46, 482
Withrow, Samuel, 46
Wolf, Jacob, 380
Wolf, Joseph, 467
Wolfe, Gov., 89, 95, 255
Wood, B.L., 414
Wood, C.B., 119
Wood, Rev., 324

Wood, Wm. Wilson, 324
Woodburn, Harriet, 153
Woodrow, A.S., 323, 330, 332
Woodruff, Jessie, 258
Woods, John S., 175
Woods, Rev., 181
Woods, Robert, 68
Woodward, David, 100, 140
Woodward, I.C., 9, 10, 93
Woodward, Joseph, 24, 100, 103, 140
Woodward, Noble, 24, 100, 140
Woodward, Ralph, 24
Woolsey, Wm., 459, 460
Work, Alexander, 328
Work, Belle, 328
Work, Clara, 328
Work, George, 328
Work, James, 328
Work, Jane, 328
Work, Margaret, 328
Work, Martha, 328
Work, Sallie, 328
Worley, John, 461
Worrel, Nathan, 371
Worrell, Jennie, 350
Wright, Ezra, 218
Wright, Hugh, 218
Wright, J.E., 68
Wright, J.W., 367, 432
Wright, James, 218, 469
Wright, John W., 305, 358
Wright, John, 64, 218, 357
Wright, Joseph, 218
Wright, Judge, 218
Wright, Phillip, 218
Wylie, Miss, 385
Wylie, Nathan, 184, 207
Wylie, Norman, 154
Wylie, William, 473
Wythe, Geo., 91
Wythe, George, 250

Y

Yant, Harvey, 195
Yerty, John D., 390
Yohe, ____, 103, 106
Yohe, D.D., 64
Yohe, Isaac, 429
Yohe, James, 429

Yohe, John, 264
Yohe, Michael, 16
Young, Ad., 374
Young, Alcinus, 125, 126, 335, 341
Young, Anna, 131
Young, E.S., 374
Young, J.F., 374
Young, John, 148, 381
Young, R.H., 131

Z

Zeh, J.B., 313, 347
Zimmerman, J.J., 344, 345

www.ingramcontent.com/pod-product-compliance
Lightning Source LLC
Chambersburg PA
CBHW020633300426
44112CB00007B/98